Italy by Train

Tim Jepson

is a writer and journalist who has lived in Rome for five years. He is the author of the Foder's Exploring Guides to Rome and Italy; *The Rough Guide to Canada*; *The Rough Guide to Tuscany and Umbria*; *Umbria: The Green Heart of Italy*; and *Wild Italy: A Traveller's Guide* and *The AA Explorer Guides* to Rome and Italy. He currently lives in London, frequently visiting Italy where he leads walking tours through Tuscany and Umbria.

D1636980

Fodor's

ITALY
by
TRAIN

BY TIM JEPSON

Fodor's Travel Publications, Inc.
New York • Toronto • London • Sydney • Auckland

Copyright © 1993 Tim Jepson

Published in the United States by Fodor's Travel Publications, Inc.

Published in the United Kingdom by Hodder and Stoughton, a division of Hodder and Stoughton Ltd.

Fodor's is a registered trademark of Fodor's Travel Publications, Inc.

ISBN 0-679-02827-7

First Edition

Library of Congress Cataloging-in-Publication Data
Jepson, Tim.
    Fodor's Italy by train / by Tim Jepson.—1st ed.
        p.   cm.
    Includes index.
    ISBN 0-679-02827-7
    1. Italy—Guidebooks.   2. Railroad travel—Italy—Guidebooks.
I. Fodor's Travel Publications, Inc.   II. Title.   III. Title: Italy
by train.
DG416.J47   1994
914504'929—dc20   94-6639
                                                        CIP

Text designed by Tim Higgins
Maps by Ruth Hodkinson

Photoset by SX Composing Ltd, Rayleigh, Essex

Special Sales

Fodor's Travel Publications are available at special discounts for bulk purchases for sales promotions or premiums. Special editions, including personalized covers, excerpts of existing guides, and corporate imprints, can be created in large quantities for special needs. For more information, contact your local bookseller or Special Markets, Fodor's Travel Publications, 201 E. 50th Street, New York, NY 10022. Inquiries from Canada should be directed to your local Canadian bookseller or sent to Random House of Canada, Ltd., Marketing Dept., 1265 Aerowood Drive, Mississauga, Ontario L4W 1B9.

MANUFACTURED IN THE UNITED STATES OF AMERICA

10 9 8 7 6 5 4 3 2 1

Contents

Introduction 7
How to Use This Book 8

General Information
Before You Go Climate 10; When to Go 10; Passports,
Visas and Red Tape 10; Customs 11; Money 11;
Health and Insurance 12; Information and Maps 13
Getting to Italy By Train from the United Kingdom 14;
By Train from the Continent 15; By Air from the
United States 15; Rail Passes 17;
Student and Youth Travel 19
In Italy Finding a Place to Stay 19; Eating 23; Museums,
Galleries and Archaeological Sites 24

The Train Network
Trains 25; Couchettes and Night Trains 27; International
Services 31; Tickets and Rail Passes 32; Stations 36;
Timetables 42; Public Holidays 44; Timekeeping 45;
On the Train Food and Drink 46; Overcrowding 46; Hazards 47;
Smoking and Non-Smoking 48

1 Piedmont, Valle d'Aosta and Liguria
Turin 52; *Turin—Aosta—Pré-St-Didier* 57;
Turin—Cuneo—Ventimiglia 64; *Ventimiglia—
Genoa: The Riviera di Ponente* 68
Genoa 70; *Genoa—Cinque Terre—La Spezia* 73

2 Lombardy and the Lakes
Milan 80; *Milan—Pavia* 87; *Milan—Bergamo* 90;
Milan—Lago Maggiore—Domodossola 93; *Domodossola—Re—
Locarno* 96; *Locarno—Lugano—Como—Milan* 99; *Milan—
(Como)—Lecco—Sondrio—Tirano* 103; *Brescia—Edolo* 105

3 Venice and the North-East

Verona 112; *Verona–Trento–Bolzano* 116;
Bolzano–Fortezza–Brunico–San Candido 123;
Verona–Vicenza–Padua 126
Venice 131; *Venice–Trieste* 144; *Trieste–Aquileia* 147; *Trieste–Udine–Cividale* 149; *Padua–Ferrara–Ravenna–Rimini* 154
Bologna 161

4 Tuscany and Umbria

Florence 170; *Florence–Siena* 182; *La Spezia–Pisa* 190;
Pisa–Lucca 194; *Lucca–Castelnuovo di Garfagnana–Aulla* 197;
Pisa–Volterra–(Massa Marittima)–Orbetello 198; *Florence–Arezzo–Cortona–Castiglione del Lago–Orvieto* 203; *Terni–Todi–Perugia–Città di Castello–Sansepolcro* 209; *Orte–Narni–Spoleto–Trevi–Foligno* 212; *Foligno–Spello–Assisi–Perugia* 218

5 Rome, Lazio and Abruzzo

Rome 230; *Rome–Frascati* 256; *Rome–Ostia Antica* 257; *Rome–Tivoli* 259; *Rome–Palestrina* 260; *Rome–Cerveteri–Tarquinia* 262; *Rome–(Tivoli)–Tagliacozzo–Sulmona* 265;
Sulmona–L'Aquila 267; *Sulmona–Alfedena–Castel di Sangro* 270

6 The South

Naples 277; *Naples–Herculaneum–Pompeii–Sorrento* 283;
Battipaglia–Paestum–Tropea–Reggio di Calabria 288;
Reggio di Calabria–Metaponto–Taranto–Rossano 292; *Cosenza–San Giovanni in Fiore* 294; *Cosenza–Catanzaro* 294; *Foggia–Trani–Bari* 295; *Bari–Altamura–Matera* 300; *Bari–Brindisi–Lecce* 302; *Bari–Alberobello–Martina Franca–Taranto* 305;
Lecce–Otranto–Gallipoli–Lecce 310

7 Sicily and Sardinia

Sicily
Palermo 315; *Messina–Milazzo–Cefalù–Palermo* 321;
Palermo–Roccapalumba–Agrigento 324; *Agrigento–Gela–Noto–Ragusa–Siracusa* 327; *Siracusa–Noto–Ragusa* 328; *Palermo–Enna–Catania* 333; *Circumetnea: Catania–Randazzo–Riposto* 336; *Catania–Taormina–Messina* 339
Sardinia *Cagliari–Mandas–Arbatax / Mandas–Sorgono* 342
Index 346

Introduction

In many countries the constraints of train travel make for dull traveling. Railways force you to visit tiresome towns and cities, steering clear of smaller villages and spectacular natural scenery. Italy's trains, however, stop in virtually all of the country's most historic cities, and allow you to enjoy some of Europe's most breathtaking scenery – from the Alpine lakes to the rolling plateaus of Sicily.

In Italy, where there's so much to see, railways provide travelers with tailor-made itineraries of the best the country has to offer. Routes in this guide combine journeys to historic cities with rides through beautiful countryside, thus combining the two main reasons for leaving home – traveling to arrive and traveling for its own sake. One needn't be a slave to trains, of course, and so we also suggest easy-to-make excursions to places of note off the rail network.

Since this is a book for train lovers, we don't keep you too long in any one place. Only the most worthwhile trips are suggested. Since few people work religiously through a city's sights, we concentrate only on the essential museums and monuments – as well as the bars, beaches, restaurants and backstreets that are as much a part of a trip as churches and galleries.

Equally as important as the places you visit are the experiences you'll have on trains, episodes that should remain in your memory long after the statues and paintings have faded. Train travel always has an air of romance, and in a country like Italy it goes without saying you'll have more than your share of adventure. Italian trains are sociable places, their traditional six-seat compartments almost designed for intimacy and conversation. Italians are also some of the most friendly of people, particularly in the south, where you're invariably invited to share the food and wine of fellow passengers. Openness and the odd smile take you a long way, even if your Italian's not up to much.

In summer, moreover, the railways are full of travelers from all over Europe. Friendships are struck, stories swapped and addresses exchanged. Don't, therefore, treat trains merely as a way to get from place to place; treat them as a way to travel. Italy is Europe's most beautiful and fascinating country. Trains are the best way to explore it.

How to use this book

ITALY BY TRAIN is divided into nine chapters, the first two covering general background, the rest rail journeys divided into seven regions. If you don't know Italy, the first chapter, *General Information*, describes some of the basic information you will need before visiting the country. It also explains how to get to Italy, and the various rail **tickets and passes** that can be bought before you leave home.

The second chapter, *The Train Network*, covers the practical aspects of Italian train travel. Much of the information is common sense, much of the detail more than you'll probably need. It's worth flicking through, however, particularly if this is going to be your first journey on Italian railways. Some of the vocabulary might be useful, and odd tips will save time and money.

As for the main chapters, the aim is to help you decide what to see, how to see it, and how and where to spend the night. Each chapter has a brief **introduction**, designed to point out what a region has to offer. This is followed by a summary of the **routes**, indicating how you might fit trips together within a chapter. It also suggests journeys you can make for their own sake – for the scenery alone, for example, or excursions which will take you to the area's best beach or place of interest.

Each chapter starts with a **major city**, often the center of the rail network for the whole region, with details of the important things to see in each city and all the practical information you'll need.

Outside the city, once you've chosen an itinerary, turn to the specific **journey**. Each journey opens with a brief description of **the route**. This outlines the towns or scenery you'll see, together with recommendations of the best places to stay overnight. This is followed by a short section on **trains**, giving the frequency of services on the route and the length of the journey in time and distance, and details of **the journey** itself – sometimes a narrative (usually on scenic trips), sometimes accounts of one or more towns. All the routes are self-contained and follow lines with through-trains requiring no changes.

Most town accounts – as well as the main city entries – have a separate **Practicalities** section. Look first at the entry for the railway station. This tells you how to reach the town center, either by walking or by catching a bus. Then look for the tourist office entry, which should be your first port of call for maps or help with accommodation. Entries also recommend a selection of hotels, together with suggestions of the nicer or nastier parts of the town to start looking on your own. Restaurants and – occasionally – bar selections are also given, together with a miscellany of information about foreign exchange, buses, travel agents and so forth.

Some journeys contain **excursions** – less detailed accounts, or pointers, to short trips (usually by bus) you can make from railheads. Some visit towns, some individual buildings; others suggest outstanding walks in a particular area.

Finally, if you do nothing else while traveling around Italy, **be sure to buy the** *Pozzorario*, a detailed timetable of all Italian train services. It's published twice-yearly in two pocket-sized volumes (North-Central Italy and South Italy). You can buy copies at any newsagents or station kiosk.

General Information

Before You Go

Climate

Italy's climate is hospitable at most times of the year, although there are dramatic regional and seasonal variations, with the north generally temperate, the south more firmly Mediterranean. Visits in high **summer** may be unavoidable, but it can be unsufferably hot – particularly in the south: July and August aren't the best months to be caught in a sweltering train compartment. Humidity in cities can also be unpleasant in late spring and early autumn. Mountain areas, however, are cooler in these periods, and you might avoid the worst of the heat by traveling at night or in the early morning and reserving the hotter part of the day for sightseeing, lounging on beaches or siestas. Persistent rain is rare in summer, although there can be powerful thunderstorms.

Winters can be as bleak as they are in the northern States, with severe weather in the mountain areas of the Alps and northern Apennines. Generally, though, Italian winters are mild and short-lived. In the south, spring is often in evidence from March. Rain and fog distinguish the plains of Lombardy and Emilia–Romagna, forlorn places from November to March.

When to Go

To avoid crowds and find good weather, aim to visit Italy around April–June and September–October. Other spring and autumn months are often fine, but you take a chance on days of sheer misery as well. Crowds are at their worst, and the trains busiest, during July and August – months when the main tourist cities seem populated almost entirely by visitors. Italians take their holidays en masse in August, and seaside resorts in particular are packed as a result.

Passports, Visas and Red Tape

Nationals of EC countries, the United States, Canada and Australia require a valid passport to enter Italy. For United Kingdom citizens, a temporary *British Visitor's Passport*, valid for one year and available over the counter at post offices, is also sufficient for entry. EC citizens can stay for unlimited periods, but other nationals must apply for a *Permesso di Soggiorno* if they stay for more than three months. In practice, passports are rarely stamped and virtually no one bothers to apply for permission to stay longer. If you plan on working in Italy, however, you should think more carefully about documentation; apply to the nearest town hall or *questura* for a *permesso* and be prepared for bureaucratic wranglings.

As a result of some fossilized piece of legislation, visitors of any nationality are in theory supposed to register with the police within three days of arrival in Italy. If you book into a hotel, this is done for you – registration forms then go to the local police station. Otherwise it's unheard of for people to present themselves, and ordinary visitors shouldn't bother – the police will be amazed if you do.

Customs

Customs police (*Guardia di Finanza*) and border guards are a fearsome looking bunch – with big dogs, smart uniforms and sub-machine guns – but they're a deterrent to drugs and arms smugglers rather than a nuisance to visitors to Italy.

There are two levels of duty-free allowances for visitors to Italy.

For goods obtained anywhere outside the EC or for goods purchased in a duty-free shop within an EC country, the allowances are: (1) 200 cigarettes or 100 cigarillos or 50 cigars or 250 grams of tobacco (these are doubled if you live outside Europe); (2) 2 liters of still table wine plus (3) 1 liter of spirits over 22% volume or 2 liters of spirits under 22% volume (fortified and sparkling wines) or 1 more liter of table wine; and (4) 50 milliliters of perfume and 250 milliliters of toilet water.

For goods obtained (duty and tax paid) within another EC country, the allowances are: (1) 300 cigarettes or 150 cigarillos or 75 cigars or 400 grams of tobacco; (2) 5 liters of still table wine plus (3) 1.5 liters of spirits over 22% volume or 5 liters of spirits under 22% volume (fortified or sparkling wines) or 3 more liters of table wine; and (4) 75 milliliters of perfume and 375 milliliters of toilet water.

Officially, two still cameras with 10 rolls of film each and one movie camera with 10 rolls of film may be brought in duty-free. Other items intended for personal use are generally admitted, as long as the quantities are reasonable.

Money

Italy is no longer a cheap country. In most respects prices are slightly higher than in cities like New York. Happily, train travel is one area where there are obvious savings on U.S. prices. In the touristy areas, especially Rome, Florence, and Venice, costs can be much higher all round, and they're bound to make a dent on budgets. Generally the south and Sicily are cheaper, though with common sense you can save money throughout the country. A bottom line budget for the backpacker – sleeping on trains, camping and buying food from shops and markets – is $20 per day; a more realistic **daily budget** – eating out once a day and staying in an average one- or two-star hotel – would be in the region of $50 per day (excluding train fares).

Currency The Italian currency is the *lira* (plural *lire*), abbreviated to L. The rate of exchange hovers around L1,700 to the U.S. dollar. Notes come in denominations of L1,000, L2,000, L5,000, L10,000, L50,000 and L100,000; coins as L50, L100, L200, L500 with a tiny number of L5 and L10 coins still (just) in circulation. There's also a telephone token (*gettone*) worth L200 and used as a coin.

It's unusual these day to be given sweets in lieu of change – as happened in the not so distant past – but presenting L50,000 and L100,000 notes can still cause problems.

Be careful with change and with notes – it's easy to be confused by all the zeros.

Cash and Traveler's Checks Try to carry some Italian lire with you to cover emergencies, delays, closed banks and so on. To avoid lines at airport currency-exchange booths, arrive in Italy with some lire in your pocket. Thomas Cook Currency Service (630 Fifth Ave, New York, NY 10111, tel. 212/757-6915) supplies foreign currency by mail.

Credit Cards Although Italy's banking system is slowly dragging itself into the twentieth century, it's still a country where cash reigns supreme, and **credit cards** (*carta di credito*) are only accepted in the biggest and more expensive hotels and restaurants. In the south they're all but useless. It's also almost impossible to pay for goods – least of all gas – with them. Many outlets which have credit card stickers do not take them when it comes to the crunch – so double check before you make your purchase, eat your meal or book your room. Also check the zeros on all receipts.

Banks A visit to an Italian **bank** (*una banca*) can be a sobering and frustrating experience. Pen-pushing, queues and forms in triplicate are still the norm. To change money look for a bank with a Eurocheque sticker or *cambio* (exchange) sign. You'll probably get a worse rate but far quicker service from an exchange kiosk – most tourist towns have one. Outside banking hours big city railway stations often have exchange facilities open at weekends and in the evening. Larger hotels may also change money, but at poor rates. In desperation visit the *cambio* at the nearest airport, usually open most hours.

Banking hours are Monday to Friday mornings 8.30 am – 1 pm. A few banks may also open for an hour in the afternoon (generally 3 – 4 pm).

Health and Insurance

While it used to be said that the best medical treatment in Italy was to take a plane home, today medical care – while often still rough and ready – is generally well-intentioned and usually fairly efficient. This is less true in hospitals south of Rome, which can still be medieval in appearance if not outlook.

Most tour operators, travel agents, and insurance agents sell specialized health-and-accident, flight, trip-cancellation, and luggage insurance as well as comprehensive policies with some or all of these features. But before you make any purchase, review your existing health and home-owner policies to find out whether they cover expenses incurred while traveling.

For minor complaints go to an Italian **chemist** (*farmacia*). Italian pharmacists are well-trained, usually able to diagnose problems, and armed with a battery of over-the-counter drugs – many of which are only available on prescription in the States. Chemists' shops operate on a rotating basis, so one is always open somewhere close at hand. When a pharmacist is closed a list on the door will name the nearest open outlets.

For more serious medical complaints seek out the local **doctor** (*medico*) – every town and village has at least one. Many have a basic grasp of English. Other minor cases and first aid problems are usually dealt with free and promptly at the local public hospital (*ospedale, ambulatorio*); head for the **casualty** section, the *Pronto Soccorso*. In emergencies or cases of serious illness phone 113 and ask for the *ospedale* or *ambulanza*.

Disabled Travelers Italy is making a concerted effort to improve its provisions for disabled travelers but there's still a long way to go. The Italian State Tourist offices in the U.S. have useful material and a list of hotels which are accessible by wheelchair. Most of the new Italian railway rolling stock have special doors for wheelchairs. Otherwise station staff are generally helpful.

Information and Maps

Before you travel to Italy visit or write to the **Italian Government Travel Office** at 630 5th Ave., Suite 1565, New York, NY 10111, tel. 212/245-4822; 500 N. Michigan Ave., Chicago, IL 60611, tel. 312/644-0990; 12400 Wilshire Blvd., Suite 550, Los Angeles, CA 90025, tel. 310/820-0098. They provide a wide range of information, town and regional maps, leaflets, accommodation listings, as well as tips and advice. In particular ask for the annually updated *Travellers' Handbook*, crammed with information and current prices on all aspects of the country. In Italy itself, virtually every town of any size has a **tourist office**, often known as an *Azienda Autonoma di Soggiorno e Turismo* (AAST). In the text the address of each is given in the *Practicalities* section for each journey. Tourist offices are dealt with in more detail under 'Sleeping' below.

Maps of the train routes in this book are good for basic planning, but it's worth carrying a general map of Italy as well. Michelin produces a single 1:1,000,000 map of the country but the best overall sheets, published by the Touring Club of Italy (TCI), are available in most travel bookshops. They cover Italy in two 1:800,000 *North* and *South* sheets and also issue excellent 1:200,000 regional maps. A handful of detailed 1:50,000 maps – mainly in the *Kompass* or *Multigraphic* series – suitable for **walking** tours are also available.

The best maps for general planning and touring are the Touring Club Italiano (TCI) 1:200,000 sheets. Local shops provide detailed hiking maps for all areas of the Alps and Dolomites. Other areas are less well served, notable exceptions being the Italian Lakes, Cinque Terre, the Amalfi coast, and Tuscany and Umbria (the Alpi Apuane in particular), where map series like *Kompass* and IGC provide excellent coverage.

Getting to Italy

By Train from the United Kingdom

There are two basic **rail routes** from Britain to Italy: the more important one is via Paris, Dijon, Modane, Turin and Rome; the other runs via Lille, Strasbourg, Switzerland and Milan. **In you're in Britain, call Victoria Station's International Rail Centre on 071-834 2345.**

London–Paris–Italy Traveling to Italy via Paris is the cheapest route with the most connections but it takes six hours longer than the other routes. Journey time from London to Rome is 26 hours, and the **current price** (1993) of a second class single ticket is $160, return $264. The discounted under-26 fare is $138, return $255. If you are in a hurry, these prices compare unfavorably with prices for flights (see below). Reservations and couchettes are available for all sections of the journey.

Tickets bought in London for travel to Italy are valid for two months from the date of issue and allow you to make stopovers at any point en route – an advantage over taking a plane. You should revalidate your ticket after French stopovers by clicking it in the orange machine at the entrance to platforms. Note that if you make a stopover in Paris, you can make Italian soil in a day by taking an early high speed TGV train to Lyon and changing to a Lyon–Modane–Turin express. You arrive in Turin at 5.30 pm, and a connection gets you to Rome just after midnight. Similarly, TGVs reach Geneva in three and a half hours; about six trains daily then run directly to Milan (four hours).

The main **disadvantage** of the Paris route is that you must change trains *and* stations in Paris. Trains connecting with boats at Calais and Boulogne arrive in Paris at the Gare du Nord. Trains leaving for Dijon, Italy and the south leave from the Gare du Lyon and the stations are on opposite sides of the city. If you take the scheduled boat train from London Victoria in the morning, this leaves you with just over an hour to cross Paris. The tube (Metro) ride takes about 25 minutes and involves one change. Be sure to have a little French money to buy a Metro ticket. If the Channel is rough or there are delays, it's often tight making the connection. Usually there are no problems, but to be sure you might take an earlier train from London – perhaps paying a little more to take the quicker *Sea Cat* crossing.

London–Switzerland–Italy The beauty of the route to Milan via **Switzerland** is that you don't have to change trains. It's a quicker and more expensive route. Journey time from London to Milan is 20 hours. The **current price** of a second class single is $194, the return $314. The discounted under -26 single is $160, return $285.

This is also the more scenic of the two routes, with a spectacular early morning ride through the Alps and past the Italian lakes into Milan. Tickets are also valid for stopovers – and the cities en route are also arguably more interesting (Strasbourg, Basle, Lucerne). If you miss the through connection to Milan, or want to take your time, trains from Calais run to Lille and Strasbourg and from there to Basle where you pick up several connections for Milan.

By Train from the Continent

If you have a **EurailPass** (see below) or are using the two month stopover facility of standard tickets, the chances are you'll be approaching Italy from a country on mainland Europe. Cities like Paris, Basle and Munich have regular daily services to Italy, as well as regular night trains with couchette and sleeper accommodation. Use the *Thomas Cook European Timetable* to plot routes to Italy from more obscure towns.

As a guide to the **direct trains** operating, look under **International Trains** (below) for departures *from* Italy to other countries. There are 17 through departures from France to Italy, seven of them from Paris (to Rome, Milan, Florence, Turin, Brindisi and towns in between); 35 from Switzerland (Basle, Bern, Geneva, Zürich) to Milan, Rome, Venice, and Naples; 24 from Germany (Dortmund, Munich, Stuttgart, Cologne); ten from Austria (Vienna, Salzburg and Innsbruck); four from the former Yugoslavia; two from Holland; and one each from Belgium, Budapest, Poland, Greece and Russia.

By Air from the United States

Flights are either nonstop, direct, or connecting. A nonstop flight requires no change of plane and makes no stops. A direct flight stops at least once and can involve a change of plane, although the flight number remains the same; if the first leg is late, the second waits. This is not the case with a connecting flight, which involves a different plane and a different flight number.

Airlines serving Italy nonstop from the United States are Alitalia (tel. 800/223-5730), Delta (tel. 800/241-4141), and TWA (tel. 800/892-4141), which all fly to Rome and Milan, and American (tel. 800/624-6262), which flies to Milan only. These flights land at Rome's Leonardo da Vinci Airport, better known as Fiumicino (from its location outside the city) and at Milan's Malpensa Airport.

The flying time to Rome from New York is 8½ hours; from Chicago, 10-11 hours; from Los Angeles, 12-13 hours.

The Sunday travel section of most newspapers is a good source of deals. When booking, particularly through an unfamiliar company, call the Better Business Bureau to find out whether any complaints have been registered against the company, pay with a credit card if you can, and consider trip-cancellation and default insurance. *The Airline Passenger's Guerrilla Handbook*, by George Albert Brown ($14.95; distributed by Slawson Communications, Inc., 165 Vallecitos de Oro, San Marcos, CA 92069, tel 619/744-2299 or 800/752-9766), may be out of date in a few areas but remains a solid source of information on every aspect of air travel, including finding the cheapest fares.

Most scheduled airlines offer three classes of service: first class, business class, and economy or coach. To ride in the first-class or business-class section, you pay a first-class or business-class fare. To ride in the economy or coach section – the remainder of the plane – you pay a confusing variety of fares. Most expensive is full-fare economy or unrestricted coach, which can be bought one-way or round-trip and can be changed and turned in for a refund.

All the less expensive fares, called promotional or discount fares, are round-trip and involve restrictions. The exact nature of the restrictions depends on the airline, the route, and the season and on whether travel is domestic or international, but you must usually buy the ticket – commonly called an APEX (advance purchase excursion) when it's for international travel – in advance (seven, 14, or 21 days are usual). You must also respect certain minimum- and maximum-stay requirements (for instance, over a Saturday night or at least seven and no more than 30, 45, or 90 days), and you must be willing to pay penalties for changes. Airlines generally allow changes in the dates of the outbound or return leg of the trip for a fee. But the cheaper the fare, the more likely the ticket is nonrefundable – it would take a death in the family for the airline to give you any of your money back if you had to cancel. The cheapest fares are also subject to availability; because only a certain percentage of the plane's total seats will be sold at that price, they may go quickly.

Consolidators Consolidators or bulk-fare operators – also known as bucket shops – buy blocks of seats that scheduled airlines anticipate they won't be able to sell. They pay wholesale prices, add a markup, and resell the seats to travel agents or directly to the pubic at prices that still undercut the airline's own promotional or discount fares. Consolidator fares are not as low as charter fares but they tend to be lower than APEX fares, and even when there is not much of a price difference, the consolidator ticket may be available without the advance-purchase restriction. Moreover, although tickets are marked nonrefundable so you can't turn them in to the airline for a full-fare refund, some consolidators sometime give you your money back. Read the fine print detailing penalties for changes and cancellations carefully. If you doubt the reliability of a company, call the airline once you've made your booking and confirm that you do, indeed, have a reservation on the flight.

The biggest U.S. consolidator, C.L. Thomson Express, sells only to travel agents. Well-established consolidators, selling to the public include UniTravel (Box 12485, St. Louis, MO 63132, tel. 314/569-0900 or 800/325-2222); Council Charter (205 E. 42nd St., New York, NY 10017, tel 212/661-0311 or 800/800-8222), a division of the Council on International Educational Exchange and a longtime charter operator now functioning as a consolidator; and Travac (989 6th Ave., New York, NY 10018, tel. 212/563-3303 or 800/872-8800), also a former charterer.

Charter Flights Charters usually have the lowest fares and the most restrictions. Departures are limited and seldom on time, and you can lose all or most of your money if you cancel. (Generally, the closer to departure you cancel, the more you lose, although sometimes you will be charged only a small fee if you supply a substitute passenger.) The charterer, on the other hand, may legally cancel the flight for any reason up to 10 days before departure; within 10 days of departure, the flight may be canceled only if it becomes physically impossible to operate it. The charterer may also revise the itinerary or increase the price after you have bought the ticket, but if the new arrangement constitutes a ''major change,'' you have the right to a refund. Before buying a charter ticket, read the fine print for the company's refund policy and details on major changes. Money for charter flights is usually paid on to a bank escrow account, the name of which should be on the contract. If you don't pay by credit card, make your check payable to the escrow account (unless you're dealing with a travel agent, in which case, his or her check should be payable to the escrow account). The Department of Transportation's Consumer Affairs Office (I-25, Washington, DC 20590, tel 202/366-2220) can answer questions on charters and send you its "Plane Talk: Public Charter Flights" information sheet.

Charter operators may offer flights alone or with ground arrangements that constitute a charter package. Well-established charter operators include Council Charter (205 E. 42nd St., New York, NY 10017, tel. 212/661-0311 or 800/800-8222), now largely a consolidator, despite its name, and Travel Charter (1120 E. Long Lake Rd., Troy, MI 48098, tel. 313/528-3570 or 800/521-5267), with Midwestern departures. DER Tours (Box 1606, Des Plains, IL 60017, tel. 800/782-2424), a charterer and consolidator, sells through travel agents.

Discount Travel Clubs Travel clubs offer their members unsold space on airplanes, cruise ships, and package tours at nearly the last minute and at well below the original cost. Suppliers thus receive some revenue for their "leftovers," and members get a bargain. Membership generally includes a regular bulletin or access to a toll-free telephone hot line giving details of available trips departing anywhere from three or four days to several months in the future. Packages tend to be more common than flights alone, so if airfares are your only interest, read the literature before joining. Reductions on hotels are also available. Clubs include Discount Travel International (114 Forrest Ave., Suite 203, Narberth, PA 19072, tel. 215/668-7184; $45 annually, single or family), Moment's Notice (425 Madison Ave., New York, NY 10017, tel. 212/486-0503; $45 annually, single or family), Travelers Advantage (CUC Travel Service, 49 Music Sq. W, Nashville, TN 37203, tel. 800/548-1116; $49 annually, single or family); and Worldwide Discount Travel Club (1674 Meridian Ave., Miami Beach, FL 33139, tel. 305/534-2082; $50 annually for family, $40 single).

Rail Passes

For those planning on doing a lot of traveling by train, rail passes can be a bargain. They allow unlimited travel within a given period of time and they usually come in versions for first- and second-class travel. They are generally available only to foreign travelers visiting a country and sometimes must be bought before you leave the U.S. Their validity begins on the first day of their use, which must be validated by a station official.

Italy has three rail passes, which can be bought at main train stations in Italy or in the U.S. through travel agents or the official representative for Italian State Railways, CIT Tours Corp. (342 Madison Ave., Room 207, New York, NY 10173, tel. 212/697-2100 or 800/248-8687 for orders). In the past, you saved money buying the passes in the U.S., but at present time, with an improved rate of exchange for the dollar, it was more economical to buy them in Italy. A few lire prices are given for purposes of comparison.

The Italian Tourist Ticket (BTLC) – the country's basic unlimited-travel rail pass – is an excellent value because it covers the entire system, including Sicily. The pass is available in a first-class version for periods of 8 days ($236 in U.S./269,000 lire in Italy), 15 days ($294), 21 days ($340), and 30 days ($406). For second-class travel, the prices for the same periods are $162 (or 179,000 lire), $200, $230, and $274.

A variation on the BTLC is the Italy Flexi Railcard, which entitles purchasers to four days of travel within nine days of validity; eight days of travel within 21 days; and 12 days of travel within 30 days. Rates for the three types for first-class travel are $180 in the U.S. (220,000 lire in Italy), $260, and $324; for second-class travel, $126 (148,000 lire), $174, and $220.

The third Italian rail pass is the Italian Kilometric Ticket, which is a good bet for families. It is valid for 20 train trips, up to a total of 3,000 kilometres (1,875 miles) of train travel, within a two-month period, and it can be used by up to five people (related or not). Children under 12 are counted for only half the distance, those under 4 travel free. A first-class ticket costs $274 and a second-class ticket $166 if bought in the U.S., or 312,000 lire and 183,000 lire if bought at main train stations and CIT offices in Italy.

The EurailPass, valid for unlimited first-class train travel through 17 countries, including Italy, is an excellent value if you plan on traveling around the Continent. The ticket is available for periods of 15 days ($460), 21 days ($598), one month ($728), two months ($998), and three months ($1,260). A Eurail Saverpass, a 15-day pass good for two or more people traveling together, costs $390 per person (between April 1 and September 30, you need a minimum of three in your group to get this discount). For those under 26 (on the first day of travel), there is the Eurail Youthpass, for one or two months' unlimited second-class train travel at $508 and $698.

The Eurail Flexipass is another option. It provides 5 days ($298), 10 days ($496), or 15 days ($676) of first-class travel over a 60-day period of validity. There is also a Eurail Youth Flexipass, good for 5 days ($220), 10 days ($348), or 15 days ($479) of second-class travel over the same 60-day period. Ask also about the EurailDrive Pass, which lets you combine four days of train travel with three days of car rental (through Hertz or Avis) at any time within a two-month period. Charges vary according to size of car, but two people traveling together can get the basic package for $298 per person.

The EurailPass is available only if you live outside Europe or North Africa, and it *must* be bought from an authorized agent *before* you leave for Europe. Apply through your travel agent, through CIT Tours (see above), or through Rail Europe (230 Westchester Ave., White Plains, NY 10604, tel. 800/4-EURAIL or 800/345-1990, fax 800/4321-FAX; or 2087 Dundas East, Suite 105, Mississauga, Ontario L4X 1M2, tel. 416/602-4195), a one-stop shopping center for European rail tickets or passes. CIT also sells point-to-point tickets for travel in Italy and elsewhere in Western Europe, but cannot make seat reservations.

Once in Italy, travelers under 26 who have not invested in any of the above passes should inquire about the Carta Verde, or Green card (40,000 lire for one year), which entitles the holder to a 20% discount on all first- and second-class tickets. Travelers over 60 are entitled to similar discounts with the Carta d'Argento. Those under 26 should also inquire about discount travel fares under the Billet International Jeune (BIJ) scheme. The special one-trip tickets are sold by EuroTrain International (no connection with EurailPass) at its offices in various European cities, including Rome, and by travel agents, mainline rail stations, and youth travel specialists (*see* Centro Turistico Studentesco, *below*).

Student and Youth Travel

Travel Agencies The Centro Turistico Studentesco (CTS) is a student and youth travel agency with offices in major Italian cities; CTS helps its clients find low-cost accommodations and bargain fares for travel in Italy and elsewhere and also serves as a meeting place for young people of all nations. The main Rome office is at Via Genova 16, near the railroad station (tel. 06/467-9271). CTS is also the Rome representative for EuroTrain International.

The foremost U.S. student travel agency is Council Travel, a subsidiary of the nonprofit Council on International Educational Exchange. It specializes in low-cost travel arrangements, is the exclusive U.S. agent for several discount cards, and, with its sister CIEE subsidiary, Council Charter, is a source of airfare bargains. The Council Charter brochure and CIEE's twice-yearly *Student Travels* magazine, which details its programs, are available at the Council Travel office at CIEE headquarters (205 E. 42nd St., New York, NY 10017, tel. 212/661-1450) and at 37 branches in college towns nationwide (free in person, $1 by mail). The Educational Travel Center (ETC, 438 N. Francis St., Madison, WI 53703, tel. 608/256-5551) also offers low-cost rail passes, domestic and international airline tickets (mostly for flights departing from Chicago), and other budgetwise travel arrangements. Other travel agencies catering to students include Travel Management International (TMI, 18 Prescott St., Suite 4, Cambridge, MA 02138, tel. 617/661-8187) and Travel Cuts (187 College St., Toronto, Ont. M5T 1P7, tel. 416/979-2406).

Discount Cards For discounts on transportation and on museum and attractions admissions, buy the International Student Identity Card (ISIC) if you're a bona fide student, or the International Youth Card (IYC) if you're under 26. In the United States the ISIC and IYC cards cost $15 each and include basic travel accident and sickness coverage. Apply to CIEE (*see above*, tel 212/661-1414; the application is in *Student Travels*).

In Italy

Hotel prices *in this guide are indicated by stars and refer to the cost of a double room with bathroom (where available). Remember that hotels will often have rooms without bathrooms at cheaper rates.*

No star	up to L25,000		
☆	L25–50,000	☆☆☆	L70–100,000
☆☆	L50–70,000	☆☆☆☆	over L100,000

Finding a place to stay is potentially the biggest problem you'll face in Italy. In the major cities of Rome, Florence and Venice hotels are heavily booked for the best part of the year and the major tourist resorts are full most of the summer.

When booking or looking for a room, a single room is *una camera singola* and a room with a double bed *una camera matrimoniale*; for a room with twin beds ask for *una camera doppia*. At the reception remember that you will by no means be offered the cheapest room of the type you have asked for. If necessary ask for something cheaper (*meno caro*), or without a bathroom *(senza bagno)* and the chances are you will be tucked away in a perfectly good, cheap room at the top of the hotel.

Tourist Offices If you're arriving bedless in big cities, especially in peak season, try to arrive in the morning. By late afternoon the empty rooms will have been snapped up. In most cities it's worth making for the station's tourist office. These usually operate a room-finding service and will book you into hotels for a small fee. The offices are in daily contact with hotels and know what rooms are available. They may also have lists of rooms in private houses, places which are often hard to find simply by walking around the streets. Queues for the service, however, can be horrendous, and obviously you have no chance of looking at the room or the area in which the hotel is located. Hotels may also be out of town.

The best overall option is to visit the local *tourist office*, usually in the town center and quieter than the station office. These go under a variety of names – *Azienda Autonoma di Soggiorno e Turismo* (AAST), which is the basic tourist office in most towns, also sometimes called the *Azienda Promozione di Turismo* (APT). A *Pro Loco* is a more modest office in small towns and villages. The *Ente Provinciale per il Turismo* (EPT) is the main tourist office for each province within a region. Each of these has lists of hotels, rooms and prices within their town or district. Some, but not all, operate a booking service. They're also responsible for regulating prices and hotels, so if you have any complaints, take them to the tourist office.

Hotels

Hotels in Italy, known as *alberghi* or *pensioni* – these days there's little difference between the two – are strictly regulated and divided into **five categories** (one-star the cheapest, five star the most expensive).

Prices vary within a category depending on the location – doubles in a Sicilian one star hotel may start under L20,000; in Florence you may not find anything for less than L35,000. Generally the more rural the area, or the further south, the cheaper the hotel. Facilities often don't change much between two and three stars – the higher rated hotels simply have a lobby, or a telephone in each room. The average for a two star double is about L55,000, for a three star equivalent about L70,000.

All prices are set by the local tourist board, and by law the price for *each* room in a hotel must be displayed on the back of the door; omissions or discrepancies should be reported to the tourist office. High and low season rates, if applicable, are also shown, as is the price of breakfast – which is usually cheaper outside the hotel. Occasionally hotels include breakfast on the bill whether you take it or not. In popular areas – sea, lakes and mountains – they're also allowed to insist on half board (*mezza pensione*) or full board (*pensione completa*). In cheaper hotels you sometimes have to pay a supplement for a shower – check on arrival with reception. Air conditioning, too, sometimes attracts a surcharge.

Stars and price, of course, bear no relation to charm, location or atmosphere, so use them only for a rough idea of what facilities to expect. Recommendations in the text usually give a brief summary of what is in store. For a single expect to pay about two-thirds of a double – and watch that you are not charged a double room rate if as a single you are put in a double. To add a third bed to a double costs an extra 35 per cent. Many hotels offer discounts for children.

As a general rule, and especially if you are traveling on a tight budget, establish the full price of a room before accepting it. The checklist is – the price of the room; with or without private bathroom; whether it includes all taxes; whether breakfast is included; whether a bath or shower is included; and whether three or four people can use a double room (and the extra to be paid). Also confirm the check-out time on the following day to avoid paying for another night's accommodation.

Youth Hostels

There are 52 youth hostels (*alberghi per la gioventù*) and numerous unofficial student hostels dotted over Italy. They vary greatly in quality, but **prices** tend to be around L10–15,000 for a single-sex dormitory bed. This isn't always a saving on a cheap double room in a hotel, which won't have the hostels' curfew restrictions (most close from 10 am to 4 pm and at midnight). Hostels are also usually some way out of town, so in choosing a hostel allow for the cost, time and inconvenience involved in traveling to and from it. For single travelers, however, they're probably the cheapest option overall. Kitchen, laundry and washing facilities can cut costs further.

An International Youth Hostel Federation (IYHF) membership card is the key to more than 5,300 hostel locations in 59 countries. Contrary to what might be assumed, given the names of the organizations running them, IYHF-affiliated hostels are open to guests of all ages (an exception is some German hostels, for those up to 26 years of age only). Sleeping quarters are sex-segregated, largely dormitory-style, but there are some rooms for families; rates are from $7 to $20 a night per person. Membership is available in the United States through American Youth Hostels (AYH, 733 15th St. NW, Washington, DC 20005, tel. 202/783-6161), the American link in the worldwide chain, and costs $25 for adults 18-54, $10 for those under 18, $15 for those 55 and over, and $35 for families. Volume 1 of the two-volume *Guide to Budget Accommodation* lists hostels in Europe and the Mediterranean, including Italy ($13.95, including postage). IYHF membership is available in Canada through the Canadian Hostelling Association (CHA, 1600 James Naismith Dr., Suite 608, Gloucester, Ont. K1B 5N4, tel. 613/748-5638) for $26.75.

During July and August try to book a hostel place in advance, either by calling at least 15 days in advance, or by using the **International Multi-Lingual Booking Cards**. These cost about 30 cents and are available from youth hostels or the YHA head office. You post the cards with an International Reply Coupon (available from post offices). Reserved beds are held until 6pm. Youth hostels are listed in the text, but for full details buy the IYHF *Handbook* (available in bookshops and from YHA head office).

Unofficial hostels have fewer restrictions – open to all, no curfews, mixed rooms – but prices are generally higher and facilities poorer.

Camping

Although it has the 'great outdoors' ring of romance about it, camping in Italy is neither a practical nor particularly cheap way of seeing the country. Official campsites are expensive. They're also far removed from the romantic notion of camping, often being swamped by excitable adolescents or Italian families in huge tents with all mod cons. Crowds, cars and queues for the showers are all disincentives to a night under canvas. Seafront campsites – the most common in Italy – can also be booked solid in the peak months. City campsites are invariably miles from the city center and difficult to reach.

Prices range from L3,000 to 7,000 daily per person, plus L4,000 to 7,000 for each RV or tent and another L5,000 per vehicle.

Tourist offices have details on local sites. Full lists are also published in the annually updated *TCI Campeggi e Villaggi Turistici*, widely available in Italy (price L30,000).

Italy's countryside, however, offers plenty of opportunities for free camping, a memorable way of seeing the country. Travel with a good light tent, small stove, utensils, thin insulating mat and sleeping bag. Be discreet, don't light fires and where possible ask landowners for permission to stay on their land – the chances are you'll be made welcome.

Agriturismo

Agriturismo is a cheap and increasingly popular way of staying in farmhouse or other rural accommodation. As they're stuck out in the country, however, they're of limited use to rail travelers. Tourist offices carry details of local options. Most offer self-contained accommodation by the week, though it's usually also possible to turn up and take a room for the night. Prices can be as low as L5,000 nightly, and there's usually the chance to enjoy home cooking, farm produce and activities like swimming, fishing or horseback-riding.

Refuges

Several routes in the text take you into the mountains, and superb walking country is sometimes within a short bus ride from the stations. Most national parks and areas in the Alps and Dolomites have a system of refuges, cheap, friendly and often dramatically situated places to spend the night. Most open from mid-June to mid-September, and a few at weekends during the rest of the year. All offer food – whether you're staying or not – and dormitory beds at around L15,000 a night. None will turn you away, which means in summer you may end up sleeping on the floor in the more popular places. A sleeping bag helps, but sheets and blankets are provided if you need them. Tourist offices in mountain areas carry full details of the refuges.

Eating

The differences between types of Italian restaurants are becoming increasingly blurred. The text aims to recommend non-touristy, traditional places where the locals eat. It offers a choice in cities, but in smaller towns nails its colors to the mast and plumps for the best place (on the basis that you're probably not going to spend several days in one place). If you find somewhere you like, it pays dividends to return there – this is especially true of a country like Italy; you'll almost certainly receive a warmer welcome and better service.

Common sense will take you far if you're trying to choose a place. Check prices and see if the restaurant's full of Italians. Watch out for tourist menus – the food's usually poor and the portions small. Lunch isn't the blow-out it used to be (though pretty much everything in the country still stops from 1 to 4 pm). Most Italians eat dinner at home around 8 pm, or 8.30 pm if they're eating out. As for **types of restaurant**, a *pizzeria* sells pizzas, but may also offer a limited range of main dishes. A *trattoria* is a restaurant by any other name. If anything, it may be a touch more basic than somewhere styling itself a *ristorante*. Standards, ambience and prices can run the gamut in both categories. A *rosticceria* tends to serve more meat dishes. A *birreria* is as informal as a *pizzeria*, usually attracting a young clientele and selling basic dishes and snacks (and beer).

Prices naturally vary according to what you eat. In a pizzeria you should be able to have a pizza, salad and beer for around L10,000–15,000. Elsewhere, the recommendations in the text concentrate on middle-ground places where a full meal should cost around L30,000. At lunch (*pranzo*) or dinner (*cena*) this would include a starter (*antipasto*), pasta or soup (*il primo*), main meat or fish course (*il secondo*), with salad (*insalata*) or vegetables (*contorni*), and a dessert (*dolce* or *frutta*). A plate of pasta on its own, of course, would come in at much less (anything from L5,000–8,000). (And unless you're in a smart restaurant don't be scared to order one dish – many Italians these days don't order all the courses.)

On the bill (*il conto*) expect to pay *pane e coperto*, a cover charge (usually L1,500–L3,000) and possible service (*servizio*). If you get a scrap of paper as a bill and feel you're being ripped off, ask for *una ricevuta* – restaurants are breaking the law if they don't give you one.

Don't forget **snacks and breakfasts**. Italian breakfast (*la prima colazione*) is a cappuccino (around L1,200) and a sweet croissant type roll known as *una brioche* or *un cornetto* (L1,000). Hotels often offer breakfast, but they're always cheaper and more fun in bars. Most bars offer sandwiches (*tramezzini*) or rolls (*panini*). Most cost L2,000–3,000. Food shops (*alimentari*) will often make you up a roll if you buy ham or cheese from them (some sell bread too; otherwise buy rolls from the bakers (*un panificio*). Most towns also have a place selling pizza by weight or by the slice (*pizza taglia*). An *etto*, or 100 g, is the basic weight when ordering food in shops. Fast food, for better or worse, is also a feature of many larger towns.

If you're after **ice cream** (*gelato*), aim for a specialist *gelateria* (in preference to bars). The best is usually easy to find – just follow the crowds (or the schoolkids). Many Italians round off a meal or their evening stroll (*la passeggiata*) with an ice cream. The choice is usually a cone (*un cono*) or a cup (*una coppa*). You specify the amount by price (rising in L500 bands usually from L1,500).

Remember **in bars** it's almost always cheaper to stand up. Sitting involves waiter service (though once you've paid to sit you can stay put for hours if you want to). If standing, remember to pay for what you want first at the *cassa* (cash-desk) and then take the bill (*lo scontrino*) to the bar and repeat your order. A L100 or L200 coin slapped down as a tip often gets you prompt service.

If you're not having an *espresso* (simply *un caffè* in Italian), other **drinks** include beer (*una birra*), always cheaper on tap (*una birra alla spina*); fruit juice (*un succo di frutta*); milk (*latte*), though fresh milk is still not common in much of Italy, especially in the south; tea (*tè*), either with milk (*al latte*) or lemon (*al limone*) – remember to specify which; freshly-squeezed juice (*una spremuta*); mineral water (*acqua minerale*), either fizzy (*gassata*) or still (*non gassata*). Coke, Fanta and the like are all known by their brand names. Lemon Soda is increasingly popular. Wine, of course, is *vino*, either red (*rosso*) or white (*bianco*). You don't have to buy it by the bottle – in restaurants the house wine (usually perfectly okay, especially in the south) is often available in 25 cl jugs (*un quartino*) or in half litres (*mezzo litro*).

Museums, Galleries and Archaeological Sites

Admission prices for museums, galleries and sites are currently being increased across the board in Italy and are not given in the text. At present in small town galleries and minor archaeological sites you can expect to pay about L3,000. At more major museums such as the Uffizi in Florence, or the sites such as the Forum in Rome, the more usual price is L8,000–10,000. Remember that there are often reductions for students (an ISIC card is required) and for those under 12 and over 60. A handful of museums (including the Uffizi and Vatican museums) are free on a couple of specified weekends each month.

The Train Network

The Italian State Railway revolves around six main lines. Between them they link Italy's major cities and provide the arteries from which the network's spurs and branch lines operate. Trains often run the entire length of one or more of these lines – from Turin to Palermo, for example – allowing you to cover huge distances without changing.

- *Turin–Milan–Verona–Venice–Trieste*
- *Turin–Genoa–Pisa–Rome*
- *Milan–Bologna–Ancona–Foggia–Bari–Lecce*
- *Milan–Bologna–Florence–Rome*
- *Bolzano–Verona–Bologna–Florence–Rome*
- *Rome–Naples–Reggio di Calabria–Palermo*

Trains

The Italian state network has seven categories of train: *Super Rapido (R)*, *Rapido* (R), *Intercity* (IC), *Eurocity* (EC) *Espressi, Diretti*, and *Locali*. As well as these designations every train has a number: many also have a name. Timetables and station Tannoy announcements give all this information. Check or listen carefully as the type of train determines not only how long a journey will take but also whether you'll need to reserve seats or pay a ticket supplement (see under 'Tickets' below).

Super Rapido are the fastest trains, stopping only at the most major cities, but are used on only a handful of routes. Ultra modern high speed trains known as the ETR 450 operate most of the services, though the best known is the fast *Pendolino*, the leaning train which runs twice daily between Rome and Milan. Seating is first class only, with free meals, magazines, and an airline type approach to service. Tickets cost about 30 per cent more than the standard first class fare, and reservation of seats, for which there is a charge (currently L2,500) is obligatory. Trying to board the train without a booking is very difficult.

Rapido trains are more numerous, stop at slightly more stations en route, and may offer second as well as first class seating. Reservations are obligatory but are free, and ticket collectors are more likely to let you board a train without them if there is room.

Intercity trains are increasingly common on the major routes. These trains are the Italian railway's answer to its reputation for appalling time-keeping. Lesser trains give way to them, often held in sidings for hours on end, and you can claim refunds if the service runs late. Most of the rolling stock for both first- and second

The Italian Railway Network

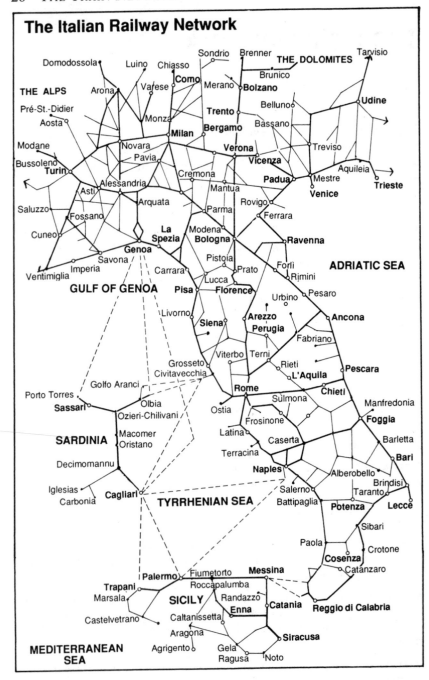

class is new, and there's usually a restaurant service. Stops are restricted to the largest towns and cities. In the majority of cases, they provide an excellent service and are totally reliable.

Eurocity are simply *Intercity* trains which cross into neighboring countries. Supplements are payable for Italian sections of the journey but are waived if you have a through ticket to a destination outside Italy.

Espressi are the best of the non-supplement trains. They have first and second class compartments, run on most major routes, often parallel to *Intercity* trains, but stop at more stations. Although they're often timetabled to take the same time as *Intercity* services over some routes, in practice they are more prone to delays. Ironically, however, as more people plump for the *Intercity* services, the *Espressi* have become less crowded on the main lines. If you're on a budget and time isn't tight, these can be the best way to travel between the big cities.

Diretti, a slower version of the *Espressi*, are not direct at all and usually stop at all but the smallest stations. Trains can be excruciatingly slow and are prone to delays.

Locali, also known as *accelerati*, stop at every station, and if you're not in the mood, or are in any sort of hurry, they can be a nightmarish way to travel. Expect trips to take twice as long as faster trains over the same route and always allow for delays. At the same time, however, the often charming stations en route, and the antiquated rolling stock usually consigned to the lowly *locali*, can make the journey a pleasure if you're not traveling simply to arrive. They're great for soaking up scenery, and you'll probably also sample a more rustic slice of Italian life into the bargain. In the south, including Sicily and Sardinia, they form the majority of services.

Couchettes and Night Trains

An advantage of traveling by night is that it solves the accommodation problem and effectively adds a day to your journey by allowing you to arrive first thing in the morning. This can be important if you are on a budget or want to exploit a rail pass to the maximum. Journeys can be extremely long, with some of the longest routes served by a multitude of night services. Nationwide there are in the region of one hundred departures daily with sleeping accommodation. These allow you to make some long trips without stirring – direct from Venice to Palermo, or from Turin to Lecce, for example. In addition there are regular night trains to numerous international destinations.

But the chief disadvantage to night travel is that you miss the scenery en route. Night trains also travel slower than the daytime equivalents and you take longer to reach your destination. Though you may gain a day, you probably won't have a terribly good night's sleep. Earplugs are a priceless investment.

When you're eventually tempted – or forced – to travel overnight on an Italian train there are four ways of passing the night: in an ordinary seat; in a pull-down seat which allows you to stretch out; in a couchette; in a sleeper.

The Seat

These do not recline and are free, but unless you're a great sleeper, or have become a practiced seat sleeper, you arrive with a stiff neck and in no state to face the following day. A small inflatable neck cushion might make all the difference here. Carriages can be very crowded, with a lot of coming and going through the night. At least try to reserve a seat when buying your ticket. Double check on timetables that your train has these ordinary seats; many overnight trains have sleeper and couchette coaches only, or carry only first class seating. If you board a train in the middle of the night, you may have to incur the wrath of sleepers in several compartments before finding a seat. As ever, don't be intimidated, but ask if there is a place (*c'è un posto?*) and watch out for bags occupying empty seats.

The Pull-down Seat

Free, and a godsend when you find them and when the compartment is more or less empty. In older rolling stock – the familiar maroon carriages with brown vinyl seats – opposing seats pull out to meet in the middle and allow you to stretch out, offering a better chance of sleep. With all six seats pulled out the compartment becomes one large bed. You'll be lucky to achieve this, however, though wily Italians in pairs do it, and then pull the curtains, turn out the light and jam the door. If seats are hard to find, have the courage to open a few doors and make room for yourself.

Couchettes

A cheap and convenient way to travel by night in a degree of comfort, couchettes (*cuccette* in Italian) are seats by day but pull down to provide proper berths during the night. Most Italian couchettes are rough and ready by the standards of French and German equivalents, though as elsewhere on the network, the introduction of new rolling stock is quickly raising standards.

Couchettes must be booked in advance (see page 34). The current price is L16,800 for both first and second class couchettes, but you must, of course, also have a normal, valid ticket for the journey in addition to the couchette voucher. In theory you can reserve a place up until five hours before the train leaves, but in practice try to book at least the day before, and in high summer, weekends and before public holidays two or three days in advance. Only quite rarely can you buy a couchette on the train itself (see below).

Each voucher shows the time, number and route of the train, the number of the carriage containing your couchette, and the number of your couchette within the carriage. It also states whether the compartment is non-smoking – though smoking is banned in all compartments once seats are pulled down to sleep. It may also say whether the berth is at the top, middle or bottom; if not, window seats are top berths, corridor seats bottom berths. Sometimes you may be able to try and request one or the other. Top berths are less claustrophobic, less stuffy and offer a little more privacy. Bottom berths have less room because of the arm rests at either end.

There are six berths to a compartment in second class, four in first class. None are segregated, but for women traveling alone this is rarely a problem as the compartments are usually full. Where they are not, the attendant responsible for each carriage usually tries to put women together. If you have doubts about the person or people in your compartment, and there's room elsewhere, the attendant, who will have checked your ticket on arrival, will usually move you elsewhere on request. Women alone should avoid compartments with a male majority and look for families or other women traveling together.

If the train's leaving late, the seats may already be pulled down. For your L16,800 each berth has a pillow, blanket and disposable sheet. There is also an individual reading light. Use the toilets or washroom at the end of each carriage for washing up. It's obviously a good idea to have the things you need for the night, plus music, books and so forth, in a separate bag so that you can stash away your main bag or pack. Always carry your valuables with you, however, and keep them under very close scrutiny. Berths also have a small personal luggage rack – not the place for money and the like.

After departure, the attendant will come and take your tickets. If you're crossing a national border, don't be alarmed when he also takes your passport. This is so you don't have to be disturbed during the night by customs and frontier officials, although checks are still sometimes made. For some peculiar reason it is standard practice for attendants to take passports even for internal journeys. Crossing borders you may also have to fill in a customs declaration.

Buying a couchette on the train is possible, though don't rely on it. Your best chance is if you're picking up the train at its station of departure. Approach the attendants of one or more carriages and let them know you are looking for a couchette (*C'è per caso una cuccetta libera? –* Is there by any chance a spare couchette?). During busy times the chances are that all will be booked. Remember that officials are likely to be busy, so be patient, try all the carriages, smile a lot and be persistent. If you hang around, attendants will see that you mean business, will remember your face and so be more likely to offer you a couchette if there's one available. If he doesn't dismiss you out of hand, the attendant will tell you to wait until immediately before the train leaves. If, as frequently happens, people haven't arrived to take up their place – L16,800 isn't a fortune for some people to throw away – it can safely be given to you. Have cash to pay for the seat as attendants generally won't mess about with traveler's checks or credit cards.

If you're boarding partway through a journey you have a more hectic job of running up and down the carriages and quizzing attendants, although by this time they have a better idea of the space available and the number of non-arrivals. Once you're on the train, it's also obviously harder for them to turn you down.

Sleepers

This is a dream of a way to travel if you can afford to. Italy's *Wagons-Lits* sleeping cars are much more comfortable and much more expensive than couchettes. Eighteen internal daily services have sleepers. They come first and second class, and again you must hold a valid ordinary ticket as well as the sleeping car voucher but they must be of the same class. You can also pay extra for a single compartment to yourself; otherwise there are two berths per compartment. Prices vary from $30 to $75, depending on whether you're sharing and the distance you're covering.

Reservations must be made in advance, and attendants take more of a dim view of people trying to buy a sleeper on the train than when they're chasing a couchette. Vouchers are marked with train time, number and route, carriage and sleeper number, and the procedure for boarding is the same as for couchettes.

Safety on Trains

Although hair-raising events certainly happen, most of the horror stories that circulate about people being drugged and robbed in their sleep are either apocryphal or exaggerated. The majority of night journeys are completely uneventful. As basic precautions in any situation, however, you should ensure the door to the compartment is locked from the inside once everyone is bedded down. Keep money and valuables – literally – close to your chest in a pouch or money belt. Don't flash money and cameras around. Be more wary if you have only a seat rather than a couchette, especially of people who stumble 'accidentally' into your compartment. Don't accept food or drink if you're at all unsure of a person. Remember that in a couchette you can usually ask the attendant to move you if you are worried.

Food and Drink on Night Trains

Intercity and *Eurocity* night trains usually have a buffet car, and occasionally a restaurant car. The more prestigious international sleepers like the *Simplon Express* and *Palatino* to Paris can usually be relied on to have refreshment cars. All close around midnight and may have been removed from the train altogether by the time you wake up next morning. Prices, of course, are high, and food of variable standard. To find out if your train has a buffet car, check the small print on the platform timetable.

The majority of night trains have no food or drink on sale at all. Occasionally there may be a **trolley service**, but this usually comes round only once in the course of the evening, and not at all in the morning when you're desperate for coffee and most in need of it. Prices are high and quality low. Buy all your picnic provisions before boarding the train, preferably at a supermarket rather than from the expensive platform sellers.

Night trains become stuffy and dry – nightmarishly so in high summer in the south – and it's essential to carry a bottle of water with you. Water in the toilets and washrooms isn't drinkable (*acqua non potabile*), but most stations have a tap or drinking fountain. Wine is great for helping you sleep, but hangover effects seem doubly worse after a night on a train. As a last resort buy from the children who board trains at main stations selling *panini* and soft drinks. The prices are vastly inflated but they're prices they know many unprepared unfortunates will be more than willing to pay.

International Services

Once a week two battered green carriages belonging to the old Soviet Union, complete with samovars and dusty lace curtains, are hitched up to an express train that leaves Rome for Moscow by way of Venice, Vienna and Warsaw. While other international train departures from Italy are less far-reaching, it's still possible to take a direct train from many Italian cities to almost any country in Europe. Italy has long prospered from its position between northern Europe and the Mediterranean, and as a corridor from western Europe to the Balkans and the near East. Rail travelers still benefit from this position at the crossroads of Europe. With a EurailPass or its equivalent, Italy is the ideal country for a period of in-depth exploration before you move on to the easily reached countries nearby.

Destinations

To the obvious onwards destinations of France, Switzerland, Germany, Austria, the former Yugoslavia, Greece and Spain – all served by through trains from Italy – can now be added the eastern European countries of Hungary, Czech Republic, Romania and Poland, all of which can be reached with just one change from Venice and northeast Italy. You need not, however, feel that foreign jaunts from Italy require a special pass or plenty of time. You can, for example, leave Rome in the morning and be in Vienna early the same evening; Geneva is just four hours from Milan, Paris six hours from Turin, Monaco and the south of France a few minutes over the border, Innsbruck four hours from Verona, Munich six hours from Verona and so on.

Planning

For detailed planning *Thomas Cook's European Timetable* is the best source of information. The *Pozzorario* also gives all the international trains leaving Italy, though the end destinations are usually buried in the small print at the bottom of each timetable (see pages 37–8). Mainline stations sometimes have individual leaflets on specific routes, and station platform timetables identify international departures (in red type).

Remember that **tickets** for international departures are usually sold from a separate window at the ticket office. If possible make a **reservation**, especially in summer or near public holidays, and book a couchette in good time. **Check** to see if trains have seating carriages; many are couchette and sleeper accommodation only.

Train Splitting

Before boarding a train for another country check the **destination board** on the side of each carriage. Trains on European routes make complicated journeys and often contain a hotchpotch of rolling stock belonging to several countries. Trains are split up as they leave Italy and at key stations en route with perhaps only one or two carriages making the through journey to the timetable's end destination. Be sure you're in the right compartment and stay in it religiously. Nothing is worse than strolling down a train during a long wait at a station to find that your carriage has been shunted off to be hitched on to another train. Carriages carry stickers or cards inside as well as the boards outside. All have the starting destination of the carriage, the main stops en route and the end destination of the *carriage*, not necessarily of the train.

Tickets and Rail Passes

The ticketing system on Italian railways is straightforward, unburdened by the savers, super-savers and off-peak periods that befuddle the British Rail network. The only potential complication is the supplements payable on certain fast trains. On top of the standard **single** and **return** tickets (first and second class) there are two specific **rail passes**, the travel-at-will *Biglietto Turistico Libera Circolazione* (BTLC) and the less flexible *Biglietto Chilometrico*. Certain reductions are also available for **families** traveling together.

Fares

Tickets are some of the cheapest in Europe. Prices are determined according to distance traveled. The FS timetable and the *Pozzorario* (see pages 42 and 44) give the distance in kilometers between stations on every route, so by using the price bands included with the timetables – and in the state tourist board's annual *Traveller's Handbook* – it's easy to work out in advance how much your journey is going to cost. As a rough idea of the figures involved, 100 kilometer journeys currently cost about L7,500; 200 kilometers L15,000; 300 kilometers for L22,000; 400 kilometers for L30,000; and 500 kilometers for L37,500. **First class** tickets are roughly two thirds as expensive again as these second class fares. **Reductions** of 50 per cent on first and second class tickets are available for children under 12 and for people over 65.

For journeys up to 100 kilometers, prices rise in bands every 10 kilometers; between 100 and 350 kilometers the bands are 25 kilometers; from 350 to 1,000 kilometers the bands are 50 kilometers; over 1,000 kilometers prices rise in bands every 100 kilometers.

As an example the second class single fare for the 316 kilometer (200 mile) journey from Rome to Florence is L22,000. First class between Rome to Florence costs L37,400. At the other extreme, the second class single from Turin to Palermo in Sicily, one of the longest direct journeys you're likely to make – a distance of 1,581 kilometres (988 miles) – is currently around L78,700; the first class fare is L133,800.

Reductions are available for people under 26 years, but you must buy a Green Card pass, a *Carta Verde*, from any main station. This gives a 30 per cent discount on tickets (20 per cent in peak season – Easter and Christmas holidays and June 25 – August 31). Senior citizens (men over 65, women over 60) can buy a Silver Card, a *Carta d'Argento*, for L10,000, bringing them a 30 per cent concession on fares.

Single and Return Tickets

A standard, **one-way ticket** in Italian is *un biglietto andata*; a **return ticket** is *un biglietto andata e ritorno*. First class is *prima classe*, second class *seconda classe*.

Thus for a second class return ticket to Rome you'd ask for *un biglietto andata e ritorno a Roma, seconda classe.*

Day and Period Return Tickets

Generally return tickets (*andata e ritorno*) are simply the price of two single tickets for each leg of the journey. The only exceptions are for **day return** and **three day return tickets**, both of which are of very restricted availability.

Day returns are only available for round journeys of 250 kilometers or under – useful for short excursions from a city, but of limited value for any substantial outing. Savings anyway are fairly modest – a mere 15 per cent. The only other saving – again of 15 per cent – is on a **three day return** for journeys over 250 kilometers and up to a maximum of 850 kilometres. Their obvious virtue is for weekend trips leaving on Friday and returning on Sunday.

Assuming your journey falls within these parameters, you should make clear, if you can, when buying your ticket that you are returning the same day (*andata e ritorno per tornare oggi* – a return ticket to return today) or within three days (*andata e ritorno per tornare entro tre giorni*). The ticket office staff might assume the latter, not the former.

Ticket Supplements

Supplements of around 30 per cent above the price of a normal ticket are payable on *Super Rapido*, *Rapido* and *Intercity* trains in addition to the normal first and second class fares. After grumbles when the concept was introduced, Italians now appear more than willing to pay these extra charges, and *Intercity* trains – once rather exclusive – can be crowded at peak times on the main routes. You may pay your supplement and still find yourself standing in the corridor even in first class.

If you know you're catching an *Intercity*, ask for the supplement (*un supplemento rapido*), which is issued separately when you buy your ticket (though it looks just the same as a ticket). You can board the train without it, but you will be charged even more for the privilege of buying it on the train. Charges for children aged between 4 and 12 are half the adult supplement.

Like tickets, **the price of supplements** is calculated according to distance on the same kilometric banding. Supplements can add an appreciable amount to the price of a journey – usually about as third as much again. Current prices are also given in the FS timetable and *Pozzorario*. As an example the supplement on the L22,000 second class single from Rome to Florence is L7,500. First class supplements are about two thirds as much again – L12,800 on the L37,400 Rome to Florence first class fare. The second class supplement for the Turin to Palermo journey is L25,800, first class L43,800. Reductions of 50 per cent are available on supplements for children under 12 and for people over 65.

Validity of Tickets

Tickets for distances up to 250 kilometers are valid only on the day that they are issued – or for the single day of the date which appears on the ticket. Distances and dates are printed on each ticket. If you are making a short journey and buying a ticket in advance, it is therefore essential to specify when you wish to travel. Give the date or ask for a ticket to travel tomorrow (*per viaggiare domani*) or the day after tomorrow (*dopo domani*). If you have problems, write the date down.

Tickets gain an extra day's validity for every additional 200 kilometers over 250 kilometers up to a maximum of six days. Thus a journey of 400 kilometers is valid for two days, one of 600 for three days, and so on.

Reservations

A reservation (*una prenotazione*) may mean you have to queue all over again after buying your ticket – at big stations you make them at a separate ticket window – but on busy routes in summer they could save you hours standing in the corridor. The present fee is L2,500, and bookings can be made up to six hours before the departure of the train. To avoid the worst of the queues visit ticket offices at the quietest times (usually 3–5 pm) and not at weekends or lunchtimes when they're besieged. Be sure to specify first or second class, smoker (*fumatore*) or non-smoker (*non fumatore*) and window (*la finestra*) or door (*la porta*). Couchettes must also be reserved, usually at separate windows.

Most large towns and cities also have **travel agents** which act as ticket agents for the state railways – look for *Biglietti* FS stickers on the windows. Where relevant, these are listed in the text. In smaller centers these can be friendly, efficient places, but in cities they tend to be well known, and the queues – or more often than not, the scrum around the booking desk – can be more frustrating than queuing at the station. Most large towns and cities also now have **student travel agencies** which issue domestic and international tickets, reservations and couchettes for students and non students alike; CTS is the best known.

International Tickets

Italy occupies a nodal point on the European train network, and it's possible to take trains from several Italian cities directly to Spain, France, Switzerland, Holland, Austria, Germany, Greece and the former Yugoslavian republics. Standard first and second class tickets, as well as couchette and sleeper reservations, are easily available over the counter from most mainline stations – usually from a separate window in the ticket office. Some big city stations also have separate offices which deal specifically with BIJ and other reduced under 26 fares. If not, visit the nearest CTS student travel agents for discounted tickets. Addresses are given in the text.

You may have problems buying a through ticket to the United Kingdom – simply because the international window of smaller ticket offices may not have the boat coupon part of the ticket that is needed to cross the English Channel. If this is the case, grit your teeth and queue at one of the big city stations – Rome, Milan, Turin, Venice and Florence – or try CTS and main street travel agents.

Ferry Tickets

As well as operating a rail service, the Italian FS also runs a fleet of *traghetti* or **car ferries**. The two most important routes run from Civitavecchia, 45 minutes by rail north of Rome, to the ports of Golfo Aranci and Olbia Marittima on **Sardinia** where they link to the island's rail network. Although they're by no means the only company to operate services to the island, the FS fares are some of the cheapest available and have the advantage of tying in with connecting trains on both the island and the mainland. Through tickets incorporating rail and ferry passages are available and can be bought at travel agents and at separate ticket windows – usually marked *Traghetti FS* – at big city stations. To take a car across, or to be sure of a cabin in high season, you'll have to book months in advance, though as a foot passenger you should have few problems.

The other FS ferry routes are from Villa San Giovanni and Reggio di Calabria to Messina on **Sicily** – tickets bought to Sicilian destinations automatically include the crossing and you need worry no further – and from Piombino on the Tuscan coast to Portoferraio on the island of **Elba**. Like the trip to Sardinia, the Elba crossing becomes busy in summer.

Buying a Ticket

Unless you're buying Italian rail passes before you set off (see below) you'll probably buy tickets from the **ticket office**, or *biglietteria*, at the railway station. In most stations this is a straightforward undertaking. Where there are specific difficulties – usually at offices in the stations of the big cities – these are detailed in the relevant section of the text.

The most common problem is long, slow-moving **queues** – so allow plenty of time before your train is due to leave. Friday evening, Saturday morning and Sunday evening are notoriously bad at mainline stations. Aim to buy your tickets in the middle of the afternoon, when most Italians are taking a siesta, or in the evening for travel on the following day (and remember to specify the day you're traveling). You can also buy tickets on most trains, but you'll pay a surcharge for the privilege.

Payment for tickets must usually be in **cash**. Try not to tender large denomination notes as change is sometimes a problem in Italy. Visa, Access and other **credit cards** are only accepted at the larger stations, and often only at special windows with flashes showing that credit cards are accepted. Check all the windows before joining a queue to ensure cards are accepted.

Italian Rail Passes

Biglietto Turistico Libera Circolazione One of the most useful and most popular of the European rail passes, the *Biglietto Turistico Libera Circolazione* (BTLC) allows you unlimited travel on the whole Italian FS rail network for 8, 14, 21 or 30 days. It's possible to extend the validity of the passes on all but the 8-day ticket. They're available for first or second class travel, are valid even for *Rapido* trains, and free you from paying supplements on *Rapido, Intercity* and *Eurocity* services. Only InterRail or Eurail passes offer the same flexibility, but with these you still have to pay the supplements on fast trains. Remember you must have the pass stamped with the dates of validity at the first station of use. There's a reminder of this on the pass itself.

Buying BTLC passes is easy, though they're only available to tourists resident outside Italy. They can be obtained at major Italian railway stations (take your passport as proof of residence), from *Citalia* (or CIT) offices in Italy, and before you go from Cit Tours (tel. 800/CIT-TOUR).

Prices for second class passes are currently $152 for 8 days, $190 for 15 days, $220 for 21 days and $264 for 30 days. Children under 12 qualify for a discount of 50 per cent.

Biglietto Chilometrico The *Chilometrico* ticket is valid for 3,000 kilometres (1,875 miles) of travel spread over a maximum of twenty separate journeys within two months. The **current price** is $156 second class and $264 first class. There are no age restrictions, and it can be used by up to five adults at a time. Thus five people could travel together with one *chilometrico* ticket on a journey of 600 kilometers; two people could make ten journeys of 150 kilometers, and so on.

In practice, the ticket is only of real value if you're traveling in a group. Three thousand kilometers is a lot to use up on your own, and in most cases it's cheaper to invest in a BTLC ticket, or simply to buy ordinary tickets. Five standard second class singles for journeys of 600 kilometers each, for example, cost a total of L179,500 – just L22,000 more than the *Chilometrico*.

To buy the tickets call at any major Italian railway station, at the CIT offices of large towns and cities, or the *Citalia* Croydon office in the UK before you travel.

Flexi Card Pass Similar to the BTLC ticket, the *Flexi Card* offers 4 days unlimited travel within a 9 day period (second class, $116) 8 out of 21 days ($164) or 12 days out of 30 ($210). These fares include exemption from supplements.

Family Travel Passes If you intend to travel as a family for any significant length of time, it could be worth buying the **Rail Europe Family Card**, known in Italy as the *Carta Rail Europ F*. Valid on all Italian services, it allows a maximum of eight people discounts of up to 50 per cent for all adults bar one (who must pay full fare) and 75 per cent for children under 12. Bear in mind, though, that it may occasionally be cheaper or more convenient instead to use the *Chilometrico* ticket.

Italy also has its own family pass, the *Carta Famiglia*, which entitles families of at least four traveling together to claim discounts of 30 per cent on the full fare for adults, and 65 per cent for children under 12.

Stations

Italian railway stations range from the soaring, cathedral-like cavern of Milan – perhaps the greatest piece of railway architecture in Europe – to the tiny, sun-baked single platforms of rural Sicily. Much of your time may be spent negotiating these worlds-within-a-world. Arriving to the bustle and apparent chaos of places like Rome or Naples can also be initially intimidating, and this section aims to make the business of stations as straightforward as possible.

Ticket Offices

The **ticket office**, or *biglietteria*, of any station is usually obvious. If not, look for signs saying *Biglietti*. Remember that reservations, couchettes, ferry and international tickets are often purchased at a different ticket window – sometimes away from the main ticket office – so check the heading above each window and make sure that you are standing in the right queue. Offices are usually open daily from 5.30 am to midnight, longer at main line stations.

Train Information

Train information offices, marked with a blue letter **i**, are found in the largest stations. Some mid-size stations may have a separate window in the ticket office dealing with information queries. In the smallest stations the ticket office or station master or mistress can usually find time to help with information. Quizzing the staff in the ticket office of larger stations usually elicits a fairly sullen response. More and more mainline stations are installing high-tech automatic information units – either computer screens or so-called *Digiplan* machines – where you type in your query and wait for an on-screen answer or printed reply. Few of these, however, are ever working.

Station Timetables

When information offices are open they are invariably packed with people arranged in very disorderly queues. You can, however, usually find the information you need either in the current *Pozzorario* (see page 42) or the white FS timetables often pasted to rotating boards near the ticket office. In main stations these may cover the entire FS network. The lists in smaller stations are usually restricted to timetables for lines and stations in the immediate vicinity.

Most of the time, though, all you need are the large station timetables posted up on boards at various points on the platforms, waiting rooms and main foyers of stations. These show all the arrivals and departures from the station in question. There are usually separate sheets for arrivals, headed *Arrivi* (on a white background) and departures, headed *Partenze* (on a yellow background). It's vital, of course, to make sure you're looking at the right poster. This may sound obvious, but in the rush for a train it's often easy to glance at the wrong one.

Each major town and city entry in the main text includes an information section that deals briefly with the railway station. It contains its address and telephone number, and also how to walk or bus to the center of town and the main tourist office. Where appropriate it also deals with orientation; where to find tickets, train and tourist information; left luggage and lost property; eating and drinking; shops, services, foreign exchange, baths, showers and waiting rooms.

Time and Train Category Timetables run chronologically on a twenty-four hour clock from 0 hr to 24 hr. On the left of each timetable entry is the time of the train's arrival or departure. For *Super Rapido, Rapido, Intercity* and *Eurocity* trains the entire entry is marked in red type; for *Espressi, Diretti* and *Locali* the entries are in black type. Alongside the time of the train is its category (R = *Super Rapido*, R = *Rapido*, IC = *Intercity*, EC = *Eurocity*, Espr = *Espresso*, Dir = *Diretto*, Loc = *Locale*). If no category is given assume the train is a *locale*.

Train Number and Name With the category is the number of the train. With fast or long distance trains there may also be the name of the train, as in the 212– *Palatino*, the Rome–Paris night train, the 617–*Donatello*, the Turin–Florence express, the 791–*Freccia del Sud* (The Southern Arrow) and so on.

Always check any other symbols and small print on this section to see if reservations are necessary (*Prenotazione obbligatoria*); whether a supplement is payable (*supplemento rapido*) – remember they always are on R, R, IC and EC trains; whether, in rare circumstances, the train is first class only (*1cl.*); or, vitally important, whether the train carries couchettes and sleeping cars only (it'll say *Solo CC* and have a small bed symbol). It's all too easy to turn up with an ordinary ticket and find your train is a sleeper with no normal seating carriages. Unless there's room and you can buy a couchette from the conductor – usually only possible in the last few minutes before a train leaves – you'll not be allowed to board.

The Route To the right, alongside the time, name, number and category of the train, is the route of the train with the main stops and, in brackets, the time of arrival for each stop. These are not, however, necessarily the **only** stops the train makes en route. To the right of this list is the point of origin of the train (on arrivals timetables) and the end destination (on departure timetables).

Platform Number On the right of each entry is the number of the platform (*binario*, abbr. *Bin*) on which the train is arriving or from which it is leaving. In large stations in particular, this in practice is sometimes not the right platform. Late trains, operating difficulties and other such euphemisms mean platforms may be changed. Changes are announced, but if you can't follow the Italian, simply follow the crowds as they change platforms. Otherwise double check with the information screens at the head of each platform, or with the station's general departures and arrivals board.

Left Luggage

Italy's bigger stations have a manned **left luggage** depot, or *Deposito Bagaglio*, invaluable institutions that allow you to wander a city unencumbered, whether to look for a room, or get in a day's sightseeing before picking up a train in the evening. Most depots open around 5 am and close at midnight, although times can vary according to the season, especially in the more popular tourist cities such as Rome, Florence and Venice. Make sure you have everything you need out of your bags before leaving them; you'll not be able to remove them to dig out a forgotten toothbrush – at least, not without paying. It's unwise, of course, to leave valuables, tickets or passport in left luggage.

You're given a ticket for each bag which you hand in when reclaiming your luggage and you will be charged a fee for every piece of luggage, so don't expect to get away with tying innumerable plastic bags and holdalls to your backpack or suitcase to create a 'single' bag. You also pay by the day, so that even a portion of a day counts as a full 24 hours. Fees are roughly L1,500 per day per piece of luggage.

Stations may also have automatic **left luggage lockers**, sometimes in addition to the manned depots. Clearly these are the solution if your train leaves while the depot is closed. Lockers come in several sizes, so make sure your bag or pack is going to fit before paying to open the locker.

Lost Property

Most mainline stations have a lost property office, usually annexed to the left luggage depot. In smaller stations or in emergencies ask station staff and go to the top – it's always the best way to get results in any Italian public sector concern. The Station Master's Office is the place to make for. Look for signs saying *Capo Stazione* or similar. In theory he or she is responsible for trains rather than passengers, but as the head of the station they're the ones who can get things done in a real emergency.

Toilets, Washrooms and Waiting Rooms

Toilet facilities (*il bagno*) vary greatly; generally they are fairly atrocious, though in some city stations where they are looked after by attendants they can be spotless. Sometimes you're expected to pay, or leave a small tip in the bowl provided at the entrance. On small stations they may be off the bar, or, more usually, at the furthest end of the main platform; look for a blue WC symbol. It's always an idea to be equipped with your own supply of toilet paper (*carta igienica* in Italian).

Big city stations often have an institution known as an *Albergo Diurno*, or 'day hotel', a less sordid proposition than it sounds. They offer **bath and shower** facilities where you can buy or rent towels, soap and shampoo. Baths cost around $2.50, showers about $1.75.

Waiting rooms are usually soulless affairs and are sometimes divided into first and second class, though in practice no one takes much notice of the division.

Assistance

Big stations have **first aid posts** (*pronto soccorso*), as well as station staff listed as qualified first aiders. If you obviously need help, concerned Italians will usually take you to the appropriate spot. In emergencies or where there is no obvious help, head for the Station Master's office.

If you need them, members of one of Italy's two main police forces – the *polizia* or the semi-military (and more efficient) *carabinieri* – patrol on or near most larger stations. Bigger stations usually have a Catholic chapel on site, where at the worst you may be able to find a sympathetic ear.

Emergencies *Emergency telephone numbers:* **112** *for the police (Carabinieri);* **113** *for any emergency service;* **115** *for the fire brigade (Vigili di Fuoco).*

Eating and Drinking

Prices for **food and drink** in station bars and restaurants are relatively expensive, and in bigger stations it can be a battle to get served. Ideally you should try to buy provisions in shops or markets away from the station. Counter service in **bars** is always cheaper – although often there's nowhere to sit. Generally you have to pay for what you want at the cashdesk (*la cassa*) and then take your till receipt (*lo scontrino*) to the bar. Hand this to the barman and repeat your order. Prices are always listed either behind the bar or at the cashdesk.

If there are tables, simply sit down and wait for the waiter. You'll pay roughly twice as much this way, but if things are quiet you also buy the right to sit at the table for hours – useful if you have time to kill between trains. In smaller stations with the odd bar table, and no waiter, you can usually buy from the bar and sit down without paying extra. If in doubt, order and then ask at the bar (*posso sedermi?* – can I sit down?).

All bars serve coffee, tea, alcoholic and soft drinks and various rolls and sandwiches (*panini*). Bigger stations may have a self-service restaurant, or a glorified bar which sells a limited variety of hot meals. Bars also often sell **tickets for the shuttle buses** which connect the station with the town centre. If, as is usually the case, the bus terminal itself is outside the station, the bar may also operate as the general ticket office. In smaller stations, the bar is also home to telephones, toilets, shop and news-stand.

Most stations also have **licensed vendors** selling nuts, fruit, sweets, crisps, *panini*, water and soft drinks from trolleys. These are expensive, but useful in emergencies. More expensive still, and to be avoided unless you're desperate, are the kids with baskets of beer, sandwiches and soft drinks who wander through carriages uttering the words, '*birra, panini, coca . . . birra, panini, coca . . .*' You'll find them most on long haul trains without buffet facilities.

Shops and Foreign Exchange

City stations always have **news-stands** (*edicole*), usually selling timetables and a selection of English-language newspapers and magazines, and there is also often a **chemists**, and a next-to-useless souvenir and electrical shop. Prices are always higher than in their downtown equivalents.

Most large stations also have **foreign exchange** facilities (outlined in the information sections where appropriate). Rates are invariably poorer than in banks and queues may be long, but they have the advantage of being open on weekends (unlike banks) and outside normal banking hours during the week.

Telephones

All stations have telephones – look for a yellow or red telephone symbol. In small places the telephone is usually in the bar, and may only take L200 tokens known as *gettoni* (available from bars, *tabacchi* and often given as change) or L100, L200 coins. The state telephone company, SIP, is updating most public phones to take L500 coins and phone cards (*schede telefoniche*), available in L2,000, L5,000 and L10,000 denominations from SIP offices, *tabacchi* and news-stands.

While phone cards are useful for long-distance calls, the best option for calling home is a *telefono a scatti*, usually a sound-proofed cabin where you dial normally and pay for the call afterwards. Bars in some stations have these, as do the odd town bars, hotels, tourist offices, or the sleek new SIP offices increasingly appearing in Italian town centers. To make a collect or **reversed charge call**, dial 10 for the international operator and say *vorrei chiamare gli Stati Uniti con pagamento a destinazione* – I would like to make a reversed charge call to the United States.

Post

Most stations have a letter box (small red boxes fixed to walls), and in larger cities may boast a fully-functioning post office. Opening hours are usually Monday–Friday 8 am–6.30 pm; Saturday 8 am–noon. Main post offices are listed in the information sections. **Stamps** (*francobolli*) can also be bought in *tabacchi* and in the odd gift shop in some tourist resorts.

Buses

The location of a town or city's main **bus terminal** are given in the Practicalities section for each town. Often they're outside the station itself. Where they're not, there's almost always a shuttle bus which runs to the town center. This is especially true in the hill-towns of central Italy where the station is often miles from the town it serves. **Tickets** usually cost between L700 and L1,000 and are often sold at the station bar or news-stand. Information sections also give details of longer haul buses that might occasionally be useful for excursions. Generally you can't get on to a bus without a ticket.

Taxis

Taxis naturally congregate outside mainline stations. Never take rides from people who approach you in the station itself and only take a ride in a registered cab. Make sure the meter is zeroed and running, and be prepared to pay legitimate surcharges for luggage, and weekend, holiday and late-night fares. By law there should be a list of such surcharges in the taxi. For very long journeys try to fix a price beforehand (*Quanto costerebbe per andare a . . . ?* – How much would it cost to go to . . . ?). If in doubt, ask the driver to write the price down. In the case of any dispute stay calm and polite and aim to find a policeman.

At smaller stations you may have to call a taxi. Often a variety of numbers will be posted near the public telephones. If not, ask at the bar.

Car Rentals

In most big cities there are car rental (*autonoleggio*) offices close to main-line stations. Look for advertising within the station, ask at the bar or ticket office, or look through the local Yellow Pages (*Pagine Gialle* in Italian).

Timetables

Investing in a timetable will whet your appetite for travel, allow you to plan your routes – or embellish those suggested here – and save you an immense amount of time queueing for information. It's important to remember that all European rail networks, except for British Rail, move from winter to summer schedules on the last Sunday in May, and from summer to winter schedules on the last Sunday in September. When buying a timetable, especially in Italy, be sure you are purchasing a current timetable – either June to September or October to May.

There are two basic schedules which are invaluable if you intend to spend any time traveling by rail.

Thomas Cook's European Timetable

The first is *Thomas Cook's European Timetable*, the bible of European rail travelers, and an essential handbook if you have a Eurail Pass. It contains the timetables for all mainline trains and a few minor services on all the European rail networks. There are also lists of ferry services. Published monthly, it currently costs $24.95 plus shipping from Forsyth Travel Library (tel. 800/FORSYTH).

The June to September issues contain the full European summer schedule, and from February to May there are forecasts of the summer timetables to come, thus allowing you to indulge in some pre-planning. The winter schedules are covered in the October to May issues, with forecasts in the preceding August and September.

You might also think about buying the *Thomas Cook Rail Map of Europe* ($9.95 plus postage).

The Pozzorario

The *Pozzorario*, literally 'the well of timetables', is an absolutely essential buy if you're traveling on Italian trains. Pocket-sized, and a distinctive yellow-orange color, it's issued twice yearly at the beginning of June and the beginning of October to coincide with the FS summer and winter schedules.

The *Pozzorario Generale* costs L8,500 and contains every train service in Italy, international services from Italy, and a map of the entire Italian rail network (including private lines). It also has summaries of the mainline services, lists of trains with sleepers and couchettes, bus timetables (for routes once served by rail where the line has been closed), and, most importantly, all the **current ticket prices** (first and second class) for all journeys between 1 and 3,000 kilometers, as well as the present cost of *Rapido*, IC and EC supplements.

It's also possible to buy the smaller *Pozzorario: Nord e Centro Italia* for

149 — Napoli-Salerno-Battipaglia-Potenza Inferiore

Dist. Km	12363 Loc 1.2	6071 Dir 2cl	3451 Dir 1.2 ✗	863 2cl	6073 2cl	3453 Dir 1.2	6075 2cl	12369 Loc 2cl ✗	12371 Loc 2cl	3491 Dir 1.2	6077 2cl	12373 Loc 2cl ✗	3455 Dir 1.2	6079 2cl	6079 2cl	6079 2cl	12377 Loc 2cl	687 IC 1.2 ✗	8023 Loc 1.2	6079 2cl	12381 Loc 2cl	779 Expr 1.2 ✗	6081 2cl
0 Napoli C. p			515					608										825				1100	
– Napoli P.G. p								608	620	635	710		725	805				825	a955			1100	1135
9 Portici-Ercolano			526					620	632	650	721		739	816			840	P	1010			1121	
23 Torre Annunz. C.			538					631	650	708	731		756	826			859	E				1143	
26 Pompei			542					637	657	713	735		801	830			904	L				1149	1157
37 Nocera Inferiore			553					647	715	737	745		818	840			922	O				1215	
46 Cava dei Tirreni			607						726	752			831	849			935	R				1227	
54 Salerno a	506		620	621				657	738	805	755		845	900			950	1051				1240	1218
74 Battipaglia p	527	535	640	645	645	716	735	748	806		814	830	903	925	930	930	930	T 1053	1105		1140	1221	1250
80 Eboli	545			657	657		748					842			942	942	942	A	1130		1152	1239	
99 Contursi Terme	2861		6071				2863				6077						1020	N per				2865	
105 Sicignano d. Alburni	615			727								912			1012			O Pa-			1222		
120 Romagnano-V.-S.	2cl	640	2cl	751	2cl							2cl					1036	lermo				2cl	
127 Balvano-Ricigliano			per														1036						
134 Bella-Muro	500		650	710							900				1042						1210		
137 Baragiano-Ruoti	504		655 Ta- ranto	714							904				1046						1214		
149 Picerno	524		713	733							923				1103						1233		
166 Potenza Inf. a	555	740	745	805	850	805	855				955	1010			1135	1130					1315	1305	1410

Dist. Km	3385 Dir 1.2	3457 Dir 2cl	6083 2cl ✗	3493 Dir 1.2 ✗	12385 Loc 2cl	3387 Dir 1.2	12387 Loc 2cl	3461 Dir 2cl	775B Dir 2cl	3389 Dir 1.2	3463 Dir 2cl	9 ✗ 1.2	3391 Dir 1.2	3495 Dir 2cl	6091 ✗ 2cl	12395 Loc 1.2	563 IC 1.2	3393 Dir 2cl	3395 Dir 1.2	3465 Dir 2cl	6093 2cl	2347 Dir 2cl	6095 ✗ 1.2
0 Napoli C. p	(1)(2) 1200	1210		1310	1330	(1)(2) 1402			(2)✗			(2) 1705							(3)✗				
– Napoli P.G. p							1420	a 1423	1430	1455	1510	1530	1705	1710		1720	a 1744	1748	1840	1905		2015	
9 Portici-Ercolano		1222		1321	1345		1436				1531		1721			1735	1757		1852				
23 Torre Annunz. C.		1233		1331	1404		1454	1457			1535		1731			1754		1808	1902	1926		2042	
26 Pompei	1222	1237		1335	1409		1458		1519	1535		1727	1735			1759			1906	1930	2046		
37 Nocera Inferiore	1233	1247		1345	1428	1431	1517	1509	1527	1545		1736	1745			1818		1820	1915	1939	2055		
46 Cava dei Tirreni		1259		1441	6085	1530			6087		6089	1756			1831		2867	865	1950	2104			
54 Salerno a		1302		1355	1403	1520	1543	1521		1605		1807			1843	1832			2003	2115			
74 Battipaglia p		1323	1330	1357	1414	1420	2cl	1523	1542	2cl	1606	2cl	1808	1824	1830		1835	1826	2005	2118		
80 Eboli			1342			1432				1540	1547	1624	1630	1842			1850	1900	2025	2030	2136	2145	
99 Contursi Terme	6081			1412		1502				1559		1642			6089		1912	1922		2042		2157	
105 Sicignano d. Alburni	2cl		1412			1502							1712		2cl	1912	6091			2112	2227		
120 Romagnano-V.-S.			1435											1936		2cl				2137			
127 Balvano-Ricigliano												per Ta- ranto						per Ta- ranto					
134 Bella-Muro	1315								1640				1810			1920	2012		2230		2320		
137 Baragiano-Ruoti	1319								1644				1814			1924	2016						
149 Picerno	1338								1703				1833			1943	2035						
166 Potenza Inf. a	1410		1535		1620				1735	1705		1735	1810	1905	2030		2015	2105	2030		2230		2320

a Napoli Mergellina.

(1) Nei giorni festivi questo treno potrà essere sostituito con autobus. Consultare gli eventuali avvisi affissi in stazione.
(2) Prosegue per Benevento (q. 152).
(3) Prosegue per Avellino (q. 152).
(4) Sospeso nel giorno prefestivo, il 25 e 26.XII, 11.IV e 1.V.
(5) ASPROMONTE. Roma T.-Reggio C.C.
Per il servizio da Napoli a Battipaglia vedere anche quadro 144.

150 — Taranto-Bari

Dist. Km	12622 Loc 2cl	12624 IC 1.2 ✗	568 IC 1.2	3586 Dir 2cl	8352 Loc 1.2	2368 Loc 1.2	3804 Dir 1.2	12626 Loc 2cl	12628 Loc 1.2	698 IC 1.2 (2)	12630 Loc 2cl	12632 Loc 2cl	12634 Loc 2cl	558 IC 1.2	12636 Loc 2cl	3588 Dir 1.2 (4)	8354 Loc 1.2	850 Dir 1.2	1974 IC 1.2	628 Expr 1.2	11638 Expr 1.2	714 Expr 1.2 (7)
0 Taranto C. p		507	600	612	628	708	854	1136	1230	1308	1333	1425	1518	1617	1713	1809	1930	2037	2050	2128	2146	2223
61 Gioia del Colle a	453	615	643	706	749	813	952	1233	1337	1401	1425	1526	1617	1713	1817	1901	2045	2132	2155	2220	2253	2316
115 Bari C. a	551	711	726	758	845	920	1043	1335	1437	1444	1548	1642	1726	1742	1909	1948	2143	2220	2242	2301	2345	2355

(1) BRERA. Taranto-Milano.
(2) PITAGORA. Villa S. Giov.-Bari.
(3) Prosegue per Roma.
(4) Prosegue per Torino con il treno 732.
(5) MAGNA GRECIA. Reggio C.C.-Bari.
(6) Si effettua nei giorni 4,5,8,11 e 12.XII; dal 18 al 23.XII, il 29 e 30.XII; dal 3 al 5.I; dal 7 al 9 e dal 12 al 14.IV. Solo letti e cuccette. Prosegue per Milano.
(7) Prosegue per Milano.

151 — Paola-Cosenza

Dist. Km	2347 Dir 1.2	9875 Loc 2cl	9877 Loc 2cl	813 Expr 1.2 (1)	9879 Loc 2cl	3669 Dir 1.2	3707 Dir 2cl	9881 Loc 2cl	12661 Loc 2cl	9883 Loc 1.2	12745 Dir 2cl (3)✗	9885 Loc 2cl	3807 Loc 1.2 (4)	9887 Loc 2cl	9889 Loc 2cl	3493 Dir 1.2	9891 Loc 2cl	633 IC 1.2 (5)	9893 Loc 2cl	9895 Loc 2cl	9897 Loc 2cl	9899 Loc 2cl	565 IC 1.2 (6)
0 Paola p	001	415	531	553	537	700	720	750	912	1100	1200	1337	1350	1422	1526	1618	1656	1735	1810	2001	2001	2202	2312
7 Castiglione C. a	015	431	553	608	642	720	741	805	927	1112	1215	1346	1405	1437	1542	1638	1709	1750	1810	1833	2017	2110	2217	2325
Castiglione C. p	016	432	554	609	643	721	741	806	928	1113	1216	1347	1406	1438	1543	1639	1710	1751	1811	1834	2018	2111	2218	2326
26 Cosenza a	021	437	558	614	648	726	747	811	933	1118	1221	1352	1411	1443	1547	1644	1715	1756	1816	1839	2023	2116	2223	2330

(1) Prosegue per Sibari-Crotone.
(2) Proviene da Reggio C.C. via S. Lucido. Parte da S. Lucido Marina ore 7.23.
(3) Si effettua fino al 22.XII, dal 7.I al 7.IV e dal 14.IV.
(4) Prosegue per Taranto.
(5) MAGNA GRECIA. Reggio C.C.-Cosenza (via S. Lucido)-Bari.
(6) SILA. Roma-Cosenza.

L5,500. This contains all the information on ticket and supplement prices but contains only timetables for services in north and central Italy (north of Rome).

The *Pozzorario* is available from virtually every newsagent and station kiosk in the country. To obtain a copy by post write to Editrice Pozzo Gros Monti SpA, Via Cernaia 59, Moncalieri, Torino, enclosing an international money order for L17,000.

The Orario delle FS
Bulkier and more expensive, but with no more real information than the *Pozzorario*, the *Orario delle FS* is the official state railway timetable. It's issued twice yearly in two volumes; *Nord Centro Italia* and *Sud Centro Italia*. Mainline stations occasionally hold leaflets detailing individual routes and a small national pocket book of limited use, *Principali Treni* (free), which covers only the major trains on the main lines.

The *Orario delle FS* is harder to pick up than the *Pozzorario*. It retails in the kiosks of larger stations and bookshops and tends to sell out quickly.

Reading a Timetable
Please refer to pages 37–8 for reading station timetables. For an at-a-glance guide to some of the symbols you'll encounter see the timetable on page 43. Pay particular attention to the train category – whether it's a slow *locale* or an R, R, EC or IC train which requires a supplement (and sometimes obligatory reservations). More important still, check the small print for the days and dates on which services run. *Feriale* means the service operates daily; *festivo* means a train only runs on Sundays and holidays. It's easy to get the two mixed up. Be aware of different time zones if you are taking a train out of Italy and watch out for the days on which clocks go back or forward one hour.

Some trains operate only at Easter, in July and August, or before any big public holidays like *Ferragosto* on August 15. *Periodico* suggests the service is seasonal, and you should look out for the words *Si effettua dal . . . al . . .* (effective from . . . to . . .) plus numbers and Roman numerals to denote the date. Thus *Si effettua dal 13–VII al I–IX* means the service only runs from July 13 to September 1.

Public Holidays

Trains either side of public holidays are much busier than normal, and there are likely to be far more reservations. Christmas, Easter and around August 15 are especially hectic periods. Extra trains are usually laid on, some of which are listed in timetables or are posted at main line stations. On the holidays themselves there are fewer trains, and on smaller lines, often no service at all. Trains which

Public Holidays in Italy
January 1, January 6 (Epiphany), Easter Monday, April 25 (Liberation Day), May 1 (Labour Day), August 15 (Assumption), November 1 (All Saints Day), December 8, December 25, December 26.

do run are often full. Watch out for the Italian habit of the *ponte* or 'bridge', whereby days or half days either side of an official holiday also become days off, especially if the holiday falls on a Tuesday or Thursday. If you're traveling close to a national holiday check with the station for changes, try to make a reservation of your own, and arrive earlier than usual for your train.

Timekeeping

Everybody knows Mussolini made the trains run on time, but in truth it's only recently that Italian railways have made real advances in timekeeping. This is partly because new lines such as the link between Rome and Florence have relieved the pressure on the busiest routes, but also because of the introduction of *Intercity* trains, services that allow you to set off confident that you'll arrive close to the time promised. Confidence in these services, which now run on most of the main line routes, is such that refunds are offered if trains arrive more than a certain time over target. On the whole the Italian railway's once appalling reputation for chaos and confusion is no longer deserved.

On more pedestrian trains, however – *espressi, diretti* and *locali* – delays still occur, though here too improvements are increasingly being made. Unexplained lapses still characterize the odd trip, however, particularly at night when delays of an hour in pitch darkness miles from anywhere are standard or on long haul trains where delays accumulate and the chances of encountering problems are obviously greater. Sunday travel, when repair work is carried out, can also be difficult.

Strikes (*scioperi* in Italian) are the main bugbear of Italy's traveling public. Imminent industrial action is widely advertised in newspapers, though it's often necessary to take the Italian media's built-in propensity for over-stating the case with a degree of caution: shots of deserted stations and forecasts of the country being *paralizzato* and traveling made an impossibility usually turn out to be sensationalized. So-called national strikes often turn out to be localized, or to affect only porters, and while minor services may be affected, long haul expresses usually continue to run.

Recently wild-cat strikes have become more common – again usually localized affairs among single sections of the workforce. This follows the growth of the so-called *cobas*, small and impromptu shop-floor unions that have become disenchanted with the increasingly out-of-touch union monoliths that dominate Italian labor relations. A local *cobas* call to action is often more effective than a nationally sanctioned dispute, the latter a weapon that's been blunted through overuse.

If you're worried about the potential seriousness of a strike, look on the inside pages of one of the more sober papers like *Corriere della Sera*, which will list the time and areas affected by the action. If your Italian is up to it, ask whether trains are likely to run when buying your ticket.

On the Train

Food and Drink

A meal or snack on a train can be a pleasure worth treating yourself to at least once – particularly if you're looking out on great scenery. Most restaurant cars are sleek air-conditioned carriages geared more to the microwaved snack than a full-blown Italian lunch. On trains to and from other countries – Austria, Germany, France and Switzerland in particular – the buffet cars of other national railways are often hitched to Italian trains. In these food and wine can be of good quality. You should be able to have a modest three-course lunch for about L25,000. Buffet cars can also be a good place to take refuge if the rest of the train is crowded.

Most *Intercity* and international trains have either a fully-fledged restaurant car or a buffet/cafeteria. To find out, check your train on the platform timetables for the appropriate symbols. Such carriages are often at the head of a train. If you're on board, ask the ticket collector if there's a restaurant (*C'è un ristorante sul treno?*), or wait for the steward to walk down the train tinkling the bell that announces lunch or dinner. On newer trains there may be a crackly announcement over the address system.

Overcrowding

The bad old days of rampant overcrowding on Italian trains are largely a thing of the past. Far more trains now run – especially on the Rome–Milan line, the busiest route of them all – and trains are longer. Around big holidays and in high summer when tourists swell the numbers, however, there can still be scenes of high chaos. On key high speed trains the fact that you've paid a supplement won't necessarily save you from standing in the corridor.

Avoidance There are several ways to escape the problem, at least partly. The most obvious are to make a reservation and to avoid traveling on Friday and Sunday evening, or mid-morning on Saturday. Try to take a train that starts at your station, and arrive as early as possible to be sure of a place. Italians haven't cast off the habits ingrained by the overcrowding of the past and still arrive a good hour before departure and park themselves on a seat.

In finding a seat remember you're competing against the Italians, second only perhaps to the American commuter in the wiles and brazen-faced audacity they use to beg, borrow or steal a seat. The most important thing is to forget all codes of queuing and good behavior. The Italians won't think you're rude if you join the scrum; they'll simply think you're stupid if you don't. Anything, or almost anything goes, short of outright violence. Everyone is in the game, and the harmless-looking little old ladies in black are usually the most determined competitors.

Simple courtesy, however, can sometimes be sufficient. Three Italians sprawled in a carriage built for six are masters at making it look as if every place is taken. Papers, magazines, handbags and briefcases will be liberally spread over the free seats. If you peer into the compartment hopefully they will simply peer back and not move a thing. Actually ask if there is a place (*C'è un posto per favore?* – Is there a place please?) and they will make room – just break the ice and don't be timid. The same applies, only more so, if there seems to be only one free seat. Remember that the buffet car has seats which are often free when the rest of the train is packed. The price of a cup of coffee lets you sit in peace for a good while.

If there are two or more of you with a lot of luggage, it makes sense to send one person to fight through the bedlam around a carriage door unencumbered by bags. They can grab seats and you can follow at leisure with the luggage. Also try the obvious tricks of standing at the far ends of the platforms where the crowds waiting to get on tend to be thinner. Don't be too disheartened by the vast numbers of people often waiting for trains at big stations. Not all of them are traveling. Many are families – this is Italy, remember – on hand to wave off a son, daughter or relative. Trains, of course, also empty at the big termini.

Hazards

Theft of luggage, money or passport is the obvious hazard you face as a rail traveler. In Italy the danger is the same as elsewhere, and while not as much of a problem as word of mouth and reputation often make out, you should be extra careful on overnight trains and at stations such as Palermo or Naples. Crowded streets and markets, obvious tourist traps, and the larger cities of the south also provide rich pickings for *scippatori* or 'snatchers'. They're usually artful thieves and accomplished pickpockets, but also make less subtle grabs at handbags, wallets and jewelery – sometimes from the back of a scooter.

For the most part common sense will see you out of danger. Be discreet and don't parade anything of value. Don't carry money in wallets bulging out of back pockets – keep it in a money belt or something similar – and keep it on your person, especially at night, which is when most thefts occur. Keep a close eye on bags and packs, especially at stations and during the confusion of getting on and off trains. Putting a bag on the platform and turning to take another one from a friend is all the time someone needs to make the snatch. Stick to well-lit parts of stations if you're forced to be in one late at night. Keep a firm hand on your camera or carry it in a strong bag. Women should carry handbags or shoulder bags as the Italians do, slung across the body.

On trains be extremely careful when **leaning out of windows** to cool off or to admire the view. At best you may receive the fruit of someone's visit to the loo further up the train, at worst bottles and cans thrown out of windows. Air conditioning has replaced opening windows on many newer trains. Also be extremely careful about falling from **unsecured doors**, especially if you're forced to stand in the corridor.

In emergencies, or if you need to report a theft, go first to the ticket collector on a train. He will summon the man in charge of the train, the *capo treno*, who in turn will alert the police. On stations go to the Station Master's office (*Capo Stazione*), contact a policeman on the station, or call 112 for the police or 113 for other emergency services.

Women Travelers On trains and elsewhere in Italy women alone or in pairs can expect the usual sexual harassment from Italian men. This is almost always irritating, but rarely carries any violent intent. Generally it becomes worse the further south you travel. Indifference and self-confidence are the best deterrents. Using some rehearsed Italian invective is not. Swearing either encourages or antagonizes, and can turn a frustrating experience into a potentially unpleasant one. By far the best way to avoid unwanted attentions on trains is to ally yourself with an Italian woman, preferably of the kindly grandmother variety. Introduce yourself and explain as best you can why you want to share her compartment. Most will understand immediately. Many Italian women traveling alone do the same. To be safe also overdress, especially in the south – no mini-skirts, shorts, skimpy tops – even if Italian women don't. Foreigners are looked on differently.

Smoking and Non-Smoking

Italian carriages aren't solely either smoking or non-smoking. Rather they're divided in half, with smoking compartments (*Fumatore*) at one end and non-smoking (*Non fumatore*) at the other. The only exceptions are very old rolling stock and the new open plan carriages without compartments. Here whole carriages are set aside specifically for smokers and non-smokers.

Italians aren't quite the smokers they once were, and attitudes are changing gradually. Nonetheless people puff away far more wholeheartedly than they do in the States. Corridors in any section of the train are the smokers' main refuge: unless you shut the compartment door you'll not escape the smoke. It's unusual these days for people to light up in a non-smoking carriage; if they, do a polite sign or word is often enough to move them to the corridor.

1 Piedmont, Valle d'Aosta and Liguria

Piedmont, the 'foot of the mountains', may well be your first taste of Italy. Trains from France wind through the region after breaching the Alps, rushing down past high snow-covered peaks through emerald alpine valleys to meet the mist-shrouded plains of the Po, Italy's greatest river. At its heart lies **Turin**, the region's largest city, best known as the home of Fiat and the Italian motor industry. An elegant Baroque city of refined cafés and shaded arcades, it was also the cradle of Italy's unification movement and home to the Savoys, the old dukes of Piedmont and first kings of a united Italy. Outside the city the main thing to see are the mountains, most notably the *Alpi Marittime*, strung along the French border on Piedmont's southern border.

The area's French bias, though, is most strong in the **Valle d'Aosta**, a tiny semi-autonomous region wedged hard up against the Alps. Hemmed in by three of Europe's highest mountains, Mont Blanc, Monte Rosa and the Matterhorn, it contains one of the country's most spectacular national parks, the **Parco Nazionale del Gran Paradiso**, and a host of peaks, waterfalls, green-damp forests and a succession of deep-cut glacial valleys. Down on the valley floors stand looming castles, ringed around by meadows and vineyards, but also occasionally blighted by the small factories and new roads which have opened up the region to trade and tourism in the last twenty years.

Historically it's long been the doorway out of Italy into France and Switzerland, initially by way of the Great St Bernard and Little St Bernard passes, and latterly via the Mont Blanc and St Bernard tunnels. It was first settled in the 3rd millennium BC and later by a Celtic tribe, the Salassi, who eventually succumbed to the Romans. They in turn built **Aosta**, still the region's main town today. The Saracens pushed this far north in the 10th century, though as in Piedmont it was the Savoy who left their stamp most clearly – though the Aostans preserved a degree of autonomy within the Savoy orbit right through to the 18th century. Today the region's still quietly self-sufficient, owing allegiance neither to France nor Italy, and most towns are officially bi-lingual.

Liguria is the oddest-shaped of regions, running in a narrow crescent of coastline from the French border to Tuscany. Inevitably it's long nurtured a seafaring tradition, best exemplified by Christopher Columbus,

Piedmont and Valle D'Aosta

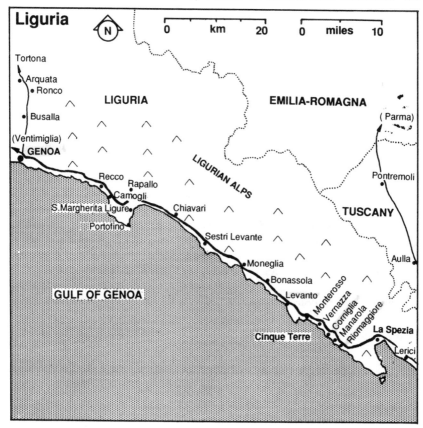

who was born in **Genoa**, still the area's capital and maritime focus. The sea's served the region well in other ways, combining with the Ligurian Alps, which arc around the region parallel to the coast, to produce one of Italy's mildest climates. Olives, vines and flowers thrive in the balmy air, and the sun's long attracted visitors, from the elegant foreign exiles of the 19th century to the hordes of less well-heeled holidaymakers that throng its long string of resorts today.

Routes Turin
Turin−Aosta−Pré-St-Didier
Turin−Cuneo−Ventimiglia
Ventimiglia−Genoa
Genoa
Genoa−La Spezia

As the focus of rail services in north-west Italy it's hard to avoid **Turin**, *though it's a gently-paced and good-looking city you could happily spend a day exploring.* **Genoa**, *by contrast, is a more dynamic but generally more sleazy metropolis, with plenty of streetlife but far less in the way of things to see. Nor is it somewhere you particularly want to spend the night.* **Turin−Cuneo− Ventimiglia** *is by far the best of the* **scenic routes**, *and one you could easily ride for its own sake, though a bus excursion from Cuneo will enable you to hike in one of Italy's newest and least-known national parks. Much the same goes for the* **Turin−Aosta−Pré-St-Didier** *journey, which cuts to the heart of the Alps. Mountain-ringed Aosta is good for an hour or so, though you should definitely aim to take a short bus ride to nearby Cogne to see the Gran Paradiso National Park at first hand. If you're after beaches and dramatic coastal scenery, make for the Cinque Terre on the* **Genoa−La Spezia** *route, well placed to head south into Tuscany.*

Turin

History

Turin has a comparatively uneventful early history, amounting to little more than a modest Roman colony (*Taurinorum*) and medieval university town until 1574 when the **dukes of Savoy** – reputedly Europe's most ancient royal dynasty – moved their capital from Chambéry in France to Turin and Piedmont (the Italian portion of the Savoy duchy). By 1713 the Savoys had acquired a royal title, and by the mid-19th century – in the hope of greater glory – had allied themselves with the liberal politicians of Italy's nascent Unification movement. The most notable of these was Camillo Cavour, who for his part needed the family to lend weight to the aims of the **Risorgimento**, or 'resurgence'. A guerrilla leader with experience in South America, Giuseppe Garibaldi provided the movement's military genius. With the connivance of foreign powers, his army brought Sicily and most of southern Italy into the Savoy orbit by 1860. Only Rome held out until 1870. When it fell the new country's capital was moved from Turin to the Eternal City.

Turin then reverted to the genteel and refined backwater it had been for centuries and still largely remains. Only the founding of **Fiat** in 1899 brought it the industrial edge that has also made it one of the country's major manufacturing centres. Fiat today is the world's sixth largest corporation and is presided over by the **Agnelli family**, Italy's equivalent of royalty and the lay successors to the Savoy monarchy which was rejected in a popular referendum after the war. The company's factories have always been a place of political foment: **Antonio Gramsci**, the leading light of the Italian Communist Party, cut his teeth with occupations of the shop floor during the First World War.

It was after the Second World War, however, that the city's face changed most radically, when it was swamped by some half million impoverished immigrants from southern Italy, encouraged to move north to service the factories then riding high on Italy's post war economic boom. The sudden population explosion brought with it a rash of social problems, one reason the notorious *brigate rosse*, or **Red Brigades** – the left-wing terrorist groups of the Seventies – found Fiat's vast Mirafiori works a fertile recruiting ground. Social tensions are still high, reflecting a growing trend on the part of northern Italians to look down on the *terroni* (peasants, or literally 'people of the land') from the south – even 40 years on.

What to See

Museo Egizio

Turin's two key sights are gathered under one roof in the Palazzo dell'Accademia delle Scienze, a Guarini-designed palace at the corner of Piazza San Carlo, a broad rectangular piazza down Via Roma from the railway station. The first, the **Museo Egizio** (9 am–2 pm, closed Mon) is ranked as the second most important Egyptian museum in the world after that in Cairo and was the first ever such museum to be founded (1824). Created first as a hobby by Carlo Emanuele I around 1628, later kings of Savoy made a more systematic collection of artifacts, added to in this century by two major expeditions and donations from the Egyptian government as thanks for the museum's part in the Aswan Dam salvage digs.

Monumental sculpture forms the core of the ground floor collection together with rooms full of mummies, paintings, textiles and much more. The real highlight, though, is the Tomb of Khaie and Merie, a 14th-century BC grave of an architect and his wife discovered in 1906. Other things to make a point of seeing include a papyrus 'Book of the Dead' and a 13th-century BC statue of Ramses II.

Galleria Sabauda

The Galleria Sabauda (daily 9 am–2 pm, closed Mon) fills the palazzo's top floor and houses paintings built around the Savoys' private art collection. The royal predilection was as much for Flemish and Dutch art as it was for Italian, and there's a variety here that you don't find in many second rank Italian galleries.

If you want to know more about the *Risorgimento*, or the Unification of Italy – which, after all, had its capital if not its finest moments in Turin – visit the *Museo Nazionale del Risorgimento* in the Palazzo Carignano opposite the Galleria Sabauda, a grandiose Baroque palace fronted by a diverting façade of statues and white marble reliefs (9 am – 7pm, Sun 9 am – noon; free on Sun). Home to the first Italian parliament (March 14th, 1861), it now contains the best overall run-through of the characters and events of Unification, with an especially interesting look at its hero, Giuseppe Garibaldi.

Piazza Castello

Via Roma pushes on past Piazza San Carlo to end in Piazza Castello, Turin's main square, a less than appealing expanse of traffic-clogged chaos, but the home of a couple of palaces and a pair of sights that merit a quick visit while you're in the centre of town. The plain-faced and apricot-coloured **Palazzo Reale** at the head of the piazza was the seat of the Savoys from 1646 to 1865, and is nowadays a monument to their fairly execrable taste: it's hardly worth taking the guided tours around the red and gilt-coloured interior and its tackily decorated rooms (daily 9 am – 1 pm, closed Mon) – though it contains an outstanding collection of Chinese porcelain vases. You'd perhaps be better off snoozing or wandering in the palace's lovely gardens, the **Giardino Reale** (1697), designed by Louis de Nôtre, better known for his gardens at Versailles (gardens open daily 9 am – 6 pm, free).

Palazzo Madama across the square is an altogether better proposition, gilded with a riotous Baroque façade by Juvarra, an eighteenth-century architect responsible for the piazza and many of its surrounding streets. Inside is the recently facelifted **Museo Civico dell'Arte Antica**, an eclectic collection that runs from Oriental ceramics, early Christian jewellery and illuminated manuscripts to a unique collection of 15th-century painted glassware and miscellaneous paintings.

On the piazza's north side, its arcades hide the **Armeria Reale**, one of the world's finest collection of arms, guns and armour – not only from Italy but from as far afield as Turkey and Japan (Tues and Thur 3 – 7 pm, Wed, Fri and Sat 9 am – 1 pm, closed Sun and Mon). Also on the corner is the Savoy's former chapel, **San Lorenzo** (1668 – 80) whose featureless façade conceals an immensely ornate interior by Guarini.

The Duomo and the Turin Shroud

Just off Piazza Castello and to the left of the Palazzo Reale is Turin's 15th-century Duomo, one of Italy's more disappointing cathedrals, though home to one of its most famous relics, the Turin Shroud. Brought to the city from the Savoy's old capital, Chambéry, in the 16th century, the four metre length of linen is reputedly the shroud used to wrap Christ after the crucifixion. It was installed in a huge and frothy chapel, the *Cappella della Sacra Sindone* (1667 – 90), a masterpiece of Baroque frippery by the priest and architect, Guarini (Tues – Sat 9 am – noon and 3 – 6 pm; Sun 9 am – noon).

The shroud's only recently become famous worldwide, thanks – or no thanks – to the research work by three leading universities (in Italy, the United States and the UK) whose carbon-dating exploits have exposed the cloth as a forgery probably created between 1260 and 1390. What they haven't been able to explain so conclusively is how the medieval forgers achieved the shroud's striking image – the front and back views of a bearded man with a crown of thorns and wound in his side

Science has done little to undermine the credulity of the Church, however, and the shroud is only brought out of its iron and silver casket in the chapel on rare occasions. What you can see is a full-scale photograph and an account (in English) of the various scientific investigations that have scuppered the shroud's credentials.

Above the main door is Luigi Gagni's *Last Supper*, a persuasive copy of Leonardo's Milanese masterpiece. Outside the duomo are Turin's main monuments to its Roman age, the remains of a Roman theatre and the **Porta Palatina**, flanked by two eccentric 16-sided towers. Beyond the cathedral to the north, Piazza della Repubblica (also designed by Juvarra) holds the city's main daily market, best seen on Saturdays when it's augmented by the 'Balon' antique and flea market.

The Mole Antonelliana

West of Piazza Castello take Via Giuseppe Verdi towards Turin's key landmark, the Mole Antonelliana, a towering folly at Via Montebello 20 which for a while was the world's tallest building and whose bizarre outlines can be seen from most of the city. Designed first as a synagogue in 1863 by an oddball local architect, Alessandro Antonelli, it languished half-finished until 1897 when the city took things in hand and completed it as a monument to Italian unity (compare Rome's Monumento Vittorio Emanuele, a similar white elephant also designed to celebrate Unification). In its way the building is a marvel, combining the lines of a Greek temple, glass pyramid and star-topped pagoda (illuminated at night) and at some 167 metres a fine belvedere for dizzying views over the city and distant Alps (daily 9 am–7 pm).

Parco del Valentino

Turin's main park, the Parco del Valentino (1856), flanks the River Po in the city's south-east corner – not far away from the railway station (turn right on Corso Vittorio Emanuele). It's one of Italy's biggest and most beautiful city parks, crammed with spots to take time out and dotted with places to rent bikes and rowing boats. While you're out here look at the **botanical gardens** and the 1660 Castello del Valentino, designed to emulate a French 16th-century château and another Savoy palace, used mainly for family weddings and extravagant parties. Give most time, though, to the rather barmy but still appealing **Castello e Borgo Medioevale**, a surprisingly convincing mixture of fake castle and village built in 1884 (Tues–Sat 9 am–6 pm, Sun 9 am–12.30 pm, closed Mon; free on Fri). The idea was to combine the cream of Piedmont's castles and houses using original designs, materials and building methods.

Practicalities in Turin

Tourist Office There's a small information kiosk at the main railway station (011/531.317) and a larger provincial tourist office at Via Roma 222 on the corner of Piazza San Carlo (011/535.181 or 535.901).

Railway Station Porta Nuova (011/517.551). Turin's main station, Porta Nuova, is at the southern end of Via Roma, the city's main street. There are 4 other stations, but the only one you're likely to see is Porta Susa in the west of the city on Corso Inghilterra. This is used by most trains en route for Porta Nuova.

Buses Corso Inghilterra 3 (011/446.431). Most of Turin's sights are within walking distance of Porta Nuova, but if you need a bus or tram, buy tickets from *tabacchi* – there's one at Porta Nuova.

Useful routes include bus number 1 (from Porta Nuova to Porta Susa); bus number 4 (north from Porta Nuova to Piazza della Repubblica and the Duomo via Via XX Settembre); bus number 60 (between the two stations via the bus terminal); bus number 52 (to the youth hostel from Porta Nuova and Corso Vittorio Emanuele).

Foreign Exchange Porta Nuova station (Mon–Fri 7 am–2 pm & 3–9 pm; Sat and Sun 8 am–1 pm and 3–8 pm).

Budget Travel CTS, Via Camerana 3 (011/534.388). 2 streets left of the station as you exit, and one block off Corso Vittorio Emanuele.

Day Hotel Clean and smart *Albergo Diurno* for showers and toilets immediately outside Porta Nuova station on the left as you leave.

Post Office Via Alfieri 10.

Bike Rental Viale Matteotti, in the Parco del Valentino. Turn right out of the station and it's 15 min from the station on Corso Vittorio Emanuele.

Hospital *Maria Vittoria*, Via Cibrario 72; in emergencies call 5747.

Taxis Tel: 5730 or 5737.

Police Corso Vinzaglio 10 (011/512.444).

Where to stay

There are plenty of cheap places to stay in the dingy area around Via Nizza close to the station (turn right on Corso Vittorio Emanuele and then first right for Via Nizza). Pricier and more salubrious spots cluster in the streets directly in front of the station on and around Piazza Carlo Felice, though the nicest spots of all are west of Piazza Castello.

Youth Hostel *Ostello Torino*, Via Alby 1, off Via Gatti (011/660.2939). Turin's IYHF youth hostel is near Piazza Crimea in a hilly residential area (bus number 52 from Corso Vittorio Emanuele; get off at the third stop over the river). Closed Jan and daily 9 am–6 pm.

Hotels ☆*Bellavista*, Via Galliari 15 (011/669.8139). Just to the right and a little behind Porta Nuova station as you leave: airy rooms and fairly peaceful.

☆*Pensione San Carlo*, Piazza San Carlo 197 (011/553.522). Ideally situated for central sights, but also set back a little from the chaos and noise of the piazza; good rooms and management.

☆☆*Castagnole*, Via Berthollet 3 (011/669.8678). Clean and recently refitted hotel off Via Nizza.

☆☆*Campo di Marte*, Via XX Settembre 7 (011/530.650). Large and convenient if charmless hotel a block from the station near Piazza Carlo Felice.

☆☆*Europa*, Piazza Castello 99 (011/544.238). Good position but popular, so book rooms well in advance if possible.

☆☆*Magenta*, Corso Vittorio Emanuele 67 (011/542.649). Just left of the station and the smartest in its price range: wide variety of rooms and rates.

☆☆*Victoria*, Via Nino Costa 4 (011/553.710). Quiet and simple hotel with garden.

Camping *Riviera sul Po* (011/638.706). The most central year-round site, on the east bank of the Po south of the youth hostel: take bus number 67 from Corso Vittorio Emanuele.

Where to eat and drink

Cafés Turin's elegant turn-of-the-century cafés are famous: try *Elorio*, Via Po 8 and *Pepino*, Piazza Carignano 8, both known for their ice cream, the lovely *Mulussano* in Piazza San Carlo, or the refined *Baretti & Milano* for afternoon tea in Piazza Castello. Top Turin institution in this mould is probably the *Caffé Torino*, Via Roma 204 on Piazza San Carlo.

Restaurants *Arcadia*, Galleria Subalpina 16. Central trattoria popular at lunchtime.

Brek, Piazza Carlo Felice. Good, popular self-service across from the station with tables inside and out. Salads, soups and fresh bread snacks for a quick, cheap meal.

Cossolo, Via Roma 68. One of a citywide chain for sandwiches, slices of pizza and other cheap snacks.

Da Giuseppe, Via San Massimo 34 (011/812.2090). Lots of Piedmontese specialities and popular with locals so arrive early or book a table.

Taverna Fiorentina, Via Palazzo di Città 6. Compact, family run trattoria off Piazza Castello.

Outlying Sights

It's almost inevitable that a car town like Turin should have a motor museum. The **Museo dell'Automobile** is Italy's only such offering and may well appeal even if you're not a car fetishist (daily 10 am–6 pm, closed Mon). At a push you could walk there from the Parco del Valentino: it's about three kilometres south along the river at Corso Unità d'Italia. Alternatively take bus number 34 from Via Nizza. The history of the Fiat, of course, is well-documented, and there are mouth-watering examples of classic cars from Lancia, Bugatti, Maserati and Alfa Romeo.

For great views of the city take tram 15 and the shuttle bus to the **Basilica di Superga**, a fine Baroque church and widely considered Juvarra's masterpiece (daily 8 am–12.30 pm and 3–5 pm; free). The tram leaves from Via XX Settembre, and if you don't then take the bus, you can instead pick up a great little cable railway at Stazione Sassi for a scenic 20-minute ride to the basilica (hourly June–Sept).

To complete a tour of Juvarra's works, and for another glimpse into the erstwhile lifestyle of the Savoys, take bus number 41 from Corso Vittorio Emanuele. You pass the Fiat works and the drab suburbs of Mirafiori – purpose built for the southern immigrants who came to work in the factories – before arriving at the **Palazzina di Caccia di Stupinigi** (10 am–noon and 3–5 pm, closed Mon & Fri). This was a royal hunting lodge, and though now rather battered on the outside the interior still preserves a wealth of glorious *trompe l'oeil*, luxurious fittings and furniture.

Turin–Aosta–Pré-St-Didier
The route

The Turin–Aosta–Pré-St-Didier line takes you into some of Italy's finest alpine country and in particular to the **Gran Paradiso National Park**, whose main village, **Cogne**, makes an ideal base for walking and camping. It's easily accessible by bus from Aosta, the area's main town and the obvious place to stay the night if you're not tempted by Cogne. The route follows the line of the **Valle d'Aosta**, both the name of the valley which scythes north-west from Turin through the mountains, and also the name of Italy's smallest and possibly most beautiful region. You might leave the train en route at towns along the valley, transferring on to the buses that journey up some of its more deepcut side valleys like the **Val di Gressoney**, the **Valtournenche** and the famous **Valle del Gran San Bernardo**.

As for the railway, the best of scenery closes in after Aosta, culminating just short of Courmayeur, one of the country's premier ski-resorts, lying in the shadow of Monte Bianco – Mont Blanc. You can make a great excursion here by taking the cable cars over the mountains to Chamonix and then returning by bus to Courmayeur.

As for an **onward itinerary** you have little choice but to return to Turin, no hardship given the frequency of connections and its proximity to Aosta.

Trains

About 15 trains daily run from **Turin Porta Nuova** *to Aosta (129 km, 2 hr). Only 6 daily run on from Aosta to Pré-St-Didier (32 km, 45 min).*

The journey

It's often a melancholy experience riding a slow train through a city's suburbs. Clanking out of Turin's fringes is no exception. The carriages wind slowly through industrial fringes heavy with old and decayed factories, the ruined legacies of Italy's 'Fifties boom rather than the modern, robot-run car factories which Fiat keeps hidden far from the city centre. Countryside invariably follows quickly upon city in Italy, however, and it's an advantage of train travel that it never confines you to a view – good or bad – for too long.

Sure enough, the train's soon running eastwards along the River Po, pushing into rich farming land that seems a world away from the pinched and improvised look of agriculture in central Italy. Unlike Tuscany's pastoral vignettes of vine and olive, and its skylines of cypress and avenues of cedars, Piedmont and the north-west are characterised by large prairie-like fields, lines of wistful-looking poplars and the gridiron of high-tech irrigation schemes. This is farming as big business, far removed from the centuries-old grind of the peasant smallholder raking a living from stony terraces.

At **Chivasso** the line branches north across the plain that lends Piedmont its name – *piede dei monti* – the foot of the mountains, the first peaks beginning to appear abruptly on the northern horizon. Most trains stop at **Pont-St-Martin** about an hour out of Turin, which marks both Piedmont's border with the Valle d'Aosta and the start of the mountains proper. Only the village's vineyards and their fine wines are of any note, though its huddle of houses centres around a 1st century BC Roman bridge, apparently given to St Martin by the devil. This type of legend's a well-worn story in rural areas, and invariably involves the devil bartering a bridge in return for the first soul to cross it – and just as inevitably sees the devil outwitted, in this case by St Martin, who sent a dog (it's usually a dog) to sacrifice its presumably more worthless canine soul.

Minutes beyond Pont-St-Martin stands the brooding profile of **Forte di Bard**, the first of the romantic-looking castles for which the Valle d'Aosta is famous. Now closed to the public, it's a 19th-century reconstruction of an 800-year old fortress that belonged to the Savoys. In 1800 when Napoleon entered Italy via Aosta, he had to sneak his heavy artillery pieces past this castle under cover of darkness. Ten years later, recalling this inconvenience, he had the old castle razed to the ground.

Excursion from Pont-St-Martin

The Val di Gressoney

A bus ride from Pont-St-Martin leads up the meadow-green valley beyond, the Val di Gressoney, unfolding some cracking views and eventually coming up to the glacier-hung crags of Monte Rosa, at 4,634 metres one of the Alps' biggest peaks. People in the geranium-hung wooden houses here speak neither French nor Italian, nor the lilting patois mixture of the two common elsewhere in the Valle d'Aosta. Instead they gabble *Walser*, a German dialect handed down from their ancestors who migrated here from the Swiss Valais in the 12th century.

Practicalities in the Val di Gressoney

6 buses daily run from Pont-St-Martin up the Val di Gressoney as far as Gressoney-la-Trinité (1 hr 15 min). There are tourist offices at Gressoney-la-Trinité (0125/366.133) and Gressoney-St-Jean, the valley's other resort 6 km south (0125/355.185). Contact them for details of hiking routes, and note that cable cars and ski-lifts operate in the summer if you want to reach the valley's upper bastions without too much effort. La-Trinité is the nicer place to stay: try the ☆☆*Argentina* (0125/355.944) or the central ☆☆*Castore*(0125/366.131). To camp use *La Pineta* at St-Jean (0125/355.370).

A short way on a tantalising glimpse of dazzling side valley flashes by to the west, a deep 'V' cutting into a mountain wilderness, quickly followed by **Verrès**, castle number two, though it's a long stiff walk to its ramparts, and one for enthusiasts only. If you leave the train at Verrès, though, you could more easily stroll into **Issogne**, just across the river from the station. The castle here's a lot less impressive from the outside, but the interior remains much as it must have been in the Middle Ages. (9.30 am – noon and 2–4 pm; guided tours every half hour).

Back on the train the railway hugs the river, a white-water torrent heavy with the glacier ground silt that lends it its distinctive milky-blue hue. With the motorway it lurches suddenly west, arching past St Vincent, a spa for the idle rich and home to one of Europe's largest casinos. Soon after it clanks into **Châtillon**, the region's second town after Aosta, but too begrimed with industry to be of much appeal. It's always one of the Alps' stranger juxtapositions, this eye-level, valley bottom squalor – a mangled skein of road, rail and factory – and the sun-dazzled snow, limpid skies and jade-cool forests that rise pristine in the mountains above.

Châtillon's the place to pick up a bus (9 daily) if you want to pay homage to the Matterhorn, known as the *Cervino* in Italian, which rises in its famous sabretooth profile at the head of the **Valtournenche**, the valley north of the town. There's plenty of walking on offer here, helped by ski-lifts which'll take you high into wilderness, though Breuil-Cervinia, the main centre, is a depressing and expensive ski-resort that rather takes the edge off the mountains' splendour; hold out for the Val di Cogne if you want to don the walking boots (see below).

After Châtillon the castles come thick and fast, the best at **Fenis**, for which you'll have to jump the train at Nus (2 km away) though with Aosta barely 15 minutes away you could easily resist its fairytale towers and battlements, armoury and well-utensiled medieval kitchen in favour of the town.

Aosta's a good place to leave the train and perhaps potter around for an hour. Once you've seen it think about taking a bus either to Cogne (50 mins), a good overnight stop (longer if you want to walk) or up the Valle del Gran San Bernardo for the superb scenery en route (1 hr 15 min).

Aosta

It's easy to be put off by Aosta's dull suburbs and industrial detritus, but beyond them the mountains rise to provide one of the finest backdrops to any Italian town. Furthermore, the centre possesses plenty of sedate charm and a pleasing handful of Roman and medieval monuments to boot. The town was founded by the Romans in 25 BC, who conquered the local Salassi tribe then promptly sold them off as slaves. It was then christened *Augusta Praetoria* in honour of Augustus (the name Aosta is a medieval corruption of Augustus) and quickly became an important military camp straddling the intersection of consular roads from the Rhône and Isère. Ever since it's been at the crossroads of France, Italy and Switzerland, a strategic position that's been much bolstered by the building of the Mont Blanc and St Bernard tunnels. During the Middle Ages it was ruled by the Challant nobility and then by the Dukes of Aosta, allies of the royal Savoys, though if anything the town now leans more towards France than Piedmont and you're as likely to hear a French dialect on the streets as you are Italian.

Practicalities in Aosta

Tourist Office Piazza Chanoux 8 (0165/ 35.655). From the station head straight down Via Conseil des Commis. If you're making excursions from town pick up the *Orari*, a summary of all local bus, train and cable car timetables.

Railway Station Piazza Manzetti (0165/ 362.057). Left luggage (9 am–noon and 2–6 pm).

Buses Buses leave from Piazza Narbonne close to Piazza Chanoux, Aosta's main square. Information (0165/362.287). To Cogne (9 daily, 50 min); Great St Bernard Pass (2 daily, 45 min); Fenis (5 daily, 30 min); Courmayeur (12 daily, 1 hr); Valtournenche (7 daily 2 hr 15 min); Valgrisenche (2 daily mid-June–mid-Sept Mon, Tues and Sat only); Val di Rhêmes (3 daily, weekdays only June–Sept).

Foreign Exchange *Banco Valdostano*, Piazza Chanoux 49 (weekdays 8.20 am–1.20 pm and 2.20–4 pm).

Post Office Piazza Narbonne.

Hotels ☆*La Belle Epoque*, Via d'Avise 18 (0165/362.276). Central, good rooms and the first choice amongst the budget hotels.
☆*Mancuso*, Via Voison 32 (0165/34.526). Turn left from the station and then left again

under the railway for a quiet and friendly place with the bonus of a reasonable restaurant.
☆☆☆*Europe*, Piazza Narbonne 8 (0165/ 236.363). Old-fashioned and cosy central hotel.

Camping *Camping Valle d'Aosta* (0165/ 32.878). 1 km from Aosta at the hamlet of Les Fourches (open June–Sept); *Camping Milleluci* (0165/44.274) 1 km from town at Roppoz (open year round).

Where to eat

To each cheaply use the self-service restaurant at the station, one of the town's many pizzerias, or the Standa supermarket on Via Torino and the food shops on Via Porta Pretoria and Via de Tiller for picnic supplies. Good snacks can also be had from the local bakers.

Restaurants *Praetoria*, Via San t'Anselmo 9 near the Porta Pretoria. Intimate atmosphere, good food and easy on the wallet.
Vecchia Aosta/Ba-i-bor, Via Porta Pretoria. Close to the *Praetoria*, but more expensive – it's built right into the old Roman walls.
Cavallo Bianco Via Aubert 15. If you've money to burn treat yourself in what's widely acknowledged as the area's best restaurant.

Excursion from Aosta

Cogne and the Parco Nazionale del Gran Paradiso

If you decide to leave the train at Aosta it's definitely worth making the 50-minute bus journey to Cogne for a first-hand look at the forests, mountains and glaciers of the **Parco Nazionale del Gran Paradiso**. The second largest of Italy's five national parks, the Gran Paradiso started life in the 19th century as a hunting reserve for the Savoys. In 1919 Vittorio Emanuele II donated the area to the state, thereby helping to preserve the ibex (or *stambecco*), a deer-like creature which his ancestors' shooting had pushed to the edge of extinction. There are now about 3,500 ibex in the park, many of them usually easy to see, along with chamois, marmots and a wide range of flora and fauna, although it's the grandiose scenery which ranges around the central peaks of Gran Paradiso itself (4,061 metres) which provides the biggest lure.

Three main valleys push into the park from the Valle d'Aosta – the **Val di Rhêmes**, **Valsavaranche** and **Val di Cogne**. Of these the Val di Cogne is the busiest but also the easiest to reach on public transport. **Cogne** is its main town, a pleasant place surrounded by open meadows and jagged mountains, full of reasonable hotels and literally within walking distance of some of the best scenery. Visit the tourist office for an excellent guide to local walks.

As usual in the Alps, most of the paths are well marked and well worn and there are hikes to suit most abilities. Ski-lifts also operate during the summer in and around the town to whisk you quickly into the mountains. Summer-only shuttle buses also connect with some of the small villages in the Val di Rhêmes if you want to broaden the scope of your exploration. Most hikers walk a couple of kilometres south of Cogne to the tiny village of **Valnontey** where there's a small **botanical garden**, the *Giardino Alpino*, most of which you can see from the outside (15 June – 15 Sept, 9 am – 12.30 and 2.30 – 6 pm). From the village the best walk follows trails 36/106 west to the *Rifugio Vittorio Sella*, a superb if steepish and popular hike (3 hr; 900 m of ascent), with a loop back to Valnontey possible if you follow the path south-east from the refuge towards the head of the valley and then walk back down the valley itself to Valnontey. The best cable car trip is to Montseuc at 2,100 metres for great views (open all year except May, Oct & Nov).

Practicalities in Cogne

Tourist Office Via Bourgeois 34, Cogne (0165/74.040).
Hotels Cogne has plenty of accommodation, although a lot of the hotels close off-season (Sept – Dec and April – June). In July and August it's advisable to call ahead to check rooms are available. Use the tourist office if you get stuck – there are plenty of private rooms to rent – and remember that places even a short walk from the centre tend to be cheaper and emptier.
☆*Stambecco*, on the road south to Valnontey

(0165/74.068) and ☆*Du Soleil* on the main road into town (0165/74.033) are the cheapest options. Try also ☆*Vallée de Cogne*, Via Cavagnet 7 (74.079), the nearby ☆☆*Petit Hotel* (0165/74.010), or ☆☆☆*Miramonti* (0165/74.030). At **Valnontey** use the ☆☆*Herbetet* (0165/74.180) but be sure to call ahead as it's a popular spot.
Camping Lo Stambecco (0165/74.137; June – mid-Sept) near Valnontey is the nicest and most popular site and there's also *Camping Gran Paradiso* (0165/74.105; June – Sept).

Roman Aosta

Aosta has a brace of Roman monuments that's earned it the overpitched title Rome of the Alps. Only the town's main Roman gateway really impresses, the **Porta Pretoria** (Via Porta Pretoria), just east of Aosta's main square, the Piazza Chanoux. Beyond the gate runs Via Sant'Anselmo, named after St Anselm who was born in Aosta and later became Archbishop of Canterbury in England. It runs to another arch, the **Arco di Augusto**, raised in 25 BC to celebrate the defeat of the Salassi, and now topped off with an anomalous 18th-century roof. Immediately past it a single-spanned Roman bridge arches over the dried-up River Buthier, still in use, though the river was diverted as long ago as the 13th century.

Off Via Porta Pretoria 50 metres before Porta Pretoria a lane winds off left to the remains of the **Teatro Romano** (daily 9.30 am–noon and 2.30–6.30 pm). A lofty 22 metre-high chunk of the façade has survived, its four tiers of arches and windows still impressive, together with a few of the 3,000 original seats that made up the *cavea*, or auditorium. In the courtyard of the convent of Santa Caterina just to the north are just seven arches of the original 60 that formed the basis of the **Anfiteatro Romano** once capable of seating 20,000 people.

Excursion from Aosta

Valle del Gran San Bernardo

The Great St Bernard Pass (closed Nov–May) at an incredible 2,473 metres has always been one of the most heavily used of the alpine passes, despite its bleakness and its appalling weather (there's usually snow on the ground for 12 months of the year). Having linked Italy to Switzerland from time immemorial, it's been used by Roman legions to march between Rome and Geneva, by Charlemagne, by Henri IV and by Napoleon, who stormed over in 1800 with 40,000 troops in tow on his way to defeat the Austrians at the Battle of Marengo. These days a motorway and new six-kilometre tunnel cut under the pass. Buses from Aosta, however, still make an extremely spectacular run up the old road and there are a trio of villages en route if you want to stop over.

Up at the Pass the most famous sight after the fantastic views is the *Ospizio*, or **Hospice of St Bernard** (just in Switzerland, so bring your passport), a large monastery founded according to legend by Bernard, Archdeacon of Aosta in 1050, and run by monks from Martigny in Switzerland. Part of their vocation involves ministering to lost and weary travellers struggling over the pass, and to this end they bred the famous Saint Bernard dogs. A few impressive specimens are still on show – very obviously kept mainly for their tourist appeal – and there's no end of china, plastic and fluffy versions in the souvenir kiosks. There's even a doggy museum and a stuffed individual – the famous 'Barry', a legendary lifesaver but now decidedly dog-eared. The present monastery dates from 1837.

Practicalities in Valle del Gran San Bernardo

Buses 4 buses daily run to the Pass (the first out at 8 am, the last back at 4.30 pm; 1 hr 15 min): buy a return ticket. You can also take a bus over the Pass to Martigny for even more scenery (45 km from the Pass; 4 daily; 3–4 hr with a stopover at the Pass).

Hotels Try the ☆*Mont Velan* at St-Oyen 15 km below the Pass (0165/78.226) or the nearby ☆*Des Alpes* (0165/780.196) in St-Rhémy. **Camping** *Camping Pineta* (0165/78.113; year round) on the river in St-Oyen.

Excursion from Aosta

Courmayeur and Mont Blanc

Although, for the scenery, you could happily chug along the railway to its conclusion at Pré-St-Didier and then return to Aosta, there's a great day's outing if you take a bus on to Courmayeur, five kilometres north of the station, and take a ride on the renowned cable car up and over Mont Blanc across the French border to Chamonix.

The ride on the *Funivia del Monte Bianco* starts from **La Palud** 3.5 kilometres north of Courmayeur (3 buses daily or taxi). The full crossing takes 1 hr 30 min, but can often be delayed or cancelled during bad weather. Remember to take warm clothes, and bear in mind that if the weather turns bad the return cable cars may be cancelled and you'll have to spend the night in Chamonix (3 buses daily, though, return to Courmayeur via the Mont Blanc Tunnel).

The car rises in stages to **Punta Helbronner** (3,321 m) on the Italian–French border in an astounding if occasionally stomach-churning journey that abounds in exceptional views. The first car leaves at 8 am, the last at 4.20 pm. To proceed from the shelter and viewpoint you'll need a passport as the next stage – which is the most breathtaking – crosses into France. The so-called 'cableway of the glaciers' passes over a kilometre above the Géant Glacier before arriving just below **Aiguille du Midi** (3,843 m). A gallery here leads to the terminal for the last stage of the journey, the descent on the **Chamonix-Mont Blanc** cableway to Chamonix. The cost of the last two French stages is about 160 francs. Several buses daily return from Chamonix to Courmayeur.

North-west of Piazza Chanoux lies Piazza Giovanni XXIII, site of the old Forum, though there's little to see except for a large underground passage, the *cryptoporticus*, whose purpose remains unclear (excavations are in progress to try and shed more light).

Cattedrale

Aosta's lumpen-looking cathedral also stands in Piazza Giovanni XXIII, fronted by an uninspiring Neoclassical façade (1848) and flanked by two Romanesque towers, all that survives from an original 11th-century church that's been rebuilt several times. The late 15th-century Gothic interior is more worthwhile, boasting some elaborately carved **choir stalls** (1468), and a pair of fine mosaics. Beyond the choir through the glass doors is the newly re-opened **Treasury Museum** (daily 10 am–noon and 3–6 pm, closed Mon) home to jewel-encrusted and ritzy reliquaries, glass, enamels, gold and silverware, tombs, caskets, a 13th-century Crucifix removed from the Arco di Augusto, and a magnificent ivory diptych dating from 406 decorated with the image of the Roman Emperor Honorius.

Sant'Orso

Aosta's finest church lies on Via Sant'Orso which strikes off left from Via San Anselmo between Porta Pretoria and the Arco di Augusto. Like the cathedral its façade is a dull affair, enlivened only by a Romanesque campanile (1161), though it too hides a more interesting interior. Parts of the crypt, the burial place of Orso, Aosta's patron saint, and important patches of fresco in the upper gallery date from the 10th century, and there's a lovely choir carved with a menagerie of animals, bats and monkeys. The 1133 **cloister**, though, and its 40 carved columns stand out as the church's showpiece. The sculpture's some of the best in the region.

Turin–Cuneo–Ventimiglia
The route

This is a journey to take for the scenery – not the agricultural and occasionally industrial plain south of Turin, but the mountains of the Alpi Marittime south of Cuneo which make this one of the most attractive railway journeys in Italy. After breasting the mountains at **Limone Piemonte** (1,009 m) the line passes into France for about 70 kilometres before dropping back into Italy at Ventimiglia on the coast. This last stretch of the line – an engineering marvel – was only reopened in 1979 after being badly damaged in the Second World War.

Cuneo is the line's only town of any substance, though not necessarily the place to stay if you're going to break your journey. If you want to take time take a bus south from the town to the villages of Valdieri, Sant'Anna or Entracque, which act as springboards into the **Parco Naturale dell'Argentera**. Protecting a large area of the Alpi Marittime, this is one of northern Italy's least known and most beautiful mountain enclaves, with exhilarating possibilities for hiking and camping. Alternatively you could stray less far from the train and stay at Limone Piemonte or any of the mountain villages over the border in France.

As for an onward itinerary, at Ventimiglia you can pick up trains for the French Riviera and Marseilles, or follow the Italian Riviera south towards Genoa and Pisa.

Trains
8 trains daily make the journey right through from Turin to Ventimiglia (187 km, 2 hr 50 min); another 6 go as far as Limone Piemonte. The journey time to Cuneo is 1 hr 10 min, departure point for the trip's best excursion.

The journey

The train shuffles out of Turin's southern suburbs, crossing the Po – already a bilious and poisonous-looking river – and then breaks through a tight web of motorways and ring roads to emerge on to the wide open spaces of the Piedmontese plain. Aim to be on a fast train to Cuneo otherwise you'll stop at every rather dilapidated rural town en route. None of these, nor the strangely somnambulant countryside hereabout, really diverts although at Savigliano, 35 minutes out of Turin, a branch line hives off west to **Saluzzo**, once the capital of a marquisate that managed to retain its independence (and print its own stamps) right through to the 19th century.

Saluzzo

Although it's hedged in by a thicket of modern houses, Saluzzo's medieval quarter remains a charming collection of cobbled streets and medieval buildings, all gathered together under a steep hillside crowned with a 16th-century castle (now a prison). A nice spot to wander – even to stay – the best part of town lies within easy reach of the station; to find it simply turn right along Corso Roma and left along Via Martiri. Try to see the austere Gothic church of **San Giovanni** (1280), below the castle and known for its frescoes, choir and cloisters. It also contains the tomb of Ludovico II (1475–1504), a full-blown Renaissance man – scholar, architect, patron of the arts – even the founder of a school of surgery. He also built the first alpine tunnel – albeit only 75 metres long – through the mountains to the west to improve trade with France. Close to the church stands the heavily restored **Casa Cavassa**, home to the Museo Civico (9 am–noon and 3–5 pm; closed Mon, Tues and Jan–Feb). The building itself is a treat, the cloister in particular, and houses furniture and paintings from Saluzzo's medieval heyday. Pride of place goes to a *Madonna della Misericordia* (1499) which shows the Virgin sheltering Ludovico, his wife and Saluzzo's population under the folds of her cloak.

Practicalities in Saluzzo

Tourist Office Via Griselda 2 (0175/46.710) in the council building, the Municipio, a couple of streets below the Casa Cavassa.
Access For the excursion to Saluzzo some 14 services daily, plus several additional buses, ply the 15 km from Savigliano (15 km, 12 min).

Afterwards you can return to the main line at Savigliano or pick up a tiny branch from Saluzzo to Cuneo (5 daily, weekdays only; 34 km, 35 min).
Hotels ☆*Luna* (0175/43.707) or ☆☆*Perpoin* (0175/42.552), both on Via Martiri.

Excursion from Saluzzo

For a closer look at the mountains take a bus west up the Po valley to Revello (8 km) and the alpine resort of **Crissolo**, 32 kilometres from Saluzzo, the best base and place to stay if you want to walk locally. Above the Piano del Re at the head of the valley is the pass over which Hannibal is supposed to have brought his elephants in their famous passage over the Alps.

At **Cuneo** the railway curves high over the river, carried by an impressive Thirties viaduct, the Viadotto Solieri, into what is a surprisingly grand station for so small a town. Tree-lined promenades lead from its forecourt into the town centre, though this isn't a town worth exploring. If you're simply after a bus for an excursion into the mountains they leave from the bays directly in front of the station. If not you can stay on the train and sit back to enjoy the scenery. The long

Practicalities in Limone

Tourist Office Via Roma 30, Limone (0171/92.101)

Hotels ☆*Mignon*, Via San Giovanni 3 (0171/92.363). 7 small rooms and a good little restaurant.

☆☆☆*Principe*, Via Genova 45 (0171/92.389). Big, comfortable hotel in a scenic position (open June–Sept & Dec–April).

Camping *Luis Matlas*, Corso Torino 39 (0171/927.565).

Excursion from Limone

Parco Naturale dell'Argentera

The Argentera National Park is the largest and most accessible of three reserves (Valle Pesio and Palanfré are the other two) that protect a good portion of the Alpi Marittime, the Italian side of the French Riviera's Alpes Maritimes. Its mountains are the most southerly in Italy to have snow year round and contain the Maritime Alps' highest peaks, some half a dozen of which are over 3,000 metres (the Serra dell'Argentera is the highest at 3,297 m). Like the Gran Paradiso National Park it was created around an old Savoy hunting lodge and today is one of the wildest, least known and best-managed of all the protected areas in the Italian Alps. As well as having tremendous scenery and plenty of opportunities for hiking, it's well-known for its incredible variety of wild flowers, an abundance which stems from a serendipitous set of conditions: abundant rainfall, high mountains, and a warm maritime climate, all of which create a lush transitional region embracing both alpine and Mediterranean vegetation zones.

You can get to the park by bus from Cuneo. The best place to aim for as a base is **Sant'Anna di Valdieri**, which has a single hotel and small hostel, or **Terme di Valdieri** based around an old royal hunting lodge – though here the accommodation is more expensive. By far the best day walk is from the Terme up the Valle di Valasco, an idyllic upland meadow surrounded by an amphitheatre of jagged peaks. From here you can continue to a coronet of small lakes and then descend on path number 22 back to the Valle and thus the Terme. Maps are available from shops in Cuneo, Valdieri or Sant'Anna, and there's a park information centre at Valdieri. Paths are all good, and usually well-marked and in summer there's a chain of cheap mountain refuges if you want to spend time in the heart of the mountains.

Practicalities in Valdieri

Information Park Centre, Valdieri (0171/97.937).

Maps Buy the 1:50,000 IGC (Istituto Geografico Centrale) sheet 8 *Alpi Marittime e Liguri*.

haul across the plain suddenly gives way to the mountains with the abruptness that's typical of Piedmont.

From Cuneo (534 m) the train struggles up to **Limone Piemonte** (1,000 m) in only 20 kilometres, doubling back on itself at one point in a spiral tunnel, the first of several extraordinary feats of engineering that guide the line through the mountains. Limone is the place to stop if you want to stay overnight in Italy or ride the resort's ski-lifts in summer to tackle some upland walking. People here speak Provençal but the town's name derives from *leimon*, the Greek for 'meadow', after the flower-strewn fields that wrap around the village. Much of the place is given over to modern ski facilities, but there's an old quarter with a creaky little Romanesque church that's worth seeing, **San Pietro in Vincoli**.

After Limone the train spends several dark minutes in the bowels of the mountains shuddering through the five kilometre Tende Tunnel. It then emerges in France before cutting back almost immediately into another series of galleries that carry the line through the twists of the Roya valley. After about 15 minutes when you have only tantalising glimpses of high wooded slopes and glorious valley scenery the line finally escapes from its tunnels at **Saorge**.

Ventimiglia is still 30 kilometres away, leaving you another 40 minutes of craggy mountains, deep-cut side valleys and broad swathes of forest as the line follows the course of the dipping and unspoilt main valley. Vegetation becomes ever more lush as the sheltered maritime effects of the approaching coast make themselves more felt and the high alpine scenery is left behind.

After these rural delights the coast, and Ventimiglia especially, is a rude awakening. Bar the old quarter's winding streets, Ventimiglia's a thoroughgoing border town just 11 kilometres from the French border. The streets are peppered with duty free shops and dreary hotels, mostly catering to the traffic that's scuttled across from France to enjoy Italy's cheaper prices. Aim to keep moving, and take advantage of the fast trains from Ventimiglia that'll carry you along the Italian Riviera to Genoa and beyond in a few hours. If you do want to take time off in the town to catch your breath there are plenty of hotels: if you simply want to stretch your legs leave the station, cross the road and follow Via della Stazione to intersect with the town's main streets, Via Cavour and Via Roma – most of what counts in town is in this area.

Practicalities in Ventimiglia

Tourist Office Via Cavour 61 (0184/351.183).
Foreign Exchange In the station (daily 7 am – 8 pm) and at Via della Stazione 3a, outside the station (Mon – Sat 8 am – 12.30 and 2.30 – 7 pm).
Hotels ☆*XX Settembre*, Via Roma 16 (0184/351.222). Cheap, amiable and has a reasonable restaurant.
☆*Lido*, Via Marconi 11 (0184/351.473). Reliable seafront option below the old town.

☆*Cavour*, Via Cavour 3 (0184/351.366). Adequate rooms and quietly run.
☆☆*Sea Gull*, Via Marconi 13 (0184/351.726). Comfortable waterfront hotel with small garden and private beach.
Camping *Camping Roma*, Via Peglia 5 (0184/33.580).
Restaurant *Cuneo*, Via Aprosio 16. Fish and pasta specials (closed Wed).

Ventimiglia–Genoa: The Riviera di Ponente

The route

Liguria's 350-kilometre crescent coastline, known as the Italian Riviera, divides into two distinct sections to either side of Genoa (Genova in Italian). To the east is the Riviera di Levante (the 'rising sun'), to the west the Riviera di Ponente (the 'setting sun'). Coming from Spain and the south of France you cross the border at **Ventimiglia**, the town which kicks off the Riviera di Ponente and sets the tone for an almost unbroken ribbon of resorts that in summer are packed solid with Italian holiday-makers. Less showy and expensive than the French Riviera – though by Italian standards most things are still costly – few spots on the Ponente stand out, the better beaches mostly being on the Levante. As a result this is a good region to see from the vantage point of a train. You could happily ride right through to Genoa, but if you wanted to pick just one resort to stay in make it Finale Ligure, and if you want to stretch your legs jump train at Albenga. Alassio and Varazze also have broad, sandy beaches.

The obvious onward journeys from Genoa are to Milan or to La Spezia.

Trains

This part of the coast is extremely well-served by **local trains,** *and by* **international services** *from France. 15 trains run daily from Ventimiglia to Genova (151 km, 2 hr, 30 min) with the occasional through train and plenty of connections at Savona for Turin. Into France there are 10–25 trains daily to Monte Carlo (25 min), Nice (40 min) and Cannes (1 hr) and Marseille (9 daily; 3 hr 15 min).*

The journey

Out of Ventimiglia the landscape quickly settles into Italian mode: the colours are more pastel and the atmosphere more relaxed than across the border. The look of apartment blocks, the cars and the languid demeanour of people in the carriages all suggest Italy's louche version of the Latin; a far less precious version than its Gallic counterpart around the coast. Many of the images associated with the French Riviera, though, also have a place. Purple bougainvillea climbs up whitewashed walls, and palms grow everywhere in defiance of latitude, nurtured by a mild maritime climate and the curving mountain chains behind the coast which cut out the worst of the northern weather. The sea is a constant presence, its aquamarine balm a soothing contrast to the relentless progression of resorts. The area's also one of the most important flower-growing regions in Italy, neat rows of greenhouses and nurseries having supplanted virtually every other type of agriculture on the hills above the coast.

The first stop out of Ventimiglia is **Bordighera**, one of the more refined coastal towns, and one of the first places to attract British emigrés in the last century. Many still pitch up to winter here, keeping alive such home-country institutions as afternoon tea. If you're going to take a look head for the seafront Lungomare Argentina, the street on which the town parades during the *passeggiata*, and which offers good views to the distant Côte d'Azur. The beach is also good and the old town even has a clutch of medieval buildings, though it lacks the kitsch character of its more famous near neighbour.

San Remo was once the jewel, the Nice, of the Italian Riviera, its parks, gardens and genteel air long a favoured spot for such as Tchaikovsky, Edward Lear and the cream of European aristocracy. These days it's on its uppers, but if the place now lacks the glamour of other resorts it's still a part-ritzy, part-sleazy character-filled spot. There's not much to do here, and the beach ranks fairly low, but an hour or two's stroll in its exotic gardens or broad avenues to soak up the atmosphere isn't going to hurt. The most famous promenade is the palm-lined Corso dell'Imperatrice, and the most famous sight the early-morning flower-market on Via Garibaldi (arrive before 6.30 am for the best of the action). San Remo is the capital of the coast's flower towns, the so-called 'Riviera dei Fiori', and something like 20,000 tonnes of rose, carnations and mimosa – amongst others – change hands here every year. From San Remo you can also take the cable car up to **Monte Bignone** (1200 m) from Corso degli Inglesi in the centre of town. On good days you can see as far as Cannes.

Back on the train you can let **Imperia** glide by, and only stop off at **Alassio** off-season – in high summer it's one of the busiest spots on the coast. By general consent it claims Liguria's best beach – three kilometres of good sand – but prices, people and crowds conspire against it. **Albenga**, by contrast, has a pebbly beach with few takers, its main attraction being its old walled quarter, by far the most historic and appealing spot on the Riviera di Ponente. Chief things to see are the 5th-century **Baptistery** – Liguria's most important early Christian building – the cathedral, the Museo Igauno, the small Piazza dei Leoni, and the Palazzo Peloso-Cipolla, which contains finds from a Roman galley sunk in the 1st century BC. If you want a respite from the train and the string of coastal towns, plenty of buses ply country lanes to the mountain villages of the interior.

Finale Ligure hoves into view just before the railway arcs inland and starts an odyssey through a series of long tunnels to emerge at industrial Savona. Hop off at Finale beforehand, though, which despite being a touristy spot is just about the most pleasant place to stay on the coast. It's most famous for its caves, which contain some of Europe's most important prehistoric finds. They're currently closed for excavation, though you can see a little of what's been uncovered in the **Museo Archeologico**, secreted away in the cloisters of a 14th-century Dominican convent, Santa Caterina (10 am–noon and 3–6 pm; closed Mon). The town divides into the area around the beach (the *Marina*) and the old town, *Finalborgo*, about a kilometre from the station which is crowned by the impressive ruins of the Castel Gavonea. Both are spots you can flop down in for an hour or so or pass a night in before pushing on.

Practicalities in Bordighera

Tourist Office Via Roberto I (0184/262.322). From the station turn left on Via Vittorio Emanuele, the town's main street, and Via Roberto is the first right.

Hotels In summer hotels may want you to stay several nights and expect you to take full or half pension. Try ☆☆*Villa Miki*, Via Lagazzi 14 (0184/261.844), just 100 metres from the station, or ☆☆*Nagos*, Piazza Eroi della Libertà (0184/260.457).

Restaurants *La Reserve Tastevin*, Via Arziglia 20. A casual and traditional trattoria almost on the beach with top-notch seafood and good views (closed Mon & Sun pm).
Le Chaudron, Piazza Bengasi 2. A stone-walled and rustic interior which apes a French Provençal look: mainly Ligurian and seafood specialities and moderate to expensive prices (closed Mon).

Practicalities in Albegna

Tourist Office Via Martiri della Libertà 17 (0182/50.475) on the road between the rail and bus stations (also home – with the seafront – to most of the town's hotels).

Hotels ☆*Italia*, Via Martiri della Libertà 10 – which also has a good restaurant (0182/50.405); ☆*Bucaniere*, Lungomare Colombo 8

(0182/50.220); ☆☆*Sole e Mare*, Lungomare Colombo 15 (0182/52.752).

Camping Five minutes on the local bus to Alassio brings you to *Camping Delfino*, Via Aurelia 23 (0182/51.998), with straw pergolas for shade and a seafront setting.

Practicalities in Finale Ligure

Tourist Office Via San Pietro 14 (019/692.581). *Associazione Alberghi* (019/694.252). A small office opposite the station which helps with finding a room (open 9.30 am –8 pm, June–Sept 15).

Railway Station Piazza Vittorio Veneto (information 019/692.777).

Bus Station Via Aurelia 28 (outside the station and turn left).

Youth Hostel *Castello Uvillermin*, (IYHF), Via

Generale Caviglia (019/690.515). In an old castle above the railway station (April–Oct).

Hotels *Albergo Cirio*, Via Pertica 15 (019/692.310). Friendly, central old town location and the first choice amongst the cheap hotels. ☆*Ferrando*, Via Barrili 31 (019/692.355). ☆☆☆*Park Hotel Castello*, Via Caviglia 26 (019/691.320).

Restaurant *Torchi*, Via dell'Annunziata 12 (closed Tues).

Genoa

Few tourists visit **Genoa**, which is mainly known – if at all – as the birth-place of Christopher Columbus (though even this is disputed, despite the great 1992 razzamatazz surrounding the 500th anniversary of his voyage). Perhaps it's because there's nothing terribly famous to see – no Leaning Tower, no outstanding art gallery – or because it's difficult to make any sense of the city's complicated geography, which is all hills, alleys, rumbustious port, meandering old centre and sprawling suburbs. At the same time it's a vibrant place rather in the manner of Naples, full of teeming streets that are worth wandering for their own sake, particu-larly around the port and *centro storico*. Lifts and little cog railways link the many different levels. Its sights are minor and eclectic – mainly small churches and palaces – but they still take up a morning's outing. There's also plenty of cheap if charmless accommodation if you want to stay; if you don't the city's many rail connections make it an easy city to move on from.

History

Genoa started its medieval heyday in thrall to other maritime powers such as Pisa and Venice, but by the 13th century its port and strategic position had made it one of Italy's most powerful cities. Its wealth derived from an empire that stretched as far as North Africa, Syria and the Crimea and was bolstered by lucrative trading and outfitting during the Crusades. The city's prosperity was made manifest by its leading noble families, who built parks and palaces and endowed them with outstanding patrician art collections.

After contesting power in the eastern Mediterranean with Venice, it was eventually defeated in 1380, and thereafter turned its attention to financial as well as mercantile endeavours. Within a couple of centuries Genoa had become one of Europe's leading economic centres, aided in no small part by **Andrea Doria** (1468–1560), one of the greatest admirals of his day. He drove the French from the city and entered into a lucrative alliance with the Spanish under Charles V. Decline came as the city's colonies were lost once more to the Venetians and the Ottomans, and as other ports increasingly grabbed a share of Mediterranean trade. In 1815 Genoa and Liguria joined Piedmont and became embroiled in the unification movement: **Giuseppe Mazzini**, a key mover in the movement was born here, and Garibaldi set sail from here for Sicily with his famous army, the 'Thousand'. Today Genoa's known by its old nickname, *La Superba*, 'the proud', and ranks as one of Italy's largest and most dynamic ports.

What to See

Via Garibaldi

Via Garibaldi is Genoa's most famous street, and amongst Italy's most impressive thoroughfares. Laid out in 1558 as the *Strada Nuova* (the 'new road'), it was designed to accommodate merchants grown plump on the city's 16th-century golden age who were eager to escape the cramped streets of the medieval quarter. Many of Genoa's wonderful *palazzi* have long since been converted to office use, or house impossibly grand antique shops, but a Renaissance air still pervades the streets and the frescoes, fountains and gardens of the vast individual courtyards are as grand as ever.

The grime-covered **Palazzo Bianco** at Via Garibaldi 11 belies its name (the 'White Palace'), but it contains the city's best art collection (Tues–Sat 9 am–1 pm and 3–6 pm; Sun 9 am–noon). Across the way, the **Palazzo Rosso**, Via

Practicalities in Genoa

Tourist Office The main provincial office is at Via Roma 11 (010/591.407 or 581.371) but the smaller city office at Via Porta degli Archi 10 off Via XX Settembre (010/541.541) is of more practical use for the city (both Mon–Thur 8 am–1 pm and 3–5 pm; Fri–Sat 9 am–1 pm.) There are information kiosks at Principe (010/262.633) and Brignole (010/562.056), both open daily 8 am–8 pm.

Railway Stations Genoa has 2 main railway stations: trains from Savona and the north mostly stop at **Stazione Principe** in Piazza Aquaverde (010/284.081); trains from La Spezia and the south stop at **Stazione Brignole** in Piazza Verdi (010/284.081). Through trains often stop at both. Bus numbers 33 and 37 connect the two stations and there's usually a train connection about every 25 mins.

To reach the centre of the city at **Piazza de Ferrari** take bus number 40 from Brignole and 41 from Principe.

Buses City services are run by AIM (010/59.971); provincial services by Tigullio (010/313.851). Long-haul buses depart from both Piazza della Vittoria near Brignole and from Piazza Aquaverde near Principe.

Ferries Ferries to Corsica (010/585.496), Sardinia, Sicily and Tunisia (010/258.041), and Spain (010/284.181). Tickets are widely available from travel agents.

Budget Travel CTS Via San Vicenzo 117r (010/564.366) off Piazza Verdi close to Brignole for discount air tickets, ferries and trains.

Addresses Genoa has a double street numbering system; red for commercial, black for office or residential addresses.

Post Office Piazza Dante behind Piazza de Ferrari and branches in Principe and across the street from Brignole.

Foreign Exchange At both stations.

Police Via Diaz (010/53.661).

Chemist Piazza Acquaverde (near Principe).

Hospital San Martino, Viale Benedetto XV 10 (010/35.351); ambulance (010/595.951)

Where to stay

If you do decide to stay in Genoa it's worth going a touch up-market as most of the plentiful cheaper hotels are pretty grim. The best bets are around Stazione Brignole – steer clear of the *centro storico*. City campsites are uniformly unpleasant and you're better off heading down the coast to the towns of the Riviera di Levante.

Hostel *Casa del Giovane*, Piazza Santa Sabina 4, near Piazza Annunziata (010/206.632 or 281.802). Excellent hostel for women only that's clean, safe and reasonably priced.

Hotels ☆*Carletto*, Via Colombo 16, off Via XX Settembre (010/546.412). In a good neighbourhood not far from Brignole.
☆*Mirella*, Via Gropallo 4 (010/893.722). Off Piazza Brignole; good, clean rooms and friendly management; try also the ☆ *Valle* a couple of flights up in the same block.
☆☆*Agnello d'Oro*, Vico delle Monachette 6 (010/262.084). Forty recently renovated rooms just 100 metres from Principe.
☆☆*Della Posta*, Via Balbi 24 (010/262.00). The best of several *pensioni* in this block.
☆☆☆*Vittorio Orlandini*, Via Balbi 33–45 (010/261.923). A better class of hotel close to Principe.

Where to eat

You'll have no trouble finding a cheap trattoria either in the old centre or around Brignole, where Borgo Incrociate, in particular, is loaded with small traditional restaurants. Make a point of having fish or Genoa's most famous pasta sauce, pesto (oil, basil, pine nuts, cheese and garlic). Chickpeas also feature heavily, either as soup (*zuppa di ceci*) or *farinata*, a type of pancake.

Restaurants *Bakari*, Vicolo della Fieno 16r, off Piazza Soriglia. Old medieval centre restaurant with 6 different fixed-price menus; especially popular at lunch.
Da Colombo e Bruno, Borgo Incrociate 44r. Extremely cheap traditional trattoria.
Sa Pesta, Via Giustiniani, 16r near Piazza Matteotti. Popular with everyone from bankers to dockers for its range of fair-priced Ligurian specialities.

Garibaldi 18 (same hours) contains works by Caravaggio, Dürer and the masterpiece of Genoa's own Bernardo Strozzi, *La Cuoca*, though the palace's overwrought decoration – great mirrors, frescoed ceiling and glittering chandeliers – is as captivating as any of the paintings.

The Centro Storico

Genoa's old 'historic centre' is a teeming medieval labyrinth of narrow alleys (or *caruggi*), washing strung across streets, wayside shrines, teetering houses and dark corners, all of which conspire to make it a superb area to wander in aimless exploration. It's also the haunt of addicts, prostitutes and assorted lowlife, and well worth avoiding after dark or on a quiet Sunday when there aren't many people about.

The **duomo**, San Lorenzo, is a Gothic affair built in the black slate and white marble combination that's common all over Liguria. It dates from the 9th century, though most of the present building went up between the 12th and 16th centuries. Most interest revolves around a bizarre collection of relics, notably a bomb from the Second World War which miraculously failed to explode after crashing into the church. The Museo del Tesoro, or Treasury, on the left side of the church, contains a hoard of the gold and silver ware for which Genoa was once renowned. Amongst the pieces are a pair of plates, one said to have been used at the Last Supper, the other the platter on which John the Baptist's head was supposedly served up to Salomé.

Behind the cathedral lies the city's quaintest square, the **Piazza San Matteo**, once home to the Doria family, the city's medieval overlords, and beyond it Via San Luca, the old town's main thoroughfare. All you can really do round here, though, is wander at will, stumbling across palaces like the **Palazzo Spinola** (Piazza Pellicceria), home to a small art collection, or the church of **Santa Maria di Castello**, an old Crusaders' hostel and one of the city's oldest religious houses: look out for the *Crucifixion* to the left of the high altar on which Christ's beard reputedly grows longer every time a crisis hits the city. A little to the east head for **San Donato**, a fine-looking 12th-century Romanesque church in Piazza San Donato off Via San Bernardo.

To see the ivy-covered house in which **Columbus** reputedly spent his childhood head for Piazza Dante.

Genoa–Cinque Terre–La Spezia
The route

This journey has some of the best coastal scenery you'll see from a train in Italy. Unlike the Riviera di Ponente, the Levante is somewhere you should consider stopping off whether it's for beaches, walking or summer nightlife. The train flashes in and out of dark tunnels, offering glimpses of turquoise sea, terraced vineyards, wooded cliffs and tiny pastel-coloured fishing villages. Although beautiful and romantic, it's not escaped the weight of mass tourism and most of its villages and resorts are popular in summer. The most famous spot is **Portofino**, one of Italy's more exclusive little resorts, accessible by bus from **Santa Margherita**

Ligure, the latter probably the most reasonable base on the northern part of the journey. The **Cinque Terre** – literally the 'five lands' – run a close second, however: five wonderful villages of which three are accessible only by train or by spectacular coastal footpaths. Between the Cinque Terre and Santa Margherita lie **Rapallo** and **Sestri Levante**, the two most developed spots on this part of the coast.

Trains

You have no worries about access on this route – numerous trains run between Genoa and La Spezia (90 km, 1 hr 20 mins). Most Intercity trains stop only at Santa Margherita Ligure, though espressi *also take in Rapallo and Sestri Levante. The bulk of services, however, are slow* locali, *and there's at least one service an hour between the stations of the Cinque Terre on the service between La Spezia and Sestri Levante.*

The journey

The first taste of the Levante is **Recco**, a bland and modern centre raised on the ruins of the old town which was almost completely destroyed by bombing in the Second World War. Immediately beyond you run into **Camogli**, little changed since Dickens described it as the 'saltiest, roughest, most piratical little place'. It takes its name from a contraction of *casa moglie* ('wives' house'), after the length of time husbands were away at sea and only women and children were left in the village. Today it's a relatively sleepy spot surrounded by olives and pine trees, with ranks of tall, green-shuttered houses clustered around a charming little harbour. You could tumble out of the train and either spend time on a pebbly beach – separated from the port by a narrow promontory – or visit the small maritime and archaeological **museum** on Via G. B. Ferrari 41 (9 am–noon; free) which has finds from a nearby Iron Age camp and artifacts from the town's seafaring heyday (when it had a fleet of over 700 boats which it leased all over Europe – more than Genoa – and saw off a naval attack by Napoleon).

Practicalities in Camogli

Tourist Office Via XX Settembre 33 (0185/ 771.066) on your right as you leave the station. It offers a room-finding service.
Hotels ☆*Selene*, Via Cuneo 16 (0185/ 770.149); turn left from the station; best overall choice is ☆☆*La Camogliese*, Via Garibaldi 55 (0185/771.402) on the seafront and just down the stairway in front of the station; ☆☆*Augusta*, Via P. Schiffiano 100 (0185/770.592) is at the opposite end of town.
Eating The many seafront restaurants are mostly bland, expensive or both; try the restaurant at the hotel *La Camogliese*, *Da Fallù*, Salita Priaro (the flight of steps up from the harbour) or the popular *Revello's*, Via Garibaldi 183 for some great snacks, notably the *camogliese* rich chocolate-filled choux pastry.
Ferries *Golfo Paradiso*, Via Scala 2 (0185/ 772.091). Up to 12 boats daily to San Fruttuoso May–Sept.

You could also take a **ferry** for a closer look at the cliffs and seascapes or walk to San Fruttuoso (see below), a hike of about three hours on a well-marked path (follow the double blue dots); the tourist office publishes a free guide to this and other local trails.

The train's next shuddering halt is at **Santa Margherita Ligure**, a pleasant and palm-shaded spot from which to explore the more expensive and precious villages up and down the coast – even if nothing much happens here.

Practicalities in Santa Margherita Ligure

Tourist Office Via XXV Aprile 2b (0185/ 287.485). Turn right from the station on to Via Roma and then right on to Via XXV Aprile; room-finding service and foreign exchange available.

Railway Station Piazza Raoul Nobili at the top of Via Roma (0185/286.630).

Buses From Piazza Martiri della Libertà; *Tigullio* services to Camogli and Portofino.

Ferries *Tigullio*, Via Palestro 8/1b (0185/ 284.670). Boats leave from the dock at Piazza Martiri della Libertà to Portofino, San Fruttuoso and the Cinque Terre (July–mid-Sept only).

Hotels ☆☆*Albergo Fasce*, Via Luigi Bozzo 3, off Corso Matteotti (0185/286.435); the best option, but call to make sure there's room and be prepared to pay a (reasonable) half-pension in August; ☆☆*Annabella*, Via Costasecca 10, Piazza Mazzini close to the town's small pebbly beach (0185/286.531); ☆☆*Moras*, Via Roma 18 (0185/286.758), down the hill from the station; ☆☆*San Giorgio*, Via Cuneo 59 (0185/ 286.770) is small and quiet but a little out of the centre; ☆☆☆*Conte Verde*, Via Zara 1 (0185/287.139) is central and close to the sea.

Eating *Trattoria San Siro*, Corso Matteotti 137; a simple, old-fashioned place with barrel-vaulted ceiling and plenty of locals; *Da Pezzi*, Via Cavour 21 has good local specialities and a separate snack and take-out service if you don't want to sit down;*Cesarino*, Via Maragliano 7 is the top restaurant in town if you want a treat.

Excursion from Santa Margherita Ligure

Portofino and Monte Portofino

An idyllic and romantic-looking fishing village, but long a haunt of the well-heeled, **Portofino**'s prices and exclusivity mean that if you're travelling on a budget it can only realistically be seen as a day-trip. Even then it's not a journey you'll necessarily want to make: so many people come in summer to enjoy the village's intimate charms by proxy – gawping at the expensive boutiques and lines of yachts – that you may want to avoid the scrum of sightseers. For a good overall view of the surroundings walk up the little lane to the church of San Giorgio (sign-posted from the bay) or to the gardens on the way to the castle. The 20-minute stroll out to the lighthouse also has breathtaking panoramas (look for the path marked '*Al Faro*'). By far the best thing to do, though, after an amble around the bay and a drink at one of the bars (worth it, just once, despite the inflated prices) is to escape the crowds by walking on to the **Monte Portofino** (610 m) headland beyond the village. Protected as a nature reserve since 1935, it consists of a lovely tranche of Mediterranean coastline, ringed by cliffs and full of *maquis*, wild flowers (over 700 species), olives, cypresses and herb-scented paths. None of the hikes are terribly difficult, but they're all beautiful and long enough to feel you've had a good jaunt. The most obvious walk strikes out for **San Fruttuoso** (2 hr 30 min), a fishing hamlet midway round the headland between Portofino and Camogli. In summer this, too, is a busy spot, though most people come in by ferry (taking the boat back after the walk is the obvious way to round off a day's outing): off-season, however, it's a peaceful spot to while away the hours or wander around the recently overhauled **Abbey** of San Fruttuoso di Capo di Monte (10 am–1 pm and 2–6 pm). Portofino's tourist office has information on the other paths that criss-cross the promontory.

If you want somewhere to swim locally try **Paraggi**, three kilometres north of Portofino on the road back to Santa Margherita.

Practicalities in Portofino

Tourist Office Via Roma 35 (0185/269.024). Maps and brochures in English, plus hiking information.
Buses *Tigullio* buses run to Portofino from Santa Margherita every 30 mins.

Hotel Portofino has only one reasonably priced hotel, the central ☆☆*Eden*, Vico Dritto 21 (0185/269.091), but you'll have to book ahead most of the year to snaffle one of its nine rooms.

Rapallo is one of the coast's big resorts, still wrapped around the harbour and surrounded by the exquisite countryside which first brought it to the attention of expatriates such as W. B. Yeats and Ezra Pound. Again, in summer it's far too busy and plush if you're on a budget to do anything but pass through. Only the castle and cobbled streets of the old town manage to fend off some of the sense of creeping commercialism and rampant development that have all but killed off the rest of the town. There are walks into the hills to the rear, though, where you can lose the tourists, as well as bus rides to inland hill villages such as Montallegro and San Maurizio di Monti; details from the **tourist office** in Via Diaz 9 (0185/51.282).

Small towns like Chiavari and Lavagna flash by, neither of them remarkable, but each with reasonable beaches, a foretaste of **Sestri Levante**, laid out around a gracious curving peninsula, but almost as grimly developed as Rapallo and just as touristy. If you want time out on a beach head for the second of the town's two bays, the *Baia di Silenzio* ('Bay of Silence') east of Piazza Matteotti (the one furthest away from the railway station). Bars are lively and nightlife racy, as they are in most large Italian resorts in summer, so you may want to spend a little time here if this is what you are after (see the **tourist office** in Via XX Settembre 33 (0185/41.422) for details of the town's many hotels).

For more intimate pleasures and more dramatic coastal scenery try to hold out for the **Cinque Terre** about 20 minutes down the coast. These little villages are increasingly well-known, and have a well-deserved reputation. A self-contained enclave, they were all but cut off from the outside world until the coming of the railway. If you've not taken care to board a stopping train all you'll see are the briefest glimpses of sea and pastel stucco houses as the train emerges for an instant from the tunnels which characterise the line as far as La Spezia. The mountains and cliff-edged coast cramp the villages so much that there's only a couple of carriages on each train where you can step off on to the station platform. Otherwise you have to climb down on to special galleries cut into the tunnels and walk through the gloom to the station.

Any of the fishing villages makes a fine place to stop – preferably outside July and August – and with each only a minute or so away from its neighbour by train it's easy to explore all five. You'll soon discover your own favourite. A special daily tourist ticket is available on the railway which gives unlimited travel between the five villages.

From north to south you'll find **Monterosso**, the largest and least charming, but with the biggest and best beach and a relatively large number of hotels; **Vernazza**, with picturesque if perhaps slightly self-conscious charm – a place to visit for the day as there are only two well-hidden hotels. The tourist office in the Castello is especially good and there's a proper sandy beach and plenty of flat rocks by the harbour for swimming and sunning; **Corniglia**, home to a long pebbly beach, though at weekends you can walk through a disused railway to a gorgeous (largely nudist) beach close by; **Manarola**, perhaps the most genuine village, and with no beach but excellent swimming from the rocks either side of the harbour; and **Riomaggiore**, incredibly picturesque, with lots of private rooms to rent, and a small pebbly beach complemented by good swimming from the rocks.

Many people stay in **Levanto**, just to the north of the five villages, because it has plenty of hotels, a stunning mountain backdrop and plenty of charm – though this is something all the villages possess in abundance. There's also a small beach and prices are perhaps a touch lower than in the villages themselves. Be sure to visit the **tourist office** near to the seafront at Piazza C. Colombo 2 (0187/808.125). You should also try to walk along some of the dramatic coastal paths that link each village, or venture along the network of far more remote trails that weave up amongst the craggy countryside and myriad tiny terraces in the mountains behind them. All the tracks are well-worn and many have been marked by the Italian Alpine Club (CAI), although it's still a good idea to have decent footwear. Boats as well as trains connect all the villages if you don't want to walk back – and remember that while distances look short on the map there's plenty of up and down to stretch out the walks.

After the palms, lemon trees and fairy-tale quality of the Cinque Terre the blunt and prosaic arrival of La Spezia is something of a shock. It's a busy commercial centre and Italy's main naval port, but there's no need to stop here, unless you're completely stuck for accommodation further north or want to catch a ferry to Corsica.

Practicalities in La Spezia

Tourist Office Via Mazzini 47, La Spezia (0187/36.000). Turn left out of the station on Via Siffredi for the office and the centre of town.

Hotels Most of the cheap hotels are immediately left of the station; try ☆*Flavia*, Vicolo dello Stagno 7, off Via del Prione (0187/ 27.465); ☆☆*Terminus*, Via Paleocapa 21 (0187/37.204); ☆☆*Firenze & Continental* (0187/31.248) and ☆☆*Parma* (0187/20.754) both on Via Fiume.

Ferries *Corsica Ferries*, Molo Italia (0187/ 21.282) run daily summer services to Bastia on Corsica (5 hrs).

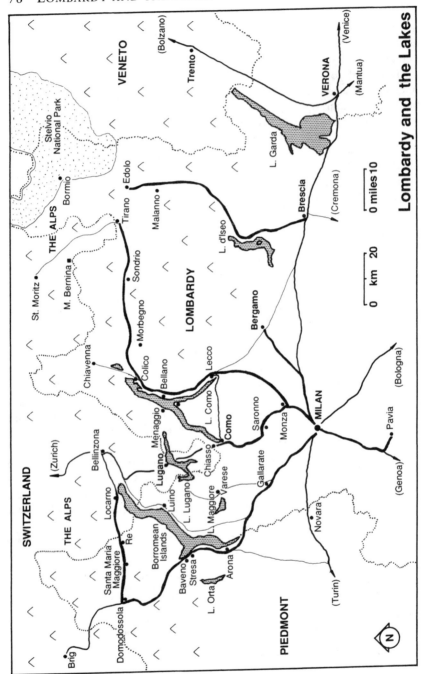

Lombardy and the Lakes

2 Lombardy and the Lakes

Italy's richest region, **Lombardy** is a perfect balance of city and country-side. Like Piedmont it is divided between the plains of the Po valley and the mountains of the high Alps. At its heart lies **Milan**, the powerhouse of Italy's financial and fashion worlds. Elsewhere a coronet of small cities like Pavia, Bergamo and Brescia combine old medieval centres with flour-ishing industrial hinterlands. North of Milan several vast **lakes** push into the mountains, areas celebrated for centuries for their natural beauty. A wave of prosperity washes over much of the region, partly as a result of its position – close to the mountain passes linking it with northern Europe – and partly because of an intense work ethic seemingly less pre-valent elsewhere in Italy.

Politically the region is coming increasingly under the sway of the new 'leagues', influential parties that exploit a popular dissatisfaction with the government in Rome. They argue the case for splitting Italy, separat-ing the north and its powerful economy from the south, a region whose corruption and inefficiency they say is holding the country back. The argument has historical precedents. Lombardy has frequently looked north – to Europe – rather than to the south. As early as the 4th century Milan was capital of the Roman Empire, Rome itself having become a city of decadence and sloth. Outsiders often saw Milan as the *de facto* capital of the Italian peninsula: Charlemagne and Napoleon, for example, both came here to be crowned. And for centuries before Uni-fication in 1860 the region was ruled by the French and Austrians: both powers left a northern stamp on its culture. Even Lombardy's name has northern roots, deriving from the Lombards, a Teutonic race who settled the region in 568 after the collapse of Rome. From the 9th century the region was officially part of the Holy Roman Empire, ruled from Ger-many and later Austria, though numerous independent city states were to develop in the course of the Middle Ages.

Milan makes the obvious starting point from which to explore the area. As a city in its own right it has relatively little to see. Most people, moreover, find its busy modern face less appealing than the more obvious historical cities of Florence or Venice. The duomo, however, the Brera art gallery and Leonardo's *Last Supper* are all things you should try to see. Another point in the city's favour, of course, is its excellent rail links.

Fascinating spots like **Pavia** and **Bergamo** are less than an hour away by train. Better still, lakes and mountains are just as close, surprisingly easy escapes from the city.

Lakes Como and **Maggiore** easily merit a visit, romantic if popular spots renowned for their lakeside villas, glorious gardens and spectacular scenery. Towns and villages dotted around the shores offer respite from the heat and hustle of the plain-bound cities. Trains also take you surprisingly close to pristine mountain scenery, in many cases a short bus ride from great walking country.

Routes Milan
        Milan–Pavia
        Milan–Bergamo
        Milan–Lago Maggiore–Domodossola
        Domodossola–Re–Locarno
        Locarno–Lugano–Como–Milan
        Milan–(Como)–Lecco–Sondrio–Tirano
        Brescia–Edolo

One obvious circuit presents itself if you want a good taste of both lakes and mountains. **Milan–Domodossola** *strikes to the heart of the Alps, running alongside Lago Maggiore en route. At Domodossola you can pick up the* **Domodossola–Locarno** *line, one of the most scenic mountain routes in the country. At Locarno it's an easy matter to connect with the* **Locarno–Como–Milan** *route, the best way to see Lago di Como, the most dramatic of all the Italian Lakes.*

    Milan–Sondrio–Tirano *is a less-travelled ride that also takes you into the Alps, providing the chance to ride Europe's highest and most spectacular railway (to St Moritz).* **Brescia–Edolo** *is the most disappointing of the mountain routes, though it comes good at Edolo, ringed by the mountains and glaciers of the Stelvio National Park.*

    Beyond Milan *frequent connections run to all corners of the country, the three principal lines serving to* **Turin, Venice** *and* **Bologna.**

Milan

Italy's capital of fashion and high finance also contains a welter of churches, palaces and galleries, a bewildering prospect for anyone determined to do the traditional tourist round. The problem of what to see somehow seems worse here than in Rome or Venice, perhaps because the city appears both much larger and more modern than most Italian centres. In truth, though, Milan is not as much fun to wander around as some historic spots, and once you've sifted out its many take-it-or-leave-it sights, the essential stop-offs boil down to half a dozen places all within reasonable walking distance of one another. The key destinations are the central **Piazza del Duomo** and its great cathedral; the **Scala** opera house; two major **art museums** – the Brera and Poldi-Pezzoli; the **Castello Sforzesco** and its museums; Santa Maria delle Grazie and **Leonardo's** *Last Supper*; and the church of **Sant'Ambrogio**, one of Milan's most important early Christian churches.

History

Milan's strength is its position, which places it at the crossroads of trade routes from the east and west and between the northern Alpine passes and the rest of Italy. It's also right at the heart of the Lombard plain, close to three major navigable rivers (the Po, Adda and Ticino), in their day all key arteries in a system of canals and waterways that gave access to most of northern Italy. A Roman colony, *Mediolanum*, as early as the 3rd century BC, it became the main seat of the Roman army and the Empire's effective capital from AD 286 to 403. The army was quartered here, and Constantine's famous edict of 313 recognising Christianity was delivered from the city. Thereafter every major-league European invader plundered the colony, including the Gauls, Goths, Franks and Lombards.

The charismatic **St Ambrose**, Milan's first bishop (in the 4th century), helped paper over divisions in the early Church, and established the city as a major religious centre which remained largely independent of Rome until the 11th century. During the Middle Ages it became one of Italy's earliest and most powerful independent *comuni*, later passing to the famous **Visconti** family, whose most prominent member, Gian Galeazzo (1351–1402), figures larger-than-life in many of the city's annals. Next came the **Sforzas**, under whom the city earned the title of the 'New Athens' after the artists and scholars attracted to their court (Bramante and Leonardo da Vinci among them). France took the city in 1499, ushering in around four centuries of foreign domination which included rule by the Spaniards, the Austrians (1712) and a brief appearance by Napoleon.

In more recent times Mussolini started his journalistic career in Milan before moving on, returning once in power to inaugurate the city's tremendous railway station. He was also strung up here after being captured and executed by partisans near Lake Maggiore.

Today Milan seems to be largely at odds with the rest of Italy, at least on the surface, making it as much a city to see for its divergence from the Italian mainstream as for its sights. Whereas Rome is often described as a 'northern suburb of Cairo', Milan is a 'southern quarter of Paris', that's to say worldly, European, forward-thinking and efficient. It's Italy's economic hub, and the country's big deals and political arm-twisting are as likely to take place in its sleek skyscrapers as they are in the corridors of Rome's crumbling bureaucracies. Materialism is rife, though, and there's something just a little distasteful in the opulence of expensive cars, clothes and trinkets that are the *sine qua non* of the wealthier Milanese. Recently the city has also been rocked by all sorts of nefarious corruption scandals involving the great, good and not-so-good. Its woes are compounded by smog and some of Europe's highest pollution levels.

What to see

Piazza del Duomo

Few Italian cathedrals are as immediately eye-catching as the fantastically over-decorated bauble at the heart of Milan's central piazza. Italy's largest Gothic cathedral, and Europe's third largest church after St Peter's, Rome and Seville's cathedral, the **Duomo** was started in 1386 by Gian Galeazzo Visconti in the hope that Heaven would reward him with a male heir. (It did, though Visconti's son, the degenerate Giovanni Maria, was assassinated soon after coming to power.) Over the next four centuries the building was loaded with an enormous weight of decoration – 2,245 statues, 135 spires, 96 gargoyles and about a kilometre of tracery. Work was only completed (on Napoleon's insistence) in 1809, by which time the church had become an impressive but fantasmagorical conglomeration of Gothic, Renaissance and Baroque elements. The whole thing became so far-fetched that there were even plans at the end of the last century to tear the whole thing down and start again.

Rather like St Peter's the **interior** bludgeons you primarily with its dimensions, appearing as a vast canopy spread over five aisles and propped up by some 52 colossal columns. It can accommodate around 40,000 worshippers, and according to the poet Shelley, was the most fitting place to read Dante. Persuasive works of art are thin on the ground, though the **stained glass windows** are some of the world's largest and the enormous bronze candlestick is an important medieval work. Look out for the world's largest sun dial (1786), bedded in the floor near the entrance, and for the wonderful 16th-century statue of San Bartolomeo, whose horrific martyrdom – he was flayed alive – is sculpted with gruesome anatomical explicitness. The large Crucifix high above the altar contains one of the main nails from the True Cross, and is suspended on a pulley system designed by Leonardo da Vinci.

Near the church's main entrance steps lead down to the fascinating remains of an ancient baptistery containing the font used to baptise St Augustine on his conversion to Christianity.

From the **cathedral roof** (entrance outside the left, or north transept), take a closer look at the fairytale domain of spires and turrets, and note the views which – smog allowing – extend over the city as far as the Matterhorn. The **Museo del Duomo** in Palazzo Reale on the piazza's right side, consists mostly of casts taken from the cathedral's statues and gargoyles, and models of 19th-century schemes to design a new façade. Upstairs is a good collection of (mostly Italian) modern art contained in the **Museo Civico d'Arte Contemporanea**. (9.30 am–noon and 3–5.30 pm, closed Mon; free).

Galleria Vittorio Emanuele

Immediately off Piazza del Duomo's north side (to the duomo's left) stands the **Galleria Vittorio Emanuele**, a beautiful glass-domed gallery designed in 1865 that marks the apotheosis of Belle Epoque splendour. Its creator, Giuseppe Mengoni, fell through the roof and was killed a few days before it was inaugurated. The Milanese call it the city's *salotto*, or living room, its shops, cafés and offices making it a great place to people-watch. Bite the bullet and pay the surcharge for the privilege of sitting down with a coffee to take it all in. If you're feeling in poor shape, look over the zodiac mosaic under the main cupola and stand on Taurus's testicles – it's meant to bring good luck.

La Scala

Walk through the Galleria and you emerge on to Piazza Scala with the famous **La Scala** opera house on your left. Named after a church which used to stand on the site, Santa Maria della Scala, the auditorium was inaugurated in 1778, though the present building largely dates from after the Second World War, when it was rebuilt following bomb damage. The **Museo Teatrale alla Scala**, entered through a door on the left of the main entrance (9 am–noon and 2–6 pm, closed Sun from Oct–April) offers much opera memorabilia – Verdi's top hat and pencils of great composers included – and you can peek into the 2,800-seat auditorium, best known for its famous chandelier.

Museo Poldi-Pezzoli

Beyond La Scala runs Via Manzoni, one of the city's most fashionable and frenetic streets. About a 100 metres up on the right at Via Manzoni 28 stands a 17th-century palace that belonged to erstwhile local bigwig, Giacomo Poldi-Pezzoli, and which now holds the art collection that he left to the State in 1879 (daily 9.30 am–12.30 pm and 2.30–7.30 pm; closed Mon and Sun afternoons April-Sept). Some of this consists of oddments such as jewellery, clocks and cutlery, but in the Salone Dorato, or 'Golden Room', which looks on to a lovely garden, are many outstanding paintings including works by Antonio Pollaiuolo, Piero della Francesca, Mantegna, Botticelli, Guardi, Giovanni Bellini, Raphael and many more, all complemented by a worthy collection of Islamic metalwork, Persian rugs, Flemish tapestries, Murano glass, bronzes and suits of medieval and Renaissance armour.

Accademia Brera

Walk another 200 metres up Via Manzoni and you come to the junction of Via Monte Napoleone, Milan's main collection of fashionable shops – great for window shopping but probably not for purchases. Turn left here (or return towards La Scala and turn right on Via Verdi) and after about ten minutes you come to the Accademia Brera, Via Brera 26, located in one of Milan's more appealing quarters and by far the city's most important museum. It's a big place, though and one in which to pick out highlights unless you're prepared to make several return visits (weekdays 9 am–6 pm; weekends 9 am–1 pm; closed Mon; free 1st and 3rd Sun and 2nd and 4th Sat each month).

Much of the collection, ranked one of Italy's best, is down to Napoleon, who ransacked northern Italy's churches and palaces to create a Louvre-type central collection for Milan, the capital of his short-lived Cisalpine Republic. It opened to the public in 1809. The best tidbits amongst a feast of paintings are Raphael's *Marriage of the Virgin* and Piero della Francesca's last work, the *Pala di Urbino*, which includes the famously hook-nosed Federigo of Montefeltro amongst its cast of characters. There are also outstanding works by Mantegna, the Venetians Giovanni Bellini, Tintoretto, Veronese and from the 17th century Caravaggio, El Greco and Rembrandt.

There is also the small but sharp little collection of modern Italian offerings by such as Modigliani, Carlo Carrà and De Chirico.

Castello Sforzesco

The rebuilt, red-brick Castello Sforzesco closes off the western edge of the Brera district. It's one of the city's best-known landmarks – if only for its tremendous size, imperious towers and fortified walls. Started, almost inevitably, by the Viscontis, its first incarnation was razed to the ground in 1447 by mobs railing against the family's regime. Rebuilt by the Sforzas soon after, under Ludovico Sforza it became the seat of Europe's leading court, a by-word for wealth and ostentation, and a home to artists including Bramante and Leonardo da Vinci. Decline set in following Milan's drubbing by the French in 1499, the castle becoming little more than a barracks for successive armies of occupation until the 19th century when it was converted into a series of museums. Its most recent pounding came from air raids in the Second World War.

The vast interior is built around three courtyards, one of which, the Corte Ducale originally formed the core of the residential quarters and now contains the entrance to the **Museo Civico d'Arte Antica del Castello** and the **Pinacoteca** upstairs (9.30 am–noon and 2.30–5 pm, closed Mon). The museum's rather a mish-mash, devoted mostly to sculpture, of which the highlight is undoubtedly Michelangelo's unfinished *Pietà Rondanini*, believed to be the sculptor's last work.

In the impressive gallery itself the first room offers a 15th-century fresco cycle and works by Giovanni Bellini, Mantegna, Crivelli and Filippo Lippi (an especially impressive *Madonna and Angels*), as well as a surfeit of offerings by Vincenzo Foppa, Milan's leading light before Leonardo arrived to steal his thunder.

Before leaving the castle aim for the third of its courtyards, the lovely Bramante-designed Cortile della Rocchetta (left of the Corte Ducale), whose basement houses a neat Egyptian collection and prehistoric miscellany gathered from Lombardy's various Iron Age sites. Equally appealing is the charming **museum of musical instruments** on the upper floor, with a beautiful display of string and wind instruments spanning five centuries.

Santa Maria delle Grazie and 'The Last Supper'

Milan's most famous painting is a strange affair. *The Last Supper* is one of the world's best known images, and yet in the flesh its faded and badly damaged surface makes for chastening viewing. Aldous Huxley called it 'the saddest painting in the world'. It's housed in the old refectory of Santa Maria delle Grazie, on Piazza di Santa Maria delle Grazie and Corso Magenta, ten minutes' walk west of the Castello Sforzesco. The Renaissance church is worth a look in its own right. Its famous fresco, outstanding dome, cloister and choir – designed by Bramante – add to the fact that it was intended as a grand family mausoleum for the Sforzas. Most people, though, aren't interested in the church, and hurry to see Leonardo's masterpiece, which is housed in Santa Maria's old monastery refectory (daily 9 am – 1.15 pm).

For all its bleached grandeur, the *Last Supper* remains a powerful work, capturing the moment Christ announces that one of His disciples will betray Him. Gestures and expressions, where they can be made out, are caught in almost photographic detail.

The painting's poor condition stems directly – though not solely – from Leonardo's determination to forgo accepted fresco procedure. Instead of applying pigment to wet plaster, a fast-drying and long-lasting technique, he painted onto a dry plaster surface in oil and tempera. This allowed him far more flexibility in colour and tone, but the price was impermanence, and within five years moisture was already causing the mural's deterioration. Restorers worked on the wall with a vengeance over the centuries, with mixed and usually detrimental results. According to a 19th-century source monks at one point simply whitewashed part of the wall. Worse still, when Napoleonic troops were billeted here they used the wall for target practice, and in 1943 a bomb destroyed the building, leaving only the wall containing the *Last Supper* intact. Modern restoration is now trying to put right the errors of the past, so be prepared for the scaffolding which you may find obstructing chunks of the painting.

Close by, you may want to see the slightly tired displays of the **Museo della Scienza e della Tecnica**, in blocks to the north at Via San Vittore 21. Unless you want to wade through the wide-ranging science exhibits, make straight for the Leonardo da Vinci gallery which displays models and explanations of the master's machines and inventions (daily 9.30 am – 5pm, closed Mon).

Sant'Ambrogio

Founded in 379 by St Ambrose, Sant'Ambrogio was to provide the prototype for many of Italy's Lombard-Romanesque churches, making it one of the most

Practicalities in Milan

Telephone Code 02.

Tourist Office Palazzo del Turismo, Via Marconi 1 (809.662), just off Piazza del Duomo to the right of the cathedral (Mon–Sat 8 am–8 pm, Sun 9 am–12.30 pm and 1.30–5 pm).

There's also a branch office at the Stazione Centrale (669.0532, Mon–Sat 8 am–6 pm). Neither will book rooms, but they will – albeit reluctantly – phone around to check for vacancies. For extra hotel information and reservations call the **Hotel Reservation Milano** (7600.6095).

Railway Stations Milan has four main stations (Centrale, Lambrate, Nord and Garibaldi), but you're only likely to use the vast Centrale in Piazza Duca D'Aosta – it has left luggage, shops, post office, exchange, baths and showers and a wide range of miscellaneous facilities.

Train Information Stazione Centrale, on the far left of the station as you face the platforms (222.441; daily 7 am–11 pm).

Metro Milan has an extensive, straightforward and efficient underground system, by far the best way of getting around the city.

Foreign Exchange *Banco Nazionale delle Communicazioni* at the Stazione Centrale (Mon–Sat 8 am–6.30 pm, Sun 9 am–2.30 pm).

Post Office Stazione Centrale or Piazza Cordusio 4, near the Duomo (Mon–Fri 8.15 am–7.40 pm, Sat 8.15 am–5.40 pm).

United Kingdom Consulate Via San Paolo 7 (803.442).

Emergencies Police (77.271); *SOS for Tourists* (545.6551).

Where to Stay

Milan is not a place you want to spend a lot of time, and there's a good argument for staying elsewhere and coming here on a day trip. Pavia or some of the towns around lakes Como and Maggiore make good bases. If you do need a hotel there are plenty of cheap and charmless places between Centrale and the city centre (walk straight out of the station and head for the streets across the large piazza to the left). Try the tourist offices first if you arrive without a bed. All the places below are near the station or around Corso Buenos Aires to the east. Aim to book in early or call in advance to be sure of room – though in cheap places a telephone booking doesn't necessarily mean they'll keep you a room.

Youth Hotel *Ostelle Piero Rotta* Via Martino Bassi 2 (3926.7095). Large, modern IYHF hostel in north west suburb: take metro line 1 to Lotto.

Hotels ☆☆*Pensione Valley* Via Soperga 19 (669.2777). Good, safe rooms and a bargain at the price: try also the *Soperga* in the same block, 278.228).

☆☆*San Marco*, Via Piccinni 25 (204.5396). Restful air and friendly management.

☆☆*Canna* (2952.0219) and *Kennedy* (2940.0934). 2 of several budget hotels in the same block at Viale Tunisia 6.

☆☆*Aurora*, Corso Buenos Aires 18 (204.9285). Grim-looking from the outside but the rooms inside are modern and clean.

☆☆*Due Giardini*, Via Settala 46 (2952.1093). Turn left out of the station on Via Scarlatti and Via Settala is the fourth on the right.

☆☆*Pensione Londra* (228.400) and *Parva Domus* (204.1138). Two popular spots at Piazza Argentina 4.

☆☆☆/☆☆☆☆*Solferino*, Via Castelfidaro 2 (657.0129). Be sure to book if you want to grab 1 of the 11 rooms in a hotel whose facilities and fittings are good at the price.

Where to Eat

Finding small back-street pizzerias and cheap trattorias presents no problems in Milan unless you're in town during August. Then the whole place shuts down for the normally workaholic Milanese to take their holidays. For the less touristy and less tawdry spots start looking away from the station, however. Snack and fast food places proliferate and there are street markets galore for cheap picnic provisions.

Bar Magenta, Via Carducci 13, at Corso Magenta. A venerable Milan institution and popular busy bar; good lunchtime snacks and busy evening drinking.

Bottega del Vino, Via Victor Hugo 4. Good for stand-up lunch, and then lie-down siesta – there are 200 wines available by the glass.

Brek, heavily-patronised self-service chain with excellent value main course and good salads aimed at the city's hard-pressed office workers; further outlets at Via del Duca 5, Corso Italia 3 and Via Lepetit 20 near the station.

Ciao Another good, city-wide chain with fine, cheap food; branches at Piazza del Duomo, Via Dante, Corso Europa 12, Corso Buenos Aires and Via Fabio Filzi, near the main station.

Flash, Via Bergamini 1 at Piazza Santo Stefano. Great snacks and pizzas in a crowded spot near the Duomo.

Grand Italia, Via Palermo 5. Bargain spot in the Brera bars and nightlife district; good for pizzas but also has a limited pasta and main course menu.

La Bruschetta, Piazza Beccaria 12. A good location close to the Duomo and great pizzas

make this a packed spot; you'll probably have to queue for a table but it's worth it.
La Piazzetta, Via Solferino 25. A Brera restaurant popular with journalists, actors and politicians.

Viel, Via Luca Beltrami. Another chain, this time responsible for the city's best ice cream and milkshakes. There's a second outlet at Via Marconi 3e near the tourist office, well-placed to eat your goodies near the Duomo.

influential and important of the city's religious buildings. Little of the original church survives, though the saint's body still resides in the crypt, an important set of relics for many Milanese, who still refer to themselves as 'Ambrosiani'. You may remember the ill-fated Banco Ambrosiano headed by Roberto Calvi who was found hanged under London's Blackfriars Bridge.

Inside, the **interior**'s rib-vaulting was revolutionary in its day, while the arched women's gallery, or *matroneum*, is a feature found only rarely in Italian churches. The chief treasures are a superb **pulpit**, amongst Italy's finest Romanesque works, an 11th-century mosaic in the apse, the sanctuary's 12th-century *ciborium* and an extravagant 9th-century gold, silver and gem-studded altar. In the seventh chapel on the right you'll find the Cappella di San Vittore, part of the 4th-century church, distinguished by its cupola's glittering 5th-century mosaics. Notice the figure of Ambrose and his lop-sided face, a deformity researchers believe was caused by a deep-set tooth, a detail discovered during an autopsy on his remains, now laid out in the crypt alongside two martyred Roman soldiers.

Milan–Pavia

The route

Little in the 25 minute train ride from Milan to Pavia excites attention: it's **Pavia** that you've come to see, and the **Certosa di Pavia** in particular, one of Lombardy's greatest buildings. Think of the town as a good day trip from Milan or even as a base from which to explore Milan itself.

Trains

More than 20 trains a day run from Milan's Stazione Centrale to Pavia (35 km, 25 min).

Pavia

Although a delightful medieval city at heart, Pavia's heyday came as early as the 5th century when it was the capital first of the Goths and then of the Lombards, who between 572 and 774 made it the head of the *Regnum Italicum*, the most important of their three Italian duchies. It remained pre-eminent until the 11th century, and both Charlemagne (774) and the Emperor Frederick Barbarossa (1155) were crowned within its precincts. In the Middle Ages it was known as 'the city of a hundred towers' (one of the grandest, the Torre Civica, collapsed in 1989 killing four people). Its independence was surrendered to Milan in 1359, the city becoming a fiefdom of the Viscontis. Today it's famous for sewing machines and its university, founded in 1361, but with earlier roots in a Roman law school.

Piazza della Vittoria

Most of Pavia's downtown appeal lies in wandering its streets and stumbling from one church and sleepy piazza to another. Start at the central Piazza della Vittoria and the **duomo**, currently in the throes of long-term restoration after the collapse of the tower which flanked its west face. It's a strange Renaissance dog's-dinner, made up of ingredients suggested by at least a dozen architects. Some of these were illustrious names like Bramante and Leonardo da Vinci, others people like Pavia's own half-crazed Giovanni Antonio Amadeo (whose work you'll also see at the Certosa di Pavia). At its inception in 1488, the building was to have been the region's most ambitious creation, but design by committee, lack of funds and general apathy meant it was only properly completed this century. The building alongside is the rebuilt 12th-century Palazzo del Comune, known locally as the **Broletto**.

San Michele

San Michele, the town's best church, stands less than five minutes' walk from the duomo in Via Cavallotti. Founded in 661 it was rebuilt in the 12th century following destruction either by lightning or by earthquake – the stories vary. The lumbering façade uses heavy yellow sandstone, an unusual medium in Italy, which lends it a lovely honey-coloured warmth but not the best stone with which to carve its friezes and capitals. Inside all is pretty sombre, making it hard to believe that this was long a venue for royal coronations. Take note of the unusual *matroneum*, or women's gallery, used to segregate the congregation, the carvings of the capitals, a series of 14th-century bas-reliefs, and the church's chief treasure, a 7th-century silver Crucifix (found in the chapel to the right of the main altar).

Castello Visconteo

One of Pavia's two main streets, the Strada Nuova, a hangover from the town's old Roman grid, ends in the huge Castello Visconteo, fringed by a grassy moat and bristling with a crop of sturdy towers. Started in 1360 by Galeazzo II Visconti, it was added to by the Sforzas and then partially destroyed after the Battle of Pavia in 1525 (a dénouement at which Emperor Charles V captured Francis I of France). Size apart there's little going for the place, simply a modest art gallery and museum full of Roman remains, sculptures and mosaics (10 am–noon and 2–4 pm, Aug, Dec and Jan 9 am–1 pm only).

Behind the castle in Via Griziotti lurk the low, rounded outlines of Pavia's second-ranking Romanesque church, **San Pietro in Ciel d'Oro** (1132), or 'St Peter's of the Golden Sky', named after its once gilded ceiling, so beautiful that it merited a mention in Dante's *Paradiso*. Its finest work now is a 14th-century altarpiece built over the bones of St Augustine, whose remains were brought to Pavia – then the Lombard capital – in 710 from North Africa by way of Sardinia.

Excursion from Pavia

Certosa di Pavia

Certosa in Italian, Chartreuse in French and Charterhouse in English, all mean the same thing – a Carthusian monastery. Jacob Burckhardt called the Certosa di Pavia, eight kilometres from Pavia, the 'greatest decorative masterpiece in all of Italy', which is perhaps pitching things a little high, though by any standards the Carthusian Charterhouse and erstwhile mausoleum of the Viscontis marks the highpoint of the Lombard Renaissance and a glittering record of artistic endeavour over three centuries (Tues– Sun 9–11.30 am and 2.30–5.30 pm, 4 pm in the winter; free – try to avoid weekends when the complex becomes crowded).

Gian Galeazzo Visconti laid the first stone in 1396 hoping to inaugurate a building to match Milan's cathedral and – more to the point – one that would be a fitting monument to the glory of the Visconti clan. He died from the plague in 1402, though, and never saw the finished project. He was, however, the only Visconti interred here, some 75 years after his death. No expense was spared during construction, marble being brought from Carrara over 250 kilometres away. Craftsmen were diverted from Milan's duomo to work on its early stages, though by the time it was finished over a century later it bore the stamp of Pavia's own Antonio Amadeo – especially noticeable in the fantastically decorated façade.

The **interior** decoration is no less sumptuous, combining statues, tombs and paintings, and 14 side chapels festooned in virulently-coloured marble swathes. Some is mere Baroque froth, some outstanding, most notably Solari's **tomb of Lodovico il Moro** and his child bride, Beatrice d'Este. Lodovico was a Sforza, the seventh duke of Milan, and the man who commissioned Leonardo's *Last Supper*. He married his 16-year-old bride when he was 40, and they shared six happy years together before Beatrice died giving birth to a still-born child. The sculptor's brief was to design a tomb expressing the happiness of the marriage. These days, though, it's empty, the bones having disappeared during a move from Milan's Santa Maria delle Grazie. The tomb originally stood in front of the church's altar, but the Dominicans offered it for sale – the Carthusians made the highest offer.

Other artworks to look out for include Bergognone's five statues of saints (in the sixth chapel on the left), the tomb of Galeazzo Visconti, and the old sacristy's 15th-century ivory altarpiece, a Florentine triptych whose 94 figures and 66 bas-reliefs describe the lives of Christ and the Virgin Mary.

You can see the church unaccompanied, but for a look at the rest of the monastery complex you have to team up with a worthwhile guided tour under the leadership of a Carthusian monk – specially released from the Order's strict vow of silence. The tours start from inside the church about every 45 minutes.

To reach the Certosa take a **bus** from Piazza Piave opposite Pavia's railway station, or one of the less than frequent **trains** from the station (6 daily, 7 min). From the station serving the Certosa turn left and walk around the monastery's walls until you reach the entrance, a beguiling 1.5-kilometre walk up a tree-lined avenue. The surrounding parkland was part of a Visconti hunting reserve that ran as far as Pavia's Castello: it was also the site of the Battle of Pavia where Charles v defeated the French, laying open Italy and leading ultimately to the infamous Sack of Rome in 1527.

If you've the stomach for more churches hunt out the Gothic **Santa Maria del Carmine** (1390s), hidden behind a typical Lombard façade and rose window, or the more plain **San Lanfranco**, noted for its *Arca di Lanfranco* (1498), another sculptural diversion by G. A. Amadeo.

Practicalities in Pavia

Tourist Office Via F. Filzi 2 (0382/22.156). Turn left from the station on Via Trieste and then right on Via F. Filzi.

Railway Station Pavia's station is in the modern west end of the town, connected to the old centre by Corso Cavour (straight on from the forecourt). Bus numbers 3 and 6 make the journey if you don't want the 10-minute walk.

Hotels ☆*Splendide*, Via XX Settembre 11 (0382/24.703). Friendly but down-at-heel – probably a last-resort choice only.

☆☆*Regisole*, Piazza Duomo 2 (0382/24.739). Clean, friendly and perfectly placed opposite the duomo.

☆☆☆*Aurora*, Via Vittorio Emanuele 25 (0382/23.664). A smarter spot close to the station.

☆☆☆☆*Ariston*, Via A. Scopoli 10d (0382/34.334). Central, comfortable hotel and better value than anything at the same price in Milan.

Camping *Camping Ticino*, at Bagno Chiosso, Via Mascherpa 10 (0382/525.362; May – Sept); bus number 4 from the station.

Eating Pavia is known for its cuisine (rabbit and frogs are the main specialities) and as a consequence you'll find plenty of good if fairly pricey restaurants. Top of the pile is the *Vecchia Pavia*, near the duomo at Via Cardinale Riboldi 2. For something cheaper try *Osteria della Madonna*, Via Liguri 28, or cheaper still, *Da Andrea*, Via Teodolina 23 (off Piazza del Duomo). If you're after a pizza repair to the homely and busy *Marechiaro*, Piazza della Vittoria 9. *Bar Vittoria* at Strada Nuova 8 has a huge choice of sandwiches.

Milan–Bergamo

The route

The main point of this easy trip is to see hill-top Bergamo, one of northern Italy's loveliest cities, home to the Piazza Vecchia and the Accademia Carrara, amongst the greatest art collections in northern Italy. Although the quickest main line route is from Milan there's no reason why you shouldn't incorporate the town into other itineraries from either Brescia to the east or Lecco and the Lakes to the north. Bergamo offers only a day's worth of sightseeing, but if you want or need to stay longer there's no problem finding a place to stay.

Trains

Surprisingly few direct trains – only 6 daily – run from Milan's central station to Bergamo by the most direct route via **Treviglio** *on the main line to Verona (56 km, 45 min). More run from either the central station (4 daily) or from Porta Garibaldi (10 daily) on the longer route via* **Monza and Carnate** *(70 km, 1 hr). If you're coming from* **Brescia** *there are 15 daily through connections (50 km, 1 hr) and about the same from Lecco on Lake Como (33 km, 40 min).*

Bergamo

Bergamo divides decisively into two parts: **Bergamo Alta** (the 'Upper City'), a compact medieval quarter, and **Bergamo Basso**, 'Lower Bergamo', a modern sprawl you need have little to do with – except for the fact it's home to the railway station and has some of the cheaper hotels. To reach the old town from the station walk straight up Viale Giovanni XXIII, cross the wide expanse of Piazza Matteotti, follow Viale Vittorio Emanuele and then take the **funicular** (every

15 mins) after the street bends right up the hill. Alternatively take bus number 1 or 3 from the station either all the way to the old town, or as far as the funicular for the fun of riding it up.

Piazza Vecchia

Bergamo's central square has received almost unqualified praise over the centuries from architects as distinguished as Le Corbusier and Frank Lloyd Wright and from the writer Stendhal, who called it 'the most beautiful place on earth'. Much of what you want to see lies on or close to it magnificent ensemble of medieval and Renaissance buildings. Of these the most overawing is the **Palazzo della Ragione**, started in 1199 – making it one of the world's oldest town halls – and built in a Gothic mode heavily overlaid with the look of Venice (the Venetians ruled the city for over 350 years). To its right rises the colossal **Torre della Civica**, whose 15th-century clock still tolls a 180-peal curfew at 10pm (the Germans threatened to melt down the bell in the Second World War to make arms). If it's open, you can ride to the top by lift.

Piazza del Duomo

Through the inviting nooks of the Piazza Vecchia's arcades you're easily seduced into the adjoining Piazza del Duomo, where the lacklustre Neoclassical duomo on the left is overshadowed by the tumultuous Renaissance decoration of the **Cappella Colleoni** (1476). The chapel's riotous medley of twisted columns, coloured marbles and miniature arcades was designed for Bartolomeo Colleoni, a leading Venetian *condottiere*, or mercenary, by Giovanni Antonio Amadeo, the Pavian architect responsible for the similarly exuberant Certosa di Pavia (see page 89). Inside, the chapel is almost equally sumptuous, from the ceiling frescoed by Tiepolo down to Colleoni's (empty) tomb, a double-decker sarcophagus bursting with reliefs and statuettes, and topped by an equestrian statue of Colleoni looking in fine fettle.

Next door is the church of **Santa Maria Maggiore**, begun around 1137 to a Romanesque plan, but now graced with later accretions such as the colourful Gothic porch and its series of statue-filled loggias. Inside the interior's a Baroque bran-tub of dubious taste and considerable excess, distinguished by the kitschy tomb of Donizetti, the Bergamo-based composer who died here in 1848 from syphilis.

The square's final eye-catching component is a 14th-century octagonal **baptistery**, removed from Santa Maria Maggiore in the 17th century when baptisms were transferred to the duomo. Behind it are the old Aula della Curia, (the Bishop's court), scattered with 14th-century frescoes, and to the rear of the church, the Tempietto di Santa Croce, a little relic from the 10th century.

The Cittadella, Castello and Walls

To complete a look at Bergamo's historic kernel walk from Piazza Vecchia along the centre's main pedestrian street, Via Colleoni, to the **Cittadella**, a Visconti military stronghold which now holds two modest museums devoted to archaeology and natural history. Beyond the Cittadella and its views over the Colle Aperto (the 'open hill') a fine little walk along a narrow lane leads towards the **Castello** where you're rewarded with an even better panorama. If you're in the mood for further walking you could make a circuit of the town's impressive walls. The full round takes about two hours, but if you only want a taster the best stretch is the southern half round from the Colle Aperto to Porta San Giacomo.

Galleria dell'Accademia Carrara

The Accademia Carrara (9.30 am–12.30 pm and 2.30–5.30 pm, closed Tues) and its superlative art collection lie just below the upper town in Piazza G. Carrara. To reach it get off the bus from the station at Porta Agostino where it enters the old walls and take Via Noca on the right about 150 metres: from Piazza Vecchia simply walk the length of Via Porta Dipinta (about 1 km), or drop down at the right moment whilst you're walking round the walls.

The Venetian, and to a lesser extent, the Lombard schools are best represented in the gallery's 15 rooms, but there are works also by Brueghel, Dürer, Van Dyck and El Greco; a Medici portrait by Botticelli; and outstanding canvases by Crivelli, Raphael, Giovanni Bellini, Mantegna, Titian and many more top names.

Practicalities in Bergamo

Tourist Office Vicolo Aquila Nera 4, off Piazza Vecchia in the old part of the city (035/232.730).
Railway Station Piazza Marconi. Information (035/247.624). Left luggage (daily 6.30 am–9.30 pm). Bus number 1 runs up to Bergamo Alta.
Buses Local and long distance buses leave from Piazza Marconi in front of the station to Milan (half-hourly); Cremona (half hourly); Como (11 daily); Brescia (8 daily); plus services to Lake Iseo, Edolo and the Bergamask valleys.
Foreign Exchange Banca Nazionale di Lavoro, Via Petrarca 12, off Viale V. Emanuele near Piazza della Libertà.
Police Via Monte Bianco 1 (035/276.111).
Youth Hostel Ostello Città di Bergamo (IYHF), Via G. Ferraris (035/342.349; closed Nov 15–Feb 15). Take bus number 14 from Porta Nuova, which lies straight up Viale Giovanni XXIII from the station, in the direction of Santa Colombana and get off after about 15 min, by the modern church. It's a good, up-to-date place, though the surroundings are suburban and soulless.
Hotels ☆*Leon d'Oro*, Via P. Paleocapa 6 (035/218.151). Close to the station – take the third

left off Viale Giovanni XXIII.
☆*Sant'Antonio*, Via Paleocapa 1, on the corner of Via Giovanni XXIII (035/210.284). Handy for the station but can fill up quickly – call ahead – and has a cheap restaurant in the basement.
☆*Mammagrande*, Via N. Sauro 7 (035/218.413). Close to the Accademia Carrara and to the *città alta*.
☆☆*Agnello d'Oro*, Via Gombito 22 (035/249.883). Housed in a 17th-century building and one of the few reasonably priced hotels in the old city – the restaurant's not bad either.
☆☆*Sole*, Via B. Colleoni 1 (035/218.238). On the corner of Piazza Vecchia, so a little noisy, and not as appealing as the *Agnello d'Oro* – but still a cheap central choice.
Eating Barnabo, Via Colleoni 31. Super and reasonable trattoria just beyond Piazza Vecchia (closed Thur and Aug).
Tre Torri, Piazza Mercato del Fieno 7a (035/244.366). Turn left off Via Gombito heading away from Piazza Vecchia for a highly popular and mid-priced spot – arrive early or book if possible.
Vineria Lozzi, Via Colleoni 229. A wine bar with over 300 wines and good cold snacks.

Milan—Lago Maggiore—Domodossola
The route

This journey takes you quickly from the heat and city bustle of Milan along the shores of Lake Maggiore and then down the Dossola valley into the heart of the Alps. At Domodossola close to the Swiss border you can either return to Milan via Lake Orta and Novara, continue into Switzerland via the Simplon Tunnel (to Brig) or – best of all – take the small private railway to Locarno and then head south to Lugano and Como (see below).

Arona on the southern tip of Lake Maggiore is the first town of note, though towns further north, such as **Stresa** and **Baveno**, are more scenic and more amenable places to stop overnight. From Stresa it's definitely worth braving the crowds and finding time for an excursion out to the beautiful **Isole Borromee** (the Borromean islands). If Maggiore appeals it's easy to take buses and boats to other points on the lake, but with the train you're edged westward towards the Swiss border into the high mountains around **Domodossola**, a not unpleasant spot from which to explore.

Trains

Numerous trains, fast and slow run from **Milano Centrale** *to* **Domodossola** (125 km, 1 hr 30 min). About eight **Intercity** *trains operate, most of which stop at* Arona (69 km, 45 min) *and* Stresa (87 km, 1 hr). *Several* locali *daily also run from Milan's* **Porta Garibaldi** *station.*

The journey

The closeness of the Alps is a considerable mark in Milan's favour. On clear days their distant snow-capped and sun-tinged ridges can easily be seen from much of the city. In well under an hour by train you can slip into lake and mountain scenery that makes the cars and stifling heat seem like a bad dream. Losing what you don't want for something different, if not necessarily better, is one of the great advantages of train travel. Not that you should crank your hopes too high. The Italian Lakes come with a considerable baggage of expectation, and their villas, gardens, dulcet waters and refined old world resorts still have their charms – as well as the romantic beauty that's brought torrents of purple prose from writers over the centuries. At the same time, though, roads and new buildings have done their bit to sully the verdant banks and tumbling green mountainsides, not to mention the advent of mass tourism which brings the often elderly burghers of northern countries south in swarms during the spring and summer.

This said, railways run to all the lakes north of Milan, and combined with the odd boat trip, or perhaps a walk or cable car ride into the mountains, make one of the best ways of casting a quick look over a large and varied area. The first glimpse of **Lake Maggiore**, though, some 40 minutes out of Milan, is less than prepossessing – still as flat and dreary as the tangle of roads and factory-fringed towns that have dogged the line since the city's main station. The tone of things soon changes as the railway starts to hug the shore and the hills pull closer to the lake.

Arona on its own doesn't amount to much, but if you're determined to explore the lake in high summer when beds can be scarce this – like other less exalted towns and small villages – offers more chance of easily finding somewhere to stay. Even if you're only passing through it's hard to miss the whopping statue of **San Carlone** above the old town, a 23-metre effigy of Charles Borromeo (1538–84), a leading light in the important medieval Borromeo family (they're important still, owning the lake's islands and all its fishing rights – as they have for almost 500 years). The 22-year old Borromeo was made Archbishop of Milan by his uncle, Pope Pius IV, in a classic piece of nepotism (nephew in Italian is *nipote* from which we derive nepotism). In time he became a prime mover in the Council of Trent and vociferous in his calls for Church reform – neither of which made him popular. In one episode he escaped an assassination attempt only because the bullet bounced off his heavily brocaded vestments. You can walk up to the statue and peer through its eye and ear sockets for a broad view over the lake.

Although already a good third of the way up the lake, **Stresa** marks the start of its real scenic fireworks, a lovely and placid place famous for its waterfront views, lush gardens – all palms and orange blossom – and the mild climate that has

---

Practicalities in Arona

Tourist Office Piazzale Stazione (0332/243.601).
Hotels ☆*Ponte* (0322/45.317); *Antico Gallo*, (0332/243.137; ☆☆☆*Giardino*, Corso della

Repubblica 1 (0332/242.401).
Camping *Lido* (0332/243.383). On the lakefront a short walk from the station.

Practicalities in Stresa

Tourist Office Via Principe Tomaso 72 (0323/30.150 or 30.416). Turn right from the station on Via Carducci and follow the signs.
Train Information 0323/30.472.
Events *Settimane Musicali di Stresa*. A music festival from the last week of Aug to the third week of Sept which collects some of the world's finest orchestras and soloists. Information and ticket office Palazzo dei Congressi, Via R. Bonghi 4 (0323/31.095).
Hotels ☆*Orsola Meuble*, Via Duchessa di Genova 45 (0323/31.087). Just downhill from the station; some rooms have terraces.
☆*Hotel Mon Toc*, Via Duchessa di Genova 67-69 (0323/30.282). Also handy for the

station.
☆*Paradiso*, Via R. Sanzio 7 (0323/30.470). Quiet rooms above the town.
☆☆*Italia e Suisse*, Piazza Marconi 1 (0323/30.540). Close to the lake and steamer landing.
☆☆*Hotel du Lac*, Via Gignous 1 (0323/30.355). A pleasant villa in a nice wooded setting.
☆☆☆*Primavera*, Via Cavour 39 (0323/31.191). A refined and friendly spot with balconied rooms.
Eating *Taverna del Pappagallo*, Via Principessa Margherita 40. Good pizzas and pasta in one of the town's more affordable restaurants.

brought visitors streaming in since the opening of the Simplon Tunnel in 1906. Once you've mixed it with the affluent pensioners in the cafés and souvenir shops, or strolled the cobbled streets and sedate lakeside promenade, your next move is either to take a trip into the hills or organise a ferry over the water. A cable car runs from Stresa Lido at the western end of town (to find it come out of the station and turn left at the lake shore), climbing up to **Monte Mottarone**, (1,491 m), a popular picnic spot with tremendous views over the lake, the Lombardy plain and a wide sweep of the Alps from Monte Rosa above the Valle d'Aosta round to the Adamello way above Lake Garda.

Excursion from Stresa

The Borromean Islands

This coronet of three almost over-idyllic islands lies in the middle of the lake north of Stresa, and though their crowds can be horrendous, it's worth putting up with the elbows, indignities and high admission prices to savour the beauty of their villas and gardens. Boats run out from Stresa's Piazza Marconi or Piazzale Lido, and from other towns including Baveno to the north and Verbania on the lake's opposite shore. Consider buying a daily excursion ticket which enables you to skip around the islands at will.

Two of the three islands can be visited – Isola Bella and Isola Madre: the third, San Giovanni, is closed to the public. A fourth island, Isola Pescatori, is – to all intents and purposes – part of the same archipelago, but it's so touristy and twee that it's only worth spending time here to find an outbound ferry.

Isola Bella is the best known of the group, little more than a stump of rock until 1670 when Count Carlo III Borromeo decided to turn it into a garden for his wife, Isabella (hence the name). A more salacious story claims he bought it as a hideaway for his mistresses. Tons of soil were brought over from the mainland and used to transform the island into ten terraces of orange and lemon trees, together with a wonderfully theatrical garden thick with camellias, magnolias, box trees, laurel and cypresses. Sadly the island's artificial grottos and much of the villa's excessive Baroque 'art' is little more than kitsch, though it's hard to quibble with the views and the creamy lushness of the gardens (Mar–Oct daily 9 am–noon and 1.30–5.30 pm).

The **Isola Madre** is larger and less visited but possibly even more appealing, especially if you want a couple of languorous hours doing not very much at all. Several generations of Borromeos laboured to produce the island's louche little villa, crammed today with family portraits and a noted collection of dolls. It's a good deal more tasteful than its neighbour across the water. A luxuriant botanical garden crammed with exotic flora and a perfect classical Italian garden round things off (same hours and admission as the Isola Bella).

Out of Stresa the railway only has a short way to run along the lake before slicing into the mountains, pulling first into **Baveno**, a fashionable resort since Queen Victoria bestowed a royal seal of approval by staying here in 1879. These days it's quieter than Stresa, squeezed between crags and a small lakefront beach, and though the package tour operators have got their teeth into the town it's still a promising place to hunt out overnight accommodation.

Practicalities in Baveno

Tourist Office Corso Garibaldi 16 (0323/924.632).
Hotels ☆☆*Villa Ruscello*, Via Sempione 62 (0323/923.006). A small villa on the lakeside.

☆☆☆*Simplon*, Via Garibaldi 52 (0323/924.112). Comfortable hotel with pool, tennis court and lake outlook.
Camping *Lido*, Via Piave 66 (0323/924.775).

The railway then quickly pulls over the River Toce and the small flood plain that has trapped the minuscule Lago di Mergozzo behind its low wall of silt. Thereafter the line bends with the Dossola valley as it enters a realm of high mountains, including the vast dome of Monte Mottac and the Val Grande to the east, one of the central Alps' wildest and most inaccessible corners. Milan now seems a long way away. **Domodossola** stands on a broad, mountain-ringed plain, almost Italy's last gasp before Switzerland, and – for all its size – a doughty Alpine town in character that makes a pleasant base and starting point for more scenic trips east by rail (see Domodossola–Re–Locarno). The town's position at the intersection of valleys from all points of the compass, and the proximity of the Simplon Pass, made it an important centre from its earliest days as a Roman settlement. Napoleon built the road over the Pass to link Geneva with Lombardy in 1805, but the town owes its recent relative prosperity to the Simplon Tunnel (19.8 kilometres long). After its opening in 1908 the Paris–Istanbul *Orient Express* promptly changed its route to take advantage of what in effect was the first major link between west and south-eastern Europe.

If you're in town make for the old centre, and the arcaded and irregularly shaped **Piazza del Mercato**, bordered by fine medieval houses, robust porticoes and looping loggias. Also visit the eclectic little **Museo Galletti**, loaded with paintings, natural history displays, exhibits on the building of the Simplon Tunnel and finds from a Roman acropolis in the nearby Val Cannobina.

Practicalities in Domodossola

Tourist Office Via Romita 13 (0324/481.308).
Hotels ☆☆*Sempione*, Via Galletti 53 (0324/43.869).

☆☆☆*Europa*, (0324/481.032). Take a taxi from the station to Calice 4 km from the town for a quiet, comfortable hotel with good views.

Domodossola–Re–Locarno

The route

It's a long way to come for a relatively short journey, but this journey rates as one of the most scenic mountain railway routes in Europe – and one of the least known. Following the Val Dossola's most beautiful side valley, the **Val Vigezzo**, the line heads east from **Domodossola** into the thick of the Alps and then crosses into Switzerland before dropping down to **Locarno**, the largest Swiss town on Lake Maggiore. There's little to do, but plenty to see from the train, and unlike so many potentially appealing

Trains

16 trains daily leave Domodossola, but of these only 8 go right through to Locarno (53 km, 1 hr 35 min). The rest stop at **Re** *(26 km, 1 hr). The last through train leaves at around 8 pm. Onwards from Locarno there are plenty of connections to* **Bellinzona** *just 20 min to the east, which is on the main line between Zürich–Lugano–Como–Milan. Note that you can buy through tickets to Italian destinations from Locarno – you don't need separate tickets for the different legs of the journey. If you don't fancy taking a quick train back to Como or Milan, a local service connects to Italian* **Luino** *on the east bank of Lake Maggiore. Here you can pick up trains along the lake shore either to Novara (4 daily, 1 hr 30 min) or Milan's Porta Garibaldi (10 daily, 1 hr 40 min).*

---

trips, this one isn't spoilt by modern developments along the way. The best places to break a journey are at **Santa Maria Maggiore** (50 mins from Domodossola), or **Re** (1 hr), the last big village in Italy before the border.

The fact that you enter Switzerland is no problem, as this is part of the Ticino, an Italian speaking canton. It's rare for there to be any passport or customs controls at the border, and you can use Italian money to buy tickets back into Italy (see below). If you need Swiss francs there's an exchange right opposite the ticket office at Locarno.

The journey

At Domodossola's mainline station you leave the platform and take a subway under the tracks into a smart underground complex of subtle lighting, polished marble and sleek new trains. This is the domain of the private *Ferrovie Domodossola*, operators of the railway, who've miraculously found the finances to keep open what must be a mind-bogglingly expensive line to operate and maintain. After a slow crawl across the valley floor the blue two-carriage train starts a smooth, gliding climb up the most extraordinarily steep gradient. It almost seems happier on the hill than when trundling across the plain. Views open up down to Domodossola as the train negotiates tight bends, its wheels squealing in protest and the carriages swaying gently as if at sea. Old stone houses with slate roofs pass by, surrounded by velvety green meadows sprinkled with orchids and walnut trees. Trontano station, the second station, is a vision, like most halts on the line, arboured with trailing roses and a trellis of vines. A short way on a grassy footpath leads from the rustic halt at Marone to a perfect little hamlet of stone houses, and at Malesco the *Old Train Bar* on the platform and *Hotel Panorama*, hard up against the quaint station, are nostalgic little hangovers from the last century.

For about half an hour the line leans perilously over huge gorges, pinning itself to the sides of chasms and trailing over old-looking viaducts that curve over crashing whitewater rivers way below. Work is in progress at several points, particularly at several ominous-looking spots where banks and cuttings have slipped into the abyss. Across the valley snow-capped mountains rear up from dark swathes of forest, their lower slopes broken every now and again by another perfect village of geranium-hung houses. This area's beauty has attracted and produced so many artists that the Val Vigezzo is also known as the 'Valley of the Painters'. One of its inhabitants is also credited with inventing Eau-de-Cologne, another with being the first to swim the English Channel.

At **Santa Maria Maggiore** the line levels out somewhat, having climbed well over 500 metres in the 20 kilometres from Domodossola. Alongside the tracks pastoral and pristine meadows have replaced the precipitous cliffs, and there's even more of an open view up to the high Alpine ridges above the valley floor. The village – where there's a small art gallery and, of all things, an umbrella museum – makes a good spot to stop, or failing that, at Re some 15 minutes beyond. From the station at Re, which appears at first to be in the middle of nowhere, take the little lane up right to the village, which is just five minutes' walk away. You're greeted with a vast hotel on the left, rather like a castle, and an even bigger grey stone church, the Santuario della Madonna del Sangue. Both are madly out of place in so tiny a spot, and cater to pilgrims who come from far and wide to celebrate an apparition of the Virgin here in the last century.

Beyond Re sit on the right hand side of the train to enjoy the best views of the journey, as the scenery once more becomes dramatically Alpine in outlook. A spectacular gorge, lake and ice-clear river make their appearance shortly after the border (though car registration plates apart, and perhaps a general overall tidiness, you'd hardly know you had changed countries).

What does change is the vegetation, which becomes more lush as the train drops towards the mild-weathered margins of Lake Maggiore. Palms put in a rather perverse appearance, together with monkey-puzzle trees and the increasingly neat gardens of Locarno's outlying suburbs. By now there are also likely to be more people on the train, the carriages humming with a lively babble of Italian, Swiss-Italian and Swiss-German.

Locarno's small underground terminus is even smarter than its Domodossola equivalent, preparing you for the lively and cheerful demeanour of the main station and town up above. Here you definitely feel in a different country, and it's well worth ambling around the streets for a while before picking up a train to take you back to Italy.

Practicalities in Santa Maria Maggiore

Tourist Office Piazza Risorgimento 100 (0324/9091).
Hotels ☆☆*La Jazza*, Santa Maria Maggiore (0324/91.471).

☆☆☆*Casa Barbieri*, Via Roma 6, Re (0324/97.019). Large, quite smart and recently renovated hotel.

Locarno–Lugano–Como–Milan
The route

This route comes south from Locarno, following on neatly from the Domodossola–Re trip above. This allows you to look at Switzerland's **Lake Lugano** and **Lugano** town, home to an outstanding art collection and close to a short rack railway which climbs above the lake for some excellent views. The journey's main stops, though, are **Lago di Como** – Lake Como – historically the most famous and most popular of the Italian lakes, and the town of **Como**, which makes the obvious departure point if you want to explore the lake more fully. At the same time you could just as easily take a train to Como from Milan – a journey of only 40 minutes – and treat the town and its lake as a straightforward day trip.

Trains

Once you've caught the 20-minute shuttle from Locarno to **Bellinzona** *you're in line to pick up any of the 20 daily expresses that hurtle into Italy from as far afield as Brussels, Amsterdam and Zürich. From Bellinzona to Lugano takes just half an hour; from Bellinzona to Como is 1 hour. If you're approaching from* **Milan** *(Stazione Centrale) there are 20 fast trains daily (47 km, 40 min) and 10 locali from Milan Porta Garibaldi (1 hr).*

The journey

The small shunt from Locarno to Bellinzona on the olive green trains of the Swiss railways runs through manicured garden suburbs, enlivened by views of the lake but occasionally blighted by the odd dash of light industry. At Bellinzona's busy station pale northern faces peer out of the long straggling trains on the last leg of their journeys from colder climes. For much of the summer on this line you have to do battle with the rucksacks and dozing army of Teutonic students funneling into Italy for a sip at the 'beaker of the warm south'. If you're standing it's only a short haul in the corridor to Lugano, however, where hordes of commuting Italians get on but scarcely anybody gets off.

Lake Lugano seems somehow a deeper blue than other lakes, and its steep mountainous shoreline more immediately pleasing to the eye. It's also a smaller and more cramped sheet of water, surrounded by clusters of villas rather than the luxuriant sprawl afforded by the bigger lakes and their broader valleys. In **Lugano**, which is as popular a resort as any in the region, the main sights revolve around paintings – primarily the private collection of Heinrich Thyssen-Bornemisza in the **Villa Favorita**, but also the frescoes of Bernardino Luini in the 16th-century church of **Santa Maria degli Angeli**, an artist the arch-Victorian critic John Ruskin considered 'ten times greater than Leonardo'. The former contains an extravagant roll call of Italy's foremost painters – Veronese, Uccello,

Titian, Caravaggio, Giovanni Bellini and others, not to mention El Greco, Holbein, Goya, Bosch, Van Eyck, Dürer and Velàzquez. As an antidote to art take a bus or local train the 15-odd kilometres south to **Capolago** where a rack railway clanks up to the summit of Monte Generoso (1,223 m) for some great views over the lake and its surroundings.

Beyond Lugano the railway crosses the lake, whose twists and turns seem unfathomably disorientating, arriving soon afterwards at **Chiasso**. This is a prominent town on northern Italian timetables and train boards, simply because it's the town which straddles the Swiss–Italian border. The chances are you'll spend a lot of time camped here in or just outside the station waiting as border guards prowl up and down the carriages.

Como's homely station is barely a passport's length beyond Chiasso, the town it serves providing enough to see and do for a couple of hours: thereafter you should pick up one of the regular ferries (or many buses) which run out to points on **Lake Como**, either for the ride, or to put up at one of the smaller resort villages around the lake.

Como

Como's proximity to Milan makes it a busy place with weekenders, but also with package holidaymakers who've made this lake above all others their home from home. Traditionally famous for its silk, these days there are next to no homespun silk-worms at work, and instead Chinese thread is imported to be spun and dyed to the whim of Milan's fashion designers. The town became a Roman vassal as early as the 2nd century BC, having been wrenched from the Gauls, and was the birthplace of both Pliny, author of *Natural History*, and his nephew, Pliny the Younger, whose letters provide one of the chief sources of information on the cultured day-to-day life of the period. It emerged as an independent commune for a brief spell in the 11th century, a time when its craftsmen – particularly its sculptors and stone masons – became renowned throughout Europe, spreading the work of their Lombard forebears all over Italy and as far afield as Sweden. Inevitably, though, the town soon fell under the Visconti yoke, remaining in thrall to Milan from 1335 through to Unification.

To reach Como's main square, **Piazza Cavour**, walk from the station through the forecourt's gardens to Via Gallio, a street which then becomes Via Garibaldi: then cross through tiny Piazza Volta, carry straight on and you're home and dry (it's about an 800 m walk). The tourist office is here, as well as a spread of pricey cafés, good refuges to idle away an hour watching the ferries' comings and goings.

As for sights, Como only really lays on a couple of first division quality. The first is the superlative **duomo**, about fifty metres back from the piazza on Via Plinio. Started in 1396, finished over 300 years later by Juvarra, it's considered the finest architectural mixture of Gothic and Renaissance styles in Italy. The Gothic is uppermost in the capricious pinnacles and rose window, leaving the Renaissance responsible for the portals and their ornate carvings (the work of the local Rodari brothers, who devoted most of their working lives to the church). The figures to either side of the main door are Pliny the Elder and Younger, prime examples of medieval Christianity's desire to include even pagan worthies within its pantheon. Neither had terribly much to do with religion, though Pliny the Younger is supposed to have ordered the death of two deaconesses and in his capacity as governor of Anatolia wrote to the Emperor Trajan asking what he should do with his local Christians. Trajan thought he should leave them well alone. The tapestry-hung **interior** contains more mixing of styles, its Gothic aisles competing happily with a Renaissance choir and transept.

Close by along Via Vittorio Emanuele, the town's main street, the 12th-century church of **San Fedele** (the town's first cathedral) boasts a Lombard-inspired altar and blind arcade – strikingly similar to the old Byzantine churches of Ravenna – together with a unique pentagonal apse and a bevy of chubby medieval carvings, most notable of which is on the exterior of the door on the north transept. Two blocks down the street on the left you stumble across the **Museo Civico** (10 am–noon and 3–5 pm; closed Mon and Sun afternoon), a potpourri of artifacts dating from Neolithic times to the Second World War.

While you're in this corner of town take the funicular up to the little hill-top resort of Brunate for views of the lake, and also a good point to kick off some easy hikes. Its lower station is on the waterfront about ten minutes walk right (east) of Piazza Cavour at the end of Lungo Lario Trieste.

Como's other premier attraction is another church, **Sant'Abbondio**, a kilometre's walk on Via Regina if you turn right outside the railway station. This is one for church enthusiasts only, though, for the building languishes in a more-than-dreary industrial corner. In the languid 11th-century interior, however, you can easily forget the outside world, and enjoy the five serene aisles and their splendid 14th-century frescoes.

Practicalities in Como

Tourist Office Piazza Cavour 16 (031/274.064). If you're camping pick up the excellent list of campsites around Lake Como. There's also an information kiosk in the station and an office nearby at Piazza S. Gottardo (031/267.214).
Train Information 031/261.494
Buses SPI services leave from Piazza Matteotti on the waterfront just east of Piazza Cavour. For information (031/304.744, Mon–Fri 8 am –noon and 3–6 pm, Sat 8 am–noon). Buses serve most towns on the lake including Menaggio, Bellagio, Gravedona, and Bergamo.
Youth Hostel *Ostello per la Gioventù* (IYHF), Via Bellinzona 6 (031/573.800, open Mar–Nov only). Walk for 20 minutes along Via Borgo Vico (left out of the station) or take bus number 1, 2, or 6 from the centre.
Hotels ☆*Sole*, Via Borgo Vico 91 (031/559.854). Tidy doubles off a small courtyard – turn left out of the station to find it.

☆☆*Albergo San Antonio*, Via Coloniola 10 (031/262.042). Behind the bus station; decent rooms and a cheapish restaurant downstairs. ☆☆*Canova*, Viale T. Gallio 5 (031/22.100). Good central choice. ☆☆☆*Barchetta*, Piazza Cavour (031/3221). Como's top hotel if you want to push the boat out; recently renovated rooms, many with balconies looking over the lake.
Eating and Drinking Como's smartest old-fashioned bar if you want to drink in style is *Belli*'s on Via Vittorio Emanuele; *Bolla*'s on Via Pietro Boldini is the place for ice cream. *Geral*'s, Via Bianchi Giovani 8 (off Piazza Cavour). Well-known and efficient take-away if finances are tight, with rock bottom meals at lunch only. *Sant'Anna*, Via Filippo Turati 3 (031/502.266). Probably the town's top restaurant, but be prepared to say goodbye to a fair sum.

Excursion from Como

Lake Como

Europe's deepest lake, and a favourite with visitors over two millennia, Lake Como is bedecked with grandiose villas, luxuriant gardens and lushly wooded promontories, and edged with a romantic blend of history-steeped villages, gentle shores and unassuming mountains. Artists and poets from Pliny onwards have been moved to rapture by its charms, none more so – inevitably – than the English Romantics. For Wordsworth it was a 'treasure which the earth keeps to itself', while Stendhal, a confirmed Italophile, thought it simply 'the most beautiful place in the world'. Verdi, Rossini, Bellini and Liszt, amongst others, were inspired to some of their best work by its surroundings.

Few places in Italy, sadly, have lived through the 20th century with their charms wholly intact. Lake Como is no exception, though it still has some fine moments. To avoid its harsher contemporary realities (pollution, crowds and rampant modern development) either stick to the ferries which ply the lake from Como, or plump for visits to its central portion and two best resorts; **Menaggio** and **Bellagio**. These, like many spots on the shores, are targets for a curious mixture of visitor, from Milanese weekender and the raucous windsurfing fraternity, to the retired English or German. Avoid the crowds by coming off-season, or failing that, on weekdays.

The lake's most popular single sight is the **Villa Carlotta**, wedged between two of the most rampantly English enclaves on the west shore, Tremezzo and Cadenabbia. (Mar–Oct 9 am–noon and 2–4.30 pm; April–Sept 9 am–6 pm). Built in 1747 it passed to Princess Carlotta of the Netherlands in the 1850s as a wedding present from her mother. Carlotta took her mind off married life by laying out a magnificent 14-acre garden, a formal collection which is at its best during the spring flowering of its thousands of azaleas, camellias and rhododendrons. Amongst its 500 or more species are exotics such as orchids, sequoia, palms and banana trees. Attractions within the villa, a pink and white Neoclassical confection, are confined largely to an indigestible feast of 19th-century sculpture, its pride of place going to Canova's mouthwatering *Cupid and Psyche*.

Easy-going **Menaggio** has a little beach to the north and is a place to think about staying (see below). It's liable to be a little less busy and expensive than **Bellagio**, the 'prettiest town in Europe', whose position at the point where the lake's twin arms divide gives it some of the area's best views. Despite its popularity it's managed to remain a genteel spot, characterised by a cypress-backed harbour and pastel-shaded houses. Ambience and panorama aside, it lures visitors with two villas, the neoclassical Villa Melzi (daily April–Oct, 9 am–6 pm) and the Villa Serbelloni, owned by the Rockefeller Foundation and believed to be built over the site of a villa belonging to Pliny (2hr guided tours of the gardens April–Oct, 10 am–4 pm).

Practicalities in Menaggio

Tourist Office Piazza Garibaldi 8 (031/32.924).
Ferries Frequent boats and hydrofoils leave daily to all lake towns from the piers along Como's Lungo Lario Triese east of Piazza Cavour (information, 031/273.324 or 260.234).
Youth Hostel Ostello la Primula (IYHF), Via IV Novembre 38 (0344/22.017; open Mar–Nov). Friendly, well-run, cheap meals and cooking facilities.
Hotels ☆*Lario* (0344/32.368); ☆*Alpino*, Via Carlo Comozzi (0344/32.082); ☆☆☆*Bellavista*, Via IV Novembre 21 (0344/32.136; April–Oct).

Practicalities in Bellagio

Tourist Office Piazza della Chiesa 14 (031/950.204).

Hotels ☆☆*Giardinetto*, Via Roncati 12 (031/950.168); ☆☆*Roma* Via Salita Grande 6 (031/950.424); ☆☆*Florence*, next to the port (031/950.342). ☆☆☆☆*Du Lac*, Piazza Mazzini 32 (031/950.320). In the centre of the village by the landing stage.

Milan–(Como)–Lecco–Sondrio–Tirano
The route

This route has two main scenic ingredients: the long eastern shore of Lake Como, and the mountain-enclosed and mostly unspoilt valley of the **Valtellina**. At Tirano you can pick up the *Bernina Express*, one of the world's greatest rail rides, a line which climbs higher than any in Europe (reaching 2,323 metres) on its way to St Moritz in Switzerland. En route it passes through a wilderness of valleys, Alpine meadows, sapphire lakes and the huge glaciers of the Bernina massif. It's feasible to make this a round trip from Tirano, and then pick up a bus to **Edolo** (via Aprica), where you can connect with the line to Brescia (see the route Brescia–Edolo below). And note that if you're in Como a short line links from the town to Lecco so there's no need to start this trip from Milan.

If Alpine scenery leaves you cold, neither of the main towns on this route – Lecco and Sondrio – are worth your while on their own. That said, there are plenty of decent villages along the lake and a small branch line to **Chiavenna** from Colico – a good little excursion – just before the main line bends into the Valtellina.

Trains

Services run roughly hourly from Milan's Stazione Centrale to **Sondrio** *(130 km, 2 hr), and there are additional much slower* locali *which leave from Milan Porta Garibaldi about every 2 hours (3 hr). Most but not all of the quick services to Sondrio continue to* **Tirano** *(26 km, 30 min beyond Sondrio). If they don't, hourly shuttles connect with trains at Sondrio for the last little leg.*

If you're cutting across from Como to Lecco there are just 6 trains daily (43 km, 1 hr), but you could give yourself more options by taking the main Como–Milan *line to Monza and then picking up the hourly expresses on the* Milan–Sondrio *route.*

The journey

After the run through Milan's suburbs and the Grand Prix town of Monza, your first view of the eastern leg of Lake Como is through the industrial edges of **Lecco**, a town known to Italians as the birthplace of Alessandro Manzoni. His novel, *I Promessi Sposi (The Betrothed)* is a 19th-century Italian classic. Every school child in Italy is expected to wade through what in truth is a somewhat turgid tome. If you've ever read it then Lecco is a place of literary pilgrimage full of Manzoniana – the tourist office at Via Nazario Sauro 6 (0341/362.360) has a special Manzoni brochure detailing related sights.

Otherwise sit tight on the train, being sure to be on the left for the best views of the lake and its largely unspoilt shores. Towers and castles crown little tree-fringed headlands most of the way down, complemented by jutting crags, green terraces and great pyramid peaks and rock pinnacles reminiscent of the Dolomites to the north. The forests are thicker and the climate less benign here than on Como's west bank, but palms and olives still flourish, and there's no shortage of the region's distinctive orange-tiled houses and tightly clustered villages.

Excursion from Colico

Chiavenna

At Colico at the lake's northern end you can pick up a battered brown two-carriage connection to Chiavenna (9 daily, 27 km, 30 min). The attractions are various: you could get off the train at Novate Mezzola (13 km, 15 min) and walk up the delightful Val Codera – the path starts close to the station at Mezzolpiano, climbing about 500 metres to Codera (4 km), a hamlet accessible only by foot. Alternatively you could wander around the superbly situated village of Chiavenna, best known for its natural rock cellars, or *grotti*, whose

steady year-round temperatures are ideal for ripening cheeses, hams and wines. Have a look, too, at the 11th-century church of San Lorenzo, the *Paradiso* botanical garden, and the tranquil Marmitte dei Giganti park, home to deep-cut glacial potholes – 'giants' kettles' in local parlance. For a glimpse of more grand mountain country, take one of the buses that run up the valleys above the town; one over into Switzerland and St Moritz, the other north to the skiing and walking centre of **Madesimo**

As the train swings round into the **Valtellina**, the valley of the River Adda, the scenery changes dramatically for the better. The valley stretches away broad and fertile, miraculously uncluttered by industry and housing. Steep forested slopes rise up to snow-tinged peaks, sheltering tiny villages which stand wedged into clefts on the valley sides. Distant waterfalls drop in thin white threads through the woods. The most distinctive feature, though, are the millions upon millions of vines, strung over thousands of terraces which lie scattered over the valley's craggy sides. Over the centuries these have been carved out by hand, the soil often having to have been carried up by mule. Even today the terraces are too steep for any sort of machinery. None of it looks like wine country, but the vintages eked out of the stony earth and tough little vines are excellent. You won't find many outside the region, so look out for some of the better tipples – names like *Sassella, Grumello, Valgello* and *Inferno*.

If you've time to linger up here, it's well worth coming off the train at **Morbegno** – all trains stop here – and taking a bus into the pair of idyllic Alpine valleys south of the village. The best of the two is the more easterly **Val Tartano**, a lost corner of great beauty whose road was only built in 1971, and even today leaves many of the local hamlets accessible only on foot or by mule. In Tartano you can **stay** at the ☆☆*La Gran Baita* (0342/645.043) or at the ☆☆*Margna*, Via Margna 24 (0342/610.377) in Morbegno if you prefer to be closer to the train.

The Valtellina's main town, **Sondrio**, is a largely modern place, harmless enough, but not somewhere you need spend any time. If you need help choosing between its many accommodation options visit the **tourist office** at Via C. Battisti 12 (0342/512.500). If you're trying to reach **Edolo** (46 km) to pick up the Brescia line, turn right out of the station, cross under the subway and the bus station is on your right on the other side of the tracks. Take a bus for Aprica (3 daily) and then pick up an Edolo bus (3 daily). Otherwise stay on the train to **Tirano**, located hard up against the Swiss border and the terminus for the **Bernina Express**.

Excursion from Tirano

The Bernina Express

The Bernina Express and its distinctive scarlet carriages run between Tirano and Chur in Switzerland (via St Moritz). It receives strangely little attention in guides, strangely because it has many claims to being the most spectacular rail journey in Europe. From a height of 400 metres at Tirano the line climbs − without the aid of rack and pinion − to well over 2,000 metres at the Passo di Bernina, the highest altitude reached by any railway in Europe. The quality of the scenery throughout the journey is matchless, reaching a highpoint with the views over the Morteratsch Glacier and the ice-crowned peaks of the Bernina mountains (whose highest point is 4,049 metres). Elsewhere the trip's an unrelenting medley of lakes, forests and pristine Alpine meadows.

Most people make the trip to St Moritz and back (take a passport for the border), but the line continues in equally spectacular fashion to Chur, a distance of 145 kilometres in all. It follows an extraordinarily engineered line, the pinnacle of which is the Albula Tunnel, the highest tunnel − road or rail − in the Alps.

The line is run by the *Ferrovia Retica* (or *Rhätische Bahn*). 12 trains daily operate during the peak season (June 2−Oct 27), and in July and August, weather allowing, special open 'panoramic' carriages are hitched up to provide 360 degree views. Enquiries and bookings through the FS station at Tirano (0342/701.353).

Brescia−Edolo

The route

The private little line that runs up and down the **Val Camonica** between Brescia to Edolo isn't the scenic adventure of other Alpine lines. Although increasingly grand mountains flank the valley as you move north, too much of the valley floor is spoilt by light and not-so-light industry, as well as a succession of rough-edged towns and busy roads. This said, the last stretch to Edolo is magnificent, as the line shadows the border of the **Parco Nazionale dello Stelvio**, one of Italy's five national parks, and skirts the mountain fastness of the Adamello range, amongst the Central Alps' greatest massifs. Moreover, the entire valley has been designated by UNESCO as a World Heritage Site in recognition of its 180,000 ancient **stone carvings** – the best such engravings in Italy – the most impressive of which are seen at **Capo di Ponte**, two hours from Brescia, in the **Parco Nazionale delle Incisioni Rupestri Preistorichi**.

This line also neatly fills in a link in a logical train route through the Lakes and Central Alps region. It's worth plodding up (or down) this line to connect at Edolo with buses over to Tirano for the 'Red Train' (see the Milan–Como–Sondrio–Tirano route), or to other Alpine destinations like Bormio, the main centre for the Stelvio National Park.

Trains

Only 7 daily trains run between Edolo and Brescia (2 hr 30 min), and all but a couple stop at every station.

The journey

Although Brescia is Lombardy's second city after Milan, there's less to the city in the way of sights than there should be. As a result it's deservedly ignored by most visitors, who push on to Venice. But while you shouldn't devote a day trip to the town you could give it an hour or so before jumping on the train towards Edolo. Take shuttle Bus C from the station to the centre, or follow Viale Stazione from the top left of the station forecourt to Piazza della Repubblica and then follow Corso Martiri della Libertà and Via Porcellaga straight to the centre. (For the **tourist office** look out for Corso Palestro, a right turn off Via Porcellaga – the office is on the right about 300 metres after the street becomes Corso Zanardelli.)

Brescia's main problem is its lack of immediate charm, nowhere more apparent than in its main square, **Piazza della Vittoria**, your first view of the city centre and as grim a piece of Fascist architecture as you can imagine. Hurry on to the **Piazza della Loggia** to its north for a more gracious Renaissance offering (Titian and Palladio had a hand in designing the eponymous loggia) and to nearby **Piazza del Duomo** which has two cathedrals – a drab 16th-century Mannerist model and more pleasing circular Romanesque affair. Neither has any single outstanding work of art on which to pounce – a lack which is repeated throughout the city. Instead you have to make the most of fragments and take your pleasure in the medieval streets.

Brescia was once a Gaulish settlement, *Brixia*, from the Celtic *brix* or hill, named after the Cydnean hill which now holds the city's 15th-century Visconti fortress, a nice spot for a picnic if you don't fancy the castle's museum of arms and military effects (it's Italy's largest, and a nod to the arms industry which has long been the city's dubious economic bread and butter). *Brixia* eventually became a Roman colony, and it is tracing the odds and ends from the city's Roman heyday that'll keep you most busy. The era's most impressive legacy is the **Capitolino** (daily 10 am–1 pm and 2–6 pm; closed Mon), the remains of a temple from 73 AD within which there's an excellent archaeological museum, the **Museo Civico Romano.**

Just down the street (Via dei Musei) the 16th-century church of Santa Giulia on the left harbours a pretty good museum of Christian art and artifacts, its prize draws a jewel-encrusted Lombard Crucifix from the 8th century and a 4th-century ivory chest (the *Lipsanoteca*) carved with Biblical scenes (daily 10 am– 8 pm). Brescia's best paintings languish in the **Pinacoteca Tosio-Martinengo** (daily 9 am–12.30 and 2–5 pm, closed Mon), whose 22 sombre rooms contain a good summary of local bigshots such as Moretto, Foppa, Moroni, Romanino and Ceruti, as well as more familiar names like Raphael, Tintoretto, Tiepolo and Clouet. Musicians might want to find time for the **Museo della Chitarra**, a guitar museum at Via Trieste 34 (Mon–Tues and Thur–Fri, 2.30–7 pm; free).

Practicalities in Brescia

Tourist Office Corso Zanardelli 34 (030/ 43.418).

Railway Station Piazza Ovest. Information kiosk (8 am–noon and 1–8 pm; 030/52.449). Left luggage lockers (24 hrs).

Buses Services from in front of the train station to a wide variety of destinations on Lakes Garda, Iseo and Idro; also to Mantua, Cremona, Verona, Trento (via Riva di Garda), Bassano del Grappa, Belluno, the Euganean hills, Turin and Milan. Ticket office (Mon–Sat 6 am–8 pm, Sun 7–11 am and 3–6 pm). Information (030/44.061).

Hotels *Servizio della Giovane*, Via Fratelli Bronzetti 17 (030/55.387). Fantastic value and superb rooms in a women-only place run by nuns; kitchen facilities available; 10 pm curfew. Close to the station: take Viale Stazione to Piazza della Repubblica and then Via dei Mille off its right hand corner; Via F. Bronzetti is the second intersection.
☆*Stazione*, Vicolo Stazione, off Viale Stazione (030/521.128). Functional hotel close to the station.

☆*Albergo Vellia*, Via Calzavellia 5 (030/ 290.425). Between main streets Via Dante and Corso Mameli three blocks west of Piazza Vittoria. If it's busy, use the ☆*Calzavellia* on the same street (030/290.425).
☆☆*Regina e Due Leoni*, Corso Magenta 14 (030/59.276). On the street north of the Pinacoteca and close to the tourist office.
☆☆☆☆*Vittoria*, Via delle X Giornate 20 (030/ 280.061). Centrally placed top-of-the-range hotel opposite the duomo; 65 newly-refurbished rooms in a converted 16th-century *palazzo*.

Eating *Da Walter*, Via San Faustino 35 (north of Piazza Loggia). Good mid-priced spot for Brescian specialities like kid, stews, polenta and skewered meat.
Ristorante Mameli, Corso Mameli 53. Reasonably priced food with a take out service downstairs and restaurant upstairs.
La Sosta, Via San Martino della Battaglia 20. Brescia's smartest restaurant, lodged in a converted 17th-century stable; dress up and expect to pay up to L50,000.

Outside Italy's deep south, few of the country's railways have the appealing if forlorn small-line feel of the *Ferrovie Tranvie*. The carriages are mud-covered orange and cream affairs, the tracks rusted rails and ancient wooden sleepers. It seems appropriate its little platform is hived off from the main FS station at Brescia. It's nevertheless a busy service, at least over the first stretch to Lake Iseo, full of excitable schoolkids and harassed commuters. Initially the train curves out of town through a pastoral plain of wheat and maize shaded by limes and maples. Set back in the haze-filled distance are the faint outlines of the pre-Alps, the first hilly ripples before the Alps buckle suddenly into fully-fledged mountains.

Lake Iseo comes as a surprise, a pleasant one initially before you take in its tawdry resorts and faintly industrial hinterland. Plenty of Italians in holiday mood get out here but you should sit tight for a good hour or more while the train clears the succession of tough, improvised-looking towns which clutter the valley. These are functional, working places with the dreary weather-beaten feel of so many big Alpine settlements.

Capo di Ponte comes hard on the heels of Breno, whose spectacular castle grabs the eye on its crag in the centre of the valley. Capo di Ponte itself is the one place to step out en route, thanks to its rock carvings and their small park, which is 15 minutes' walk from the station (daily 9 am–sunset, closed Mon). The earliest incisions may date from as early as 5000 BC, though most start around 2200 BC, and are the work of the *Camuni* tribe. They settled here to escape northern invaders and used the local glacier-smoothed sandstone to carve a bewildering variety of animals, weapons, religious ceremonies, hunters, Bronze Age burials, solar discs and mysterious figures and geometric designs. They're beautiful, clumsy and peculiar by turns, but all are archaeologically significant, primarily because of the long period of their gestation – a broad time-scale which offers an insight into how customs and ways-of-life, never mind artistic styles, varied and developed over 25 centuries.

Beyond Capo di Ponte you can settle back to enjoy the scenery, from the mad dashing river funnelled between rocky tree-hung banks to the tremendous view that suddenly unfolds at **Malonno**. Here the broad flat valley is patchworked with cut meadows and small haystacks, while in the forests above – lovely mixtures of deep green pines and emerald chestnuts – small fields lie dotted amongst the trees where they've been carved out to provide oases of high pasture. This is a delightful pastoral spot, framed behind by the huge snow-capped and serrated rocky peaks of the Adamello.

Edolo and the end of the line lie a few minutes on, the mountains and forests now closer, lending the town a superb backdrop. In the Middle Ages the area was famous for producing weapons and armour, a strange activity given the rural setting. It was based on the iron ore mines which still serve up raw materials to the Val Camonica's small steel industry – hence the valley's desecration towards Brescia. Small, neat and scenic, Edolo's a good place to stay, and if you stop over for a couple of days the town's perfectly placed for walks into the high country on all sides.

Practicalities in Edolo

Tourist Office Piazza Martiri della Libertà (0364/71.065). For the centre of town walk up the tree-lined street in front of the station and turn right at the main 'T' junction at the top.
Hotels ✰✰*Aurora*, Via Monte Colmo 8 (0364/ 72.644). Perfectly adequate hotel just across from the tourist office over a bar and restaurant and overlooking the river.
✰✰✰*Eurotel*, Via G. Marconi 40 (0364/ 72.621). Modern, central hotel.
Eating There's a shortage of places to eat in town, giving the cosy *Le Alpi*, two doors left of the tourist office, a virtual monopoly on meals.

3 Venice and the North-East

Three regions and one great city make up north-east Italy, the country's most ethnically diverse corner. **Venice** needs little introduction, a rival to Rome for the attentions of most visitors. Around it stretches the **Veneto**, a region ruled for centuries by the Venetian Republic, embracing city-studded plains in the south and spectacular Dolomite mountains in the north. The area's finest city – after Venice – is **Verona**, an appealing historical treasure house, followed by **Padua**, known for the magnificent fresco cycle by Giotto, and **Vicenza**, renowned for its surfeit of Palladian architecture.

North of the Veneto lies a curious hybrid region, **Trentino-Alto Adige**. The more northerly Alto Adige is a German-speaking enclave, ceded to Italy from Austria at the end of the First World War. To the south, Trentino is Italian through and through. Over the years, ethnic differences have created inevitable tensions and extremism on both sides. These days matters are in hand, at least in the Alto Adige, where a large measure of autonomy has kept the lid on separatist ambitions. Both provinces are loaded with mountains, the **Dolomites** in particular, 30 or so individual massifs slightly detached from the main ridges of the Alps. Few areas in Europe are as spectacular, thanks to the mountains' unique medley of rocky pinnacles and stark, soaring summits. Their key city is **Bolzano**, interesting in its own right, though you should aim to tackle some walking if you come up here: paths, maps and facilities are the best in the country.

East of Trentino-Alto Adige stretches an equally jumbled region, **Friuli-Venezia Giulia**, a cocktail of Italian, Slav and central European cultures that fills Italy's north-east corner. A strange and potentially rewarding area, it's nonetheless one of the least-visited of any in the country. Geographically it shares the split between mountains (in the north) and plain (in the south) that distinguishes all of Italy's northern regions. Trains here, though, are more useful for seeing towns than enjoying the scenery. The old Austro–Hungarian port of **Trieste** is the best (and best-known) centre, though **Cividale**, an old Lombard capital, and Roman **Aquileia**, also deserve to feature on any itinerary.

Finally, the chapter includes a city and clutch of towns that don't fit easily elsewhere. Most trips south by train pass through **Bologna**, renowned for its politics and cuisine, but wrongly overlooked by most tourists. Florence and Tuscany tempt strongly beyond the city, but it's worth taking time to see **Ferrara** and **Ravenna**, the former a Renaissance jewel of a town, the latter home to probably the world's greatest Byzantine mosaics. South of Ravenna the coast stretches away in a succession of resorts and lacklustre scenery to virtually the tip of the Italian 'boot'. For a taste of beach culture, however, in all its sleazy glory, **Rimini** is without equal.

Routes   Verona
Verona–Trento–Bolzano
Bolzano–Fortezza–Brunico–San Candido
Verona–Vicenza–Padua
Venice
Venice–Trieste
Trieste–Aquileia
Trieste–Udine–Cividale
Padua–Ferrara–Ravenna–Rimini
Bologna

Although **Venice** *is the region's obvious base,* **Verona** *is the more convenient city to stay in if you are travelling by train. You can visit Venice, Padua and Vicenza from the city. The* **Verona–Trento–Bolzano** *route leads to the heart of the Dolomites, the* **Bolzano–San Candido** *branch offering a self-contained scenic ride through the mountains (and straightforward access into them if you want to walk). At Dobbiaco on the Bolzano–San Candido route, a short, scenic bus ride takes you to Cortina d'Ampezzo and then Pieve di Cadore. At Pieve you can ride a train back to Venice, thus completing a neat circuit without any need for backtracking.*

Please note the Pieve–Belluno–Treviso route is not described in the text: generally it's spectacular in its early reaches, following a mountain-hemmed valley for about 30 minutes, then rather mundane beyond Vittorio Veneto when it breaks through to the plains.

Most of the region's main lines lead into other countries, making it difficult to construct neat circular routes. This is especially true if you ride out from **Venice–Trieste** *(though to avoid repetition you can easily arrange to return to Venice by way of Udine and Cividale). Similarly, following the* **Padua–Ferrara –Ravenna–Rimini** *line leaves you stranded on the east coast. Either you can return to* **Bologna,** *for connections to* **Florence** *(one hour away), or, more interestingly, you can take the small, delightfully pastoral line that connects* **Faenza** *(between Rimini and Bologna) with Florence (by way of Borgo San Lorenzo and Pontassieve).*

Venice and the North East

Verona

Rose-coloured and romantic, Verona is north-east Italy's second city after Venice. Plenty of people come here, and there's a lot to see, but a refined and relaxed air permeates the city making this one of the region's most pleasing spots to visit. Today it's amongst the country's most prosperous cities, thanks mainly to its position at the intersection of east –west and north–south trade routes. A wealthy Roman settlement for the same reasons, it's hardly ever known bad times, either in its period as a city state or during the reign of the Scaligeri family, who dominated Verona's history throughout most of the 13th century. Milan's Viscontis moved here following the Scaligeris' demise, making way for the Venetian Republic in 1405 which continued to rule the city until the arrival of Napoleon. Thereafter it followed the fortunes of the Veneto in general, falling under Austrian control before incorporation into Italy in 1866.

What to See

The Arena

Only the Colosseum and Capua's amphitheatre are larger than Verona's **Roman arena**, the centreplace of the Piazza Brà and the city's most majestic single monument. Built in the 1st century AD, it's survived remarkably intact, only the third and upper tier having been lost to a tumultuous earthquake in the 12th century. Nonetheless the measurements are still impressive – 152 metres long by 123 metres wide, and with 44 ranks of stone-tiered steps designed to seat upwards of 20,000 people. In the 16th century the city organised a special committee to protect the structure – in marked contrast to the Colosseum where huge amounts of stone were carted off to help build Rome's Renaissance churches and palaces (interior open 8 am–6.45 pm, closed Mon; Jul & Aug 8 am–1.30 pm).

Most evenings in July and August the amphitheatre is a magical setting for spectacular **opera** productions. Tickets can be bought either from touts outside the arena most afternoons – at very little over the odds – or directly from two offices within the arches. The cheapest tickets buy you a place in the upper gallery – actually the best place to sit (the more expensive seats have less of a view) but arrive early to stake your place on the stone tiers – there are no reservations. It is advisable to hire a cushion and it's also worth taking a sweater because the evenings get cold. The atmosphere isn't one for purists, with drinks sellers and carnival high spirits in evidence throughout. As dusk falls thousands of tiny candles are lit to welcome the orchestra.

Piazza delle Erbe

Walk down the pedestrianised Via Mazzini from Piazza Brà, lined with smart stores and legions of determined shoppers, and you come to **Piazza delle Erbe**, site of the old Roman Forum and the real heart of the city. For so prime a piece of real estate, it's odd that a market still operates here, occupying virtually the entire square. It's a pulsating affair, and great to wander around, although it no longer sells the herbs, flowers and vegetables suggested by its name. These days it proffers a wide range of cheap clothes, tacky souvenirs and expensive antiques.

An array of superb period buildings rings the piazza, easily missed behind the awnings and market babble. The best are the **Domus Mercatorium** (on the corner of Via Pellicciai), built in 1301 as an exchange and merchants' warehouse; the Torre del Gardello (1370); and the Casa Mazzanti. Also hunt out the marble *Berlina* at the centre of the square: in the 16th century convicts were tied to this and pelted with rotten fruit.

Piazza dei Signori

Even as you walk around Piazza delle Erbe you have tantalising glimpses of another bewitching square – the **Piazza dei Signori**, once Verona's main public piazza. It's entered under the Arco della Costa, the 'Arch of the Rib', after the whale rib hung from it: legend has it that the rib will fall if a married virgin walks underneath. Here also is a magnificent medley of medieval buildings, most notably the Palazzo degli Scaligeri, facing you as you enter, principal home of the Scaligeri dynasty. To your left is the Loggia del Consiglio (1493), the assembly chamber of the city council prior to Scaligeri rule. Close by is the grey-stoned Palazzo della Ragione ('Reason'), the old law courts (1193), also known as the Palazzo del Comune. For a view of the whole area turn sharp right in the square and climb the 12th-century **Torre dei Lamberti** (8 am–6 pm, closed Mon).

The Scaligeri Tombs

Leave Piazza dei Signori through the arch at its far end and you come to the modest Romanesque church of Santa Maria Antica, next to which are the odd but beautiful *Arche Scaligeri*, the outdoor tombs of the leading Scaligeri and some of the finest Gothic monuments in northern Italy. By the church's side entrance an equestrian statue of Cangrande I ('Big Dog'), godfather of the Scaligeri, lords it over his tomb. Lesser family worthies lie grouped together in the canopied tombs enclosed within a wrought iron palisade. Notice the ladder motifs, the family's emblem, which derives from the clan's proper name, the 'della Scala' (*scala* means steps or ladder). Other members of the dynasty mouldering here, all with canine-obsessed nomenclatures, include Mastino I ('Mastiff'), the family's founder; Mastino II and Cansignorio ('Top Dog').

Juliet's House

You're going to have to see the so-called *Casa di Giulietta*, or Juliet's House sometime, so it's worth popping down to Via Cappello from the Scaligeri tombs to see what all the fuss is about. Shakespeare's *Romeo and Juliet* is set in Verona. Although the families in the play existed – as the Cappello and Montecchi, rather than the Bard's 'Capulets' and 'Montagues' – the young starring protagonists were fictional inventions. Try telling this to the hordes who swarm into the little courtyard at Number 23, Via Cappello. The lovely house was built in the 14th century, and certainly has a persuasive little balcony, but the Capulets, much less any daughter, never lived here. The whole thing's a rather transparent tourist scam. You can wander through the house, and stand in line to be photographed on the balcony, but perhaps the most intriguing thing here is the vast amount of lovers' graffiti covering the arched entrance to the courtyard (8 am−7 pm, closed Mon).

Basilica di Sant'Anastasia

Just east of Piazza delle Erbe on the river stands Verona's largest church, the Dominican Sant'Anastasia, built between 1290 and 1481. Gothic in overall appearance, with odd touches of Romanesque, the plain exterior doesn't delay you for long. Take time, however, to look at the 14th-century carvings of New Testament scenes around the door. Inside art jumps out at every turn, the star piece being Pisanello's *St George Freeing the Princess* in the Cappella Giusti at the end of the left transept (you may have to ask the sacristan to open up to see the work). The church's other big painting is the fresco by Altichiero (1395) in the second apsidal chapel on the right. The Florentine terracotta work on the altar is also impressive; the stooped hunchbacks supporting the stoups for the holy water add a bizarre touch.

The Duomo

Walk to the left of Sant'Anastasia on Via Duomo and you come to the city's duomo, rather a long way from the centre of things by the standards of most Italian cathedrals. The lower reaches of the red and white marble striped exterior are Romanesque, dating from 1187, the best sections being the carvings around the two doorways; try to identify the story of Jonah and the Whale on the southern portal, and the statues of Roland and Oliver, two of Charlemagne's generals, on the other.

Inside, the columns and some of the side chapels chapels have some wonderful architectural touches – the Cappella Mazzanti especially (last on the right) – and there's a big artistic draw as well; an *Assumption* by Titian in the first chapel on the left, its grandiose frame the work of Sansovino, who also designed the choir.

While you're in this part of town it might be worth hopping over the river on the Ponte Pietra (behind the duomo to the right) – either to take in the much-restored Roman theatre immediately on your right, or to climb up to the Castel San Pietro to its rear. Views of the city from here are magical, particularly at dusk.

The Castelvecchio and Ponte Scaligero

By far the most beautiful of Verona's 15 bridges, the **Ponte Scaligero** dates from 1355−75, and was built on the orders of Cangrande II. Although the Germans blew the bridge up in 1945 it's since been painstakingly restored using salvaged materials. Be sure to wander over to the **Parco dell'Arsenale**, the city's best park, and ideal if you feel like a break from sightseeing.

The bridge derives much of its scenic impact from the great fortress at one end, the **Castelvecchio**, perhaps Verona's most important medieval building. Also built by Cangrande II, it served time as the family seat, became a museum in

Practicalities in Verona

Tourist Office Via Dietro Anfiteatro 6b (045/
592.828; Mon–Sat 8 am–8 pm; Sun
9 am–2 pm) and Piazza delle Erbe 38
(045/803.0086), plus a small office in the
railway station. All help finding
accommodation, though don't make
reservations.

Railway Station Piazza XXV Aprile
(information 045/590.688). Linked with Piazza
Brà and the centre by Corso Porta Nuova – a 15
min walk. Take bus number 1 or 8 (51 or 58 in
the evening) from the ranks outside for Piazza
Brà. Left luggage 24 hr.

Buses ATP services leave from Piazza XXV
Aprile. Information (045/800.4129) opposite
the railway station – links to Riva del Garda,
Brescia, Sirmione, Montagnana and most other
north-east destinations.

Foreign Exchange At the railway station
(7 am–9 pm); *American Express*, at Fabretto
Viaggi, Corso Porta Nuova 11 (045/594.700);
Cassa di Risparmio, Piazza Brà on the
corner of Via Roma.

Budget Travel CTS, Largo Peschiera Vecchia
9a, near the Scaligeri tombs (045/30.951) or
CIT, Piazza Brà 2 (045/591.788) for student
and IYHF hostel cards, and cheap fares for
planes, buses and trains including Transalpino
and BIJ.

Emergencies Police (045/596.7770); special
foreigners' office with interpreter available
(*Ufficio Stranieri*), Lungoadige Porta Vittoria
(Mon–Fri 8.30 am–12.30 pm).

Where to stay

Youth Hostel Salita Fontana del Ferro 15 (045/
590.360), on the north bank of the river behind
the Teatro Romano (walk from the centre, or
bus number 2 or 20 go close). One of Italy's
nicest and best-run hostels, located in a
wonderfully restored 15th-century building
complete with original frescoes. Good, cheap
meals; camping is also available in the garden.
Rooms open at 6 pm, but you can drop bags off
and register earlier. Curfew at 11 pm, but with
allowances for opera-goers.
Casa della Giovane, Via Pigna 7 (045/596.880),
off Via Garibaldi and on the number 2 bus
route; clean double and triple rooms for women
only. Closed 9 am–6 pm, and 10.30 pm curfew
unless you're off to the opera. Advance
bookings taken.

Hotels Verona's hotels are especially busy
during the July and August opera season.
☆*Locanda Catullo*, Vicolo Catullo 1, off Via
Mazzini (045/800.2786). Some lovely rooms, a
few newly renovated and with terraces.
☆*Albergo Rosa*, Vicolo Raggiri 9, off Piazza
delle Erbe (045/800.5693).
☆*Al Castello*, Corso Cavour 43 (045/
800.4403).
☆*Elena*, Via Mastino della Scala 9 (045/
500.911).
☆☆*Aurora*, Via Pellicciai 2 (045/594.717).
Camping *Campeggio Castel S. Pietro*, Via
Castel San Pietro 2 (592.037; open mid-June–
mid-Sept). Take bus number 3 to Via Marsala
on the north side of the river beyond the castle.
Hot showers, bars and shops.
Campeggio Romeo e Giulietta, Via Bresciana
54 (045/851.0243). 5 km from the
centre – take APT bus for Peschiera and tell the
driver you want the *campeggio*; hot showers,
shops and plenty of room.
  Camping places are also available at the
youth hostel at Salita Fontana del Ferro 15
(see above).

Where to eat and drink

Bars *Bottega del Vino*, Vicolo Scudo di
Francia, off the north end of the Via Mazzini.
Verona's local wines are Soave, Valpolicella
and Bardolino, though this old bar offers a
selection from all over Italy. For another wine-
obsessed place try *Osteria delle Vecete* in Via
Pellicciai, near Piazza delle Erbe.
Restaurants Verona's city centre restaurants
are fine, but generally more expensive than their
neighbours across the river in the university
district.
Fontanina, Piazzetta Chiavica 5, near the
Scaligeri tombs. Cheap food with streetfront *al
fresco* dining.
Dal Ropeton, Via San Giovanni in Valle 46
(045/30.040). A very busy spot below the youth
hostel; reservations can be a good idea,
especially to secure the much-in-demand
courtyard tables.
Da Salvatore, Corso Porta Borsari 39. Pizzas.
Nuova Grottina, Via Interrato dell'Acqua
Morte 38, off Via Carducci near the Ponte
Nuovo. Cheap pizzeria and restaurant popular
with local students.

1925, and also suffered during the Second World War (8 am–7 pm, closed
Mon). The interior's maze of courtyards and corridors is worth the admission
alone, simply for the pleasure of wandering the labyrinth, but it also plays home
to an excellent collection of weapons, jewellery and the best of the city's fine art.

Pride of place goes to the equestrian statue of a grinning Cangrande I – removed from the Arche Scaligere (the statue at the tombs is a copy). The best of the paintings include Tintoretto's *Nativity* and *Concert in the Open*; Tiepolo's *Heliodorus* and the *Talents of the Temple*; Veronese's *Descent from the Cross*; a pair of Madonnas by Giovanni Bellini; the *Madonna of the Passion* by Carlo Crivelli; and Pisanello's *Madonna della Quaglia*. Almost equally seductive, though, are the myriad paintings and sculptures dotted about by the region's anonymous or little known medieval artists.

San Zeno Maggiore

San Zeno Maggiore languishes some way from the centre of things and has been under restorative wraps for years. Neither fact should deter you from walking through the Parco dell'Arsenale or following the river for a look at what ranks not only as Verona's greatest church, but also perhaps the greatest Romanesque church in northern Italy (daily 8 am–noon and 3–7 pm). San Zeno Maggiore started life as a chapel in the 5th century, built over the tomb of Zeno, Verona's patron saint, but the present brick building and finger-thin campanile went up in the first half of the 12th century. Decoration and refinements then continued to accumulate over the next 200 years.

Worth close scrutiny on the **exterior** are the ivory-coloured façade, the rose window (a medieval 'wheel of fortune') and the main portal, in particular its carvings (1138) which illustrate episodes from the months of the year and scenes from the life of St Zeno. The **door**'s 48 12th-century bronze panels are more extraordinary still. The first such bronzes attempted in Italy since antiquity, they ushered in an Italian-wide trend for bronze portals. Byzantine influences infuse the panels, most of which portray vignettes from the life of St Zeno and stories from the Old and New Testaments.

The **interior** is no less captivating, its airy, peaceful space partly mapped by patches of fresco and overarched by a wooden 'keel' roof. The **crypt** is tightly packed with 42 ancient columns, and note the work above the church's high altar – an important triptych of the *Madonna and Saints* by Andrea Mantegna (1459).

Verona–Trento–Bolzano

The route

Taking the main line from Verona towards the Brenner Pass and Austria is the most direct way of jumping to the heart of the **Dolomites**, one of Europe's most spectacular mountain ranges. Spread over a broad swathe of north-east Italy, they comprise some 30 or more self-contained massifs, most of them distinguished by the pinky orange Dolomia limestone after which they are named. **Hiking** possibilities are excellent and straightforward, thanks to first-rate maps and well-worn and well-signposted paths. Accommodation is also easier to find than anywhere else in the Alps, with even the tiniest hamlets offering several hotels.

At **Trento**, the one main stop on the route, you can pick up a bus for Madonna di Campiglio, a resort in the shadow of the Dolomiti di Brenta, perhaps the Dolomites' most dramatic and best-known massif. Trento is also worth an hour or two's wander in its own right, as is German-speaking **Bolzano**, a city which makes a good forward base for expeditions to further mountain enclaves. If you want to leave the walking to others, this is a fine journey for the scenery alone, particularly if combined with the line between Bolzano and San Candido (see Bolzano–Fortezza–Brunico–San Candido on page 123).

Trains

More than 20 trains daily run on the busy route between Verona, Trento (92 km, 1 hr 5min) and Bolzano (148 km, 1 hr 50min). Many services ply the line having started from cities like **Bologna** *or* **Milan**, *so if you're coming from further afield you may not have to change trains.* **International** *expresses connect with Innsbruck, Munich, Cologne, Dortmund and Utrecht. The Spree Alpen Express runs from Verona as far as Berlin.*

The journey

After leaving the plain around Verona you're quickly into the Adige valley, a beautiful flat-bottomed vale, hedged in by craggy mountains that should whet your appetite for the Dolomite peaks further north. Along its western flank the long chiselled ridge of **Monte Baldo** runs for some 20 kilometres, blocking out the view of Lake Garda which nestles in a trough to the west. Rising well over 2,000 metres, its slopes are one of Europe's premier botanic treasure troves, thanks to the proximity of the lake, which ensures a mild micro-climate, and to its position between Mediterranean and Alpine vegetation zones. Conditions are thus ideal for plants from both northern and southern climes. To see the mountain at first hand either walk up from the station at Avio or take a cable car from Malcesine on Lake Garda's east shore (accessible by bus from Verona). Over on the valley's eastern margins are the **Monti Lessini**, scene of some of the bitterest fighting during the First World War, when battles raged between Italy and Austria throughout the mountains of the north-east. As on the Western Front, the conflict here was largely one of stalemate and attrition. 460,000 men died and 947,000 were wounded on the Italian side alone.

As you proceed further up the valley the overwhelming image is of fruit trees – thousands of apples and pears in particular – and more especially of vines, which are trained in vast trellises to create what appears to be an unbroken canopy of green across the valley floor. Immediately out of Verona you're in Bardolino and Valpolicella wine country, a source of cheap and cheerful plonks for the most part, though higher up the Adige vineyards are producing ever-improving vintages. The cooler climate at these altitudes and latitudes is well-suited to crisp, fruity whites, the best examples of which hail from zones like Casteller, Sorni and Teroldego.

After less than half an hour the train leaves the Veneto and enters into Trentino, the southern and decidedly Italian part of the Trentino-Alto Adige. Beyond Trento you start to hear German spoken more frequently, but for now there's little hint of the linguistic and cultural shift to come. **Rovereto** rolls by to the east, famous for its silk industry and home to the Museo Storico della Guerra, Italy's largest museum relating to the First World War.

Trento

A few minutes beyond Rovereto, Trento makes a more worthwhile stop, and given the number of trains on this line you'll have no trouble picking up another connection after an amble round town. Failing that you could head for the bus terminal just 100 metres from the station and make the **excursion** to Madonna di Campiglio and the Dolomiti di Brenta.

Trento itself is best known as the setting for the Council of Trent, a meeting of the Catholic hierarchy between 1545 and 1563 which debated ways of turning Europe's rising tide of Lutheranism. Its opening and closing sessions took place in the **duomo** in Piazza del Duomo, heart of the present town and the centre of the former Roman colony, *Tridentum*. Loggias to either side soften the austerity of the cathedral's 13th-century exterior, while inside the most eye-catching details are traces of fresco and a pair of twin-arched steps cut into the walls of the nave. Outside on the building's east (Via Garibaldi) side look out for examples of Trento's famous 'knotted columns', a convoluted testimony to the skill of its medieval stone masons.

A medieval crypt and the remnants of a 6th-century Paleochristian basilica were discovered beneath the duomo in 1977, almost certainly the burial place of St Virgilo, Trento's third bishop. Entrance to the excavations is via the **Museo Diocesano Trentino** in the neighbouring Palazzo Pretoria, a small museum which traces the duomo's history (mid-Feb to mid-Nov Mon–Sat 9.30 am–12.30 pm and 2.30–6.30 pm).

Leave Piazza del Duomo on the Renaissance-era Via Belanzani, turn right on Via G. Manci and you soon come up against the blank outer walls of the **Castello del Buonconsiglio**, Trento's other main attraction. Adapted over the centuries by the bishop-princes who ruled the city from the 10th to 18th centuries, it comprises three distinct sections; the battlemented 13th-century Castelvecchio, the Magno Palazzo added in 1536, and the 17th-century Albertine. Within its walls you'll find a tranquil courtyard and the **Museo Provinciale d'Arte**, a mish-mash of art, archaeology and social history (castle and museum 9 am–noon and 2–5 pm, closed Mon).

The other spot you might want to pop into before moving on is **Santa Maria Maggiore** (at the end of Via Cavour off Piazza del Duomo), best known for the mighty marble balustrade (1534) supporting the organ and a large altarpiece

Practicalities in Trento

Tourist Office Via Alfieri 4 (0461/983.880), located diagonally across Piazza Dante and the gardens outside the station. The office for the province of Trentino in general is at Corso III Novembre 132 (0461/980.000).
Railway Station (0461/823.671). For the town centre turn right out of the station on Via A. Pozzo and continue straight on Via D. Orfane and Via Cavour.
Buses (0461/983.627). On Via A. Pozzo 100 metres right of the railway station. Services to Rovereto and Calliano (hourly 40 min); Riva del Garda (hourly, 1 hr); Madonna di Campiglio (4 daily, 1 hr 30 min); Molveno (6 daily, 2 hr); Cles & Malè (12 daily, 1 hr); Belluno (1 daily, 2 hr 40 min); Canazei via Cavalese, Predazzo & Vigo di Fassa (3 daily, 2 hr 40 min); San Martino via Imer, Mezzano & Piero di Primiero (3 daily, 3 hr).
Budget Travel CTS, Via Cavour 21 (0461/981.533).
Bike Rental Rental points at Castello di Buonconsiglio, Torre Vanga, Piazza Mostra and Piazza Garzetti.
Youth Hostel *Ostello Giovane Europe* (IYHF), Via Manzoni 17 (0461/234.567). Walk straight down the street in front of you outside the station (gardens on your right) until you reach Via Torre Verde and turn left on Via Manzoni. Check-in from 7.15 am; lock-out 9 am—5.30 pm.
Hotels ☆*Albergo Mostra*, Piazza Mostra 12 (0461/980.223).
☆☆*Al Cavallino Bianco*, Via Cavour 29 (0461/231.542). Good-sized rooms close to the duomo.
☆☆*Hotel Venezia*, Piazza del Duomo 45. A safe choice, some rooms with views of the duomo; note the sister hotel of the same name around the corner.
Campsite *Camping Trento*, Lungoadige Braille (0461/823.562; April—Sept). A 20 min walk up the river or take bus number 2 from the station.
Eating *Pizzeria Duomo*, Piazza del Duomo 22. Good, cheap and unpretentious spot in the centre of the town.

Excursion from Trento

Dolomiti di Brenta

Perhaps the Dolomites' most spectacular massif and some of their most straightforward walks are just an hour and a half's highly scenic bus ride from Trento. Four buses daily run to **Madonna di Campiglio**, a pleasing little resort in the lee of the **Dolomiti di Brenta**. The huge pinnacles, crags and glaciers of these mountains rear up with a splendour almost unequalled in western Europe, crossed by excellent trails and dotted with wonderfully sited refuges.

Madonna itself amounts to little more than a ski-resort, but it makes an excellent base. Plenty of trippers come here to admire the mountains from below, but August is the only month you might have problems finding a reasonably priced room. The town's about 1,500 metres high, which leaves you little to do in the way of climbing to reach the best scenery. In addition, several ski-lifts operate in summer.

There are all sorts of walks you can do in a day. The easiest is to take the Grosté ski-lift to the *Rifugio G. Graffer al Grosté* (2,438 m) and follow path number 316 to the *Rifugio del Tuckett* (2,272). From here you can follow paths number 317 or 328/318 back down to Madonna. Alternatively you can walk from Madonna to the *Rifugio Vallesinella* (an easy hour's stroll on a gravel road, number 375) and then climb up to *Rifugio dei Brentei* (path number 317/318). From here you can follow path number 318 up the breathtaking Val Brenta Alta to the *Rifugio Pedrotti* (2,491 m) – and then double back the same way to the *Brentei*, or drop down into the Val Brenta and back to Madonna on trail number 323 or 391.

When you've done with the Brenta, there are plenty of hikes in the peaks and lakes of the Adamello range west of the town (also with ski-lift short-cuts), or the beautiful Val Genova to the south-west.

Practicalities in Madonna di Campiglio

Buses Four daily from Trento bus terminal to Madonna di Campiglio (1 hr 30 min).

Tourist Office Centro Rainalter, in the main square at Madonna di Campiglio (0465/42.000).

Refuges Refuges open from mid-June to late-Sept, and are far less rustic than their name might suggest. The atmosphere is lively and friendly – only the washing facilities are a little spartan. All provide meals and snacks if you're passing through. Accommodation is in shared dorms and costs are reasonable. Though refuges can't turn you away it's as well to call and book (especially in August) if you want to be sure of a bed rather than a space on the floor. Details from tourist offices.

Hotels In summer many hotels may require you to take half- or full-pension, which isn't always a hardship as there are next to no restaurants in Madonna. There are dozens of central hotels, many of which offer large discounts outside the July and August high season.

from 1534. For real train buffs and for another dose of fine mountain scenery, note the little private **branch line** that runs from Trento to **Malè** (10 trains daily, 1 hr 25 min). It's a slow run, but at Malè there are plenty of walking opportunities close at hand in the Val di Rabbia and Val di Pejo.

Bolzano

Capital of the mostly German speaking Alto Adige (the *Südtirol*), Bolzano is a relaxed and congenial place from which to explore the mountains on all sides. The town developed thanks to its position at the junction of the Isarco and Talvera rivers. It also enjoyed good trading links along the Adige valley to the south and across the Brenner Pass to the north. During the Middle Ages these advantages led to the growth of four annual markets, renowned jamborees that attracted traders from all over Europe. Historically the town's also been something of a political football, booted backwards and forwards, first between the Counts of Tyrol and the Bishops of Trento, and then between Bavaria and the Hapsburg rulers of the Austro-Hungarian Empire. In 1809 the Austrians ceded the area to the Napoleonic kingdom of Italy, only for it to be returned to Austria until the end of the First World War when it was again handed back to Italy.

What to see

It's a simple 300 metres walk from the station on Viale Stazione to Bolzano's main **Piazza Walther**, a tidy, appealing square named in the last century after a 12th-century Tyrolean troubadour, a symbolic act designed to assert a German cultural identity in the polyglot Hapsburg Empire of the day. The piazza's 14th-century Gothic **duomo** was badly damaged in the Second World War, but has been well restored, neatly combining modern altars with patches of medieval fresco. Its most eye-catching features are the elaborately carved spire and the colourful green and yellow-tiled roof, but look out also for the fine sandstone pulpit (1514) and the so-called *porta del vino* (the 'wine door') off the apse. This is decorated with vines and farmers tending the grapes, commemorating a special licence granted to the church to sell wine in 1387.

Just off the piazza along Via Posta stands the **Chiesa dei Domenicani**, a 15th-century monastery and the traditional place of worship for the town's Italian-speaking community. Like the duomo it, too, was rebuilt after bomb damage, though it managed to hold on to Bolzano's finest paintings; the Giottoesque frescoes (c. 1340) in the Cappella di San Giovanni. More frescoes from the same era, and probably by the same Paduan school, stand in the Cappella di Santa Caterina and in the Gothic cloister next door (entered from the street at number 19a).

Head north from the right-hand corner of Piazza Domenicani and you come to **Piazza dell'Erbe**, site of a daily fruit and vegetable market and a great little spot to hole up and watch the world go by. The statue in the square is of Neptune and

Practicalities in Bolzano

Tourist Office Piazza Walther 8 (0471/975.656 or 970.660). Excellent office for accommodation lists and help with hikes long and short (Mon–Fri 8.30 am–12.30 pm and 2–6 pm, Sat 9 am–12.30 pm).

If you're exploring more of the region be sure to visit the close-by provincial tourist office for the area (EPT) at Piazza Parrocchia 11 (0471/993.809). This has info on all accommodation in Alto Adige, as well as help in finding your way around the region's labyrinth of hiking possibilities (weekdays 8.30 am–12.30 pm and 3–5.30 pm).

Railway Station Piazza Stazione (0471/974.292). Information 8.30–noon and 2.30–5.30 pm. Left luggage 24 hr.

Buses From Via Perathoner 4 (0471/975.117) on the left between the station and Piazza Walther; main services to Siusi (7 daily, 50 min; Brunico (8 daily, 1 hr 45 min); Collalbo (5 daily, 50 min); Cortina d'Ampezzo (4 daily, 3 hr 30 min); Merano (3 daily, 1 hr); Silandro (4 daily 1 hr); Selva and the Val Gardena (4 daily, 1 hr 30 min); Fiero di Primiero via Predazzo and San Martino (1 daily, 3 hr 45 min); Corvara (2 daily, 1 hr 15 min); Val d'Ega, Carezza al Lago and Passo Costalunga (2 daily, 1 hr) continuing to Vigo di Fassa & Canazei.

Foreign Exchange *Banca Nazionale di Lavoro*, at the end of Viale Stazione on Piazza Walther.

Budget Travel CTS, Via Rovigo 38 (0471/934.146) or CIT, Piazza Walther 11 (0471/978.516).

Bike Rental Viale Stazione, near Piazza Walther.

Hiking Information *Club Alpino Italiano* (CAI), Piazza delle Erbe 46 (0471/978.172; weekdays 11 am–12.30 pm and 5–7 pm); or *Alpenverein Südtirol* (AVS), Via Bottai 25

(0471/978.729; weekdays 3.30–7.30 pm).

Camping *Sportier*, Via dei Portici 37a.

Hotels Remember that cheap hotels, rooms and refuges in great mountain locations are only a bus ride or walk away from Bolzano should the town or its hotels leave you cold. The town's cheaper options are plentiful, but often gloomy. Call ahead in August to check the availability of rooms. At other times you should have few problems.

☆*Collegio (Kolpinghaus)*, Via dell'Ospedale 3 (0471/971.170). A hostel in all but name two minutes' walk from Piazza Walther.

☆☆*Hotel Regina Angelorum*, Via Renon 1 (0471/972.195). Hard up against the station and a reliable last resort if other choices are full.

☆☆*Croce Bianco* (0471/27.552) and ☆☆*Figl* (0471/978.412), both on Piazza del Grano immediately north of Piazza Walther.

☆☆*Klaus*, Via della Mostra 14 (0471/971.294). About 1 km from town and takes some getting to, but worth it for the surroundings. Turn right out of the station on Via Renon, right under the tracks and over the river to the Kohlerbahn cablecar (20 min walk); ride the car to the hamlet of Colle. The *Klaus* is one of several hotels on the same road.

☆☆☆*Herzog*, Piazza del Grano (0471/26.267).

Camping *Moosbauer*, Via San Maurizio 83 (0471/918.492, open year round). Take bus number 8 from the station (last one leaves at 8.30 pm).

Eating *Spaghetti Express*, Via Goethe 20, just off Via dei Portici. About the town's liveliest spot; young, fun and noisy atmosphere, with numerous pasta specialities.

Weisses Rössl (Cavallino Bianco), Via dei Bottai 6. Authentic Austrian *bierkeller* ambience, with plenty of local specialities and standard Italian menu items.

marks the place where local miscreants were pilloried in the 18th century. East off the piazza runs **Via dei Portici**, a wonderfully dark and narrow street of medieval houses lined with oriel windows and stylish shops.

A minute's walk north of the piazza, by contrast, brings you to the leafily set 14th-century church of the **Francescani** (on Via Francescani). Of note are the lovely carved altarpiece (1500) in the Cappella della Vergine and the Gothic cloisters.

Around Bolzano

Around Bolzano are a couple of straightforward excursions, the easiest a ride up in the *funivia*, or cable car to **Monte Renon** (1,221 m). The hill just to the north-east of Bolzano gives a faint taste of the views to be had if you're prepared to tackle a bit of walking in the Dolomites. The cable car starts from the end of Via Renon, reached by turning right out of the station and following Via Renon for about a kilometre. The *funivia* stops at Soprabolzano, literally 'over Bolzano', and from here a tiny **tramway** takes you another seven kilometres to the hamlet of **Collalbo**.

From here you can walk or rent a bike (see 'Practicalities') and cycle out to one of several castles in the Valle Sarentina north of the town. **Castello Roncolo** (13th–19th century) is the closest and most impressive, and allows visitors on guided tours into its rooms, most of which are decorated with 15th-century frescoes portraying scenes from courtly life (10 am–noon and 3–5 pm, closed Sun and Mon). Bus number 1 also comes out here from the station.

Excursions from Bolzano

A range of mountain enclaves lie within easy reach of Bolzano by bus, the closest being the **Parco Naturale dello Sciliar** to the north-east. Services run to three villages on its fringes. Tires in the south, Fiè to the west and Siusi to the north, where you can stay. Moderately easy walks from any of these centres take you into the park, the best spots to aim for being the *Rifugio Bolzano*, just below the summit of the Sciliar (2,563 m), a great flat-topped, sheer-sided mountain (4 hrs from Tires or Fiè) and the *Rifugio Bergamo* (3 hr 30 min east of Tires). En route you'll wander over the famous **Alpe di Siusi**, a beautiful if much-tramped expanse of Alpine meadows – one of the largest such areas in the Alps – noted in spring for its myriad wild flowers.

Slightly less accessible uplands await in the **Parco Naturale di Tessa** above Merano, about half an hour north-east of Bolzano by bus or train (note that currently the train service beyond Merano to Malles is suspended). The park contains some of the most interesting areas in the central Alps, with plenty of flora and easily seen fauna (including numerous chamois), and many walking possibilities long and short. The only problem here, though, is that the trailheads are further from easy points of access unless you take a taxi from Merano.

Bolzano–Fortezza–Brunico–San Candido
The route

This is the best journey if you want to see the Dolomites from the train, and amongst the most scenic mountain railway routes in the country. The line strikes north along the Isarco valley as if heading for the Brenner Pass, but branches east shortly after the historic town of **Bressanone** to follow the **Val Pusteria** towards the Austrian border. Closing the Val Pusteria to the north are the central Alps, the best slice of which, the **Valle Aurina** (Italy's northernmost point) can be seen as an easy excursion from **Brunico**, the Val Pusteria's main centre and its nicest overnight base. To the south lie three Dolomite massifs, each protected by parks – the Puez-Odle, the Fanes-Sennes-Braies and the Dolomiti di Sesto. Buses run from Brunico to villages which can be used as centres to explore all these areas.

Superlative mountains await whichever direction you choose, providing almost unlimited **walking** possibilities. To get you started we've given a couple of suggestions in the Valle Aurina and in the Dolomiti di Sesto, easily reached from almost the last station on the line at **Dobbiaco**.

Accommodation is cheap and plentiful in all the villages of the Val Pusteria, and even in the tiny hamlets north and south – but of course it's easy to return to Bolzano if you don't want to hike around the mountains. To continue onwards, one train daily runs across the border to Vienna through more great scenery. Otherwise you might take a bus from Brunico south to Corvara and thus back to Bolzano, or a bus from Dobbiaco to Cortina d'Ampezzo and Pieve di Cadore to link with the railway lines from Pieve di Cadore to Padua and Venice.

Trains

3 trains daily run from Bolzano directly to San Candido (113 km, 2hr 15min) via Bressanone (38 km, 35 min) and Brunico (81km, 1 hr 30 min). This doesn't sound many, but if you take a main line train from Bolzano to the Brenner (15 daily) and change at **Fortezza**, *north of Bressanone, then more frequent shuttles operate along the Val Pusteria between Fortezza and San Candido (9 daily).*
1 express daily, the 'Val Pusteria' runs on the route **Innsbruck–Brenner–Fortezza–San Candido–Vienna** *(and vice versa). Comprised of Austrian rolling stock, it's a hangover from the days when this was all the Südtirol, and thus Austrian territory.*

The journey

Out of Bolzano the railway picks up the Isarco valley as it cuts its way through the mountains towards the Brenner Pass eighty kilometres to the north. Initially the valley's a little spoilt, but soon jagged peaks and mist-wreathed forests drop down on each side, laced with rushing streams and tiny villages of wooden houses. **Ponte Gardena** is the first substantial stop, marking the spot where the Val Gardena drops down to the main valley, one of the few corridors where roads are able to penetrate the Dolomites' central massifs. Here, or at **Chiusa**, the next station north, are the best places to catch trains to Ortisei and Selva, both bases for hotels, paths and ski-lifts if you want to explore the Puez-Odle mountains.

Bressanone

The only town you want to look at for its historical offerings is **Bressanone**, an ancient bishopric whose bishop-princes fought constant battles with the Counts of Tyrol, ruling the region on and off for over a thousand years. Come out of the station and turn left up Viale Stazione to reach the old centre, about ten minutes' walk away. Piazza del Duomo's 13th-century cathedral received a drastic 18th-century re-modelling, but the paired columns and 14th-century frescoes of the cloister to the right are still enchanting. Off the square stands the church of San Giovanni Battisti, decked with more fine early frescoes and a small cathedral treasury loaded with the ornate vestments of Bressanone's erstwhile bishops (daily 10 am–noon and 1–5 pm). Alongside the duomo stands the old bishop's palace, now the grandly furnished Museo Diocesano (daily 10 am–5 pm), crammed, rather perversely, with numerous 18th- and 19th-century crib scenes, as well as examples of the Romanesque and Gothic wood carvings common all over the Alto Adige. Also look at the Casa Pfaundler on the other side of the duomo, an odd mixture of Italianate and Teutonic architectural ideas; and at the Gothic church of San Michele, whose tower, the Torre Bianca, lends the town its distinctive skyline. For the best of the streets, wander down Via dei Portici Maggiori, an evocative if sombre corridor of 16th-century houses.

Practicalities in Bressanone

Tourist Office Viale Stazione 9 (0472/22.401). **Hotels** ☆☆*Schwarzer Adler*, Via Ortici Minori 2 (0472/22.327). ☆☆*Gasthof Grauer*, Mercato Vecchio 27 (0472/22.472).

Camping Two campsites at Varna, 5 km north of Bressanone (bus); one at Oberdof 130 (0472/32.169), the other at Brennerstrasse 13 (0472/23.216).

At Fortezza the line's cosy little trains are shunted around for their trip up the **Val Pusteria**. People read German newspapers, the faces and quiet manner a world away from the Latin looks and Mediterranean high spirits of lands further south. The names of villages and streets are bi-lingual, but this seems a sop to the Italians rather than to the Tirolese. In virtually every other respect this is clearly a land that owes next to nothing to Italy.

Outside the scenery is gloriously alpine, with views over meadows of hay to emerald green forests and the pinnacles of pinky-stoned mountains. Hardly any industry or housing blights the outlook, and it's a pleasure just to sit back and take in the countryside. Hills and distant snow-stopped ridges roll by, growing ever more invigorating until **Brunico** (Brixen), a busy little town and the hub of all the smaller valleys in the area.

The station's at the top of Via Europa, which curves to the tightly-knit streets of the centre past the bus station and the tourist office (and is the site of a vibrant

Practicalities in Brunico

Tourist Office Via Europa 22 (0472/85.722; weekdays 8 am–noon and 3–6 pm; Sat 8 am–noon). Helpful staff and excellent information on the numerous accommodation possibilities both in town and in the Valle Aurina and Dolomite villages to the south.
Railway Station Via Europa (information 0474/85.826).
Buses Via Europa 22, downstairs from the tourist office. SAD run buses all over the region, often to tiny villages that don't look as if they merit a service.
Bike Rental *Velo*, Via San Lorenzo, a continuation of Via Michael Pacher.
Hotels *Pension Notburgaheim*, Via Bruder Willram 4. Central location on the river with views of the castle; shared bathrooms; breakfast included.
☆*Ragen Haus*, Via Bruder Willram 29 (0474/ 84.818). Close to the *Notburgaheim*, but rooms have private bathrooms. Breakfast included.
☆☆*Blitzburg*, Via Europa 10 (0474/85.723). Handy for the station, buses and town centre.
Eating Most hotels in the Dolomites have a dining room, usually serving a mixture of pastas and more robust Austrian fare – watch out for those dumplings – and eating reasonably, if unexceptionally, is no problem. For the cheapest deal in town go for the *KVW Mensa* on Via Tobl (lunch only), invariably packed with locals and workmen.

Excursion from Brunico

The Valle Aurina

Whether you want to walk or not, it's well worth taking a bus to the Valle Aurina, the mountain-swathed valley which strikes north from Brunico to the so-called *Vetta d'Italia* – the 'roof of Italy'. And at the top of the road you're at the country's northernmost point, surrounded by a stunning basin of rocky crags and hanging glaciers. Buses run all the way up the valley.

From there it's easy to plan any number of spectacular **day walks** up on to the ridges above the valley. **Predoi** (Prettau) or **Casere** (Kasern) close to each other near the valley's head make good starting points: from Casere try the obvious loop east on path number 11 up the Rotbach valley which climbs from 1,595 m to 2,590 m before dropping down the

Windtal valley on track number 12 back to Casale. To the west leave Casale on paths 15 and 15a to the Lago di Selva from where you're able to climb right up to the main ridge – and put one foot in Italy, the other in Austria (path number 13/ the *Lausitzer Weg*). Tracks return to Predoi or the village of San Pietro (a little further south down the valley). These are just two excellent walks; possibilities in the valley as a whole are myriad.

You'll also have no problems staying locally, as every hamlet has at least one hotel, usually cosy ski places with excellent summer rates. **Campo Tures** is the main centre, but higher up the valley Lutago, Cadipietra, San Giacomo, San Pietro, Predoi and Casere – all with hotels – lie closer to the meat of the mountains.

market every Wednesday morning). Looming over everything is the Castello di Brunico, perched on the 'Schlossberg', a weighty fortress built in 1250 on the orders of the Bressanone bishops, and the germ of the present town. It suffered alterations in the 16th century, but still looks the part of a castle from a Grimm's fairy story. It's occasionally open if you want to peer at its chapel and royal rooms (times from the tourist office). Also leave a few minutes to see the parish church, which contains a crucifix by a leading Gothic woodcarver, Michael Pacher, whose home was in Brunico.

If you want to see the mountains the lazy way take the **cablecar** to the Pian de Cornes immediately south of the village (2,273 metres). Any bus south to places like Corvara or Cortina offers some jaw-dropping scenery, and there are all sorts of canny bus itineraries you can organise to give you day tours of this part of the Dolomites (returning to either Brunico or Bolzano). Brunico also offers plenty of **walking** both close to the town, or in the mountains north and south.

Beyond Brunico the train courses through the best of the valley's already stunning landscapes, hedged in tight to the valley floor by the looming mountains and dark tunnels of pines to either side. Trains stop at **San Candido**, where you've no choice but to turn round and come back unless you're continuing into Austria. To the south, though, you'll probably already have seen the outlying bastions of the Dolomiti di Sesto, one of the most awe-inspiring of all the Dolomite ranges. The views are irresistible. You can see them from closer to by taking a bus from **Dobbiaco** to Cortina (32 km), or better still to **Sesto** (12 km from Dobbiaco).

Idyllic Sesto, or its little near neighbour, San Giuseppe, both have hotels you can use as bases to explore the well-worn paths into the Sesto group. The obvious day hike follows paths number 5/102 up the Bachen valley south of San Giuseppe to the Rifugio Locatelli, where there are extraordinary views of some of the Dolomites' most-photographed peaks, the Tre Cime di Lavaredo. You could then loop back towards Sesto on path number 105, or stay up high for a more demanding day exploring paths number 101 and 104.

Verona–Vicenza–Padua

The route

Although it's hard to resist Venice's siren call, try to spend a couple of hours in Vicenza and Padua, two lesser but nonetheless diverting towns conveniently placed on the main line between Verona and Venice.

Trains

*About 20 trains daily run between Verona and **Venice** calling at Vicenza (52 km, 30 min) and Padua (82 km, 55 min). Services on this stretch of line can be busy year-round, and particularly in summer when everyone heading for Venice from the north, west and south meets at Verona or Padua for the last leg of their journey.*

Vicenza

Wealthy Vicenza has grown fat on the back of Europe's largest textile industry and a booming electronics sector, but to most visitors it's known for one man – Andrea di Pietro della Gondola, better known as **Palladio** (1508–80). One of the Renaissance's most influential architects, his stamp now lies over most of his adopted city. Born in neighbouring Padua he moved to Vicenza aged 16 to become a stonemason, later entering the pay of a local nobleman, Giangiorgio Trissino, who influenced his architectural grounding, gave him a suitably Classical-sounding name, and introduced him to the city's wealthy patrons.

Reworked Renaissance Classicism can be a cold and bland affair, but Palladio's version of the genre is in a league of its own. Even if you'd normally not give architecture from this era the time of day, it's well worth sampling his cluster of palaces around the city to see what all the fuss is about.

Piazza dei Signori

Piazza dei Signori was the main forum during the city's Roman heyday, its drawing-room during the period of Venetian domination, and finally the setting for Palladio's masterpiece, the **Basilica**. For years the old Palazzo della Ragione had defied the attempts by architects to prop up its crumbling exterior. In 1546 Count Trissino backed his protégé's plans to shore up the building with a cleverly designed twin loggia of Ionic and Doric columns. This in effect was to act as a monumental frame that would buttress the 15th-century Gothic palace. It was Palladio's first major project and secured his reputation – though he continued to add refinements until his death (9.30 am–noon and 2.30–5 pm; Sun 9.30 am–noon, closed Mon; free).

Across the piazza stands another Palladio venture, the unfinished **Loggia del Capitano**, designed as a residence for the city's Venetian military commander. Only the three bays and four massive pairs of columns, though, are the work of the master. Its reliefs portray scenes from Venice's victory over the Turks in 1571 at the Battle of Lepanto.

Immediately south of the piazza is the **duomo**, a disappointing affair, largely because it was flattened in the Second World War and painstakingly reconstructed to dead and gloomy effect.

Piazza Matteotti

Leave Piazza dei Signori with the Loggia on your left and you come to Corso Andrea Palladio, Vicenza's main street, an arrow-straight thoroughfare lined with palaces (now mostly shops and offices) that cuts through the heart of the old city. Turn right and you come to **Piazza Matteotti**, home to a trio of sights. On the left is **Santa Corona**, a 13th-century Dominican church, repository for two great paintings by Giovanni Bellini and Veronese. (For a third artistic *tour-de-force* visit the nearby Baroque church of **Santo Stefano** and Palma Vecchio's *Madonna and Child with SS George and Lucy*.)

On the piazza's righthand back edge stands the **Museo Civico**, housed in another imposing Palladian pile, the **Palazzo Chiericati** (begun 1550), whose first floor holds the city's art collection (daily 9.30 am–noon and 2.30–5 pm; Sun

10 am–noon, closed Mon). Note that you can buy a combined ticket for the museum and the nearby Teatro Olimpico across the way (see below).

Also worthwhile is the **Teatro Olimpico** to the left of the tourist office, Europe's oldest indoor theatre, another clever piece of Palladiana derived from the architect's reading of classical texts and his studies of Roman buildings (daily 9.30 am–noon and 3–5.30 pm, Sun 9.30–noon).

Palladio's other palaces dot the old city, none of them more than a couple of minutes' walk from the Corso or the two main squares. For the best, pick up a map from the tourist office and make for Palazzo Valmarana-Bragna, Corso Fogazzaro 16, and Palazzo di Porta-Festa (considered by Vasari the best of Palladio's works, despite its being unfinished), Palazzo Porta-Barbara and Palazzo Thiene, all on Contrà Porti.

Practicalities in Vicenza

Tourist Office Piazza Matteotti 12 (0444/ 320.854) next to the Teatro Olimpico.
Railway Station Piazza Stazione, at the end of Viale Roma (0444/325.045). Left luggage 6 am–10 pm.
Buses The bus terminal is at Viale Milano 7 (0444/544.333) on the left outside the station. EIV services run to most towns and villages in the Veneto.
Hotels ☆*Villa Marzia*, Via Mure Pallamaio 96 (0444/227.055). A basic and reliable central hotel.
☆☆*Milano*, Stradella dei Servi 5 (0444/ 238.643). With the 2 hotels below, a reasonable, central choice.
☆☆*Due Mori*, Contrà Do Rode 26 (0444/ 221.886). Recently refurnished and sparkling rooms.

☆☆*Palladio*, Via Oratorio dei Servi 25 (0444/ 221.072).
☆☆*Hotel Vicenza*, Stradella dei Nodari, off Piazza dei Signori (0444/321.512). Clean and central but potentially noisy rooms.
Eating and Drinking Vicenza's daily outdoor market takes place in Piazza delle Erbe to one side of the Basilica. Thursday sees a larger market spread through much of the city centre.
Antica Casa della Malvasia, Contrà delle Morette 5. Busy, popular and unassuming restaurant; good prices and an appealing bar.
Vecchia Guardia, Contrà Peschiera Vecchia 11. A touch smarter than the *Antica Casa*, but still deservedly popular.
Al Grottino, Piazza delle Erbe 2. Great cave-like *enoteca* for a cool glass of wine near the Basilica.

Excursion from Vicenza

The Villa Rotonda

Palladio's famous villas scattered around the Veneto countryside aren't the easiest places to reach without a car or fairly determined use of public transport. One of the best and most famous, though, lies within easy striking distance of the city. Goethe considered the much-imitated Villa Rotonda (also known as the Villa Capra) one of Europe's greatest architectural achievements, and few have bothered to argue the point. The interior's open only once a week, but it's well worth

trying to see, both for its sumptuous decoration and to appreciate the full subtlety of the architect's design. To reach the Villa take bus number 8 or 13 from near the station (open March 15–Oct 15 Wed only 10 am–noon and 3–6 pm).

About ten minute's walk from the Rotonda you might also visit Vicenza's other main peripheral sight, the **Villa Valmarana** (daily 3–5 pm), a fairly dull house but known for Tiepolo's superb decorative frescoes.

Padua

Padua's once impeccable historical credentials, not to mention many of its sights, were tarnished during the Second World War when bombing razed much of the old city to the ground and brought about the frenzy of modern development that greets you as the train pulls into town. This said, you should definitely stop off here, if only to see the **Cappella degli Scrovegni**, which has the advantage of being only ten minutes' walk from the station. Most guides try to make out a case for the rest of the place – which undoubtedly has its moments – but the only other spot to devote time to is the **Piazza del Santo** and its monuments to St Antony of Padua, one of Italy's most important saints.

The Cappella degli Scrovegni (The Arena Chapel)

The Cappella degli Scrovegni is one of the most treasured points of artistic pilgrimage in Italy, thanks to an astounding **fresco cycle** that is believed to have been completed by the Florentine artist, Giotto. Walk straight out of the station down Corso del Popolo and the chapel is about 600 metres down on the left, close to where the Corso del Popolo becomes Corso Garibaldi (April–Sept daily 9 am–7 pm; Oct–Mar daily 9 am–6 pm, closed Mon). There's often a tight scrum of bodies battling for a view of the paintings, so try to come early or late to avoid the worst of the crowds.

The chapel was commissioned in 1303 by Enrico Scrovegni in an attempt to buy Heavenly favour for his father, whose usurious habits were so extreme that he was forbidden a Christian burial. The provenance of the frescoes has been debated by art historians for years although their importance is not disputed: they moved Italian painting away from the stilted strictures of Byzantine art – which was all lifeless, flat-faced Madonnas – and introduced depth into compositions and naturalism into characters.

The strikingly large church just south of the chapel and the dull Museo Civico is the **Eremitani**, whose tremendous fresco cycle by Mantegna was all but destroyed by bombing in the Second World War – one of the greatest blows ever dealt to Italy's artistic patrimony. What's left is a sad collection of salvaged fragments.

The Basilica di Sant' Antonio

It's hard to know why St Antony of Padua, patron saint of the lost and found, is such a popular figure – perhaps it's because his brief embraces lost love. Whatever the reason, hordes of people come to pay homage to his body in Piazza del Santo's Basilica di Sant' Antonio (daily 6.30 am–7 pm; free). To get here it's a good kilometre's walk south from the Eremitani, first on Via della Zaberella out of Piazza Eremitani and then on Via del Santo.

As a mark of his considerable standing, Antony was canonised within just eighteen months of his death. The weight of pilgrims who then came to venerate his remains led to the building of the Basilica, a faintly daft medieval extravagance of domes, octagonal campaniles and offbeat minarets that took from 1232 to the mid-14th century to complete. The chapel containing the body (in the left transept) is worth a visit both for its irresistibly kitsch if undoubtedly heartfelt collection of votive offerings, and for an insight into the extent that saints and their relics still have a place in the Catholic church.

The chapel's nine carved panels represent some of Italy's most important 16th-century relief sculptures, and describe episodes from the life of St Antony. The basilica's other artistic treasures include seven bronze sculptures (1443–53) by **Donatello** on the high altar; the 14th-century frescoes in the Cappella del Beato Luco (two chapels down from the saint) and in Cappella di San Felice (in the right transept). Also make a point of finding the bizarre little reliquary in the apse containing St Antony's jaw and tongue.

Piazza del Santo

Outside, to the right of the Basilica, the rest of the Piazza del Santo contains the **Oratorio di San Giorgio** and the **Scuola Santa**. The Oratorio, originally a mortuary chapel, is best known for the frescoes by Altichiero di Zevio and Jacopo Avanzi (1377), two followers of Giotto: the Scuola has a handful of paintings, four of which are said to be early works by Titian (both open daily 9 am–

Practicalities in Padua

Tourist Office There's an excellent tourist office in the railway station (049/875.2077) with exchange facilities and an accommodation-finding service: you'll find another office in the bus station. Pick up the free and massively detailed *Padova Welcome* booklet (in English) for a full run down on the city and its province.

Railway Station Piazza Stazione (049/875.2077). Left luggage 7 am – 1.30 pm and 3 – 9 pm.

Buses ATP buses operate from Via Trieste 42 (049/820.6811) reached from the station by walking 300 metres down Corso del Popolo and then turning left on Via Trieste (5 min). Services to Venice (half hourly, 45 min); Vicenza (half hourly, 30 min); and Bassano del Grappa, Abano Terme, Montegrotto Terme and other local towns. Long distance routes connect to Milan, Genoa, Trieste, Treviso, even to Vienna.

Budget Travel CTS, Via Santa Sofia 94 (049/875.1719).

Post Office Corso Garibaldi 25.

Bike Rental Piazza del Municipio at the Comune di Padova.

Youth Hostel *Città di Padova*, Via A. Aleardi 30 (049/875.2219). Take bus number 3, 8 or 12 from the station and get off at the Basilica or Prato della Valle, about 10 min walk from the hostel. It's a good but busy place, with large, clean rooms, and a friendly bar-restaurant. Open 8 am – 11 pm to register and drop off luggage, but there's a loosely observed 9.30 am – 6 pm lockout.

Hotels Many people choose to use Padua as a base from which to explore Venice. This saves money and a considerable amount of hassle. The city has plenty of cheap accommodation options – if you need help contact the tourist office in the station.

☆*Pace*, Via dei Papafava 3 (049/875.1566). A small street with several cheap places one block south of the duomo.

☆*Pavia*, Via dei Papafava 11 (049/661.558).

☆*Bellevue*, Via L. Belludi 11 (049/875.5547). On the street off the southwest corner of Piazza del Santo; lovely rooms looking over an ivy-decked courtyard.

☆☆*Al Santo*, Via del Santo 147 (049/875.2131). Between Piazza del Santo and the Cappella degli Scrovegni.

☆☆*Casa del Pellegrino*, Via Cesarotti 21 (049/875.2100). A basic and clean 162-room pilgrim hotel near the Basilica.

☆☆*La Perla*, Via Cesarotti 67 (049/875.8939). Close to the Basilica and the *Pellegrino*, but it has just 5 rooms.

Eating and Drinking Padua's large student population means there's no shortage of cheap snack places and reasonable trattorias. Try *Al Pero*, Via Santa Lucia 72, near Via Dante, or *Al Traguardo* on Piazza Petrarca. Bars stay open later (much later than Venice); look up the *Alexander*, Via San Francesco 38.

12.30 pm and 2.30–5 pm). Alongside the Scuola stands the **Pinacoteca Civica**, the civic art gallery, home to mainly Venetian paintings from the 14th–18th centuries.

The statue in the centre of the piazza is Donatello's **Gattamelata**, or 'The Honeyed Cat' (1453), the nickname of Erasmo da Narni, an eminent mercenary known for his nobility and the agility and ferocity which earned him his nickname. This was the first large bronze sculpture cast during the Renaissance. For a break from art, saints and statues, follow the little lane to the right of the Scuola to the **Orto Botanico**, one of Europe's first botanical gardens (1545) and probably the best spot in town for a siesta or quiet picnic (Mon–Sat 9 am–1 pm and 3–6 pm). Little has changed since the plot was laid out, least of all a large palm planted in 1585 (Goethe came to see it in 1786) and still flourishing.

Venice

It's no use pretending you'll be able to do any justice to Venice's many churches, palaces and miscellaneous treasure trove of sights. Most of the time, you'd be best advised to enjoy the city simply by wandering its alleys and canals at random – and the further from the main sights the better. The sights below are a straightforward roll-call of the essential landmarks, aiming to cut through what in many guides is usually either a bewildering gazetteer of names, or impossibly complicated itineraries through a city which thoroughly defies any attempt to break it into convenient components.

Brave the endless battalions of tourists to see the **Piazza San Marco**, and its key elements, the **Basilica di San Marco** and **Palazzo Ducale**. For art move on to the **Galleria dell'Accademia**, and for the top churches and more paintings visit **Santa Maria Gloriosa dei Frari** and the adjacent **Scuola Grande di San Rocco**. For another convenient pairing, see the **Colleoni statue** and church of **SS Giovanni e Paolo** on Campo San Zanipolo. Be sure to ride up the central Grand Canal by *vaporetto*, and think about longer boat trips to the islands of **Torcello**, **Murano** and **Burano**.

History

The banks of the Venetian lagoon were probably first settled around the time of Christ, but concerted population of the area only took place during the Barbarian invasions. By the 6th century a loose confederation of groups on the islands had developed. Initially these owed allegiance to Byzantium and were more or less ruled from Ravenna. In 726, though, the settlers elected a provincial government and nominated a leader – the first doge.

By the 10th century the city had established trading links with the East, its prosperity increasing in the wake of the Crusades. Not only looted treasures flowed back to Venice, but also a great deal of territory, so that by the 13th century she owned a string of ports stretching to the Black Sea and 'one quarter and one half quarter' of the old Roman Empire. On its own back door the city concentrated on subduing Genoa, its main 14th-century rival, and in building up a mainland empire (present day Veneto and beyond) which remained intact more or less until the arrival of Napoleon.

Venice's rise inevitably brought it into conflict with the Papacy and with other European powers. In 1508 the League of Cambrai united almost every foreign power against the Venetians as a prelude to attacking the Turks, a rising influence in Venice's old power bases (Constantinople had fallen to the Turks in 1453). The Venetians held out, though lands and cities were sacked, and the state treasury all but exhausted. Elsewhere the opening up of the Americas diverted the balance of world trade to the West, away from Venice's traditional markets in the East.

After the Sack of Rome in 1527 all of Italy except for Venice came under the control of the Holy Roman Emperor Charles v. Thereafter, stranded on the periphery, the city declined. The Turks ate away at the Empire overseas, taking Crete, its last stronghold, in 1669. Napoleon brought things to an end in 1797, dismantling what in any case was a moribund state and leaving Venice what it has since largely remained – a city renowned as a playground of casinos, brothels and perpetual festivities. After a further short interval of French occupation, Venice passed to the Austrians, who held the city until the Unification of Italy in 1866. The Austrians subsequently moved most of their trade through Trieste, further removing any chance of Venice reasserting itself as a port. Tourism developed instead, followed – as the 20th century progressed – by the growth of industrial Mestre and Marghera on the mainland. The city's population is now just 70,000 (down from 180,000 in 1945). But for some 20 million visitors a year, the city might well be a ghost town.

What to See

Piazza San Marco

Venice's magnificent main piazza these days is not so much Europe's 'drawing-room', as Napoleon called it, but more the melting pot for the tourists of several continents. It's always been a meeting place, whether as a centre for trade or for conversation in one of the coffee houses which sprang up in the 18th century. A couple survive, the most famous being *Florian*, which at L6,000 plus for an *espresso*, must be generating profits that'll ensure its survival for centuries to come. Far more prosaically, though, and a sign of the way things are going, is the *Wendy's* burger joint nearby. Several of the city's foremost sights sit in the square, however, so you'll have to put up with the shoals of visitors, at least for a while, before striking into the more restful back streets for peace and quiet.

The best place for an overview of the square is the reconstructed **Campanile**, which started life as a lighthouse in the ninth century, was modified for centuries thereafter and collapsed spectacularly on July 14th, 1902. The views are superb, and better, incidentally, than those from the square's other tower, the Torre dell'Orologio (daily 9.30 am–hour before dusk).

The short, west side of the piazza contains the **Museo Correr**, home to collections of coins, weapons and the like, and to the **Quaderia**, whose collection of mainly Venetian paintings should whet the appetite for the artistic feast to come in the nearby Accademia.

To the right of San Marco, between the square and the waterfront (known as the *Molo*), stretches the Piazzetta, home to two masterworks by Sansovino; the **Zecca** (Venice's mint, built in 1547), and the **Libreria Sansoviniana**, arguably the city's finest Renaissance building. Its second floor has frescoes by Veronese and Tintoretto, amongst others, and contains the Museo Archeologico, an outstanding collection of Roman and Greek antiquities – but in the context of Venice, one that can come fairly low down your list of priorities (daily 9 am–1 pm, closed Sun).

The Basilica di San Marco

St Mark was reputedly moored on Venice's lagoon, en route for Rome, when an angel appeared and told him he would be laid to rest in the city. When he died, however, he was buried in Alexandria. In 828 two Venetian merchants took it upon themselves to fulfil the city's destiny and stole the body, packing it in pork to smuggle it past Arab officials. The church, built to house the saint's relics, was modelled on Constantinople's Church of the Twelve Apostles (the borrowing is most obvious in the five bulbed domes) and like the old St Peter's in Rome, given a cruciform plan, both devices being a deliberate ploy to rival the great churches of Rome and Byzantium. Modified and embellished over the centuries, to a bewildering and spectacular degree, the result is a unique blend of Arab, Byzantine and western architecture, and since this was primarily the doge's private chapel rather than the city's cathedral it's topped off with pieces of bounty looted on his behalf from all corners of the Empire.

Amidst the **exterior**'s vast surfeit of detail and decoration the outstanding features are the main portal's Romanesque carvings, and the mosaic above the doorway on the far left which depicts the story of St Mark's abduction and the *The Arrival of the Body of St Mark* (1260). The four horses above the door are replicas of the original Hellenistic bronzes, now inside the basilica to shelter them from the elements. The staircase to the main door leads also to the **Loggia dei Cavalli** (or *Galleria*), home to the horses, and a lovely spot to cast an eye at closer range over the basilica's carvings and mosaics (daily 10 am–5 pm).

The **interior** is mainly about mosaics – 4,000 square metres of them – a twinkling kaleidoscope of colour and encyclopaedia of Biblical anecdote. All of them are set off by the beautiful 12th-century inlays of glass, marble and porphyry of the church's intricate geometric pavement. Take a few of the panels in at a time and pop back for several visits to avoid mosaic fatigue. Around the church's main body pay special attention to the rood screen (1394); its flanking pulpits; the 10th-century icon of the Madonna di Nicopeia, Venice's most important icon (housed in the chapel on the right side of the north transept); and to a lovely 15th-century fresco cycle on the *Life of the Virgin* in the adjacent Cappella della Madonna dei Mascoli.

Also be sure to see the **Pala d'Oro**, the basilica's top treasure, kept in the Sanctuary off the south transept. Commissioned in 976 in Constantinople as a gold altar panel, it was restudded with jewels over the centuries to almost gaudy effect and now groans under the weight of 83 enamel plaques, 74 roundels, 38 carved figures, 300 sapphires, 300 emeralds, 400 garnets, 15 rubies, 1,300 pearls and a vast assortment of lesser stones. Close by in the transept a door leads into the **Treasury**, an incredible repository of gold and silver chalices, reliquaries and the like, most of them removed to Venice during the Fourth Crusade.

The Palazzo Ducale

Between the basilica and the lagoon stands the Palazzo Ducale, almost as much of a hybrid of styles as San Marco, but above all a triumph of 14th-century Venetian Gothic. The home not only of the doge – Venice's effective ruler for almost five centuries – it also housed a complex coterie of councils, committees and civil servants designed to administer the Empire (the bureaucracy was also designed to limit the power of any single individual, doge included).

Not all of the palace, by any means, is going to interest you, so it's worth picking out the highlights. As ever in Venice, try to arrive soon after opening to avoid the worst of the crush, and be prepared for parts of the building being under wraps for restoration.

The main entrance, the **Porta della Carta**, is the city's premier Gothic concoction, but thereafter the appeal is more artistic, starting with the Tintorettos and Veronese of the **Anticollegio**, a waiting room for visiting dignitaries hoping to see the doge and his cabinet. The Sala di Collegio alongside has more works by Veronese, a painter who crops up again in perhaps the palace's most renowned room, the **Sala del Maggior Consiglio**. His *Apotheosis* stands above the doge's dias, backed by an immense panel of *Paradiso* painted by Tintoretto near the end of his life with the help of his son, Domenico. The portraits around the walls are pictures of the first 76 doges, the single blank space being for Doge Falier, who was effaced after being executed in 1355 for conspiring against the state. Amidst the other rooms, which are sometimes sumptuous to the point of cloying bad taste, hunt down, in particular, the chamber of the Council of Ten, Venice's much feared equivalent of the KGB.

The Galleria dell'Accademia

Venice's art is a lifetime's study, but if you haven't the time or patience to winkle out the paintings scattered amongst the city's churches and palaces, the Galleria dell'Accademia is a shortcut to the glories of Venice's artistic patrimony and probably enough of a feast to satiate anybody's cravings for fine art (Tues–Sat 9 am–2 pm, Sun 9 am–1 pm). It's on the Grand Canal west of San Marco, reached by *vaporetti* number 1, 2, and 4.

One of Europe's finest galleries, it traces the development of Venetian painting from the 14th to the 18th century, charting a roughly chronological course through its 20-plus rooms. Room 1 kicks off with the city's earliest known indigenous painters, notably Paolo and Lorenzo Veneziano (early 14th-century) before moving on a century or so in Room 2 and works by Carpaccio (notably the *Crucifixion and Glorification of the Ten thousand Martyrs*), Cima da Conegliano and Giovanni Bellini (see especially the *Pala di San Giobbe*).

Rooms 4 and 5 are two outstanding sections, with more Bellinis (Giovanni and father, Jacopo), an early Piero della Francesca, Mantegna (*St George*) and the star turns, Giorgione's *La Vecchia* and the *Tempest*, one of the strangest and most famous of Italian paintings.

Room 6 ushers in the Venetian High Renaissance and the era's biggest names; Titian and Tintoretto (*The Madonna dei Camerlenghi*, 1566), as well as a supporting cast of characters like Room 7's Lorenzo Lotto and his fine *Young Man in His Study* (1528). The climax comes in Room 10 with Veronese's overwhelming *Christ in the House of Levi*, a notorious painting that enraged the Inquisition who railed at its presumed irreverence: "Does it appear to you fitting," they asked, 'that at our Lord's Last Supper you should paint buffons, drunkards, German dwarfs and similar indecencies?' The painter stood firm, and simply changed the picture's title to placate his accusers. Also in the same room are more Titians, notably a gloomy *Pietà*, believed to have been intended for his own tomb, and a clutch of Tintorettos that show the painter in his best light.

Room 11 moves on to Tiepolo, leading light of 18th-century Venice, followed by a rather duller succession of rooms that's interrupted by the paintings of Carpaccio and Gentile Bellini in Room 20. The following room has an exceptional cycle of pictures, again by Carpaccio, illustrating the *Story of St Ursula* (1490-94). Ursula was a Breton princess betrothed to Hereus, a British prince, though she refused to marry until Hereus converted to Christianity; she also undertook a pilgrimage in the company of 11,000 virgins, a sojourn which ended in a massacre near Cologne – an event foretold to Ursula in a dream. Titian's Presentation of the *Virgin* in Room 24 rounds things off.

I Frari

The church of I Frari may not, at first glance, be much to look at from the outside, but its collection of paintings and sculptures makes it one of the city's unmissable points of artistic pilgrimage. It includes a pair of Titians (an *Assumption*, arguably one of his greatest works, and the *Madonna di Ca' Pesaro*). Titian's tomb is in the nave, together with that of Canova, two overblown monuments erected in the 19th century. The highlights are two tombs flanking the *Assumption* – monuments to the doges Tron and Francesco Foscoli by Antonio Rizzi and Antonio Bregno respectively; Donatello's *St John the Baptist* in a chapel to the right, while the sacristry altar is the background for Giovanni Bellini's *Madonna and Child with Saints*, one of the most captivating paintings in the city.

The Scuola di San Rocco

The Scuola di San Rocco lies behind I Frari and dates from 1515, built on the proceeds from the donations of people invoking the aid of San Rocco, the saint against infectious diseases – and the plague in particular. His body was brought to Venice in 1485.

Today the Scuola's great appeal lies in its **Tintoretto paintings**, the earliest of which on this site reside in the **Sala dell'Albergo**. In 1564 the Scuola instigated a competition for the commission to paint the building's first picture. Tintoretto won by producing a finished piece (other artists came up only with sketches) which he hung in the centre of the ceiling – the spot chosen for the winning entry. Most of one wall is now covered by a mighty *Crucifixion*, a painting 'beyond all analysis, and above all praise', in the judgement of the Victorian critic, John Ruskin, and in which Tintoretto managed – in his own words – to combine 'the colour of Titan with the drawing of Michelangelo'. Other parts of the room contain only slightly less striking scenes from the *Passion*.

After eight years in the Sala, Tintoretto moved to the main upper hall of the Scuola, executing three large ceiling panels whose Old Testament themes were oblique references to the organisation's charitable works.

Still more works by Tintoretto adorn the church of **San Rocco** alongside the Scuola.

Campo San Zanipolo

After Piazza San Marco, the Campo San Zanipolo is Venice's finest square (San Marco, you'll notice, is the city's only open space accorded the status of a 'piazza'). The name is a contraction of Santi Giovanni e Paolo, after the square's church, the main, but not sole reason for a walk up here. Also on show are the **Colleoni statue**, one of Italy's best equestrian monuments and the **Scuola Grande di San Marco**, which though it may not have the Scuola Grande's artistic lures, has the loveliest façade of any of Venice's many *Scuole*.

Bartolomeo Colleoni, a leading mercenary or *condottiere*, began his career with the Venetians in 1429, later defecting to Milan, the first of several transfers before he signed up with his home city for good in 1448. This was a time the city had recently conquered mainly territory in Lombardy and the Veneto, though Colleoni found himself called upon only once more in the 25 years up to his death in 1475. In his will he left a large legacy to the state, though only on condition that they raised a statue to him in front of the Basilica di San Marco. The Republic refused to grant so important a site to a single individual, but with typical cunning twisted the will so that they built a monument in front of the Scuola Grande di San Marco and still kept the money: the name was almost the same, only the location was different.

The commission for the statue (1481–88) went to the famous Florentine sculptor, Andrea Verrocchio, who produced one of the Renaissance's unqualified masterpieces – though the enterprise was not without its ups and downs. Having all but completed the horse, he heard that another artist was being approached for the figure, and promptly defaced the sculpture and scuttled back to Florence. All was soon soothed over, however, and work proceeded quietly until Verrocchio's death in 1488, after which the Venetian Alessandro Leopardi was called in to finish the work and construct a plinth.

Colleoni's backdrop is the lovely façade of the **Scuola Grande di San Marco** (1487–95), painted several times by Guardi and Canaletto, and the work of three of the city's foremost artists: Pietro Lombardo, Giovanni Buora and Mauro Coducci.

Santi Giovanni e Paolo

Santi Giovanni e Paolo, or San Zanipolo when rendered in Venetian, was built by the Dominicans between 1246 and 1430 as a simple affair consisting of a single nave and two aisles. Within the looming brick interior the impression is of huge size, its inherent plainness disturbed by numerous tombs and monuments. No fewer than 25 doges were buried here, though only a handful of their monuments are worth making a special effort to see: try to hunt out the tombs on the western wall (the entrance wall), which belong to the Mocenigo clan, the finest that of Doge Pietro Mocenigo (d. 1476) by Pietro Lombardo and his sons. Ruskin thought the tomb of Doge Michele Morosini (d. 1382) in the chancel 'the richest monument of the Gothic period in Venice'.

Tombs aside, the church creaks under the weight of its fine art, notably Giovanni Bellini, Lorenzo Lotto and a ceiling by Veronese in the Cappella del Rosario. At the head of the aisle the Cappella di San Domenico is noted for its ceiling by Piazzetta (1726) and a choice little relic, the foot of St Catherine of Siena, one of Italy's first division saints. Most of her body resides in Rome, bar her head, which is in Siena.

The Ghetto

Turn left out of the station and pass through its tawdry environs, and the tight district of the Ghetto is one of the first tempting areas of the city you come to. This was the world's first Jewish ghetto, the word itself possibly deriving from *getar* (to found) or *geto* (foundry), after the iron works that occupied the area until 1390. Jews were segregated here from 1516, sealed in at night, and forced to wear distinguishing caps and badges. Injunctions against them, however, were generally lighter than elsewhere in Europe at the time. As a result many Jews expelled from Spain (1492) and Portugal (1497) made their way to Venice (where their religion was at least tolerated). Today there are five synagogues catering to the faithful of different countries (the Scola Levantina, Scola Spagnola and Scola Tedesca are open to the public). At its peak the Jewish population reached about 4,000, all of whom had to be crammed into a designated area, hence the area's tall, multi-storeyed houses. Napoleon removed the ghetto's gates in 1798, and relaxed some of the restrictions constraining Jews, only for the Austrians to replace them a year later. Full parity with other Venetians didn't come until Unification with Italy in 1866. For an insight into Jewish life in the city past and present visit the **Museo di Arte Ebraica** in Campo Ghetto Nuovo (10.30 am–12.30 pm and 3–5 pm, closed Sat).

Wandering around north-east of the Ghetto make a beeline for the church of **Sant'Alvise**, home to an outstanding Tiepolo, *The Road to Calvary*, and then head east through archetypal Venice backwaters towards **Madonna dell'Orto**, an interesting piece of transitional Romanesque, Gothic and Renaissance architecture. Inside, sadly, the church has been reworked along 19th-century lines, but it's the resting place of Tintoretto, buried in a chapel to the right of the high altar. Fittingly, he's surrounded by some fine examples of his work.

The Rialto

The Rialto is one of Venice's best known names after San Marco, and – like the Ghetto – it's best to wander aimlessly rather than hunt out specific targets. The lagoon's earliest settlers were attracted to the upper bank, or *riva alta*, of what was to become the Grand Canal. In time the Rialto developed from this area – and adopted a corruption of its name. While political power centred on San Marco, commercial interests and trade were concentrated on the Rialto. Europe's first central bank was founded here in the 12th century, together with the bureaucracy which eventually developed to oversee maritime trade. The exchequer was transferred to the new Palazzo dei Camerlenghi in the 16th century, perfectly placed – like all of the Rialto – to take advantage of the area's 11,000 or so prostitutes, who had the sense to station themselves where money flowed and business was brisk.

For about 400 years markets on the Rialto traded not only in flesh, but also in just about anything that could be bought and sold: the spices of the Orient, gold, silver, textiles, silks and much besides. Today there are still markets locally, some of the city's most bustling spots (and relatively free of foreign babble). You'll find souvenir trash and fruit around Campo San Giacomo, meat and vegetables on Campo Battisti, as well as a fish market and a plethora of cheese and general food shops. Visit the church of **San Cassiano** on your way out of the area, home to three Tintorettos, including one of the city's premier paintings, a *Crucifixion* from 1568.

The Lido

Immortalised, after a fashion, by Visconti's film *Death in Venice*, the Lido is now a shadow of its elegant former self. One of the lagoon's southern islands, it was mostly unspoilt sand banks until the turn of the century when it became probably Europe's most fashionable bathing spot. Most people have heard of the area's beaches and reputation, which only makes it as well to know the reality, which is cheek-by-jowl hotels on the sea front (the *Grand Hotel des Bains* is the Belle Epoque landmark), massive crowds and ludicrous entry fees for the privilege of staking a stretch of decent sand on the mostly private beaches. The only public spots are at the Lido's northern and southern ends, where the sand and water are so filthy that you won't want to risk your health in their pursuit. It's best to save the sand and sea experience for elsewhere in Italy.

Torcello, Murano and Burano

Venice has two main groups of islands to the north and south of the city. You could visit all of them by *vaporetto* simply for the enchantment of the journey, or to escape the worst of the centre's madding crowds. For something to do when you get there, however, the northern archipelago is the most interesting. It's reached on *vaporetto* number 12 (and 5 for Murano), which leaves every 15 minutes for the 45 minute trip from the Fondamente Nuove.

San Michele is largely a cemetery island – Stravinsky and Diaghilev are buried here, amongst others. Meditative and relatively rural Torcello is visited mainly for Venice's first cathedral, Santa Maria Assunta, a magnificent building founded in the 7th century and known for its 11th- and 12th-century mosaics.

Better known than either island, though, is **Murano**, synonymous these days with its **glass industry**. The city's glass-blowing artisans moved here in 1291 as a safety precaution, the furnaces having been deemed a fire risk. Over the centuries they've jealously guarded their industrial secrets – for a long while, for example, they were the only people in Europe capable of producing glass mirrors. As a result of their expertise they won many privileges from the state.

Most of the island's shops sell pure tourist tat, although most people come here to wander through the numerous **workshops** to see the blowing process at first hand. Entry is free as the expectation is that you'll buy something at the end of the tour, though you'll rarely find that there's much pressure to part with your money. On Fondamenta Cavour take time to visit the **Museo Vetrario** housed in the Palazzo Giustinian (Mon, Tues and Thur–Sat 10 am–4 pm; Sun 9 am–12.30 pm), a fascinating look at glassware and glass-blowing from Roman times.

While on the island look at its two other main attractions, the church of **San Pietro Martire**, known for its fine Bellini, *Madonna and Child with Saints*, and the more impressive **Santi Maria e Donato** (7th to 12th century), home to a sumptuous mosaic floor (1141) and to four 'dragon's bones' above the altar, relics from a creature slain by St Donato's holy spittle (Donato's remains are kept here).

Where Murano is about glass, **Burano** is about lace – at least for the women; the men are largely kept busy by fishing, and though there's still a hint of the fishing village about Burano, it's a place that inevitably caters heavily to tourists. This said, it's still worth dropping into the **Scuola dei Merletti** (the 'Lace School'), opened in 1872 to breathe life into a dying craft and now a small museum as well as a school. Lace made here is the real stuff, in contrast to the product in the shops which is largely machine-made and imported.

Practicalities in Venice

A word of warning You can't miss Venice, of course, but you might not want to spend as long as you imagined in the city, particularly if you're unlucky enough to be visiting in the madcap and hyper-thronged months of July and August. It might sound a heresy, but at peak times – and even outside them – you should give careful thought to the idea of taking a room away from the city (in Padua, Vicenza, Treviso, or even Verona) and make day trips to the city. This will save you money, hassle and ultimately time, as well as the headache of trying to secure a room in the face of fierce summer competition.

Arrival Arriving in any big city can be traumatic; dropping off the train in Venice can be doubly so, firstly because of the strangeness of emerging into a place with no cars and roads, and secondly because of the sheer number of people.

To get straight to Venice's key spot, Piazza San Marco, board the water bus (*vaporetto*) number 1 or 2, which leaves every ten minutes between 7 am and 11 pm from in front of the railway station (see 'Transport'). To walk, turn left out of the station on to the street Lista di Spagna and follow the signs. It's about a 40 minute hike, the route shadowing the Grand Canal for most of the way.

Districts Note that when you're looking at addresses you'll see streets and alleys followed by the name of a district. The area around and north of the station is **Cannaregio**; across the Grand Canal from the station is **San Polo**; **San Marco** includes the central area around and to the west of Piazza San Marco; the **Castello** in the region east of Piazza San Marco. **Dorsoduro** refers to the small arm of land across the Grand Canal from San Marco. The **Giudecca** is the separate and outlying 'island' south of Dorsoduro.

Telephone Code 041

Tourist Office The office at the railway station is helpful, but likely to be besieged by hordes of people (719.078), so too the summer-only office in Piazzale Roma, the frantic square just left of the station where the road from the mainland ends (522.7404). There may be fewer queues at the main office in Piazza San Marco, housed under the arcade at the far end of the square from the Basilica (522.6356; Mon–Sat 8.30 am–7 pm). Pick up the useful *Un Ospite di Venezia*, a free weekly full of current events, timetables and entertainment listings.

Accommodation Offices To save tramping the canals for hours if you arrive without a room, several booking offices will organise a bed in either a 1- or 2-star hotel (not in any of the hostels). They take a booking fee, deductible from your first night's stay. Offices open 9 am–9 pm at the railway station (alongside the tourist office) and in Piazzale Roma 540d (522.7402) and both are kept busy, so be prepared to wait.

Railway Station The Stazione di Santa Lucia, also known simply as the *Ferrovia*, is at the western end of the city right on the Grand Canal. Information (715.555, 7 am–9 pm). Left luggage: 24 hrs in theory, not always in practice; be prepared for long queues. Bar and Buffet 6 am–9 pm. Lost property (716.122).

Day Hotel The *Albergo diurno*, or 'day hotel', lets you have a shower and brush up during the day. Located in the station next to Platform 1 (daily 7 am–8 pm).

Trains The first thing to check when heading for Venice is that trains go to the city's Santa Lucia station. Through trains may stop at Venezia Mestre on the mainland: if you're on one of these there's likely to be a connecting train to Santa Lucia around every 15 min (look for the separate timetable and infoboards at Mestre for details).

Direct mainline services to Padua (every 15 min, 30 min); Bologna (14 daily, 1 hr 30 min); Milan (18 daily, 2 hr 30 min); Florence (6 daily, 2 hr 30 min–3 hr); Rome (4 daily, 5 hr 15 min). Don't forget the many sleeper trains out of Venice if you're travelling the length of the country, or the many connections at Bologna if you're heading down the Adriatic coast to Brindisi (for ferries to Greece).

Daily international services from Venice (Mestre/S.L.) run to Vienna, Munich, Zürich and Paris, either direct or with connections at Milan or Verona.

Foreign Exchange Change money beforehand outside the city, if at all possible, to avoid queues and poor rates at the railway station and exchange booths and banks around the city. The station exchange opens Mon–Sat 8 am–7 pm and Sun 8 am–1 pm.

American Express Off Piazza San Marco at the end opposite the Basilica – follow the Amex signs on the pavement (520.0844; exchange office opens Mon–Sat 9 am–7 pm).

Emergencies Police: (113) or Piazzale Roma, (523.5333); the *Questura* for reporting thefts, passport problems and the like, is on Fondamenta San Lorenzo, Castello (520.0754); Hospital: *Ospedale Civili Riuniti di Venezia*, Campo SS Giovanni e Paolo (529.4517); Ufficio Stranieri/Foreigners' Office (520.0754); United Kingdom Consulate, Dorsoduro 1051, by the Accademia (522.5996).

Transport In a city as compactly beautiful as Venice it obviously makes sense to do most of your travelling on foot. You can cross the whole city in an hour, and all the main sights are close together. Once you've got your bearings and a map, orientation isn't as bad as it might first appear. Most of the main districts and landmarks are also well sign-posted from some distance (in yellow on the sides of buildings). Thus if you're disorientated, head back to a base by looking out for **signs** to San Marco, Piazzale Roma, the Accademia or the *Ferrovia*.

It's equally as captivating – and often extremely practical – to take a water bus, known as **vaporetti**, or the slightly quicker **motoscafi**. The main routes run mostly up and down the Grand Canal; the others you're unlikely to need unless you're going out to the islands, but you might want to ride them anyway for the views. Boats aren't always clearly numbered, which can be initially confusing, but the routes don't really take too much working out.

Tickets are available from landing stages in front of *vaporetti* signs, from shops displaying an ACTV sign, or from the main ACTV offices at the Piazzale Roma and Rialto stops. Buy several at one go, as some booths at stops aren't always open, preferably in a block of ten (*un blochetto*). You can also buy tickets on board from the conductor with a surcharge, or an unlimited 24 hr *biglietto turistico*. Services run about every 10 min during the day, and much less frequently through the night in the city centre.

No. 1 The so-called *accelerato*, but actually the slowest boat on the system: Piazzale Roma – Stazione S.L. – Rialto – San Marco – Lido (with eight intermediate stops along the Grand Canal).

No. 2 The quickest way from the station to Piazza San Marco: Rialto – Stazione S.L. – Piazzale Roma – Accademia – San Marco – Lido (no intermediate stops).

No. 4 The *Turistico*: limited stop summer service along the Grand Canal and across the Lido.

No. 5 The *Circolare*: two services in opposite directions along the same route, the *Destra* and *Sinistra*: San Zaccaria – Giudecca – Piazzale Roma – Stazione S.L. – Fondamente Nuove – Murano (and reverse).

No. 12 Runs to the northern islands from the Fondamente Nuove: Fondamente – Murano – Burano – Torcello – Treporti

Where to eat and drink

Restaurants Too often in Venice you're on a hiding to nothing when it comes to restaurant meals. Food is usually expensive and tourist-orientated. Bar snacks and picnics may be a much better alternative (see below). Most places advertise a *menù turistico*, which means you can rely on the price, but not always on the food, the quantities or the service. It's almost always a bad idea to eat in and around San Marco: the further you get from here the more chance you have of a reasonable meal. Perhaps the best area of all to find reasonable trattorias is Dorsoduro. You should find some small local place of your own. Watch out for extras like *coperto* (cover) and *servizio* which can add several thousand lira to the bill.

Venetian specialities include fish and seafood (prawns, squid, crab and octopus as *antipasti*; salt cod, cuttlefish and eels as main courses). **Risotto** in many forms is a Venetian staple, along with *polenta*, a maize-based porridge eaten all over northern Italy when times were hard, and now inexplicably becoming fashionable – it's perhaps the blandest food in Europe. It needs an accompaniment, and in Venice this usually means liver (*fegato*). For puddings the ubiquitous *tiramisù* was invented in Venice, so there's a chance of getting a good one. Otherwise sweet tooths are well catered for by the city's predilection for **cakes and pastries** in all shapes and sizes.

Aciugheta, Campo Santi Filippo e Giacomo, Castello. Bar, restaurant and pizzeria if you must eat close to San Marco. Closed Wed.

Ai Promessi Sposi, Calle d'Oca (off Campo SS Apostoli), Castello. Traditional fish specialities; friendly bar and good pastas. Closed Tues.

All'Anfora, Lista Vecchia dei Bari, San Polo. Easy-going local spot with pizzeria, trattoria and good home-cooking.

Al Masceron, Calle Lunga Santa Maria Formosa, Castello, north-east of San Marco. A trendy, arty spot popular with Venetians and a touch more expensive than some places, but great food and ambience. Closed Sun.

Alla Madonna, Calle della Madonna, San Polo (near the Rialto). Top-notch Venetian food and often full despite its reputation for abrasive service. Closed Wed.

Alla Rivetta, Ponte San Provolo, off Campo Santi Filippo e Giacomo, Castello. Close to *Aciugheta* and another reasonable and not overly-touristy spot close to Piazza San Marco. Closed Mon. Try also the welcoming *Chinellato* close by on Calle Albanesi.

Alle Burchielle, Santa Croce. A spot to consider if you're trapped close to the station; off the corner of Piazzale Roma, over the bridge to Campazzo Tre Ponti. Local dishes served up on the canal's edge. Closed Mon.

Casa Mia, Calle dell'Oca (on the same street as the *Ai Promessi Sposi*), Castello. Popular with locals who tend to go for the pizzas rather than the pricier trattoria menu. Closed Tues.

Da Bruno, Calle Lunga San Barnaba, Dorsoduro. Nicely rough-edged and well-patronised place. Closed Thur lunch and Sun.

Donna Onesta, Calle della Madonna (near I Frari), San Polo. Friendly, popular and generous portions. Closed Sun.

Vini da Gigio, off the right hand side of the Chiesa San Felice, off Strada Nova. Fish dishes and no English menus – usually a good sign. Closed Mon.

Where to stay

During high season unless you've booked your accommodation in advance there's little chance of a room unless you arrive early in the morning and do the rounds of the hotels and hostels. Prices have levelled out to other big city levels, though don't be fooled by the apparent bargains offered by hotel touts at the station. Use the tourist offices and accommodation offices if you need to hunt out a room (see 'Information').

Hostels Ask at the tourist office for the annually updated list of the city's hostel accommodation. It's usually possible to find a bed in a dormitory somewhere, even in peak season. Most places have an evening curfew and lock you out during the day.

Youth Hostel *Ostello Venezia*, Fondamenta delle Zitelle, Giudecca 86 (523.8211). Take *vaporetto* number 5 (sinistra) from the station (25 min) and get off at Zitelle and walk right. Open June – Sept. No phone bookings are taken, so arrive early to join the queue to book in at 6 pm (doors open at noon). Ask at the tourist office first to see if they're already full. IYHF cards needed. There's a large overspill annexe in a local school, and often there's room for one or two even when all seems lost. No kitchen but meals available. Curfew 11 pm.

Archie's House, Rio Terrà San Leonardo, Cannaregio (720.884). Tightly run spot (no 'rowdies' or people under 21). Rooms have 3-5 beds and price varies depending on time of year, the length of stay and the number in your party.

Domus Cavanis, Rio Terrà Foscarini, Dorsoduro(528.7374). A Catholic-run spot with separate male-female dorms on the street to the left of the Accademia. Clean rooms, though not the cheapest hotel prices; meals are reasonable.

Domus Civica, Calle Campazzo, San Polo (522.7139). Women only. Between I Frari and Piazzale Roma, (follow yellow signs from the Piazzale to the Rialto) on the corner of Calle Chiovere, Calle Campazzo and San Rocco. Curfew 11.30 pm; check out 7.30 – 10 am. Open June – July and Sept to mid – Oct.

Foresteria Valdese, Santa Maria Formosa, Castello (528.6797). *Vaporetto* number 5 or 8 to San Zaccaria, 5 min walk to Santa Maria Formosa, then along Calle Lunga, over the bridge and the hostel – an 18th-century palace – is straight ahead. Check in at 9.30 am – 1 pm and 6 – 8.30 pm. Dorms for 8, 12, or 16, but inquire about a pair of much in demand apartments.

Istituto Ciliota, San Marco (520.4888). Near San Marco and the Accademia in Calle delle Muneghe, off Calle delle Botteghe and Campo Morosin. Singles and doubles. Open mid – June to mid – Sept).

Suore Cannosiano, Fondamenta del Ponte Piccolo (522.2157). Nun-run place for women only. Take *vaporetto* number 5 to Sant'Eufemia and walk left when you get off. Lockout 8.30 am – 4 pm, though you can leave your bags any time of the day. Curfew 10.30 pm. Dorms or 5-bed rooms.

Hotels

Cannaregio – Stazione to the Rialto

As in any city, the station is the breeding ground for a rash of cheap and usually not terribly salubrious hotels. Turn left on to Lista di Spagna, though, and at least the places here are convenient and there's plenty to choose from. The selections below are some of the better ones. Prices are a category lower in most places for rooms without a bathroom.

☆☆☆*Adua*, Lista di Spagna 233a (716.184). Quiet for the area, and spacious if bizarrely decorated rooms.

☆☆*Al Gobbo*, Campo S. Geremia (715.001). Second large piazza on the right 200m down Lista di Spagna, and a little more elegance and higher prices than the *Adua*.

☆☆*Casa Carettoni*, Lista di Spagna (716.231). Amongst the most appealing of the area's cheap hotels.

☆☆☆*Locanda Rossi* (715.164). Follow Lista di Spagna 100 m from the station, turn left on Calle della Procuratie before Campo San Geremia. Quiet and modern, if slightly characterless rooms.

☆☆*Locanda Antica Casa Carettoni*, Lista di Spagna 130 (716.231). Venerable 'truly Venetian' rooms; open Mar – July and Sept – Jan.

☆☆*Orsaria* (715.254). Rooms on Calle Priuli about 50 m from the station; turn left after the small Chiesa Scalzi; clean, well-kept and handy for new arrivals and early departures. Also 3- and 4-bed rooms available.

San Marco and Castello

☆☆*Albergo Bernardi-Semenzato*, Calle dell'Orca, close to Campo SS Apostoli (522.7257). From Strada Nuova, the main route from the station to the San Marco, take

Calle del Duca and the first right which is Calle dell'Orca. Helpful English-speaking management.

☆☆*Caneva*, Roma della Fava (522.8118). Just 2 min from the Rialto: take Calle Stagneri from busy Campo San Bartolomeo, cross the bridge and hang a right after Campo della Fava. Peaceful, with inner courtyard and the bulk of the 23 rooms look over a canal.

☆☆*Casa Petrarca*, Calle delle Colonne, San Marco 4394 (520.0430). West of San Marco: go south on Calle dei Fuseri from Campo San Luca, take the second left and then turn right on to Calle Schiavone. Very friendly at reception and delightful rooms. English spoken. Call first, as there are only 6 rooms.

☆☆*Pensione Casa Verardo*, Ruga Giuffa, Castello 4765 (528.6127). Follow Rimpetto la Sacrestia from Campo SS Filippo e Giacomo (east of San Marco) and across the bridge. Probably the best choice in this part of town.

☆☆*Rio*, SS Filippo e Giacomo, Castello 4356 (523.4810), something of a steal given its proximity to Piazza San Marco (2 min walk).

☆☆*San Samuele*, Piscina S Samuele, San Marco 3358 (522.8045). Take Calle delle Botteghe from Campo Santo Stefano and turn left on Salizzata San Samuele. Small, standard rooms, but not as dowdy as some in this range – and the manager's amiable.

☆☆*Silva*, Castello 4423 (522.7643). Take Calle dell'Anzolo alongside Piazza San Marco, take the second right, cross the bridge and left when you meet Fondamenta del Rimedio. Canal-situated, lots of room and well-tended. The ☆☆*Canal* next door is okay too (523.4538).

Dorsoduro, San Polo and Santa Croce

☆☆*Ca'Foscari*, Calle della Frescada, Dorsoduro 3888 (522.5817). An alley on Calle della Frescada, which is at the foot of Calle Crosera where it meets Calle Marconi. Easy-going, family-run and well-appointed 10 rooms.

☆☆*Casa dei Stefani*, Calle Traghetto San Barnaba, Dorsoduro 2786 (522.3337). Convenient and some of the 18 rooms in this 16th-century palazzo have fine frescoed ceilings.

☆☆*Montin*, Fondamenta di Borgo, Dorsoduro

1147 (522.7151). Just 7 high-reputation rooms and a noted (but pricey) restaurant.

☆☆☆*Stefania*, Fondamenta Tolentini, S. Croce 181 (520.3757). Close to station and Piazzale Roma; off Fondamenta San Simeone Piccolo. Convenient, but slightly odd and gloomy building, though rooms are large – look out for the murals.

Eastern Districts

☆☆☆*Locanda Sant'Anna*, Corte del Bianco, Castello 269 (528.6466). Take Via Garibaldi off Riva del VII Martiri, east of Piazza San Marco. Follow it on to Fondamenta Sant'Anna, turn left on Fondamenta Sant'Anna and right at Corte del Bianco. It's a longish walk, but you could take *vaporetto* number 1 or 4 to Giardini. Far from the crowds, but still well-known, so call ahead; 3- or 4-bed options.

☆☆*Belvedere*, Via Garibaldi, Castello 1636 (528.5148). Off the beaten track, so a good chance of room at short notice except during Aug.

☆☆*Toscana-Tofanelli*, Via Garibaldi, Castello 1650 (523.5722). Advantages of *Belvedere*, but more basic, though the position and en suite trattoria are excellent.

Camping All the city's camping options require boat trips, and when this is added to the generally expensive cost of pitches you're not getting much of a bargain. The days of dossing down outside the station or on the beach at the Lido are now long gone, although people still try.

Litorale del Cavallino This litoral offers an unbroken line of campsites along the Adriatic coast east of the city with a combined 60,000 places. The *vaporetto* number 14 plies the coast, stopping near the *Venezia* (Via Montello 6, 966.146; April–Sept; minimum stay of 3 days; *Miramare* (966.150; April–Sept), and many more.

The Lido site is the 150-pitch *San Nicolo*, Riviera San Nicolo (767.415).

Another option is to take bus number 5 or 19 from the bus station back over to the mainland and stay on the bus until you see a site which takes your fancy. Prices here are much lower, but the views can be grim and mosquitoes voracious.

Venice–Trieste
The route

This journey takes you to northern Italy's least explored corner, and to Trieste, one of its most atmospheric and little-known cities. It's unlikely, though, that you'll want to stop off en route as the train curves around the flat land and lagoons of the northern Adriatic. The best additional stops are made from Trieste itself, as easy train excursions to Udine and to **Cividale**.

Trains

About 15 trains daily run between Venice (Santa Lucia) and Trieste (157 km, 2 hr).

Trieste

Trieste's position has been both its making and its undoing. Captured by the Romans in 178 BC, it emerged as a colony, *Tergeste*, and a leading Adriatic port. Little of its Roman legacy survives, however, in fact little of anything prior to the 19th century appears to survive. The overwhelming majority of the city's architecture belongs to the late Baroque and Neoclassical periods. Most of it is concentrated in the *Borgo Teresiano*, or city centre, named after Empress Maria Theresa (1740–80), who was largely responsible for initiating the project. Some years earlier, in 1719, Charles VI of Hapsburg had conferred the title of 'free port' on Trieste, then just a few hundred houses grouped around the hill, or *Colle*, of San Giusto. This was in reply to Venice, who had claimed sovereignty over the whole Adriatic. Over the years the city was built up to act as the major southern port for the Austro–Hungarian Empire, a process that came to an abrupt halt following the Hapsburg defeat after the First World War. The break-up of the empire destroyed Trieste's markets and hinterland at a stroke. It also left Trieste at the very edge of Italy, a position which further weakened it economically. Worse, it made it a bone of contention between Slavs and Italian nationalists. Yugoslavia and the allies fought over it until 1954 after the Second World War, and a final border was only agreed as late as 1975. After decades in the doldrums, the opening up of eastern Europe may herald the resurgence of Trieste as a port – though the troubles in ex-Yugoslavia can only make the traditional divisions between Slavs and Italians more acute.

Colle San Giusto

If truth be told there's not an awful lot to see in Trieste. Its main appeal is its otherworldliness, and the weight of its historical associations. This said, you can still spend a morning seeing the sights before simply wandering to take in the atmosphere. The Colle San Giusto and its **Fortezza** and **duomo** are the two key draws, both easily reached on bus number 24 from the station if you don't first want to walk through the city. The fortress is the last stop and leaves you having to climb the 265-step Scala dei Giganti up the hill from Piazza Goldoni. Before diving into the cathedral, notice the column with the melon and the halberd, the city's two symbols, and the odd fragments of a basilica from the old Roman forum.

The present **duomo** was largely created in the 14th century, and owes its irregular plan to the fact that it joined two earlier buildings dating from about the 5th century (churches dedicated to San Giusto and Santa Maria Assunta respectively). The righthand apse of the lop-sided **interior** contains 15th-century frescoes and superb mosaics depicting Christ and San Giusto (late 14th century), mirrored by earlier mosaics and frescoes in the apse on the opposite side of the altar.

As for the **castle**, it was built between 1470 and 1630 on the site of an earlier Venetian fortress, and though perfectly impressive there isn't a lot to see – though you should take a walk around the ramparts and perhaps drop into its small museum for its modest collection of weapons and furniture (daily 9 am–1 pm, closed Mon). Within the walls is a large outdoor stage which hosts theatre and cinema performances during the city's summer festival cycles.

Museums

Less than a hundred metres from the duomo stands the **Museo di Arte e Storia**, primarily dedicated to the city's history, but also home to a busy little collection of Roman, Greek and Egyptian artifacts from places other than Trieste (daily 9 am–1 pm, closed Mon).

The city's main museum, the Revoltella on Via Diaz, has been shut by bureaucratic squabbling for years, leaving the **Civico Museo Morpurgo** at Via Imbriani 5 to mop up with displays of traditional regional costumes and the 19th-century house contents of Signor Morpurgo, the merchant and banker who left a *palazzo* of prints, pictures and furniture to the city (daily 10 am–1 pm, closed Mon). Museum duties are wrapped up by the **Museo Sartorio** in Largo Papa Giovanni XXIII, which comprises mainly gloomy private rooms loaded with dark Venetian paintings, but is redeemed by 270 drawings by Tiepolo and a noted ceramics collection.

Risiera di San Sabba

One of the city's understandably less-publicised areas – you hesitate to call it a sight – is the Risiera di San Sabba, which has the unfortunate distinction of having been the only concentration camp in Italy during the Second World War. Once a rice factory, it was converted into a death camp in 1943 under the supervision of Erwin Lambert, also responsible for the design of the more notorious Treblinka death camp in Poland. The numbers of people who met their death in the camp are not known, though 20,000 identity papers were found when the area was liberated by the Yugoslavs on May 1st, 1945. Sad to say, the camp commandant was a local man, the region's history having provided a fertile breeding ground for enthusiastic rather than lip-service Fascists. To see the camp take the number 10 bus south to Via Valmura (daily, 9 am–1 pm, closed Mon).

Practicalities in Trieste

Tourist Office The office in the railway station (040/420.182) has adequate information on the city, but there's another office in the Castello di San Giusto (040/309.298). Both provide accommodation details – which can be handy, as small *pensioni* often fill surprisingly quickly with students and itinerant workers.

Railway Station Piazza della Libertà, (040/418.207). At the city's northern end; walk down Via Cavour along the quays to reach the centre (15 min). Left luggage 24 hr.

Buses Leave from Corso Cavour (040/370.160) on the edge of Piazza della Libertà to the right as you leave the railway station. Left luggage 6.30 am – 9 pm. Services to Udine (7 daily); Belluno (1 daily); Cividale (2 daily); Duino (hourly); Gorizia (5 daily); Grado (3 daily); Pordenone (3 daily); Rijeka/Fiume (5 daily).

Foreign Exchange Banca d'America, Via Roma 7. Also provides cash advances on Visa.

Post Office Piazza Vittorio Veneto 1.

UK Consulate Vicolo delle Ville 16 (040/302.884).

Budget Travel Aurora Viaggia, Via Milano 20 (040/60.261), travel and accommodation information.

Where to stay

Youth Hostel Ostello Tegeste, Viale Miramare 331 (040/224.101). Fine hostel with seafront view, but accepts IYHF members only. Take bus number 6 from the stop outside the station opposite the tourist office and ride it to the end of the line. Then pick up bus number 36 to the hostel. Registration noon – 11.30 pm; lock-out 9.30 am – noon; curfew 11.30 pm. Cheap meals.

Hotels ☆*Pensione Venezia*, Via Genova 23 (040/68.480). Clean and friendly budget choice.

☆*Centro*, Via Roma 13 (040/64.408). In the grid of streets immediately south of the station off Via Ghega.

☆*Julia*, Via XXX Ottobre 5 (040/68.247).

☆*San Nicolo*, Via San Nicolo 2 (040/366.532). Follow Corso Cavour from the station and the hotel is off its continuation, Riva III Novembre.

☆☆*Hotel al Teatro*, Capo di Piazza G. Bartoli 1 (040/64.123).

Camping *Camping Obelisco* (040/299.264). Nearest site to the centre, but still 7 km distant in the suburb of Opicina; take a local train or the old cable tramway (the *tranvia*) from Piazza Oberdan. The site is not on the beach. *Marepineta* (040/299.264). Further down the coast than *Obelisco* in Sistiana (hourly buses from the bus terminal), but more facilities and a beachside location (May – Sept).

Where to eat and drink

Trieste's cuisine inevitably has an eastern European flavour – plenty of dumplings, goulash and potato noodles – but is also noted for its fish and for its coffee, this still being Europe's largest coffee-importing port. If you want picnic purchases the open air market is in Piazza Ponterosso (Tues – Sat 8 am – 5.30 pm), by the canal in the grid of streets south of the station.

There are plenty of smart bars for snacks and coffee – try *Caffè degli Specchi* in Piazza dell'Unità d'Italia – and more simple *osterie* where you can find good, simple food and sample wine straight from the barrel. The champagne-like *prosecco* is the drink in Trieste, but you should also try the red *terrano*, a rougher novelty found only in the countryside around the city. *Osterie* worth hunting out include the *Bar Tevere*, Via Macanton and the dens at Via delle Settefontane 13 and Via Veneziana 11.

Cafés *Caffè San Marco*, Via G. Battisti. Trieste's premier café is a wonderful 80-year-old Liberty-style spot full of mirrors, gilt, mahogany and marble-top tables.

Caffè Tommaseo, Piazza Tommaseo. The city's other top spot, with top-notch prices, though some of its old world charm has recently been removed by restoration.

Pipolo, Viale XX Settembre. A key stop-off for ice cream during the evening *passeggiata*.

Restaurants *Antica Trattoria Suban*, Via Comici 2. Well-deserved reputation as the city's top eatery, but inevitably pricey; a nice garden for summer eating.

Allo Squero, Viale Miramare 42. The best of Trieste's seafood spots tend to be on this long, broad street; turn left and sharp left again out of the station.

Trattoria dell'Antica Ghiacceretta, Via dei Fornelli. Popular place and dependable food.

Pizzeria Barattolo, Piazza Sant'Antonio 2. Fine pizzeria at the end of the canal on Via G. Rossini, a street which cuts back from the end of Corso Cavour.

Miramare

The most popular local trip from the city is to Miramare, seven kilometres up the coast, which isn't to say it's the most deservedly popular. Triestini come out here in hordes during the summer to swim and sunbathe, but the main draw for outsiders is the kitsch castle built by Archduke Ferdinand Maximilian between 1856 and 1870 (Ferdinand was the younger brother of Franz Josef, the Austro-Hungarian emperor). Ferdinand had been forced to take shelter here during a storm and resolved to buy the spot and build a **castle** on the site. In the event he never saw his fantasy realised. Having embroiled himself in imperial politics, he took himself off to become 'Emperor of Mexico' and was promptly assassinated. His wife, Charlotte, then went mad, thus giving rise to a legend that anyone spending a night in the castle would come to a bad end. The prophecy was lent further weight by the fact that Archduke Ferdinand spent a night here in 1914 before the assassination at Sarajevo.

The **interior**'s well worth the admission if only to revel in its display of glorious bad taste – look out especially for the bedrooms and the 'Monarch's Salon' with its parade of regal portraits (daily 9.30 am–1 pm and 2.30–6 pm, Mon 9.30 am –12.30 pm). To reach Miramare take bus number 6 to the end of the line and transfer to bus number 36.

Grotta Gigante and the Carso

Other easy and worthwhile trips from the city include the Grotta Gigante, the largest publicly accessible cave in the world – 107 metres deep by 208 metres wide. Stairs wind around the interior, which the brochures claim could accommodate St Peter's with room to spare (guided visits every 30 min daily 9 am–noon and 2–7 pm, closed Mon; hourly Nov–Feb 10 am–noon and 2.30–4.30 pm). It's 15 kilometres from the city centre, best reached by taking the old tramway from Piazza Oberdan (every 20 min 7.30 am–8 pm) to the suburb of Opicina and then the number 45 bus to Borgo Grotta Gigante.

While you're in the area you could also explore part of the **Carso**, the harsh, bone-white limestone uplands that back the city and run in narrow ridges down into Slovenia. This is one of northern Italy's richest regions for naturalists, with over 1,600 plant species, thanks to the area's position at the crossroads of Balkan, Alpine and Mediterranean vegetation zones. It's also home to pockets of fine walking country, notably the Val Rosandro and to the wetlands around Lago Doberdo, a haven for local birdwatchers.

Trieste–Aquileia

The route

A sleepy agricultural town, **Aquileia** languishes on the broad, dull flats of the Laguna di Marano about 40 kilometres west of Trieste. Little about its position or appearance today suggests its former importance, or the fact that this is one of the most significant archeological sites in northern

Italy. Come out here – either as a day trip or en route for Venice – if you want to see its superb **Basilica** and interior mosaics, and the remains of what in its day was the Roman empire's fourth most important city in Italy after Rome, Milan and Capua.

Trains

You can make the bulk of the journey from Trieste by **train,** *riding any of the mainline services from Trieste to Venice (15 daily) as far as the combined station of Cervignano–Aquileia–Grado (45 km, 35 min from Trieste).* **Buses** *then connect every half hour from the station to* **Aquileia** *8 kilometres to the south. Note that if you've taken a train up to* **Udine** *from Trieste (see below), you could make a neat circular loop back towards Venice by taking a bus from Udine to Aquileia (hourly, 40 min), see the town, and jump back on the train at Cervignano.*

Aquileia

Founded in 181 BC, Roman Aquileia was in a perfect position for trade and defence, commanding routes to the Empire's northern and eastern reaches. By 10 BC and the reign of Augustus it was capital of the region, now the Veneto and Istria. The so-called Patriarchate of Aquileia was founded in 313, and under its first patriarch, Theodore, (a mixture of prince and glorified bishop) saw the construction of the town's first basilica. The area declined during the barbarian invasions, and lost the seat of the patriarchate to nearby Grado, which was better protected by its surrounding lagoons. It then moved again, this time to Cividale (see below). Things picked up by 1019, when Aquileia wrested back regional control, and Patriarch Poppo rebuilt the basilica, along with the campanile, a landmark visible for miles around. Power eventually passed to Venice, and in 1751 the patriarchate moved to Udine, ultimately fizzling out into a toothless archbishopric.

The Basilica

The basilica (daily 7.30 am – 7.30 pm) has suffered a little over the years, notably from an earthquake in 1348, but it's still a remarkable building which despite its solid Romanesque exterior is crammed with an artistic legacy spanning many centuries. The interior's pointed arches lean heavily towards the Gothic, a result of the rebuilding which followed the earthquake. The ribbed ceiling is a 1526 addition, though it's unlikely to command more than a glance once you've seen the nave's extraordinary **mosaic pavement.** Western Europe's finest early Christian mosaic, it dates from the building's first flush under Theodore in the 4th century, extending in almost perfect condition over 700 square metres, and rippled with brilliant colour and a wealth of Christian and pagan decorative themes. More mosaics of a similar age have recently been discovered around the campanile (access from inside the basilica). Also have a look at the **Cripta degli**

Scavi, on the left as you enter, where excavations have turned up three levels of flooring, corresponding to three eras in the building's history (daily 9 am–2 pm, closed Mon, ticket also valid for the Museo Archeologico).

Elsewhere, the crypt beneath the altar dates from the 9th century and contains lovely Byzantine-tinged frescoes depicting scenes from the life of Christ and Aquileia's early Christians (Mon–Sat 9 am–3 pm, Sun 9 am–1 pm). The Gothic chapel of St Ambrose at the end of the right aisle contains four large sarcophagi, the tombs of several patriarchs.

The rest of the town

A crop of yellow signs and a good map from the tourist office make the rest of Aquileia's sights easy to find. Behind the basilica to the left follow the cypress-lined **Via Sacra** (nicer than walking on Via G. Augusta), which winds for 15 minutes past excavations of the old Roman harbour, to the **forum** and then to the **Museo Paleocristiano** (daily 9 am–1 pm; free). Here there are more moss-covered mosaics and part of another large 5th-century Christian basilica. For a more general survey of the artifacts dug up locally make for the **Museo Archeologico** in Via Roma on the crossroads to the basilica's right. The objects here run the gamut of Roman life, with a special emphasis on the glassware, amber and engraved stones that formed the colony's staple trading commodities. Perhaps the most outstanding item is a 1st-century BC bust of Livia Augusta. If you're obsessive about Roman remains, the town is littered with fragments of baths, houses, sepulchre and Roman amphitheatre.

Practicalities in Aquileia

Tourist Office Piazza Basilica (0431/91.087; open April–Oct). Good maps and details of the town's scant accommodation if you need to stay.
Hotels ☆*Aquila Nera*, Via Roma/Piazza Garibaldi (0431/91.045) with reasonable restaurant.
☆☆*Roma*, Via Roma (0431/91.008).

Camping *Camping Aquileia*, Via Gemina 10 (0431/91.042; May–Sept). Turn left along Via G. Augusta as you face the basilica and then third left after 500 metres on Via Gemina; the site is another 300 metres on the right. Comfortable, shady and has a swimming pool (plus 2-person caravans and wooden chalets to rent).

Trieste–Udine–Cividale

The route

Italy's north-eastern corner isn't an area many people get to, but both Udine, the region's second town, and Cividale, its most historic, are easily seen and surprisingly interesting stops. Udine, with its squares, canals and Tiepolo works of art is a mere hop from Trieste, while Cividale is at the end of a short branch line from Udine. After seeing one or both of the towns there's no need to double back to Trieste – though they're easy day trips from the city. Instead pick up the main Vienna–Venice line at Udine to return to Venice.

Trains

It is possible to take a direct train from Trieste to Udine – even if it doesn't appear so from a map of the rail network. The route runs via Gorizia, and there are 14 trains daily (83 km, 1 hr 5 min). Services between Udine and Cividale run roughly hourly (16 km, 15 min).

Numerous trains run from Udine to **Venice** *(136 km, 1 hr 35 min), and several run directly to Milan, Florence, Rome and Naples (notably the* Romulus, **Vienna–Udine–Venice–Bologna–Rome;** *and the* Freccia delle Dolomiti, **Udine–Vicenza–Milan***).*

Udine

Udine sits at the foot of a low, castle-topped hill which legend says was built by Attila the Hun's army using their helmets as buckets. The idea was to provide a platform for their leader to admire the sight of Aquileia burning away to the south. In fact the hill is a natural mound made up of glacial deposits, and from the earliest times provided an ideal lookout over the wide plains towards the distant Alps. With the neighbouring towns of Cividale and Zuglio, Udine became one of the bastions of the Roman Empire's northern frontier. Its real rise to regional dominance, though, came only during the 13th century, when Patriarch Bertoldo di Andechs transferred some of Cividale's power and privileges to Udine. The rights of citizenship and, more importantly, the right to hold two markets put the town firmly on the map (the markets were held in Via Mercatovecchio and Piazza Matteotti, the latter still the local market place). After a brief period in thrall to Austria, the town fell to Venice in 1420, and in its look and feel still bears something of the Venetian stamp. Venetian rule continued until 1797 and the arrival of Napoleon.

Today the town is a prosperous spot, and though it has only half Trieste's population, it's thought by many to be on the way to overtaking its neighbour's role as regional capital. It's also at the heart of the region's tri-cultural melting pot, mixing Balkan, central European and Italian manners and mores. As a result you'll hear a mixture of Italian, German, Serbo-Croatian and snatches of the old Friulian dialect, *friuliano*, a derivative of the old and equally obscure Swiss Romansch.

Piazza della Libertà

Collect your thoughts in Piazza della Libertà, Udine's main square, before embarking on a stroll around one of Italy's more urbane and airy little towns. The piazza's dominated by the Palazzo del Comune, which owes much to the Gothic influences of Venice, as does the clock tower (1527) across from the palace, whose lions and twin Moors striking the hours borrow directly from Piazza San Marco's Torre dell'Orologio.

The Castello

Across the square, in the clock tower corner, walk through the Arco Bollani (1556), a passageway designed by Palladio to cut through the walls enclosing the

Castello. Continue up past the striped **Loggia del Lionello**, another elegant Venetian legacy, and you soon come to the **Castello** itself, once home to the city's Venetian governors. It houses a forceful little gallery, the **Museo Civico**, recently restored after the tumultuous earthquake of 1976 which ravaged huge areas of Friuli–Venezia Giulia (Tues–Sat 9.30 am–12.30 pm and 3–6 pm, Sun and Mon 9.30 am–12.30 pm). There are paintings by Tiepolo, Caravaggio, Carpaccio and Bronzino, amongst others, and frescoes by more minor local artists.

The Duomo

North of Piazza della Libertà runs Via Mercatovecchio, the town's main shopping street. You'll find more historical interest south of the piazza in the shape of the duomo, a Romanesque-Gothic creation with a Baroque refit. Its main distractions are paintings by Tiepolo. To the duomo's right the 18th-century **Oratorio della Purità** contains a good crop of Tiepolo frescoes (painted with the aid of his son, Giandomenico). Drop the duomo's sacristan a small tip and he should open it up and show you around.

Tiepolo's finest Udinese works, though, hide in the **Palazzo Arcivescovile** (weekdays 9 am–noon; free), 200 metres north of the duomo (take the alley to the left of the post office on Via Vittorio Veneto).

The rest of the town

Elsewhere in town try to visit the church of **San Francesco** off Piazza xx Settembre, immediately south of the duomo – a Renaissance gem – and the Friulian crafts, costumes and folk art collected in the **Museo Friuliano delle Arti e Tradizioni Popolari** (Tues–Sat 9.30 am–12.30 pm and 3–6 pm, Sun 9.30 am–12.30 pm, closed Mon). The **Galleria di Arte Moderna**, out on the town's north-

Practicalities in Udine

Tourist Office Piazza 1 Maggio (0432/295.972). Take Via Manin out of Piazza della Libertà to find the office, a pink-fronted building crammed with information and good free maps.
Railway Station Viale Europa Unita (0432/503.656; information office Mon–Sat 8 am–noon and 3–7 pm). Left luggage 8 am–10 pm. To walk to the centre take Via Roma from the forecourt, carry straight on down Via Carducci and turn left on Via V. Veneto (15 min): or take bus number 1, 3 or 8 from outside the station to Piazza della Libertà
Buses Viale Europa Unita (0432/203.491). Right out of the station and the bus terminal is one block down on the left. Services throughout the region including Trieste (9 daily, 1 hr); Venice (2 daily, 2 hr); Aquileia (16 daily, 40 min); Cividale, 20 daily, 30 min).
Post Office Via V. Veneto 42.
Police Via Prefettura 16 (0432/502.841).

Hotels ☆☆*Al Vecchio Tram*, Via Garibaldi 15 (0432/502.516).
☆☆*Manin*, Via Manin 5 (0432/501.146). Very central – just off Piazza della Libertà and a reasonably priced first choice.
☆☆*Piccolo Friuli*, Via Magrini 9 (0432/507.817). In the west of town near Via Poscolle (take Via Cavour from Piazza della Libertà).
Eating *Da Arturo*, Via Pracchiuso 75. Perhaps the most popular of Udine's restaurants. On the street between Piazza 1 Maggio behind the castle and Piazza Oberdan in the town's northeast corner.
Zenit, Via Prefettura 15. Faintly drab canteen atmosphere, but okay if you want quick and cheap self-service food.
Pizzeria Ai Portici, Via V. Veneto. A choice between cheap pizzeria or smart restaurant under one roof in the town centre.

western edge in the Palazzo delle Mostre, Piazza P. Diacono 21 offers a collection of most of the major Italian 20th-century masters, plus pieces by Picasso, Chagall and De Kooning (daily 9.30 am–12.30 pm and 3–6 pm, Sun 9.30 am–12.30 pm, closed Mon).

Cividale del Friuli

Cividale del Friuli is a jewel of a town, prized by locals but all but unknown to the passing tourist. It's important primarily as one of the few places in Italy where there're some tangible remains of the Lombards. It's also a lovely town to wander around in its own right, graced with a serenity that remains unmoved by the Italian predilection for the frenetic.

Tradition has it that Julius Caesar founded the town around 50 BC when he was in command of the army up here. Certainly the frontier post had developed into a thrusting Roman colony, *Forum Iulii*, by the time the Lombards invaded Italy in the spring of 568. A Teutonic warrior race who had descended from Scandinavia to occupy the Lower Danube, the **Lombards** had a reputation as the fiercest of the 'Barbarians' who fed off the Roman empire in its dying days. Led by their king, Alboino, they arrived in Italy with 40,000 men, women and children in tow, as well as countless slaves, wagons and livestock. They easily remained in control of the country until defeated by the Franks in 774. During the period of their ascendancy they organised three separate dukedoms in Italy. The first was established with Cividale as its capital after Alboino awarded the town to his nephew, Gisulfo (the other two were in present day Lombardy – with its capital at Pavia – and in central Italy, where the capital was Spoleto). In 737 the bishop-patriarch of Aquileia, Callisto de Treviso, moved to Cividale, making it the region's epicentre until power shifted to Udine in the 13th century.

Piazza del Duomo

Cividale's historic kernel lies on Piazza del Duomo, home to two of the town's key attractions. The first, the **duomo**, started life along Venetian–Gothic lines in 1457, before Pietro Lombardo welded on some large scale Renaissance additions in 1528. Inside there are several first-rate works of art, notably an early 13th-century *pala* or silver **altarpiece**.

Off the right hand aisle lies the entrance to the **Museo Cristiano**, known for two extraordinary artifacts: foremost of the pair is the **Altar of Ratchis**, carved in 749 and one of the few surviving masterpieces from the Lombard era. The museum's other piece is the **Baptistery of Callisto**, an extraordinary octagonal work – made partly from 5th-century Lombard fragments – commissioned by Cividale's first patriarch. It once stood alongside the duomo (Mon–Sat 9.30 am –noon and 3–7.30 pm; Sun 9.30 am–noon; free).

To the left of the duomo, on the Piazza's northern edge, lies the **Museo Archeologico** (daily 9 am–1 pm, closed Mon), home to a tantalising hoard of Lombard exhibits – weapons, jewellery, tools, domestic ware and odd manuscripts.

The Tempietto Lombardo

The best of the town's Lombard heritage, and amongst the finest of such works in Italy, stands beyond the old medieval quarter of Borgo Brossana above the banks of the River Natisone (just 100 metres behind the duomo, but reached rather circuitously – there's good signposting – from Piazza San Biagio).

The so-called 'little temple' or Tempietto Lombardo dates from the 8th century, but incorporates pieces from earlier buildings and was extensively restored following two of the area's bigger earthquakes (in 1222 and 1976). Its core is an exquisite stucco arch cradling a sextet of saints, figures that represent some of the period's finest sculptural work, and the 14th-century wooden stalls and faded frescoes, not to mention the temple's river and mountain view, are also sublime.

Before leaving town be sure to wander Cividale's tight tangle of old streets, paying special attention to the old bridge just off Piazza del Duomo, the **Ponte del Diavolo**, and the 14th-century church of San Francesco which boasts a smattering of early frescoes.

Practicalities in Cividale del Friuli

Tourist Office Largo Boiani 4 (0432/731.398). The office is on the building's first floor. Largo Boiani is immediately off Piazza del Duomo.
Railway Station Viale Libertà. For Piazza del Duomo take the wide Viale Marconi from the forecourt, turn left at Borgo San Pietro, go through the gate (Porta San Pietro) and turn right out of Piazza Diaz for Largo Boiani (a total distance of 450 m).
Buses The bus terminal is close to the station on Viale Libertà; regular services run to Udine if no train is due.
Hotels ☆*Pomo d'Oro*, Piazza San Giovanni (0432/731.489). The best budget bet; walk out of Piazza del Duomo on Corso Mazzini and turn left through Piazza Diacono into Piazza San Giovanni.
☆*Belvedere*, Via San Pietro (0432/727.057). Midway between the station and the centre.
☆*Al Vescovo*, Via Roma 67 (0432/726.015).
☆☆*Castello*, Via del Castello 18 (0432/734.015). You'll need to walk or take a taxi 2 km north of town on the road to Tarcento and Faedis for this fine little 10-room hotel with great views, sunny terrace and reliable restaurant.

Where to eat and drink

Cividale's speciality is *gubana*, a fig and prune filled pastry soaked with *grappa* – a good, home-baked version comes from the bakery at Corso d'Aquileia 16 close to the Ponte del Diavolo. The town's open air **market** takes place on Sat in Piazza Diacono.

Restaurants *Al Fortino*, Via Carlo Alberto 46. Moderately priced meals – strong on game and mushroom dishes – in an old castle with vaulted ceilings and open hearth (closed Tues).
Frasca, Via de Rubeis 10. Top spot for local specialities (truffles, dumplings) on the corner of Corso Mazzini just north of Piazza del Duomo (closed Sun and Mon).
Da Renzo, Stretta Stellini 18. Smartish spot (it has an Italian minor celebrity autograph collection), but home made pasta and a nice roof terrace that looks over the church of San Francesco (closed Mon).

Close to Cividale are the vineyards responsible for *Picolit*, perhaps Italy's most fabled dessert wine, made in tiny quantities – yields and production restrictions are some of Italy's tightest – and difficult to find outside the region. Aim to drink DOC Picolit only – it's expensive, but non-DOC wines may well be substandard and still pricey. Cividale is also at the heart of one of Friuli's more general leading wine areas, the Colli Orientali del Friuli DOC. Look out in particular for *Verduzzo* wines, made from an ancient vine indigenous to the area, and for Riesling Renano, Refosco and Cabernet Sauvignons.

Cividale's smartest bar if you just want a glass of something is the *San Marco*, under the town hall's loggia opposite the tourist office. See the tourist office for details of visits to local vineyards and free tastings.

Padua–Ferrara–Ravenna–Rimini

The route

Instead of rushing to Bologna or Florence from Venice, it's worth taking time to visit two towns on and just off the main routes south. **Ferrara** is a superb walled town full of medieval remnants, while **Ravenna** has some of the greatest Byzantine and early Christian mosaics in the world. Both are also comparatively under-visited spots, and make appealing places to wander and spend the night. Rail links from each lead easily on to Bologna for onward travel, and there are various more circuitous back-door routes to Florence and the Adriatic coast.

For sheer beachside excess, **Rimini** rates as Europe's premier resort: not its smartest, by any means, but its biggest and most bustling. Italian, German and Scandinavian students come here in their droves, together with what sometimes seems like every family in Italy. The coast is packed with discos, clubs, bars and hotels, a combination found most of the way down the Adriatic, though nowhere is the cliché of sun, sea and sex (Rimini is a byword for the latter) so thoroughly realised.

Think again if you're thinking of an excursion to the unaccountably famous Republic of **San Marino**, reached by bus from Rimini. It's a tacky, tourist-filled rip-off with almost nothing to recommend it save the views from its hilltop site.

Trains

Trains run from Padua to Ferrara (76 km, 50 min) roughly every half hour, though watch out for the locali *which take an excruciating 1 hr 25 min. At Ferrara change to the self-contained service (12 trains daily) to* **Ravenna** *(74 km, 1 hr) and* **Rimini** *(124 km, 2 hr 20 min). Note that extra* locali *also run between Ravenna and Rimini about every hour (50 km, 1 hr 5 min).*

Ferrara

Ferrara was dominated by a single noble clan, **the Este**, from 1208 to 1598, who in the manner of medieval big shots spent half their time intriguing against one another and the other half becoming enlightened Renaissance patrons. Their bustling court attracted painters such as Mantegna, Pisanello and Titian, amongst others, and poets like Ariosto and Petrarch. The family's most influential member was Ercole I d'Este, who succeeded to the throne in 1441, following on his father's heels – who was reputedly poisoned. He eliminated pretenders and rivals with a ruthlessness that earned him the names of 'Diamond' and 'North Wind'. While the blood flowed, however, Ercole was also responsible for organising the city's elegant northern district – the so-called 'Herculean

Addition' – a planned quarter that saw Ferrara dubbed Europe's first 'modern city'.

After marrying into some of Europe's premier families (Lucrezia Borgia and the daughters of the kings of France and Spain became Este wives), the family's nemesis ironically came in its eventual inability to produce an heir. This left Ferrara to fall into the hands of the Papacy, whose somnambulant rule saw the city collapse into virtual ruin. Its canals became malarial swamps and so much weed choked the streets that Stendhal wrote in 1817 that, 'The Papal legations could feed half a cavalry regiment on the grass that grows in the streets.' Today the town is more prosperous, thanks largely to its huge fruit-growing hinterland.

The Castello Estense

In the plumb heart of the city sits the looming mass of the **Castello Estense**, built in the 14th century not so much to defend the Este from rival clans, as from their own subjects, who'd embarked upon one of their periodic uprisings against the family (daily 9 am–1 pm and 2–6 pm, closed Mon). It still reverberates with faint echoes of the Estes' past, some rooms preserving grand frescoed ceilings. The overall atmosphere, though, is windblown and chill. The darker side of life under the Estes is seen to best effect in the atmospheric dungeons, where, amongst others, Parisina Malatesta, the wife of Nicolo III d'Este, was murdered for having an affair with her step-son Ugolino. The episode is said to have inspired Robert Browning's marvellous poem, *My Last Duchess*.

The Duomo

Just a few steps south of the Castello and past the Palazzo Comunale is the duomo, a blending of Gothic and Romanesque elements that's worth a visit for the **Museo del Duomo** upstairs (10 am–noon and 4–6 pm, closed Sun; free). The collection offers illuminated manuscripts, tapestries and paintings by Ferrarese artists. Pride of place goes to a set of bas-reliefs portraying episodes from the *Months of the Year* removed from the exterior of the cathedral.

Piazza dei Diamanti

Off Corso Ercole I, Ferrara's main north-running street, make for the Palazzo dei Diamanti, the cream of the city's old ducal residences (*diamanti* refers to the diamond-shaped bricks and indentations on the façade). It's home to a dullish museum devoted to Unification and the Resistance, and to the more enticing **Pinacoteca Nazionale** (daily 9 am–2 pm, Sun 9 am–1 pm, closed Mon) which offers the best of the Bolognese and Ferrarese schools.

The rest of the town

After the main sights, Ferrara's key pleasure, of course, is ambling around its streets. The atmosphere's romantic and melancholy by turns, but the overall effect is of a lovely little backwater that deserves a good morning's stroll.

The best of the medieval town lies south of Viale Cavour and Corso della Giovecca, the most evocative single street being Via delle Volte. Corso Ercole I, by contrast, shows Ercole d'Este's planned Renaissance quarter off to best effect. Make a point, too, of heading to the town's south-east corner for a couple of

Practicalities in Ferrara

Tourist Office Piazza Municipio (0532/ 209.370). Directly opposite the duomo, with a well-briefed staff and fully-stocked shelves.

Railway Station Viale della Costituzione (0532/37.649). Lies just west of the city's impressive set of walls a 10-minute walk from the centre – follow Viale della Costituzione left from the forecourt and then take Viale Cavour straight to the Castello Estense. Alternatively take bus number 1, 2 or 3 from the forecourt.

Buses Many services run both from outside the station (buy tickets from the *Bar Fiorella* opposite), and from Piazza Castello and the main terminal at Via Rampari San Paolo.

Post Office Viale Cavour 27.

Police Corso Ercole I d'Este (0532/207.555).

Youth Hostel *Ostello Estense* (IYHF), Via Benvenuto Tisi da Garofalo 5 (0532/21.098; open April–Oct). Call ahead before you walk here to check there's room – follow Viale Cavour and take the fourth main turn on the left, Via Ariosto. This isn't one of Italy's best or best-scrubbed hostels, but the beds are the cheapest in town.

Hotels ☆☆*San Paolo*, Via Pescherie Vecchie 12 (0532/762.040). This hotel's in the tangle of streets south-east of the duomo, home to the bulk of Ferrara's cheap accommodation. The *San Paolo* is the area's best, blessed with new rooms and a peaceful location. Call ahead to book if possible.

☆☆*Stazione*, Piazza Castellina 1 (0532/ 56.565). Opposite the station.

☆☆*Casa degli Artisti*, Via Vittorio 66 (0532/

35.210). In the medieval quarter.

☆*Raiti*, Via Della Scienze 13 (0532/464.156).

☆☆*Nazionale*, Corso Porto Reno 32 (0532/ 209.604). One of several hotels on this busy and rumbustious street south of Piazza Municipio. Try also the ☆*Tre Colonne* at number 70 (0532/35.207) and the *Garibaldi* at 77 (0532/26.318).

Camping *Estense*, Via Porta Catena (0532/ 52.791; open Easter–Oct) is the city campsite off the ringroad just outside the city walls; take bus number 4 and get off at Piazzale Giochi.

Eating and Drinking Ferrara's market is in Via Mercato, off Via Garibaldi near the duomo. The city's considered something of an eating centre, and there are plenty of restaurants – many pretty pricey – and quite a few local specialities: look out for *caelletti*, a ravioli type pasta; *salame al sugo*, a rich sausage marinated in wine and served hot in its own juices; and a chocolate-smothered almond and fruit cake.

Trattoria da Giacomo, Via Garibaldi 135. Amongst the best cheaper spots in town; closed Sat and Aug.

Al Postiglione, Vicolo Chiuso del Teatro 4. Off Piazza Martiri della Libertà between the *castello* and the duomo. Full meals, plus toasted sandwiches, cheap wine by the glass and plenty of different beers. Closed Sun.

Al Brindisi, Via G. degli Adelandi 11. Claims to be Italy's oldest *osteria* (founded 1435); meals, sandwich snacks and 600 different types of wine.

---

outstanding palaces that are open to the public. **Palazzo Schifanoia**, Via Scandiana 23, Ferrara's first Renaissance building and an Este property, has some captivating frescoes (daily 9 am–7 pm; free on the second Sun and Mon of the month). Close by on Via XX Settembre is the **Palazzo Ludovico II Moro**, distinguished by a gracious courtyard and an archeological museum of local Roman and Greek finds. To round off a tour of the top palaces, nip into the **Casa Romei**, Via Savonarola 30, a typical 15th-century aristocratic home, loaded with frescoes and beautifully decorated rooms (Tues–Sun 9 am–2 pm). Perhaps also leave a little time for the **Palazzina di Marfisa d'Este**, Corso della Giovecca 170, a rather more gloomy abode, but again, scattered with frescoes and period fittings (daily 9 am–12.30 and 3–6 pm).

Ravenna

Ravenna's historical heyday came almost by accident and eventually proved to be something of a false dawn. In 402 the Roman Emperor, Honorius, chose it as the Empire's new capital, prompted by Rome's stagnation and the march of barbarian armies encroaching from the north. Surrounded by marsh and easy to defend, the town was also close to **Classe**, the Romans' main port on the Adriatic coast. Buildings sprang up to house the trappings of the Empire, and the boom continued even after the city fell to the barbarians in 473. The Byzantines took the burgeoning city in 540 and the Ostrogothic king Theodoric dominated Italy from Ravenna. He, too, continued to build and embellish, accounting for most of Ravenna's present day sights. Decline then set in fast, as the port silted up and the coast receded. Things perked up briefly under Venice's ascendancy in the 16th century before falling away under the dead hand of Papal rule.

Today smart shops and the even smarter Ravennese themselves testify to the place's current prosperity, the result largely of an industrial resurgence that accompanied the discovery of natural gas close by. Ravenna boasts some of Italy's oldest and best-preserved **mosaics** – ranked the finest Byzantine monuments outside Istanbul – but even if this sort of thing leaves you cold, the town's still a surprisingly appealing and compact little place of restrained medieval flavour and pleasingly low-key tourism.

Basilica di San Vitale

Although you'll probably be tempted by Ravenna's neat squares and streets, the best of the city from the mosaic point of view lies about ten minutes' walk from the centre or 20 minutes from the station. The Basilica di San Vitale on its own is superb, never mind its decoration: an obviously Byzantine-inspired church, octagonal in plan, with a large central dome and an eerie atmosphere of extreme antiquity. It was started by Theodoric in 525 and completed in 548 by the Byzantine Emperor, Justinian (daily 8.30 am – 7 pm).

The **mosaics** cover much of the interior and are incredibly well-preserved. All sorts of rules governed the artistic precepts behind them; the higher up and further east a subject, for example, the more important or holy the item. And if hierarchy needed to be emphasised further, a gold background gave added weight to a subject's stature or holiness. The bulk of the panels describe Old Testament scenes, though look out for two anomalous panels on the lateral wall of the apse. These show *Justinian and His Court* and *Theodora and Her Court*, both out and out Byzantine creations that contrast with the more classical leaning of the Biblical scenes.

Theodora was Justinian's wife, and one of history's juicier characters, known for a ruthlessness that quickly disposed of anyone who got in her way. Later accounts of her life tell of a youth spent as a child prostitute and circus performer, followed by time served as a courtesan and actress in deviant live sex shows. Needless to say a stir ran round court circles when she took Justinian's fancy, and the emperor had to wait until his mother died before he could take her on as his wife (and as an ally in a reign of rampant corruption).

Mausoleo di Galla Placidia

Just across the grassy piazza around San Vitale stands the Mausoleo di Galla Placidia, a tiny chapel in the shape of a Latin Cross that's studded with perhaps Italy's most breathtaking mosaics – small in extent, but old (pre-450) and executed in some of the most vivid colours imaginable (daily 8.30 am−7 pm; same ticket as for the Basilica).

Galla Placidia had almost as remarkable a career as Theodora. The daughter of Theodosius I (father of Honorius), she was kidnapped when the Goths sacked Rome, but promptly married one of her kidnappers − Ataulfo − who was subsequently assassinated. She then returned to Rome and took refuge with Honorius, her half-brother, but was forced into a marriage − still only 27 − with a Roman general, Constantius. She succeeded in having her husband made joint-Emperor with her brother, and then, when she was widowed a second time, wangled her son, Valentinian III (aged 6), into place as Emperor with herself as Regent. She thus managed to be the daughter, sister, wife, widow and mother of various emperors. She died in Rome around 450 aged about 60, and was buried there, leaving open the question of who instigated her mausoleum in Ravenna.

Before leaving the Basilica you might want to drop into the **Museo Nazionale**, quartered in the cloisters of the ex-convent attached to the Basilica (daily 9 am− 1 pm, closed Mon). There's something here from just about every epoch of Ravenna's history; Roman, early Christian, Byzantine and medieval.

Piazza del Popolo

Even in the town centre the mosaics are far from over, though there are plenty of medieval backstreets in which to wallow for a time. The Piazza del Popolo is the focus of the town's best old streets, lined with great period buildings and plenty of bars with the all-important outside tables. A little way to the south alongside the church of San Francesco is the **Tomba di Dante** − Dante's tomb, the remains of the country's premier scribe being a cause for considerable local pride. Dante died here in 1381 having been chased out of Florence and having just completed *The Divine Comedy*.

Piazza del Duomo

From Piazza del Popolo stroll a couple of minutes west to Piazza del Duomo, not so much for the duomo, which is a dull Baroque rework of a 5th-century original, but for the **Museo Arcivescovile** to its left (daily 9 am−noon and 3−6 pm). Various early mosaic fragments from around the city have been gathered here to sit alongside the building's own 6th-century **Oratorio di Sant'Andrea**, a chapel decorated with a mosaic showing Christ decked in the armour, cloak and leather skirt of a Roman soldier. The collection's most impressive piece, though, is ranked as the greatest piece of ivory sculpture in the Christian world; a highly ornate throne from Alexandria owned by Bishop Maximilian in the 6th century.

Next door on Via Battistero stands the **Battistero Neoniano**, a simple 6th-century octagonal baptistery that previously served time as a Roman bath-house (daily 7 am−noon and 3−6 pm). Fairly badly preserved mosaics from its older Roman sections sit low down, contrasting with the better-looking Christian work higher up. It's worth comparing these with the mosaics from the town's other baptistery, the **Battistero degli Ariani** (Arian Baptistery) on Via di Roma, where 6th-century mosaics also show the *Baptism of Christ* and a *Procession of the Apostles*.

Practicalities in Ravenna

Tourist Office Via Salara 8 (0544/35.404). Slightly tucked away in the corner of town by San Vitale. From the top right corner of Piazza del Popolo take Via Muratori to Piazza XX Settembre. Take Via Matteotti north out of the square, turn left on Via Cavour and Via Salara is first right. Good maps, hotel information and rarely busy.

Railway Station Piazza Farini (0544/36.450). On the eastern edge of town; for the old centre follow Viale Farini from in front of the forecourt and then walk straight down Via Armandio Diaz to Piazza del Popolo.

Buses Local and long-haul services depart from outside the railway station.

Foreign Exchange Plenty of banks on Via A. Diaz between the station and Piazza del Popolo.

Post Office Piazza Garibaldi 1, off Via A. Diaz to the left before Piazza del Popolo.

Police Piazza del Popolo (0544/33.212).

Where to stay

Youth Hostel *Ostello Dante*, Via Aurelio Nicolodi 12 (0544/420.405; closed Oct–Mar). A 10-minute walk from the station or take bus number 1. An institutional sort of spot – and potentially noisy – but meals are good and you can rent bikes on the premises.

Hotels ☆*Hotel Ravenna*, Viale Maroncelli 12 (0544/212.204). One of several cheap choices in the slightly fetid area around the station (turn right as you exit); this is a hygienic and stolid little place. If it's full try the ☆*Minerva* (0544/213.711) across the street.

☆☆*Albergo Al Giaciglio*, Via Rocca Brancaleone 42 (0544/39.403). Reasonably handy for the station; to reach it walk along Viale Farini and take the first right through

Piazza Mameli. Quiet, carpeted and clean rooms, and good meals if you take the reasonably priced half-board.

☆☆☆☆*Bisanzio*, Via Salara 30 (0544/27.111). An excellent and central top-end-of-the-market hotel.

Camping All Ravenna's nearby beach towns have big campsites, though the coast locally isn't one of Italy's best. Take an ATM bus from Piazza Farini to Punta Marina, Marina di Ravenna or Casal Borsetti. Punta Marina's *Campeggio Pineta*, Via Spallazzi (0544/445.152) is perhaps the pleasantest pitch.

Where to eat and drink

The city's central covered **market** is just up Via IV Novembre from Piazza del Popolo for picnic purchases (Mon–Sat 7 am–1.30 pm).

Ca' de Vin, Via V.C. Ricci 24. A lovely *enoteca* and the best place for an indoor drink of wine and a snack; Via C.V. Ricci runs south out of Piazza del Popolo.

Guidarello, Via Gessi 7 (off Piazza Arcivescovado alongside the duomo). A big, bustling spot with keen prices that operates as a pizzeria downstairs and pricier restaurant upstairs.

La Gardenia, Via Ponte Marino 3. Leave Piazza del Popolo on Via IV Novembre and this excellent and popular trattoria is at the top near the junction with Via P. Costa.

Mensa Il Duomo, Via Oberdan 8 (off Piazza del Duomo). Rock-bottom cheap self-service place for lunch only (Mon–Fri, noon–2.15 pm; closed Aug). Arrive early to grab a full meal for under L10,000.

Excursion from Ravenna

Sant'Apollinare in Classe

If you've still not overdosed on mosaics, Ravenna has more, this time about 5 kilometres from the city centre at Sant'Apollinare in Classe (one stop south of the city by train, or take the number 4 bus every half an hour from the train station). It's about all that survives of the old Roman port of *Classe*, other buildings

having either been pillaged for stone or sunk beneath the ever-encroaching silt. The spot, consecrated in 549, survived because it was the burial-place of Ravenna's patron saint. These days, though, it's in pretty unprepossessing surroundings. Once past the 10th-century campanile and into the interior, however, the mosaics are as good as any in the city.

Sant'Apollinare Nuovo

The town's last major call is **Sant'Apollinare Nuovo** on Via di Roma, which you can easily see on the way back to the station. Here, too, it's mosaics – amongst Ravenna's finest – that take the plaudits. The building was started in the 6th century by Theodoric, an Ostrogoth, and therefore an Arian, an early branch of Christianity eventually stamped out partly for political and partly doctrinal reasons – Arians, for example, didn't believe in Christ's absolute divinity. Images of Theodoric were eventually removed from the mosaics, and the church rededicated to St Martin, a well-known scourge of heretics.

Rimini

Hourly trains cut south from Ravenna to Rimini, whose beach resort nirvana is preceded by easeful countryside and row upon row of vines and peach trees. The town revolves around good and mostly harmless fun, and miraculously manages to avoid tackiness – though late at night there's a fair sprinkling of hetero-, homo- and trans-sexual prostitutes mingling none too discreetly with the revellers. The beach is only 15 minutes from the station, so you could feasibly sit out in the sun for the day and pile back on to the train in the evening. For the town's much vaunted club, disco and beachfront scene, though, which stretches along 20 kilometres of the coast, you'll obviously want to stay over. If you're on a rock-bottom budget, people do bed down on the beach (but be careful of theft and so on): otherwise go to the tourist office for help with accommodation. They'll also fix you up with a full list of current clubs and events. Be warned that you'll have next to no luck with hotels in the first two weeks of August unless you've booked, and that most places demand full board unless it's way out of season – a period when the town's fairly dead and unappealing.

Finally, don't forget the **old town**, on the west side of the railway tracks away from the modern resort. Surprisingly quiet and charming, its cobbled streets centre around **Piazza Cavour**, though by far the main thing to see is the **Tempio Malatestino** on Via IV Novembre. Built as a Franciscan church, it was transformed in 1450 into a masterpiece of Renaissance architecture for Sigismondo Malatesta (1417–68), head of Rimini's long-term leading family and reputedly one of Italy's most evil men. He intended the church as memorial both to classical hedonism and to his fourth wife, Isotta degli Atti. As a result there's plenty which isn't terribly Christian about the church – the lovers' entwined initials on every

Practicalities in Rimini

Tourist Office Piazza Battisti 1 (0541/27.927). Outside the station to the left (8 am – 8 pm); there's also an office on the sea front at Piazza dell'Indipendenza 3 (0541/24.511).
Hotels *Promozione Alberghiera*, at the train station and Piazza dell'Indipendenza 3 (0541/52.269). Further help with finding a room, but

make it clear how much you're prepared to pay.
Railway Station Piazza Battisti (0541/53.512). For the beach turn right along Piazza Battisti, right through the tunnel (with yellow signs saying *al mare* – 'to the sea') and then follow Via Principe to the beach.
Police Corso d'Augusto 192 (0541/51.000).

surface, flying elephants and scenes of bacchanalian excess, for example – all of which led Pope Pius II to condemn it as 'a temple of devil-worshippers'. Malatesta (literally 'headache') was damned by the Pope and his effigy burnt on the streets of Rome for what the Papal charge described as 'murder, violation, adultery, incest, sacrilege and perjury'.

Bologna

You're almost bound to wind up in Bologna. Five mainline railway routes meet here. Whether you should get off the train, though, is a moot point. The city's more about look, feel and reputation than any excess of churches or galleries. The food here is supposed to be Italy's best, hence one of its nicknames, *La Grassa* ('the fat'), while its university is Europe's oldest (founded in 1076) – its other appellation is *La Dotta* ('the learned'). Dante, Petrarch and Copernicus are just some of the worthies to have passed through its doors. Bologna is also the spiritual home of the Italian Left, and a showpiece of efficiency and good government for the erstwhile Communist party (now the renamed 'Democratic Party of the Left') who've ruled the city for years. Hence the right-wing bomb attack at the railway station in 1980 which killed over 80 people in Italy's worst ever terrorist outrage.

Whatever your politics it's hard to fault the city's cultural pazzaz – it hums with theatres, cinemas, music and summer events – nor the prosperous air pervading its red-bricked houses and the elegant colonnades of the old *centro storico*. Walking or people-watching here is as good as anywhere in Italy, and the bars, cafés and nightlife some of the country's best.

The flip side is the price of everything, the cost of living being as high, if not higher, than in Milan or Florence. Then there's the weather, which can be stiflingly humid in summer, and relentlessly misty and miserable in autumn. For all its surface gloss, the city also has an underside, manifest in its junkies and a few streets you'd not want to be alone in at night. And while there's certainly no shortage of worthwhile monuments and oddities, nothing in the city really ranks as unmissable. You could see the sights below in a day.

Trains

No other northern Italian city has the edge over Bologna in terms of rail connections. Trains run roughly hourly to and from the following cities; Milan (219 km, 2 hr–2 hr 30 min); Venice via Padua and Ferrara (160 km, 2 hr–2 hr 30 min); Verona (114 km, 1 hr 50 min); Rome (413 km, 3 hr–3 hr 30 min); and every half hour to and from Florence (97km, 1 hr–1 hr 30 min).

What to see

Piazza Maggiore

Bologna's beating heart lies in the central Piazza Maggiore and adjacent Piazza del Nettuno, the best starting points for a logical tour of the city's sights, all of which are within easy walking distance of their broad, bustling margins.

Piazza Maggiore is a social meeting place, crammed with cafés, home to an early-morning market, and the rendezvous for the evening *passeggiata*. Although the buildings here are impressive, most of them bludgeon with their bulk, rather than impressing with architectural finesse. The chief pile is the **Palazzo Comunale** on the square's west flank, built between the 13th and 15th centuries – hence its potpourri of styles – as the seat of the city's medieval comune: it's still Bologna's main council chamber. It houses a handful of paintings, including good Renaissance offerings by Tintoretto and Luca Signorelli, though the best reason for a visit is the views over the square from its upper rooms (Mon and Wed–Sun 9 am–1 pm). Notice the windows here, designed by one of the city's top Renaissance architects, Fiorvanti, whose son, Aristotele, remodelled the Palazzo del Podestà across the piazza (built in 1484) and then went on to design the Kremlin in Moscow.

Next to the Palazzo del Podestà is the **Palazzo del Re Enzo**, named after King Enzo of Sardinia who was imprisoned here from 1249 – after waging war on Bologna – until his death 23 years later in 1272. Criminals traditionally received the last rites in the palace's courtyard chapel before being taken out for execution in Piazza Maggiore.

The bronze **statue** and fountain in front of the palace is *Neptune and Attendants*, one of the city's symbols – though an odd one given Bologna's distance from anything remotely maritime. Cast in 1566 by Giambologna, it's known locally as '*Il Gigante*' ('The Giant'). Giambologna actually designed it in the hope of winning a competition for a fountain in Florence. Water seems to gush from every corner, even from the breasts of the mermaids at Neptune's feet.

Basilica di San Petronio

San Petronio, dedicated to Bologna's 5th-century bishop and the city's largest church, was initially intended to be bigger than St Peter's but the Church ordered money for the project to be diverted to build the nearby Palazzo Archiginnasio. The financial shortfall left the church decidedly asymmetrical, though Antonio da Vincenzo's original Gothic plan (1390) still makes this one of Italy's top 14th-century brick buildings. Work continued on the church for 300 years, but still left things unfinished, most notably on the **façade**, which lacks a marble facing and whose upper two thirds is missing its intended geometric patterning. The main portal, though, is topped by an eroded but striking sculpture of the *Madonna and Child* by the great Sienese artist, Jacopo della Quercia (1425–38).

The **interior** is big and was intended to be bigger – you can still see the columns outside intended to support another aisle on the church's eastern flank. The financial profligacy here was said to have been instrumental in turning Martin Luther against Catholicism. Several of the side chapels contain outstanding works of art.

Museo Civico Archeologico

The Museo Civico Archeologico lies to the left of San Petronio, across Via dell'Archiginnasio (daily 9.30 am – 1 pm, closed Mon) and offers a comprehensive, if poorly displayed, collection of Egyptian and Roman remains, together with plenty of prehistoric pieces and finds from *Felsina*, Bologna's Etruscan incarnation, some of the best Etruscan-era material outside the more famous museums of Rome and Lazio.

Archiginnasio

The Archiginnasio just behind San Petronio and the archeological museum mark the probable site of Bologna's university, though the present building was only built in 1565 on a space previously ear-marked for San Petronio. One theory is that the Church wanted to centralise students under one roof at a time when the Reformation seemed to threaten political and social unrest. The medallions over the walls are coats of arms belonging to its more famous graduates. Lectures still take place here, though the bulk of the building is now given over to the university's library. The main sight, if you can get the porter to open up, is the Teatro Anatomico, the old medical faculty's dissection theatre.

San Domenico

San Domenico rises just south of the Archiginnasio off Via Garibaldi, and is Italy's most interesting Dominican church – chiefly because it contains the remains of St Dominic himself. The saint died here in 1221. His tomb, the *Arca di San Domenico*, is decorated, as would be expected, at different times and by a posse of prominent artists including Michelangelo, Nicolo Pisano and his assistants and Nicolo di Bari (1473), who was so chuffed with his contribution that he changed his name to Nicola dell'Arca to recall his work in the chapel (he provided the canopy). The reliquary behind the sarcophagus contains the saint's head (1383).

The unfortunate King Enzo of Piazza Maggiore fame is also buried here – a tablet in the right transept marks the spot. The odd tomb outside the church, the one raised on pillars, belongs to an eminent 14th-century lawyer, Rolandino dei Passegeri.

Santo Stefano

Walk back up Via Garibaldi from San Domenico and left on Via Farini and you're soon at Santo Stefano, four (originally seven) Romanesque churches jigsawed together under one roof. Walk through the first, the rather shabby Crocifisso, to the polygonal **San Sepolcro** – the best of the four – whose wonderfully tasteless centrepiece is the tomb of San Petronio. Outside in the courtyard is an unlikely bath-sized basin, reputedly the one used by Pilate to wash his hands and absolve himself of responsibility for Christ's death. Alongside San Sepolcro stands **SS Vitale e Agricola**, the oldest of the group, and the oldest church in Bologna. The fourth church and its small museum you can happily skip.

Instead of walking up Via Santo Stefano to reach Bologna's famous towers (see below), detour right on Via Santo Stefano and take Via Guerrazzi (third on the left) to the church of **Santa Maria dei Servi**. A lovely thoroughbred Gothic

Practicalities in Bologna

Telephone Code 051.
Tourist Office The office in the railway station is near the main exit to the street (246.541). Use it to book rooms and save yourself hours of walking. The city's central infocentre is in the main square at Palazzo Comunale, Piazza Maggiore 6 (239.660).
Railway Station Bologna Centrale, Piazza delle Medaglie d'Oro (246.490). Information 8 am – 8 pm. Reservations 7 am – 9.45 pm. Foreign exchange 7.30 am – 12.30 pm and 3 – 7.30 pm; after 7.30 pm go to ticket booth number 1. Left luggage 24hrs. Cafeteria-Restaurant 7 am – midnight.

It's a 1.5 km walk from the station to Piazza Maggiore – turn left in the forecourt station and then first right at Piazza XX Settembre to follow Via dell'Indipendenza to the central piazza. Otherwise take bus number 25 or 30 from Piazza XX Settembre to Piazza Maggiore.
Buses Local ATC and long distance services leave from the terminal on the far side of Piazza XX Settembre 250 metres left of the station (248.374).
Budget Travel CTS, Via delle Belle Arti (264.862). A popular and efficient travel agents close to the Pinacoteca Nazionale; arrive early to avoid queues. Cheap tickets, IYHF and ISIC cards.
Post Office Piazza Minghetti, two blocks east of Piazza Maggiore.
American Express Piazza XX Settembre 6 (220.477).
Police Piazza Galileo 7 (113 or 278.846). *Ufficio Stranieri* (Foreigners' office) 337.473.
Hospital *Ospedale Traumatologico*, Via Boldrini 2 (224.965).

Where to stay

Youth Hostel *Ostello di San Sisto* (IYHF, but non-members accepted), Via Viadagota 14 (519.202). Situated in a park-surrounded villa, but 6 km north-east from the centre – and it's difficult sorting out buses to reach it; ask at the tourist office which has a leaflet of specific instructions. Bus number 93 from Via dei Mille or Via Irnerio (the first main right off Via dell'Indipendenza from the station) should take you to the door, though it stops running at 8.15 pm Mon – Fri and 2.15 pm on Sat, when you should take bus number 19 from Via Irnerio and walk the last 1.5 km.
Hotels Hotels can be surprisingly full much of the year, thanks to the large number of students and the huge number of trade fairs which bring business people into the city. Use the tourist office as the first resort if you arrive with nowhere to stay. After hours the office in the

station often posts up lists of the latest vacancies. Most hotels listed below are around the station, but other concentrations of hotels can be found in the University area and close to the centre.
☆☆*Pensione Marconi*, Via G. Marconi 22 (262.832). Turn right from the station and then first left up Via G. Amendola which becomes Via G. Marconi. Reliable and clean and there's someone on duty all night if you arrive late.
☆☆*Albergo Minerva*, Via de' Monan 3 (239.652). Adequate spot off Via dell'Indipendenza about half way to the centre and about 10 min walk from the station.
☆☆*Arcoveggio*, Via Spada 27 (355.4360). Behind the train station off Via Matteotti (left and first left from the forecourt); new place with spotless rooms and amiable management.
☆☆☆*Il Guercino*, Via L. Serra 7 (369.893). Turn left out of the station, first left on Via Matteotti, left again on Via Tiarini and then first right onto Via L. Serra for a quiet, comfortable but well-known budget hotel.
☆☆*Apollo*, Via Drapperie 5 (223.955). Reasonable central rooms off Via Rizzoli which runs from Piazza Maggiore to the 2 towers in Piazza di Porta Ravegnana.
☆☆*Accademia*, Via delle Belle Arti 6 (232.218). Relaxed spot in the University area close to the Pinacoteca.
☆☆*Farini*, Via Farini 13 (271.969). Close to the towers.
☆☆☆*Orologio*, Via IV Novembre (231.253). The best choice in the centre for a cheapish room; it's in a pedestrian zone just off Piazza Maggiore – but it's very popular, so call ahead to secure one of the 32 newly-renovated rooms (top floor choices have good views).
☆☆☆☆*Corona d'Oro*, Via Oberdan 12 (236.456). Good central choice if you want to push the boat out a little without going overboard on price. The hotel's been in business over a century, and has original Art Nouveau décor but 35 decent modern rooms. On the street off Via Rizzoli just north of the towers.

Where to eat and drink

Almost any of Bologna's many restaurants should give you a good meal – the more humble in appearance, probably, the better the food. Especially good hunting grounds for cheap and traditional trattorias include Via Piella, Via Augusto Righi and Via Saragozza – and of course the University area in the city's north-east corner.
Da Marco, Via Broccaindosso 71d, off Strada Maggiore. Popular spot for lunch only (noon – 3 pm, closed Aug & weekends).

Antica Trattoria Spiga, Via Broccaindosso 21a.
A single-roomed old-style place with perfectly
good food (closed Sun).
Bertino, Via delle Lame 55 (522.230). It's
worth booking for a table at this popular and
unpretentious spot (closed Aug and Sun).
Clorofilla, Strada Maggiore 64, near the
towers. Good and right-on whole food and
predominantly vegetarian restaurant.
Pizzeria Piedigrotta, Via Santo Stefano 40f.
Probably Bologna's top pizza spot; aim for an
outside table in summer (closed Aug and Tues).
Caffè Rinascimento, Via G. Oberdan 4a (closed
Sun). Tasteful modernised interior; lively and
comfortable, with a variety of warm snacks and
limited menu meals at reasonable prices; good
for lunch or teatime.
Da Carlo, Via Marchesana (closed Tues). In the
heart of the market area of the *centro storico*
and graced with a large and unusual patio.
Reasonable and recommended.
Terisina, Via Oberdan 4. Intimately secluded
down a passage off a busy pedestrianised street
close to Via Rizzoli; you can eat out in the
passage in summertime; easy and pleasant
atmosphere.

Torre di Galluzzi, Corte de'Galluzzi. Located in
a hidden courtyard in the centre; housed at the
base of a medieval tower just behind San
Petronio. Pretty expensive, but excellent food.
Don't miss *Atti's*, a superb patisserie, and *A. F.
Tamburini*, a sumptuous delicatessen, both on
Via Caprarie.

Wall-to-wall students in Bologna mean there's
no shortage of bars and nightlife. For lively
drinking holes and cheap drinking places make
for the University area, especially Via Zamboni,
and around Via delle Belle Arti and Piazza
Verdi. *Osterie* – pub-like places with snack
food – are a Bologna institution.

Markets Bologna's markets are fun places to
look over the raw ingredients of its noted
cuisine. The indoor *Mercato delle Erbe*, Via
Ugo Bassi 2 (closed Thur & Sat afternoon) is
appealing, with smaller affairs at Via Clavature
(same closing) and Piazza Aldrovandi on Strada
Maggiore. The big outdoor market is in Via
Pescherie Vecchie, off Piazza Maggiore. The
local **flea market**, La Montagnola, is held in
Piazza VII Agosto each Fri and Sat.

church, it contains the bonus of a thrilling *Maestà* by Cimabue – Vasari's 'father
of Italian painting'. It hangs in the left hand chapel behind the altar.

Piazza di Porta Ravegnana

Piazza di Porta Ravegnana isn't famous on its own account, but for Bologna's
best-known sights, the **Torre degli Asinelli** and **Torre Garisenda**. The twin
towers were both built in 1488, and are two of only a dozen or so survivors from
the 200-plus towers that once filled the city's medieval skyline. They were top-
ranking towers even in their own day, both being mentioned in Dante's *Inferno*.
The Garisenda was shortened in the 16th century as a safety measure – it still
leans about three metres – leaving its 97-metre partner fourth overall in the
league of Italian towers (after Cremona, Siena and Venice). It, too, leans
ominously from the vertical. Be sure to climb the 500 steps of the Asinelli for a
great view of the city (daily 9 am – 1 pm and 3 – 6 pm).

Immediately right of the towers, on the corner of Piazza di Porta Ravegnana
and Strada Maggiore, stands the church of **San Bartolomeo**, worth a quick visit if
only for its famous Guido Reni *Madonna* (it's in the left transept).

San Giacomo Maggiore

San Giacomo Maggiore is a couple of hundred metres up Via Zamboni from the
towers, a skilful blending of Romanesque and Gothic styles whose chapels offer
a selection of passable paintings. The main reason to drop by, though, is the
ambulatory's **Cappella Bentivoglio**, home to the vaults of a medieval Bolognese
family.

Pinacoteca Nazionale

the Pinacoteca at Via Belle Arti 56 stands on the fringes of the rambling university quarter, which like any student enclave, is a warren of bookshops, cheap bars and lively restaurants. The highly-ranked gallery devotes itself mostly to the works of Bolognese painters, most notably to the school's 16th-century greats, Guido Reni, the Carracci family and Guercino. Leavening the local mix, though, are works such as a Giotto altarpiece, Raphael's celebrated *Ecstasy of Santa Cecilia* and Perugino's *Madonna in Glory* (daily 9 am–1 pm, closed Mon).

Museo di Anatomia Umana

Long after you've forgotten Bologna's churches and paintings, the chances are you'll remember its nicely grotesque medical waxworks, the Museo di Anatomia Umana, at Via Irnerio 48 on the main street immediately north of the Pinacoteca (weekdays 9 am–noon and 3–6 pm). Although the bits and pieces of human anatomy were used in the 19th century as teaching aids, there's an appealing artistry and clinical goriness about their almost perversely illustrated detail. Florence has a similar waxworks, but there casts of limbs, organs and bones were taken to mould the wax: in Bologna every last detail was lovingly sculpted.

4 Tuscany and Umbria

Tuscany is Italy for many people. Its landscapes are a pastoral idyll of soft-edged hills and vineyards, its main cities – **Florence** and **Siena** – Europe's greatest repositories of Renaissance art. **Umbria**, by contrast has lived in its shadow, its brace of fascinating hill towns overlooked, its dulcet landscapes all but ignored. Both regions, rightly, are likely to occupy much of your time in Italy. Both, thankfully, have railways which visit the key sights. Better still, most towns are close together.

Florence's siren call is hard to resist, its artistic treasures a vortex which sucks in as many tourists as anywhere in Europe. This makes it something of a scrum in summer, and it's as well to be prepared for the crowds. Its galleries and art-crammed churches, however, more than compensate – though the fabric of the city itself isn't as attractive as you might expect. For civic architecture and medieval ambience head for **Siena**, similarly rich in art, but generally more beautiful and appealing than its neighbour.

Beyond these two beacons, Tuscany is crammed with lesser cities – none perhaps as charming as Siena, but all worth a day of anyone's time. Little-known **Lucca** comes in third, as graceful and civilised a place as you'll find in Italy. Most people pass it by in favour of **Pisa**, drawn by the Leaning Tower, certainly something you have to see – along with its surrounding medieval ensemble. More intimate, but no less visited, is **San Gimignano**, with its walls and towers the epitome of a medieval hill-village.

After the main cities, travelling around by train soon reveals sides to the Tuscan landscape that transcend the pastoral clichés of the popular imagination. Railways pass through some of the most striking, ideal ways to enjoy the region's lesser known facets. Heading down the coast from La Spezia, for example, you pass the **Alpi Apuane**, a dramatic mountain range of saw-toothed Alpine peaks. A little branch line strikes through the heart of the region from Lucca. South of Pisa, almost all the way down the coast, the main line to Rome crosses the **Maremma**, a flat yet evocative coastal plain edged by bare hills. Two towns here, **Volterra** and **Massa Marittima**, are also well worth visiting. All down the coast, of course, are plenty of moderate resorts if you want to take time out on a beach. Finally, south of Siena, you can ride a looping line through the

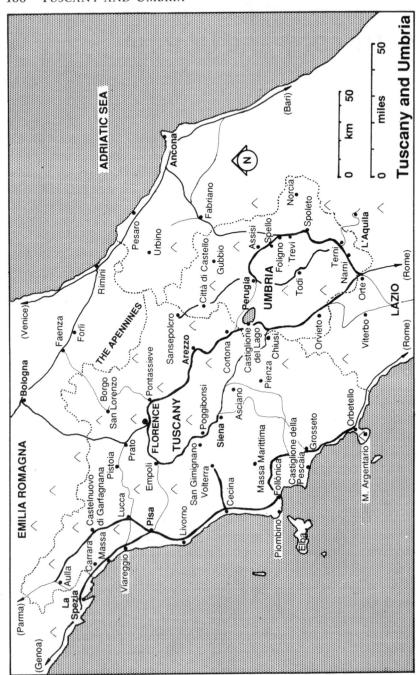

Tuscany and Umbria

crete, the Sienese 'badlands'; bare and sunbaked hills with an eerie atmosphere all of their own.

And when you've had your fill of Tuscany, you can move south to Umbria, not for more of the same, but for a subtle and self-contained region as varied as any in Italy. The obvious way into the area is the main line to Rome from Florence, a route that touches two final, worthwhile Tuscan destinations; **Arezzo**, home to *The Story of the True Cross*, one of Italy's most famous fresco cycles, and **Cortona**, an ancient town of long views and historic monuments.

Perugia is Umbria's capital, an initially off-putting place, its large modern suburbs entirely untypical of the region. Come back to it – and its fine historic centre – after some of the other hill towns, places like **Spoleto**, amongst central Italy's most appealing towns, or smaller villages like **Spello**, **Narni** and **Trevi**. Each has its own distinct character, and each is easily seen from the train. Save most of your time, however, for

---

Routes Florence

Florence–Siena

La Spezia–Pisa

Pisa–Lucca

Lucca–Castelnuovo di Garfagnana–Aulla

Pisa–Volterra–(Massa Marittima)–Orbetello

Florence–Arezzo–Cortona–Castiglione del Lago–Orvieto

Terni–Todi–Perugia–Città di Castello–Sansepolcro

Orte–Narni–Spoleto–Trevi–Foligno

Foligno–Spello–Assisi–Perugia

Routes are less important than the towns they visit in Tuscany and Umbria (though remember some of the scenic options outlined above). The regions also have more lines – and more historic towns – than are covered in this chapter, which concentrates on the most famous (in **Tuscany***, for example, you might look at* **Prato** *and* **Pistoia** *on the Florence–Lucca line; in Umbria, try* **Gubbio***, a medieval gem just off the main Rome–Foligno–Ancona line).*

The order in which you explore this area will depend on your approach. **Florence** *(from Bologna) is the most obvious starting point, though if you're coming from Genoa and La Spezia, you might want to kick off with the cities of Pisa and Lucca (***La Spezia–Pisa** *and* **Pisa–Lucca***). Nevertheless, many centres conveniently fall on the same routes, notably* **Pisa–Volterra–Massa Marittima–Orbetello** *and* **Florence–Arezzo–Cortona–Orvieto***. In Umbria, especially, trains are the perfect way to see the region (***Orte–Narni–Spoleto–Foligno** *and* **Foligno–Spello–Assisi–Perugia***).*

Assisi, birthplace of St Francis, and – for all the tourists and pilgrims – easily Umbria's most rewarding destination. Finally, no visit is complete without a morning in **Orvieto**, enough time to enjoy its incredible setting and breathtaking duomo, the finest Gothic cathedral in Italy. It also leaves you perfectly placed for heading south to Rome.

Florence

Florence is a city-sized shrine to the Renaissance, its churches, palaces and museums crammed with enough art to last a lifetime. With this in mind you should take your time, and on a first visit at least restrict yourself to the highlights outlined below. You might also prepare yourself for the city's downside: crowds, traffic, restoration, busy hotels and high prices (most museum and gallery admissions were recently doubled). It's also something of a surprise to find the city's not as beautiful at street level as you might expect. The dour *palazzi*, for example, have none of Siena's rose-coloured charm, the monuments none of Rome's immediacy. And you're hard-pressed to find anything of Venice's fairytale quality in the gloomy streets.

If this argues against the notion of Florence's artistic pre-eminence, it's to emphasise that the city – a few notable exceptions aside – is an indoor experience. The two main squares are points of departure rather than places to linger. **Piazza del Duomo** leads to the **duomo** and **Baptistery**, **Piazza della Signoria** to the main galleries and points south of the river (the *Oltrarno*). Amongst the galleries, three main ones stand out; the **Uffizi** (paintings), the **Bargello** (sculpture) and the **Museo dell'Opera del Duomo** (sculpture). Church interiors, of course, also contain individual works of genius, notably **Santa Croce** (Giotto), **San Marco** (Fra Angelico), **San Lorenzo** (Michelangelo), **Santa Maria del Carmine** (Masaccio and Masolino) and **Santa Maria Novella** (Masaccio, Ghirlandaio and Filippino Lippi). Other key sights include the **Accademia**, home to Michelangelo's *David*; the Romanesque jewel of San Miniato; the sculpture-filled façade of **Orsanmichele**; and the jumbled collection of the city's second-ranked picture gallery, the **Palazzo Pitti**.

These are only the unmissable spots. You could easily spend at least an hour in some, and a good morning or more in most. This said, as in Venice, the sheer crowds and difficulty in finding a bed, especially if you arrive late in the day, mean you should think about seeing Florence as a succession of day trips. Somewhere like Arezzo makes a good base, just half an hour and a few thousand lire away by train.

History

Florence had a standard early Italian history: Etruscan roots (in the shape of Fiesole, a town in the hills above Florence) and then time as a Roman colony (*Florentia*, established in 59 BC by Julius Caesar). It emerged from the Dark Ages as an independent city state at the beginning of the 12th century. Fighting between noble factions continued apace as it did in much of the country. Despite internal strife, however, the city prospered through banking, trade – in wool and cloth particularly – and the conquest of neighbouring towns. It then passed through various periods of rule, first by mercantile elements (the *Primo Popolo*) and then by leading guilds (the *Secondo Popolo*). By 1293, though, it had developed a sophisticated form of republicanism, the *Signoria*, a council drawn from the major guilds.

Many towns in the 14th century, however, gradually came under the sway of a single clan. In the case of Florence it was the **Medici**, a banking family who exerted political control over the city through several generations. Giovanni was its patriarch, the man responsible for making the initial fortune. His financial legacy conferred legitimacy on his son **Cosimo**, who with his grandson, **Lorenzo il Magnifico** (1449–92), provided the enlightened patronage that formed one of the motors of the Renaissance. This unparalleled artistic flowering sprang not only from money but also from the city's dynamic and cosmopolitan atmosphere combined with an upsurge in classical scholarship and humanist thought. Medici control faltered around 1490, with the failure of the family bank, then stuttered to a halt with the surrender by Lorenzo's son, Piero, to the French army of Charles VIII. Until 1498 the city was in thrall to **Savonarola**, a charismatic monk eventually ousted by the Papacy. The Medici returned in 1512, though with reduced power, only to be removed in 1527 when Emperor Charles V's army overran Rome. The Pope at the time, Clement VII, was a Medici. Two years later, however, the family were back, under another Cosimo, who took control of all Tuscany (the Medicis styled themselves Grand Dukes of Tuscany from 1570).

The last Medici died in 1737, and under the terms of a family treaty, handed Florence to Francesco of Lorraine, the future Emperor Francis I of Austria. The city remained under the Austrian yoke until Unification in 1860 (bar an interlude of 15 years, when it was controlled by Napoleon). Subsequent events in its history stood out for the wrong reasons. First came the events of 1944, when the retreating Nazis dynamited all but one of the city's bridges. Then came the famous flood of 1966, when three days of rain on top of a wet autumn saw the Arno burst its banks. The ensuing deluge killed several people and ruined countless artistic treasures – a catastrophe which brought substantial international aid into the city.

What to see

The Duomo

Florence's duomo, Santa Maria del Fiore, is Europe's fourth largest cathedral. Started in 1294 to a design by Arnolfo di Cambio, it was only consecrated in 1436 after the work of several more architects, in particular Filippo Brunelleschi, who tackled the thorny problem of raising one of the largest domes ever built. The finished product was a miracle of medieval engineering, and stands as one of the city's symbols, still the dominant feature of the Florentine skyline.

The **façade** is almost as impressive, but it's largely a 19th-century copy of a Gothic model, albeit one that uses the same stone as the original (white marble from Carrara, red from the Maremma and green from Prato). The free-standing **campanile** was designed by Giotto in 1334, though later architects altered his specifications and only the first storey is as originally planned.

The **interior** appears empty, impressive more for its size than any works of art, most of which have been removed to the Museo dell'Opera del Duomo (see below). Its two main paintings, however, defy movement, both being painted on the wall. One commemorates Sir John Hawkwood (1436), a famous English mercenary, painted by Uccello (on the left wall); the other – just beyond – is a portrait of Niccolo da Tolentino (1456) by Castagno. The panel beyond them is Michelino's *Dante Explaining the Divine Comedy* (1465).

Be sure to climb the **dome** (463 steps), an occasionally back-bending experience that has you weaving between its two stone shells. The views, needless to say, are superb (daily 10 am–5 pm); entrance on the left wall close to the transept.

The Baptistery

Florence's oldest building, the octagonal **Baptistery** (*Battistero*) stands immediately in front of the duomo. It dates from around the 6th century, though Roman fragments incorporated inside are clearly from an earlier era (legend has it this was the site of a Temple to Mars). Inside the main features are a marvellous marble floor and 13th-century **mosaic ceiling** (created by Venetian craftsmen, because the mosaic art had 'died out' in Florence). Also outstanding is a prized early Renaissance **tomb** of 15th-century Pope John XXIII by Donatello and pupils (Mon–Sat 1–6 pm, Sun 9.30 am–12.30 pm and 2.30–5.30 pm; free).

The building's best known feature, however, is its **bronze doors**, considered by many to mark the start of the Florentine Renaissance. One set of the three doors required was already in place (cast in 1336 by Andrea Pisano). A competition was then announced to design the remaining pair. The 20-year-old **Lorenzo Ghiberti** (1378–1455) produced the winning entry, fighting off challenges from five other sculptors (including Brunelleschi and Siena's Jacopo della Quercia). The resulting bronzes now decorate the north and east doors. (Note that the panels are replaced by replicas and the originals moved to the Museo dell'Opera del Duomo.)

The Museo dell'Opera del Duomo

The Museo dell'Opera is one of the city's finest collections of sculpture, containing works removed from the duomo, campanile and baptistery. You'll find it by leaving the duomo from the right aisle exit and turning left towards Piazza del Duomo (Mon–Sat 9 am–7.30 pm, Sun 10 am–1 pm). Pride of place on the mezzanine goes to a *Pietà by* **Michelangelo**, one of the artist's last works, a sculpture he once attacked with a hammer, removing Christ's left arm and leg in the process. A pupil patched things up, completing the figure of Mary Magdalen (notice the distinct contrast in styles – and ability). Signs of the artist's frenzy, though, are still evident.

Upstairs the star turn is **Donatello**'s *Mary Magdalen*, a tortured, naked figure wrapped in her own hair, and a pair of contrasting *cantorie* (choir-lofts) by Donatello and Luca della Robbia.

Piazza della Signoria

Florence's main square, **Piazza della Signoria**, leads on to three key Florentine sights – the Palazzo Vecchio, Uffizi and Orsanmichele. The piazza itself, though, is rather spoilt by some doughty 19th-century buildings. It's also had a traumatic few years of restoration: the chances are that the piazza's rubble, fences and building site will still be there when you visit.

It was here in 1497 that the famous 'Bonfire of the Vanities' took place, a sermon in which **Savonarola** urged his followers to cast off and burn their worldly possessions. Less than a year later he himself was burned as a heretic – a bronze plaque marks the exact spot of execution. Otherwise look out for the **Loggia della Signoria** at the square's western edge and its two famous statues – Benvenuto Cellini's celebrated *Perseus* and Giambologna's equally flamboyant *Rape of the Sabine Women*. Other statues around the square are less successful, in particular Ammanati's *Neptune Fountain*, proof that size isn't everything and that Florence isn't without its duds.

Palazzo Vecchio

Not one of the city's most graceful buildings, the **Palazzo Vecchio** and campanile on the east side of Piazza della Signoria date from 1299, built to house the *signoria*, the heads of the seven major guilds and top tier of the city's government. Each guild took a month in office: the palace's rooms served as living quarters during each monthly shift. Most of the paintings and interior decoration date from the Medici's nine-year tenure in 1540. Cosimo I then moved on to the Palazzo Pitti (weekdays 9 am–7 pm, Sun 8 am–1 pm).

Many of the palace's rooms are worth a look, but the main interest revolves around the **Salone dei Cinquecento** and Vasari's second-rate murals (1570). The **Sala dei Gigli** features frescoes by Ghirlandaio and a newly-restored *Judith and Holofernes* by Donatello.

Orsanmichele

The church of Orsanmichele lies two blocks off Piazza della Signoria on Via dei Calzaiuoli, one of the city's main streets, and the principal promenade for its *passeggiata*. The church's interior contains a vast and gorgeously detailed 14th-century Gothic **tabernacle** by Andrea Orcagna, but it's the exterior that commands most attention. Once a granary, the building became a trade hall for the city's guilds, and then in 1380 was given over primarily to religious functions. Each guild, however, undertook to decorate one of the new church's fourteen exterior niches. Most of the resulting sculpture is outstanding, in particular Ghiberti's *John the Baptist* and Donatello's *St Mark*.

The Uffizi

The Uffizi is easily found – it's the building ringed by queues of people off Piazza della Signoria. Europe's most famous art gallery is one of the most tourist-thronged sites in Italy, and you'll do yourself no favours by attempting to do battle with the hordes. If you can't come off-season, aim to be in place when the doors open, or visit in the couple of hours before the gallery closes (Tues–Sat 9 am–7 pm, Sun 9 am–1 pm; free on the first and third Sat and second and fourth Sun of the month).

Most of the collection was accumulated by the Medici and bequeathed to the city by the family's last scion, Anna Maria Ludovica (1667–1743). Despite the hefty admission fee it's well worth giving yourself a couple of days to take in the many well-known paintings. Invest in a guide for a detailed tour around the gallery. Most are Florentine pieces arranged in chronological order with the odd excursion into the Sienese, German and Venetian schools. These are simply the absolute highlights.

Room 2 has three majestic altarpieces of the Madonna Enthroned (*Maestà*) by Cimabue, Duccio and Giotto, arranged to allow comparison of similar works by three early Italian masters. **Room 3** looks at Siena in the 14th century, with works by the Lorenzetti brothers and Simone Martini's *Annunciation* the chief attractions. **Room 5** is a brief nod to the 'International Gothic', an ornate and courtly style exemplified by Gentile da Fabriano.

Room 7 is the first to move on to more familiar Renaissance ground, with names like Fra Angelico and Masolino, but dominated by three masterpieces; Domenico Veneziano's *Madonna and Saints*, one of only twelve known works by the artist; Piero della Francesca's portraits of *Federigo da Montefeltro and Battista Sforza*; and Paolo Uccello's *The Battle of San Romano*. Filippo Lippi, Botticelli and Pollaiuolo adorn Rooms 8 and 9 before the run of five rooms (**Rooms 10–14**) given over almost entirely to famous paintings by Botticelli, most notably the *Birth of Venus*.

Room 15 shifts to Leonardo da Vinci and Room 18 to sculpture and portraits, followed by the Signorellis and Peruginos in the next room. German art takes over for a couple of rooms (Holbein, Memling, Dürer and others), together with Venetian painters like Giovanni Bellini. Subsequent highlights are Michelangelo's *Doni Tondo* in **Room 25**, his only complete easel-painting. Its vivid colouring and twisted gestures were studied by the Mannerist masters who follow – Bronzino, Pontormo and Rosso Fiorentino. Raphael makes an appearance around half-way, so too Titian (see his erotic *Venus of Urbino*), as well as a host of famous names often over-looked by the scrum which tends to form around the earlier paintings. Tintoretto, Parmigiano and Veronese fly the Italian flag, and there are works by foreigners such as Goya, Rubens, Rembrandt (a fine *Self-Portrait*) and Van Dyck. Caravaggio is given **Room 43** (with an outstanding *Bacchus* its centrepiece). Don't overlook the **Corridoio Vasariano** which you can see on a guided tour (see the main gallery office on the third floor). It offers some nice views of the city and a long corridor of portraits by a bevy of illustrious 16th-, 17th- and 18th-century artists.

The Bargello

The Bargello, or Museo Nationale del Bargello, is Florence's second most important museum (after the Uffizi) and Italy's single finest collection of sculpture (Tues–Sat 9 am–2 pm, Sun 9 am–1 pm). Built in 1255, the palace was home to the *Podestà*, the city's magistrates, and later became a prison. It took its present name in the 16th century when it housed the *bargello*, or chief of police.

The first room is given over largely to **Michelangelo**, the works including a *Bacchus* (carved when he was 22), a bust of *Brutus*, an unfinished *Apollo* (or *David*), and a tondo of the *Madonna and Child*. Close by are pieces by **Cellini** and **Giambologna**, the latter's *Mercury* being especially noted (see also his *Oceanus* in the courtyard outside) and a cheerfully awful *Adam and Eve* by Bandinelli.

Upstairs see **Donatello**'s bronze *David* (c.1435), the first free-standing nude carved since antiquity and the glazed terracotta Madonnas by **Lucca della Robbia**.

Also look out the **Sala dei Bronzetti**, a room devoted to small bronzes, the best a menagerie of small animals made by Giambologna for a Medici garden grotto. Busts and sculptures in subsequent rooms include items by Mino da Fiesole, Verrocchio and a host of others.

Santa Maria Novella

The church of Santa Maria Novella is almost the first thing of note outside the station – its rear elevation confronts you across the forecourt. Founded in the 11th century, the church became the Florentine headquarters of the Dominicans, though the order never got round to organising its **façade** in any coherent way. As a result the 14th-century lower section reflects the Gothic taste of the day, in marked contrast to the upper tiers added by Leon Battista Alberti around a hundred years later.

The **interior** is sombre, but it conceals several premier works of art, the most famous *The Trinity* by **Masaccio** (1428), one of the first paintings in which the tenets of Classical art and the vagaries of perspective were mastered.

The **Cappella di Filippo Strozzi** (1486–1501) to the right of the altar is lavishly frescoed by **Filippino Lippi**. The area around the altar itself glows with narrative panels by **Ghirlandaio** (1485); the Gondi chapel to their left contains a famous *Crucifix*, apparently carved by Brunelleschi as a lesson for Donatello (who was apparently so overwhelmed when he saw it he dropped a basket of eggs).

Be sure to visit the **cloisters**, entered to the left of the façade, the most heavily decorated of any in the city (daily 9 am–1 pm, closed Fri). Uccello and his assistants produced the frescoes in the righthand Chiostro Verde (the 'green cloister'), Andrea da Firenze the cycle in the Cappella degli Spagnuoli (1360s).

San Lorenzo

Founded in the 4th century, **San Lorenzo** served time as the city's cathedral for several centuries. In its present guise it was the work largely of the Medici, becoming in effect their family parish church. Brunelleschi drew up plans for their new chapel in 1416, and Michelangelo later struggled to design a façade, efforts which came to nothing as you can clearly see in the bare brick frontage. The **interior** features two sizable **bronze pulpits** by Donatello, who's represented elsewhere in the church in the Sagrestia Vecchia.

A door at the top of the left aisle leads to the **Biblioteca Laurenziana**, the Medici library, an architectural tour-de-force designed by Michelangelo in 1524 (Mon–Sat 8 am–2 pm; free). Notice his famous staircase, in particular. More famous still is the artist's contribution to the **Cappelle Medicee** (Medici chapels), part of the San Lorenzo complex, but entered from Piazza Madonna degli Aldobrandini (Tues–Sat 9 am–2 pm, Sun 9 am–1 pm). Most people ignore the marble mausoleum and head straight down to the **Medici tombs** (in the Sagrestia Nuova). Michelangelo sculpted two of the tombs – those of Lorenzo and Guiliano de' Medici, grandson and son of Lorenzo the Magnificent respectively.

Take time to wander the **market** around San Lorenzo, a maze of street stalls selling all manner of clothes, bags, belts and shoes. Although prices are keener elsewhere, it's fun taking in the streetlife and local colour (watch your valuables). Better still, walk around the covered **Mercato Centrale**, the city's fantastic main food market (weekdays 7 am–1 pm, Sat 8 am–1 pm and 4–8 pm).

San Marco

The ex-Dominican monastery of San Marco is one of Florence's more peaceful spots, and may end up being your favourite amongst the city's churches. During Medici-funded rebuilding in 1437 (the monks were not meant to own property), **Fra Angelico**, one of the Renaissance's most sublime artists and himself a Dominican, frescoed much of the building as an aid to the monks' contemplation. In effect, the former monastery, now the **Museo di San Marco**, is a museum to the work of the painter (Tues–Sat 9 am–2 pm, Sun 9 am–1 pm).

The church's Ospizio dei Pellegrini or the Pilgrims' Hospice, contains about twenty works, some brought from other churches around the city (look out for an especially lovely *Last Judgement*). Across the cloister, the chapterhouse, or Sala Capitolare, has two masterpieces; a *Crucifixion* and an *Annunciation* (at the top of the stairs). Around the monastery's upper floor are 44 little cells, each frescoed either by Fra Angelico himself, or with the help of pupils (cells 1, 3, 6 and 9 and most on the left file are solely by the artist). One of the cells belonged to Savonarola, another couple – the largest – to Cosimo de' Medici, who came here on retreat.

The Galleria dell'Accademia

People come to the Accademia for one thing – Michelangelo's *David*, one of art's most familiar images and a veritable symbol of Florence and the ideas of Renaissance endeavour (Tues–Sat 9 am–2 pm, Sun 9 am–1 pm). So many people come here, however, that seeing the statue, never mind studying it close up, can be all but impossible. As with the Uffizi, which the Accademia at times rivals for sheer pandemonium, aim to visit first thing in the morning.

The commission was issued in 1501 by the Opera del Duomo, a type of Cathedral Public Works committee. Michelangelo was 26 at the time. He was to work on the statue for three years, using a leftover piece of marble, a massive piece of stone all but ruined by a previous sculptor. Looking at the statue's poise and monumental dignity, it's worth remembering it was intended as a work of public sculpture, not a museum piece (it stood in Piazza della Signoria until 1873). This partly explains why so many of the proportions are deliberately wrong: the hands are far too large, for example, the arms too big for the torso, and the head disproportionate to the body. The distortions were primarily designed to emphasise the statue in a large open space. They were also, however, deliberate attempts by Michelangelo to defy prevailing standards of sculptural form. Close to the *David* don't overlook Michelangelo's *Slaves*, a series deliberately unfinished, designed to embody the sculptor's dictum that carving was the liberation of form already within the stone.

The Accademia also has a fine collection of paintings, including numerous 14th- to 16th-century altarpieces and a clutch of canvases by **Botticelli**.

Santa Croce

Santa Croce is one of the city's key churches. As well as a compendium of paintings, including frescoes by **Giotto**, it contains the tombs of some of Florence's most illustrious personalities. It was started by the Franciscans in 1294, possibly to a design by Arnolfo di Cambio (also responsible for the duomo) and deliberately placed as far from San Marco and the order's Dominican rivals as possible. The campanile and façade are 19th-century additions, the result of a scam by an architect who persuaded city officials his scheme borrowed from a set of bogus original drawings.

The **tombs** start immediately you enter. Vasari's mausoleum of **Michelangelo** is on the right by the entrance, a spot personally chosen by the artist, it's said, because the first thing he'd see on the Day of Judgement would be Brunelleschi's dome through the portals of Santa Croce. His body was brought back to the city from Rome in July 1574. **Galileo** lies opposite, clasped in a tomb built in 1737, a century after his death. Previously the scientist had been denied a Christian burial, the consequence of his 'heretical' idea that the earth was not the centre of the universe. **Dante**'s Neoclassical tomb in the right aisle lies empty, for the poet – exiled by the Florentines – died in Ravenna and the body was not returned. The remains of Machiavelli, Lorenzo Ghiberti and some 260-odd tombs of lesser worthies lie dotted elsewhere in the nave.

Giotto's frescoes occupy two adjacent chapels to the right of the main altar (the Cappella Peruzzi and Cappella Bardi). One cycle describes the *Life of St*

Francis, the other episodes from the lives of St John and St John the Baptist. Many of the surrounding frescoes owe much to Giotto, whose naturalistic style was revolutionary at the time. **Taddeo Gaddi**, a long-term assistant of Giotto, painted the Cappella Baroncelli (the chapel at the end of the right transept) with scenes from *The Life of the Virgin*. The chapel alongside is the work of Taddeo's son, **Agnolo Gaddi**.

Elsewhere, look for the famous *Annunciation* by **Donatello** (on the right wall, two thirds of the way down the nave) and his *Crucifix*, criticised by Brunelleschi because it made Christ look like a peasant (in the chapel at the end of the left transept). Also make a point of paying to see the **Cappella dei Pazzi**, a harmonious architectural gem designed by Brunelleschi at the end of Santa Croce's first cloister. Off the cloister you'll also find a small **museum**, whose centrepiece, Cimabue's *Crucifixion*, was one of the prime victims of the 1966 flood. The deluge produced a six metre tide of water in Santa Croce, ripping paintings from the wall and creating damage whose effects can still be seen.

The Ponte Vecchio

At some point you'll want to cross the River Arno to round up the major sights in the distinct area known as the **Oltrarno** ('across the Arno'). The main crossing point is the **Ponte Vecchio**, an evocative bridge laden with old shops perched over the water's edge. Built in 1345 to replace an earlier wooden bridge, it was the only Florentine bridge not mined by the Nazis during their retreat from the city in 1944. Originally the shops embraced a miscellany of butchers, grocers and blacksmiths, all ejected in 1593 by the Medici Duke Ferdinando I. His private corridor between the Medici offices (the Uffizi) and personal palace (the Palazzo Pitti) crossed the bridge and he objected to the slabs of meat and unseemly produce that often blocked the ducal passage. Ever since the bridge has been the preserve of more up-market jewellers and goldsmiths (and these days all sorts of dubious tourist trash). Look, but don't buy.

Just over the bridge pop into the little-visited church of **Santa Felicità** to see one of the city's finest Mannerist paintings, a *Deposition* by Pontormo. It's in the Cappella Capponi, inside the door on the right.

Palazzo Pitti

Now home to six **museums**, the colossal Palazzo Pitti (1460) was originally built for the Pitti family in a forlorn attempt to rival the Medici. The Medici bought it in 1549 and made substantial alterations, all of them grandiose in scale and modest in architectural achievement. If anything, the palace's gardens, the **Giardino di Boboli** (9 am−dusk; free) are as rewarding as the museums, providing the only large area of open space in the city centre. Climb away from the gardens' entrance, which tends to be crowded, and head up to the gate leading to the **Forte di Belvedere** (daily 9 am−8 pm; free). A fort built in 1590, it serves mainly as belvedere for the city.

By far the best of the museums is the **Galleria Palatina**, one of Europe's first public galleries when it opened in 1833. Now Florence's largest gallery after the Uffizi, it consists of several Medici apartments (in fairly execrable taste), most stacked high with 16th- and 17th-century paintings. Stacked here is the operative word, for the canvases are crammed on to the walls with little sense of order. They were left in this state by the Medici, clearly ones for conspicuous artistic consumption. Nonetheless, there are some outstanding moments. Most of the best items are in the front rooms overlooking the piazza, in particular paintings by Raphael, Titian, Rubens and Andrea del Sarto.

The other museums are for more specialist tastes. The **Museo degli Argenti** presents a collection of silverware and household treasure that verge from the tacky to the sublime (the antique vases are exceptional). The **Galleria d'Arte Moderna** is a thorough-going display of mainly Tuscan modern art from the last 2 centuries; the **Galleria del Costume** is just that, a gallery of costumes; the porcelain museum is open by appointment only; the coach museum has carriages from the Houses of Savoy and Lorraine. The **Appartamenti** on the first floor alongside the main gallery offer a selection of state rooms decorated in the last century.

All the museums open Tues–Sat 9 am–2 pm, Sun 9 am–1 pm.

Santo Spirito

Piazza Santo Spirito is slightly seedy, making it a rather apt setting for the church of Santo Spirito. Nothing in the unfinished façade supports the claim of Baroque genius Bernini that this is 'the most beautiful church in the world'. The assertion's based more on the interior, which is lauded as a gem of Renaissance architecture but may strike you as no more than cold and gloomy. It was one of a pair of church interiors designed by Brunelleschi (the other was San Lorenzo), and its importance rests on the architect's harmonious and deftly proportioned work – all squares, cubes and mathematical regularity – a precursor of numerous churches to follow.

Santa Maria del Carmine

Santa Maria del Carmine is one of Florence's must-see churches, known above all for the **Masaccio fresco cycle** in the Cappella Brancacci at the end of the right transept (daily 10 am–5 pm, Sun 1–5 pm; closed Tues).

Three painters contributed to the frescoes in all. Masolino started work in 1425, and was soon joined by Masaccio, initially as a pupil but soon as a peer. The paintings marked a turning point in Renaissance art, displaying a new perspectival sense, increased drama and naturalism, and – above all – a masterful handling of light and space. Immediately adjudged a masterpiece, artists flocked to admire and learn from the cycle.

By 1428 Masaccio was dead, aged just 27, and the commissioning agents, the Brancacci family, were about to be expelled from the city. It was 50 years before the finishing touches were applied by Filippino Lippi.

San Miniato al Monte

Brave the long walk, the bus ride (number 13 from the station), the tourist hordes – whatever it takes – to reach **San Miniato al Monte**, which perches in verdant surroundings above one of the city's premier viewpoints, the **Piazzale Michelangelo** (sunset offers the most memorable panoramas). Started in 1013, the church – an erstwhile Cluniac monastery – gradually evolved into the city's finest

Practicalities in Florence

Telephone Code 055
Tourist Office Main offices at Via Cavour 1r,
north of the duomo (276.0382) and Chiasso dei
Baroncelli 17 – 19r (230.2124) for adequate
maps and information, hotel advice, but no
booking service.
  At the railway station use the *Consozio* ITA
(283.500) between platforms 9 and 10 who will
find you a room in a given price range (plus
commission): also try the kiosk, *Informazione
Turistica*, the red and white booth by the exit at
platform 16. Expect both station offices to
be busy.
Railway Station Santa Maria Novella, Piazza
della Stazione. Information (278.785; open
8 am – 9 pm). Foreign exchange (poor rates and
long queues). Left luggage 24 hr. Late night
pharmacy.
  It's an easy walk from the station to Piazza
del Duomo, but if you want to bus take the
number 7 (for Fiesole) or the 10 (which
continues beyond the duomo to San Marco).
Buses Several companies operate from
different parts of the city. SITA run most
services from the terminal Via Santa Caterina
da Siena, which is on the corner immediately
right of the station.
  Tickets for ATAF orange city buses can be
bought at the station or from *tabacchi*.
Post Office Via Pellicceria, off Piazza della
Repubblica.
American Express Via Guicciardini 49r
(278.751; weekdays 9 am – 5.30 pm, Sat 9 am
– 12.30 pm). Over the Ponte Vecchio before the
Palazzo Pitti.
Budget Travel CTS, Via Zanetti 18r
(292.088). Train, boat and air tickets.
Bike Hire *Ciao & Basta*, Via Alamanni,
opposite the railway station; in summer also at
Palazzo Pitti and Fortezza di Basso.
Taxis Ranks at the station and Piazza della
Repubblica; radio cabs call 4798 or 4390.
Tickets Box Office, Via dei Neri 46r (283.747).
Tickets for gigs, shows, concerts and theatre
(Mon – Sat 10 am – 8 pm).
Emergency Ufficio Stranieri (office for
foreigners), Via Zara 2 (49.771).
First Aid and Doctor First aid at *Misericordia*,
Piazza del Duomo 20 (212.222); Tourist
Medical Service, Via Lorenzo il Magnifico
(475.411).
UK Consulate Lungarno Corsini 2 (284.133).

Where to stay
Hostels *Istituto Gould*, Via dei Serragli 49
(212.576). In Oltrarno over the Ponte alla
Carrara. Excellent hostel and very popular –
reserve by post 3 months ahead to be sure of a
place.

Ostello Villa Camerata (IYHF), Viale Righi 2
(601.451). Half hour bus journey (number 17b
from the station or Piazza del Duomo). Smart,
popular and beautifully sited in 16th-century
villa with loggia, frescoed ceilings and gardens.
Postal bookings only, but call ahead to see if
they have room (2 – 11.30 pm – aim to be on
site at 2 pm). Midnight curfew. There's also a
basic 60-pitch **campsite** in the grounds.
Pensionato Pio X, Via dei Serragli 106
(225.044). Rock-bottom cheap, and despite
religious slant, relaxed and with amiable staff.
Aim to arrive for 9 am; no reservations;
midnight curfew; two day minimum stay; 35
beds in 2-, 3- and 4-bed rooms.
Santa Monaca, Via Santa Monaca 6, in
Oltrarno near S.M. del Carmine (268.338). A
non-IYHF hostel – crowded and poor security,
but the only central dorm rooms. No
reservations, just turn up and hope; 8 – 9.30 am
& 4 – 11.30 pm.
Suore Oblate dell'Assunzione, Via Borgo Pinti
15 (248.582). A convent taking in men and
women; open mid-June to Sept; midnight
curfew.
Suore Oblate dello Spirito Santo, Via Nazionale
8 (298.202). Run by nuns who take in women
and families only; clean, secure and close to the
station; midnight curfew (July to mid-Oct).
Camping *Italiani e Stranieri*, Viale
Michelangelo 80 (681.1977). Great facilities –
kitchens and a good if expensive shop – and
superb view of Florence, but always packed
solid – arrive early; take red or black bus
number 13 from the station (15 min). Open
6 am – midnight mid-Mar to Nov.
Panoramico, Via Peramonda 1 (599.069). Well
out of the city in Fiesole; take bus number 7
from the station.

Hotels
Station
The area around the station is packed with
well-known cheap hotels. One group centres on
Via Faenza to the north, the other on Via della
Scala to the south: Via Fiume, Via Nazionale
and Via Guelfa also have many *pensioni*. The
cheapest places, be warned, are pretty seedy,
and at night this isn't one of the best areas to be
walking. Even so there are a lot of travellers
chasing the rooms. You'll have to do a lot of
walking to find a space, and it's often no good
phoning ahead at these places. Aim to head for
the fringes of the district, and go upmarket or
leave well alone if you're unsure – some spots
are unlicensed. The worst spots tend to be the
ones with 'agents' touting for punters at the
station – to be ignored.
Santa Maria Novella
☆☆*Elite*, Via della Scala (215.395). Friendly

manager and just 8 rooms; send deposit or phone and arrive by noon to be sure of a place; no curfew.

☆☆*Giacobazzi*, Piazza S.M. Novella 24 (294.679). Just 7 rooms often snapped up by Italian visitors.

☆☆*La Romagnola*, Via della Scala 40 (211.597), with the *Gigliola* at the same address the best choice in this area; simple, friendly and with 42 rooms, so often a good chance of finding space.

☆☆*La Mia Casa*, Piazza S. M. Novella 23 (213.061). Good location and free nightly films (in English) and invariably busy. Generally better than the ☆☆*Isis* at no. 22 (239.6735).

☆☆*Ottaviani*, Piazza Ottaviani 1 (296.223). Try for rooms looking over the piazza – the others are ropey. Try also the ☆☆*Visconti* at the same address (213.877).

☆☆*Universo*, Piazza S. M. Novella 20 (211.484). Functional rooms, though some look over the piazza.

☆☆/☆☆☆☆*Aprile*, Via della Scala 6 (216.237). Near the station, but way above the league of most places close by; an old 15th-century Medici palace complete with frescoes and paintings, plus small courtyard for fresh air.

City Centre

☆☆*Bavaria*, Borgo Albizi 26 (234.0313). A good choice – quiet, old-fashioned and kindly – but students often snap up the rooms.

☆☆*Firenze*, Piazza Donati 4 (241.203). Clean, personable and convenient.

☆☆*Brunori*, Via del Proconsolo 5 (289.648). Lovely setting and central, plus friendly owners – though it can be noisy and rooms are past their best.

☆☆*Davanzati*, Via Porta Rossa 15 (283.414). 10 small, bright rooms in great location near the river; good value and welcoming management.

☆☆*Esperanza*, Via dell'Inferno 3 (213.773). Rooms with period furniture (a few with balconies) in a peaceful area.

Orchidea, Borgo degli Albizi 11 (248.0346). 7 fine and excellent value rooms in a 12th-century building, some overlooking a quiet garden; ☆☆/☆☆☆☆*Aldini*, Via Calzaiuoli 13 (214.752). Reliable choice if you're preparing to spend a little more; newly updated rooms, but with period fittings preserved (antique fireplaces especially).

☆☆☆☆*Hermitage*, Vicolo Marzio 1 (287.216). Bookings essential to secure one of the 14 cosy rooms close to the Ponte Vecchio, the more so if you want a room with a view of the river. Some bathless ☆☆☆ rooms; nice roof terrace.

☆☆☆☆*La Residenza*, Via Tornabuoni 8 (284.197). Near the Palazzo Strozzi (it looks over the gardens) on one of the city's ritziest streets; similar price range as the *Hermitage* and also a roof terrace for views of the streetlife below.

Oltrarno

Fewer people make it over the river, which makes this quiet area a slightly more likely district to find rooms.

☆☆*Sorelle Bandini*, Piazza Santo Spirito (215.308). An excellent first choice spot if you're lucky enough to get in; airy rooms on a quiet square; tasteful décor and marble fireplaces; and a three-sided loggia for enjoying the views. Reservations recommended.

☆☆*La Scaletta*, Via Guicciardini 13 (283.028). Similar to the *Bandini* but in a noisier, more central spot and more expensive; roof terrace with views of the Boboli gardens and the city skyline.

☆☆☆☆*Annalena*, Via Romana 34 (22.402). Legendary old-world *pensione* popular with writers and the like over the years; in a 14th-century *palazzo* near the Boboli gardens; furnished with art antiques, rooms with high ceilings, sizable garden and friendly ambience.

Eating

Cafés *Zatti*, Borgo degli Albizi 19r. Superlative *pasticceria* for coffee and cakes.

Manaresi, Via de' Lamberti 16r. Contender for the best coffee in the city.

Gilli, Piazza della Repubblica 39r. Grandest of the city's cafés, and one of several venerable and expensive, rather touristy spots on this piazza.

Giacosa, Via Tornabuoni 64r. Birthplace of the *negroni* cocktail and favoured spot for the smarter of the city's youth.

Rivoire, Piazza della Signoria 5r. Highly expensive café, but popular with Florentines and tourists alike.

Ice cream *Vivoli*, Via Isola delle Stinche 7r, near Santa Croce. Follow the crowds – the best ice cream in Florence, and perhaps the best in Italy.

Restaurants Good eating doesn't come cheap in a tourist town like Florence. If your budget's tight, however, there are plenty of bar snacks and pizza-slice places. Also remember the Mercato Centrale for picnic provisions.

Station, Santa Maria Novella and University
Antichi Cancelli, Via Faenza 73r. Cheap, basic food.

Da Giorgio, Via Palazzuolo 100r. More cheap hearty food at some of the city's keenest prices.

Da Mario, Via Rosina 2r. Big wooden tables crammed with students and market traders – so be prepared to queue; amiable atmosphere and reasonable prices.

Il Contadino, Via Palazzuolo 69r. Close to *Da*

Giorgio; a well-known backpackers' favourite; solid, unfancy and cheap.

Mensa Universitaria, Via San Gallo 25a. Bustling place with the city's cheapest meals – but remember you need an ISIC card (closed mid-July to mid-Sept).

Pizza Nuti, Borgo San Lorenzo 39r. Pizzas and more at good prices in one of the city's oldest restaurants.

Za-za, Piazza del Mercato 26r. Popular canteen-type place with a good reputation – but in unlovely surroundings. Soups are a speciality here.

City Centre

Acqua e Due, Via Vigna Vecchia 40r. Trendy amongst Florence's young and consequently always packed.

Benvenuto, Via dei Neri 47r (Santa Croce area). Fine food in what appears from the outside like a delicatessen.

La Maremmana, Via dei Macci 77r (Santa Croce area). Nice presentation – tablecloths and cut flowers – plus good food, generous portions and affordable prices. Good set price menus.

Le Mossacce, Via del Proconsolo 55r. Former Bohemian haunt, now known for its top quality food.

La Stazione di Zima, Via Ghibellina 68r (Santa Croce area). Probably the city's most popular vegetarian restaurant.

Oltrarno

Angiolino, Via Santo Spirito 22. Often busy with locals, though standards vary; restricted menu with lots of daily specials.

Cantinone del Gallo Nero, Via Santo Spirito 6r. Downstairs in a converted wine cellar (the door's easily missed); particularly known for its wine, though the *crostini* starters are house specialities.

Casalinga, Via Michelozzi 9r, near Piazza Santo Spirito. Perhaps the first-choice for genuine Tuscan cooking at an affordable price; always crowded but the atmosphere's easy-going.

Romanesque building. It was built in honour of San Miniato, a 3rd-century Christian whose martyred corpse was apparently observed carrying its head across the Arno and up the hill to the site of the present church.

The beautiful multi-coloured marble façade dates from the end of the 11th century, its patterning a deliberate echo of the Baptistery (the mosaic of *Christ and the Virgin* was a glorious 13th-century afterthought). The **interior**'s raised choir and crypt strike you immediately (both are rare but not unique features), closely followed by patches of 15th-century frescoes and fragments of ancient marble floor. Perhaps the single most important sight, however, is the chapel dedicated to James of Lusitania, a Portuguese cardinal who died in Florence in 1459 (he was a nephew of the King of Portugal, who paid for the monument). It's a combined work by sculptor Rossellino, painter Baldovinetti, and the brothers Pollaiuolo (and located off the left aisle). Luca della Robbia took care of the ceiling. Look out also for Taddeo Gaddi's paintings in the crypt, and note the parapet, pulpit and 13th-century mosaic up in the choir.

Florence–Siena

The route

Patches of classic Tuscan countryside mingle with less salubrious light industry and road-spoilt valleys on this route. At the end of the line, **Siena**'s a more appealing town than Florence, more mellow and more medieval than its Renaissance neighbour. The pace of life is slower, the crowds less frenetic, making it a lovely place to spend at least a couple of days. The past is also more firmly part of the present, a feeling best expressed by the *Palio*, Siena's famous horse race. Horses, jockeys and the town's *contrade* compete against one another twice a year in Italian's most dynamic *festa*. *Contrade* are the city's seventeen medieval divisions, each with its flag and animal motif (emblazoned all over on streets and buildings), its own sense of neighbourhood identity, and even its own church, social centre and museum. (The *Palio*'s held twice yearly on July 2 and August 16.)

Trains

Trains to Siena usually leave from platform 1 at Florence station. They're often crowded, though much of the jam loosens at Empoli where most people get off. There are 14 through services daily (63 km, 1 hr 40 min) and an additional 5 services if you change trains at **Empoli**. *Three expresses daily run from Florence direct to Siena, continuing to* **Grosseto** *on the west coast (for connections on the* **Rome–Pisa** *main line). Remember there are also connections to Siena from* **Chiusi** *on the* **Rome–Florence** *line.*

Siena

Tradition has Siena founded by Remus, brother of Romulus, the legendary founder of Rome, a tall story recollected in the city's many statues of the two brothers being suckled by the she-wolf. The city probably dates from around the birth of Christ, but only entered the reckoning in the 13th century, when its banks, wool industry, trade routes and quasi-democratic *commune* made it one of Europe's most important cities. Rivalry with Florence continued throughout the period, power swinging first one way – when Florence catapulted excrement and dead donkeys over the walls to induce a fatal plague in 1254 – and then the other, most notably in the period after Siena's victory at the Battle of Montaperti in 1260. Although power gradually tilted towards Florence, Siena still prospered, and from 1287 to 1355 under the rule of the so-called Council of Nine enjoyed a building boom and artistic flowering that saw its artists at the cutting edge of Italian art.

The plague of 1348 turned the tide decisively, wiping out around 70,000 of the city's 100,000 population. Political chicanery over 2 centuries saw Siena's virtual surrender to Florence, culminating in its absorption into the Grand Duchy of Tuscany in 1554. Florence then deliberately kept the city down, its decline into a rural backwater being one of the reasons for its survival as the medieval town you see today.

Piazza del Campo

Siena's curving amphitheatre of a piazza, the Campo – literally 'the field' – is probably Italy's greatest square. Shaped like a vast half shell, it's long been the centre of civic life, being used as a racetrack for the *Palio*; a soapbox for San Bernardino (the town's premier saint); as an arena for bullfights, boxing matches and public executions; and as a focus for all the town's wandering and social intercourse. Construction began in 1347, centring on the old marketplace, the point at which the city's *contrade* converged (and therefore a neutral spot in a fiercely competitive city). The Council of Nine divided the square into nine segments, aiming to be as even-handed as possible. Even the paving stones were in nine-piece sections (or so it's claimed – you can actually count eleven).

The square's most dominant feature is the **Palazzo Pubblico**, which closes its lowest edge (see below), flanked by a huge sceptre-like tower, the **Torre del Mangia**. The idea was to build a tower on behalf of the city which no noble or clergyman could start to challenge. Two Perugian architects were commissioned – men from a city that at the time bristled with towers – and came up with the second tallest structure built in medieval Italy (Cremona's *Torrazzo* claims first place). Its name supposedly comes from the glutton (*mangia*) who served as the tower's first watchman-cum-bellringer. The entrance is off to the left of the palace's internal courtyard (daily 10 am–7 pm; closes 1 hr earlier Nov–May).

In front of the *palazzo* stands the small **Cappella di Piazza** a modest stone loggia commissioned in 1348 to celebrate the end of a plague which claimed half the city's population. It took around a hundred years to build, hence the marked transition of styles between its upper and lower levels. At the Campo's highest point the **Fonte Gaia** adds a Renaissance dash to the medieval arena, a piece designed by Siena's own Jacopo della Quercia. The panels are reproductions, the eroded originals now sitting in the rear loggia of the Palazzo Pubblico.

The Palazzo Pubblico

Hustle past Siena's citizens on council business in the Palazzo Pubblico – which is still the city's town hall – and be sure to see the **Museo Civico**, an excellent museum and art gallery which meanders through several of the palace's public apartments (Mon–Sat 9.30 am–6.45 pm, Sun 9.30–12.45 pm; Nov–Mar Mon–Sun 9.30 am–12.45 pm).

Its early rooms are little more than a prelude to the famous **Sala del Mappamondo** (Room 10) – though en route make time to see the frescoes of Taddeo di Bartolo and Jacopo della Quercia's wrought-iron screen in the Cappella del Consiglio. Named after a damaged series of astrological frescoes, the *Mappamondo* is renowned for two majestic works of art; the first, Simone Martini's *Maestà* (1315), one of the great Italian paintings; the second, his now disputed *Portrait of Guidoriccio da Fogliano* (1328) a wonderful courtly image of the *condottiere* on horseback.

Equally famous frescoes wait in the next rom, the **Sala dei Nove**; Ambrogio Lorenzetti's *Allegories of Good and Bad Government*, and don't miss the handful of other fine paintings in the adjoining **Sala della Pace**.

The Duomo

Not many cathedrals match the exuberance of decoration on Siena's duomo, banded in black and white marble and loaded with sculptures, tracery and mosaics added over several centuries. Much of the lower façade is the work of Giovanni Pisano and pupils, though most of what's on show are copies. The originals reside in the Museo dell'Opera (see below).

More or less completed by 1215, the building nonetheless sprouted many half-finished additions over the years. The largest stands round the corner to the right (as you face the façade). The stone shell here formed part of a scheme to enlarge the church – the idea was to rival Florence's cathedral by building a completely new nave. Under the plan the original (and present) nave was to have been a transept, producing what would have been Italy's largest church outside Rome. Money and enthusiasm dried up following the plague of 1348.

The **interior** is tinged with a dusky light that illuminates a decorative riot to rival that of the façade. Some of the best work lies in the **pavement**, covered in 56 marble panels, each a self-contained episode designed by forty artists between 1349 and 1547. Many are kept covered for protection, though enough are revealed to suggest the overall effect and variety of themes. Perhaps the interior's most eye-catching effect, however, is the dozens of sculpted heads atop the pillars of the nave (each represents a pope). The best single work of art is the **pulpit**, carved around 1265 by Nicola Pisano and Arnolfo di Cambio, and there is more fine sculpture, chiefly the **Piccolomini altar** half way up the left aisle. Donatello has a bronze pavement in the north transept (*The Tomb of Bishop Pecci*, 1426) and a statue of *John the Baptist* in the left of the two circular transept chapels.

Midway down the left hand side of the church is the entrance to the **Libreria Piccolomini**, famous for its decorative frescoes by Pinturicchio, a leading Umbrian painter (daily 9 am–7 pm, winter 10 am–1 pm and 3–5 pm). The cycle was commissioned by Pope Pius III (who reigned for just 10 days) to commemorate his uncle, Aeneas Piccolomini, Pius II, one of the Renaissance's larger than life figures (he was a poet, philosopher, religious reformer, diplomat, geographer, town planner and so on).

Museo dell'Opera del Duomo

The cathedral museum, the Museo dell'Opera is more than an afterthought to the duomo itself: the art on show here ranks alongside the best in the city. Walk right as you face the cathedral façade and left into Piazza del Duomo and the museum is straight ahead, under the arches in a corner of the duomo's unfinished extension (daily 9 am–7.30 pm; off season 9 am–1 pm). The lower floor houses Pisano's façade sculptures, some of the foremost carving of the period in Italy. Upstairs is a spread of excellent works by Simone Martini, Sano di Pietro and Pietro Lorenzetti, all overshadowed by one of the greatest of all Sienese paintings, Duccio's *Maestà* (1311). Beyond the museum, off Via Monna Agnese and behind the cathedral, be sure to drop down the steps to see the duomo's often-overlooked **Baptistery** (daily 9 am–1 pm and 3–6 pm). Behind an unfinished Gothic façade its centrepiece is an early Renaissance font (1417–30), decorated with bronze panels including contributions from Lorenzo Ghiberti (*The Baptism of Christ* and *John the Baptist Imprisoned*), Donatello (*Herod's Feast*) and Jacopo della Quercia (*The Angel Announcing the Birth of John the Baptist*).

Pinacoteca Nazionale

The **Pinacoteca Nazionale** provides a thorough grounding in the art of Siena, its hundreds of works running the gamut of all the city's leading (and lesser)

Practicalities in Siena

Tourist Office Via di Città 43 (0577/280.551), plus another small office nearby on Piazza del Campo. Excellent maps, money exchange, bus, train and boat tickets and help with hotels as well as a list of rooms for rent.

Railway Station Piazza Rosselli. About 2 km from the centre; take a taxi from the ranks outside, or almost any of the buses across the street (the number 15 is quickest) which drop you at Piazza San Domenico or Piazza Matteotti. The Campo is signposted from here on. Foreign exchange is available at the station ticket office.

Buses TRA-IN and LAZZI services to Florence, Rome and most main Tuscan destinations leave from Piazza San Domenico (0577/221.221) where there's plenty of information and you can buy tickets on the spot.

Post Office Piazza Matteotti 36.

Police Via del Castoro, near the duomo.

Youth Hostel *Ostello della Gioventù Guidoriccio* (IYHF), Via Florentina 89 (0577/52.212). About 2 km north-west of the centre in the suburb of Lo Stellino: take bus number 4 or 15 from the station, 10 or 15 from Piazza Matteotti, but remember there's a reasonable chance of cheap rooms closer in. Curfew 11 pm.

Pilgrim hostel ☆*Casa del Pellegrino*, Via Camporeggio 31 (0577/44.177). Old nun-run hostel open to all, behind San Domenico with clean rooms, some with good views; they prefer reservations, so call ahead.

Hotels ☆*Locanda Garibaldi*, Via Giovanni Dupre 18 (0577/284.204). Eight good budget doubles close to the Campo (off the righthand side of the Palazzo Pubblico). Midnight curfew.

☆☆*Tre Donzelle*, Via Donzelle 5 (0577/280.358). Centrally placed off Banchi di Sotto 5 min from the Campo; big and fairly basic, though singles tend to be taken by long-stay students; try also the smaller, smarter ☆☆/☆☆☆*Etruria* (0577/280.358) just 30 metres down the street.

☆☆*La Perla*, Via delle Terme (0577/47.144). Another central option with plenty of rooms, hard against the Campo on a street parallel to Banchi di Sopra.

☆☆☆*Il Palio*, Piazza del Sale 19 (0577/281.131). Intimate hotel with comfortable rooms, nice location and accommodating management.

☆☆☆*Hotel Continentale*, Via Banchi di Sopra 85 (0577/41.451). A grand-looking hotel in 16th-century *palazzo* that's known better days, and given its position on one of the main streets, potentially noisy, though there are some great rooms and an appealing air of faded elegance.

☆☆☆*Hotel Duomo*, Via Stalloreggi 34 (0577/289.088). The best of the city's middle-priced hotels – follow Via di Città south of the duomo – but often full, so call ahead or arrive early.

☆☆/☆☆☆*Palazzo Ravizza*, Pian dei Mantellini 34 (0577/280.462). Quiet 17th-century townhouse close to the duomo with 30 doughty, old-fashioned rooms, though many have new bathrooms. Lovely little garden and view, and vaulted dining room in which you'll have to take half-board from Mar–Nov.

☆☆/☆☆☆*Santa Caterina*, Via Piccolomini 7 (0577/221. 105). Under the same management as the *Ravizza* and only a hotel since 1986, so rooms are modern and comfortable, with garden and veranda for breakfast; ten minutes' walk from the Campo out of Porta Romana.

Cafés and Ice Cream Drinks, it goes without saying, are expensive in the bars that line the Campo, but splash out all the same. Don't touch the restaurants, here, however. *Nannini*, Via Banchi di Sopra 22–24. By far Siena's top bar (other branches in the city), owned by leading local family (the son was a racing driver, the daughter's a pop star). Good for drinks and snacks on the hoof. *Nannini Gelateria*, Piazza Matteotti/Via Banchi di Sopra. Top ice cream. *Gelateria Artigiani*, Via di Città/Via dei Pellegrini just off the Campo. More ice cream.

Restaurants *La Torre*, Via di Salicotto 7. Tiny, friendly and averagely-priced place behind the Palazzo Pubblico; a definite first choice – if you can get one of the 10 tables (closed Thur). *Garibaldi*, Via Giovanni Dupre 18. Under the eponymous *locanda* near the Campo; good, basic and cheap (closed Sat). *Le Logge*, Via del Porrione 33 (0577/48.013). Certainly the most pleasing old-world interior in town, good food – pricier than most – and very popular, so it's essential to book or arrive early. *Ai Marsili*, Via del Castro 3 (0577/47.154). In all the guides as the city's top spot, but quite expensive and standards can vary – it's currently on an up. Located in a 900-year-old wine cellar, with elegant brick-vaulted dining area.

Excursion from Siena

San Gimignano

The little hill town of San Gimignano and its famous crop of towers is the best if most tourist-choked destination between Florence and Siena. Few places suggest so well how a medieval town must have looked to contemporaries. Now its churches and palaces are stacked with excellent paintings, which combined with its quaint, rural feel (crowds notwithstanding) make it a place to spend at least a day. Come off-season, if possible, or stay overnight, and then you can enjoy the atmosphere free of the trippers.

Access is straightforward. Leave the Florence–Siena train at Poggibonsi. Buses run to San Gimignano from immediately outside the railway station. The bus drops you either at the village's southern end (near Porta Giovanni) or its northern extremity (Porta San Matteo). In either case orientation is easy – you simply walk through the gates and up the main streets to the central Piazza del Duomo.

Note that one ticket can be bought to take you into most things worth seeing, available at the tourist office or individual sights. Opening times have been synchronised accordingly (April–Oct daily 9.30 am–12.30 pm and 3.30–6.30 pm; Oct–Mar same hours except closed Mon).

The Towers San Gimignano's towers need no pointing out – there are 14 of them, survivors of 72 that once jostled for space on the medieval skyline. Similar towers sprouted in most Italian towns during the 12th century, partly because nobles wanted physical symbols of their prestige – and aimed to build higher than their rivals – and partly because they served bonafide defensive purposes (they were useful as grain stores, for example, or as redoubts from which to dribble boiling oil on enemies).

On a larger scale, the town – once a player in the regional power game – fought wars with the likes of Volterra and Poggibonsi. Collapse and an increasing if reluctant reliance on Florence followed the Black Death of 1348. Under Florentine control the town ceased to be torn apart by internal feuds, and as the towers posed no military threat they were largely left alone. For a less than romantic portrait of the village's more recent state, come armed with E. M. Forster's novel *Where Angels Fear to Tread*, whose fictional Monteriano is based on San Gimignano.

If you want to climb a tower, only one is available for the purpose; the **Torre Grossa**, the highest surviving specimen. It's rooted immediately to the right of the Palazzo del Popolo in Piazza del Duomo. Views from the top, of course, are exceptional.

The Collegiata The Collegiata is San Gimignano's cathedral by any other name. Its glowing Romanesque interior must rate as one of the region's most comprehensively frescoed churches. There are three main cycles – one on the rear wall and one on each side wall (plus a separate sequence in a side chapel on the right).

The rear wall's faded display is *The Last Judgement* by Taddeo di Bartolo (1393), which makes up for its condition with some of the most gruesome snapshots ever painted of what awaited sinners in the final reckoning. The separate figure of St Sebastian low down is by Benozzo Gozzoli, painted to commemorate the passing of a plague in 1464.

The left wall contains episodes from the **Old Testament** by Bartolo di Fredi (c. 1367), again filled with appealing narrative eccentricities (see Noah exposing himself, for example, in *The Drunkenness of Noah*). The right wall has scenes from the **New Testament**, though their authorship is disputed: Barna di Siena is usually given credit, but he probably died falling from scaffolding in the church (in the 1350s). The pieces may have been completed by Lippo Memmi, brother-in-law and collaborator of Simone Martini.

The best of the church's art, though, was painted when the side chapels were reorganised in the 15th century. Domenico Ghirlandaio was brought in to fresco the **Cappella di Santa Fina**, a chapel dedicated to St Fina, who at the age of 10 made the mistake of accepting an orange from a boy. Castigated by her mother, she vowed to repent her sins by lying on a plank of the kitchen table. There she remained during the 5 years to her death (at which point the table reputedly blossomed with violets). The story may not be up to much but the frescoes are superb. The baptistery through the arch to the left of the Collegiata has a loggia also frescoed by Ghirlandaio.

Palazzo del Popolo Still in Piazza del Duomo, drop into the Palazzo del Popolo, where the first room off the courtyard, the Sala di Dante, is the place where in 1299 Dante – speaking as a Florentine ambassador – attempted to win San Gimignano over to the Florentine cause. Early Sienese works and hunting scenes line the walls, outshone by Lippo Memmi's *Maestà* (1317), widely acknowledged as the artist's masterpiece. Upstairs the **Museo Civico** fields a fine crop of Florentine and Sienese paintings, including pieces by Filippino Lippi (an *Annunciation*), Pinturicchio (a lovely *Madonna*), Girini (another look at St Fina) and Taddeo di Bartolo's *Life of San Gimignano*. Be sure to look out Memmo di Filipuccio's cycle of paintings, a sequence that follows a courtship through scenes such as shared bath and wedding night frolics.

Out of the Palazzo and a few steps above the Piazza you might want to stroll up to the **Rocca**, a belvedere for extensive views over the Tuscan countryside.

Sant'Agostino Curve north on Via San Matteo away from the Piazza del Duomo and its attendant throng and you hit **Sant'Agostino** hard up against the town walls. Inside is another mesmerising fresco cycle, this time by **Benozzo Gozzoli**, a pupil of Fra Angelico. This great little cycle relates episodes from *The Life of St Augustine*. There are bonus paintings in the shape of Bartolo di Fredi's *Life of the Virgin* and Sodoma's *St Sebastian*, amongst others.

Practicalities in San Gimignano

Tourist Office Piazza del Duomo 1 (0577/ 940.008). Provides a list of limited local hotel accommodation and of the numerous options for beds in private rooms. Foreign exchange facilities and bus tickets.
Cooperative Turistiche Via Giovanni 125, just inside Porta San Giovanni (0577/940.809). Operates a room-finding and booking service; as does the *Agenzia Simona* nearby at Via San Giovanni 985 (0577/941.848). Expect a booking fee.
Buses TRA-IN buses leave from Piazza Martiri outside Porta San Giovanni for Poggibonsi (20 min). Timetables are displayed in Piazza del Duomo and you can buy tickets at the tourist office.
Youth Hostel *Ostello della Gioventù*, Via delle Fonti 1 (0577/941.991). Good location in the northern part of town; friendly staff, good bar and views. Call ahead to check availability. Reception open 7.30–9.30 am and 5–11.30 pm; 11.30 pm curfew.
Convent *Convento di Sant'Agostino*. Piazza Sant'Agostino, first left inside Porta San Matteo (0577/940.383). 20 good rooms in a working monastery: in summer you'll need to book or write well in advance for a place (though the monks try to squeeze you in if it's possible).
Rooms 15 or so people rent out rooms at ☆☆prices: wander around the village looking for signs (*camere*) or enquire at the tourist office or letting agents listed above.
Hotels San Gimignano has 4 fairly up-market hotels within the walls, plus a couple of guest houses.
☆☆*Il Pino*, Via San Matteo 102 (0577/ 940.415). Basic place above a restaurant.
☆☆*Le Vecchie Mura*, Via Piandorella 15 (0577/940.270). Rooms above one of the better town restaurants; on the first left coming up Via San Giovanni from the outer walls.
☆☆☆*Leon Bianco*, Piazza della Cisterna (0577/ 941.294). Reliable and refined hotel located in an old *palazzo* near the main square.
☆☆☆*La Cisterna*, Piazza della Cisterna 23 (0577/940.328). Oldest and swishest hotel in town.
☆☆☆☆*Antica Pozzo*, Via San Matteo 87 (0577/942.014). Town's top decor and top prices.

Camping *Il Boschetto*, at Santa Lucia (0577/ 940.352). 3 km down the hill from Porta San Giovanni on the not unpleasant road to Volterra (buses go past the site). Has on-site pizzeria, bar, shop and hot showers (open April–Oct; reception closed 1–3 pm and 8–9 pm).

Drinking San Gimignano's tipple is *Vernaccia*, a long-established white wine that's recently

been revamped and smartened up (though standards vary).

Eating *Chiribi*, Via San Giovanni. First left after you enter Porta San Giovanni; fine cheap snacks, pasta *primi*, take outs and small pizzas (closed Mon).

Le Vecchie Mura, Via Piandorella 15. Pizzas and often superlative main meals.

---

painters including Duccio, Simone Martini, Pietro and Ambrogio Lorenzetti and Taddeo di Bartolo, (daily 8.30am–2 pm, Sun 8.30 am–1 pm).

The rooms follow a chronological order, and you should be looking out in particular for the early pieces by Guido da Siena (Room 2), perhaps the first purely Sienese painter, whose Byzantine-tinged works and broad gilt backgrounds were to be a staple of those who followed. Duccio (1260–1319) in rooms 3 and 4, is in the Sienese top tier, together with Simone Martini (a *Madonna* in Room 6 stands out), and the brothers Pietro and Ambrogio Lorenzetti (in rooms 7 and 8). Midperiod high points come with Bartolo di Fredi (1353–1410) and his pupil Taddeo di Bartolo (1362–1422), who you may see again if you take a trip out to San Gimignano (Rooms 9 to 11). Further down the line, the paintings display the influences of mainstream Italian art – which is to say Florentine art – noticeable in the portraiture naturalism and perspectival experimentation of painters like Sassetta. There's a throwback to the old style, however, in Giovanni di Paolo, Sano di Pietro and Matteo di Giovanni, painters who appeared during the Siena school's dotage (Rooms 12–16).

The churches

San Domenico should be the first church on your list, primarily for Sodoma's eye-opening frescoes on the life and ecstasy of St Catherine. They're in a chapel on the church's south side, together with a reliquary containing her head. Look out, also, for her portrait by Andrea Vanni, a contemporary and friend (on the church's right-hand side as you enter). Elsewhere the highlights are frescoes by Pietro Lorenzetti (fourth chapel on the right) and lesser painters like Matteo di Giovanni (first chapel on the right) and Sano di Pietro (first chapel of the left transept).

San Francesco is a gloomy, cavernous spot, but has a couple of Lorenzetti frescoes (first and third chapels of the north transept). In the piazza alongside – the Oratorio di San Bernardino (ring bell at number 22 for entrance) are more frescoes by Sodoma. **Santa Maria delle Nevi** (Via di Camollia) has a celebrated altarpiece by Matteo di Giovanni (1477).

La Spezia–Pisa
The route

The flashing glimpses of sea and fishing villages on the Ligurian coast give way beyond La Spezia to the more drab coastal plain of the **Riviera della Versilia**. One image stays in the mind from this stretch of rail: the ubiquitous presence of marble, either as rough-hewn blocks or the fine dust that settles over the region's towns and villages. Some is imported to be worked by local craftsmen, whose fund of expertise – accumulated over two millennia – is second to none. The bulk, though, is blasted from the *Alpi Apuane*, whose saw-toothed ridges run along the coast for 40 kilometres. The main marble towns are **Carrara**, which has something to recommend it (a quaint medieval centre) and **Massa**, a modern place, which doesn't. Both offer bus links to the mountains, which are served by refuges and detailed maps if you want to walk.

The coast's other main draw is its resorts, busy and unpretentious places for a dip and a few hours of ultraviolet. Most guides rubbish the area, but the beaches aren't as black as they're painted. Trains stop at most points, and the stations are invariably close to the sea. There's little to choose between towns, though the smartest spot is **Forte di Marmi**, the most popular **Viareggio**. All have plenty of hotels in all price ranges, cheap off season, bursting in August. Most have private beaches (*stabilimenti*) where you pay to sit on groomed sand and enjoy bars and shower facilities. Public beaches, though, dot the strand as well.

If you want to ride out the beach and outdoor activities, art and architecture await in **Pisa**, most famously in the Leaning Tower and its surrounding medieval ensemble. Like the coast, however, the city's no more than a half-day's outing, so be prepared to push on elsewhere into Tuscany or beyond.

Trains

Genoa to Rome expresses thunder along this route, though after La Spezia they usually stop only at Pisa (6 daily, 75 km; 50 min), and occasionally at Viareggio (4 daily, 54 km; 30 min from La Spezia). Slower trains are more numerous, with 18 services daily which stop at all or most of the stations en route (average journey La Spezia–Pisa 1 hr 10 min).

Pisa

You catch a glimpse of perhaps Italy's most famous image before the train pulls into Pisa Centrale. There's the tower, and yes, it certainly leans. From the station, though, you have a clearer idea of what the rest of Pisa is like – a quietly provincial city with a modern face, the result of rebuilding after Second World War bombing. Once the city was amongst Tuscany's most powerful, its 11th-century empire embracing Corsica, Sardinia and the Balearics. It rivalled Genoa, Amalfi and Venice in its seafaring endeavours, growing rich by ferrying men and supplies to the First Crusade. In its heyday, local artists forged the stamp that was to leave its mark over much of the region, particularly in the sculpture of Nicola and Giovanni Pisano, and more especially in the distinctive striped marbles and blind arcades that distinguish Pisan–Romanesque churches across central Italy. Decline came fast, precipitated by naval defeats and the silting up of the harbour. The Florentines took over in 1406, in the process rejuvenating Pisa's famous university, one of the Renaissance's intellectual engine houses (Galileo was amongst its professors). Later the city was host to the likes of Byron and the Shelleys, eminent names in almost five centuries of what was otherwise virtual obscurity. Industry, an international airport, and a booming trade in tacky tourist souvenirs have all helped to re-establish the modern city.

The Campo dei Miracoli

The Campo dei Miracoli (the 'Field of Miracles'), also known as the Piazza del Duomo, contains Pisa's beautiful historic core: the Leaning Tower, Duomo, Baptistery and Camposanto. Even the belt of souvenir stands which girdles it fails to detract from an ensemble which would be exceptional even without the novelty of a tilting tower.

It's 20 minutes' walk to the Campo from the station, so you're better off taking bus number 1 which leaves regularly from the station forecourt (5 min). Tickets can be bought from the kiosk on your left as you leave the station building.

The Leaning Tower

Started in 1173 as a campanile for the duomo nearby, the Leaning Tower, or *Torre Pendente*, began to go awry almost from the word go. Architect Bonanno Pisano had reached the third of its eight levels – a height of about 10 metres – when the area's unstable sandy subsoil made itself felt: the tower took a 10-centimetre lurch from the vertical. Bonanno is said to have fled the city in fear of his life. Over the next 180 years various architects came to finish the job, each distorting the building's line in attempting to compensate for the lean. Tommaso di Andrea completed the work, rounding things off with a bell-tower in 1350. 600 years on the slide continued, the tilt having now reached an incredible 5 metres. The lean's sheer magnitude – even if pictures have prepared you – is one of the tower's most breathtaking features.

It comes as no surprise to learn that the point of no return is at hand. Having tipped by a millimetre a year for the last couple of decades, it's now lurching by the same amount almost every month. Measures to close the tower in 1989 were initially resisted by the Pisans, who fear losing the enormous windfall generated by visiting tourists. Things never happen quickly in Italy, not least when money and bureaucracy are involved. Only the collapse of a medieval tower in Pavia – when 3 people died – brought closure in January 1990. Numerous schemes have been dreamt up to save the tower, most of them fairly unworkable. Such situations in Italy usually produce a compromise unsatisfactory to everyone. This seems one occasion, however, where there's no way to muddle through. Major cracks are already appearing in the 14,000-odd tonnes of marble. Whatever eventually happens, however, the tower looks set to remain closed for years to come.

The Duomo

Hordes of people visit the Campo and see nothing beyond the Leaning Tower, casting an eye over the duomo only in so much as it forms a backdrop for the central attraction. In fact the cathedral is one of Italy's finest. Begun in 1064, it formed the first of the Campo's buildings, though it's been added to substantially since. The first addition came from Bonanno, the tower's first architect, who cast a bronze doorway, the **Portale di San Ranieri** (since moved opposite the tower). The entrance is now framed by doors from the workshop of Giambologna.

Much of the old **interior** was lost to a fire in 1595, but several masterpieces escaped the flames, notably traces of the pavement; Cimabue's *Christ in Majesty* (1302), now in the apse; and a group of paintings by Ghirlandaio (on the right wall). The best work by far, however, is Giovanni Pisano's **pulpit**, the last and greatest of several important sculptures executed by Giovanni and his father, Nicola.

The Baptistery

Begun in Romanesque mode in the middle of the 12th century, Italy's largest baptistery was rounded off by Nicola and Giovanni Pisano after a financial shortfall brought work to a halt. Their additions – a dome, tracery, gables and a riot of pinnacles – bring a Gothic note to the arcaded lower storeys. After the exterior's exuberance the interior disappoints, though its plain walls create superb acoustics, the finer points of which a custodian demonstrates at regular intervals. More tangibly, there's another extraordinary **pulpit** (1260), sculpted by Nicola Pisano 50 years before his son's work in the duomo (daily 9 am–1 pm and 3–7 pm. shorter pm hours in winter). Note that an all inclusive ticket is available valid for the Museo dell'Opera del Duomo, Camposanto and Museo delle Sinopie.

The Camposanto

The Camposanto is a cemetery – but not just any cemetery: it's been called the most beautiful graveyard in the world. Before Allied bombing destroyed its frescoes, it had also been described as one of Italy's three most valuable buildings (the other two were the Sistine Chapel and Venice's Scuola di San Rocco). It lies behind a wall of white marble to the left of the duomo, behind which is enclosed soil supposedly brought from the Holy Land during the Crusades. Apparently it's able to rot down a corpse to a skeleton in 24 hours (May–Sept daily 8 am–8 pm; Oct–April 9 am–5 pm).

Wander the lawns to study the Pisan way of death, or at least that practised by its wealthier burghers. To the left of the entrance take in the patches of fresco by

Benozzo Gozzoli, virtually all that survived an incendiary attack in 1944. The cloisters once boasted 2,000 square metres of frescoes, now only remembered in fragments and pre-war photographs at the entrance. Some further idea of what's been lost comes from the frescoes arranged in the Cappella Ammanati opposite the entrance, painted by an anonymous 14th-century hand.

Museo dell'Opera del Duomo

Behind the tower in the Campo's south-eastern corner the newly updated **Museo dell'Opera del Duomo**, or cathedral museum, collects together works of art gathered from the duomo, baptistery and Leaning Tower (daily summer 9 am–1 pm and 3–7 pm, winter closes 5 pm). Like many such miscellanies, the works are a mixed bag, though the highlights – sculptures by Andrea and Nicola Pisano – are exceptional.

The rest of the city

You could be forgiven for heading to the station after the Campo dei Miracoli: Pisa has only a medley of minor sights, chief of which is the **Museo Nazionale di San Matteo**, where you can ponder paintings by Simone Martini, Masaccio, Gozzoli, Fra Angelico and Pietro Lorenzetti. The museum's on the Arno next to Ponte alla Fortezza (Tues–Sat 9.30 am–7 pm, Sun 9 am–1 pm).

Make sure your return walk takes in **Piazza dei Cavalieri**, a large square lined with Renaissance palaces, the best – the Palazzo dell'Orologio – distinguished by

Practicalities in Pisa

Tourist Office Piazza della Stazione 11 (050/ 42.291). Friendly office on the left as you leave the station; good map but no accommodation service. There's another office in the north-east corner of the Campo dei Miracoli near the Leaning Tower (050/560.464).
Railway Station Piazza della Stazione (050/ 42.291 or 41.385). Located in the south of the city, well away from the Campo; take bus number 1 from the right of the station forecourt. Left luggage (24 hr).
Buses APT and LAZZI services leave from Piazza Vittorio Emanuele or the adjoining Piazza San Antonio immediately north of the station forecourt; useful links to Volterra, Lucca, Pistoia, Prato, Florence and La Spezia.
Foreign Exchange Use the bureau at the railway station, and ignore the rip-off kiosks around the Campo dei Miracoli.
Post Office Piazza Vittorio Emanuele 8.
Hostel *Casa della Giovane*, Via Corridoni 31 (050/22.732). Nice staff and clean rooms (2-, 3- and 4-bed) for women only; turn right out of the station and you're on Via Corridoni – it's a 10 min walk; reception 7.30 am–10.30 pm; 10.30 pm curfew.
Hotels Not many people stay over in Pisa, but cheap places still fill up with university students

– so call ahead. Hotels cluster around the station, Piazza Dante and Piazza dei Cavalieri, though the best spots are obviously those near the Campo dei Miracoli.
☆*Serena*, Via d. Cavalca 45 (050/24.491). Off Piazza Dante in the heart of the old quarter; popular with students despite the slightly depressing rooms (so check availability).
☆*Rinascente*, Via dell Castelletto 28 (050/ 502.436). Another popular student-filled place housed in an old *palazzo* near Piazza dei Cavalieri.
☆☆*Milano*, Via Mascagni 14 (050/23.162). In a side street off Piazza della Stazione and one of the better places handy for the station.
☆☆*Albergo Gronchi*, Piazza Arcivescovado 1 (050/23.626). Definite first choice, with elegant old-world air and gardens just behind the Leaning Tower.
☆☆*Pensione Helvetia*, Via Don G. Boshi 31 (050/41.232). Two minutes from the Campo; tidy if sparse rooms and welcoming owners.
Campsites *Torre Pendente*, Viale Cascine 86 (050/561.704). 1 km west of the Campo – follow signs from Piazza Manin immediately west of the Baptistery. A big and well-run site, with lots of facilities, but it can be hot and desperately crowded in summer.

its archway and clocktower. Here in 1208 the Pisans imprisoned one Ugolino, wrongly accused of treachery in the Battle of Meloria, which Pisa lost to the Genovese. He was starved to death, along with his sons and grandsons, an event described by Shelley in the *Tower of Famine* and by Dante in the *Inferno*. Ugolino, on the horns of a dilemma, is condemned by the poet to the eighth circle of hell for eating his own children to ward off starvation (to no avail).

Amongst the churches, detour to take in **Santa Maria della Spina** on the river at Lungarno Gambacorti, a tiny Gothic jewel, and **San Nicola** on Via Santa Maria, famous for its altarpiece of San Nicola (Pisa's patron saint) shielding the city from divine ire (fourth chapel on the right).

Pisa–Lucca
The route

After Florence and Siena you could make out a good case for **Lucca** as Tuscany's finest and most likeable city – and a place that's still relatively undiscovered. Few places are as delightful to wander. Clasped within tree-lined walls and surrounded by a swathe of grass and gardens, the quiet Roman grid of streets is dotted with tiny Romanesque churches, palaces, and enticing nooks – the sort of place, according to Henry James, that's 'overflowing with everything that makes for ease, for plenty, for beauty, for interest and good example'.

In the past it was the city in which Caesar, Pompey and Crassus formed the Triumvirate that ruled Rome in 56 BC. It was also the first Tuscan town to accept Christianity. Under the Goths and Lombards Lucca was the capital of the entire region (then known as *Tuscia*). Banking expertise and a flourishing trade in silk brought immense prosperity between the 11th and 13th centuries, mirrored by a territorial expansion that swept Pistoia and Pisa into the city's orbit. Florence might also have fallen, but for the death of Lucca's leading general, Castracani. Centuries of inconsequence followed, interrupted by the arrival of Napoleon, when the city was handed to the Emperor's sister, Elisa Baciocchi. In time the Bourbons assumed control, remaining in charge until Italian Unification. Today the city flourishes once more, thanks largely to its lingerie industry and the

Trains
A shuttle runs roughly hourly from Pisa to Lucca (24 km, 30 min), though bear in mind you can also reach the city directly either from **Viareggio** *(23 km, 30 min), Florence (78 km, 1 hr 10 min) and points in between on the 15 trains that ply the* **Florence–Prato–Pistoia–Lucca–Viareggio** *line.*

produce from its agricultural hinterland, one of the richest in Italy ('half-smothered in oil and wine and corn and all the fruits of the earth,' thought James).

Lucca

San Michele in Foro

On paper Piazza San Michele doesn't rank as Lucca's central piazza – that honour goes to the Piazza del Duomo or the characterless Piazza Napoleone close by (see below). In the flesh, however, the site of the old Roman forum (*foro*) is far and away the place in town you'll come back to most often, not least for the church of San Michele in Foro, whose façade must be one of the most astounding in Italy. Like most Lucchese churches, it's inspired by the banded marble that distinguishes most Pisan-Romanesque buildings. Here, though, the poetic confection of tiny loggias, blind arcades and wonderfully varied pillars reaches virtual perfection.

The **interior** forms a more muted contrast, partly the victim of a cash shortfall that saw the main body of the church left largely unfinished. Its main work of art is Filippino Lippi's majestically-framed *SS Jerome, Sebastian, Roch and Helena* at the end of the right nave.

The Duomo di San Martino

Lucca's marvellously asymmetrical **duomo** is the third in the city's triumvirate of important Romanesque churches (San Martino and San Frediano are the other two). It embraces some key Renaissance works, kicking off in the atrium and main **portal** with some outstanding bas reliefs by Nicola Pisano, complemented by panels in between by Guidetto da Como, the façade's chief architect.

In the more sombre **interior** your eye's soon caught by the **Tempietto**, a gaudily overdecorated octagon and home of the *Volto Santo* (Holy Face), a not altogether convincing cedar wood crucifix said to be a true effigy of Christ (reputedly carved by Nicodemus, an eye-witness to the crucifixion). Both its parentage and the means by which it came to Lucca in the 8th century are dubious. Nonetheless, it brought considerable power and kudos to the medieval church – the purpose of many a relic – and still commands immense reverence, as a spell watching some of the desperate acts of devotion performed in front of it will confirm.

Of rather more appeal to lay visitors is the **Tomb of Ilaria del Carretto** (1410), situated beyond the Tempietto on the left in a broad alcove. One of the Renaissance's most exquisite masterpieces, it's the work of the great Sienese sculptor Jacopo della Quercia.

Finally, take note of the paintings around the interior, many by leading Italian artists.

San Frediano

Out of Piazza San Michele aim to follow **Via Fillungo**, Lucca's pivotal street, through the city's medieval core. Watch out for the façade of San Cristoforo (now deconsecrated and inscribed inside with the names of Lucca's war dead), and the famous *Caffè di Simo* (at number 58), noted for its evocative turn-of-the-century ambience. This was a favourite haunt of opera-ace Giacomo Puccini, born in the city at Via di Poggio 30 close to San Michele. The house is now a museum of Puccini memorabilia (daily 10 am–4 pm, closed Mon; free).

Keep straight as the street veers right and you quickly come to Lucca's third Romanesque masterpiece, **San Frediano**, dedicated to a 6th-century Irish saint said to have saved Lucca from flood. Unlike its peers, the church's façade is free of Pisan-inspired loggias, and instead relies for its decorative impact on a vast polychrome mosaic (a 13th-century vision of *The Ascension*). This provides a stunning introduction to an equally arresting **interior**, its dim and venerable basilica home to more first-rate artistic treasures. Foremost of these is the beautiful **Fonta Lustrale**, a weighty 12th-century font carved by three different craftsmen.

The rest of the town

You can't walk a street in Lucca without seeing a poster showing **Piazza del Anfiteatro**, an arena of medieval buildings that still partly incorporates arches and columns from the city's old Roman amphitheatre. It's an evocative and unspoilt spot, even if the bulk of the theatre long vanished to build the city's palaces and churches. Two blocks east, pop into **San Pietro Somaldi**, another fine little Romanesque church, graced with the usual exterior details and a sumptuous *Assumption* in an otherwise whitewashed interior.

For the city's oddest sight follow the streets south to the austere **Case Guinigi**, a rambling labyrinth of interconnected 15th-century palaces built by the city's leading noble family. Aim for the **tower** on Via Sant'Andrea, distinguished by the holm tree incongruously sprouting from its pinnacle. You can climb the 230-odd steps for a look at the tree (and the roots in the room below), as well as great views over the city to the hazy outlines of the Apuan Alps in the distance (April–Sept Mon–Sat 9 am–7 pm; Oct–Mar 10 am–5 pm).

Lucca's not without museums, though you can safely skip the indifferent Pinacoteca Nazionale on Via Galle Tassi. The Villa Guinigi's **Museo Nazionale Guinigi** is more generally appealing, and makes up in quantity what it lacks in quality. It presents a hugely varied collection of furniture, sculpture and paintings, with a special nod towards Romanesque-era artifacts. Lucchese and Sienese artists, archeological finds, and works by della Quercia and Matteo Civitali (Tues–Sun April–Sept 9 am–7 pm; Oct–Mar 10 am–4 pm).

Having trawled Lucca's streets, leave time to amble the four-kilometre ring of **walls** girdling the old city. Built between 1500 and 1650, the ramparts were designed to take account of the advances in siege weapons, though in the event the only battle they saw was the struggle to hold back the flood waters of the River Serchio in 1812. The green space beyond them shields the old centre from the modern world, the result of a decree that cleared all vegetation in a 200-metre swathe to prevent giving cover to attacking forces. Strolling here is a great way to look down on the old streets, shaded by lines of lime, plane and chestnut trees planted atop the walls.

Practicalities in Lucca

Tourist Office Piazza Verdi (0583/53.592). A brand new office just inside the walls on the city's western edge: they rent bikes as well as providing copious amounts of information. Currency exchange is available Mon–Sat 9 am–1 pm and 3–7 pm. There's another small office off Piazza Napoleone at Via Vittorio Emanuele 40 (0583/493.639).
Railway Station Piazza Ricasoli, off Viale Cavour outside the walls (0583/47.013). For the centre (Piazza Napoleone) turn left on Viale Cavour and take the first gate on your right (Porta San Pietro, off Piazza Risorgimento); turn left on Via Carrara and second right on Via Vittorio Emanuele. For Piazza Verde climb up onto the walls and follow them left to Porta V. Emanuele.
Buses Piazza Verde. There are two separate companies and two different ticket offices. LAZZI (0583/584.876) long distance coaches leave from the square's east (righthand) edge, serving Rome, Florence, Siena, La Spezia, Pistoia, Prato, Pisa, Empoli, Viareggio; CLAP local buses leave from the southern side and run throughout northern Tuscany (0583/587.897). City buses leave from Piazza Napoleone.
Post Office Via Vallisneri, off Piazza del Duomo.
Youth Hostel Via del Brennero (0583/953.686; open Mar–Oct). About 3 km out of town – take bus number 7. Reception 6 am–11 pm; midnight curfew.
Hotels Lucca has a relative shortage of hotels, and though it's not Tuscany's busiest tourist town, places still seem to fill up. If you're stuck, backtrack to Pisa or Viareggio, or call at the CIV-EX agency at Via V. Veneto 28 (0583/56.741). The tourist office's accommodation leaflet has a good map showing the location of all hotels.
☆☆*Albergo Diana*, Via del Molinetto 11 (0583/490.368). Best choice in town, located just a block west of the duomo.
☆☆*Cinzia*, Via della Dogana 9 (0583/41.323). Around the corner from the *Diana*, close to the duomo; both quiet and relaxed.
☆☆*La Pace*, Corte Portici 2 (0583/44.981). Intimate and central – one block south of San Michele off Via Calderia.
☆☆*Ilaria*, Via del Fosso 20 (0583/47.558). Quiet spot on the canal, with friendly and studently feel and small but serviceable rooms.
☆☆☆*La Luna*, Corte Compagni. (0583/43.634). Appealing location west of Piazza del Anfiteatro.
☆☆/☆☆☆*Universo*, Piazza Napoleone/Piazza Del Giglio 1 (0583/493.678). Lucca's traditional top hotel.
☆☆☆*Hotel Rex*, Piazza Ricasoli 19 (0583/955.443). A well-fitted but dull hotel right outside the station.
☆☆☆*Celide*, Viale G. Giusti 27 (0583/955.443). One of the smarter hotels, with amiable front desk; outside the walls – turn right from the station and walk five minutes on Viale G. Giusti.
Eating The covered **market** is in Piazza del Carmine, close to Piazza del Anfiteatro, where there's an outdoor market on Wed and Sat (8 am–1 pm).
Da Giulio, Via del Tommaso 29. Probably the city's best-known and busiest mid-price trattoria, so arrive early to avoid a long wait.
Margherita, Via Sant'Andrea 8. Old, basic trattoria with no tourists, easy 'Fifties atmosphere, friendly owners, and cheap, moderately exciting food. Also a few dingy rooms to rent upstairs (closed Sun).
Da Leo, Via Tegrimi 1, behind Piazza San Salvatore off Via degli Asili. Good value food with *al fresco* eating options in summer (closed Sun).
Il Buca di San Antonio, Via della Cervia 1 (0583/55.881). Booking essential in this top-quality restaurant (closed Sun and Mon).
Festivals The *Settembre Lucchese* is a series of mostly classical music events in Sept, usually featuring at least one Puccini opera. Every third weekend of the month, Piazza del Duomo hosts one of Italy's biggest antiques markets.

Lucca–Castelnuovo di Garfagnana–Aulla

The route

The little line that strikes north from Lucca is one to ride for the scenery alone as it pushes into a little-known region of Tuscany, the **Garfagnana**.

Trains

Ten trains daily run between Lucca and Aulla (91 km, 1 hr 45 min);
Castelnuovo di Garfagnana is 45 km and 1 hr from Lucca. At Aulla 10 trains
daily run to La Spezia (20 km, 20 min) for frequent connections to Genoa or
Pisa, including four through services to Pisa daily (1 hr 10 min).

The journey

The line follows the Serchio valley virtually to its source, bounded on one side by
the ridges of the **Alpi Apuane** and on the other by the higher but more rounded
slopes of the **Orecchiella**. Both are beautiful and all but unknown mountain enclaves, each protected by regional nature parks. Both offer fine walking
possibilities, being well-mapped and criss-crossed by marked trails. For the full
brief on hiking stop off at the area's main town, **Castelnuovo di Garfagnana**,
where the tourist office by the small castle (Via F. Testi 10), or the excellent Com-
unità Montana in Piazza delle Erbe (open all year; 0583/65.169) advise on maps,
refuges and trails.

Otherwise, sit back on the train and let the mountains and broad, verdant valley roll by. A long tunnel at the head of the Serchio brings you into a still wider
and less known region, the **Lunigiana**. The train stops at **Aulla**, where you pick
up connections to La Spezia (or Parma) and the main Genoa–Pisa–Rome line.

Pisa–Volterra–(Massa Marittima)–Orbetello
The route

Most people sit back and grit their teeth for the 3 hour run between Pisa
and Rome. The scenery hardly changes for most of the journey, confined
largely to coastal plains and rippling wooded hills. This route takes you
as far as **Orbetello**, about an hour from Rome (see Rome–Cerveteri–
Tarquinia on page 262 for the run to the capital). Despite appearances,
however, the coast offers a couple of good reasons to stop, though in
both cases they require short and convenient bus excursions from the
railway. The old Etruscan hill-top town of **Volterra** is the first, somewhat
bleak in feel, but with great views, plenty of medieval streets and one of
the country's best Etruscan museums.

The second stop is **Massa Marittima**, the finest historic town in south-
western Tuscany, reached by bus from the station at Follonica. As for
Orbetello, more and more people are coming here for the beaches, curved
around the sandpits enclosing its lovely lagoon. More monied Italians
have long known about the **Argentario** to its rear, a rocky knuckle of land
with two developed and fairly chic resorts, Porto Santo Stefano and
Port'Ercole. Buses connect both of these to Orbetello (connected in turn
to its station, four kilometres distant). For easier access to **beaches**, how-

ever, you could try the brash and popular resort of San Vincenzo, or the string of more intimate places to its north – though with these you'll have to ride a slow train. Finally, if you want to go all out for beach culture and turquoise seas, take the branch line to Piombino for ferries to **Elba**. Volterra's the nicest place to **stay** en route: Massa Marittima scarcely has a hotel to its name. In emergencies the coastal resorts have plenty of modern places where you should have few problems finding a bed. Orbetello is likely to have fewer vacancies, likewise the Argentario towns, which are also more expensive than most.

The obvious **onward route** at Orbetello is to continue to Rome, but at Grosseto (north of Orbetello) a handful of trains daily run through southern Tuscany via Buonconvento to Siena – a neat way of heading across country.

Trains

Numerous trains daily ply between **Rome** *and Pisa, but be sure to catch one that stops at* **Cecina** *(54 km, 45 min) for the connection to Volterra. 7 services daily ply between Cecina and Volterra (30 km, 30 min), but 4 of these are run by buses. For* **Massa Marittima** *you'll need a train that stops at* **Follonica** *(106 km, 1 hr 30 min). 5 trains daily operate between* **Grosseto and Siena** *(101 km, 1 hr 30 min), 2 of which (the* Freccia dell'Argentario*) continue directly to* **Florence**.

The journey

Out of Pisa the train sidles across the Arno's broad alluvial plain, soon pushing into low green-tinged hills. The shapeless modern town of **Cecina** marks the beginning of the **Maremma**, the general name given to the entire coastal plain that stretches to Orbetello and beyond. Once an area of marsh (the two words are connected), it was drained by the Etruscans and then largely left to disintegrate under the Romans and through the Middle Ages. By the 19th century it was a malaria-infested region, inhabited only by charcoal burners, migrant shepherds and the famous *butteri*, or cowboys. These hardened types tended the area's indigenous white cattle and semi-wild horses (today some are hired to ride in Siena's *Palio*). Malaria was banished in the 1950s, and drainage is now all but redundant. Nonetheless, there's still something a little forlorn and melancholy about the region, particularly on grey and windswept days when the clouds are driving in off the sea. At the same time it's a distinctive and often startling landscape, distinguished by beautiful dawns and long avenues of cypress trees striding across emerald fields.

Small pockets of the old Maremma, complete with its distinctive flora and fauna, have been preserved as reserves, notably at **Bolgheri**, ten kilometres south of Cecina. Turn right out of the station and the *Rifugio Faunistico di Bolgheri* is a kilometre or so south, just past the cypress-lined lane to the village (open Fri and Sat Oct 15–April 15). Even if it's shut you could visit the huge beach at **Marina di Bibbona**, where you can walk for miles through the dunes and glorious *pineta* (pine woods) that also typify the Maremma.

Volterra

While the Maremma's natural enclaves are of marginal interest, Volterra makes a more generally rewarding stopover. Few Tuscan towns are as dramatically situated, its old centre sitting astride a lofty plateau high above bare and brooding volcanic hills. This was the sort of position favoured by the Etruscans, whose settlement here, *Velathri*, became one of the leading members of the Etruscans' 12-city federation. The town owed its pre-eminence to mineral resources and to its impregnable position (a position reinforced over the centuries by three rings of walls, large segments of which are still extant).

During the Middle Ages the town's population shrank to a third of its Etruscan figure. Worse, its mines attracted the attention of Florence, which by 1472 – following an appalling siege – managed to capture the town. This turnabout marked the beginning of the end, though Volterra's economic slide these days has been halted by its wearisome trade in alabaster (every other shop sells the stuff). It's more literal slide continues, however, in the shape of the *balze*, the eroded cliffs girding the town, whose subsidence every now and again swallows a chunk of the medieval town.

The Piazza dei Priori

Volterra's main charm lies in its cobbled and stone-slabbed streets, and the medley of arched gateways and dark-coloured palaces dotted around its medieval heart, the **Piazza dei Priori**. Two heavy *palazzi* flank the square, the 13th-century Palazzo Pretorio and the Palazzo dei Priori (1208–54), said to be Tuscany's oldest civic palace. It's known for one of its towers, the Torre del

---

Practicalities in Volterra

Tourist Office Via G. Turazza 2, just off Piazza dei Priori (0588/86.150).
Railway Station At Saline di Volterra 9 km from the town centre; 8 daily buses meet trains and run to Piazza Martiri della Libertà or Piazza XX Settembre, both about 5 minutes from Piazza dei Priori.
Youth Hostel Via Don Minzoni, at the east end of town close to Porta a Selci and signed on Via del Poggetto (0588/85.577). Excellent non-IYHF hostel in a converted mansion with a verdant garden and fine views from some rooms; reception 8 am–10.30 and 6-11 pm; curfew 11.30 pm.
Convent Convento Sant'Andrea, Piazza Sant'Andrea (0588/86.028). On the town's north-east outskirts – a short walk out from

Porta Selci or Porta a Marcoli. Cheap, peaceful converted monastic cells, some with views; open to men, woman and couples.
Hotels ☆☆Hotel Etruria, Via Matteotti 32 (0588/87.377). Central location on the town's main street.
☆☆☆Villa Nencini, Borgo Santo Stefano 55 (0588/86.386). Hotel with pool and garden outside Porta San Francesco.
☆☆☆☆San Lino, Via San Lino 26 (0588/82.250). Volterra's top hotel – swimming pool and all the trimmings – located on the street leading from Porta San Francesco.
Restaurants Osteria dei Poeti, Via Matteotti 55/57. Perhaps the town's most popular eaterie (closed Thur).

Excursion from Volterra

Massa Marittima

Ready yourself to leave the train at Follonica if you want to make the excursion to Massa Marittima, about 19 kilometres inland and accessed by half-hourly connecting buses from the station. Massa's likeable chiefly for its cathedral and central piazza, but it also boasts a mining museum and split level centre (the *Città Nuova* and *Città Vecchia*), both good for at least an hour's wandering. Once the second city of the Sienese Republic, it rode a wave of prosperity produced by its silver and copper mines. Under Siena's thumb from 1335 it enjoyed a century of high times, before subjugation by Florence and decline to a virtual ghost town. The plague, malaria and a downturn in mining all hastened its demise. Revival came with the drainage projects of the 1830s, schemes eventually completed by Mussolini. These days the town preserves a pleasing air of provincial obscurity – and by Tuscan standards doesn't see too many visitors.

The Duomo Massa is a small place and even if you overshoot the bus stop on Via Corridoni – get off when you see the duomo's campanile – it's only a short walk from the bus terminal to the central square, **Piazza Garibaldi**. One of Italy's finer medieval ensembles, the piazza's dominated by its exhilarating 13th-century **duomo**, half raised on steps and set at a deliberately oblique angle to the rest of the square. Its striped marble façade harks back to the architecture of towns further north, but it's far more than simply derivative, thanks to a capricious collection of spires, tiny columns and blind arcades (and a rather more blunt campanile).

The bare-stoned **interior** is equally appealing. The first thing you see is a vast baptistery and font (1267), carved from a single slab of marble, sheltering an equally impressive 15th-century tabernacle. Just around the corner stand some primitive, almost pagan looking sculptures from the 11th century and next to them, in marked contrast, an ancient and polished Roman sarcophagus. At the top of the left nave is a glorious *Madonna delle Grazie* by Duccio. Behind the main altar look for the *Arca di San Cerbone* (1324), a series of bas-reliefs on the life of San Cerbone, a 6th-century bishop famous for his way with animals – you'll see a flock of geese that followed him when he was summoned to Rome on heresy charges (and the bear he tamed when Totila the Hun threw him into a pit of wild animals). The main door outside has more panels on the saint's life.

The Museo Civico Before leaving Piazza Garibaldi look into the Palazzo del Podestà, the leftmost of the 2 palaces across the square to the right of the duomo. Home to a small tourist office, it's also the seat of the **Museo Civico**, worth the admission just for Ambrogio Lorenzetti's *Maestà* (1330), one of Tuscany's finest altarpieces (Tues–Sun 10 am–12.30 and 3.30–7 pm, shorter winter hours).

The rest of the town Follow your nose around the town rather than the 'tourist itinerary' laid out and signed by the town council (which takes in some pretty dull spots). Aim primarily for Via Moncini, a steep and attractive street that climbs to the walls and great arch that formed part of the old medieval defences (wander some of its alley off-shoots for their charming gardens and distant views). Across Piazza Matteotti at the top there's a small **museum** of fossils and archive photos, best seen in conjunction with the bigger and better **Miniera Museo**, situated 5 minutes from Piazza Garibaldi off Via Corridoni. A full-blown affair, the museum's 700 metres of galleries provide a chronological account of the area's mining methods and traditions (guided tours 10 am–12.30 pm and 3.30–6 pm). The **Antico Frantoio** on Via Populonia is an 18th-century oil press, accompanied by displays describing how oil was extracted (Tues–Fri 10am–noon; weekends 10 am –noon and 4–6 pm).

Practicalities in Massa Marittima

Tourist Office Piazza Garibaldi; look in also at the travel agents at Piazza Garibaldi 18 who sell bus tickets for all local destinations.

Buses If you're not heading back to the train, buses run from Massa to Siena via the abbey of San Gargano (2 daily at 8.30 am and 5.30 pm, 1 hr 30 min), as well as to Follonica and Piombino.

Hotels ☆*Cris*, Via Roma 9-10 (0566/903.830). As yet the only central hotel – though others are being built; the downstairs restaurant is also one of the cheaper places to eat in town. ☆☆*Duca del Mare*, Via Massetana Sud 25 (0566/902.284). Modern hotel on the approach road to town.

Restaurants *Da Alberto*, Via Parenti 35. Nice outdoor garden for *al fresco* eating, and one of the better of the tourist-oriented restaurants on this street (behind Piazza Garibaldi). *La Torre*, Piazza Matteotti. Quiet and attractive bar-pizzeria with a few outside tables overlooking the old town fortifications.

Porcellino (the 'Piglet's Tower') after the little porker carved on its façade. Inside, its main sight is an *Annunciation*, a sizeable fresco on the first floor by Orcagna (Mon–Sat 9 am–1 pm).

The black and striped **duomo** close by isn't one of Tuscany's best, though the rather desultory interior has some attractive medieval carvings, a pulpit attributed to the Pisanos (of Siena and Pisa pulpit fame), and a sweeping fresco of *The Magi* by Benozzo Gozzoli (in the oratory left of the entrance). The old baptistery in front of the duomo stands over the site of a pagan temple, but it's closed for longterm restoration.

The **Pinacoteca**, up Via Buonparenti from the piazza, is more promising, and contains one of Tuscany's greatest paintings, Rosso Fiorentino's bizarre *Descent from the Cross* (1520). Full of virulent colours, it's particularly notable for the bilious green used for the figure of Christ. Other notable exhibits include Taddeo di Bartolo's *Madonna and Saints*, a Signorelli *Annunciation*, Ghirlandaio's *Christ in Glory* and a fine mix of early sculpture, many carved in Volterra's local alabaster (daily 9.30 am–1 pm; June-Sept only 9.30 am–6.30 pm).

Out of the piazza on Via dell'Arco aim to see the **Arco Etrusco**, a 3rd-century BC Etruscan arch, the blackened sculptural blobs on its cyclopean ramparts variously described as old Etruscan deities or the heads of executed enemy prisoners. Otherwise stroll down Via Marchesi to the inviting green shade of the **Parco Archeologico** (daily 10 am–noon and 4–7 pm; free).

In the other direction out of the square, north of the art gallery, Porta Fiorentina takes you to a surprisingly well-preserved **Roman theatre** and **bath complex** (still being excavated), while a long walk along Borgo San Giusto to the west provides spectacular views over the plunging cliffs of the *balze*.

The Museo Guarnacci

Etruscan museums aren't to every taste, especially ones with endless rows of funerary urns – and Volterra's **Museo Guarnacci** at Via Don Minzoni 15 has 600 of them (most of them poorly displayed). Yet one or two star turns stand out, the most famous the faintly disturbing *Gli Sposi*, a carved husband and wife pairing whose peculiar embrace features on postcards all over the town. Another highlight is the **Ombra della Sera** (the 'Shadow of the Evening'), a feathery bronze figure whose limbs seem to follow the floating contours of a man's shadow. Otherwise the best of the urns are those sporting carved bas-reliefs (in terracotta, alabaster or volcanic *tufa*), most of which date from the 4th to 1st centuries BC. They're arranged mostly by subject – usually hunting scenes or voyages to the underworld.

Florence–Arezzo–Cortona–Castiglione del Lago–Orvieto

The route

A day's enough to see 2 out of 3 big-draw towns on this route. Choose, therefore, between **Arezzo** and its famous fresco cycle; the views, old streets and art gallery of **Cortona**; and the Umbrian hilltown of **Orvieto**, home to Italy's greatest Gothic cathedral. **Castiglione del Lago**, by contrast, is a quietish spot on Lago Trasimeno, Italy's fourth largest lake, ideal for swimming or swanning around on modest beaches for a couple of days.

Orvieto and Cortona both make good accommodation bases, with Cortona, on balance, the most pleasant place to spend the night. Arezzo is more impersonal, though there's a good chance of finding a bed here.

Onward routes are fairly varied. Most people head for Rome, though at Orte, a few minutes beyond Orvieto, you might pick up trains into Umbria (see Orte–Narni–Spoleto–Trevi–Foligno on page 212). At **Terontola** close to Cortona, a line strikes east towards Perugia and Assisi (see Foligno–Spello–Assisi–Perugia on page 218). **Chiusi**, a major stop south of Castiglione del Lago, offers an intermittently pretty branch line to Siena (8 trains daily, 89 km, 1 hr 30 min).

Trains

This route is a segment of the old main line between Rome and Florence, now superseded by a new high speed line. However, it still carries plenty of diretti and espressi trains on the **Rome to Florence** *run. Trains run hourly to Arezzo (88 km, 40 min), and a touch less frequently to Camucia–Cortona (116 km, 1 hr 15 min), Castiglione del Lago (133 km, 1 hr 35 min) and Orvieto (2 hr 10 min). Orvieto is an hour from* **Rome**. *Two locali services also run on the route, from Orte–Chiusi and from Chiusi–Arezzo.*

The journey

Arezzo

No-one's pretending **Arezzo** is a place to spend the rest of your life, but it's worth thinking about as a quiet base if you can't face staying in Florence. And whether you're overnighting or not, it's definitely worth an hour off the train for one of the region's most important fresco cycles, Piero della Francesca's *Legend of the True Cross*. These days the town's material well-being derives from its jewellers and goldsmiths, but in the past its position at the crossroads of trade routes over the Apennines brought it fame and prosperity. It ranked highly in the Etruscan federation of cities, and maintained a high profile under Roman rule. In 1348, however, after centuries of independence it fell into Florentine clutches.

San Francesco

Piero della Francesca, born in nearby Sansepolcro, has his masterpiece in the church of **San Francesco** (daily 7 am – 12.30 pm and 3 – 6.30 pm; free). Started in 1457, the cycle took as its theme the story of the Cross used to crucify Christ. In tracing its story from seed to crucifix, though, it also addressed the story of humanity's redemption from the starting point of original sin. This said, the sequence of events in the panels follows an artistic rather than a narrative logic. Its various battle scenes, for example, are faced off against each other, not placed in their rightful historical position. As a painter, Piero della Francesca was much concerned with the mathematics of perspective, fusing them with pale colours and enigmatic figures to produce measured but almost mystical compositions.

If the fresco's story is too much to follow, then take pleasure in simple details,

---

Practicalities in Arezzo

Tourist Office Piazza della Repubblica 22 (0575/377.678). A summer-only office outside the station on the right; the main EPT office is up from the forecourt on the first right off Via G. Monaco at Piazza Risorgimento 116 (0575/ 23.952).
Railway Station Piazza della Repubblica. Leave your bags in left luggage and walk up Via G. Monaco from the forecourt for the town centre. San Francesco and the Piero frescoes are to the right when you reach Piazza del Popolo.
Hotels Finding a room's difficult on the first weekend of the month, when Arezzo's full for a renowned monthly antiques market; otherwise things shouldn't be too tight. Most places are near the station.
Hostel *Piero della Francesca*, Via Borgo Unto 6 (0575/354.546). Private hostel near Piazza Grande.
Hotels ☆*Milano*, Via Madonna del Prato 83 (0575/26.836). Most central of the cheap options.
☆*Michelangelo*, Viale Michelangelo 26 (0575/

20.673). Decent rooms a minute from the station, but aim for beds away from what can be a noisy road.
☆☆*Cecco*, Corso Italia 217 (0575/20.986). Central, functional hotel.
☆☆*Astoria*, Via Guido Monaco 54 (0575/ 24.361). Small rooms and moderate décor, but it's big and there's always the chance of space.
☆☆☆*Europa*, Via Spinello 45 (0575/357.701). Modern and plain, but air-conditioned and just over from the station.
Restaurants *Otello*, Piazza Risorgimento 16. Opposite the tourist office and close to the *Milano*; a trendy, nicely decorated place with excellent if unadventurous food (closed Tues).
La Buca di San Francesco, Piazza Umberto I. The one the tourists know next to San Francesco, but the food's okay and the prices reasonable if you stick to basic (closed Sun and Mon).
La Torre, Piazza Grande 5. Lively unaffected pizzeria-trattoria.

such as the dawn portrayed on the righthand wall where troops opposing Constantine flee before the sign of the cross. Sir Kenneth Clark described it as 'the most perfect morning light in all Renaissance painting'.

The rest of the town

After the frescoes the next port of call is the 12th-century **Pieve di Santa Maria**, one of the region's finest Romanesque churches and – oddly – one whose arcaded façade belongs to the Pisan-inspired architecture more often found in western Tuscany. Notice the vivacious carvings above the main portal (1210) an allegory of the months of the year, and the 14th-century campanile, known locally as the 'tower of a hundred holes' after the windows on all sides. Inside the raised presbytery holds a much-restored Pietro Lorenzetti polyptych, a *Madonna, Child and Saints* (1320). Behind the church stretches the Piazza Grande, an impractically steep piazza ringed by some of the town's more diverting architecture.

You could pop quickly into the **duomo**, no great shakes, though another Piero della Francesca fresco, a *Magdalen*, graces the Tarlati tomb beyond the organ. Close by, the mainly 13th-century church of **San Domenico** is dotted with colourful frescoes and a large *Crucifix* by Cimabue (1260). There's more to the town, of course, but the other sights are more for specialists – Vasari's house in XX Settembre and the Museo Archeologico near the station being the most prominent – though if you've time, take a picnic up to the Fortezza Medicea for views of the town and the forest-covered hills of the Casentino region off to the east.

South of **Castiglion Fiorentino**, wrapped within its walls, the train enters the Valdichiana, a broad bottomed continuation of the Tiber valley to the south. Low hills on either side hold odd towns of evocative promise – like Città della Pieve, birthplace of the painter Perugino – but the scenery is only moderately pastoral, all too often spotted with light industry. **Cortona**, however, towering over its surroundings, more than lives up to its distant promise. Its nearest station is at Camucia-Cortona, from where a bus grinds through the gears on the 5 kilometre climb through terraces of vines and olives to the old town's Piazza Garibaldi.

Cortona

Views from Cortona stretch over Lago Trasimeno and the Valdichiana, sweeping across the plains to the south and mountains to the rear. Ancient in look and feel, the town's said to be as old as Troy, and was already a thriving settlement when commandeered by the Etruscans in the 8th century BC. Its latter heyday came as a Florentine vassal in the 15th century. Today it's a good place to stop over, thanks to its medieval ambience, a couple of cracking restaurants and superb nighttime view over the twinkling lights below. Only beware the increasing numbers of tourists.

What to see

Padding and panting around the town's precipitous streets is the best way to explore (Via Jannelli, Via Guelfa, Via Maffei and Via Ghibellina are some of the best). Otherwise make for **Piazza della Repubblica**, the town centre, dominated by the Palazzo Comunale, a favourite for locals to while away the early evening. The Palazzo Pretorio to the rear in Piazza Signorelli contains one of the town's two museums, the **Museo dell'Accademia Etrusca**, a mish-mash of coins, carvings, furniture and early medieval paintings. Its high spots, though, are two fascinating rooms of Etruscan remains, dominated by Cortona's most famous relic, a vast bronze chandelier (or *lampadario*). Its 15 sculpted lamps date from the 5th century BC (daily 10 am – 1 pm and 4 – 7 pm, closed Mon).

Close by, in Piazza del Duomo, however, stands a still finer museum, the **Museo Diocesano**. A small, punchy gallery, it boasts fine works by Luca Signorelli, Il Sassetta, Pietro Lorenzetti, and – its highlight – a magnificent *Annunciation* by Fra Angelico, executed during his ten-year sojourn in Cortona's Dominican monastery. Another work from this period, a *Madonna, Child and Saints*, is also on display (daily 9 – 1 pm and 3 – 6.30 pm, closed Mon).

Elsewhere, head for the church of San Francesco, near Piazza della Repubblica, and to **San Nicolo**, a Romanesque gem with a *Deposition* by Signorelli (over the main altar). Ring the bell on the lefthand side wall if the church is closed. If the custodian's on hand you may see the deft little mechanism that turns the panel round to reveal Signorelli's *Madonna and Saints* on the other side.

Also make a big effort to climb to the **Fortezza Medicea**, the castle above the town. Though often closed, its surroundings offer astounding views over the town's rooftops and across the valley and distant hills. En route you'll pass pieces of Etruscan and Roman walls, part of an ancient temple to Mars and plenty of

Practicalities in Cortona

Tourist Office Via Nazionale 72 (0575/ 603.056). Stuffed with maps and leaflets, and willing to help find accommodation.

Railway Station LFI buses run about half hourly from the station and drop you in Piazza Garibaldi outside the city wall's main gate; go through this and follow Via Nazionale (the tourist office is on your left) to Piazza della Repubblica.

Youth Hostel *Ostello San Marco* (IYHF). Via Maffei 57 (0575/601.392; March – Oct; reception closed 1 – 5 pm). Pleasant, cosy and central; cheap meals; 1 am curfew.

Hotels 6 hotels serve the centre of town, with less appealing alternatives near the stations at Camucia and Terontola. Often these aren't enough to meet demand, kept high by tourists and students.

☆☆*Athens*, Via S. Antonio (0575/603.008). Good budget choice with decent-sized rooms and nice views – though it's always busy.

☆☆*Italia*, Via Ghibellina 5 (0575/603.264). The town's only other budget option.

☆☆☆*Sabrina*, Via Roma 37 (0575/630.397). Smallest and cheapest of the more up-market hotels.

☆☆☆*San Michele*, Via Guelfa 15 (0575/ 603.348). Nicely situated on one of the town's most picturesque streets.

☆☆☆*San Luca*, Piazza Garibaldi 2 (0575/ 603.787). A simple, adequate hotel; some rooms with fine views.

Restaurants La Loggetta, Piazza Pescheria 3 (0575/603.777). A definite first choice for a small treat; a lovely position above Piazza della Repubblica; tasteful if slightly self-conscious medieval interior and excellent food at moderate prices (closed Mon).

Zerolandia, Via Ghibellina 3. Zappy, youthful and popular restaurant-pizzeria (closed Wed). *Grotta di San Francesco*, Piazzetta Baldelli 3, just off Piazza della Repubblica. More homely atmosphere and lower prices than *La Loggetta* but the food's every bit as good (closed Tues except July and Aug).

winsome picnic spots. Aim, too, to join locals in their easy-going, early-evening *passeggiata*, when the town's views, tinted with sunset, are at their most beguiling.

A few minutes on and the train curves around the reed-lined shore of Lago Trasimeno, sublime and grey-veiled with haze in sunshine, melancholy and windswept on more overcast days. **Castiglione del Lago**'s beaches are the main reason for hopping off the train (a good 15 minutes from the station), though they're being discovered by foreigners and Italians alike. The campsites are thronged in high summer, but off season the town's a nice escape from the rigours of big city sight-seeing. Most of the beaches dot the promontory below the fortified old town (the best sand is on the headland's southern edge). There are a few bars and several lakefront trattorias, otherwise the beachlife is calm and uncommercialised. You can also take boat trips and visit the idyllic little **Isola Maggiore**, busy in season, but dotted with plenty of wooded nooks if you want a touch of privacy.

Practicalities in Castiglione del Lago

Tourist Office Piazza Mazzini 10, in the old town's main square (075/952 184). Helps with accommodation and has a money exchange and boat schedules to the lake's islands.
Hotels ☆☆*Miralago*, Piazza Mazzini 6 (075/951.157). Bang on the main square, and with views of the lake to the rear.
☆☆☆*Trasimeno*, Via Roma 174 (075/952.194).
Campsites Most of the lake's many campsites are signed off the main road south of the town. The lakefront *Lido Trasimeno* (075/954.120), north of the castle, is the most central.
Restaurants *La Cantina*, Via Vittorio Emanuele 89a. Excellent – good, simple food and large, relaxed dining room.

Orvieto

The ancient Etruscan town of Orvieto hoves into view half an hour south of Castiglione, spread over the *rupa*, a cliff-edged table of rock that rises over 300 metres from the valley floor. The station is at Orvieto Scalo, an ugly new town at the foot of the cliff, linked by bus and funicular to the ramparts above.

The duomo

All streets in the old town lead sooner or later to the **duomo**, fronted by one of the most breathtaking façades of any church in Italy. It was built ostensibly to celebrate the Miracle of Bolsena (1263), in which a German priest travelling to Rome – and troubled by religious doubts – found blood dripping from the Host on to the altar cloth as he celebrated Mass. A miracle was declared and the idea for a new church launched, though it was to be 300 years before work was completed. Building was hampered by the violence of medieval Orvieto – the worst in Italy, according to Dante – and by the foot-dragging of the planners (it took 30 years just to come up with a first draft). Constant changes of style over three centuries didn't help.

The **façade** is overwhelming, a mixture of coloured mosaics, sculptures, bronzes, spires, bas reliefs, columns and dozens of capricious decorative details. Pride of place goes to 4 **pillars** alongside the doors, a highpoint of 14th-century Italian sculpture. Most are by the Sienese architect Lorenzo Maitini, also responsible for guiding the construction of the building through its most crucial phase. The reliefs describe episodes from the Old and New Testaments, but look in particular at the pillar on the extreme right, a graphic and intricately carved account of the damned being packed off to Hell.

The **interior** appears bare by comparison. In the side chapel on the right, however, is one of central Italy's finest fresco cycles, **Luca Signorelli**'s *Last Judgement* (1499–1504). The dozens of figures and sordid goings-on make compulsive viewing, particularly in the panels where the dead drag themselves from the ground. The ceiling vaults, painted 60 years earlier, are by **Fra Angelico**.

The chapel opposite, the **Cappella del Corporale**, was more modestly but still wonderfully frescoed with episodes from the Miracle of Bolsena by a local 14th-century painter, Ugolino di Prete. Frescoes in the apse are also by him.

The rest of town

Orvieto is more dour than some Umbrian hill-towns, but is still good for an hour or so's walk. Opposite the cathedral is the **Museo Faina** (9 am–1 pm and 3–

Practicalities in Orvieto

Tourist Office Piazza del Duomo 24 (0763/ 41.772). Good maps, detailed listings and a room finding service.

Railway Station It's too far to walk from the station to the centre. Instead, either take bus number 1 from the forecourt to Piazza Cahen (then follow Corso Cavour to the centre), or take the half-hourly orange shuttle bus which drops you in Piazza del Duomo. Another good way up is to take the newly restored 19th-century funicular which runs from the forecourt to Piazza Cahen. Buy bus and funicular tickets from the station bar.

Buses Services from Piazza Cahen, though the bulk of inter town buses also stop in front of the station where there's a full timetable of services. Daily buses to Todi and Perugia, and to Narni, Amelia, Terni and Viterbo.

Foreign Exchange Use the booth at Via del Duomo 7 in preference to the banks.

Hotels Rooms are easy to come by, but aim to stay in the old town rather than the characterless modern hotels in Orvieto Scalo.

☆☆*La Posta*, Via Signorelli 18 (0763/41.909). Top ranking cheap choice, with central location, much character and a small rear garden.

☆☆*Duomo*, Via Maurizio 7 (0763/41.887). Down the steps to the left of the duomo; with neat, spacious rooms.

☆☆☆*Virgilio*, Piazza del Duomo 5/6 (0763/ 41.882). Appears to have a perfect position, but only a handful of rooms have views of the cathedral.

☆☆☆*Italia*, Piazza del Popolo 13 (0763/ 42.065). Large old-style hotel and likely to have rooms when other places are full.

☆☆☆☆*Maitini*, Via Maitini 5 (0763/42.011). Best of the up-market choices.

Camping The *Orvieto* is the town's nearest campsite, 10 km away on the shores of Lago di Corbara (0744/950.240; Easter–Sept 30), reached by bus to Baschi and Civitella del Lago.

Restaurants *CRAMST-San Francesco*, Via Maitini 15 (closed Sun). Popular co-operatively run pizzeria, self service and restaurant with places for 450 (and some outside tables in summer). Walk down Via Maitini opposite the duomo for 50 metres, turn left and follow the signs.

Bottega di Buon Vino, Via della Cave 26. A charming *enoteca* annexed to a small restaurant; a good place to sample Orvieto's famous white wine; ask the owner to show you around his Etruscan well.

Grotta, Via Signorelli 5. Off Via del Duomo and close to the *Posta* hotel; a sound choice for reasonably-priced Italian staples in a friendly, old-style trattoria.

7 pm, closed Mon), a predictable collection of Etruscan remains (with great head-on views of the duomo's façade from its top floors). It's best seen in conjunction with the 6th-century BC **tombs**, situated outside town off the road back to the station (9 am–dusk; free). Alongside the duomo on the right is the **Museo dell'Opera del Duomo** (9 am–1 pm and 4–7 pm), a miscellany of artistic junk and gems given to the duomo over the centuries. Amongst a clutter of jewellery, religious vestments, pottery and stone fragments are paintings by Simone Martini and early wooden sculptures by Andrea Pisano and Arnolfo di Cambio.

Pick up a map from the tourist office opposite the cathedral and head for **San Giovenale**, a striking amalgam of a Gothic church and earlier Romanesque chapel (1005). Inside, the interior's completely covered in 14th- and 15th-century frescoes. Hunt out the tiny chapel of **San Lorenzo di Arari** (1291) a humble Romanesque antidote to the grandeur of the duomo, decorated with four frescoes in an otherwise bare interior. Also aim to walk round the walls and the edge of the cliffs for tremendous views over the surrounding countryside. Otherwise passing pleasures include the street market and 13th-century Palazzo del Popolo in Piazza del Popolo (off Corso Cavour, the town's main shopping street) and the **Pozzo di San Patrizio**, a 62-metre well sunk in 1527. Thanks to a fine piece of medieval engineering, spiral staircases woven into the stone allow you to walk to the bottom of the well; in its day water was brought up by donkeys (daily 9 am–7 pm).

Terni–Todi–Perugia–Città di Castello–Sansepolcro

The route

The *Ferrovia Centrale Umbra* (FCU) is a wonderfully scenic private line that runs through the heart of the Umbrian countryside. For most of its route it follows the river Tiber towards its source, threading past historic hill towns such as Perugia, the regional capital, and **Todi**, one of the region's most charming towns, before arriving in Città di Castello and nearby Sansepolcro. All points en route are crammed with interest, Sansepolcro being especially notable for the subtle and unsettling paintings of Piero della Francesca.

The journey

Like so many small lines, the Ferrovia Centrale belongs to another age. Stations are tiny affairs, beautifully kept, and decorated with palms and baskets of geraniums. Train interiors make few concessions to comfort – seats are hard and rustic, home to farmers, school children and country women making their weekly shopping trip to town. People know each other up and down the line;

Trains

The FCU fills crucial gaps in the state network, and for this reason remains economic to operate. You can join the line on the FS network either at **Terni** *(where the FS and FCU share a station), or at* **Perugia**, *where there is a shared station at Ponte San Giovanni (about 8 km from Perugia), or at the separate Sant'Anna FCU station in Perugia itself. Not all trains are through trains from Terni to Sansepolcro (many halt at Perugia), but services operate about once hourly. There is much stopping and starting – and buses occasionally replace trains – so study the jumbled timetable and its small print carefully. FS tickets are not valid on the line, though you can buy tickets from a separate window at Terni's FS station. Tickets are otherwise available at all FCU stations or on the trains themselves.*

gossip is exchanged, mail delivered; and odd packages, animals and farming supplies unloaded at leisurely halts en route. Scheduled stops are few, but you can ask the guard – or even the driver – to drop you at almost any point on the line.

Terni, though backed by the first mountains of the Apennines, is of little interest, and soon left behind as the single-track line hugs wooded slopes and open fields, the blue, two-carriage train rattling through one-horse hamlets and flower-filled meadows. **Acquasparta**, a quietly charming spa town, is the first stop, though you might ask to be let off at the earlier halt of San Gemini. Turn left from the station and follow the road a kilometre to the Roman ruins at **Carsulae** (they're Umbria's largest). Little-visited, but once known as the 'Pompeii of central Italy', the colony's remains are impressive, with a stretch of the original Via Flaminia still visible – complete with ruts made by chariots – along with arches, gateways, bath-houses and much more.

Todi

Todi is the main target on the line, however, a high and magnificently-situated hill town, long impervious to the 20th century, but now becoming increasingly well-known by Italians and tourists alike. Its medieval piazza is amongst the finest in Italy, home to a lovely cathedral – with one of the country's most beautiful carved choirs – and ringed by a gaunt collection of houses and palaces straight out of the Middle Ages. Make a point of exploring the narrow streets around the piazza, and notice the rings of walls which mark the town's Etruscan, Roman and medieval limits.

Churches make up the other highlights, notably **San Fortunato**, a Romanesque-Gothic masterpiece with an extravagant carved doorway and a bright, airy interior of captivating simplicity. Better known **Santa Maria della Consolazione** lies just outside the town, its design inspired by Bramante (architect of St Peter's in Rome), and considered by many to be the finest Renaissance church in Italy. Spend some time also in the public gardens to the right of San Fortunato, full of shady nooks, little walkways and views across half of Umbria.

Practicalities in Todi

Tourist Office Located under the arches in the main square, Piazza della Repubblica 23 (tel: 075/43.788).
Railway Station Todi's station is 5 km from the town. Buses meet some, but not all of the trains. You may need to wait 40 minutes for a connection. There are no taxis. Return buses to the station leave from in front of San Fortunato (tickets from the fruit shop in Piazza Jacopone nearby).
Hotels ☆*Zodiaco*, Via del Crocifisso 23 (tel: 075/882.625). Cheapest and most central hotel (though it's still outside the walls).
☆☆☆*Bramante*, Via Orvietana 48 (tel: 075/884.8381). Comfortable, converted 13th-century convent 100 metres past S. M. della Consolazione.
Restaurants *Cavour*, Via Cavour 21. Friendly and old-world place just off the main square.
Umbria, signed under the arches to the left of the tourist office in the main square. Magnificent outside terrace, but rather pricy and service can be slow.

Halts beyond Todi will depend on whether you're interested in ceramics or wine. **Deruta** has produced Italy's finest pottery since Roman times, and many pieces by its medieval craftsmen are now scattered around the world's museums. Avoid the roadside stalls near the station if you're buying, and browse instead in the numerous workshops of the new town beyond. If you've time, wander to the old town on the hill and look at the *pinacoteca*, a small art gallery which also traces the history of the area's ceramic tradition.

The last stop before the ugliness of Perugia's suburbs is **Torgiano**, home to the vineyards of Giorgio Lungarotti, one of the most celebrated of Italy's new breed of wine producers. His label on any bottle invariably guarantees a good wine. While you may not want to drink in the village – his wines are available throughout most of Italy – you may want to visit its wine museum, a fascinating look at viticulture through the ages (Palazzo Graziano, Via Bramante 6, closed Mon).

Depending on your itinerary you'll now want to return to Terni, continue northwards, or stop off in Perugia (see Foligno—Spello—Assisi—Perugia route). Beyond Perugia, the valley of the Tiber begins to close in, the hills of the Altotiberini coming down to meet green-golden fields of wheat and tobacco (the area is one of Italy's most important tobacco growing regions). Scenery aside, the attractions from here on are artistic, starting in **Città di Castello**, a town which sprawls across the valley floor with only a handful of monuments to hint at its Roman and medieval roots. Its art gallery, however, merits a halt, crammed with Umbrian and Florentine works, and the grid of streets in the centre is good for an hour or so of happy wandering.

Practicalities in Città di Castello

Tourist Office Via Raffaele de Cesare 2b (tel: 075/855.4817).
Hotels ☆*Umbria*, Via dei Gallanti 4 (tel: 075/855.4925).
☆☆☆*Tiferno*, Piazza R. Sanzio 13 (tel: 075/855.0331).

A few minutes on brings you to **Sansepolcro**, perched on the Tuscan-Umbrian border. Quiet and modest, the town nonetheless owns two superlative paintings by **Piero della Francesca**. People make long pilgrimages to see these works – the *Resurrection* and *Madonna della Misericordia* – both of which are found in the town's small art gallery in Via Niccolò Aggiunti 65. If you have time you might bus or taxi out to the small cemetery chapel at Monterchi (5 km west of the town) to see another famous piece by the same artist – the *Madonna del Parto*, the only depiction of the pregnant Madonna in Italian Renaissance art.

Piero's masterpiece is the fresco cycle in Arezzo (see Florence–Arezzo–Cortona–Castiglione del Lago–Orvieto). You might continue your journey by taking one of the buses which depart from outside Sansepolcro's station to Arezzo (the last bus leaves at 20.00 hrs and the journey takes an hour. In Arezzo you can pick up fast trains to Rome and Florence and points in between.

Orte–Narni–Spoleto–Trevi–Foligno
The route

This route strikes to the heart of Umbria's pastoral countryside, taking in three of the region's finest hill towns on the way: **Spoleto**, an unmissable spot, and the unvisited gems of **Narni** and **Trevi**. You could see all three in a day, but may well want to spend more time in Spoleto, the ideal place to **stay**. Foligno – a modern but not unattractive provincial town – has more beds and makes a good accommodation standby.

As for onward travel, the rail network in this part of the country offers a myriad of possibilities. If you go through to Foligno the obvious follow-up is to take in Perugia and Assisi, Umbria's leading towns, following the line to Terontola on the Rome–Florence run (see Foligno–Spello–Assisi–Perugia on page 218). Alternatively, after Spoleto you could double back to Terni, a major rail junction, and head either into the Abruzzo (see Sulmona–L'Aquila on page 267) or ride the rattling carriages of the private FCU line to Todi, the best of Umbria's middling hill towns (with an option to continue to Perugia and beyond: see Terni–Todi–Perugia on page 209).

Trains
Most trains on the main Rome to Florence line stop at **Orte**. *About 15 trains daily – fast and slow – operate between* **Orte** *and* **Foligno** *(83 km, 1 hr 10 min), about half of them services on the main* **Rome–Foligno–Ancona** *line.*

The journey

After ear-popping tunnels and a monotonous ride if you're headed from Rome, Orte marks the border with Umbria and the beginning of more amenable

The Italian Railway Network

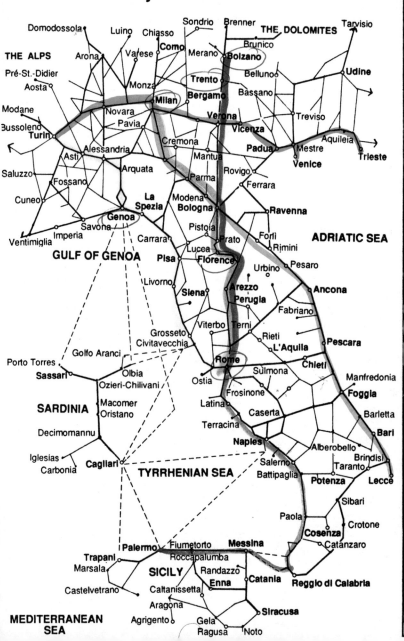

countryside. Steep-sided and oak-covered hills begin to rise from the Tiber valley and wheat fields and paddocks of white oxen replace the flat and factory-pocked plains of the Roman *campagna*. Orte itself lies away from its station, a town of Etruscan foundation set on a high rocky outcrop – the sort of site favoured by the Etruscans. Though dramatic in profile from a distance, you're better off passing over its tangle of medieval streets for the Umbrian hill towns to come. Beyond Orte the line for Foligno swings east, trundling into Umbria through the lower reaches of the Nera valley, an important tributary of Rome's great river, the Tiber. It's an inauspicious start to a region renowned for its countryside. Steel and chemical mills were introduced into the area in the 19th century, and though only a few industrial pockets remain, they're still a grim introduction.

Ten minutes or so from Orte, however, the train enters a dramatic canyon, a spectacular interlude that ends with the hilltown of **Narni**, a place of perfect medievalism tiered on a rocky ledge that edges into the gorge. As the train pulls into **Narni Scalo**, the ugly new town in the valley below, look out for the ruined arches of the **Ponte Augusto**, the remnants of a Roman bridge on the Via Flaminia, an important consular road between Rome and Ravenna.

Narni

Etruscan *Nequinum*, present-day Narni, changed its name in 229 BC under the Romans, taking on a vital strategic role as a colony on the new Via Flaminia. In guarding the Nera Gorge it controlled the major road between Rome and the Adriatic coast. As in many hill towns, its main pleasure today – and one few tourists have discovered – is walking the streets and exploring its medieval nooks and crannies (all shielded, incidentally, from the factories below).

The duomo

Buses from the station drop you in **Piazza Garibaldi**, the town's lively hub, hard up against the old medieval walls. Under an entrance arch a single main street, Via Garibaldi, bends around the 12th-century **duomo**, a gloomily atmospheric church squashed under a cramped portico. Fragments of medieval fresco dot the walls, though the most captivating works of art are two 15th-century marble pulpits and the *Sacello dei SS Giovenale e Cassio*, a Renaissance stone screen decorated with Romanesque and early Christian sculptures. Look also for the age-blackened chapel on the right, all that remains of an earlier church on the site.

Piazza del Popolo

Initially narrow and cobbled, Via Garibaldi soon widens into **Piazza del Popolo**, a gem of a square, edged with a graceful fountain (filled with goldfish), and two medieval civic palaces, the Palazzo del Podestà and Palazzo dei Priori. The former is distinguished by four small bas reliefs, wedged above the door, and a single great painting, the *Coronation of the Virgin* (1486) by Domenico Ghirlandaio. Following Via Garibaldi, renamed Via Mazzini from here on, you come upon **Santa Maria in Pensole**, a tiny and beautifully simple 12th-century church.

Further down the street comes **San Domenico**, a forlorn looking church that doubles as the town's art gallery (daily 9–1 pm, closed Sun). Most of the paintings are Umbrian pieces salvaged from local churches, with pride of place going to an *Annunciation* by the Florentine artist Benozzo Gozzoli.

Unguided meanderings through the town's multitude of arches and alleys could happily detain you for a further hour. If you want some purpose to your wanderings, head out of Piazza Garibaldi up to the vast medieval castle (or **rocca**) that lords it over the town.

Practicalities in Narni

Tourist Office Piazza del Popolo 12 (0744/715.362).

Railway Station It's too far to walk from the station at Narni Scalo to the old town; buses link from the forecourt, though they don't always tie in with trains (tickets from the station newsagents).

Hotels The town's only cheap hotels are 4 unappealing spots in Narni Scalo – for emergencies only; 2 are in Via Tuderete, the road leading straight from the forecourt; the best is the –

☆☆*Fina*, Via Tuderete 419 (0744/733.648).
☆☆☆*Minareto*, Via dei Cappuccini Nuovi 32 (0744/726.343).
☆☆☆☆*Dei Priori*, Vicolo del Comune 4 (0744/726.843). Fine hotel in a medieval *palazzo* off Piazza del Popolo and the only place to stay in the old town.

Restaurants *La Loggia*, Vicolo del Comune. Annexed to but pre-dating the *Dei Priori*, this is a deservedly noted restaurant serving plenty of moderately priced local specialities in a tasteful medieval setting.

Out of Narni the train skirts more industrial dinosaurs – steel and chemical works – before sliding through the suburbs of **Terni**, a modern town that was all but destroyed by Allied bombing in the Second World War. Rebuilding has left a grid-iron and high rise sprawl of no appeal, though you might have cause to use its station for the private *Ferrovia Centrale Umbra* line (Terni–Todi–Perugia–Città di Castello–Sansepolcro) or the minor line to the mountains of the Abruzzo (Terni–Rieti–L'Aquila–Sulmona).

Beyond Terni, though, the line breaks at last into beautiful scenery, idling through heat-hazed hills and fortified medieval hamlets. Half an hour later **Spoleto** emerges to crown the ride, presenting a medieval skyline of towers, turreted castle and orange-tiled houses, the whole tempting ensemble set against a backdrop of wooded hills and distant mountains.

Spoleto

Spoleto's station is a quaint 'Thirties affair, far more in keeping with the town's easy-going and provincial air than the huge cast iron sculpture out in the forecourt. This is the first of several monuments – some good, some awful – bequeathed to the town by the *Festival dei Due Mondi* (the 'Festival of Two Worlds'), a two-week arts, theatre and music jamboree held annually in the town for the last 30 years. Whilst bringing prosperity and fame to Spoleto, it's also meant crowds and higher prices in July and August – not to mention the odd touch of cultural pretension. Little, however, detracts from the appeal of Spoleto, one of Italy's loveliest small towns.

An Umbrian settlement in the 6th century BC (with walls from the era still extant), the town rose to prominence under the Romans when it was amongst the most important colonies in central Italy. Its importance endured through to the advent of the Lombards, who made Spoleto the capital of one of their three Italian dukedoms (Pavia and Cividale were the other two). After a brief spell as an independent *comune*, the town quickly passed to the Papacy, remaining in history's backwater until Napoleon made it the capital of a central Italian *dipartimento*.

The Lower Town

If it weren't for a trio of churches, you could ignore Spoleto's **lower town** – a mantle of modern houses ringing the hill town (raised from the ashes of Second World War bombing). The easiest of these to see is the 11th-century **San Gregorio**, tucked off Piazza Garibaldi. Marked by a gleaming portico and doughty bell tower, it's an intriguing amalgam of styles, the façade made from materials filched from Roman ruins, the interior bearing the simple stamp of the Romanesque. Notice the unusual raised presbytery, and be certain to investigate the exquisite tiny-pillared crypt. Early and well-preserved frescoes near the altar round the whole thing off.

The more impressive **San Salvatore** lies ten minutes' walk from the station, signposted from Piazza Garibaldi and located in the town cemetery. Built in the 5th century by monks from the eastern Mediterranean, it's one of the oldest churches in Italy, fronted by a crumbling façade and distinguished by an intensely atmospheric interior. Bare-walled and redolent with age, the basilica's form harks back to a Roman temple, its arches filled in to prevent collapse and the apse a jumble of awkwardly-wedged Corinthian columns. Close by, **San Ponziano** diverts by virtue of its Romanesque façade, and – if it's open – an odd and interesting crypt filled with Byzantine frescoes and triangular columns.

The Upper Town

Few spots in Italy have the unmitigated charm of Spoleto's old streets. To negotiate their twists and turns pick up a map from the tourist office in Piazza Libertà (the drop off point for buses from the station). Across from the office is the most prominent of the town's Roman remains, an over-restored but still evocative 1st century **amphitheatre**. It's used for musical and dramatic events during the festival (daily 9 am–1 pm and 3–6 pm; free).

A 100 metres north, a triumphal arch from the same era, the **Arco di Druso**, frames the entrance to the Piazza del Mercato, site of the old Roman forum, and today the town's social hub and market place. Pop into the church of **San Ansano** to the right of the arch for its 6th-century crypt, partly decorated with well-preserved patches of Byzantine fresco. Afterwards, settle down in the square for a drink or snack to watch the streetlife.

Outside the square a tangle of street unwinds suddenly to reveal the **duomo**, cradled in a fan-shaped piazza and framed by hanging gardens and lovely wooded countryside. Few sights are as beautiful as its porticoed façade, studded with eight rose windows and a glittering 13th-century mosaic, *Christ, the Virgin and St John*.

The interior, burdened with a Baroque conversion in the 17th century, contains one superb **fresco cycle**, *The Life of the Virgin* (1467) by Filippino Lippi (in the apse), and a pair of painted chapels, the **Cappelle Erioli**, immediately on the right as you enter: the eye-catching painting in the first is a *Madonna and Child* by the Umbrian painter Pinturicchio.

The alley that strikes off the Piazza del Duomo hides the **Museo Civico** (10 am –noon and 3–5 pm, closed Tues), a small collection of cannonballs, costume, sculpture, and medieval ephemera. Immediately above the Piazza to the left is the wonderful 12th-century church of **Sant'Eufemia**, unique in Umbria for its *matroneum*, an arched gallery once used to segregate the congregation's women. Built over the remains of Roman and Lombard palaces, much of the bare Romanesque interior uses fragments from the earlier buildings, the most obvious the finely crafted 8th-century column in the right nave.

Exiting, the piazza to the left brings you to the Giardini Carducci, the castle and to the Via del Ponte, a shady lane offering superb views over the Tessino gorge and the grey silhouettes of distant mountains. In five minutes it brings you to the town's most famous sight, the **Ponte delle Torri**, built to supply the castle

Practicalities in Spoleto

Tourist Office Piazza Libertà 7 (0743/220.311). Large and efficient with excellent maps.

Railway Station Piazza Palvoni (0743/48.516). It's a 15 min walk to the upper town from the station; from the forecourt walk straight down Viale Trento e Trestino, turn right through Piazza Garibaldi and follow Corso Garibaldi up the hill. A regular bus also connects the station to Piazza Libertà (tickets from the station bar).

Buses Local buses leave from the station forecourt and from Piazza Libertà. Long distance services leave from Piazza Garibaldi, between the station and the old town.

Post Office Piazza Libertà 12.

Hotels ☆*Fracassa*, Via Focaroli 15 (0743/221.177). A small, cheap lower town choice: few of the 7 rooms have bathrooms.
☆☆*Pensione dell'Angelo*, Via Arco del Druso 25 (0743/222.385). Central location above a pizzeria off Piazza del Mercato – though it's small, so call ahead or drop by early.
☆☆*Aurora* Via dell'Apollinare 4 (0743/223.256). A definite first choice amongst the cheaper places; smart rooms in a courtyard (signed off Corso Mazzini near Piazza Libertà).
☆☆*Il Panciolle*, Via del Duomo 3-4 (0743/45.598). Another excellent, central option; newly fitted rooms above an easy-going local restaurant with lovely outside terrace and medieval dining room.

☆☆*Anfiteatro*, Via Anfiteatro 14 (0743/49.853). In the lower town, so handy for the station (10 min walk). The rooms are fine, though the road below can be noisy.
☆☆*Nuovo Clitunno*, Piazza Sordini 6 (0743/38.240). Probably the best of the central mid-range places.
☆☆☆☆*Gattapone*, Via del Ponte 6 (0743/223.447). Hotels don't come much nicer; if you've come into some money, this is the place.
Camping *Monteluco* (0743/220.358; open April–Sept). A small and bucolic site behind the church of San Pietro (15 min walk from Piazza Libertà).

Restaurants *Dell'Angelo*, Via del Arco di Druso 25. Best central spot for a basic, cheap pizza, though there's a pricier restaurant alongside.
Il Panciolle, Via del Duomo 3–4. Only serviceable food, but cheap, ample portions and an excellent tree-shaded outside terrace for *al fresco* eating.
Pentagramma, Via Tommaso Martini 4. Signed immediately off Piazza Libertà. The ambience is an odd mix of red-chequered tablecloths and medieval stone walls, but this is still the best place for a slightly more up-market meal with a choice of local dishes.
Sabatini, Corso Mazzini 54. Best food, ambience and service in the Upper Town – but avoid the cheese risotto, the house speciality.

with water in the 14th century. One of Italy's greatest works of medieval engineering, the vast aqueduct measures 240 metres across and 80 metres high (making it a notorious lovers' leap).

Cross the span and turn right and a two-kilometre walk brings you to the church of **San Pietro** (clearly visible from Via del Ponte). Undistinguished inside, the façade contains the region's finest medieval carving, matched only by the sculptures on the façade of Orvieto cathedral. If you turn left, however, across the aqueduct, a level track contours around the gorge, leading quickly to peaceful countryside (and offering some fine views).

Whaleback mountains rise on the right of the train, as you leave Spoleto, and a broad plain stretches hazily out on the left, all that's left of an old lake bed drained by the Romans and now a rich if rather drab agricultural oasis. Glimpses of white-stone towers and straggling villages flash by, dominated by **Trevi**, which appears on its great pyramid of a hill after 20 minutes. Seen from below, few Italian hill towns compare for sheer spectacle, and the apparently daunting inaccessibility of the place perhaps explains why few people bother to visit. If curiosity gets the better of you, take a bus up the hill and you'll find a sleepy, immediately likeable backwater. Its most eye-catching feature is the tiny mosaics of patterned cobblestones in the immaculately kept streets, but there's also a small **pinacoteca** on Piazza Mazzini, the main square (home to a Pinturicchio *Madonna*, minor paintings and archaeological bric-à-brac). The good-looking 12th century church of **Sant'Emiliano** at the crown of the hill is spoilt by its Baroque interior, but it's held on to some colourful frescoes by a local 16th-century painter, Melanzio. The town's best pictures, however, are the canvases by Perugino in the church of **Madonna delle Lacrime** (midway between the town and the station). Another nearby church, **San Martino**, also has a smattering of good Umbrian paintings.

Practicalities in Trevi

Tourist Office Piazza Mazzini 16. A small office with irregular hours.
Hotels ☆☆*Albergo Cochetto*, Via Dogali 13 (0742/78.229). 22 rooms above the town's best restaurant (closed Tues).
☆☆*La Casarecchia*, Piazza Garibaldi 19 (0742/980.343). A few rooms above the eponymous pizzeria.

When you hit **Foligno**, one of the region's few plain-bound towns, a look at its modern and quietly provincial streets should persuade you not to bother trawling around the place. Most of the old quarter was bombed flat in the Second World War, leaving only an evocative main square (with duomo, civic palace and art gallery) and a single church, Santa Maria Infraportas, as monuments to its medieval past. It is, however, a town you might find accommodation in when hotels in Spoleto (or Assisi) are full. The tourist office is at the Porta Romana (0742/60.459) about 300 metres along Viale Mezzetti from the station. There's also an IYHF **youth hostel**, the *Ostello Fulginium* at Piazza San Giacomo 11 (0742/52.852): to reach it, take bus number 1 from the station and ask to be dropped at the *ostello*.

Foligno–Spello–Assisi–Perugia

The route

Still relatively unvisited, **Spello** merits an hour or so for its handful of churches, pinky-stoned streets and a superb fresco cycle. If time is short push on to **Assisi**, the birthplace of St Francis and undoubtedly Umbria's main cultural draw. Most of the town's many visitors are pilgrims or art lovers, both keen to see the Basilica di San Francesco, burial place of the saint and home to some of Italy's greatest paintings. The rest of the town, though, is also crammed with interest, somehow retaining its charm in the face of 2 million visitors every year.

Much the same goes for **Perugia**, the regional capital which, though surrounded by ugly suburbs, possesses an old centre of medieval streets crammed with palaces, churches and galleries. At a push you could see Perugia in a day, though try to allow two days for Assisi, the best place to stay despite its many day-trippers. Spello's accommodation prospects are pleasant, but limited. Perugia is fairly frenetic, and its central hotels likely to be busy.

Itineraries beyond Perugia are easily planned: you can continue to Terontola and thus to Rome or Florence, perhaps with stops at Orvieto or Arezzo. Heading to Rome, note that Chiusi offers connections to Siena (6 daily, 1 hr 30 min). From Perugia you might also take the private FCU line to Todi (see Terni–Todi–Perugia on page 209).

Trains

Expresses on the Rome–Ancona route stop at Foligno (see Orte–Narni–Spoleto–Trevi–Foligno on page 212 for frequency). About 15 trains daily run from Foligno to Perugia (40 km, 40–50 min); all but 3 stop at Spello (5 km, 6 min) and all stop at Assisi (16 km, 25 min). Most services continue from Perugia to Terontola (43 km, 40 min).

The Journey

Foligno

Foligno's flat sprawl is an aberration in this region of hill towns. So – to some extent – are the factories dotting its surrounding plain. Within minutes of leaving the town, however, your attention is distracted by a lumbering whaleback of mountains – Monte Subasio – once the domain of a wandering St Francis, and by the lovely walled town of **Spello**, spilling down its slopes in tiers of towers, turrets and pink-stoned houses.

The town was a way station on the old Roman Via Flaminia, and the main entrance is still the **Porta Consolare**, an arched gateway from the 1st century.

Across the road to its left be sure to visit the *Bar Ennio*, supplier of the town's top ice cream (it has the awards on the walls to prove it). Up the main street, Via Consolare (which later becomes Via Cavour), it's two minutes to the church of **Santa Maria Maggiore**, its warm 12th-century façade betrayed by a dull Baroque interior. On the left, though, behind glass, is a chapel-full of frescoes by Pinturicchio, more than enough to redeem the rest of the church.

Pinturicchio – literally the 'rich painter', after his paintings' detail and glorious colouring – was the number two Umbrian artist after Perugino. He left work in the Sistine Chapel, in Siena's Piccolomini library and in churches all over central Italy. Painted in 1501, his frescoes in Spello are some of his finest. Whilst here, wander to the left hand corner of the church where there are a couple of his intimate and often over-looked *Madonnas*.

Although you should aim to explore Spello's backstreets (the Porta Venere, a Roman gateway is a good target), the town's other sights are easily seen if you continue up the main street. On the sharp left bend before Santa Maria Maggiore look out for the **Cappella Tega**, a small street-side chapel half-smothered in 15th-century frescoes. The next church up on the right, **Sant' Andrea**, is a gloomily atmospheric spot, with a kitsch crib on the left as you enter, a mass of frescoes, and a stunning *Madonna and Child* by Pinturicchio (in the right transept). Almost at the top of the street, **San Lorenzo** is a handsome mix of Baroque styles, with many incidental points of charm. The graphic statue of St Peter the Martyr, with a cleaver in his head, is the most appealing. Take time out on the terrace bar opposite the church (the *Pinturicchio*), or climb up through the arch straight ahead for the old castle walls and some fine views.

Practicalities in Spello

Tourist Office A sparse office at Piazza Matteotti 3, midway up the main street on the right (signed *Pro Loco*).

Railway Station For the centre turn left from the forecourt, right at the main road after 200 metres and then cross over to Porta Consolare ahead of you. Via Consolare leads into town beyond it.

Convent *Santa Maria Maddalena*, Via Cavour 1 (0742/651.156). Pleasant and perfectly sited cheap rooms on the main street opposite Santa Maria Maggiore.

Hotels ☆☆*Cacciatore*, Via Giulia 42 (0742/651.156). First choice for unpretentious rooms

and relaxed family-run atmosphere; glorious terrace; try for rooms with a view and call ahead to book.

☆☆☆*Bastiglia*, Via Salnitraria 17 (0742/651.277). Up the road from the *Cacciatore*: more formal, with small, comfortable rooms, all with views.

Camping Use the *Umbria*, located in the hamlet of Chiona, 2 km east of town (0742/651.772; open April to mid-Oct).

Restaurant *La Cantina*, Via Cavour 2. Best spot in town by far; local specialities, relaxed service, and medieval setting (closed Wed).

Assisi

Back on the train there's just one station before **Assisi**, the little halt of Cannara, a suitable prelude, for the hamlet is close to the spot St Francis made his famous sermon to the birds. From this point on you'll be hard pushed to lose **St Francis**, patron saint of Italy and founder of the Franciscan movement (the world's largest monastic order). A remarkable and revolutionary man, his humility and personal example turned medieval religion on its head, moving away from the gloom of the Dark Ages to return Christianity to the basics of 'poverty, chastity and obedience'. In the process he broke the Church's rigid orthodoxy, upsetting a wealthy and morally bankrupt Papacy in the process.

Even without its Franciscan baggage, however, Assisi would still be an unmissable town, thanks to its Roman monuments, a cracking castle and a plethora of immaculately kept backstreets, fountain-splashed piazzas and geranium-hung medieval streets.

The Basilica di San Francesco

Before his death (in 1226, aged 44) Francis had asked for a simple burial – to no avail. Within two years funds had flooded in from all over Europe to finance a basilica, prompted largely by Brother Elias, the Franciscans' second leader (until a bitter series of schisms and disputes saw him ousted and excommunicated). The basilica was inaugurated in front of the Pope and full entourage, though at the last moment – to Papal disapproval – Elias whisked off the body and buried Francis behind closed doors (to save his relics from desecration). The remains weren't found until 1818, and only then after more than a month's excavations.

Many visitors, of course, come to pay homage to the saint, this ranking as the second most important point of pilgrimage in Italy after St Peter's. The great majority of lay admirers, however, are here to admire the basilica's frescoes, one of the turning points of Western art. Here, painters such as Giotto, Cimabue and Simone Martini spurred one another to greater innovation, moving art away from the hidebound strictures of Byzantine painting to a more dramatic approach that took note of human emotion, the contours of buildings, subtleties of colour, and any number of naturalistic nuances that paved the way for the Renaissance over a century later.

The Lower Church The basilica consists of two churches arranged double decker fashion, a confusing concept to read about, but perfectly clear when you're on the spot. The Lower Church came first, a wonderfully decorous building designed to house Francis's tomb and to reflect the humility of his earthly life. Almost every corner of the darkened nave and its atmospheric side chapels is painted, and you need several visits to take in the wealth of art on display. Not so long ago the monks managed to keep the crowds to a respectful silence; now all attempts seem to have been abandoned. Try to come early or late, therefore, to enjoy the art in relative peace (daily 6.30 am – 7 pm; free).

The frescoes on the walls of the nave, the basilica's earliest, are by the anonymous **Maestro di San Francesco**, and recount scenes from the life of St Francis. Many have been obliterated by the entrances of later side chapels, built to accommodate the rising tide of pilgrims. The first such chapel (on the left as you walk down the nave) houses a glorious fresco cycle by **Simone Martini**. Painted between 1310–15, they describe episodes from the life of *St Martin of Tours*, the father of monasticism in France.

Equally outstanding are the paintings in the **vaults** above the main altar, allegories of *Poverty, Chastity and Obedience* by Giotto and assistants. To their left, in the transept, are superlative frescoes (1314/1324–5) by **Pietro Lorenzetti**, another eminent Sienese artist. The most powerful panels are a stark *Deposition* (Christ being taken down from the Cross) and an extraordinary *Crucifixion*, painted against a deep blue background and drama-filled crowd of onlookers. In the opposite transept, to the right of the altar, is a famous *Madonna and Child, Angels and St Francis*, including a portrait of St Francis you'll see on postcards all over town; on the wall to its left look out for the similarly duplicated image of St Clare, founder of the Clarissans, the Franciscans' female wing.

Mid-way along the nave steps lead down to a cramped crypt and Francis's tomb, though so many Masses are held down here you'll find it difficult to catch more than a glimpse of the tomb. Walk up the steps behind the altar for a look at the cloisters and the entrance to the Basilica's Treasury, the **Tesoro della Basilica**, crammed with gifts made to the Franciscans over the centuries. Amongst them are numerous fine paintings, notably the 55-canvas Perkins Bequest, including works by Signorelli, Fra Angelico, Gozzoli, Masolino, Lorenzetti and many others.

The Upper Church Entering the soaring Gothic nave of the Upper Church ushers in an experience at odds with the cloistered solemnity of the Lower Church. Intended as a celebration of Francis's Heavenly glory, these days it appears primarily a showcase for Giotto's magnificent **fresco cycle** on the *Life of St Francis* (painted c. 1296). Arranged in a 28-panel sequence, the paintings are some of the finest in Italy, all the more impressive for their unexpected scale and excellent state of preservation. Some episodes like the *The Sermon to the Birds* will probably be familiar. In others the narrative content is self-evident if you've picked up a life of the saint from the tourist office.

The church's intricately carved **choir** repays close study, as do the strangely faded frescoes in the transepts alongside. These are the work of Cimabue, an artist described by Vasari as the 'father of Italian painting' (for introducing naturalism into Italy's Byzantine artistic heritage). He was also one of Giotto's teachers (one legend says he discovered the young Giotto scratching pictures on a stone whilst tending his father's flock). The paintings' odd appearance is due to the oxidisation of a lead pigment, producing sepia-tinged images that look like a photographic negative.

Piazza del Comune

Once the site of the old Roman forum, Assisi's lively main square, **Piazza del Comune**, is now home to a trio of sights and the starting point for exploring the town's more outlying monuments. Its most eye-catching item is the **Tempio di Minerva**, a blackened but perfectly preserved six-pillared façade from a 1st-century Roman temple (though the church behind, sadly, is of no interest whatsoever). If you haven't had enough of paintings, you might want to visit the **Pinacoteca** for its neat little collection of Umbrian offerings (daily 9.30 am– 1 pm and 3–7 pm, closed Mon). It's a touch more interesting than the **Museo Civico**, tucked away on the corner of Via San Francesco, a display of Roman fragments and parts of the old forum (daily 9.30 am–1 pm and 3–7 pm, closed Mon). Be sure to pop into both the post office and the frescoed SIP telephone offices, surely the most beautiful public service buildings in Italy.

The rest of the town

You could amble around Assisi's lesser churches and streets for hours. To be sure of seeing the key sights, however, first walk out of Piazza del Comune on Via di San Rufino and make for the **duomo**. Although graced by one of the region's loveliest façades, the church sports a desperately disappointing Baroque interior. Continue up Via di Porta Perlici from the duomo and take the first cobbled alley on your left, a short-cut to the **Rocca**, the town's fortress and a belvedere for glorious views over Assisi and the surrounding countryside. It reputedly dates

Practicalities in Assisi

Tourist Office Piazza del Comune 12 (075/ 812.534). Good map (in English) and lots of accommodation information: ask about the possibilities of staying cheaply in religious houses (*Case Religiose di Ospitalità*).
Railway Station In Santa Maria degli Angeli, the drab new town on the plain, 5 km from Assisi, centred on church of Santa Maria degli Angeli (built over the site of Francis's first monastery). Buses run to the town centre (Piazza del Comune or Piazza Matteotti) every 30 min.
Buses Leave from Piazza Matteotti to Perugia (8 daily), Foligno (via Spello, 4 daily); Gualdo Tadino (1 daily) and minor villages; to Rome and Florence (1 daily).
Hostel At Fontemaggio, a hamlet 4 km east of Assisi (075/813.636); clean, single sex 10-bed dorms. Take a taxi or follow signs from Porta Cappuccini. The adjoining campsite is under the same management.
An IYHF hostel, the *Ostello della Pace*, is due to open.
Pilgrim Hostels All the places listed below are in the town centre, all take men and women. Prices vary depending on the number in a room; singles and doubles are usually available.
Casa del Terzario, Piazza del Vescovardo 5 (075/812.366).
Suore dell'Atonement, Via G. Alessi 10 (075/ 812.542).
Monastero San Giuseppe, Via Sant'Apollinare 1 (075/812.332).
Istituto Beata Angelina, Via Merry del Val 4 (075/812.511).
Hotels Finding a room can be tough during any of Assisi's big religious festivals. Easter and *Calendimaggio* (early May) are the big two.
☆*Italia*, Vicolo della Fortezza 2 (075/812.625). Neat little hotel in an alley off the north side of

Piazza del Comune (open Mar–Oct).
☆☆*La Rocca*, Via di Porta Perlici 27 (075/ 812.284). Simple place on the north (quiet) edge of town above the duomo (5 min from Piazza del Comune). The adjoining restaurant's cheap and cheerful.
☆☆*Anfiteatro Romano*, Via Anfiteatro Romano 4 (075/813.025). Similar to *La Rocca* – same part of town, large restaurant, quiet and some rooms with views.
☆☆*Sole*, Corso Mazzini 35, (075/812.373). Large, functional spot east of the Basilica di Santa Chiara.
☆☆*Palotta*, Via San Rufino 6 (075/812.307). Tiny but okay place above a noted restaurant between the duomo and Piazza del Comune.
☆☆☆*Umbra*, Vicolo degli Archi 6 (075/ 812.240). One of the best of the more up-market choices; booking is almost essential.
☆☆☆☆*Subasio*, Via Frate Elia 2 (075/ 812.206). Venerable and traditional hotel close to the Basilica. The place to go if you're doing Assisi in style.
Campsite At Fontemaggio by the hostel (see above).
Restaurants *La Fortezza*, Vicolo della Fortezza 2b. Friendly, unpretentious and popular with locals and tourists alike: probably the best place for an averagely priced and satisfying meal.
Palotta, Via San Rufino. Cheap, very cheerful and very busy, so arrive at 12.30 pm for lunch, 7.30 pm for dinner.
Il Pozzo Romano, Via Sant'Agnese 10. Off Piazza Santa Chiara; Assisi's favourite pizzeria. *Medio Evo*, Via dell'Arco dei Priori 4. Just south of Piazza del Comune past the Chiesa Nuova, site of Francis's birthplace, this beautiful restaurant is far and away the town's best place to treat yourself.

back to Charlemagne, who is said to have raised the first walls here after sacking the town. Given the rocky crag's tremendous position, however, there was doubtless a citadel here much earlier (around the 6th century BC). Most of what you see today is a restored update of a Papal castle built in the 14th century.

The streets below the castle are some of Assisi's quietest, though for more sights you need to drop back to the main square and follow Corso Mazzini to the **Basilica of St Clare**. The church marks the burial place of St Clare, daughter of a wealthy Assisi family. Appealing on the outside, inside it's bare but for some saintly relics and the Byzantine *Crucifix* said to have bowed to Francis and ordered him to 'repair God's church'.

The vision, of course, was issuing a general instruction to revitalise Christianity. Francis, however, ingenuous as ever, took it as a literal injunction to repair the ruined church of **San Damiano**. You can see the church today, though it's a steep 15-minute walk out beyond the basilica. The trek's worth it, however, for this is one of the few places in town you still feel a sense of the original Franciscan ideals of humility and poverty. Long a home to the Clarissans, the church still preserves the trappings and atmosphere of a medieval monastery. Much the same can be said of the **Eremo delle Carceri**, now an idyllically sited monastery four kilometres east of town (taxi or walk, it's well signed), but originally the site of the caves that were home to Francis and his earliest companions.

Perugia

Perugia at first glance is a dour antidote to Assisi, grim and foreboding where its neighbour is soft-toned and welcoming. It doesn't help that the train's approach lies through endless ranks of suburbs. Once safely in the old centre, though, you're back in familiar medieval hilltown territory. The town's state university and a private university for foreigners mean there's always a cosmopolitan throng on the main thoroughfare, the **Corso Vannucci**, as good a place as any in Italy to sit and watch the world go by. It's also home to the core of the city's sightseeing – Piazza IV Novembre and the Palazzo dei Priori, seat of Umbria's premier art gallery. The Corso also leaves you well placed for the rest of the town; concentrate on its sights first, then cover the area west and north (the Oratorio di San Bernardino, Arco di Augusto and surrounding churches) before returning to the Corso and heading south for San Domenico, the Museo Archeologico and San Pietro.

Piazza IV Novembre

Once a Roman reservoir, the Piazza IV Novembre closes Corso Vannucci at its northern end, backed by the unfinished façade of the **duomo** (1345–1450), an austere Gothic creation noted more for its oddities than for any convincing works of art. The Virgin's 'wedding ring' is kept here, a three-centimetre piece of agate hidden away inside 15 individually locked boxes (kept in the first chapel on the left). Two Popes are also buried locally, their tombs marked by plaques in the transepts – Martin IV who died in the city after eating too many eels, and Urban IV who was reputedly poisoned by a mixture of arsenic and pig fat.

The square's centrepiece, the **Fontana Maggiore** (1277), is perhaps Italy's loveliest fountain, sculpted by the father and son team of Nicola and Giovanni Pisano (whose work on the pulpits of Pisa and Siena cathedrals set a benchmark for medieval sculpture). The panels around the two basins are now fairly faded, but you can still make out scenes describing the months of the year, and episodes from the Old Testament, classical myth and Aesop's fables.

Up the fan-shaped steps behind lies the **Sala dei Notari**, part of the gaunt 13th-century **Palazzo dei Priori**, the latter the medieval heart of the city. Many consider it the greatest civic palace in Italy. This particular wing was the old lawyers' meeting hall, decorated with lots of colourful but not terribly prepossessing frescoes (daily 9 am–1 pm and 3–6 pm; free).

Galleria Nazionale dell'Umbria

Walk down Corso Vannucci from the Piazza and the majestic portal in the Palazzo dei Priori marks the entrance to the Galleria Nazionale dell'Umbria, a 33-room survey of mostly Umbrian art. (Climb the stairs or take the lift to the palace's fourth floor for the ticket office; daily 9 am–2 pm, Sun 9 am–1 pm, closed Mon.)

The gallery's been in the throes of restoration for years, and some paintings may still be under wraps. The highlights, though, shouldn't be missing. These start with pieces by Duccio and other Sienese masters including Guido da Siena and Taddeo di Bartolo. The gallery also holds dozens of perfectly good if not terribly outstanding altarpieces from this early period. Two paintings, however, interrupt the Umbrian procession, magnificent works that would be worth the admission price on their own; Piero della Francesca's *Madonna and Saints with Child* (1460) and a triptych by Fra Angelico (1437) painted in Perugia for the church of San Domenico. It was the arrival of artists such as Fra Angelico, Benozzo Gozzoli and Fra Lippo Lippi that gave the Renaissance spur to Umbrian art. Their influence can be seen in the middle rooms of the gallery's chronological résumé, largely given over to Perugino and his followers. Some of the more interesting painters to look out for include Pinturicchio, Ibi, Giannicola di Paolo and Eusebio di San Giorgio.

The Collegio di Cambio

Outside the gallery and back on the Corso, turn right and a few metres down is the entrance to **Collegio di Cambio**. The old seat of the Bankers' Guild, its walls are covered with **frescoes** (1496) by Perugino (they're considered the artist's masterpiece). Notice Perugino's sour-faced self-portrait on the lefthand wall as you enter. The side chapel at the rear is by Giannicola di Paolo, a pupil of Perugino. Another pupil, Raphael, is also thought to have helped his master in the Collegio. (You'll find one of Raphael's earliest works, incidentally, in the church of San Severo off Via del Sole east of the duomo). The Collegio is open daily (9 am–12.30 pm and 3–6 pm, Sun 9 am–12.30 pm, closed Mon).

A few steps up the street is the **Collegio della Mercanzia** (1390), the meeting place of the Merchants' Guild, lined entirely with stunningly carved and inlaid wooden panelling. Tickets for the Collegio di Cambio are also valid here, and opening times are the same.

The Oratorio di San Bernardino

Through the arch in the Palazzo dei Priori pick up Via dei Priori, one of the city's best medieval streets – full of towers, tiny churches and dead end alleys – and follow it to the pleasant grassy piazza which fronts the **Oratorio di San Bernardino**. On its façade are multicoloured reliefs carved by Agostino di Duccio (1461), commissioned by Perugia's council to honour Siena's San Bernardino (who'd tried to bring peace to the city). One scene shows the saint preaching the *Bonfire of the Vanities*, urging the Perugians to cast off their more decadent trappings – you can see the pile of wigs, books and hosiery they came up with in one of the lower friezes.

Bernardino had quite a job. Perugia was described by medieval historians as the most 'warlike' of cities, and had a particularly bloodthirsty passage through the Middle Ages. The worst excesses occurred during the despotic rule of the Baglioni, an infamous family who killed each other as well as rival clans.

The Arco di Augusto

From the Oratorio walk past **San Francesco**, ruined by earthquakes over the centuries, and follow Via A. Pascoli to Piazza Fortebraccio and the **Arco di Augusto**. This ponderous gateway has Etruscan foundations, virtually the only memorial to Perugia's Etruscan heyday, a period when it formed part of the 12-city Etruscan federation. The bulk of the gateway, however, is Roman, added in 40 BC when the city fell to Rome.

To return to Corso Vannucci, pass through the arch and follow **Via Ulisse Rocchi**, Perugia's oldest street (it's 2,500 years old). To the right of the arch is another famous street, **Via del Aquadotto**, a raised causeway you'll probably have seen all over the city on postcards.

Sant'Agostino and Sant'Angelo

Up Corso Garibaldi away from the Arco di Augusto stands **Sant'Agostino**, a rather wistful shadow of its former self (most of its paintings were looted by Napoleon). One or two patches of fresco and a wooden chair suggest how it might once have looked.

At the end of the Corso Garibaldi, in a peaceful crook of the city's wall, is the 5th-century **Sant'Angelo**, a beautifully plain circular church probably built over the site of a similar-shaped Roman temple.

San Domenico

From Corso Vannucci head south for the Carducci gardens beyond Piazza Italia. Views from here are tremendous, undoubtedly the site Henry James was thinking of when he described Perugia as 'the little city of the infinite views'. Dropping down to Corso Cavour you quickly meet the looming and apparently half-derelict **San Domenico**, Umbria's largest church. Its cavernous gloom is dispelled by several works of art, the first a carved arch (1459) by **Agostino di Duccio** (fourth chapel on the right), and the second a **Gothic tomb** belonging to Benedict XI, a pope who was murdered in Perugia after reigning just eight months. Who carved the tomb, one of Italy's finest, is unknown: Giovanni Pisano, Arnolfo di Cambio and Lorenzo Maitini are all possible candidates. The stained glass

Practicalities in Perugia

Tourist Office Piazza IV Novembre 3 (Palazzo dei Priori) (075/23.327). There's also a summer-only office at the railway station. Look out for the new *Digiplan* machines at the station and around town (at Piazza Italia) which print out a range of tourist information.
Railway Station FS station Piazza Vittorio Veneto (075/70.980). It's too far to walk to the centre (4 km uphill), so take bus number 26, 27 or 33-36 from the forecourt, all of which drop you either in Piazza Italia or Piazza Matteotti (on or just off Corso Vannucci). Tickets are on sale from a kiosk on the forecourt or from a machine in the station.
The private FCU station, Stazione Sant'Anna is at Largo Cacciatori delle Alpi 8 (075/23.947). Take one of the nearby escalators (*scala mobile*) to the centre.
Buses Local ASP and long distance buses, including services to Assisi and Todi leave from Piazza dei Partigiani (reached by *scala mobile* from Piazza Italia). Information (075/61.807).
Post Office Piazza Matteotti.
Foreign Exchange Most banks on Corso Vannucci have exchange facilities; also try the CIT travel agency on the corner of Piazza IV Novembre.
Budget Travel CTS, Via del Roschetto 21, off Via Pinturicchio (075/61.695).
Albergo Diurno (day hotel) Viale Indipendenza 7 (off the *scala mobile* below Piazza Italia); toilets, showers, bath and luggage storage (open 8 am – 8 pm).
Youth Hostel Via Bontempi 13 (075/22.280). A non-IYHF hostel 2 min from the centre; take the street leading right off Piazza Dante behind the duomo. Lockout 9.30 am – 4 pm and midnight curfew.
Hotels Perugia has a fair few hotels, but accommodation can be tight during the July *Umbria Jazz* festival.
✩*Lory*, Corso Vannucci 10 (075/24.266). Almost on Piazza IV Novembre, so as central as you could wish for.
✩*Etruria*, Via della Luna (075/23.730). Take the alley by Corso Vannucci 55 for this central *pensione*.

✩✩*Anna*, Via dei Priori 48 (075/66.304). Close to the Corso on one of the city's oldest streets; quiet, period rooms, some with views.
✩✩*Piccolo Hotel*, Via L. Bonazzi 25 (075/22.987). Functional but central spot off the Corso (on the west side, 4 alleys south of Via dei Priori).
✩✩/✩✩✩*Signa*, Via del Grillo (075/61.080). Off the ancient Via Ulisse Rocchi between the Corso and the Arco di Augusto.
✩✩✩*Excelsior Lilli*, Via L. Masi (075/20.241). Convenient more up-market spot off Piazza Italia.
Camping You're probably better off taking the train on to Passignano or Castiglione del Lago for campsites on Lake Trasimeno, but the nearest to the city is *Paradis d'Eté* at Colle della Trinità 5 km away on bus number 36 (075/795.117; open all year).
Cafés *Pasticceria Sandri*, Corso Vannucci 32. By far the nicest bar in town, all polished brass, old wood and frescoed ceilings.
Caffè del Cambio, Corso Vannucci 29. One of the Corso's smarter looking bars, but not too expensive; does excellent and cheap lunchtime snacks/meals to eat in or take away and there's a straightforward restaurant downstairs if you want to take more time.
Restaurants *Del Mi'Cocco*, Corso Garibaldi 12. Just up from the Arco di Augusto; rather self-conscious in its use of Umbrian dialect on menus, but solid helpings, reasonable prices and occasionally inventive local food.
La Botte, Via Volte della Pace. A cheap family-run place popular with Perugia's teenagers; handy for the hostel.
Falchetto, Via Bartolo 20. Behind the duomo and a good, simple mid-priced place for a decent meal in medieval surroundings.
Events The 10 days of **Umbria Jazz** in July is Perugia's biggest knees-up, with top international names at venues all over the city; tickets and information from the tourist office. Other notable events include the theatrical *Teatro in Piazza* (July and Aug) and the *Sagra Musicale*, a series of sacred music concerts (Sept).

windows above are Italy's second largest, bowing only to the windows in Milan cathedral.

The church's cloisters now house the **Museo Nazionale Archeologico dell'Umbria**, a museum which is to the region's Etruscan and Roman remains what the Galleria Nazionale is to its paintings (daily Tues–Sat 9 am–2 pm, Sun 9 am–1 pm; closed Mon).

San Pietro

If you visit only one church in Perugia make sure it's **San Pietro**, a few minutes beyond San Domenico on the left. Built as the city's first cathedral, it must be one of Italy's most beautifully decorated churches. By far its best single component is the **choir** (closely followed by the pulpits). The sacristy has paintings by Perugino, Caravaggio and a disputed Raphael. The puzzling fresco splayed across the back wall is a genealogical tree of the Benedictines, collecting together the most eminent members of the Order.

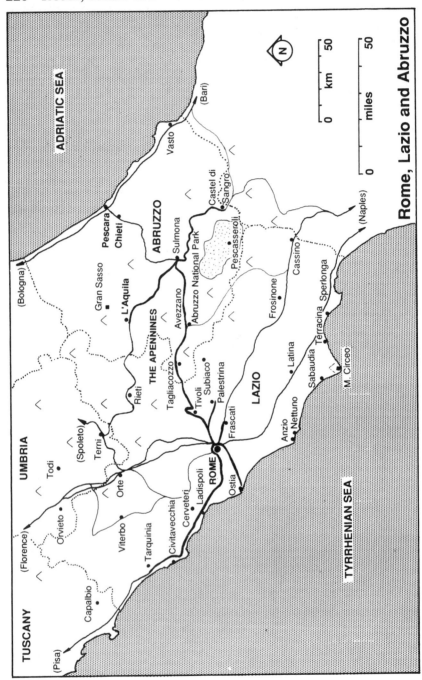

Rome, Lazio and Abruzzo

5 Rome, Lazio and Abruzzo

You probably need little persuasion to visit Rome. Unlike Florence or Venice, however, it's not a city that can – or should – be seen from somewhere else. There's so much to see you need to put down roots for a few days (but don't overdo things – it's not a place to see in one visit). Moreover, most of the incursions you want to make into **Lazio**, the region around Rome, are only sensibly made as day trips from the city. In this respect Rome's perfectly placed, with several neat branch lines pushing to sights located conveniently close to railways.

Tivoli is the most enticing, thanks to the Villa d'Este gardens and the Villa Adriana, the most sumptuous palace ever built in the Roman Empire. More vestiges of empire – if you've not had enough in Rome itself – await in **Ostia Antica**, a scarcely-visited set of ruins as good as, if not better than, any in the city. **Palestrina** has more ancient remains, though **Frascati** is a better choice if all you want is to escape Rome's cauldron for a few hours. **Cerveteri and Tarquinia** require slightly longer trips, probably of interest only to enthusiasts of Etruscan art and culture (though villages nearby offer some of the quietest beaches close to Rome).

Further afield lies the **Abruzzo**, a mountainous and backward region east of Rome. Filled with untrammelled wilderness, ancient villages and interesting medieval towns, it's a potentially fascinating area, hardly known to outsiders and still almost untouched by commercial development. **Sulmona** is its most central and useful town, especially if you're coming from Rome. It's also the departure point for trips into two of the region's finest pieces of countryside. To the north, trains run to **L'Aquila**, an appealing mountain town within a short bus ride of the **Gran Sasso**, the highest peak on the Italian peninsula. To the south, a lovely line skirts the edge of the **Parco Nazionale d'Abruzzo**, one of the country's best national parks. Both areas are great for walking, with plenty of excursions easily made from railheads.

Routes Rome

>*Rome—Frascati*
>*Rome—Ostia Antica*
>*Rome—Tivoli*
>*Rome—Palestrina*
>*Rome—Cerveteri—Tarquinia*
>*Rome—(Tivoli)—Tagliacozzo—Sulmona*
>*Sulmona—L'Aquila—Terni*
>*Sulmona—Alfedena—Castel di Sangro*

It's not so much a question of what to do around Rome as to where to go afterwards that determines the order of onward itineraries from the capital. (And it's also worth noting that you can come into the region by the back door, travelling on a quaint two-carriage train from Terni *(in Umbria) to L'Aquila via Rieti; (see* Orte—Narni—Spoleto—Trevi—Foligno *on page 212).*

After Rome it makes most sense to see Tivoli, *mainly because it's on the line that continues to Sulmona: you can see the town and then push on to the Abruzzo (*Rome—Tivoli—Tagliacozzo—Sulmona *see page 265). South of Sulmona you can plug into the complex network of tiny lines that criss-cross the south, meandering through mountain country virtually uncharted by tourists. This is the domain of the real train buff; people happy to take lines for their own sake and hang the time it takes.*

At Rome, however, you may well decide to push south *immediately, taking the main line to* Naples *(2 hr from the capital), or even pushing right down to* Sicily *(reachable in a day – just). Equally, you may blanch at the idea of the south, returning north instead towards* Florence *(2 hr) or* Pisa *(3 hr). Finally, you have the option of crossing to* Sardinia, *served by frequent ferries from Civitavecchia, north of Rome (45 min) on the* Rome—Cerveteri—Tarquinia *route.*

Rome

Rome is all the things you'd expect, and rather a lot you wouldn't. Neither built nor seen in a day, its history-soaked ruins, churches, paintings and museums would be intimidating even with a lifetime's sightseeing to spare. At the same time, however, its traffic, dreadful pollution, madding crowds and the Romans' grumpy lethargy can be intimidating in a more unpleasant manner. Rome requires you to steel yourself more than any Italian city – with the exception of Naples and possibly Palermo. This said, if you keep a firm grip on your money, avoid the heat of the afternoon, and don't attempt to see too much, then you should come away with good memories.

The sights outlined below are the tip of an iceberg, but they're the unqualified highlights. Bear in mind, however, that Rome's best moments are to be had not in staggering relentlessly from museum to monument, but in taking time out with a coffee or ice cream in one of the main piazzas. The gorgeous market-filled **Campo dei Fiori**, for example, or nearby **Piazza Navona**, make an ideal introduction to the city. They also make a good antidote to your arrival at Termini, Rome's central station, perhaps the navel of the city's sleazy underbelly. Nor should you rush headlong to the main sights: take time, instead, to acclimatise and gather your wits; leave the Colosseum, Forum and St Peter's for a while, and wander the backstreets of **Trastevere**, Piazza Navona or the old **Ghetto**. Rome is too densely packed to stick to any plan, but this sort of oblique approach will save you from the fate – which clearly befalls so many – of seeing too much of the city's present chaos and too little of its glorious past.

With a map and vague sense of direction **orientation** around central Rome isn't too difficult. Forget the famous Seven Hills which, though remembered by name have mostly been swallowed up by roads and buildings. Concentrate instead on **Piazza Venezia**, a huge traffic-filled square at the heart of the present city. Behind it rises the Monumento di Vittorio Emanuele, a huge white monument to Italian Unification (the 'altar of the Nation' in official parlance, the 'wedding cake' or 'typewriter' to most Romans). To its left is the Campidoglio, or Capitoline Hill, the nexus of the ancient city.

Roads lead to the four points of the compass from the piazza. To the east Via Nazionale leads to Stazione Termini; to the south Via dei Fori Imperiali passes the **Roman and Imperial Forums** en route for the **Colosseum** (with access to San Clemente and San Giovanni in Laterano; to the north Via del Corso strikes out towards Piazza del Popolo, passing famous spots such as the **Fontana di Trevi** and **Spanish Steps** (and the shopping area centred around Via Condotti); to the west Corso Vittorio Emanuele leads to St Peter's, bisecting the heart of medieval Rome. Most of your time will probably be spent here, or in the best of the old quarters, **Trastevere**, across the River Tiber (Tevere) south of St Peter's. Your only longer trips need be to the Villa Borghese, north of Piazza del Popolo, a large park that's home to the important museums of the **Galleria Borghese** and **Villa Giulia**.

History

Legend kicks off Rome's 2,700 year history – the story of the twins Romulus and Remus, sons of Mars and the vestal virgin, Rea Silvia. Due for ritual sacrifice, the twins were instead saved and cast adrift by their mother. They washed up beneath Rome's Palatine hill and were raised by a she-wolf. Later they returned to the site, Romulus on the Palatine, Remus the Aventine hill opposite. Both wished to form a city and both quarrelled over what it should be called (*Roma* or *Rema*). Romulus solved things by murdering his brother, becoming first king of Rome in 753 BC.

So much for legend. There was probably some sort of settlement in the hills above the Tiber marshes as early as the 12th century BC. The Isola Tiberina made a perfect spot to cross the river, and the area was on a prime trading route between the Etruscan cities to the north and the tribes of Campania to the south. Events in the city's history, however, remain hearsay until around the 4th century BC, much of it myth and conjecture put together by later writers such as Virgil and Livy. After the rule of seven Etruscan kings, the people of Rome are said to have risen up in 507 BC against the last, Tarquinius, angered by his son's attack on a Roman woman, Lucrezia (the event described in Shakespeare's *Rape of Lucrece*).

The Romans then formed the **Republic**, a system 'where the people were kings' (*res publica*). Over the next 300 years they subdued tribes to the north and south (the Etruscans, Sabines and Samnites). By the 3rd century BC the city sought to expand further, coming into conflict with **Carthage**, another great power based in North Africa. Rome eventually triumphed, defeating the Carthaginians in the three **Punic Wars** (Hannibal, Carthage's most dynamic general, was defeated during the second).

As Rome expanded, however, the ruling (patrician) classes jostled for the power, eager to snatch the wealth accruing from the spoils of an Empire (which by now extended over much of the Mediterranean). Against this background of unrest – known as the **Social Wars** – the influence of the army increased. By 48 BC, **Julius Caesar**, a leading general, came to exert dictatorial power, a power he generally used to peaceable and reforming ends. Such individualism though inevitably aroused envy and intrigue, and in 46 BC on March 15th – the Ides of March – he was murdered. Thirteen years of in-fighting then ensued before Caesar's great nephew, Augustus, proclaimed himself emperor (thus marking the start of the so-called **Imperial Age**).

The next 200 years produced many of the city's most evocative names – emperors Tiberius, Nero, Caligula, Hadrian – and many of its greatest buildings. As early as AD 275, however, the seeds of Rome's gradual decline had already been sown. In that year the emperor Aurelian was forced to build new city walls – the first for 600 years. Later, Diocletian divided the empire into east and west. No single reason, however, explains Rome's fall, rather a combination of economic stagnation, declining imperial revenues, decimated agriculture and a disintegration of political and military control. Successive invasions by the Goths, Huns, Vandals and Lombards – the so-called **Barbarians** – were simply final nails in the coffin.

Over the next 500 years the **Papacy** did much to re-establish the city. In 800 AD the Pope crowned **Charlemagne**, a Christian, head of the **Holy Roman Empire**, a domain extending over much of Europe. In the process this created problems for future popes and emperors – popes could claim emperors ruled by their consent and vice versa. This was to be the root of almost constant rivalry over several centuries (fought out in city states all over Italy – the so-called Guelph against Ghibelline confrontations). Papal fortunes hit rock bottom in 1305 when the Papacy moved itself to Avignon. By the 15th century, however, they were again in the ascendant, thanks to the wealth of the **Papal States** (the nucleus of which had been granted to the popes by Charlemagne).

Under popes like **Julius II** (1503–13) Rome entered a new phase, moving to the forefront of Renaissance endeavour. Artists such as Michelangelo, Raphael and Bramante were attracted to the city; St Peter's was built and the Sistine Chapel painted. The city's onward march was briefly interrupted by the **Sack of Rome** in 1527, when Charles V's armies ran riot, ushering in more rebuilding and a chastened Papacy. The 17th century saw the explosion of **Baroque** architecture under men like Bernini and Borromini, a period that transformed the city's churches, palaces and fountains.

During the 18th century Papal power entered a period of terminal decline. Napoleon occupied the city in 1798, establishing a republic that endured until 1815 (when the popes were restored). In 1849 an independence movement under **Mazzini** and **Garibaldi** established a further brief period of republican rule. Eleven years later the **Risorgimento** (Unification) brought modern-day Italy into being (though Rome and the popes – protected by the French – held out until 1870).

The new leaders did what every ruler before them had done: they attempted to leave their mark on Rome through grandiose building projects – new ministries, residential quarters, and roads such as Via Nazionale, Via del Tritone and Via Vittorio Emanuele. **Mussolini**, in similar mode, carved roads like Via dei Fori Imperiali through the heart of the ancient city. He also concluded the **Lateran Treaty** with the Papacy in 1929, recognising **Vatican City** and a handful of Papal properties in Rome itself as sovereign territory.

During the Second World War Rome was declared an 'open city', meaning that it was largely spared by both sides. The devastation, however, came in another guise after the war. An explosion of unplanned housing and new suburbs (the **borgate**) destroyed forever Rome's small town feel – and much of its charm – sending the population from 500,000 to something approaching today's figure of 5 million. With large-scale immigration from the south and the rural backwaters of Lazio and Abruzzo came all the traffic and social problems with which the city is still bedevilled.

What to see

Roman Monuments

Ara Pacis Augustae The Ara Pacis Augustae stands in a glass-fronted pavilion south of Piazza del Popolo close to the river. Built between 13–9 BC, the large relief-covered altar (*ara*) was intended as a memorial to the Emperor Augustus's victories in Gaul (France) and Spain, and a celebration of the peace he brought to the Empire after years of strife and civil war.

The altar stands on a tier of ten steps, with only about a third of its original carvings intact. The two-tiered **marble screen** which surrounds it, however, is far better preserved and contains some of the city's most beautiful Roman bas-reliefs. Probably the finest of the friezes is the east-facing relief, a depiction of the altar's ceremonial consecration.

Colosseo (Colosseum) You may know what the **Colosseum** is going to look like beforehand but nothing prepares you for its monumental grandeur in the flesh. It costs you nothing to admire from the outside, but it's worth paying to climb to the higher tiers for fine views of the Forum. There's also a small museum which gives you an idea of how it looked and functioned in its heyday. Aim to visit early in the morning or late in the evening to avoid the worst of the crowds (Mon and Wed–Sat 9 am–sunset; Tues and Sun 9 am–1 pm; interior free).

The arena was started by the Emperor Vespasian in AD 72, but remained unfinished at his death in AD 79. His son Titus added the finishing touches, inaugurating the 50,000-seater stadium with a gala that saw 5,000 animals slaughtered in a day; another 100 days of games and entertainments followed.

The structure was an architectural and engineering miracle, and has provided the model for large stadia ever since. Rowdy crowds could leave their seats within minutes through the 76 numbered exits or **vomitoria**. On the upper storey a huge sailcloth could be winched into place to shade spectators from the sun. Of all the surviving details, notice the half-columns on the exterior arcades, which are Doric at ground level, Ionic on the first arcade and Corinthian on the second.

Contrary to popular myth the Colosseum was not used for the mass slaughter of Christians. Its gory games and gladiatorial tussles, however, were part of the process by which – in the words of Juvenal – the Roman people sold their power in return for 'bread and circuses'. The games became ever more inventive in their desire to keep punters amused. Gladiators had originally fought in ritual combat to prepare them for battle, a practice inherited from the Samnites and Etruscans. Eventually, however, more decadent tussles saw men, women – even midgets – fight each other. If the combatants were criminals, the combat was often to the death. The arena could also be flooded to let mock sea battles take place. Spectators often exercised power of life and death, replying to a fighter's appeal for mercy (raising a finger on the left hand) with the waving of handkerchiefs (a let-off) or with the more famous down-turned thumb. Survivors usually had their throats cut anyway, and even the dead were poked with red-hot irons to ensure they weren't feigning death.

The combats were finally outlawed in AD 438 and the last recorded show involving animals took place in 523. During the Dark Ages after the Empire's fall, fires and earthquakes took their toll on the Colosseum. In 664 the metal clamps that had bound the travertine blocks together were removed, leaving the distinctive holes that pock the exterior today. Over the centuries the arena became a huge quarry, unashamedly pillaged by the Romans to build churches, palaces and bridges. Pope Benedict XIV stopped the practice in 1744, consecrating the site in memory of the Christians reputedly martyred there. Later popes began the process of restoration, something – what with traffic and pollution – which is needed today more than ever.

Immediately alongside the Colosseum stands the **Arco di Constantino**, a superb and recently restored triumphal arch. Such arches were much favoured by the Romans, and were raised to honour emperors and victorious generals. Only three in Rome preserve their former grandeur (the others are the Arco di Tito and Arco di Settimio Severo, both in the Forum). Elsewhere, however, they've had considerable influence, as London's Marble Arch and Paris's Arc de Triomphe testify.

Constantine's arch was erected in 315, one of the last great monuments built in ancient Rome. It was intended to celebrate the Battle of Milvian Bridge, an encounter where Constantine defeated his rival emperor, Maxentius. Most of its decorative reliefs are filched from earlier buildings – partly a pragmatic move (it saved carving new ones), but also an attempt to link Constantine's exploits with those of his predecessors. The most notable borrowings are the vivid battle scenes in the central arch, which show the Emperor Titus at war with the Dacians.

Fori Imperiali It's easy to confuse the Fori Imperiali with the Foro Romano (Roman Forum) close by. The former were built by emperors after Augustus as the original forum filled up, leaving too little room for business and – more to the point – the emperor's self-congratulatory building projects. Most now lie buried beneath Mussolini's Via dei Fori Imperiali, a road built partly as a stage for his own imperial triumphs – such as they were – and partly to improve the view from his office in Piazza Venezia.

On the whole there's not much to see. Julius Caesar was the first to build (54–46 BC), though two thirds of his **Foro di Cesare** lies under Via dei Fori Imperiali. Only three columns remain as its memorial (on left of road as you face Piazza

Venezia from Via Cavour). 'I found Rome brick and left it marble' was Augustus's famous boast, though little survives of his **Foro di Augusto** (to the right of Via dei Fori Imperiali and its gardens). Its best relics are three large columns from the Tempio di Mars Ultor ('Mars the Avenger'), built to commemorate the Battle of Philippi in 42 BC where Augustus defeated Brutus and Cassius (two of Caesar's murderers). The **Foro di Nerva** (AD 96–98) is now little more than a fragment, but a fine one, consisting of a temple to Minerva and lovely frieze on the corner of Via Cavour.

The best of the fora is the **Foro Traiano** (AD 107–113), mainly wistful piles of stones and columns, but redeemed by the **Colonna Traiano**. Built in AD 113, the column commemorated Rome's victory over the Dacians (a tribe from present day Romania). Its 18 marble drums contain a 200-metre frieze, its 2,500 carved figures one of the best surviving records of Roman arms and modes of warfare. The statue on the top is St Peter, replacing one of Trajan which was conveniently 'lost' in 1588 to make way for a more suitable Christian icon. You'll get your best look at this forum, however, if you walk up to the start of Via Nazionale (take the steps up the slope behind the column). At number 94 is the entrance to the **Mercato Traiano**, the well-preserved remains of a large market built as part of Trajan's forum. You can wander around about 150 booths on three levels – now in brick without their original marble facing – where all the staples and exotica of the Empire were traded. The huge curving wall or *exedra* was built to shore up the slopes of the Quirinale hill, a large spur of which was excavated to make way for the forum (Tues–Sun, 9 am–1 pm).

Foro Romano (Roman Forum) It can be confusing and disappointing to walk around the jumble of stones and overgrown ruins that make up the **Roman Forum**. It's hard to believe this was once the heart of republican Rome and centre of most of the known world for several centuries. Too much has been destroyed or plundered over the centuries to suggest its former splendour. Its small area was also developed for over 1,000 years, with the result that buildings were pulled down, altered or enlarged to leave what today is a superimposed – and still only partially excavated – mixture of monuments from different eras. Perhaps the best way to enjoy the forum is as a romantic collection of ruins, taking advantage of their better preserved fragments to assemble a picture of how it might all have looked. The forum is open 9 am–1 hour before dusk Mon and Wed–Sat; Tues and Sun 9 am–1 pm.

Originally the area was a marshy hollow between the Palatine and Capitoline hills. Later it was an Iron Age cemetery, probably known as the *forum*, or 'outside the walls'. In time it became a rubbish tip for the settlements on the hills, and eventually a marketplace for local tribes. As the Empire grew, however, it accumulated all the structures of civic, social and political life. Consuls, senators and emperors vied to outdo each other in the magnificence of their embellishments, the building frenzy only abating around the 2nd century. Then political power moved to the Palatine (see below), trade to the Mercato Traiano, and new building projects to the Fori Imperiali.

The entrance to the forum is on Via dei Fori Imperiali directly opposite where it is met by Via Cavour. Before entering, however, be sure to take in its general plan from the vantage points on Via del Campidoglio (on the northern side of Piazza del Campidoglio).

You're probably best following a roughly circular tour, starting with a right turn below the entrance on the Via Sacra (Rome's oldest and most important street). Immediately on the right are six columns and a lovely frieze from the **Tempio di Antonio e Faustina** (AD 141), built by Antonio to honour his wife Faustina, though according to Roman gossip, he was the only man in the city to remain unaware of her constant infidelities. It's been a church, San Lorenzo in Miranda, since the 11th century, one reason it's survived in such good condition.

Turning right on the still-cobbled Via Sacra the large area of stumpy columns is the site of the **Basilica Aemilia**, once a business centre and money exchange, and the Forum's first basilica – a rectangular form of building supported by rows of columns, one of the Romans' more distinctive architectural forms (it was used in numerous early Christian churches). Ahead, at the end of the Via Sacra, lie two unmistakable monuments: the dour brick blockhouse of the **Curia** and the **Arco di Settimio Severo**. The open space before them on the right was the **Comitium**, probably Rome's earliest public meeting place and the hub of its social and civic life. Processions, sacrifices and important funerals took place here, and the heads of the city's 300 districts, the *Comitia Curiata*, met to debate and cast their vote. From the law courts here the *praetor* seated on his *tribunal* handed down judgments.

The Curia was the meeting place of the Roman senate, with room for 300 senators, and probably existed in some form from Rome's earliest days. It became a church in the 7th century and lost its magnificent bronze doors (the present ones are copies) to Borromini for use in his restoration of San Giovanni in Laterano. The arch of Settimio Severo (AD 203) was built to commemorate victorious battles and ten years of the emperor's reign. Its four main reliefs show scenes from these battles, goddesses of victory and a large inscription praising Severo and his sons, Geta and Caracalla. Below the arches are the scant remains of the **Imperial rostra**, or orators' platforms, named after the bronze prows, or *rostra* of ships (used to ram other ships), used here to decorate the podiums. It was from these, supposedly, that Mark Antony made his famous 'Friends, Romans and countrymen . . .' speech following the murder of Julius Caesar. Immediately in front of the rostra is a large, lone column, the **Colonna di Foca**, raised in 608; just behind is the damaged **Arco di Tiberio** and behind that the three columns of the **Tempio di Vespasiano**, built in AD 79 by Domitian to honour his father, the Emperor Vespasian. The 12 columns to the right marked the gateway to a temple to the twelve Olympian gods, their restoration in AD 367 marking the last ever work in Rome on a pagan temple.

In front of this are eight red and grey granite columns, all that's left of the **Tempio di Saturno**, the oldest temple in the Forum (479 BC), built for the Roman god of agriculture (a deity in turn borrowed from an Etruscan god of the crops). It was the most venerated of all the early temples, probably because Rome's original power was seen to be based on agricultural acumen (possibly the reason it was chosen to house the city's state treasury).

Turning round to face back down the Forum's length, the open area of fragments on the right is the **Basilica Giulia**, once a central courthouse. At its far end is the **Tempio di Castore e Polluce**, gods revered as horsemen and the patrons of cavalry, now remembered only by three lonely columns. Immediately beyond is the large complex of ruins that mark the site of the **Tempio di Vesta**, or temple of the Vestal Virgins. The distinctive circular temple was the site of Rome's sacred flame (tended by the Vestals); the complex behind,the **Atrium Vestae**, where the Virgins lived. Only one man could enter these precincts, the *Pontifex Maximus*, or high priest, literally 'he who makes a bridge to the gods'. The cult of the flame and its guardians probably goes back to Rome's earliest tribes and the importance, literally, of keeping the home fires burning.

Only six Vestals served at any one time, chosen from wealthy Roman families before they reached the age of 14. Most remained closeted for 30 years, spending ten year periods learning, practising and then teaching the sacred rites. A Vestal's blood could not be spilt, so any lapses of chastity were punished by burial alive (male seducers were whipped or suffocated). As a reward Virgins enjoyed special privileges – none of them terribly enticing – including seats at the Colosseum and Circo Massimo (a vast racetrack still visible five minutes' walk south of the Colosseum). They could also ride in chariots in the otherwise pedestrianised Forum, extend mercy to condemned prisoners, and supervise wills and important state treaties. They were one of the last Roman institutions to die out, continuing to the end of the 4th century, well after the Empire's adoption of Christianity.

To the left of the Vestals' house (and immediately on the right of the main entrance) stands the **Tempio di Romolo**, its great columns and old bronze doors dating from around AD 309. Although superbly preserved, little's known of its history, but it may have been a temple raised by Maxentius for his son, Romulus, who died young. The Forum's last great monument is the **Basilica di Massenzio**, whose three huge coffered vaults suggest more than anything else in the Forum the monumental scope of Rome's builders.

Continuing down the Via Sacra, with the basilica on your left, you pass the church of San Francesca Romana and its distinctive campanile, entered from outside the Forum. Eventually you come to the **Arco di Tito**, framing a lovely view of the Colosseum. The arch was built in AD 81 by Emperor Domitian in homage to Emperor Titus, his brother and predecessor, and the general who captured Jerusalem in AD 70. Its bas-reliefs show several scenes of Titus's triumphal return to Rome bearing spoils from the campaign.

The Palatino (Palatine) Just before the Arco di Tito the *Clivus Palatinus*, an old Roman street, strikes off right to the **Palatino**, one of Rome's original Seven Hills and the legendary site of Romulus's first city. Today its collection of ruins is more confusing than those of the Forum (the ticket to the Forum also gains entry to the Palatine), but its beautiful gardens, groves of orange trees and numerous shady nooks make this a lovely place to wander – even if you can't make sense of the remains. During the days of the Republic this was one of the city's prime residential areas – for those who could afford it – and then the favoured area for later emperors to build their palaces. The house of Augustus, the **Domus Augustana** is here, at the top of the *Clivus*, and to its right the **Casa di Flavia**, the house of his wife, decorated with a few faded frescoes; Tiberius, Caligula and Domitian, amongst others, also built substantial properties here. The most striking ruins are Domitian's large stadium (left of the Domus Augustana) and the massive arcades of the **Domus Severiana** (overlooking the Circo Massimo). The gardens, though, which will probably take most of your time, were built over much of the area for Cardinal Alessandro Farnese in the 16th century.

The Pantheon No other monument, not even the Colosseum, gives such an idea how ancient Rome must have looked as the **Pantheon**. Built in AD 128 by Hadrian (to his personal design), the huge temple largely replaced an earlier building erected in 27 BC by Marcus Agrippa, son-in-law of Augustus. With some modesty, however, Hadrian retained the inscription still splayed across the pediment (*M. Agrippa L. F. Cos Tertium Fecit* – Marcus Agrippa, son of Lucius, consul for the third time, built this). The temple was dedicated to the 'most holy' deities, that is, the 12 Olympian gods (not 'all the gods' as the name *pantheon* seems to suggest). That it's survived almost perfectly intact is thanks to its consecration as a Christian church as early as AD 609 (the first time a pagan temple had been thus converted). Only a few pieces have gone astray over the years. The bronze gilding covering most of the dome was plundered early on and Bernini, on the orders of Pope Urban VIII, melted down the bronze of the portico's beams for the *baldacchino* in St Peter's (with enough metal left over, it's said, to furnish the Pope with 60 new cannons). Bernini also added a pair of spires to the Pantheon itself, so ridiculous that they became known as 'Bernini's donkey ears' and were removed in 1883.

The colossal **portico** is sheltered under a canopy supported by sixteen immense columns. In antiquity a ramp led up to the porch, a measure of how much street level has risen over the centuries. Inside, the **interior** is the most perfectly preserved of any ancient building in Italy. Not all of its walls and pavements are original, but their marbles conform to the earliest decorative patterns. So, too, do the eight *aedicules*, or shrines, and six recesses around the wall, which once held statues of Hadrian, Augustus and the Olympian gods. Their place these days is taken by the **tombs** of Raphael and two Italian kings, Umberto I and Vittore Emanuele I.

By far the interior's most captivating aspect, though, is the **dome**, and more particularly the nine-metre hole, or *oculus*, at its apex. This allows both sunlight and rain to pour in, but formed an integral part of the design, aiming to illuminate the interior and create a bridge between the earthly (the temple) and the divine (the heavens). The 43-metre diameter cupola itself was the largest freestanding dome in the world until as late as 1960: it was also the largest concrete construction project undertaken before this century. To ease its load, heavy travertine was mixed with concrete at the base, lighter volcanic tufa midway up and featherlight pumice at the apex. The dome's shell also became thinner towards the *oculus*, from about seven metres thick at its base to less than a metre at the crown. The distinctive coffers, or *lacunars*, indenting the dome's interior were made by pouring concrete into moulds. Note that the dome's dimensions are vital to the building's sense of harmony, its diameter being exactly equal to the height from the floor to the *oculus*; a perfect sphere, in theory, could thus be neatly fitted into the interior.

Museums and Galleries

The Castel Sant'Angelo The circular bulwarks are one of the city's more distinctive landmarks. Started in AD 130, it was intended as the tomb of Hadrian and his imperial successors, and modelled on the Mausoleo di Augusto (itself probably a copy of earlier Etruscan tombs). It continued to be used as a vault until 271 when Emperor Aurelian incorporated it into the city's defences. Thereafter it became Rome's key fortress for over 1,000 years. Once known as the *Hadrianium*, its name changed after Pope Gregory the Great's vision of an angel sheathing a sword, a sign taken to symbolise the end of a plague afflicting the city. By 847 the castle had become a Papal fortress linked to the Vatican palaces by a covered passage known as the *Passetto*. During the Middle Ages it became a prison of fearsome repute, holding such notable prisoners as Cesare Borgia, Benvenuto Cellini and Beatrice Cenci. After time as a Papal pleasure palace, and later as a barracks, the shell was restored and opened as a museum in 1933.

It's entertaining enough simply to wander the labyrinth of rooms, cells, chambers and tiny passageways that thread around the museum's four floors (Hadrian's original tombs are on the ground floor as you enter). Most of the collection has a military bent, though there are also plenty of excellent furnishings, tapestries, paintings and miscellaneous treasures amongst the lavish Papal apartments. On the second floor hunt out the façade of Leo x's chapel, designed by **Michelangelo**, and one of his less well-known works. On the third floor the Loggia of Paul III leads out on to the gallery surrounding the building, a conduit to more grand rooms and the great **Sala della Biblioteca**, a magnificent library. Be sure to climb to the terrace for superb views to St Peter's and down on to the **Ponte Sant'Angelo**, one of the city's most picturesque bridges. It's the stage for a troop of Bernini statues (1688) known as the 'Breezy Maniacs', so-called because they seem to be doing crazed battle with the wind.

The Keats and Shelley Museum (Piazza di Spagna) immediately to the right of the Spanish Steps is a must for anyone with a shred of curiosity or literary romance. Keats came to Rome for his health and died in this house in 1821, aged just 25. He's buried in the city's **Protestant Cemetery**, a beautiful spot well worth visiting in its own right (it's immediately behind the Piramide, an old Roman tomb, south of the Colosseum; take bus number 27 to Piramide). With him is what's left of Shelley, who also died in Italy, drowned off the Tuscan coast and cremated on the beach by his friends. The lovingly kept house and museum contains all sorts of Keatsian memorabilia – books, pamphlets and essays – his death mask and other literary oddities such as Shelley's half-burnt cheek bone and locks of Milton's hair (Mon–Fri 9 am–1 pm and 2.30–5.30 pm).

The Galleria Borghese (Villa Borghese) at the heart of Rome's largest and most appealing park, contains one of Rome's greatest art collections. Most of its treasures were accumulated by Cardinal Scipione Borghese, a scion of one of the city's leading medieval families and a nephew of Pope Paul V – himself a patron of Bernini, the sculptor responsible for the gallery's best exhibits. Subsidence has closed the gallery's upper floor since 1985, so opening times are somewhat haphazard until restoration is complete (Tues–Sat 9 am–1.30 pm, Sun 9 am–12.30 pm; free for duration of renovations).

Room 1 on the ground floor contains the collection's most notorious work, Canova's erotically charged statue of *Paolina Borghese* (1804), Napoleon's sister and the wife of Camillo Borghese. Rooms 2 and 3 have major works by Bernini; a *David* (whose face is reputedly a self-portrait) and *Apollo and Daphne* (1622), (considered one of the artist's masterpieces). Room 4 has a bevy of Roman busts and Bernini's *Rape of Proserpine* (1621), with a host of Classical sculptures filling subsequent rooms, the top attraction an ambiguous *Sleeping Hermaphrodite*.

Upstairs in the picture part of the gallery – if it's open – you'll see, amongst other things, a **Raphael** *Deposition*; a *Crucifixion* by Pinturicchio; a noted collection of four major **Caravaggio** paintings; Titian's highly celebrated *Sacred and Profane Love* and other pieces by Bronzino, Bernini, Giovanni Bellini, Antonello da Messina and a host of others.

The Palazzo Barberini (Via delle Quattro Fontane 13) one of Rome's grandest Baroque palaces, the Palazzo Barberini was the work of Bernini, Maderno and Borromini, three of the era's highest flying architects. It's a maze of glorious suites, apartments and sweeping staircases, but also home to the **Galleria Nazionale d'Arte Antica**, one half of the nation's outstanding 'ancient' art collection (ancient in this context means 'old' rather than Roman). The other half is in the Palazzo Corsini (see below). The Palazzo Barberini is open Mon–Sat 9 am–2 pm, Sun 9 am–1 pm.

Early rooms contain mainly high-class Renaissance paintings: works by Fra Angelico, Filippo Lippi, Piero di Cosimo, Perugino and one of the city's most famous paintings, *La Fornarina* by **Raphael**. Later rooms move on chronologically, offering more mouthwatering pictures by Titian, Tintoretto, Lorenzo Lotto, Andrea del Sarto, Caravaggio, El Greco as well as a sideshow of Flemish art dominated by Holbein's well-known portrait of *Henry VIII*. As a grand finale the palace provides the **Gran Salone**, an almost excessively decorated room over-arched by one of the masterpieces of the Baroque, Pietro da Cortona's ceiling frescoes, an *Allegory of Divine Providence*.

Palazzo Corsini (Via della Lungara 10) one of Rome's more intimate and less-visited galleries, the Palazzo Corsini houses the latter half of the Palazzo Barberini's national art collection (daily Mon–Sat 9 am–2 pm, Sun 9 am–1 pm). On display is Guido Reni's renowned portrait of *Beatrice Cenci*, supposedly painted on the eve of the poor girl's execution. Beatrice had been convicted with her mother of plotting her father's murder, allegedly driven to despair by his incestuous advances (the poet, Shelley, was just one of many inspired to creation by the story). Also on show are a rare portrait of Bernini, and panels by Fra Angelico, Murillo, Titian, Poussin, van Dyck, two Caravaggios, winter scenes by Brueghel and a noted collection of early 17th-century *chiarascuro* paintings.

Out in the palace's old gardens lie Rome's **botanical gardens** (daily 9 am – 6 pm; free), devastated by the disastrous winter of 1984, but still a lovely place for some peace and quiet amidst the din of Trastevere.

Palazzo-Galleria Doria Pamphili (Via del Corso–Piazza del Collegio Romano 1a.) Only a small part of the rambling **Palazzo Doria Pamphili** is given over to the Doria Pamphili family's artistic hoard. Nonetheless it rivals that of the Galleria Borghese as the most important of the city's old patrician collections (Tues and Fri–Sun 10 am–1 pm).

Its arrangement is haphazard, with paintings numbered rather than labelled, perhaps a ploy to sucker you into buying a guide from the ticket desk. The most treasured work is easily found, however; a portrait by **Velasquez** of *Innocent X*, a feeble and suspicious pope whose weaknesses the portrait captures perfectly. Innocent himself even commented the likeness was 'too true, too true'. Compare it with a far more flattering bust by Bernini alongside. Both are in a separate small room at the end of the third of the collection's three galleries. In the other wings the decoration alone is enough to whet appetites, but the best of the paintings – mostly in the first gallery – include two Titians (labelled 29 and 10); Raphael's *Double Portrait of Two Venetians* (23); a pair of Caravaggios (40 and 42) and Annibale Carraci's *Flight Into Egypt*.

It's also worthwhile visiting the palace's apartments, which include a decorous ballroom, chapel, Smoking Room, Winter Room and famous tapestry-hung 'Yellow Room'.

The Musei Capitolini are two museums housed opposite one another in the magnificent Michelangelo-designed **Piazza del Campidoglio** (1536). They lie to the right of Piazza Venezia's vast 19th-century 'wedding cake' memorial to King Vittorio Emanuele and the Unification of Italy. A single ticket covers both museums, which together contain some of the city's finest art and antiquities (Tues–Sun 9 am–1.30 pm, Tues and Sat also 5–8 pm; last Sun of the month free).

The **Palazzo Nuovo** on the piazza's left has the collection's smaller but richer section, kicked off by the vast statue of the river god *Marforio* in the courtyard, one of Rome's 'pasquinades' – statues to which gossipy epigrams and political graffiti were hung in the Middle Ages (usually criticising Papal corruption). The upper floor's six rooms contain some of the greatest masterpieces of Classical sculpture. Also here are 65 busts, including 'portraits' of Augustus, Caracalla, Homer and Socrates.

Across the way, the **Palazzo dei Conservatori** contains further ravishing Classical pieces, starting with the courtyard's fragments of what must have been a colossal statue of the Emperor Constantine. Upstairs stands one of Rome's most famous statues, the *Spinario*, a captivating scene of a boy removing a thorn (*spina*) from his foot. Almost as important is the *Capitoline Wolf*, an Etruscan bronze thought to date back to the 6th century BC. On the second floor there's also a high calibre **pinacoteca** with works by Titian, Caravaggio, Van Dyck, Tintoretto, Veronese, Bellini and Velasquez, amongst others.

Musei Vaticani (Vatican Museums) The Vatican museum complex is the world's largest, and you could easily spend a large part of your time in Rome wandering around its seven kilometres of rooms and galleries. Even seeing the collection's highlights might take you a couple of days. On a first visit you have to see the top attractions – the **Sistine Chapel** and **Raphael Rooms** – and then pick your way through the best of the rest before indulging the urge, if you've time or energy, to study the further-flung exhibits. It's probably not worth following the museums' four colour-coded walks, though the guide is a good investment to make the most of the collection (many works are poorly labelled).

The museums are best seen after a trip to St Peter's, about ten minutes' walk away. To reach them from Piazza San Pietro take Via della Porta Angelica right out of the square (as you face the church). At Piazza del Risorgimento turn left, following Viale Vaticano around the walls to the main museum **entrance** (Easter and June–Oct weekdays 9 am–4 pm, Oct–April 9 am–2 pm; weekends 9 am–2 pm; free last Sun of the month). You may want to charge off and see the Sistine Chapel immediately, which is well away from the entrance, but this is a roughly sequential summary of the highlights as you come to them.

Museo Gregoriano Egizio Eight well-presented rooms offer an impressive if predictable collection of Egyptian mummies, sarcophagi and monumental statues.

Museo Pio-Clementino This gives you the cream of the Vatican's gargantuan collection of sculpture, including some of the world's greatest pieces of Classical art: the Apollo Belvedere and Laocoön.

Museo Gregoriano-Etrusco Having touched on Egypt, Greece and Rome, the museums move on to the Etruscans. If the works here appeal, be sure to combine them with a visit to Rome's other great Etruscan museum, the Villa Giulia (see below).

The Galleries There's a lot of distance to cover in the museums, and much of the longer hauls involve tramping down a 400-metre triple gallery designed by Bramante. The first section is decorated with marble candelabra, reliefs and sculptures, the second with glorious **tapestries**, and the third with one of the museums' most memorable and enchanting pieces of décor: forty enormous **maps** (1580) showing Italy and the Papal states.

Stanze di Raffaello (Raphael Rooms) In 1503 Pope Julius II moved into the Vatican and commissioned the 26-year-old Raphael to decorate a suite of four rooms he could call his own. In doing so he was responsible for one of the masterpieces of the High Renaissance. Room 1, the *Stanza dell'Incendio*, was the last to be painted, by which time a new pope was on the scene, Leo X. He chose to celebrate his previous Papal namesakes – therefore the four main frescoes depict the *Coronation of Charlemagne* by Leo III; the *Oath and Self Defence of Leo III*; the *Battle of Ostia* (at which Leo IV showed mercy to the defeated Saracens in 848); and the *Fire in the Borgo* where Leo IV – actually a portrait of Leo X himself – extinguishes a fire by making the sign of the Cross.

Room 2, the *Stanza della Segnatura*, and the first to be painted, is the most renowned of the rooms. It served originally as Julius's library and the room in which Papal Bulls were signed (*segnatura* – 'signature'). The four main frescoes celebrate Theology, Philosophy, Poetry and Justice respectively. Each contains a wealth of complicated Classical and religious allusion – not to mention a cast of hundreds of eminent names connected with each discipline. Ignorance of the frescoes' finer points, however, hardly detracts from an appreciation of their beauty and virtuosity. Room 3's frescoes are allegories, each describing occasions when Divine Providence intervened to defend an endangered Christian faith. The most obvious is *Leo I Repulsing Attila the Hun* (though again, the central figure is Leo X). None of the frescoes in the last room is by Raphael, though he was responsible for some of the original drawings.

Cappella Sistina (Sistine Chapel) European art's single greatest achievement is hardly going to disappoint, but you should prepare yourself for the crowds fighting to admire Michelangelo's frescoes in the Sistine Chapel. The huge chapel was built for Sixtus IV between 1475 and 1480.

Not all the art, though, is by Michelangelo, and it's worth taking time to study the **side walls**, frescoed from 1481–3 by a collection of leading artists; Perugino, Pinturicchio, Botticelli, Ghirlandaio, Piero di Cosimo and Luca Signorelli. Panels on the left wall as you face the altar describe scenes from the life of Christ, those on the right wall episodes from the life of Moses. The finest frescoes on the left are probably Ghirlandaio's *Calling of the Apostles* (3) and Perugino's *Christ Giving the Keys to St Peter* (5); the best on the opposite wall the collaborative *Moses kills the Egyptians* (2) and Botticelli's *Punishment of Corah*.

Michelangelo's ceiling, however, is the best known of the frescoes, though it remained unpainted for 20 years after the side walls. The commission to produce a sequence of frescoes recounting Biblical stories and the history of humanity before Christ was taken up by the artist in 1508. They took four years to complete – 930 square metres of painting and 300 individual figures – painted in cramped conditions and harsh extremes of heat and cold (Michelangelo worked mainly lying down).

The rear wall contains a single majestic fresco, Michelangelo's **Last Judgement**. Perhaps even greater than the ceiling paintings, it was executed 20 years on, a time lapse that sees the artist painting in far more sombre and uncompromising mood.

Pinacoteca The Vatican's **art gallery** is the last unmissable museum of the complex, its 18 rooms crammed with what is only a fraction of the Papal collection. Early rooms open with early Tuscan, Umbrian and Sienese paintings, notably Giotto's *Stefaneschi* triptych in Room 2, which once hung in the old St Peter's. Room 3 claims Fra Angelico's *Scenes from the Life of St Nicholas of Bari* and a triptych by Lippo Lippi, Room 4 a famous portrait of *Sixtus iv* by Melezzo da Forlì. A brace of altarpieces follows, interrupted by Perugino's *Madonna and Saints* and Pinturicchio's *Coronation of the Virgin* in Room 7. Room 8 is reserved for **Raphael**, particularly his *Transfiguration*, long considered Rome's most sublime painting and chosen to hang above the artist as he lay in state. Room 9 has Rome's only Leonardo da Vinci, an unfinished monochrome overshadowed by Giovanni Bellini's lustrous *Pietà*. The subsequent room contains some fine altarpieces by Caravaggio, Guido Reni and Domenichino. The final rooms tail off with works by Titian, Caravaggio, Dutch and Flemish masters and a dreary catalogue of papal portraits.

Other museums include the **Museo Gregoriano Profano**, a collection of pagan art – mainly classical sculpture; the **Museo Pio Cristiano**, artifacts tracing the growth of Christianity; the **Museo Missionario Etnologico**, a fine, bulging anthropological collection gathered by missionary expeditions worldwide; and the **Museo Storico**, a historical record of the Papal State, full of uniforms, weapons, carriages, flags and banners.

Villa Giulia If the Etruscans are to your taste, then the **Villa Giulia** is a must. It houses the world's greatest museum dedicated to the culture that pre-dated the Romans in western central Italy (May to mid-Aug Tues–Sat 9 am–7 pm, 9 am–2 pm the rest of the year; Sun 9 am–1 pm).

The somewhat haphazard collection divides into two wings of the palace (itself a great 16th-century Mannerist creation). One takes the finds from north of Rome – Veio, Cerveteri and Tarquinia (see Rome–Cerveteri–Tarquinia on page 262), the other artifacts from the south; Nemi and Praeneste, present day Palestrina (see Rome–Palestrina on page 260). By far the most arresting piece in the museum is the **Sarcophago degli Sposi**, whose sharp-lined reliefs portray a couple wreathed in enigmatic smiles and obvious marital bliss. The other big features are the terracotta statues of **Apollo and Hercules** from Veio, and the huge array of urns and vases without which no Etruscan museum is complete. The search for some of the vases' more erotic decoration relieves the tedium, an ennui you can further lighten by seeing the **Castellani collection**, the best of all the fascinating assortment of miscellaneous objects – jewellery, bronzes, domestic utensils and the like – scattered around the museum.

Churches

Gesù (Corso Vittorio Emanuele) Built for the Jesuit order between 1568 and 1575, the **Gesù** became the model for Counter-Reformation churches all over Europe. Both the imposing façade by Giacomo della Porta, and the crushingly over-decorated interior by Vignola were to be immensely influential. The main attractions are the **Chapel of Ignatius Loyola** (1696–1700) by Andrea Pozzo and the fresco in the vaults of the nave by G. B. Gaulli, the *Triumph in the Name of Jesus*.

Sant'Andrea al Quirinale (Via del Quirinale) A tiny church with delicately carved façade, **Sant'Andrea** (1658–71) is one of Bernini's masterpieces, built for

Cardinal Camillo Pamphili, a nephew of Pope Innocent X. It's full of novel architectural conceits, from the oval interior and eight lateral chapels to the cleverly placed window that illuminates the high altar. Lavish decoration is also draped over most surfaces, its unifying theme being the story of St Andrew. The American writer Nathaniel Hawthorne loved the place, and commented, 'I only wish I could pack it in a large box and send it home.' By way of comparison, visit San Carlino designed by Bernini's great Baroque rival, Borromini.

San Carlino (Via del Quirinale) Borromini started work on this cramped and difficult site in 1634, aiming, it's said, to make San Carlino no larger than one of the four main columns beneath the dome of St Peter's. His subtle and complex interior is less immediately appealing than Bernini's Sant'Andrea, but it's as much an expression of Baroque genius. Notice, in particular, the clever three-dimensionality of the façade and the cloisters.

Santa Cecilia in Trastevere (Piazza di Santa Cecilia) Few Roman churches have as delightful an approach as Santa Cecilia in Trastevere, fronted by a Baroque gateway, lovely garden – complete with large Roman vase – gracious 18th-century façade and a 12th-century portico of Roman columns. The church was built in the 9th century on the site of a chapel that marked St Cecilia's martyrdom. She died around AD 300, the Romans having first tried to scald her in her bath. When this failed they attempted a more conventional execution. All three blows of the soldiers' swords – all they were allowed under Roman law – failed to sever the saint's head. Cecilia lived another three days converting dozens by her fortitude. She also managed to compose a song during her ordeal, and is said to have invented the organ, which is why she is the patron saint of music (her name comes from *coeli lilia* – the 'lily of heaven').

Within, the church is predominantly bad Baroque, its blandness redeemed by a famous statue of St Cecilia by Stefano Maderno, a portrait of the saint as she was found when her tomb was opened in 1599. Maderno was present at the event, and took notes, though the three nicks on the statue – the blows of her execution – are presumably artistic licence. Above the altar is a grand **canopy** by **Arnolfo di Cambio** (1293), and behind it, in the apse, a lustrous **9th-century mosaic** of Pope Paschal I. Paschal was responsible for the original church and the removal of Cecilia from Rome's catacombs in the 9th century. Her tomb is now in the **crypt**.

Although the church contains fragments of fresco (on the life of Cecilia, inevitably), the best paintings are Pietro Cavallini's *Last Judgement* (1293) in the cloister. Before the Baroque butchers got to work the frescoes covered the entire church. What's left still ranks as the masterpiece of this influential artist.

San Clemente (Via di San Giovanni in Laterano) Don't miss San Clemente, two minutes from the Colosseum, one of the city's most fascinating archaeological sites. Three distinct places of worship are layered on top of each other, neatly encapsulating three eras of religious observance in Rome. The main church (1110–30) is easily the finest medieval ensemble in the city, dominated by a stunning **choir screen**, a pair of **pulpits** and huge Cosmati **candle holder**. Behind the altar is a masterful 12th-century **mosaic**, and below it faded frescoes and a marble tabernacle by Arnolfo di Cambio. As if all this weren't enough, there are superlative frescoes on the *Life of St Catherine* (c. 1428) by Masolino di Panicale, a rare example of this influential Florentine's work.

Steps lead down to an earlier 4th-century church dedicated to San Clemente, the fourth bishop of Rome after St Peter. Much of this building was destroyed by the Normans in 1084, then filled with rubble to act as the foundations of the upper church (thus preserving much of what remained). Here you'll find important 8th-century frescoes.

Lower still, you drop into the remains of a Roman **Mithraic temple**, a dank place redolent with age. Listen out for the eerie sound of running water, thought to be an old diverted underground stream that leads to the Forum's main drain, the *Cloaca Maxima*. Mithraism was a Persian cult brought by soldiers to Rome about 50 BC, a religion that involved initiation by fire, ice and hunger, and until its outlawing in AD 395 threatened to be more popular than Christianity. Similar temples have been found as far afield as London.

San Giovanni in Laterano You'll see the huge statues atop San Giovanni from all over Rome, marking the main cathedral church of Rome (St Peter's, remember, is in Vatican City, a separate state). Its façade proclaims it the 'mother of all churches' in Italy and the world. Given to the Church by Constantine, the first Christian emperor, it housed an early *cathedra* – the bishop of Rome's throne – from which the word cathedral derives. It was the main Papal palace until the 14th century, and popes continued to be crowned here until the 19th century.

The present church retains the outlines of the original basilica, though it's been much rebuilt. The main bronze doors were brought from the original Curia or Senate House, of the Roman Forum. Most of the interior was remodelled by Borromini (1646–50), though he respected the earlier building, leaving the glorious **wooden ceiling** almost untouched. The tabernacle above the altar is reputed to contain the heads of St Peter and St Paul, though the main points of artistic appeal are the wonderful **cloister** off the left aisle, the pinnacle of the city's Cosmati tradition (the Cosmati were a family skilled in decorative marble work and their name is now given to the distinctive patterned stonework you'll see in churches all over central Italy).

Outside the church to the rear be sure to see the **Baptistery**, Italy's first, whose octagonal form was copied all over the country (in Pisa and Florence, for example). It was originally the site of the baths of Fausta, Constantine's second wife, and is the only surviving part of the earliest church. Also see the **Scala Santa**, housed across the road to the church's right, reputedly the marble staircase from Pilate's palace in Jerusalem up which Christ ascended during his trial. You gain nine years respite from Purgatory for every step climbed (on your knees).

San Luigi dei Francesi (Piazza di San Luigi dei Francesi) France's national church in Rome, San Luigi (1589) is best seen whilst walking from the Pantheon to Piazza Navona, and is known for one thing alone: three outstanding canvases by **Caravaggio**. Reviled in their time as too shockingly realistic, the pictures – on the **Life of St Matthew** – show the artist's supreme handling of light and shade to virtuoso effect.

Santa Maria d'Aracoeli (Piazza del Campidoglio) Raised over one of Rome's Holy of Holies, **Santa Maria d'Aracoeli** sits impressively near the summit of the Campidoglio, site of the city's first *Arx*, or citadel. Here the Emperor Augustus is said to have been told by a seer of a Virgin and Child who would overthrow the altar of the gods. Moved by this he set up the *Ara Coeli* (Altar of Heaven), from which the church takes its name. The altar was carved with the words *Ecce ara primogeniti Dei* 'Behold the altar of the firstborn of God' (now carved on the church's triumphal arch).

Most of the current church dates from 1260, when the Franciscans moved in, though records show a church on the site as least as early as AD 574. You'll be hard pushed to miss the impressive 120-step staircase to the entrance, built in 1348 as thanks for Rome's deliverance from the Black Death (it's traditional for newly married couples to climb the steps). The **interior**'s effect is marvellously decorative, full of gilt, grand pulpits, chandeliers, and a fine ceiling and Cosmati pavement. Its main treasures are **Pinturicchio's frescoes** on the *Life of San Bernardino* (first chapel on the right), but seek out the *Tomb of Luca Savelli* by Arnolfo di Cambio in the left transept; the 10th-century altarpiece; and Gozzoli's fresco of *St Antony of Padua* (third chapel on the left).

Santa Maria in Cosmedin (Piazza Bocca della Verità) One of Rome's few churches not to have succumbed to the Baroque, Santa Maria in Cosmedin is a sublime piece of medieval architecture, though it's known primarily on the tourist trail for the **Bocca della Verità**. This is an old Roman drain cover carved with a face and gaping mouth (situated on the left before you enter the church). The legend is that if you hold your hand in the maw and tell a lie the mouth will snap shut. Oaths and business deals were sworn here, and women suspected of adultery were forced by their husbands to take the test.

While the church has few individual treasures, overall it's one of the city's loveliest, creaking with age and solemnity. This said the Cosmati work is fine, as are the pulpits, pavement, choir screen and the oversized candleholder. Look out, too, for the masterful little crypt, the sculpted altar canopy or *baldacchino* (1294), the faded medieval frescoes and a magical 8th-century **mosaic** in a room off the right aisle.

Outside, the grassy piazza holds a couple of excellently preserved Roman temples, far better, in many ways, than anything you'll see in the Forum or on the Palatino.

Santa Maria Maggiore (Via Cavour) If you're walking from the station, **Santa Maria Maggiore** may be the first major Roman sight you see, hardly a bad introduction to the city, for it has many claims to being the most important of all Rome's many hundreds of churches. It's the largest of the 80 churches dedicated to the Virgin, one of the city's main points of pilgrimage, and one of the four so-called patriarchal basilicas (St Peter's, San Giovanni in Laterano and San Paolo fuori le Mura are the others). Moreover, it's the only place in Rome that Mass has been celebrated every day without interruption since the 5th century. The **interior** is frequently quoted as being Rome's finest, its beauty derived from 40 ancient columns, acres of decoration and two sets of **mosaics**: 36 panels in the nave dating from the earliest church (5th century) and an **apse** sequence by Jacopo Torriti (1275), considered the acme of Rome's medieval mosaic tradition. Also look at the *Cappella Sistina* (1585) off the right nave, designed for Pope Sixtus V by Domenico Fontana, and the **Cappella Paolina** (1611) opposite, designed specifically to outdo the Sistina – which it does with a surfeit of décor excessive even by Baroque standards. The altarpiece here is a much-revered work, reputedly painted by St Luke. On the high altar is the prize exhibit, five pieces of iron-bound wood said to be part of **Christ's crib**: it's brought out on the 25th day of every month. To the right and rear of the altar is the church's top **tomb**, that of Cardinal Rodriguez (1299), crafted by Giovanni Cosma, part of the great Cosmati family of masons.

Santa Maria sopra Minerva (Piazza della Minerva) Rome has just one Gothic church – **Santa Maria sopra Minerva** – so-called because it was built over a Roman temple to Minerva. Before you enter notice Bernini's famous and idiosyncratic **elephant statue** in the piazza outside. The interior boasts frescoes (1488–92) by the Florentine **Filippino Lippi** (in the Cappella Carafa at the end of the right transept); the tombs of **Fra Angelico** and St Catherine of Siena, one of Italy's national saints: both are under the main altar. Its star turn, however, is the figure of *The Redeemer* by **Michelangelo** (1519–21), an early work criticised when it was sculpted for being more like a pagan god than a figure of Christ. Its loin cloth was added later, as was the sandal, designed to prevent the stone being worn away by the hands of the faithful.

Santa Maria del Popolo (Piazza del Popolo) Santa Maria del Popolo is amongst Rome's top five churches, thanks to its interior design work – effected mainly by Bramante and Bernini – and the high count of outstanding works of art. The original church was built on the site of Nero's tomb in 1099, supposedly to redeem ground sullied by its contact with the evil emperor. The key works are **Pinturicchio's frescoes** (1485–89), painted behind the main altar (he has other frescoes in the first chapel on the left as you enter). Elsewhere, the choir has two superlative tombs by **Andrea Sansovino** (1505–7). Of the many chapels, the most famous is the **Cappella Chigi** (1513), where wealthy Sienese banker, Chigi, commissioned **Raphael** to 'convert earthly things into heavenly'. All its decoration is by Raphael, bar the altarpiece and some Bernini medallions. The best individual canvases are two masterpieces by **Caravaggio** (in the left transept's first chapel), worth comparing with the painter's main rival, Annibale Carraci, whose *Assumption of the Virgin* hangs in the chapel over the main altar.

Santa Maria in Trastevere (Piazza Santa Maria in Trastevere) Trastevere's top church – with Santa Cecilia – **Santa Maria in Trastevere** provides a colourful background for the eponymous piazza, the main focus of the area's *al fresco* social life. Rome's first church dedicated to the Virgin, it's perhaps the oldest place of Christian worship in the city, tracing its foundation to AD 222. Most of the present church is later, of course, from the main body and Romanesque campanile built in 1143 through to the artful porch added by Carlo Fontana in 1702 (Fontana was also responsible for the piazza's fountain). The façade's most eye-catching features, though, are its mosaics (mid-12th or 13th-century), a lovely coloured feature that brightens the entire piazza. It's sad to think that before the Baroque builders got to work nearly all Roman churches would have been similarly decorated. Inside, the interior has a set of mosaics which, if anything, are more stunning still, divided into two main groups: those in the upper apse, Byzantine-influenced work from around 1140, and those in the lower apse – meditations on the *Life of the Virgin* (1290), executed by Pietro Cavallini (one of the era's leading and most innovative artists). The ancient columns in the nave are Roman, and come from the Terme di Caracalla, large Roman baths, substantial remains of which you can see south of the Colosseum.

Santa Maria della Vittoria (Via XX Settembre) You visit this otherwise rather bland Baroque church for one, if not the masterpiece of Baroque sculpture, Bernini's *Ecstasy of St Teresa*. The work's a highly theatrical depiction of the vision of St Teresa (1515–82), founder of the Carmelite order of nuns. Many have seen it as a little too erotic and earthly, as if Bernini were portraying physical rather than spiritual fulfilment. These days, the scandal's largely forgotten, the piece's genius unquestioned.

San Pietro (St Peter's) You can't come to Rome and not see St Peter's, the world's largest church and heart of Roman Catholicism. Neither its immense size, nor its great historic and religious significance can fail to impress. At the same time, however, you may find its chill interior and relative lack of art leave you feeling hard done by. For many people the highlight of a visit is climbing the dome, not the church at all, for the views it offers over Piazza San Pietro and the city beyond (you have to pay and often queue for the privilege).

The original church was reputedly built over the tomb of St Peter, an Apostle and Rome's first bishop (and thus pope). He was crucified nearby in AD 64 or 67 (recent work has proved the church's high altar does indeed lie over a tomb of some sort). The first recorded church was raised in AD 326, a basilica that was to survive for almost a thousand years. In 1452, however, its parlous state caused Pope Nicholas V to consider plans for a new church. It was another fifty years, though, before Julius II gave the orders for the old building's ultimate destruction. Things then became complicated, as different architects were brought in and plans for the new church see-sawed between rival schemes. **Bramante** kicked off with plans for a design centred on a Greek cross; Antonio da Sangallo followed up in 1539, changing work in progress to incorporate a Latin cross (a nave and two transepts). **Michelangelo**, then aged 72, was called in to salvage the mess, which he did by removing Sangallo's work and altering the dome (the dome's drum and distinctive twin columns are Michelangelo's). **Carlo Maderno**

(1605) then returned to the Latin Cross, widening the façade to its present width. A few years later, Bernini mopped up in the interior and created the magnificent **piazza** outside. The church was more or less completed in 1626, the 1300th anniversary of the first basilica's original consecration.

In the broad **portico** notice the Porta Santa on the left, opened once every 25 years, and the main door (1433), salvaged from the earlier basilica. Above the main doorway are more early fragments; a fresco of the *Navicella* by Giotto showing the Apostles' ship in a storm and Christ walking on the water. The statues on the right and left are *Constantine* and *Charlemagne* respectively.

The **interior**'s size is impressive enough, but there's surprisingly little to admire amongst its acres of marble, its gloomy tombs and the huge avalanche of third-rate Baroque décor. As you walk down the nave notice the floor markers which indicate (inaccurately) the size of other churches in relation to St Peter's. The most famous piece of work is **Michelangelo's** *Pietà* (1499), kept behind glass at the beginning of the right nave (following vandalism in 1972). At the end of the aisle the unmissable statue is St Peter, whose right foot has been caressed by millions since Pius IX granted a fifty day indulgence to anyone kissing it after confession.

Equally imposing is the vast **baldacchino** (1624–33), crafted by Bernini using bronze melted down from the ancient porch of the Pantheon. It was commissioned by Urban VIII, a pope lifted from the powerful Barberini family, which is why the thing is covered in bees – the family's symbol (and one you'll see repeated in various places around the city). Behind it in the apse is another Bernini offering, the **Cathedra Petri** (1656), or the Throne of St Peter, created to enclose a wood and ivory chair supposedly used by St Peter to deliver his first sermon to the Romans. To either side are the church's best tombs: that of Pope Paul II to the left, by Giacomo della Porta, and its twin to the right, the **Tomb of Urban VIII** (1642) by Bernini. The latter was the model for countless Baroque monuments all over Europe.

San Pietro in Vincoli Close to the Colosseum, San Pietro in Vincoli is a one-stop church, its single sight **Michelangelo's** monumental sculpture of Moses (1503–13) at the top of the right hand nave. Originally intended as part of a tomb for Pope Julius II – a never to be completed work that occupied Michelangelo for years – the huge physical presence and immense spiritual power of the figure easily make this one of the sculptor's masterpieces. The church itself was founded in AD 432 on the site where St Peter was condemned to death under Nero. It houses the chains which bound Peter in Jerusalem, and later those that shackled him in Rome's Mamertine prison. Both sets miraculously fused together, and can now be seen in a casket below the altar (*vincoli* means chains in Italian, hence the church's name).

Piazzas and Fountains

Campo dei Fiori or 'field of flowers' is by far the city's most appealing piazza, thanks to its picturesque food and flower market (Mon–Sat 6 am–1.30 pm). To its rear is the more austere Piazza Farnese and the imposing façade of the Palazzo

Farnese, designed in large part by Michelangelo, and perhaps the most important Renaissance palace in Rome. Sadly, however, it's used as the French Embassy, and remains closed to the public.

Fontana di Trevi Most famous and spectacular of Rome's fountains, the Fontana di Trevi was built over an earlier fountain designed to take the waters of the Acqua Vergine (an aqueduct built for Pope Nicholas V in 1453). Constructed between 1732 and 1751, the new fountain was modelled on the Arco di Constantino alongside the Colosseum. It was built on one side of the Palazzo Poli, one reason for its fascination – it appears as though a fountain is coursing through the side of the building. The name comes from *tre vie*, or three streets, after the three lanes which converge here out of the warren of surrounding alleys. The central statue is Oceanus or Neptune: the figures to either side symbolise a storm and calm sea. The statues in niches are allegories of Health and Abundance, overseen by pediment statues that represent the Four Seasons.

The great tradition here, of course, is not to take a dip in the manner immortalised by Anita Ekberg in Fellini's film, *La Dolce Vita*, but rather to throw a coin in the fountain if you wish to return to Rome. This follows a Roman tradition of throwing coins in certain fountains to appease particular gods, later picked up by Christians who threw coins on to the (supposed) tomb of St Peter. The fountain's one of Rome's great meeting points, and can be a delightful place to while away an hour people-watching. If you want more peace, come here late in the evening when the waters are floodlit to spectacular effect.

Piazza Navona Everyone sooner or later comes to **Piazza Navona**, in many ways Rome's heart and certainly its grandest square – or in this case, ellipse, for the piazza matches exactly the outline of the *circo* or racetrack built for the Emperor Domitian in AD 86. Used for centuries, it served as an arena for jousts, horse races and so-called water games (when it was sealed off and flooded to allow boating and mock sea battles). It was transformed in 1644 when Innocent X, a pope from the Pamphili family, decided to emulate Urban VIII, a Barberini, who had recently raised family monuments all over the city. The square acquired two outstanding fountains by Bernini, the most impressive the central **Fontana dei Fiumi** (each of its four main statues representing the four main rivers of the world – Nile, Ganges, Danube and Plate – and the four corners of the world, Africa, Asia, Europe and America). Borromini, Bernini's rival, designed the church of **Sant'Agnese in Agone**, a Baroque tour-de-force, though for most people, particularly in the evening, the square is simply a wonderful place to walk, sit or sip coffee and watch the world go by.

Piazza di Spagna like Piazza Navona and the Fontana di Trevi is famous more for its beauty and the fact that people gather here than for any particular monuments. Its centrepiece is the Scalinata della Trinità dei Monti, more commonly known as the **Spanish Steps**. The steps are named after the Palazzo di Spagna, built in the piazza during the 17th century as the Spanish Embassy. In its day the square and elegant surroundings were the favoured haunt of foreign visitors on the Grand Tour. Look for the Keats-Shelley museum to the right of the Steps and the eccentric Barcaccia fountain at their foot, designed to resemble a half-submerged boat (the design is attributed to Bernini).

Practicalities in Rome

Telephone Code 06 (note that Rome is in the process of changing many of its telephone numbers).
Tourist Office At Stazione Termini (482.4078) in the front ticket hall area, though queues here are likely to be horrendous. Except *in extremis*, ignore all offers of hotel rooms from the agents who hover here.
The main office is 10 minutes' walk away at Via Parigi 5 (488.3748) – leave the station, cross the huge Piazza dei Cinquecento ahead bearing left to Piazza della Repubblica beyond. Take Via G. Gomita out of the piazza. Both places have good maps, lots of leaflets and both will help with accommodation.
Railway Station Stazione Termini – usually known as Termini – at Piazza dei Cinquecento is the main station. It can be a daunting introduction to Rome. Watch out for pickpockets, especially the swarms of gypsy children and keep an eye on your luggage at all times.
Some through expresses, especially at night, stop at Stazione Tiburtina, way out in the suburbs; Ostiense is the station for the airport and Ostia Antica. Other stations like Roma Nord, Trastevere and so on you shouldn't need to worry about.
Train Information(4775: booking office 72.80 – though don't expect much joy in dealings on the phone). Many brand-new train information booths stand near the main entrance, though they're always busy; booths have the language spoken by the staff posted above them. Staff at ticket counters, by contrast, are loath to give you information.
Station Facilities Termini is like a village, with most things you'll need – there's even a morgue – though prices, of course, are high. Left luggage is alongside platform 1 (5 am–1 pm). Foreign exchange (daily 8 am–8 pm); several banks and kiosks with poor rates and long queues again; will not give VISA cash advances, and most don't accept Eurocheques either – cash, travellers' cheques or nothing. Walk down into the subterranean concourse for most of the shops (including late night pharmacy) and the *albergo diurno* (daily 7 am–8 pm), or day hotel, where you can shower or snooze. The police are at the far end of platform 1 for lost property or to report thefts.
Tickets Buy tickets from the huge line of booths, but be absolutely sure you're in the right queue (see page 37). Allow plenty of time to get a ticket before a train leaves – 20 mins is an average time in the queue: Fri night and Sat morning are the busiest times. Several agencies around the city can sell FS tickets and BIJ and other discount tickets can be bought in kiosks on the station's main concourse. *Transalpino* have an office at Piazza Esquilino 8a (474.7605) 5 minutes from the station (turn left down Via Cavour off Piazza dei Cinquecento). The nearest general FS ticket agencies are ringed around Piazza della Repubblica.
Foreign Exchange *Frama*, Via Torino 21b. Quiet, quick and efficient, and about 10 min from Termini: Via Torino is the first main right off Via Cavour (Mon–Fri 9.30 am–12.30 pm and 3–5 pm; Sat 9 am–noon).
Post Office Piazza San Silvestro 19, near the bottom of Via del Tritone and Piazza Colonna.
American Express Piazza di Spagna 38 (72.82 or 67.641). Travel office, free maps, exchange facilities and mail collection (Mon–Fri 9 am–5.30 pm, Sat 9 am–12.30 pm).
Budget Travel CTS, Via Genova 16, off Via Nazionale on the left as you drop down from Piazza della Repubblica (446.791). Best spot for cheap student and non-student discount flights, international train tickets, ferries and student cards (Mon–Fri 9 am–1 pm and 4–7 pm, Sat 9 am–1 pm).
Bicycle Hire More outlets are opening all the time – but Rome's traffic needs careful attention; the most prominent stands are on Via del Corso.
British Embassy Via XX Settembre 80 (475.5441).
Foreigners' Office (Ufficio Stranieri), Via Genova 2 (4686.2987).
Medical Attention *International Medical Centre*, Via Amendola 7 (462.371; nights and weekends, 475.1575). English spoken.

City Transport

Buses You can walk most of central Rome, though you'll still occasionally need the odd bus (see useful routes below). Orange city buses (and occasional tram) are run by ATAC. These are as efficient and regular as the traffic allows. Virtually every service either starts or passes through Piazza dei Cinquecento outside Termini. Remember the basics: buy your ticket first (see below); get on at the back of the bus and off in the middle; cancel your ticket in the small machine at the back; be prepared to jam up against your neighbour and watch your bags and pockets (the number 64 is the most notorious thieves' and gropers' route). For a good cheap look at the city sit on the number 30 tram from the start to finish of its route. It makes a long journey past many sights.

Tickets Tickets, valid for 90 minutes, must be purchased before getting on the bus: they're available from green ATAC booths at main intersections – Piazza dei Cinquecento, Colosseum and Largo Argentina – shops with an ATAC sticker and at most *tabacchi* (bars and tobacconists with a black 'T' sign). You can save money by buying a block of ten tickets known as a *blochetto*. You can also buy a full day pass (*biglietto giornaliera*) or weekly pass (*biglietto settimanale*). The fine for being caught without a ticket is L50,000.

Information At the ATAC booth in Piazza dei Cinquecento (46.951), out of Termini and on your left across the forecourt.

Main Routes **Number 64** Termini–Piazza Venezia–Piazza Navona and Campo dei Fiori –St Peter's.

Number 27 Termini–Via Cavour–Forum–Colosseum

Number 13/130 (trams) Colosseum–Trastevere

Number 65 Stazione Tiburtina–Porta Pia–Piazza Venezia–St Peter's

Number 75/170 Termini–Piazza Venezia–Trastevere

Number 81 Colosseum–Piazza del Risorgimento (for the Vatican Museums)

Number 119 (minibus) Piazza del Popolo–Piazza di Spagna–Via Ripetta

Number 190 Termini–Villa Borghese

Where to stay

Hotels Rome's chock full of accommodation possibilities. In high summer, however, they fill up surprisingly quickly. As a first option leave your bags in left luggage and trawl around the streets close to the station. The streets to the south (on the right as you face the platforms) are crammed with cheap places – though this can be a seedy area at night (and noisy, but then most of Rome is noisy). Ideally, of course, you want to be near Piazza Navona and Campo dei Fiori, but the few good places here fill up more quickly than any. If you must accept an offer from the touts at the station, be certain to find out where the hotel is and make sure you've agreed on a price (get the price *written* down).

As in most capital cities, prices are well over what you'd pay elsewhere. Only the nastiest places have ☆ prices. All the prices below are at the top end of their rating category (that is, expensive).

☆☆*Abruzzi*, Piazza della Rotonda (679.2021). Great location near the Pantheon, though it's noisy at the front and the rooms are past their best.

☆☆*Alimandi*, Via Tunisi 8(679.9343). Near the Vatican museums, and therefore quieter than more central places.

☆☆☆*Bocca di Leone*, Via Bocca di Leone 7 (679.8661). One of the more reasonably-priced hotels in an expensive area near Piazza di Spagna.

☆☆☆*Britannia*, Via Napoli 64 (463.153). Small, recently refurbished hotel close to the station.

☆☆*Campo Marzo*, Piazza Campo Marzo 7 (651.4486). Simple rooms just north of the Pantheon.

☆☆☆*Columbus*, Via della Conciliazione 33 (686.5435). On the main approach to St Peter's, and an old-world *palazzo* setting – a favourite of visiting cardinals.

☆☆*Della Lunetta*, Piazza del Paradiso 68 (686.1080). Handy for Campo dei Fiori, but not as nice as the well-known *Sole* immediately round the corner.

☆☆☆*Doge*, Via Due Maccelli (678.0038). Some of the nicest rooms at their prices; Piazza di Spagna district.

☆☆*Edraelli*, Via Due Maccelli 28 (679.1265). Adequate rooms close to the Spanish Steps, but potentially noisy.

☆☆☆*Forte*, Via Margutta 61 (678.6109). Appealing hotel in a quiet street of galleries and artists' studios.

☆☆*Fiorella*, Via del Babuino 196 (361.0597). Popular spot close to Piazza di Spagna; book first or arrive early.

☆☆*Forti's Guest House*, Via Cosseria 2 (679.9390). Another busy place in Prati (good for St Peter's); close to the Lepanto *metro* stop.

☆☆*Imperia*, Via Principe Amedeo 9 (475.4474). One of the better places near the station.

☆☆*Le Rovere*, Vicolo Sant'Onofrio 5 (654.0739). Hidden across Ponte Aosta off the Via Giulia – quiet, friendly and efficient.

☆☆*Mimosa*, Via Santa Chiara (654.1753). 10 rooms in peaceful street near the Pantheon.

☆☆*Navona*, Via dei Sediari 8 (654.3802). 18 simple rooms close to Piazza Navona run by Italo-Australian couple.

☆☆☆*Nerva*, Via Tor de' Conti 3 (679.3764). Functional, serviceable hotel in a good location for the Forum and Colosseum.

☆☆*Perugia*, Via del Colosseo 7 (679.7200). Small, little-known place in a side-street at the bottom of Via Cavour (good for the Colosseum and Forum).

☆☆*Pomezia*, Via dei Chiavari 32 (686.1371). Cheap rooms near Piazza Navona.

☆☆☆*Sistina*, Via Sistina 136 (475.8867). One of the better choices in the smarter, middle price bracket. Good Piazza di Spagna location and a lovely terrace.

☆☆*Smeraldo*, Via dei Chiodaroli (687.5929). Good choice 2 minutes from Campo dei Fiori.

☆☆*Sole*, Via del Biscione 76 (654.0873). Very well-known bargain; busy, bright rooms immediately off Campo dei Fiori.

YWCA, Via C. Balbo 4 (488.0460). Women only hostel with rooms rather than dorms – about 10 minutes' walk from the station.

Bars and Cafés *Bar della Pace*, Via della Pace. About 100 metres off Piazza Navona and the trendiest bar in Rome for a while; peaceful in the day, when you can enjoy the lovely 19th-century interior of marble tables, mirrors and polished wood, but in the evening the outside tables are packed; see and be seen.

Caffè Greco, Via Condotti 86. Founded in 1742 and the haunt, amongst others, of Goethe, Casanova, Byron and Stendhal; more of a tourist trap these days, but the city's most famous bar. Avoid the equally famous *Babington's Tea Rooms* nearby on Piazza di Spagna – probably the costliest and worst cup of tea you'll ever drink.

Castellino, Piazza Venezia 135. Central late-nighter, but only if you're stuck in the small hours – increasingly dodgy patrons as the night goes on.

Cul de Sac, Piazza Pasquino 73. Lively wine bar, good for snacks at lunch and evening tipple.

Caffé San'Eustachio, Piazza Sant'Eustachio, Just south of the Pantheon, and one of the city's best cups of coffee; methods and décor unchanged since 1938; a couple of tables on the piazza outside. *Camilloni*, just opposite, also has its admirers.

Del Fico, Piazza del Fico. Less frantic and self-conscious than *Bar della Pace* just around the corner.

Druid's, Via San Martino ai Monti 28. Friendly and atmospheric Irish bar south of Santa Maria Maggiore; popular with ex-pats and Italians alike. Try the bigger, sister bar around the corner, the *Fiddler's Elbow*, Via dell'Omertà 43.

Enoteca, Campo dei Fiori. On the corner leading into Piazza Farnese; the hangout for Rome's poets, self-styled intellectuals, punks, their dogs and assorted lowlife.

Enoteca Cavour, Via Cavour 313. Little-known, relaxed spot for drinks and snacks, lunch and evening at the Forum end of Via Cavour.

Enoteca Piccola, Via del Governo Vecchio 75. Intimate and reasonable wine bar close to Piazza Navona; best spot for a quiet drink or romantic liaison.

La Scala, Piazza della Scala. The best and busiest of the Trastevere bars for night-time action; big, live music, cheap bar, cheerful basic food and hectic service.

Tazza d'Oro, Via degli Orfani. In a little alley immediately off Piazza del Pantheon, and by common consent Rome's best cup of coffee – it sells little else.

Tempera, Via di San Marcello 19. Behind Piazza Venezia on the way to the Fontana di Trevi, and definitely the best of the city's *birrerie* (beer halls); cheap food and drink, and amiable atmosphere.

Trastè, Via della Lungaretta 76. Cool, relaxed and arty spot for teas and cultured chat; also good cakes and light meals; nice place to while away an afternoon.

Ice Cream *Gelateria della Palma*, Via della Maddalena 20. Flashy place behind the Pantheon, but probably the city's top ice cream and certainly its biggest selection of flavours – around 120, including some weird and wonderful mixtures; lots of sweets and sticky cakes, too.

Giolitti, Via degli Uffici del Vicario 40. North of the Pantheon off Via della Maddalena; amongst Rome's most venerable bars, but best known for its ice cream; take away, or sit down and enjoy the wonderful interior and legendary grumpy service.

Pascucci, Via Torre Argentina 20. Just off the north side of Largo Argentina, this tiny hole-in-the-wall has 6 blenders turning out fresh fruit and milk/ice-shakes (*frullati*); nationally renowned.

Tre Scalini, Piazza Navona. One of the big bars on the piazza and renowned for its extraordinary *tartufo* – expensive, but the most chocolate you'll ever have in an ice cream.

Restaurants Eating is one of the great Roman virtues, though its traditional specialities take a strong stomach: tripe, offal, ox-tail, veal and brains. Most menus worth their salt will have one of these, but you'll always be able to get more standard fare as well. Prices in Rome are creeping up, but stick to basics and you can still eat reasonably. Remember bar snacks as a cheap standby. **Wine** is invariably good basic white, usually a *Frascati* clone, from the hills and Castelli Romani south of the city.

Around the station all the streets are lined with places offering a fixed *menù turistico*; avoid these unless you're desperate – there's better and/or cheaper food elsewhere. Trastevere is the traditional spot to eat, with plenty of atmospheric and outdoor spots – almost all of them, however, touristy and expensive. If you want to be adventurous and go where the students are going these days, take a bus down to Testaccio, the old slaughterhouse neighbourhood, or, more promisingly, to San

Lorenzo 5 minutes east of Termini (bus number 71 or 492) still an earthy working class district; Via Tiburtina is a good starting point.

These are tried and tested spots, all within walking distance of the centre.

Al Leoncino, Via del Leoncino 28. Off Via del Corso to the west; about as old world and authentic as a pizzeria gets; cheap, intimate and pizzas made and cooked in big oven in front of the marble bar and formica-topped tables.

Baffetto, Via del Governo Vecchio 114. Minuscule pizzeria, and a Rome institution, which means long queues, but still good fun and value.

Filetti di Baccalà, Largo dei Librari 88. Take Via dei Giubbonari east from Campo dei Fiori and this appealing, cheap glorified fish and chip shop is about 3 min on the left.

Grappola d'Oro, Piazza della Cancelleria 80. More expensive than some places, but a wonderful slice of old Rome and genuine Roman cuisine; a few paces off Campo dei Fiori.

Il Corallo, Via del Corallo 10. Bright, breezy and popular modern pizzeria-restaurant, with good and inventive food; off Via del Governo Vecchio near Piazza Navona.

Ivo, Via di San Francesco a Ripa 157. A good crust and a topping ahead of the field; *the* Trastevere pizzeria – thronged, busy and nicely frenetic; expect to queue – though turnover's quick.

La Fraschetta, Via di San Francesco a Ripa 134. A few doors down from *Ivo* on the same side of the street and much quieter; nice interior, good pizzas, but also a full range of pastas and main courses; above average desserts. If it looks full, don't overlook the room at the back.

Margutta, Via Margutta 119. Off Via del Babuino near Piazza del Popolo; not quite

Rome's only vegetarian restaurant, but its best known; rather expensive and almost over-tasteful flowers and polished wood type interior.

Mario's, Via del Moro 53. Extremely well-known Trastevere budget choice, usually full of backpackers; still cheap but service can be excruciatingly slow – though the soap opera in the kitchen offers light relief.

Nerone, Via Mecenate. Walk up the steps to the right of the underground station at the Colosseum, turn right on Via del Domus Aurea and first left; this quiet, long-established place is on the corner at the top of the street.

Pasqualino, Via dei SS Quattro. About 100 metres from the Colosseum to the east; old family place and one of a vanishing breed; aim to eat downstairs or outside – this may become your Rome favourite.

Romanesca, Campo dei Fiori 23. The place to eat on the Campo; smaller and less touristy than *La Carbonara* at the top of the square, which does, though, have plenty of outside tables that are worth the premium you pay on prices.

Markets Rome's most picturesque market, whether you're buying or browsing, is the glorious collection of fruit, fish and flower stalls in **Campo dei Fiori**; highly recommended for a cup of coffee to take in the streetlife. The city's main food and general market is more prosaic, but still worth a visit, and gathers around **Piazza Vittorio Emanuele** about 5 min east of Termini. The weekly **flea market** – Europe's largest – takes place on Sundays at Porta Portese on the eastern edge of Trastevere. Be warned, though, that the crowds can be appalling. You'll also have to keep extra special watch on your valuables.

Rome–Frascati

The route

A byword for cheap white wine the world over, **Frascati** is the best known of the Castelli Romani, a sprinkling of towns in the Albani hills to the south of Rome. It's also one of the easiest ways to escape the heat and bustle of the city. Although it offers no sights to rival Tivoli or Ostia Antica, its cooling breezes, fine views and a moderate town centre should be enough to occupy a morning's visit.

Trains

Some 11 trains daily run from Termini to Frascati (24 km, 30 min).

The journey

Condensed into the little journey up to Frascati is a summary of all that's good and bad in Rome. First come glimpses of Roman ruins – fragments of ancient aqueducts striding across the *campagna* south of the city. Next come the blighted suburbs and half-built shanty towns that have sprung up in the last 30 years. Then comes the countryside – the dark, haze-shrouded outlines of the Albani hills; old volcanic stumps whose rich soil accounts for the wine for which the area is renowned (though in most cases the deep yellow brew siphoned from the barrel of many a Rome restaurant is a basic if perfectly acceptable plonk). As the train starts to climb it winds through vineyards and bucolic pastures. By the time it reaches **Frascati**, it feels as if Rome is behind you for good. A short amble from the station brings you to the main square, Piazza Marconi, whose belvedere and adjoining gardens offer a huge panorama over the country to the south (a vista described by Goethe as 'an endless horizon, with a view of Rome in the plain and the sea beyond'). In the other direction the outlook is dominated by the **Villa Aldobrandini** (1598), one of many great estates in the Albani hills built either for the clergy or members of Rome's great patrician families (the Pope's present summer retreat is in the Papal castle at nearby Castel Gandolfo). The villa still belongs to the Aldobrandini and is closed to the public, but by applying to the tourist office in Piazza Marconi you may be able to get into the gardens – superb in places, sadly neglected in others (Mon–Fri 9 am–1 pm).

When all's said and done, however, you're in Frascati to wander or to eat and drink (the town's a favourite of Romans out for Sunday lunch). Most places sell wine and the tourist office has lists of producers that run tours and tastings. If you're here in October and November all sorts of more-or-less inebriated festivities take place to celebrate the wine harvest or *vendemmia*. Probably the only buildings worth a look are the medieval fortress and 17th-century duomo. The Germans used Frascati as a headquarters for the defence of Rome in 1944. As a result it was heavily bombed, much of its older fabric being destroyed in the process.

Rome–Ostia Antica

The route

The Ostia Antica ruins are one of Rome's better-kept secrets (not to be confused with Ostia, a vast and tawdry seaside resort close by). The remains here are as good as anything in the city itself, ranking as the best-preserved Roman town after Pompeii – though with far less commercial razzamatazz and fewer attendant crowds. They also have the added advantage of a lovely setting, the site being strewn with vines, wildflowers and creepers, the paths shaded by elegant stands of parasol pines and swathes of clinging ivy. All of this makes it a good place to spend the day, so bring a picnic and be prepared for plenty of walking.

The site's open Tues–Sun 9 am–6 pm in winter, Tues–Sat 9 am–4.30 pm the rest of the year.

Trains

Numerous local trains run from Rome's Stazione Ostiense, which is reached by underground (Metro) from Termini. Or take the Lido trains from Magliana on Metro line B. Get off at the Ostia Antica stop (one before Ostia Lido).

The journey

Ostia Antica was once Rome's leading port. According to legend it was here that Aeneas, forefather of the Latins, first landed and where in the 7th century BC, the fourth king of Rome, Ancus Martius, established a settlement at the mouth (*ostium*) of the River Tiber. In fact, Ostia probably started life as a fishing village around 335 BC. As the empire grew, though, it became Rome's main outlet to the sea, trading a host of commodities – grain in particular – from the farthest-flung imperial outposts. By the 2nd century it had also become a major naval base, with a population of around 500,000. By this time, however, it was also unable to deal with the sheer weight of imperial commerce. Worse, its harbour had begun to silt up (the site of the old docks is now Fiumicino airport, well inland). Claudius began a new port, the *Portus Romae*, to deal with Ostia's surplus, placing it on the opposite bank of the Tiber. This was greatly expanded by Constantine, leaving the old port to become a quiet residential centre. By the 5th century, and the fall of Rome, Ostia was virtually abandoned.

Excavations to uncover what had become an almost buried city began in the 19th century. Much of what was brought to light went immediately to Rome's museums, but the ruins that remain on site – accounting for about half of the original port – still offer a fascinating insight into how a Roman colony must have looked. More importantly, Ostia preserves a single urban plan, leaving it unencumbered by the medieval, Baroque and modern additions that overlay Rome's ancient monuments. Furthermore, it was also buried under mud for centuries, thus escaping the pillage that robbed central Rome of many of its treasures.

Although you can wander the ruins for the pleasure of the surroundings, it's hard to make much real sense of the site's layout without a map (guides on sale at the entrance make a good investment). Any trip starts at the Porta Romana, a gateway for the **Decumanus Maximus**, the still-cobbled main street of the old port. Innumerable alleys and streets lead off, every turn revealing the ruins of some ancient building. These include theatres, temples, shops, workshops and the famous *horreae*, the old warehouses used to store cargo. Equally interesting are the many *insulae*, the remains of Roman four- and five-storey apartment blocks. Some of the ruins to make a special point of seeing are the **Terme di Nettuno**, just inside the Porta Romana, built by Hadrian and home to a set of elaborate mosaics depicting Neptune and Amphitrite. Alongside it is the

Augustan-era **amphitheatre** from which you can look down on the **Piazzale delle Corporazioni**. This large square contained the 61 offices of the port's shipping agents. Many are still fronted by mosaics denoting the trade each one carried out. Also try to find the **thermopolium**, a Roman-era bar, complete with shelves, marble counter and a set of murals illustrating parts of the menu.

Rome–Tivoli
The route

Tivoli is the most popular day trip from Rome, offering two top sights – the Villa d'Este and its famous gardens, and the Villa Adriana, the Emperor Hadrian's personal estate. There's a lot to see so set out early.

Trains

6 trains daily run to Tivoli from **Termini** *and 8 from* **Roma Tiburtina** *on the main* **Rome–Pescara** *line (40 km, 35–55 min). If return trains are inconvenient,* **buses** *leave Tivoli's main square, Largo Garibaldi (opposite the tourist office) roughly every 30 minutes.*

The journey

After wending its way through some of Rome's poorer suburbs, the eastbound mainline begins its climb into the hills, passing one notable landmark – the reeking sulphurous springs at **Bagni di Tivoli** – before suddenly emerging into the countryside framing **Tivoli**. Take a bus from the station forecourt to the town centre, otherwise it's a long and steepish walk. (If you want to hike, turn right up Viale Mazzini to Largo Sant'Angelo – which has the entrance to the Villa Gregoriana (see below) – and then cross the Ponte Gregoriano. Thereafter follow Via Ponte Gregoriana, Via Palatina and Via di Trevio to Largo Garibaldi.)

In Roman times Tivoli, ancient *Tiber*, was known for its travertine marble and as a retirement home for prosperous Romans. There were so many villas here, said Horace, that 'the Tibertine soil no longer has ploughland'. Today it's a lively town, often made livelier by hundreds of tourists and dozens of tour buses. Most people are here to admire the **Villa d'Este**, located directly opposite the main square, Largo Garibaldi (daily 9 am–dusk).

Initially built as a convent, the villa was altered in 1550 by Piero Ligorio to create a country retreat for Cardinal Ippolito d'Este, the son of Lucrezia Borgia and the Duke of Ferrara. Nowadays his creation is no more than a shabby procession of faded rooms and bad Mannerist frescoes. Their one saving grace is the views over the surrounding gardens, whose fountains and formal terraces rank as some of the most beautiful in the world. The 500 **fountains** were to be a model for generations of gardens afterwards, particularly those of other great stately houses around Rome, including the Villa Borghese and Villa Doria Pamphili. Bernini's central *Fontana di Biccierone* is the most elegant of the fountains, but stands overshadowed by the sheer scale of the Viale delle Cento Fontane (the 'Avenue of a Hundred Fountains'). This watery caprice has as its centrepiece the *Fontana dei Draghi* (the 'Fountain of the Dragons'), built for Pope Gregory XIII, whose emblem was a short-tailed dragon. All the gardens' avenues and byways repay exploration, especially the little path which leads to the *Rometta*, a scale model of the Isola Tiberina and Rome's major sights.

Before leaving Tivoli cross to the other side of town for the **Villa Gregoriana**, centred on a pair of waterfalls and a dramatic, vegetation-covered gorge. The larger waterfall, the *Grande Cascata*, was created in 1831 when Pope Gregory XVI diverted the River Aniene to protect Tivoli from flooding. The smaller falls were engineered by Bernini.

To reach the town's other big draw you need to take the number 4 bus from Largo Garibaldi to Bixia Adriana about five kilometres from Tivoli itself. This leaves you 15 minutes' walk from the **Villa Adriana**, or Hadrian's Villa, a more peaceful spot than the Este gardens (daily 9 am—one hour before sunset). Begun in 125 AD to Hadrian's own design, the villa was completed ten years later. The emperor himself, however, spent only three years here before ill-health forced him to seek healthier climes. His intention was to recreate some of the great buildings he had seen on his travels (Hadrian was reputed to have visited every province in the Empire, at a time when it covered the largest area in Rome's history). In the end the villa and its grounds occupied a site larger than the centre of Imperial Rome, making it the largest – and most expensive – palace every built in the Roman Empire.

So many buildings were constructed that the function of many is still unknown. Before embarking on exploration, study the model near the main entrance, an attempt to suggest the villa's original appearance. Amidst the plethora of ruins – bathhouses, libraries, temples and the like – the most captivating spot is the **Teatro Marittimo**, a colonnaded palace built in the middle of an artificial lagoon. There's even a beach, once heated by steam pipes buried in the sand, as well as a series of underground service tunnels, large enough in their day to accommodate horses and carts.

Rome–Palestrina

The route

Although a less prominent feature on tourists' itineraries than Tivoli, Palestrina still merits a morning's visit – partly for its medieval streets and great views, but mainly for the remains of the **Tempio di Fortuna Primogenia**, one of Italy's greatest pre-Roman temples.

Trains

Trains stop below Palestrina at Zagarola (35 km, 30 min) on the main line south to Naples via Frosinone and Cassino.

The journey

The line out to Palestrina from Rome is more picturesque than many in the city's environs, skirting the vine-wreathed hills of the Colli Albani to the south before pushing into the pristine farming land of the Monti Prenestini. The town appears on its hill after 30 minutes, still a good way from the station. Buses up to the centre are not the world's most regular. Once ensconced within the ramparts, however, you're confronted with a place whose medieval appearance belies its long history (the longest in the region if legend is to be believed). In antiquity its Tempio di Fortuna Primogenia was the site of a famous oracle and a major temple to Fortune, mother of the gods. Myth claims it stands on the oldest site in Latium, founded by Telegonus, son of Odysseus and Circe. Archaeological evidence, though, suggests it was founded around the 7th century BC. At that time ancient *Praeneste* was already a religious centre and an important Etruscan trading centre. The Romans took the town in 338 BC and added further to its existing temple, the exact scope of which was only rediscovered after bombing during the Second World War.

Present day Palestrina is still built on six vast terraces buttressed into the hillside, ancient ledges which correspond to the six levels of the original temple. Remains of the edifice are visible at every turn, though most of its treasures are collected in the **Museo Nazionale Archeologico Prenestino** (in Piazza della Cortina), located in what would have been the sanctuary's upper level (Tues–Sun 9 am–1 pm). Its steps are adapted from an amphitheatre originally annexed to the temple's Rotonda, the possible site of the oracle itself (which was consulted by drawing out the *sorti Preneste*, or thin, carved sticks, from which priests would interpret the prophecies). Much of what's been found locally has wound up in Rome's Villa Giulia, but the museum contains a good scale model of how the temple might once have looked, bas reliefs, numerous busts, and plenty of *cistae*, or funerary headstones. Its pride and joy, though, is the outstanding 1st-century **Mosaic of the River Nile**, a highly detailed narrative which describes the story of the Nile from its source to its delta. The museum ticket also admits you to the excavations nearby, worth entering simply for the views over the surrounding countryside.

Rome–Cerveteri–Tarquinia

The route

This route north of Rome takes you to two of the region's leading Etruscan sites, Cerveteri and Tarquinia, both easily seen in a day. Each has a
good little museum and a number of ancient necropoli open to the public.
You'll also come out on this line if you're travelling to **Civitavecchia**, the
most convenient port for Rome to pick up ferries to Sardinia.

At a push you might also want to take a dip in the sea at one of the *lidos*
around Tarquinia, though few of the beaches are particularly clean or
appealing. For the best bathing possibilities stay on the train beyond Tarquinia for another 45 minutes and get off at the tiny hamlet of **Chiarone**.
Here, virtually empty beaches stretch for miles towards the rocky headland of Monte Argentario.

None of the towns in this area makes terribly appealing places to **stay**,
though you'll pay a good deal less in towns like Tarquinia than you will
in Rome. Camping is possible in a site at Chiarone, and you could camp
for free in the dunes close by. If you don't want to return to Rome, the
possibilities for **onward travel** mostly start from Grosseto, a dour
modern town to the north. Connections here run inland to Siena. Alternatively you could follow the main line north to Pisa.

The journey

Make no mistake, the ride out of Rome is not one to make for the scenery. D. H.
Lawrence described the plains and low hills en route as a 'peculiarly forlorn
coast, the sea peculiarly flat and sunken, lifeless looking, the land as if it had
given up its last gasp and was now forever inert'. He had better things to say
about the Etruscans, however, and his book, *Etruscan Places* makes a good introduction to both Etruscan art and culture. If you're not armed with a book, all
you can do otherwise for 40 minutes is sit back and watch reclaimed marshes and
the odd seaside resort flash by.

Cerveteri

Get off at the worst of these resorts, **Ladispoli** – 'desecration put upon desolation', said Lawrence – and wait for a bus in the forecourt to take you to **Cerveteri**.
Once you're in the town it's another two kilometre walk to the archaeological
site, probably the best of the many Etruscan remnants scattered around the
countryside close to Rome. Before setting off for the tombs, though, visit the
tourist office in Piazza Santa Maria Maggiore. The necropoli are signed from the
village.

The Etruscans ruled much of western central Italy between the 7th and 3rd

Trains

Plenty of trains head north on the main line to Pisa, but be sure the one you pick up stops en route. The faster services halt only at Civitavecchia (81 km, 50 min) and Grosseto (188 km, 1 hr 45 min). 10 trains daily call at Cerveteri (51 km, 40 min) and Tarquinia (101 km, 1 hr 10 min). Only a couple of trains stop at Chiarone, so check timetables carefully.

centuries BC, concentrating their culture into a loose federation of 12 city states. Where the Etruscans came from is one of history's great mysteries, though it's likely they were a mixture of indigenous tribes and foreign settlers. Where they went is less baffling, for they were conquered by the Romans, who absorbed many of their social, political and cultural traditions. In doing so they also obliterated much of the Etruscans' peculiar civilisation, leaving only the tombs and their contents as monuments to what must have been a lively and advanced civilisation.

Most of the graves' best remains have long since been removed to Rome's museums (the Villa Giulia and Vatican in particular). The graves themselves, however, still make fascinating viewing. Etruscan Cerveteri, or *Kysry* (Roman *Caere*) was an important trading centre as early as the 10th century BC, well-known to the Greeks, whose art and culture made marked impressions on the Etruscans. Eventually it figured amongst the Etruscans' top three cities, its wealth bolstered by the minerals mined from the Tolfa hills east of the town. Its decline coincided with the rise of Rome, which took the city in 351 BC.

Cerveteri's tombs are known as the **Necropoli della Banditaccia**, differing from those in Tarquinia in that they were constructed as a literal 'city of the dead'. Around 5,000 or more tombs are arranged as houses and streets in the manner of a real city (though only around 50 of the tombs have been properly excavated). Food, ornamentation and myriad everyday articles were left to provide the tombs' occupants with all they would need in the afterlife – much in the manner of the Egyptians. Wall paintings were added to remind them of life's earthly pleasures (usually scenes of feasting, dancing and swimming). All that remains today, though, are the graves themselves (real Etruscan cities were largely built of wood, another reason why so little of the Etruscan culture has come down to us). Spanning the 7th to 1st centuries BC, the tombs vary between strange pillboxes carved from the living rock to earthcovered tumuli – some over 30 metres across – that ripple all over the surrounding countryside.

The 12 show tombs cluster close to the site's entrance, wedged between the two main streets bisecting the necropolis. Not all, however, are open at the same time (Tues–Sun 9 am–7 pm, Oct–April 9 am–4 pm; under 18 free). In particular try to see the **Tomba Bella** (Tomb of the Bas-Reliefs), the **Tomba dei Capitali** and **Tomba dei Letti Funebri** (Tomb of the Funeral Beds). Round off a trip with a visit to the **Museo Nazionale Cerite**, a modest collection of Etruscan artifacts housed in the town's 16th-century Castello Orsini (May–Sept 9 am–1 pm and 4–7 pm, Oct–April 9 am–4 pm).

Tarquinia

Back on the train the line passes two appealing little resorts, **Santa Severa** and **Santa Marinella**, distinguished by their small castles and fringes of umbrella pines. Soon afterwards it crawls through **Civitavecchia**, blighted by its refineries, before arriving at the station for **Tarquinia**. Again you have to ride a bus to reach the town itself, which from a distance seems an evocative place of medieval towers and Renaissance buildings. Close to, though, the town's a strangely drab and half-derelict place, with just one church – Santa Maria di Castello – the only building to command any attention.

The only one, that is, except for the **Museo Nazionale**, a small but pithy collection of Etruscan remains. Its centrepiece – a pair of winged terracotta horses – is one of the most famous Etruscan sculptures in Italy. The museum's just up the road from the Barriera San Giusto, where the bus from the station stops, and one block up on the left from the tourist office (Palazzo Vitelleschi, Tues–Sat 9 am–2 pm, July 15–Sept 15 also 4–7 pm). Apart from the horses, which probably formed part of a temple frieze, the museum's half-dozen rooms offer some high quality jewellery, funeral urns, the usual vases, and some nicely bizarre three-legged candle sticks. In other rooms tombs have been reconstructed, primarily to display their wall paintings in controlled conditions.

As in Cerveteri the vast spread of tombs at Tarquinia are some way from the present town, scattered over the Monterozzi plateau to the east. It's a 20 minute walk to the nearest of the graves, or you can take any of the buses marked *Cimitero* from Barriera San Giusto. Tickets from the museum are valid for the tombs, and the ticket office displays a list of tombs currently open (most are open in rotation to protect their wall paintings). Trips into the tombs are in guided tours only – so you may have to wait until a large enough group assembles: the tourist office also organises trips from the museum.

The necropolis consists of some 6,000 tombs, all that remains of ancient Tarquinia, in its day a city of 100,000 people and probably the Etruscans' cultural and political capital. The graves here are less literal 'houses' than in Cerveteri – and similarly stripped of their booty – though they're distinguished by all sorts of vigorous **wall paintings**. These divide roughly into two eras: the earliest emphasise largely mythical and ritualistic scenes, the second – from the 6th to 4th centuries BC – concentrate more on social episodes, giving both an insight into the daily lives of Etruscans and a glimpse of the eastern and Greek styles which influenced the paintings (and which elsewhere have largely vanished without trace). The best of the tombs from the latter group include the Orca, Auguri, della Caccia and della Pescia graves.

Practicalities in Tarquinia

Tourist Office Piazza Cavour 1 (0766/856.384).
Hotel ☆☆*Hotel San Marco*, Piazza Cavour 18 (0766/840.813).

Camping Three large campsites at Tarquinia Lido: the *Tuscia* is the best (0766/88.294), reached by bus from the station or town centre.
Restaurants *Corneto*, Via Garibaldi 12.

Rome–(Tivoli)–Tagliacozzo–Sulmona
The route

Any trip across the Italian peninsula involves crossing the Apennines, the mountainous spine that runs virtually the length of the country. This means that any trip guarantees at least a modicum of mountain scenery. The trans-Apennine route from Rome to Pescara is no exception. This journey follows it half-way, stopping at **Sulmona**, an interesting and appealing little town and perfectly placed for short trips to L'Aquila to the north and the Abruzzo national park to the south. Unless you stop off at Tivoli en route, however (see Rome–Tivoli on page 259), little on the line merits leaving the train. Sulmona is the place to stay, though **Tagliacozzo** also makes a quiet stopover.

Trains
10 trains daily operate between Rome and Sulmona (172 km, 1 hr 30 min), half of them fast trains from **Termini** *en route for* **Pescara***, the rest painfully slow* diretti *that take a mind-numbing 3 hours to make the same journey.*

The journey

Once you've slipped through Rome's eastern suburbs most of this journey involves sitting back to look at the mountains. Tivoli passes by after half an hour, a tempting prospect if you've not already been here from Rome (see page 259). Almost immediately the hills start to rise in height, the Monti Simbruini to the south, source of much of Rome's drinking water in the days of imperial aqueducts (their name derives from the Latin for 'heavy rain'). After increasingly sylvan countryside, **Tagliacozzo** rolls into view to the south, lodged below forest-covered crags and clustered around a neat Renaissance centre. The town takes its name from the Greek muse of theatre (*Thalia*) – reputedly because it was founded by Greek settlers from Mount Parnassus. There's little to see, but the tangled streets and elegant little piazzas make it an appealing enough place to stay if you're forced to stop overnight. Contact the tourist office in Piazza Argoli for details of the town's hotels.

Twenty minutes beyond Tagliacozzo the mountains suddenly rear up to new heights, crowned by two vast peaks, Monte Velino (2,487 m) and Monte Sirente (2,349 m), two of central Italy's wildest upland enclaves. Almost as suddenly the land away to the south flattens into nothing as the line skirts the **Piana del Fucino**. This huge plain was once Italy's third largest lake. Today it's the largest lake in the world ever to have been artificially drained. Attempts to empty the lake started almost 2,000 years ago. Under the Emperor Caligula, the Romans attempted to combat the floods that ripped through the area every time the snows melted. A six-kilometre tunnel was dug to empty the lake into an adjoining valley. In the event it proved unable to cope with the volume of water it siphoned off. Thousands of spectators – the Emperor included – narrowly escaped being washed away when the gates were opened. Further attempts to re-use the tunnel failed, and the lake was only finally drained in 1875. What had seemed like a good idea for centuries, however, then came to be a cause for regret. Although the drainage released agricultural land, it also burdened the area with mist, mosquitoes and a wearing, humid climate.

Sulmona

After its easy passage across the plain and a series of meandering tunnels the train emerges in **Sulmona**, a bracing upland town surrounded on all sides by a forest-draped wall of mountains. If it's known at all, it's as the birthplace of the great Roman poet Ovid (43 BC–AD 19). *Sulmo mihi patria est*, declared Ovid, 'Sulmona is my homeland', an observation recalled ever since in the town's coat-of-arms, which bears the letters SMPE. The main street, **Corso Ovidio**, bears the poet's name, and the main square to which it leads, **Piazza XX Settembre**, boasts a statue of the scribe. Whilst you're in the square, incidentally, grab a coffee at the *Gran Caffè*, a turn-of-the century art nouveau institution.

Out on the Corso the street's full of shops selling *confetti*, a sugared-almond confection bound with wire and ribbons into elaborate flowers. The town started making them in the 15th century, since when they've played a part in Catholic and non-Catholic weddings the world over. These days, of course, it's coloured paper that's thrown (though at Abruzzese nuptials proper white *confetti* are still used).

Otherwise the place you want to see in town is the combined church and palace of the **Annunziata**, off the Corso 100 metres north of Piazza XX Settembre. Started in the 15th century, it's a harmonious blend of medieval, Renaissance and Baroque elements – rather like the town itself. Funded by the town's well-to-do, it was built to minister to the town's poor, aiming to care for the needy from cradle to grave. The palace (on the right) has a Gothic upper tier of windows and three portals below, dating from 1415, 1483 and 1522 respectively (making them interesting to compare). The church alongside is largely concealed behind a Baroque façade (built in 1700), most of whose decoration revolves around the theme of life and death.

A 100 metres south of Piazza XX Settembre stands what's left of the church of **San Francesco delle Scarpe** (literally 'St Francis of the Shoes': unlike other monastic orders the Franciscans occasionally wore shoes instead of sandals). The church's doughty portal was the only part of the original building left standing after an earthquake in 1703. Nearby is the **Fontana del Vecchio**, a fine Gothic fountain (1256) named after the carved figure of an old man at its crown. It emptied water brought to the town by an aqueduct, built not only to supply drinking water but also to power the town's mills. Behind it stretches the large Piazza Garibaldi, home to a museum devoted to the Abruzzo's shepherding traditions.

Way up at the top end of the town (follow Corso Ovidio and then Viale Roosevelt) the **duomo** is known for its magnificent 12th-century Byzantine-style relief in the crypt, the *Madonna Enthroned.*

Practicalities in Sulmona

Tourist Office Via Roma 21, off Corso Ovidio (0864/53.276).

Railway Station The town's a 2-kilometre uphill walk from the station. Bus A, however, connects to Piazza XX Settembre every 30 minutes.

Buses Buses leave for surrounding towns and villages from the Villa Comunale, the public gardens at the northern end of Corso Ovidio. Destinations include L'Aquila and Scanno, a mountain village on the edge of the Abruzzo national park that makes a good day's outing from Sulmona. Countryside and views en route are superb.

Hotels ☆☆*Albergo Italia*, Piazza Tommasi 3 (0864/52.308). The best hotel in town, just behind Piazza XX Settembre overlooking the Annunziata and with views of the mountains.

☆☆*Nuova Madrigale*, Via Paolina (0864/ 51.785). Also close to the Annunziata off Corso Ovidio, but with less character than the *Italia*.

☆☆*Stella*, Via Mazara 15 (0864/52.653). Located on the first right off the Corso north of the Fontana del Vecchio. There's a reasonable restaurant annexed downstairs.

☆☆*Da Giovanni*, Via Peligna, off Via Mazara (0864/51.397).

Restaurants *Italia-Da Nicola*, Piazza XX Settembre 22. The best of several good eating places in Sulmona, and a good place to sample genuine Abruzzese specialities.

Cesidio, Via Gramsci-Piazza Solimo, just off the north end of the Corso on Via Solimo. A popular place with locals, and a touch less expensive and self-conscious than the *Italia*.

Sulmona–L'Aquila

The route

It's only a short hop north to L'Aquila from Sulmona. The reasons for making the trip are two-fold – firstly to see L'Aquila and secondly to make an excursion to the **Gran Sasso d'Italia,** the highest point on the Italian peninsula. The journey, which follows the Aterno valley, has the additional bonus of more excellent mountain scenery.

Like Sulmona, L'Aquila is a little-visited town, and though a tad more bleak and commercially-minded it also makes a good place to stop overnight. For onward travel there's a slow branch line that connects to Terni – scenic in its early stages to Cittaducale – which offer myriad possibilities for itineraries in Tuscany and Umbria.

Trains

10 trains daily (6 at weekends) run from Sulmona to L'Aquila (60 km, 1 hr 10 min). All are locali which stop at every station.

L'Aquila

Dour in appearance at first glance, closer acquaintance with **L'Aquila** – capital of the Abruzzo – reveals a lively town that combines medieval and modern in equal measure. The region's main museum is here, together with a brace of monuments and old streets that should keep you busy for a morning. Wherever you go it's impossible to escape the city's fondness for the number 99. Even the bell of the town hall clock strikes 99 times every evening at 9.09 pm. The obsession springs from 1242, the year Emperor Frederick II reputedly created L'Aquila from 99 castles and villages in the surrounding countryside. Each village is supposed to have built its own church, piazza and fountain in the new city.

What to See

L'Aquila's most famous sight, the **Fontana delle 99 Cannelle** (1292), is another monument to its numerical fixation. It's a 99-spouted affair that spurts water (from an unknown source) out of 99 gargoyles (plus 6 undecorated taps). You'll see it at Porta Riviera if you walk from the station to the town centre.

Museo Nazionale d'Abruzzo

The Museo Nazionale d'Abruzzo (Tues–Sun 9 am–2 pm), located in the Castello (1534–49), is a Spanish-built fortress that looms over the town's north-east quarter. Constructed to keep down a rebellious population, the castle was damaged during the Second World War, after which the grounds were landscaped and the museum created. The collection's a fascinating pot-pourri, ranging from a stuffed mammoth found locally to displays of sacred art, local pottery and the cream of the region's paintings. Perhaps the best-known works

Practicalities in L'Aquila

Tourist Office The town's local office is at Via XX Settembre 8 (0862/22.306). To reach it turn right out of the station and at Porta Riviera take Via San Jacopo uphill to Via XX Settembre. The EPT which serves the whole province is more central – Piazza Santa Maria Paganica 5 (0862/410.808), located off the northern end of Corso Vittorio Emanuele. This office is particularly worth a visit if you intend to visit the Gran Sasso.

For further hiking information, maps and books, visit the Club Alpino Italiano (CAI) offices on the third floor at Via XX Settembre 15 (0862/24.342), usually only open Mon–Sat 6–7 pm.

Railway Station Piazza della Stazione – Via Santa Maria del Ponte (0862/20.497). Regular buses numbers 1, 3 or 3/5 connect to the town centre. Otherwise it's an uphill walk of about 1.5 km.

Buses Long haul SITA buses leave from Piazza Battaglione, west of the Castello, and at the northern end of Corso Vittorio Emanuele.

Hotels ☆*Italia*, Corso Vittorio Emanuele 79 (0862/20.566). Probably the most central and characterful of the town's cheaper hotels.
☆*Aurora*, Via Cimino 21 (0862/22.053). Cheap and fairly dowdy rooms off the Corso, immediately opposite Piazza del Duomo.
☆*Centrale*, Via Simonetto (0862/64.211). More basic central rooms off the Corso.
☆☆*Sole*, Largo Silvestro dell'Aquila (0862/24.041). Big, bright rooms in a quiet backstreet close to Piazza del Duomo. Cheaper rooms without bathrooms are also available.
Restaurants *Stella Alpina*, Via Crispomonti 15. Reliable choice for local dishes which include lamb, saffron, truffles and the local *chitarra* pasta – so called because it's cut into strips with what look like wires strung over a guitar. For pudding try the local nougat (*torrone*), widely available around town.
San Biaggio, Piazza San Biaggio 1. More expensive than the *Alpina*, but undoubtedly the first choice amongst locals.

are a pair of wooden doors (1132) carved with New Testament scenes, removed – like many of the exhibits – from earthquake-ravaged churches in the surrounding countryside. Its most infamous piece is a silver processional crucifix (1434), once stolen from the town's duomo and unwittingly auctioned at Sotheby's before being returned to the museum.

San Bernardino

Back from the castle follow Corso Vittorio Emanuele (the main street) south and turn left on Via San Bernardino for the church of San Bernardino. Although St Bernard (St Bernardino) hailed from Siena, he died in L'Aquila and was buried here (the Sienese traditionally visit the town on his feast day bearing gifts of Tuscan oil). Built from 1454–72, the grand three-tiered façade was added between 1527–40. Inside, the rich Baroque ceiling dates from the 18th century, a masterpiece of gilding and carving. The tomb of San Bernardino (1505) is by Silvestro dell'Aquila, a pupil of Donatello, popularly known as the 'Michelangelo of the Abruzzo'.

Excursion from L'Aquila

The Gran Sasso d'Italia

At 2,912 metres the Gran Sasso d'Italia – literally the 'big rock of Italy' – is the highest point on the Italian peninsula (Etna in Sicily and peaks in the Alps are higher). You can see its serrated profile from points around L'Aquila, but for a closer look take a 12-kilometre bus ride out of town (bus number 6 from Piazza Battaglione; 5 daily, 1 hr). Ask for an *extraurbano* ticket from the information kiosk in the piazza or from *tabacchi*.

The bus takes you to **Fonte Cerreto** (1,120 m), a hamlet at the foot of a cablecar, or *funivia*. This complex consists of little more than two hotels, a restaurant and a good **campsite**, the *Camping Funivia del Gran Sasso* (open June–Sept and Nov–April).

From here on you have several choices. From the bottom of the cable car there are several simple trails – try number 10 to Monte della Scinderella (2,230 m) for great views of the Gran Sasso and L'Aquila. Or you can simply ride the cablecar up for the view (it runs half-hourly from 8.30 am–5.30 pm, except at 1.30pm). In the summer, be warned, this is a busy spot, so don't expect mountainous solitude.

At the top of the cablecar there's a hotel, the *Albergo-Rifugio Campo Imperatore*, famous as the spot where Mussolini was imprisoned by partisans after Italy surrendered in 1942. He was sprung from the eyrie by a daring German raid, and then taken to northern Italy to head the short-lived Salò Republic. You could stay here as base for **hiking**, though it's cheaper to use the *Duca degli Abruzzi Rifugio* (July–Sept) close by. Both places sell food and drink if you're only passing through. The classic walk from here is the west-wall ascent of the Corno Grande. Many people cross over the massif, overnighting at the *Rifugio Franchetti* (0861/95.642).

If you intend to do any walking try to pick up maps and trail details at the EPT tourist office or CAI office in L'Aquila. If you intend to spend a night in any of the mountain refuges enquire at the tourist office about closing times and the likely availability of beds (most open mid-June to Sept). Outside the summer months there's lots of snow and ice, and potentially dangerous scree at all times, so only tackle the mountain if you're properly equipped.

Back on to the Corso and you're soon in Piazza del Duomo, the centre of town, though only a vibrant little daily **market** holds out any appeal. Your time's better spent exploring the steep skein of streets to the south, Via Sassa in particular, home to the tiny church **Beata Antonia**. Ring the bell at number 29a and a nun will open the door and lead you to the *affresco*, a 15th-century scene of the crucifixion covering most of one wall.

Santa Maria di Collemaggio
Santa Maria di Collemaggio is one of the most important churches in the Abruzzo, thanks mainly to its spectacular portal and pink-and-white marbled façade. Begun in 1287, the heavy rectangular church was instigated by Pietro di Morrone, a hermit who was forced from the mountains against his wishes and then encouraged to become Pope. He made the Papacy as Pope Celestino V in 1294 (following two years of deliberations by the Papal conclaves). Intended as a mere pawn, he eventually proved too simple-minded to pass muster even as a figurehead. He resigned after only five months, and was canonised posthumously for his trouble. Thieves removed his relics from the church in 1988, hoping to secure a ransom – to no avail – and the hapless monk is now back in his mausoleum (contained in the right apse). The church's big day is August 29, when a free pardon is granted to those who walk through a 'holy Door' – one of the few initiatives made by Pietro during his shortlived Papacy. Dignitaries from all over Italy come in search of absolution.

Sulmona–Alfedena–Castel di Sangro
The route
Central Italy's meandering branch lines are some of the most extraordinarily engineered railways in the country. This is mainly because they have to wend their way around the high mountains of the central Apennines. This short route offers both a taste of the high country from the train, and the opportunity to venture into Italy's finest national park, the **Parco Nazionale d'Abruzzo**. This is virtually the last redoubt for brown bears in Italy, and also home to many of the country's 200 or more wolves. It's also a superbly administered park, with many well-signed and well-mapped **footpaths** if you want to tackle some hiking – the main reason for coming here.

At Castel di Sangro the possibilities for **onward travel** become complicated. If you're happy pottering around one of the least known parts of the country, change trains (and stations) for the great little line that strikes north-east up the Sangro valley towards Lanciano and the Adriatic coast (another marvellously scenic ride). Or stay with the same line for Isernia, where one set of connections takes you to Vairano on the

Trains

Journeys are slow in this part of the world, no hardship given the scenery that passes the window. 8 trains daily run from Sulmona to Castel di Sangro (77 km, 1 hr 25 min). Only 2 run through to Isernia (although there are additional connections at Castel di Sangro).

Excursion from Alfedena

Parco Nazionale d'Abruzzo

Although the train has already carried you through some of the wildest of the Abruzzo's mountains, the area's most beautiful scenery is protected by the Parco Nazionale d'Abruzzo, immediately west of Alfedena.

Once you're off the train, the best approach to the park is by bus from Alfedena. Six ARPA services daily run between Alfedena and Avezzano (on the Piana del Fucino, so you could also pick up a bus in Avezzano and enter the park from the north; see Rome–Tagliacozzo–Sulmona on page 265). The buses stop at all the main villages en route, the biggest of which is **Pescasseroli** (an hour from Alfedena), home to the park headquarters and – though not the park's prettiest village – probably its best overall base. Plenty of trails strike out from here, but you can easily broaden the scope of your exploration by taking the bus to neighbouring villages and walking from these.

All the villages have **information offices** (at Opi, Villetta Barrea, Barrea and Civitella Alfedena, open daily during the summer 9 am–1 pm and 4.30–6.30 pm).

Only the office in Pescasseroli, however, is reliably open off season. It's at Via Piave opposite the police station (0863/910.461). Also make a point of visiting both the small Park Centre, well-signed next to the Town Hall at Via Consulatore 1 (0863/910.995), and the much larger Park Museum, 300 metres away.

If you're walking, most of the offices should stock the park's own excellent **map**. With over 100 trails, however, it's difficult to know which to choose. These are some of the best: from Pescasseroli, try trail B2 to Monte di Valle Carrara (2 hr 30 min) or C3 to the Valico di Monte Tranquillo (2 hr 30 min). Both can easily be extended. The best walk from Civitella Alfedena, and one that almost guarantees sightings of chamois, is trail 11 into the Valle delle Rose (5 hr round trip). Numerous tracks strike into the Valle Fondillo near Opi, one of the loveliest and most popular parts of the park. Another favourite is the climb from Barrea to Lago Vivo (2 hr), or the walk in the Camosciara valley to the Belvedere della Liscia (2 hr), west of Villetta Barrea.

Practicalities for Parco Nazionale d'Abruzzo

Hostels Most of the villages offer cheap hostels, but their locations vary from year to year, so check with the tourist offices for latest details.
Hotels (Pescasseroli) ☆☆*Al Castello*, Via G. d'Annunzio, off the main piazza (0863/910.757); ☆☆*Peppe di Sora*, Viale B. Croce (0863/910.908); ☆☆*Valle del Lupo*, Via Collachi, 2 km out of town (0863/910.534). (Civitella Alfedena) ☆☆*La Torre*, Via La Torre

(0864/890.121). (Alfedena) ☆☆*Leon d'Oro*, (0864/87.121).
Campsites Pescasseroli has 4 local campsites; the best is *Campeggio dell'Orso* on the main road out to Opi (open all year). The *Marsicano* is the next best option. About 2 km outside Opi (on the bus route) is the *Vecchio Mulino*; Civitella Alfedena has the riverside *Pinas Nigra* site.

main Rome–Naples line, and another puts you on yet more lines through beautiful unknown country – either to Benevento or Termoli on the Adriatic (via Campobasso).

The journey

None of the villages en route can be said to have any 'sights', but you'll have some of your best 'sit back and let the world go by moments' on this – and other – lines locally. From a height of 405 metres at Sulmona the train climbs quickly in a series of tunnels and broad hairpins to over 1,200 metres, winding around whaleback hills and offering far-reaching views of the Maiella mountains (2,793 m). Beyond Pescocostanzo, however, a picturesque village, civilisation begins to put in a reappearance, largely in the shape of alpine-type chalets aimed at winter skiers. Castel di Sangro eventually appears in the valley below, the train having to make a sweeping curve through **Alfedena** before dropping to the village.

6 The South

The south is a catch-all description that embraces four regions; **Campania, Calabria, Basilicata** and **Puglia**. Where it starts has always been a moot point. The Milanese say Florence, the Florentines Rome. **Naples**, though, capital of Campania, is probably as good a place as any; the border of the *mezzogiorno*, the 'land of the mid-day sun', an area separated for centuries from the rest of Italy by geography, history and economics. These days it's as much a world apart as ever; poorer, wilder, more backward, probably more corrupt than northern Italy. Whatever you hear about it, however – and northerners are increasingly scathing about their neighbours – the south is also one of the more interesting parts of Italy. Overall the cities and towns may have less in the way of monuments, but amongst the people, and in the feel of the place, you're more likely to find traces of the Italy of old.

This has its good side – old ideals of honour and hospitality, for example, and glimpses of a way of life that has vanished in much of Europe. Its downside, however, to generalise, is a grinding bureaucracy, a decaying infrastructure, and a numbing inefficiency. There's also a fair amount of petty crime (in cities, rarely in rural areas). Hotels and restaurants, too, are fewer and farther between, although prices and crowds are also considerably reduced. In many ways, the south's railways are a microcosm of all that's good and bad in the region. They're small and quaint – and if this is your idea of how railways should be, there are endless small lines to explore. They're also, however, slow and infrequent (though this, again, may not be a problem for train buffs). You need to allow far more time to get around than in the north and you need to read the timetables more carefully. At the same time, lines still run to the best spots – even if some meander through half-forgotten, little-visited countryside en route.

The recommended routes, as ever, take you to the highlights – although it can't be stressed enough that you should also explore some of the interior lines if time allows. Wherever you're headed, the chances are you'll start from **Naples**, the south's traditional capital. For some this chaotic, crime-ridden but overwhelmingly vibrant city is one of the most fascinating in Italy. For others it's a place to escape from as quickly as possible. Like much of the south it's been administered over the centuries by foreigners – Greeks, Normans, Angevins (the kings of Anjou), the Spanish and the French; all powers – together with the Saracens in the deep south – who've most left their mark politically and artistically on the region.

Beyond Naples, **Campania**'s highlights include a trip round **Vesuvius**, a still active volcano, or visits to **Pompeii** and **Herculaneum,** old Roman colonies buried by Vesuvius in AD 79 and now two of Italy's finest archaeological sites. Nearby, buses from the railhead at **Sorrento** allow you to explore the area around Amalfi, one of the country's most famous coastlines. Many people, though, at this point, sit tight on a train all the way down Italy's western coast en route for Sicily.

Calabria is the toe of the 'Italian boot', as impoverished and under-developed a region as any in the south, bereft of artistic treasures, but possessed of a largely unspoilt coastline and uncompromising mountainous interior. To experience the former at its best, jump train at **Tropea**; to see the latter at first hand ride one or other of the scenic lines from Cosenza. **Basilicata,** north of Calabria and the boot's 'instep', has the un-enviable distinction of being Italy's poorest region. Don't, however, be put off from taking a train through its wild, tourist-free interior. It's single unmissable sight is **Matera,** known for its *sassi*, ancient cave-dwellings burrowed into the hills in and around the town. (Though the town is better seen from Puglia.)

Puglia (Apulia) forms the heel of the boot, by far the most rewarding part of the south to explore at length (and length is the optimum word here – the region's 400 km from north to south, so don't underestimate the distances involved). Neither its interior, the *Murge* – bare, dry and rocky – nor its coast (flat and smothered in vines and olives) offer much scenically, save in the enclave of cliffs, forests and fine beaches known as the **Gargano** (a promontory that forms the 'spur' of the boot). In the towns, though, especially **Lecce, Bari** and **Trani,** you'll find stunning examples of Puglian-Romanesque architecture, and, in the case of Lecce, a showcase of Baroque buildings as well. Riding a couple of smaller lines takes you to see the *trulli*, ancient conical dwellings, and the Salentino peninsula, an area more Greek-looking than Italian.

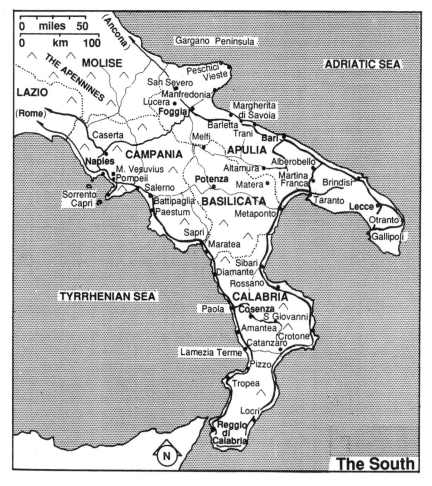

The South

Routes *Naples–Herculaneum–Pompeii–Sorrento*
Battipaglia–Paestum–Tropea–Reggio di Calabria
Reggio di Calabria–Metaponto–Rossano–(Taranto)
Cosenza–San Giovanni in Fiore
Cosenza–Catanzaro
Foggia–Trani–Bari
Bari–Altamura–Matera
Bari–Brindisi–Lecce
Bari–Alberobello–Martina Franca–Taranto
Lecce–Otranto–Gallipoli–Lecce

There are far more routes in the south than are covered in the chapter. Choice, however, is not the main problem. Your main concern is likely to be how (and when) to cross the peninsula from west to east – that is, how to see **Campania** *(Naples and* **Naples–Pompeii–Sorrento***) and then move over to explore Puglia (which has the majority of the chapter's routes). The coastal option is a long way round (***Naples–Reggio di Calabria** *and* **Reggio di Calabria–Taranto***). The* **most direct route** *is* **Naples–Caserta–Benevento–Foggia,** *though it's not the most scenic. Probably the best is* **Naples–Avellino–Spinoza–Altamura,** *or some variation, perhaps involving Potenza: the branch line options here are numerous. All involve slow journeys and lots of changes, but the little villages and empty, rolling hills make them worthwhile if you're not in a hurry (or desperate to have 'sights' en route). Remember you can access many of the south's small interior lines from the Abruzzo lines (see Sulmona–Castel di Sangro, for example on page 270).*

More specifically, the best of the **scenic routes** *are the two lines* **Cosenza–San Giovanni in Fiore** *and* **Cosenza–Catanzaro.** *These require access from the west coast route, however – (***Battipaglia***)–Paestum–Tropea–Reggio di Calabria, which rather leaves you with few options other than making straight for Sicily. If you head east, though,* **Foggia–Bari** *and* **Bari–Brindisi–Lecce** *take care of Puglia's cities;* **Bari–Matera** *gives you the one-off novelty of Matera's sassi;* **Lecce–Gallipoli** *a look at the Salentine peninsula (plus beaches near Gallipoli);* **Bari–Martina Franca–Taranto** *provides the chance to see the famous* trulli *(and* **Taranto's** *noted museum – the city's otherwise not a place to linger). Taranto also sets you up for a trip around the coast to* **Reggio di Calabria** *and thus to* **Sicily.**

Naples

Italy's most infamous city arouses fierce passions. Some find its chaos, crime and endless cacophony unendurable. Others find it compelling for the same reasons. Merely traipsing around the sights, however, won't help you make your mind up either way. You need to take your courage in both hands and explore as much of the city on foot as you can. Not for the monuments, of which there are few, but to experience its melodrama and raucous charm. Whatever else, it's like nowhere else in Italy, its inhabitants a different breed to Italians. Spend a day here, says a local saying, and you hate the place; spend a week and you'll have fallen in love; spend a year and you'll never want to leave.

Most of the myths and clichés surrounding Naples have basis in fact. It's the city of Sophia Loren, for example, a particular archetype for decades, as well as pizzas and sentimental songs (for example *O Sole Mio*, the most famous). It's also a place obsessed by football, not to mention those other Italian staples – family, food and religion. Once, too, it was a city of legendary beauty, the Bay of Naples and the backdrop of Vesuvius having provided the lure for 'Grand Tourists' (the 'Grand Tour' traditionally culminated in the city). These days, though, it has its moments of beauty – degenerate or otherwise – it's a city with the highest population density in Europe, grinding poverty, relentless bureaucratic inefficiency, high unemployment and just about every social ill you can think of. Inevitably, of course, it's also thick with petty and organised crime, from the *scugnizzi* – wily street kids who'll steal anything you've got – to the *Camorra*, the Neopolitan mafia, masters of just about everything that matters in the city.

History

The name 'Naples' comes from *Neapolis*, the 'New City', founded by Greek settlers from nearby Cumae in the 6th century BC. This presupposes the existence of an 'old city', possibly *Parthenope*, a 9th century BC colony on a hill above the city (scholars can't agree on the derivation). The colony prospered under the Greeks and then the Romans, largely escaping the decline that beset Rome after the fall of the Empire.

The city blossomed again during a brief period of Norman rule (begun in 1139), when it formed part of the Kingdom of Sicily under Roger II. The Hohenstaufens, notably Frederick II, the Holy Roman Emperor, ruled until 1269, eventually giving way to the kings of the French Anjou dynasty, who built up the city but, with the exception of Robert the Wise, generally proved ineffectual rulers. In 1422 they lost the city to the

Spanish under Alfonso I of Aragon. Spain remained in charge until 1734 when the French took over (under Charles of Bourbon). Neither period of foreign domination did much for the city, though they produced most of its monuments and important buildings. More recently, Naples' dire economic situation has not been helped by serious earthquakes – one, in 1980, claimed 4,000 lives – nor by the fact that huge amounts of financial aid from national and EC coffers has wound up in criminal hands. Worse, there have even been outbreaks of cholera, not a disease that should strike a city in one of the world's leading industrialised nations.

What to See

Naples is a complicated city which needs time and patience. It's unfortunate that **Piazza Garibaldi**, outside the station, is one of its most intimidating and dispiriting areas. Push beyond it, though, taking **no** risks whatsoever, and things improve.

The city's crammed with churches and palaces of only incidental interest (over 350 churches, in fact), places you should pop into as you pass during your wanderings. What follows is a guide to sights it's worth heading for specifically. None are terribly close to the main railway station, but as walking is the best (often the only) way to see the city, this needn't be a hardship. Greater Naples is large and sprawling and orientation is far from easy. The old historic centre, though, lies between the station and Piazza Garibaldi in the east and (north-running) Via Toledo and Via Roma in the west. Two other main streets connect the station areas to the two westerly thoroughfares: Via Tribunali and Via San Biagio dei Librai – running through Spaccanapoli ('split Naples'), heart of the historic centre.

The Castel Nuovo

Walk all the way down Corso Umberto I from Piazza Garibaldi for the Castel Nuovo (also known as the Maschio Angioino), a good-looking castle built in 1279 by Charles of Anjou to replace the waterfront Castel dell'Ovo. The latter was deemed too susceptible to attack, but still survives, sitting astride a promontory to the south. The former was later rebuilt by Alfonso I as the Aragons' royal residence. These days it's the headquarters of the Naples and Campania councils – with entry restricted as a result – though you can still see the **Arco di Trionfo** at the entrance, a triumphal arch built in 1467 to celebrate Alfonso's taking of the city. Look out for Alfonso in the central panel, riding his chariot and surrounded by fawning courtiers.

Just behind the castle is the **Teatro San Carlo** (1737), one of the finest opera houses in the world (more impressive, even, than La Scala in Milan). 'Naples is the only capital of Italy,' declared Stendhal after seeing the interior. It's a plain affair from the outside, but join one of the regular guided tours for a glimpse of what an opera house in the old style should look like. Afterwards, strike north up Via Toledo to the Museo Archeologico.

En route, though, just off Piazza Carità, drop into **Sant'Anna dei Lombardi**, a superficially unassuming church begun by Olivetan monks in 1411. If it's open – and generally it isn't – there's a wealth of Renaissance sculpture on show, plus frescoes by Vasari and a beautifully intricate set of inlaid choir stalls. The best sculptures are a *Pietà* (1492) by Guido Mazzoni (claimed by many to be the finest carving in the city). It's in the chapel at the end of the right transept. Almost as outstanding are the *Nativity* and *Tomb of Maria of Aragon*, both by Antonio Rossellino (housed in the second chapel on the left).

Museo Archeologico Nazionale

Most people who have no desire to get to grips with Naples brave the city simply to see the Museo Archeologico Nazionale, widely considered the greatest archeological museum in Europe. The labelling of exhibits is poor, and often whole sections are closed for restoration, but you should go away satisfied even if you manage to see only a fraction of what's on offer. Much of the collection comes from Pompeii and Herculaneum, so be sure to drop in if you're also intending to visit these sites. If you aim to give the place a thorough going-over, consider investing in one of the English guides on sale at the ticket office (Tues–Sat 9 am–2 am, Sun 9 am–1 pm).

The **ground floor** is devoted mainly to classical sculpture from the Farnese collection, garnered by one of Rome's leading 17th-century families from sites all over Lazio and Campania. The best pieces are the *Farnese Hercules*, a triumphant muscular figure, and the *Farnese Bull*, the largest group of sculptures to have survived from antiquity. Both came from the Terme di Caracalla in Rome: the latter was restored by Michelangelo. Other highlights include the Augustan-era *Eurydice and Hermes*; the famous *Javelin Thrower*; a figure of *Doryphorous* taken from Pompeii (one of the finest Roman copies of a Greek original); a selection of busts; and the *Venus Callipage* (the 'Venus of the Beautiful Posterior').

Further on, up the marble staircase, the mezzanine floor contains numerous **mosaics**, some of the museum's highlights, all of which are fascinating and extraordinarily well-preserved. Look out, in particular, for the *Battle of Issus*, a realistic tableau showing Alexander the Great defeating the Persians; the *Seascape* showing a squid fighting a lobster; *Street Musicians*; the *Group of Soothsayers*; and *The Meeting of the Platonic Academy*.

Upstairs, most of the rooms are devoted to **wall paintings**, most of them lifted from Pompeii and Herculaneum. These, for most people, are the museum's high-spot, and it's worth taking time to explore some of the smaller and more intimate panels. In addition to the murals are displays of various artifacts from Campanian archaeological sites, mainly glass, silver and ceramics. Look out for the 115-piece table service from the house of Meander in Pompeii, and the famous *Tazza Farnese*, a cup made of veined sardonyx. Particular attention is given to finds from the **Villa dei Papiri** in Herculaneum, mostly bronze statues and celebrated *papyri* covered with Greek inscriptions. Other Pompeii pieces include blood-curdling gladiatorial paraphernalia – helmets, swords and trumpets – and a room of carbonised items taken from lava-encrusted houses: soap, shoes, pans – even dates, olives, onions and cakes.

The Duomo

Unlike most Italian cities where the duomo is a prominently placed and grandiloquent statement in stone, Naples' cathedral languishes in a side street off Via Tribunali (walk here by turning left out of the museum to Piazza San Gennaro and then right down Via del Duomo). The façade is a drab 19th-century affair, the interior partly 13th-century Gothic, though the church is famous not for its monuments but for the relics of **San Gennaro**.

Gennaro, the city's patron saint, was martyred outside the city in 305. Legend has it that when the body was transferred to the site of the present duomo, two phials of the saint's blood liquified in the bishop's hands. Since then the phials have been expected to repeat their miraculous behaviour three times a year (at boisterous and heavily-attended Masses on the first Saturday in May, September 19 and December 16). On the rare occasions they fail, local superstition – an immensely powerful phenomenon – holds that some disaster awaits the city; anything from defeat for the local football team to an eruption of Vesuvius (the latter occurred in 1944 after one non-liquification).

On the opposite side of the church are the remains of the basilica of **Santa Restituta**, officially the oldest building in Naples, erected by Constantine in 324 using materials from an earlier temple to Apollo. Within is a baptistery built a century later, home to frescoes from the period and a primitive font crudely dug out of the floor. Excavations below the church are revealing more early finds, open to fascinating guided tours on Saturday mornings at 10.30am and 11.30am (book tickets from the tourist office in Piazza del Gesù). The nave's arches, incidentally, incorporate columns from earlier pagan temples; the frescoes above, by Luca Giordano, depict 46 saints.

San Lorenzo Maggiore

Turn left out of the duomo, then first right on Via Tribunali, and the Franciscan church of San Lorenzo Maggiore is almost immediately on your left. One of the finest examples of Neapolitan Gothic, the aisleless interior is the work of 14th-century French Provençal craftsmen. If you've read Boccaccio, this is the church in which the writer saw the girl he immortalised as Fiammetta. Petrarch also stayed in the monastery next door in 1345. Various of the chapels along the walls contain important early works of art, most notably a 14th-century *Crucifixion*; the *Tomb of Catherine of Austria* (c. 1325) by Tino di Camaino; and the *Tomb of Robert d'Artois and Giovanna di Durazzo*.

Outside the church, make a point of exploring Via Gregorio Armenio, one of Naples' more typical old-world streets. Craftsmen here make the city's famous Christmas cribs (*presepi*).

Cappella di San Severo

Although it's just one more bizarre sight in the city's catalogue of extraordinary experiences, the **Cappella San Severo** is still well worth hunting out (it's on Via de Sanctis, just north of Piazza San Domenico Maggiore – the fourth turning on the left as you walk down Via Tribunali from San Lorenzo Maggiore). The chapel was built for the de Sangro family and decorated by the 18th-century sculptor,

Practicalities in Naples

Crime Everything you've heard about crime in Naples is true. More than anywhere else in Italy you need to have your wits about you. Women and single travellers should be especially careful. Carry no valuables, watches or jewellery. Only walk on major streets and try to look confident. Don't buy anything from anyone – least of all cigarettes, which will turn out to be made of cabbage or be cartons carefully filled with sand. Don't rely on anyone, even kindly-looking couples, least of all to watch your luggage. Only use official taxis.

Tourist Office Brave the queues at the station tourist office (081/268.779) to pick up maps, brochures and the useful *Qui Napoli*. Staff also call hotels for you, but be sure to ignore the hotel touts who swarm around the office. Probably a better if less immediately convenient office is the one at Piazza Gesù Nuovo (081/552.3328).

Railway Station Naples has several big stations. Most trains on the main Rome–Sicily line stop at Napoli Centrale (081/264.644) on Piazza Garibaldi; trains to Sorrento on the Circumvesuviana leave from Stazione Circumvesuviana on Corso Garibaldi, immediately south of Piazza Garibaldi. Centrale has full facilities, including foreign exchange, left luggage and day hotel – though it's not a place you particularly want to linger.

Buses Naples' buses are crowded to the point of disbelief. Most local services leave from Piazza Garibaldi. Tickets must be bought beforehand from tobacconists. Tickets are valid on the underground (the *Metropolitana*), a more useful way of crossing the city from Centrale (stops at Centrale, Piazza Cavour – for the Museo Nazionale – Piazza Amedeo, Mergellina and Pozzuoli).

Foreign Exchange Few banks are willing to change money; those that do charge commission, so try to bring cash with you. Best bet is the kiosk at Centrale or the *Banco Commerciale* on Piazza Garibaldi, the closest bank to the station.

Budget Travel CTS, Via Mezzocannone 25, off Corso Umberto near Piazza Bovio (081/552.7060); CIT, Piazza Municipio 70-72, (081/554.5426).

American Express Piazza Municipio 1 (081/551.5303).

Post Office Piazza Matteotti.

UK Consulate Via Crispi 122 (081/663.511).

Emergencies Police (081/794.1111); English speakers are usually available. For problems also use the *Ufficio Stranieri* at the Questura, Via Medina 75, off Via Diaz.

Where to stay

Youth Hostels *Ostello Mergellina*, Salita della Grotta 23 (081/761.2346). Well away from the centre, but in a nice location, and one of the safest and cleanest budget options in the city. It's a big place (200 beds), but still check availability of rooms (2–, 3– and 6–beds) during July and August. Either take bus number 152 from Piazza Garibaldi or the metro to Mergellina, from where it's 15 min walk on Via Piedigrotta.

Hotels Never accept offers from any of the hotel touts. If at all possible avoid the cheap and invariably appalling hotels on and around Piazza Garibaldi (the best options here are listed below). The area around the university, between Piazza Dante and the duomo has a better selection of lower-priced places. The Mergellina area (which requires a metro ride) is another promising district – the more expensive hotels tend to be here. Always consider paying a little extra for comfort and safety, and always ask to see the room and agree on a final price before parting with your passport (watch out for extras such as showers and breakfasts). If you have any complaints call the EPT tourist office's special number (081/406.289).

☆*Ambra*, Via Mezzacannone 109 (081/206.896). Popular with university students.

☆☆☆*Britannique*, Corso Vittorio Emanuele 133 (081/660.933). One of the smaller and more stylish top-of-the-range hotels (if you want the best, by the way, it's the *Excelsior*).

☆*Console*, Via Mezzacannone 109 (081/282.502). Central Spaccanapoli situation; safe and economical – longer stays preferred.

☆*Casanova*, Via Venezia 2 (081/268.287). Passable budget choice off Via Milano, a street off Piazza Garibaldi.

☆☆*Corso*, Corso Umberto 1 377 (081/283.201). Convenient both for the station and the city centre.

☆☆*Crispi*, Via F. Giordani (081/664.804). Well-known place close to the Mergellina metro stop.

☆☆*Duomo*, Via Duomo 228 (081/265.988). Clean, spacious rooms.

☆☆*Fiamma*, Via Francesco del Giudice 13 (081/459.187). Large and recently renovated rooms.

☆☆☆*Lago Maggiore*, Via del Cerriglio 10 (081/320.611). Reliable, cost-effective hotel near the Castel Nuovo.

☆☆/☆☆☆*Muller*, Via Mergellina 7 (081/669.056). Close to the Mergellina metro stop. Good rooms, some with views of the waterfront.

☆☆/☆☆☆*Prati*, Via Cesare Rosaroli 4 (081/554.1802). Turn right out of Piazza Garibaldi on Corso Garibaldi and Via C. Rosaroli runs off Piazza Principe Umberto about 100 metres north. Good rooms, each with TV and fridge.
☆☆☆*Rex*, Via Paleopoli 12 (081/416.3888). Reasonably priced, convenient if slightly bland mid-range hotel.
☆☆*Trentino*, Corso Umberto I 311 (081/220.397). Close to the *Corso*.

Eating and drinking

Bars *Gambrinus*, Via Chiaia 1-2. Oldest and most famous of the city's traditional bars; not as cheap as some but worth a drink for the air of fading elegance.
Pintauro, Via Roma-Toledo 275. Founded in 1785 and perhaps the city's leading producer of *sfogliatella*, Naples' best-known cake – a ricotta cheese-stuffed pastry.
Scaturchio, Piazza San Domenico. Another city institution at the heart of Spaccanapoli.
Restaurants Naples is one of Italy's culinary highspots, and eating here is almost always reasonable and rewarding. Pizzas everywhere are cheap and excellent, and most trattorias are atmospheric, old-world places serving traditional specialities (seafood in particular, like mussels – *cozze* and clams, *vongole*). Most are family-run, and few cater to tourists, except the nasty places on Piazza Garibaldi (its side streets aren't so bad). Almost anywhere with locals in it should be okay; these are just the most famous.

Da Michele, Via Cesare Sersale 1-3, right off Corso Umberto I close to the station. Naples' most famous, traditional – and possibly best – pizzeria, serving just two varieties; the *marinara* (tomato, garlic and oil) and the *margherita* (tomato, cheese and basil).
Da Peppino Avellinese, Via S. Spaventa 31. The best restaurant and pizzeria close to Piazza Garibaldi (third left off the square out of the station). A safe, well-lit area and friendly atmosphere; popular with locals and tourists alike.
Pizzeria Trianon da Ciro, Via Pietro Colletta 44/46. Close to the station and to *Da Michele*, its great rival; a pizzeria in the old mould – marble tables and wood-burning stoves: it probably has more fans than its competitor, courtesy of a wider menu.
Bellini, Via Santa Maria Constantinopoli 80, by Port'Alba (081/459.774). Runs *Da Michele* close as the city's most famous cheap restaurant, but has a full menu, including pizzas. Service can be slow, however, and it's a touch pricier than your basic pizzeria. Book ahead.
Dante e Beatrice, Piazza Dante 44–5. Another popular restaurant, but with plenty of tables.
Da Marino, Via Santa Lucia (081/416.280). Also up there in the top-rank in the eyes of locals – book ahead; good pizzas and plenty of fresh fish.

Giuseppe Sammartino. At its centre stands the artist's *Cristo Velato (Veiled Christ)*, remarkable for the extraordinarily lifelike veil covering the prostrate figure of Christ.

Downstairs in the crypt, through a door to the right, more grisly scenes await; two 18th-century corpses preserved inside a glass case – one of them obviously a pregnant woman. They're held to be the work of Prince Raimondo, the man responsible for the chapel and a notorious 18th-century alchemist (excommunicated by the Papacy for his pagan dabblings). The veins, capillaries and most of the figures' vital organs were preserved by the prince using some mysterious elixir (others tell you that they're all reconstructions). The best legend claims the woman was Raimondo's wife, the other her lover, and that both were poisoned with a substance that accidentally preserved them (Mon and Wed–Sat 10 am–1.30 pm and 5–7 pm, Tues and Sun 10 am–1.30 pm).

Palazzo Reale di Capodimonte

Built in 1738 as the royal palace of the Bourbon King Charles III, the hill-top Palazzo Reale di Capodimonte now houses the pictorial wing of the Naples museum, the Museo Nazionale di Capodimonte (Tues–Sat 9 am–2 pm, Sun 9 am–1 pm). You could walk up here after seeing the Museo Nazionale –

though it's a fairly long way (2km) – or take a bus directly from Piazza Garibaldi outside the station (number, 110 or 127). Buses 22 or 23 also run here from Piazza del Plebiscito, the vast car park close to the Castel Nuovo. It's well worth making the effort to come up here, not so much for the palace's lacklustre royal apartments as for its outstanding second-floor collection of paintings which include some Flemish works by Pieter Brueghel and a pair of triptychs by Joos van Cleve. Most of the collection, though, is naturally given over to home-grown talent, the outstanding examples of which are by Simone Martini, Masolino da Panicale, Masaccio, Raphael, Filippino Lippi, Giovanni Bellini, Caravaggio, Coreggio and Titian. Other artists represented include Michelangelo, Perugino, Pinturicchio, Botticelli, Luca Signorelli and Sebastiano del Piombo, as well as a host of lesser known, predominantly Neapolitan painters.

Naples–Herculaneum–Pompeii–Sorrento

The route

This route takes you to two of southern Italy's most famous archaeological sites. Both **Herculaneum** (present day Ercolano) and **Pompeii** were Roman colonies partly destroyed by the eruption of Vesuvius on August 2nd, AD 79. Today they're superbly excavated spots that give a vivid impression of how a Roman town must have looked and functioned. Most of their treasures, however, have been removed to the Museo Archeologico in Naples, so aim to combine a trip to the sites with one to the museum.

It would be hard work to do justice to both towns in a day, particularly if you wanted to tackle Vesuvius, the area's other highspot. The volcano can be seen as an excursion from Herculaneum, preferably before

Trains

Trains for most destinations on this route follow the Circumvesuviana from Naples, a circular line around Vesuvius.

Services for **Ercolano** *(20 min) leave every 15 min; those for the station at* **Pompeii–Scavi–Villa dei Misteri** *about every half an hour (25 km, 30 min). Trains drop you outside Pompeii's western entrance (be sure to get off at the Scavi, not the town – and check the timetable carefully to make sure your train stops, not all of them do). Turn right out of the station and there's a* **tourist office** *in Piazza Esedra–Via Villa dei Misteri (081/861.0913). Trains to* **Sorrento** *also run every 30 minutes. If you want to make the full circuit – good for views of the volcano, but not for much else – trains run from Naples–Torre Annunziata–Poggiomarino (change trains)–Naples (2 hr).*

exploring the ruins. Perhaps the best overall approach is to see Herculaneum (and Vesuvius) and then continue by rail beyond Pompeii to Sorrento. You can then return to Pompeii as a day trip from **Sorrento**, a lively resort and good base for exploring the **Amalfi coast**. Buses from the town run to Positano and Amalfi, two of Italy's most stunningly situated coastal villages.

A neat itinerary might be to explore Pompeii and the coast from Sorrento, and then take a bus through to Salerno, where you can pick up the main Naples–Reggio di Calabria line south (see Battipaglia–Reggio di Calabria on page 288).

The journey

Herculaneum

It's extraordinary that two such famous sights should be enclosed by some of the dreariest suburbs in Italy. The train from Naples to Ercolano wends through dismal housing estates and derelict industrial estates. Ancient *Herculaneum* lies at the seaward end of modern-day Ercolano's main street, a 500-metre walk downhill from the station (daily 9am–1hr before sunset). It's well worth buying a guide to get the most from the site (the best is published by *Amadeo-Maiuri*, available in shops and bars near the entrance).

Herculaneum is smaller and generally less crowded than Pompeii, making it easier to explore; if anything it's also better preserved, if less impressive overall (perhaps making it the more manageable of the two sites to start with). Having been buried in 15 metres of volcanic mud, the town was only discovered in 1709, though excavations and preservation only began in earnest in 1927.

In its heyday the colony was a chic residential district, unlike Pompeii, which was more a commercial centre. Built to take advantage of sea breezes and views over the Bay of Naples, the houses here belonged to wealthy patrician families. As a result they were built as rambling villas, more varied and sophisticated than the neat townhouses of Pompeii's business class.

All of the site is worth exploring, so it makes little sense trying to plot a set itinerary around the ruins. On the whole there are no large civic buildings or large communal spaces, simply two main streets which intersect at what would have been the town's centre (the *Decumano Inferiore* and *Cardine IV*). About 15 of the houses are open at any one time, though attendants open others for a small tip. Where the remains score most highly is in the smaller details – the evocative pieces of carbonised furniture, for example, or the sculptures, mosaics and pieces of preserved wood panelling. Some of the larger ruins, however, are still well worth seeing. They include the **House of the Mosaic Atrium**, famous for its rippling black and white mosaics; the **House of the Wooden Partition**, still with its wooden partition doors; the **House of the Bicentenary**, the colony's best-preserved shop; the **Palestra**, dominated by a magnificent bronze fountain; and the

Excursion from Herculaneum (Ercolano)

Vesuvius

Although you can take a train around the base of Vesuvius, it's obviously far more rewarding if you can make the trip up to the crater itself. When Charles Dickens came here he was carried up the slopes in a litter borne by 15 attendants. These days there are more prosaic ways of making the ascent. The most straightforward is to take a blue *SITA* bus from outside Ercolano's railway station (6 daily, last return bus 5.50pm). Most of the buses run in the morning, so aim to tackle the volcano before seeing Herculaneum. Only take the taxis outside the station if you fix a price first.

Buses drop you at a clutch of cafés and souvenir stalls. From here you have to walk a 30 minute marked path over barren mountainside. At the top there's an 'admission fee', though it's a moot point whether you have to take one of the 'guides' to the crater's edge (they insist you do). The view down into the huge rocky bowl is breathtaking, but it takes around two hours to walk its circumference (watch your step, as the paths are crumbling and the safety fences fairly rickety).

Vesuvius is the only active volcano on the European mainland, though these days only a few wisps of smoke testify to the forces at play under the surface. A molehill alongside Sicily's Mount Etna (1,227m against Etna's 3,347m), it's still probably the more dangerous of the two volcanoes – certainly in its potential for mass destruction. Since the apocalyptic eruption of AD 79, Vesuvius has creaked into life around 100 times, the last occasion being in 1944 (when part of the old main cone was destroyed). With an average strike rate of an eruption every 30 years, the next cataclysm is clearly long overdue. When the next big bang arrives Naples and its environs will again be in the firing line. Odd, therefore, that there are no plans to deal with the aftermath of an eruption.

House of Neptune and Amphitrite, graced with another fine mosaic. The best house overall, however, is the House of the Deer, noted for its statue of the drunken Hercules and two marble groups of deer being attacked by dogs. The bath-complex, or thermae, is also superbly well-preserved.

Pompeii

Although Pompeii's now more famous than it ever was in its heyday, the former Greek and later Roman colony was nevertheless an important commercial centre before the eruption that brought its sudden demise. Despite the crowds, the site is immensely rewarding, requiring at least a morning – and preferably a whole day – to do it justice. Many of the best sights remain locked until a suitable tip has crossed the palm of the attendants. If you blanch at paying out, tag along with one of the many tour groups doing the rounds (open daily 9 am – 1 hr before sunset).

Pompeii had already been convulsed by an earthquake in AD 63, its aftermath a mere aperitif for what was to follow 16 years later. By August 24th, AD 79 Vesuvius had been spewing smoke and débris for several days. Many of Pompeii's 20,000 inhabitants had already been evacuated when the volcano finally burst its basalt plug. A huge cloud blotted out the sun, raining dust, stone and lava on the surrounding countryside. Pompeii was covered in hours by around two metres of débris, some 2,000 of its inhabitants being taken by surprise and killed (mainly by falling rocks and asphyxiating gases). A feeble light only returned to the area on the 26th, but that evening the internal walls of the volcano's cone collapsed, sending further torrents of ash and dust over the stricken town (it was at this stage, incidentally, that Herculaneum received its flood of superheated mud).

Pompeii's fate was the archaeologists' fortune. The eruption effectively caused time to stand still, preserving the town and many of its inhabitants under metres of solidified débris. Parts of the town were first discovered in 1600, partly as a result of studying ancient texts. Full-scale **excavations** began in 1748, aided by the fact that much of the covering material was relatively soft (in contrast to Herculaneum's hard mantle of tufa). Most of the site has now been revealed, providing not only the world's finest surviving Roman town, but also an unparalleled insight into the everyday minutiae of 1st-century life.

Walking the **ruins** is a fair undertaking. Some of the houses amount to little more than foundations, and after a while one ruin can look pretty much like another. It pays, therefore, to be selective (also make sure you're equipped with a map from the tourist office).

Entering from the west, the **forum** is virtually the first thing you encounter. The centre of all civic life, its surviving buildings include a basilica (used as law courts), a market place, and temples to Apollo, Jupiter and the Emperor Vespasian. Along one side, and in the **Antiquarium** close by, are the famous body casts taken from the volcanic ash. These graphically evoke the horror of Pompeii's fate, the faces twisted in agony and the figures contorted to shield themselves from the falling débris. A couple of blocks beyond the forum are the **Terme Stabiane**, a large bath complex, and close by the **Vico del Lupinare**, one of the town's main red-light areas. At the top of the street stands a small brothel, still with several bed stalls and paintings describing the various services on offer.

The finest of the public buildings, however, is undoubtedly the **anfiteatro**, Italy's best-preserved and oldest surviving amphitheatre (dating from 80 BC). Once it could accommodate almost 20,000 people, virtually the town's entire population. Probably the most artistically interesting of Pompeii's many **houses** is the **Casa dei Vetii**, an upper-class merchant's lodging, home to the best of the wall paintings not removed to Naples' archaeological museum. It's also the seat of a famously well-endowed statue of Priapus, not to mention a roomful of explicit erotica (usually closed). Phallic symbols appear all over town, probably attempts to ward off the evil eye (another theory is that they provided directions to the town's red-light districts). Largest of the town's houses, though, is the **Casa di Menandro**, graced with a lovely peristyle and several appealing frescoes. Other exceptional homes include the **Casa di Loreio di Tiburtino**, known for its terraces and courtyard (or *atrium*), and the **Casa del Fauno**, a near-perfect example of a Roman *domus* home, source of many fine paintings (most of them now in Naples).

Before leaving the site, be sure to visit the **Villa dei Misteri**, a 3rd century BC villa located outside the main ruins (but accessible on the same ticket). To reach it, return to the station and continue straight down Viale alla Villa dei Misteri). In many ways this is the grandest of Pompeii's patrician houses, known above all for its frescoes describing the initiation of women into the Dionysaic mysteries (*misteri*). Little is known of the cult (which was forbidden in the Imperial era) though the narrative thread of the beautifully executed and remarkably preserved paintings is simple to follow.

Sorrento

After Naples' dreary surroundings, **Sorrento** is virtually the first place you might want to spend any time. A bustling, attractive and unpretentious resort town, it's perfectly placed for trips to Pompeii and – more to the point – for excursions to towns like Amalfi, Ravello and Positano. If you can deal with the crowds (and prices), it's also a point of departure for boats to the famous islands of **Capri** and Ischia. Make any of these excursions and you're treated to one of Europe's finest coastlines, fabled for its immense cliffs, lush vegetation and breathtaking views.

Over and above its convenience and relative peace, Sorrento has the added advantages of rocky beaches and reasonably-priced accommodation. What it doesn't have, if truth be told, is terribly much to see. If you come here, it's to relax, sample the nightlife and take in the views. If they want to swim, most people head for the **Marina Grande** a short walk or bus ride away from Piazzo Tasso (the town centre). A little further away, try Regina Giovanna at Punta del Capo (again connected by bus), or the Villa di Pollio, a park and old Roman ruins. Both are good bathing spots.

Practicalities in Sorrento

Tourist Office Via L. de Maio 35, off Piazza San Antonio (081/878.1115). Use the travel office in Piazza San Antonio for bus and ferry enquiries.
Railway Station Located in the centre of town about 5 minutes' walk from Piazza Tasso.
Buses All SITA buses leave from in front of the *Circumvesuviana* station, with frequent services to Praiano, Amalfi and Positano (change at Amalfi for buses to Salerno, Atransi, Ravello, Scala, Minori and Maiori).
Ferries 5 ferries daily run to Capri. 2 services daily operate to Ischia (via Naples). Note that you can make connections at Capri for ferries to other points of the Sorrento peninsula.
Bikes and mopeds Sorrento *Rent a Car*, Corso Italia 210a. Biggest outfit for mopeds and scooters. *Guarracino*, Via San Antonio 19 rent bikes and tandems.
Youth hostel Via Capasso 5 (081/878.1783). To find the hostel turn right out of the station on to Corso Italia; Via Capasso is a left turn.
Hotels Sorrento has plenty of cheap, central

hotels, and finding a room should only be a problem in August.
☆☆*Mara*, Via Rota 5 (081/878.3665). First right after the youth hostel (see above); nice rooms (some with terraces) in quiet area.
☆☆*Linda*, Via degli Aranci 125 (081/878.2916). Not in the nicest part of town, but the rooms are fine.
☆☆*City*, Corso Italia 221 (081/877.2210). Central position, but can be noisy.
☆☆☆*Savoia*, Via Fuorimura 48 (081/878.2511). Handy for the station and a good chance of finding rooms during busy times.
Camping The nearest site is *Nube d'Argento*, Via del Capo 21 (081/878.1344). From the station take Corso Italia until it becomes Via del Capo. It's 10 minutes' walk and the Marina Grande is just beyond. The neighbouring town of Sant'Agnello also has numerous campsites.
Restaurant *Sant'Antonio*, Via Santa Maria delle Grazie 6. A spot favoured by locals and tourists alike.

Excursion from Sorrento

The Amalfi Coast

If you visit Sorrento, on no account miss the Amalfi Coast. Stretching along the southern side of the Sorrentino Peninsula, it's a medley of huge cliffs and precariously perched villages. Most is skirted by a corniche road, a dramatic ride by bike or bus from Sorrento. Much is also developed, albeit in an upmarket sort of way, making the chic towns expensive places to stay. This shouldn't stop you from voyeuristic day-trips. This is a sketch of the places to aim for, and what to see when you get there.

Impossibly picturesque **Positano**, an hour from Sorrento, is one of the most famous towns, dangling above the sea in a steep jumble of houses. Literary and cinematic stars past and present have villas here. It has two small beaches, ringed by overpriced bars and restaurants. Beaches and town are both frequently packed, but it's still difficult not to be seduced by their charm. Ferries run to most neighbouring towns and to Naples. The **tourist office** is at Via del Saracino 4 (089/875.067).

Praiano nearby, though less quaint, has a good beach and is similarly congested. **Amalfi** is bigger and probably better if you want to try and stay locally. In addition to its cliff-edged surroundings, it has the bonus of a marvellous **duomo** and a beautiful quayside. Make a point, also, of seeing the Chiostro del Paradiso, a beautiful 13th-century cloister next to the cathedral. You can also potter off into the hills to the rear for some peace and quiet. Again there's a beach and a good ferry network. The lacklustre **tourist office** is at Corso delle Repubbliche Marinare 19/21 (089/871.107). Use them for help with accommodation: reasonably priced hotels do exist, but don't expect any vacancies in July and August. Leave time for the 10-minute stroll (or bus ride) to the neighbouring village of Atrani.

Ravello lies inland, half an hour by bus from Amalfi. Again, the journey's worth it for the views. In the town, be sure to see the duomo, noted for its 13th-century pulpits, and two famous villas; the Villa Rufolo and Villa Cimbrone. Both have superb gardens. The tourist office is at Piazza Vescovardo 13.

(Battipaglia)–Paestum–Tropea–Reggio di Calabria

The route

This route takes in all of Italy's western, or Tyrrhenian coast from south of Naples to Reggio di Calabria. Many people sit out this entire stretch of line on their way to Sicily, content merely to look at a succession of small resorts and sea views that characterise most of the region. Only the superbly preserved temples at **Paestum** tempt from a historical point of view, together with the archaeological museum at **Reggio di Calabria**, an otherwise depressing modern town. If you fancy breaking your journey, however, **Tropea** is the best place to sample sea and sand.

Trains

Battipaglia *is 74 km and one hour south of Naples by train. It's on the main line south, with many services available as a result. Not all trains, however, run the entire route, and to access some of the smaller towns – Paestum and Tropea in particular – you need to choose a* **stopping train.** *Expresses cover the entire route in 4 hr 15 min.*

If you're planning to cross the peninsula here (on the **Battipaglia–Potenza– Metaponto** *route), it's worth noting that there's been no service for a couple of years between Battipaglia and Potenza. The train has been replaced by a bus service.*

The journey

South of Battipaglia the imminent arrival of **Paestum** is announced by the coastal flats of the Piana del Sele. Depending on the time of year the chances are its fields will be grazed by buffalo, the source of some of Italy's finest mozzarella cheese. Once off the train, little in the village suggests the existence of the country's best-preserved Greek temples. Walk a short way from the station, though, and you're confronted with three honey-coloured temples, all the more beautiful because they rise romantically from flower-strewn meadows with the sea as their back-drop. Or, as the poet Shelley put it, 'the effect of the jagged outline of the mountains through groups of enormous columns on one side, and on the other the level horizon of the sea, is inexpressibly grand.' If possible, try to be here early in the morning to enjoy the site while it's still quiet and empty.

The original settlement, *Poseidonia* (after the god of the sea) was founded in the 6th century BC by Greeks from Sybaris, a colony across the peninsula on the Ionian Sea. (Pottery remains, however, suggest possible links with Asia Minor as early as 2400–1900 BC). Bolstered by trade with the Etruscans and lands to the north, the town quickly grew, passing to the Romans in 273 BC who renamed the colony *Paestum*. Amongst other things it was famous for its roses and violets – Virgil mentions them – used in a lucrative scent industry. Unusually for so powerful a centre, though, it had no citadel, relying instead on a circuit of walls some eight kilometres in circumference (of which traces remain, together with the original four main gateways).

In time the extension of the Via Appia, a consular road from Rome to the Adriatic, meant that Paestum's trading routes were superseded. Coupled with malaria and Saracen raids, this eclipse brought about the colony's downfall. From the 9th century the site remained buried under vegetation, only being redis-covered during roadbuilding work in the 18th century.

The best-preserved of the temples is the **Temple of Neptune**, built in 450 BC and considered by many to be the greatest surviving Doric temple of antiquity. Only its roof and a few inner walls are missing. Alongside stands the double-columned **Basilica of Hera**, built a century earlier and though less well preserved, considerably larger than its neighbour (it's nine columns wide, broader by three

columns than the Parthenon). Standing somewhat apart from the others is the
Temple of Ceres (*c.* 500 BC), a smaller affair originally dedicated to Athena (it
later served time as a Christian church).

Most of the site's later Roman monuments – the forum, baths and theatres –
are now no more than rubble. The Normans despoiled many, carrying off stones
and columns to rebuild Salerno's cathedral. The excellent museum across the
road from the temples, however, fills in some of the gaps, displaying bronzes, terracottas, sculptural fragments and some fascinating wall paintings removed
from Paestum and surrounding sites.

Practicalities in Paestum

Tourist Office Via Aquila (0828/811.016).
Mon–Sat 9am–2pm.
Admission The site and museum are open daily
from 8 am until two hours before sunset.
Railway station It's a 600 metre walk to the
site from the station.
Hotels There are plenty of hotels just north and
south of the temples. The *Santa Lucia* (0828/

811.133) and the *Poseidonia* (0828/811.066)
are the cheapest, located close to the site and to
the beach.
Campsites Several campsites line the popular if
average beach 2km west of the site. There's
little to choose between them, but *Mare Pineta*
is closest to the ruins.

Beyond Paestum the train delves into the **Cilento**, a wild and thickly wooded
mountain enclave. Sadly the rustic interlude is shortlived, the line soon emerging
on to the coast and a string of largely indifferent resorts (Pisciotta and nearby
Palinuro are the best bets if you want to break the journey). Around **Sapri**, however, the line's pushed up close against some of the more spectacular cliffs on this
stretch of the coast. **Maratea** makes a fair place to stop, a pretty and spectacu-
larly-sited village, linked to the station by bus (it's inland, though – for beaches
take the station bus to Maratea Porto). Five kilometres further south, the station
at **Maratea Marina** offers more access to beaches and plenty of hotels and campsites.

A few kilometres on the train enters Calabria, the toe of the Italian boot, the
start of a fairly uniform succession of resorts, beaches and gently unassuming
countryside. Most of the towns are lively with Italian tourists in summer and all
but dead during the winter. All have hotels and campsites, and most have a quiet
old quarter and modern marina below – though not all are uniformly appealing.

Paia a Mare is okay as far as it goes, but the village of San Nicola Arcella a little
way south boasts a bigger and better beach. Let the town of Scalea pass by, and
plump instead for **Diamante**, a more than usually chic little spot astride a small
promontory. Most trains stop at **Paola** (197km and 2hr from Battipaglia), the
spot to make connections inland for Cosenza and the mountains (see Cosenza–
San Giovanni in Fiore on page 294). Beyond the town the string of resorts and
fishing villages picks up again. The best of the bunch is **Amantea**, home to a particularly popular beach.

If you only stop at one place, however, probably the best bet is **Tropea**,
perched on the edge of a broad promontory. You'll need to be on a train that

takes in the little loop around the headland, which means you may need to change at **Pizzo**, a picturesque spot in its own right (which you might use as a base for the headland as a whole). It's a breezy and cheerful spot, with a lively market and central piazza, and narrow streets of whitewashed houses. There's a busy youth hostel located in the town castle (0963/231.551), but call ahead in August to be sure of a bed. If it's full, the town has plenty of other cheap alternatives.

Skirting the promontory, don't be put off by Vibo Marina, an industrial eyesore, for Tropea's big and inviting beaches are just around the corner. Tropea itself is a fashionable but still surprisingly charming place, as yet unspoilt, despite its summer visitors and its excess of hotels and trattorias. Somehow it manages to remain one of the south's prettiest towns. The beaches are excellent, and there are modest palaces and a fine Norman cathedral if you want some sightseeing. Contact the tourist office close to the station for the full low-down, Via Stazione 10 (0963/61.475). Further fine beaches await at Capo Vaticano, a little way round the promontory.

Practicalities in Tropea

Tourist Office Via Stazione (0963/61.475). **Hotels** ☆☆*Miramonte*, Via Libertà (0963/61.570). On the sea on the road south out of town. ☆☆☆*Rocca Nettuno*, Via Annunzlata (0963/61.612). Town's best hotel in a park overlooking the sea. ☆☆☆*Virgilio*, Via Tondo (0963/61.978). **Restaurant** *Al Timone*, Piazza del Duomo.

Back on the main line the train crawls across the broad flats of the Mesima river before climbing into high country and some of the region's most spectacular coastal scenery. Sicily, too, is now clearly visible across the Straits of Messina. **Scilla** flashes by, ancient *Scylla*, home to one of the famous monsters mentioned in Homer's *Odyssey* as a threat to sailors. The other, Charybdis, is modern day Cariddi across the Straits. Both had some basis in fact, insofar as treacherous whirlpools are created here by the meeting of currents from the Ionian and Tyrrhenian seas. Even today ships must navigate with care.

If you're carrying a through ticket to Sicily, the train crosses from Villa San Giovanni. If not, and you're continuing around the coast, the grim outlines of **Reggio di Calabria** soon put in an appearance. The only possible reason for stopping here, in one of Italy's grimmer cities, is to see the **Museo Nazionale** (Tues–Sat 9 am–1 pm and 3.30–7 pm, Mon and Sun 9 am–1 pm). It's located almost immediately in front of Reggio Lido, the smaller of the town's two stations. If your train only halts at Reggio Centrale it's a simple matter of picking up one of the many buses which ply Corso Garibaldi, the long street connecting the two stations. (The Centrale has a small tourist office.) The museum documents the history of Magna Graecia, the area of southern Italy dominated by the Greeks before the rise of the Romans. Its most famous exhibits are the **Bronzi di Riace**, two Greek bronzes (5th century BC) dredged from the sea off the coast of Calabria in 1972.

Reggio di Calabria–Metaponto–Rossano–(Taranto)

The route

This route arcs around the toe of the Italian peninsula and then follows the Ionian coast to **Metaponto** and the border with Puglia. It's part of an obvious itinerary that takes you around the entire southern coast of Italy, but it's not a journey that requires much in the way of off-train excursions. It's also a long trip, so don't be fooled by what looks like an easy hop on the map.

Less developed than its Tyrrhenian counterpart, the coast attracts only a handful of intrepid German and Italian tourists – so if you want long stretches of empty beaches and modest resorts, this is the place. Scenically, however, much of the ride is unexceptional, the countryside confined to bare and empty coastal flats, views of distant mountains the only solace. Perhaps the best thing to do is sit tight until Taranto, and then explore the more rewarding lines that criss-cross Puglia.

The best of the resorts is **Soverato** (and there are also perfectly good beaches at Palizzi, Bovalino and Brancaleone). **Locri** has a smattering of archaeological finds, though the most interesting historical stop is at **Rossano**. Three of southern Italy's greatest Greek colonies graced this coast – at present-day Crotone, Metaponto and Sibari (the last the home of the Sybarites, famed for their legendary good-living). Sadly the ruins of all three are fairly lacklustre, and in the case of Sibari, still largely unexcavated. Generations of scholars have fretted over where ancient *Sybaris* might be, and it was only in the 'Sixties with the aid of aerial photography that the present site was properly identified. The hoped-for archaeological bonanza, however, has never materialised.

Trains

Try to board an Intercity train on this route. Journeys otherwise around this portion of the coast are slow, and you may find yourself having to make several connections.

Metaponto is a major rail junction, with connections north into **Puglia** *via Taranto and back to* **Naples** *by way of Potenza.*

2 fast trains daily operate from **Reggio di Calabria** *to Taranto (471 km, 5 hr 50 min) via Soverato (160 km, 2 hr); Crotone (238 km, 3 hr); Rossano (336 km, 4 hr) and Metaponto (430 km, 5 hr 20 min).*

The journey

Somnambulant **Locri** boasts a long beach, but is better known for its wide-ranging ruins, all that remains of Greek *Locris*, a powerful ally of Syracuse from the 6th century BC until the arrival of the Romans. Much of the site lies scattered over a wide area south of the town. Unless you're a ruin-fiend it's best to conjure up how it might all have looked from the comfort of the train. Much the same goes for places further north – unless you take time out at the increasingly popular resorts of **Copanello** and **Soverato** about 40 minutes beyond Locri. Neither Catanzaro Marina nor Crotone beyond merit a stop, both of them industrial centres – though Crotone in its day was one of Magna Graecia's most important cities (Pythagoras lived here for a period). Barely a stone from the period survives.

Rossano

Rossano, 30-odd mins on from Crotone, was the area's leading Byzantine city, a thriving centre of art and culture during its heyday between the 8th and 11th centuries. Today the train stops at Rossano Scalo, a bustling resort about 12 kilometres from the old hilltop village – perhaps the only place on the coast worth making an effort to visit (a bus links Rossano with the station).

What to See

Up in the old centre make first for the **Museo Diocesano** (Mon–Sat 9 am–noon and 5–7 pm; Sun 9 am–noon). Though small it packs a punch, the star of its rich little collection being the *Codex Purpureus*, an early Christian illustrated manuscript. Extremely valuable, the 188-page book contains the Gospels of St Matthew and St Mark. It seems likely that the book was brought to Italy from the Holy Land by monks fleeing the Muslim invasions. In a good copy of the original, which is kept under wraps, you can leaf through the pages, most people making for the most famous image; a depiction of the Last Supper as seen through early Middle Eastern eyes – with Christ and the disciples reclining rather than seated, and all eating from the same bowl. One page of the original manuscript is turned every year.

Equally as interesting is **San Marco** (at the edge of town on Corso Garibaldi), considered the finest Byzantine monument in Calabria. Built around AD 1000, the recently restored interior combines ancient-looking vaults and arches with patches of early fresco. Outside, the palms and the five exterior cupolas only add to the distinctive Middle Eastern flavour. As an added bonus the terrace offers a view over Rossano's gorge, still riddled in places with caves used by the town's earliest settlers. Elsewhere the small Byzantine churches of La Panaghia and Santa Maria del Pilerio deserve a look, as does the cathedral, a mixture of medieval, Renaissance and Baroque architecture. If you want to stay in town see the **tourist office** at Piazza Matteotti 2 (0983/32.137) for details of the hotel and camping options (either in town or at Rossano Scalo).

Practicalities in Rossano Scalo

Tourist Office Piazza Matteotti 2 (0983/ 32.137).
Hotels ☆☆☆*Europa Lido*, Russano Stazione (0983/22.095).

☆☆*Murcino*, Lido Sant'Angelo (0983/25.370 or 21.788).
☆☆*Scigliano*, Via Margherita 257, Rossano Stazione (0983/21.846).

Cosenza–San Giovanni in Fiore
Cosenza–Catanzaro
The routes

The only reason to come to **Cosenza** is to leave again on one of two little lines that offer great rides through Calabria's mountainous interior. Few tourists see this part of the country, let alone ride the trains, and if you like god-forsaken backwaters, you'll love both routes. Unless you're up for some hiking, however, neither has anything in the way of places you want to stop off at.

To reach Cosenza change trains on the Naples–Reggio di Calabria main line at Paola (12 daily, 30 min). If you're coming from the east coast, services run from Metaponto, with a change at Sibari – a dull run down the Crati valley (11 daily, 3 hr). Some trains arrive at a new railway station away from the centre. If so, shuttle trains and regular buses connect it to the old station, Cosenza Centrale, departure point for both routes (take bus number 5). If you need to stay here, cheap hotels gather around the station. There's a tourist office at the new station.

Trains

3 trains daily run right through to **San Giovanni in Fiore** *(76 km, 2 hr 15 min). Another 3 run as far as* **Redipiano** *(32 km, 1 hr) – though this leaves you short of the best scenery.*

6 trains operate between Cosenza and **Catanzaro** *(99 km, 3 hr). Mark well the time and distance – the train achieves an average speed of just 33 km per hour (about 20 mph).*

The journeys

The line to **San Giovanni in Fiore** cuts to the heart of the Sila, the broadbacked and forest-covered ranges that form the heart of Calabria's mountainous interior. En route the tiny one-carriage trains clamber up some fantastically engineered gradients, offering breathtaking views over some of the best scenery you'll see from a train in Italy. Lakes, forests and deep gorges punctuate the journey. If you want to spend more time up here, leave the train at **Camigliatello** (1hr 30min from Cosenza), a summer and winter resort, and head for the small tourist office, or *Pro Loco*, at Via Faigitelle (150m left of the station). They can fill you in on hikes into the surrounding hills, and on the various accommodation options around town. Try the ☆☆*Aquila and Edelweiss*, Viale Stazione 13 (0823/978.044).

Once you're in San Giovanni, not the most prepossessing of villages, there's nothing for it but to turn round and come back (though there are hotels if you're stuck). Timetabling usually means you can leave Cosenza in the morning and be back for mid-afternoon.

The scenery on the **Cosenza–Catanzaro** line is less spectacular but still worth the trip. The line also has the advantage of leaving you in Catanzaro where you can easily rejoin the main coastal line betwen Crotone and Reggio di Calabria (for connections to Sicily or Puglia). It simply makes a more interesting way of heading south than sticking to the main Naples–Reggio di Calabria line. En route you're treated to classic stretches of Calabria's lower-hilled margins, dotted with villages old and new, most of which won't have seen a tourist for years. Be warned, however, it's probably one of the slowest railways you'll ever ride.

Foggia–Trani–Bari

The route

Foggia lies at the end of one of the more direct routes across the Italian peninsula. Take one of the frequent trains from Naples to Caserta (35km, 30min), then change to one of the ten trains daily that run directly to Foggia (163km, 2hr 20min). The town's an important rail junction – and the gateway to Puglia - but it's bereft of any sights that merit further investigation. Two worthwhile excursions, however, can be made from here; one to **Lucera**, a haunting little town, the other to the **Gargano** peninsula, an increasingly popular mixture of beaches and unspoilt wooded countryside.

On the line from Foggia to Bari, **Trani** deserves a stop, principally to see one of the region's finest Romanesque cathedrals. **Bari**, by contrast, Puglia's capital, makes little play for tourists – though its atmospheric old quarter fields a pair of exceptional Romanesque monuments. Its rail connections also make it a potential base for exploring the region (many people, however, stop here to catch ferries to Greece).

Trains
Foggia is the meeting point of trains on the **Naples–Bari** *and* **Bologna–Lecce** *main lines, so there's no shortage of services in all directions. Around 25 run between Foggia and Bari (123 km, 1 hr 10 min). Only the slower* locali, *however, stop at Trani (81 km, 1 hr).*

The journey

Foggia sits at the heart of the Tavoliere, the fertile lowlands stretching from the Basilicata border to the Gargano. This is the largest tract of plain in the whole country, greater even than the Po valley (which should give some idea of the distances involved in travelling and the relative dullness of the countryside). An agricultural shangri-la for over two millennia, the region is still southern Italy's wheat bowl, providing the raw materials for a good proportion of the country's pasta. Much of Foggia itself was bombed in the Second World War, and though the modern town that rose from the ruins must be pleasing enough to live in – all spacious piazzas and broad boulevards – it's unlikely to be a place you want to spend any time in. If you do stop off here, however, the places to visit are the **duomo**, a Norman–Baroque hybrid, and the **Museo Civico**, a beautifully presented collection of archaeological fragments, stuffed birds, and items from Puglia's rustic past (looms, spinning wheels and other articles of ethnographic interest).

Excursion from Foggia/San Severo

The Gargano Promontory

Many Italians make the **Gargano** the focus of their entire holiday. You could easily spend a fortnight enjoying its beautifully diverse landscapes, from the beaches on its northern and eastern coasts – some of Italy's best – to the wild interior tracts of the primal *Foresta Umbra*. This short section merely gives you a few starting points.

Two short branch lines give you partial **access**; one from Foggia to Manfredonia on the promontory's southern edge (9 trains daily, 30min); the other from San Severo to Peschici-Calanelle, well round the northern coast (buses connect the station to Peschici proper). Most of the time, though, you're better off relying on the bus network that connects most of the towns.

From Manfredonia – a rather forlorn town with a good beach – you should bus to the lofty hill-town of **Monte Sant'Angelo**, site of four appearances by the archangel Michael in the 5th century and now one of the most important points of pilgrimage in the country. Buses from Manfredonia also leave twice daily for Vico del Gargano, a trans-promontory trip that provides a good look at the interior countryside.

Most of the coast has been fairly heavily developed, especially around Vieste, though more of the villages offer decent beaches. If you manage to resist Vieste, make for **Peschici**, by far the promontory's best all-round town. Everywhere is crowded in August, of course, but come off-season and the region's remarkably quiet.

Practicalities in Foggia

Railway station At the northern end of town, a short walk along Viale XXIV Maggio to Piazza Cavour. At Piazza Cavour take Via Landa right for Corso Vittorio Emanuele and the centre.
Hotels Note that if you're not in a hurry it's nicer to stay in Lucera (see below). There are plenty of cheap places near the station; these, though, are more appealing:
☆☆*Centrale*, Corso Cairoli 5 (0881/71.862). As good as its name – just 5 minutes from the station – and a good choice thanks to large

rooms and a recent expensive refurbishment.
☆☆*Asi*, Via Monfalcone 1 (0881/623.327). A little cheaper than the *Centrale*, and a different atmosphere – modest, old-world and full of faded elegance.
Restaurants *Del Cacciatore*, Via Pietro Mascagni 12, at the end of Corso Vittorio Emanuele (0881/20.031). Note this restaurant – the town's best – also rents out good ☆☆rooms. The *Sorrento*, Via Trieste 37 and *Santa Lucia*, Via Trieste 37 make good standbys.

Excursion from Foggia

Lucera

Once the capital of the Tavoliere, vibrant Lucera has more going for it than Foggia. Hourly buses run here from Foggia's Piazza Vittorio Veneto, across the piazza to the left of the station (the 18km journey takes about 30 minutes).

Given the town's lofty position, and its huge fortress, it's easy to see why it dominated the region for so long. During the 13th century Frederick II settled 20,000 Saracens here, allowing them complete freedom of worship (unusual at the time). Most were Arabs from Sicily (which he also ruled), unruly in the company of Christians, but often the best mercenaries when drafted into Frederick's army. Half a century later the town fell to Charles of Anjou, who in turn imported some 140 Provençal families. Both groups lived together until the arrival of Charles II of Anjou, who massacred the Arabs and razed much of the town's Islamic-influenced architecture.

Once you're off the bus it's a short walk through the arch ahead of you into the old centre. The main sight is the **duomo**, built in 1300 over the site of the Arabs' principal mosque. It was erected to 'commemorate' the removal of the Arabs. Majestic and forlorn by turn, today it ranks amongst Puglia's greatest medieval buildings. Inside, the centrepiece is a valuable 14th-century *Crucifixion*, though the frescoes, stained glass and

French Gothic detail are all outstanding. Behind the cathedral lies a modest **Museo Civico** (Tues–Sun 9 am–1 pm), full of Greek pottery, mosaic fragments and ancient terracotta heads (the tourist office is in the same courtyard). Close by, visit the church of **San Francesco** for its Gothic and Baroque frescoes.

The streets around preserve something of their Arab flavour, full of intriguing courtyards and intimate alleyways. As you wander, follow signs from the **castle**, built by Frederick II in 1230 and – at over a kilometre in circumference – the largest fortress in southern Italy (after Largopescole in Basilicata). Most of the original 24 towers are still intact, the walls offering expansive views over the Tavoliere to the Gargano and hills of the Apennines (castle open daily 9 am–1 pm; free). The panorama explains where the Tavoliere, or 'chessboard' got its name – from the chequered pattern of wheatfields stretching to the horizon. The land has changed little since the days the Romans parcelled it into neat squares for distribution amongst pensioned-off army officers.

Lucera's a good spot to stay in preference to Foggia. Of the town's two **hotels** the ☆☆*Al Passetto* is the best, Piazza del Popolo 28-30 (0881/941.124). The slightly costlier *Hotel Gioia* is nearby at Viale Ferrovia 15 (0881/945.207).

Trani

Once the train leaves Foggia it chugs gently across the Tavoliere, reaching the coast close to **Margherita di Savoia**, famous for its immense salt pans. The chances are you'll be able to see some of stockpiled salt, huge white pyramids that provide some 90 per cent of the country's saline needs. Around 20 minutes later, having ground through industrial Baretta, it reaches **Trani**, in its day one of Italy's most important medieval ports (large enough in the 14th century to rival Bari and even the imperious Venetians). Something of the cosmopolitan air it must have enjoyed then – when it had a large Jewish and international mercantile community – survives to the present day, manifest in a wealth of smart buildings and busy streets. The port's also picturesque, bobbing with fishing boats, making this a good little spot to stop in preference to Puglia's larger coastal cities.

The main sight is the **duomo**, amongst the most astounding examples of Puglia's noted Romanesque architecture. Begun in the 11th century, it's a rose-coloured building perched dramatically on the sea's edge. The façade is stark and austere, lightened by a lovely rose window, though perhaps its most startling feature is the bronze door of the central portal (1180). Equally as interesting is the fact that the site contains three superimposed churches from different eras. While the bulk of the building is Norman, the crypt contains a pair of older chapels – San Nicola and Santa Maria della Scala (whose columns are of Roman vintage), and fragments of a 6th-century paleo-Christian tomb, the *Ipogea di San Leucio*.

Other things to see around town include the castle (just west of the duomo), built by Frederick II, the Palazzo Cacetta, a unusual piece of 15th-century Gothic, and the Chiesa di Ognissanti, a 12th-century Crusader hospice. Plenty of the old quarter's streets, however, repay exploration for its own sake. One of the best is Via Ognissanti, linking Via Mario Pagano to the port area (there's a daily fish and produce market at its bottom end).

Practicalities in Trani

Tourist Office Piazza della Repubblica (0883/ 43.295). Located in the top left hand corner of the square as you approach from the station.
Railway station To reach Piazza della Repubblica from the station walk down Via Cavour, the street which leads off from the forecourt. From Piazza della Repubblica walk left on Via Mario Pagano for the old centre.
Hotel ☆☆*Lucy*, Piazza Plebiscito 11 (0883/

41.022). A good choice with large rooms near the sea and public gardens. Walk down Via Cavour from the station, straight over Piazza della Repubblica, and then follow Via Cavour on the other side to Piazza Plebiscito.
Restaurants There are plenty of good, cheap fish restaurants near the port – look for ones full of locals.

Bari

Like many a Puglian town Bari is more interesting for its ambience than for any glut of monuments. There's little to the new town, a model of 19th-century planning, and the old town is almost Arab in look and feel. Its warren of streets harbour two of Puglia's better Romanesque buildings, though they also have a reputation for petty crime (so watch your valuables and steer clear of dingier areas at night). An important trading centre since Roman times, Bari's golden age was during the 11th century, when it rivalled Venice as Italy's leading port. After Barese sailors stole the body of **San Nicola** it also became an important point of pilgrimage (he was spirited away from southern Turkey in 1087). This 'St Nicholas' is the St Nick of Father Christmas fame, as well as the patron saint of children, sailors, pawnbrokers and Holy Russia. How he gained the Santa Claus tag is open to question. One story has him saving three girls from prostitution by throwing money at their window. Another has him reviving three children butchered and bottled in brine.

His resting place, the **Basilica di San Nicola**, is one of the two main sights in the

Practicalities in Bari

Tourist Office On the right as you leave the station at Piazza Aldo Moro 33a (080/ 524.2244). Note that the *Stop-Over* service duplicates many of its functions (see below).

Stop-Over Bari runs a programme called *Stop-Over*, designed to help visitors do just that – and non-residents under 30, backpackers in particular, qualify for a range of free and discounted services all over the town. Visit the booth in the station for help with maps, cheap hotels and restaurants. If you're camping, take bus number 3 or 5 (free with *Stop-Over* qualifications) to the *San Francesco* campsite, where sites and most of the services are also free.

The booth can also fix you up with a *Stop-Over* package of up to two nights in private rooms. Call (080/521.1182) for reservations, which are appreciated though not essential. The organisation's main office is at Via Dante Aligheri, III (080/521.4538), open daily mid-June to mid-Sept 9am–8pm. For the 24-hr hotline call (080/441.186).

Railway Stations Bari has three stations; the main FS station in Piazza Aldo Moro (trains to Foggia, Taranto, Brindisi and Lecce), also the home of the *Ferrovie del Sud-Est* (Castellana Grotte, Alberobello and Martina Franca). On the west side of the square are the two stations serving the *Ferrovie Calabro-Lucane* (Altamura, Gravina and Matera) and *Bari-Nord* (Bitonto and Barletta).

Ferries Boats leave from the Stazione Marittima on the northern edge of the old city. Bus number 20 runs here from outside the main FS railway station. Services run to ex-Yugoslavian destinations; Corfu (11 hr); Igoumenitsa (13 hr); and Patras (15–20 hr). Most services run daily from July–September.

Tickets and information are available directly from the Stazione Marittima. Be prepared for port taxes on top of ticket prices. Check-in at least two hours before departure.

Hotels Bari isn't a place to stay, particularly if you can't take advantage of the *Stop-Over* scheme. If you must stop, most of the cheaper places are on Via Crisanzio, one block north of Piazza Aldo Moro and the FS station, or Via Calefati, another five blocks to the north off Via Andrea da Bari.

☆*Pensione Darinka*, Via Calefati 15a (080/ 235.049). Also try the slightly more expensive *Bristol* in the same block (081/211.503).

☆☆*Giulia*, Via Crisanzio 12 (080/521.6630). Large, clean rooms close to the station and the first choice amongst the cheapies.

☆☆*Hotel del Corso*, Corso Vittorio Emanuele 30 (080/216.100). Basic, unassuming hotel five minutes from the old town.

☆☆☆*Moderno*, Via Crisanzio 60 (080/ 213.313). Solid mid-range hotel.

☆☆☆*Plaza*, Piazza L. di Savoia 15 (080/ 54.007). Modern rooms right in the centre of town.

Bar *Stoppani*, Via Roberto di Bari 79. Amongst the most famous Art Nouveau bars in southern Italy.

Restaurants *Taverna Verde*, Largo Adua 19 (080/540.309). Located on the Lungomare N. Sauro near the Mole San Nicola (if you're walking up Corso Cavour turn left on Via Cognetti). By far the most popular restaurant with locals – and surprisingly keen prices; book, or arrive early.

Le Travi, Largo Chiurlia 12, at the end of Via Sparano. Nice stone cellar setting and extremely cheap meals.

old town (the *Città Vecchia*). Consecrated in 1197, it was a prototype for Puglian–Romanesque architecture all over the south. All four of the genre's influences coalesce in the building; Lombard in the animal carvings at the façade's base; Byzantine in the angels supporting the external arches; Classical in the rosettes of the corniche; and Saracen in the figures and patterns around the main door. The **façade** is austere in the extreme, with both flanking towers unfinished (the one of the right pre-dates the church, a hangover from a Byzantine fortress on the site). Before entering, look at the church's north side (on the left as you face the façade) for the Porta dei Leoni, a door beautifully decorated with chivalric motifs. Inside, the **ciborium**, or altar canopy, and **episcopal throne** are two of the finest such works in Italy, distinguished by some quite exceptional sculpture. Both are set off by a lovely mosaic floor in the choir. Only the Baroque ceiling detracts from the overall austerity of tone. Drop down to the crypt to see the bones of San Nicola, kept in the altar.

Close by, the **Cattedrale di San Sabino** is another outstanding if more sombre Romanesque building. It was built at the end of the 12th century in honour of the town's first patron saint (later usurped by St Nicola). Also worth a look is the huge **Castello Svevo**, constructed on the site of an earlier Byzantine–Norman fort by Frederick II in 1240.

Bari–Altamura–Matera

The route

Matera offers one of the region's more noted sights, the famous *sassi*, or cave dwellings, worth a visit from whichever direction you approach. By train it's 90 minutes from Bari, for example, though you can also get here by bus from Metaponto's railway station (10 buses daily, 1 hr; see Reggio di Calabria-Metaponto); from Potenza (1 bus daily, 1 hr 45 min); from Taranto (6 daily, 1 hr 45 min).

Trains
This line is operated by the **Ferrovie Apulo-Lucane**, *with 9 direct trains daily from Bari Centrale to Matera Centrale (77 km, 1 hr 40 min). Be sure you're boarding a Matera train; some services from Bari via Altamura take a spur to Gravina and Potenza.*

The journey

Not many tourists brave the Campanian interior. A poor and remote region, it's changed little since Carlo Levi wrote *Christ Stopped at Eboli*, still the definitive portrait of the Italian south. Large towns are few and far between. The land is poor and the landscapes barren, though the countryside has an atmosphere you won't find anywhere else in the country.

Matera

Matera is a one-off, possessed of a picturesque appeal unusual in the south. Divided into distinct halves – modern in the west, old in the east – it's unique for its *sassi*; cave dwellings dug from the living rock in the ravines (or *gravine*) in and around the town. Some form an elaborate honeycomb of streets and steps, one house supported by another below it. Many have been lived in since prehistoric times. For most of this century, however, they represented the ugly face of Italy, a maze of slums, disease and withering poverty. In *Christ Stopped at Eboli* Levi describes the scene, quoting his sister, who compared the *sassi* to Dante's *Inferno*. 'Never have I seen such a spectacle of misery,' she said, ' . . . old men, emaciated by hunger . . . faces yellowed and stricken with malaria.' Dysentery and trachoma were also rife.

Over the last 30 years the *sassi* have been cleared – often forcibly – and their inhabitants rehoused in modern apartments in the new town. Many of the caves had to be sealed up to prevent their occupants returning. Now, however, a process of gentrification appears to be underway, the *sassi* becoming the latest in designer homes for affluent *materiani*. Around 700 people now live in the caves (or never left). Many, though, are still empty.

The labyrinth of *sassi* is accessible from several points, most of them well-signposted. To get the best overview, approach them from the **Strada Panoramica**, a road specially built for the sightseers (also known as Via Madonna delle Virtù). To see some of the nooks and crannies, though, and the noted rock churches, you have to slip into some of the smaller backstreets. It's also worth paying some of the children who hang around to act as guides: their stories are pretty tall, but they take you to places you wouldn't otherwise find.

The main area divides into two districts, the **Sasso Caveoso** and **Sasso Barisano**, both skirted by the Strada Panoramica. Start at the street's eastern end and you walk first through the Sasso Caveoso. There are four types of *sassi*: the oldest are the crude niches cut into the side of the canyon (inhabited up to 7,000 years ago). The second group, concentrated in the Sasso Caveoso, date from 2000 BC. The third, mainly on Via B. Buozzi, are 1,000 years old; the fourth – the dwellings on Via Fiorentini – date back up to 750 years (though the majority are 17th century).

Make a special point of seeing the *chiese rupestri*, or **cave churches**, of which there are around 120 in all, mostly carved by monks between the 8th and 13th centuries. Two of the best lie alongside each other on the Sasso Caveoso (for the location of some of the others see the map from the tourist office). **Santa Maria de Idris,** perched on a turret of rock (Monte Errone), boasts Byzantine frescoes from the 14th century; **San Pietro Caveoso** has similar rock paintings, but is usually closed to the public. **Santa Lucia alle Malve,** a 10th century church, is also worth a visit. It, too, has frescoes, dating from 1250. Also try to cross to the other side of the ravine – it involves fording the river (enlist a guide, perhaps) – but the path leads to some fine rock churches and miscellaneous *sassi*.

To complement a tour of the caves, visit the **Museo Nazionale Ridola** at Via

Ridola 2, a nicely presented four-part collection covering prehistoric, Iron Age and Greek and Roman finds from Matera and the surrounding area. At the end of Via Ridola drop into the *Fondazione Carlo Levi* (Tues–Sat 9 am–2 pm), a collection of the writer's paintings of scenes from Basilicatan life (and blessed with a particularly good view of the *sassi*).

Elsewhere in the town make for the **duomo**, a robust little church in the Puglian–Romanesque style built in 1270. Inside, the Baroque ceiling detracts from the prevailing style, though not from the beauty of the 15th-century choir and the richly-decorated Cappella dell'Annunciazione. Look, too, for the fresco of the Byzantine *Madonna* in the first chapel on the left. Lesser churches you could make time for include **San Giovanni Battista**, a harmonious 13th-century piece of Gothic (blended with Saracen and Romanesque details) and **San Francesco d'Assisi**, a Baroque affair with a few traces of frescoes pre-dating its 1670 refit.

Practicalities in Matera

Tourist Office EPT, Piazza Vittorio Veneto (0835/211.188). Located in the new town's main square. There's a smaller AAST at Via de Viti de Marco 9 (0835/212.488), the second right turn off Via Roma as you walk from the station. For more information on the *sassi* visit the *Co-op Amici del Turista*, Piazza San Pietro Caveoso.

Railway station Piazza Matteotti (0835/211.015). To reach Piazza Vittorio Veneto from the station walk up Via Roma from the left side of Piazzo Matteotti (a distance of about 300 metres). To reach the duomo and the *sassi* leave Piazza V. Veneto on Via delle Beccherie.

Hotels Hotels in Matera are surprisingly busy, so aim to arrive early or book a few days in advance.

☆*Roma*, Via Roma 62 (0835/212.701). The cheapest and most convenient place in town – and therefore the most popular, so call ahead.

☆☆*President*, Via Roma 13 (0835/214.075). Rather characterless, but clean, modern and civilised.

☆☆*Moderno*, Via de Sariis 11 (0835/212.336). Something of a last resort – and not exactly as modern as its name suggests.

☆☆*Italia*, Via Ridola (0835/211.195). One of Matera's better hotels; recently refitted, each room having bathroom and cooking facilities; a good spot.

Restaurants *Lucana*, Via Lucana 48, off Via Roma. The best of Matera's often overpriced eateries.

Il Terrazzino, Vico San Giuseppe 7 (leave Piazza V. Veneto past the *Banco di Napoli* and follow the path past the Birra Peroni sign). This restaurant has a great location – choose between the converted *sassi* or the outside terrace. The food's pretty good too. Only the omnipresent owner detracts.

Il Cantinone, Via San Biagio 13, off Piazza V. Veneto. A popular, more downmarket place for pizzas and beer.

Bari–Brindisi–Lecce

The route

Expect plenty of backpacking company on this route. It's much-travelled by people on their way to the Greek ferries at **Brindisi**, a town which otherwise you want as little to do with as possible. **Lecce**, by contrast, is well worth your time, its easy-going pace and exuberant Baroque architecture make it one of the highlights of any trip in southern Italy. If you've

any sense, however, you'll take the more meandering inland route to
Lecce via Martina Franca (see Bari—Alberobello—Martina Franca on
page 305). This coastal route offers little by comparison.

Trains
*Around 15 trains daily run between Bari, Brindisi (111km, 1hr 40min) and
Lecce (149km, 2hr 15min).*

The journey
Brindisi

Little happens between Bari and Brindisi, the coast flecked only with a few resorts (Torre Canne probably being the best). Although, if pushed, you could
make out a case for Brindisi, leave it well alone unless you're catching a **ferry to
Greece**. Be prepared for all the trappings of a busy port: dingy modern buildings,
endless shipping offices, dereliction and thousands of exhausted backpackers
awaiting deliverance.

If you are taking a **ferry**, the port's 20 minutes' walk from the Stazione Marittima. Ignore the touts selling fake boat tickets at the station. Watch your bags at
all times, and be careful if you're alone at night (most ferries leave in the evening).
Watch out for rip-offs of all kinds, whether it's tickets, non-existent boats, or
dubious foreign exchange outlets. Aim to make friends with other travellers.
Stock up on food – what's available on the boats is expensive. When you buy a
ticket a port tax surcharge is payable. You must also have your boarding card
(issued with tickets) stamped at the police station on the first floor of the Stazione
Marittima building (be prepared for queues). Also be sure to check in at ferries
two hours before sailing (otherwise you can lose your reservation).

The most reliable of the many ticket agencies is *Hellitalia*, Via del Mare 6.
The best boats are operated by *Adriatica*. They're not the cheapest, but it's
worth paying extra for safety and reliability. (*Pattimare*, be warned, has a poor
reputation).

Lecce

Lecce is to the Baroque what Florence is to the Renaissance (the 'Athens of Apulia' is another way the guides put it). It's the one town to see above all others in
Puglia, and it's crammed with superb 17th-century architecture. Over the centuries, all sorts of invaders left their mark on the town – Greeks, Romans,
Saracens and Swabians amongst them – but it was the denizens of Hapsburg
Spain in the 16th and 17th centuries who left the most lasting stamp. During this
period, the influence of the Counter Reformation, combined with the zeal of
local aristocrats, saw the whole town receive a new decorative veneer. Rebuilding affected not only churches and palaces, but also houses, balconies,
courtyards, even humble hovels in nondescript sidestreets. Gargoyles and

garlands of fruit were draped over most available surfaces; chubby *putti* and a menagerie of stone animals found their way into all nooks and crannies. Most of the work is in Lucchese sandstone (*pietra dorata*), an amber-coloured and easily-carved medium (which has the strange quality of being malleable when first quarried, but of hardening with time). The stone's delicacy accounts for Lecce's lightness of touch, a quality not always evident in Baroque reworkings.

What to see

There's so much to see around town that the best way to tackle the place is simply to wander at random. This said, the best place to start is **Piazza del Duomo**, one of Lecce's two pivotal squares. A marvellous ensemble of buildings, it's dominated by the **duomo**, rebuilt between 1659 and 1670 by Giuseppe Zimbalo, the force behind much of the town's most prominent architecture. Alongside on the right is the **Palazzo del Seminario**, swathed in a Baroque froth in 1709 by Giuseppe Cino, a pupil of Zimbalo. Have a close look at the incredible decoration of the well inside its courtyard.

Lecce's other main squre, **Piazza Sant'Oronzo**, lies close by along Via Vittorio Emanuele. Named after the town's first bishop (martyred in the 1st century), it's overlooked by the Colonna di Sant'Oronzo, a column once topped by a bronze statue of the bishop. This was one of two which once marked the end of the Via Appia in Brindisi: it was moved here in 1666 after the saint saved the town from the plague. It's since been removed again – to protect it from smog. On the piazza's west side are the remains of the 20,000 seater **Anfiteatro Romano**, most of whose decorative reliefs have been removed to the town's Museo Provinciale (see below).

Most of the town's other architectural highlights lie close by. Far and away the most extravagent is the **Basilica di Santa Croce** (1548–1646), generally considered the apotheosis of Lecce's peculiar Baroque style. No decorative flourish was too much for this extraordinary building. Next door stands the **Palazzo del Governo**, another Cino-Zimbalo project. Other decoratively-loaded churches to make a point of seeing include Santa Chiara (1694), attributed to Cino; the plain-faced Gesù, remodelled in 1579; the Rosario, Zimbalo's last work (and as fantastically ornate as any of his earlier efforts); and the Carmine, Cino's last hurrah (1717).

Not all of the town, however, is subsumed by the Baroque. The Romans put in another appearance with the **Teatro Romano** (near Santa Chiara), the only one of its kind in Puglia, probably built during the reign of Hadrian. The church of SS **Nicola e Cataldo** provides a Romanesque respite from the prevailing Baroque mood. Initiated in 1190 by the Normans, it's crowned by a Byzantine-style dome, hinting – like the restrained arched interior – at the influence of the Saracens. The façade is part-covered by Cino-inspired Baroque decoration, though the original portal remains intact, neatly encapsulating the architectural influences that have been brought to bear on Lecce over the centuries (of the door's three friezes, the first is Byzantine, the second Romanesque, the third Islamic).

Finally, drop into the **Museo Provinciale**, conveniently situated close to the station on Viale Garibaldi (weekdays 9 am–1 pm and 3–6 pm, Sun 9 am–1 pm). Divided into three sections, it embraces an Antiquarium – mainly Puglian and Greek vases, bronzes and terracottas; a topographical display – artifacts from the region around Lecce (the Roman theatre's reliefs are amongst the most interesting); and a Pinacoteca, home to gold, silver and ivory work, a variety of paintings, and several outstanding 13th-century Gospel covers and miscellaneous holy books.

Practicalities in Lecce

Tourist Office Palazzo Sedile, Piazza Sant'Oronzo (0832/46.458).

Railway Station Piazzale Stazione–Viale Oronzo Quarto (0832/21.016). The station handles both FS and *Ferrovie Sud-Est* trains. To reach the town centre (Piazza del Duomo), 1km south of the station, walk down Viale O. Quarto. At Viale Gallipoli cross straight over and continue down Via B. Cairoli and Via Paladini.

Buses STP services to the Salentino peninsula operate from Via Adua, parallel to Via Taranto. *Sud-Est* buses run to most Puglian destinations from Via Boito.

Budget travel CTS, Via Palmieri 89 (0832/21.862).

Post Office Piazzetta Libertini.

Hostel *Ostello per la Gioventù Adriatico*, (0832/650.026; open May–Sept). Located 12km from Lecce on the beach at San Cataldo. To reach it catch a bus from Viale Brindisi or Villa Comunale (near Piazza Sant'Oronzo).

Hotels There's plenty of accommodation in Lecce, but not too much in the cheaper price brackets. If you're stuck, contact the tourist office for details of private rooms in people's houses.

☆☆*Cappello*, Via Montenegrappa 4 (0832/28.881). Walk up Viale O. Quarta from the station and take the first left, Via Don Bosco – then follow the signs.

☆☆*Carmen*, Via V. Morelli (0832/46.408).

☆☆*Faggiano*, Via Cavour 4 (0832/42.854). Fairly dowdy spot, but cheap and central.

☆☆☆*Grand Hotel*, Viale Quarta 28 (0832/29.405). Large 'Thirties hotel; not too grand, and not too expensive.

☆☆☆*Risorgimento*, Via Augusto Imperatore 19 (0832/42.125). Large – so always a chance of rooms – and reliable mid-range hotel.

Campsite Take bus number 18 to Litoranea for the *Torre Rinalda* campsite, 3km from the beach.

Restaurants *La Capannina*, Via Cairoli 13. Good food and outdoor eating in a piazza just a few minutes from the station.

Gambero Rosso, Via M. Brancaccio 16. Good, cheap *trattoria* popular with locals.

Da Claudio, Via Cavour 11. A cheap and reliable central choice (close to the *Faggiano* hotel).

Bari–Alberobello–Martina Franca–Taranto

The route

This route is the domain of the *Ferrovie Sud-Est* (FSE), a private railway that runs through some of Puglia's prettiest countryside. The journey's most interesting aspect are the *trulli*, distinctive conical buildings unique to this part of Puglia. The biggest concentrations are found at **Alberobello**, but further examples lie dotted around **Martina Franca**, a town worth a stop for its subtle medieval centre. **Taranto**, at the end of the line, is a largely modern and industrialised place, of use mainly for its train connections. It does, however, possess a good archaeological museum, a close rival to the similar museums in Naples and Reggio di Calabria.

Note that this makes a far more interesting way of travelling south towards Lecce than the Bari–Brindisi–Lecce coastal route. See Alberobello and Martina Franca, and then change at Martina Franca for a direct train to Lecce (see below).

Trains

This is a single line operated by the Ferrovie Sud-Est. *13 trains daily run from Bari Centrale to* **Taranto** *(113 km, 2 hr 20 min) via Alberobello (63 km, 1 hr 25 min) and Martina Franca (78 km, 1 hr 40 min).*

7 trains daily (except Sun) run directly from Martina Franca to **Lecce** (103 km, 1 hr 45 min).

The journey

If you've been travelling along the coast it's a relief to push into the interior, a respite from the stark contrast of dazzling sea and limestone lowlands. As the train winds inland, blankets of olives mingle with orchards and vineyards (Puglia is Italy's largest regional wine producer). This is part of the *Murge*, a desolate, bone-dry plateau that occupies much of the Puglian interior.

About 50 minutes out of Bari are the **Grotte di Castellana**, Italy's best caverns and one of the area's main tourist attractions. The caves are about two kilometres from the station (well-signed), an easy 20-minute walk. The system's entrance, *La Grave*, also the main cavern, was little more than a rubbish dump until 1938 when the rest of the underground complex was discovered. Galleries run from it for about a kilometre, ending in the *Caverna Bianca*, a spectacular amphitheatre of stalagmites and stalagtites (said by some to be the world's single most beautiful cave). 90-minute tours run roughly hourly (9 am–noon and 3–7 pm); partial tours – which miss the *Caverna Bianca* – take only 40 minutes and cost half the price.

Trulli

Beyond the village of **Putignano** the landscape becomes increasingly dominated by the *trulli*, some of Europe's most curious – and perhaps most ancient – dwelling places. Round, whitewashed buildings with tapered stone roofs, the earliest surviving example seems to date back to the 13th century. Most, however, were built in the 16th and 17th centuries. Cool in summer, they're also easily built, making use of locally available stone. Why they should occur only in this region, however, and what their ancient origins might be, is unknown. The theories, though, are legion.

For a while it was thought *trulli* were built to thwart Ferdinand I of Aragon. During his reign, he forbade the Puglians to build permanent homes. In this way he could move peasants around as they were needed. The peasants responded by constructing homes which could easily be taken down (*trulli* are traditionally made from layers of uncemented stones). Another theory was that the *trulli* aided tax evasion. The Spanish imposed a levy on individual buildings, exempting only those which were unfinished. Wily peasants were supposed to have removed their roofs at the first sign of the tax inspector.

It's likely, though, that the building's origins were more exotic. The method used to construct them is similar to that used to build the 'sugar loaf' houses near Aleppo in Syria. They also bear a striking resemblance to houses in North Africa and ancient Crete. One theory is that Puglian soldiers saw such houses during the Crusades and imported the idea. Another links them with buildings and tombs excavated at Mycenae in Greece, which would connect the *trulli* with the Greek civilisation of around 3000 BC.

Alberobello

Whatever their history, the *trulli* provide a startling and beautiful addition to the landscape. The best place to see them is Alberobello, literally the 'beautiful tree' (oak woods once blanketed the region, hence the town's earlier name, *Silva Arboris Belli*). Be warned, though, that the place is often crawling with tourists (and many of the dwellings have become chintzy shops and souvenir stalls). Restaurants and accommodation are also overpriced, so it's probably best to make this a day trip or casual stopover. For the thick of the *trulli* (the town has around 1,500 examples) turn left out of the station on Via Garibaldi. This brings you to Piazza del Popolo and the **tourist office** at Corso Vittorio Emanuele 15. Any left turn leads into *trulli* country.

Martina Franca

Trulli continue to sprinkle the landscape as the train potters slowly along the Itria valley. They're still in evidence as it pulls in to Martina Franca. Don't be put off by the highrise blocks on the town's outskirts: the centre's a lovely and little-known showcase of Baroque and Rococo architecture. Reputedly founded in the 10th century, its original inhabitants were refugees from Taranto, forced to flee the city by Saracen raids. The town only prospered, however, when Philip of Anjou granted it various tax privileges in the 14th century (hence *franca* in the town's name, meaning duty or stamp). He also built a massive defensive wall, fortified by 24 towers (12 round and 12 square). Only four of the former gateways now survive.

If you miss one of the rare buses from the station to the centre then it's an easy walk to Piazza Roma and the **tourist office**. (Turn left out of the station and follow Viale della Libertà to Corso Italia). The piazza's dominated by the **Palazzo**

Ducale (1669), most of its 300 rooms now used by the council – though a few on the third floor are open to the public (Mon–Sat 8 am–8 pm; free). You're usually left to wander at will, the tremendous decoration more than worth the time. The cream of the town's Baroque architecture lines Via Cavour – all wrought-iron balconies and curlicues of stone – though its single outstanding highlight is a church, **San Martino**. Rebuilt in the 18th century, it's fronted by a soaring Baroque façade and flanked by an older campanile, all that survives of an earlier Romanesque church. The main doorway, and its carving of *St Martin and the Beggar*, is a foretaste of the richly decorated interior.

Once you've tired of the architecture wander to what's left of the old walls for a lovely panorama of the Itria valley and its *trulli*-dotted patchwork of fields and olive groves (Viale de Gasperi offers one of the better vantage points). When you've tired of the views, head for the *Café Tripoli* in Via Garibaldi, a wonderful turn-of-the century bar. The local tipple is *Bianco neutro*, a white wine used to fortify other wines (vermouth and *spumanti* in particular).

Practicalities in Martina Franca

Tourist Office Piazza Roma 35 (080/705.702).
Youth Hostel *Ostello La Cremaillere* (080/00.052). The hostel's 7km out of town at Via Orimini 1 in the hamlet of Locando San Paolo. To get there take the FSE bus from Piazza Crispi (off Via Taranto) for Locando San Paolo and Taranto.
Hotels Martina Franca's not blessed with many cheap hotels. Most places, moreover, fill up during the town's *Valle d'Itria* festival during the last week of July. ☆☆*Da Luigi*, Via Taranto (080/901.324). The cheapest place in town.
Restaurant *La Tavernetta*, Corso Vittorio Emanuele 30. Far and away the best food in town.

Taranto

An odd mixture of port, old town and industrial city, Taranto isn't a place to make a special journey for – though its gritty ambience and unvisited air make it interesting for an hour or so. You'll also find plenty of train connections here, and a string of cheap – if dowdy – places to stay. If you do stop over, the one un-doubted attraction is the **Museo Nazionale**, crammed with artifacts from Taranto's pre-Roman heyday. For centuries ancient *Taras* was capital of Magna Graecia, boasting a population estimated at 300,000, a figure hardly reached by other cities until the Industrial Revolution. In this century, however, it was the headquarters of the Italian fleet, a status which invited heavy bombing in the Second World War. Since then any trace of *Taras*, or Roman *Tarentum*, has been confined to the *museum*.

Taranto's easily navigated, and the museum easily found. The town divides into three: a northern spur containing the station and the industry (known as the *Borgo*); a central island containing the old town (the *Città Vecchia*); and a south-ern spur containing the new city (and the museum). All three areas are linked by bridges. Pick up a map at the station's information kiosk and take any bus for the new city (watch yourself at night in the old town: for safety's sake stick to the brightly-lit seafront boulevards like Corso Vittorio Emanuele). Most buses run along Corso Umberto I in the new city, perfect for the museum which is at its junction with Corso Cavour (two blocks after crossing from the old town). The museum opens Mon–Sat 9 am–2 pm, Sun 9 am–1 pm. There's almost too much to see in one visit – the museum boasts 50,000 Greek terracottas alone (the world's largest collection). The more important exhibits, however, are picked out, with a star rating running from one to four. The lower floor rooms are largely given over to the earliest Italic tribes; the core of the museum is on the first floor, the so-called Tarantine collection.

Make first for the **Sala degli Ori**, the gallery's centrepiece, a scintillating display of goldware (mainly intricately worked jewellery). Elsewhere, the rooms document the gamut of daily life in Magna Graecia, displaying Greek statues, articles from burial grounds, decorated terracottas, and a wide range of ceramics and sculptures. Other exhibits to look out for include a pair of *kore* (statues of young girls); a series of Roman portraits; the bas-reliefs and mosaics from the town's tombs; a variety of actors' masks; and two busts of Apollo and Aphrodite. The most popular exhibit is probably the *sarcophagus*, cut from a single block of marble. In it lies the skeleton of a Greek athelete, complete with perhaps the finest set of teeth in antiquity.

Practicalities in Taranto

Tourist Office The main office is in the new city at Corso Umberto 113 (099/21.233). Take bus number 8 from the station and get off three stops after crossing from the old town. There's also a small information kiosk at the station.

Railway station Piazza Duca d'Aosta (099/411.801). The station serves both FS and FSE networks.

Buses Buy tickets for local AMAT services at the small booth outside the station. Long distance FSE and SITA buses leave Piazza Castello, a square on the southern end of the old town before the bridge for the new city.

Budget Travel CTS, Via Matteotti 1 (099/27.460). Immediately over the bridge in the new city.

Beach For sea and sand take the summer-only bus along the *lungomare* and head for the *Lido Silvana*, the region's nicest and most peaceful beach.

Hotels It's best to avoid the generally dingy hotels on Piazza Fontana in the old town, particularly if you're a woman travelling alone. The better options in this area are given below, but to be safer head for the new city.

☆*Ariston*, Piazza Fontana 15 (099/407.563). On the waterfront, with views of the sea from some rooms. Clean rooms, but many long-stay clients, so call ahead.

☆*Sorrentino*, Piazza Fontana 7 (099/471.8390). Alongside the *Ariston*. Slightly chaotic, but family run, good views and nice atmosphere.

☆☆*Pisani*, Piazza Garibaldi (099/24.087). A first choice by virtue of its central position (in the new city) and its smart new rooms.

☆☆*Bella Taranto*, Via Principe Amadeo 60 (099/22.505). A safe and popular choice, so call ahead to check on vacancies, right in the centre of the new town.

☆☆☆*Pisani*, Via Cavour 43 (099/24.087). In a quiet cul-de-sac close to the Museo Nazionale.

Restaurants Seafood's the thing in Taranto, widely available in the plethora of cheap places in the new city.

La Grande Birreria, Via Regina Margherita 43. A buzzy and popular place that combines a restaurant, pizzeria and self-service rolled into one.

Basile al Ristoro, Via Pitagora 76. First port-of-call in the new city for a proper sit-down meal; it has an easy-going atmosphere, fine food and friendly service.

Lecce–Otranto–Gallipoli–Lecce
The route

This neat little circuit allows you to explore the Salentino peninsula, the southernmost tip of the Italian 'heel'. For the most part it's a matter of enjoying the scenery (pleasant, but no more), or stopping off at the beaches and backwater towns. A trip to **Otranto**, the route's main town, gives you a taste of the area if you don't want to make the entire trip. **Gallipoli** is a quaint fishing village (with modern outskirts), a good place to rest up for a couple of days.

Trains

There's no doubt this is a journey for people with plenty of time. The private FSE *line in this part of the country is a lazy affair. Trains are slow and infrequent, so be prepared to take your time. There are 9 trains daily from* **Lecce–Zollino–Maglie.** *Change at Maglie (29 km, 45 min) for* **Otranto** *(9 daily, 18 km, 25 min). For* **Gallipoli** *(53 km, 1 hr 5 min) there are 8 direct trains daily from* **Lecce-Zollino–Nardo–Gallipoli.**

The journey

Out of Lecce the train heads inland, leaving you little to do but admire the rocky, low-hilled scenery until **Maglie**, where you change trains for **Otranto**. Greek in origin, the tiny town snuggles into its harbour, still a fishing village at heart, but beginning to fill up in summer with *Club Med* visitors and backpackers riding the ferry to Greece (its beach is moderately good).

In its day, Otranto was the capital of Byzantine southern Italy, falling to the Normans in 1070. Later it became a port of embarkation for the Crusaders. In 1480 it bore the brunt of a Turkish attempt on mainland Italy, holding out for 15 days before surrendering. Over 12,000 people perished in the encounter, but worse was to come. The archbishop was sawn in half – so the story goes – for his part in the defence. Another group of survivors who refused to convert to Islam were taken to a nearby hill and executed. The 16th-century church of **San Francesco di Paola** marks the spot, complete with a list of the slain and a juicy account of the event. The executioners' block was reputedly at the spot marked by a chapel mid-way up the church's steps. The column nearby was erected to honour Belar Bey, one of the executioners, who refused to carry out his brief and converted to Christianity.

Some of the martyrs wound up in the duomo, **Santa Maria Annunziata**, a Romanesque building begun by the Normans in 1080 and restored in 1481 (after the Turks had used it as a stable). The executioner's block is under the high altar. It's best known, however, for its extraordinary **mosaic floor**. A naïve 12th-century work, it runs the length of the nave, describing the *Tree of Life* in a beautiful patchwork of stone. Numerous themes and figures are depicted in an historical mish-mash, including King Arthur, the Queen of Sheba and Alexander the Great. Twisted into the narrative are Biblical scenes (Adam and Eve, Cain and Abel) and decorative flourishes using stone fish, serpents and mermaids. Be sure to venture into the **crypt** (1088) decorated with Byzantine frescoes and supported by 42 tiny columns taken from earlier Greek, Roman and Arab buildings (many of the columns in the main church came from the same sources).

Other places to dip into in town include the **Castello**, a massive 15th-century Aragonese fortress, and the cracking 10th-century church of **San Pietro**, decorated with Byzantine frescoes.

Practicalities in Otranto

Tourist Office Via Basilica 8 (0836/801.436).
Ferries *Roana Lines* operate a dilapidated ferry service to Corfu and Igoumenitsa (June– Sept). More information from the Stazione Marittima.
Hotels For help with finding rooms use the *Cooperazione Servizio Turismo* on Largo Cavour (near the duomo). Be prepared to make bookings in August, and to take full pension. The office also has a **bike rental** facility.
☆☆*Ester*, Via Papa Giovanni XXIII 19 (0836/ 84.169)
☆☆*Bellavista*, Via Vittorio Emanuele 16 (0836/ 86.359).
Campsite The *Campeggio Hydrusa* (0836/ 81.255) is signposted from the port.

After Otranto it's back the way you've come, retracing your steps to Zollino to pick up a train that covers a wide arc around the peninsula. En route you pass through low hills, scarcely more than ripples, and through groves of figs and olives, splashes of green against the white of limestone and golden fields of corn. **Gallipoli** was named 'beautiful city' by the Greeks (*kalli-pollis*), not a moniker that seems terribly fitting as the train plods through its uninspiring outskirts. Once in the old town, though, the reasons for the Greeks' enthusiasm become clearer. The town sits on a virtual island, connected to the mainland by a narrow isthmus. Narrow streets twist around the promontory, decked with hanging flowers and lined with low whitewashed houses (all rather Greek-looking, in fact). Once you're bored with pottering about, head for the fine beaches to the north at Santa Caterina and Santa Maria al Bagno (there are more reasonably secluded beaches south of the town as well). This is a quiet spot to rest up for a few days (as are many of the resorts on the Salentino). Rooms are in fairly short supply, but see the small tourist office for what's available (at Corso Roma 225, 0833/476.202). If you're tenting, there are several campsites within about three kilometres of town.

On the return leg to Lecce, **Nardo** is a lively little town, crammed with Baroque buildings, though probably less interesting overall than nearby **Gallatina**. Founded by the Greeks, this is another town – like Gallipoli – which retained much of its Greek culture, even traces of an ancient dialect, until this century. Great swathes of tobacco grow on all sides (this is one of Italy's leading centres of production), though the town's better known for the cathedral of **Santa Caterina**. Built in 1384, its interior's covered in frescoes by 15th-century artists from Emilia-Romagna or the Marche. When all's said and done, however, you're riding this line for the landscape, dominated back to Lecce – as it has been throughout – by vistas of vines and olive groves.

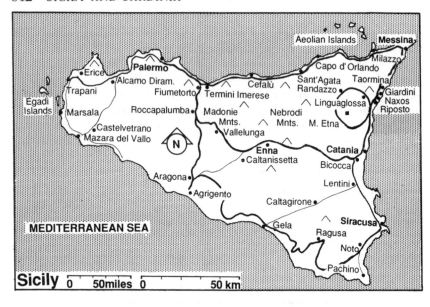

7 Sicily and Sardinia

Sicily and Sardinia are the first and second largest islands in the Mediterranean. Geographically distinct from Italy, they are also separated by history and culture from the rest of the country. As islands in their own right, however, they have almost nothing in common. Each is a world apart, with enough to occupy you for weeks. In Sardinia, though, the rail network has been pared to the bone. It's unlikely you'll want to travel there simply to ride its trains. Sicily, by contrast, is criss-crossed by charming old railways, many perfectly routed to open up the island's most interesting sights.

For centuries **Sicily** was at the heart of the known world. Plumb centre of the Mediterranean, its strategic position made it both a focus for trade and a prize for foreign powers. There are few periods in its history when Sicilians themselves have held the whip hand. Its history and therefore its cities and historic sites are rooted in the cultures of past invaders. Between the 8th–3rd centuries BC this meant the Greeks; in the 9th and 10th centuries it was the Arabs; in the 11th century the Normans. These were the epochs that most tangibly affected the island. Between times, however, it also knew the attentions of Romans, French, Spanish, Bourbons – even the British for a while. These days there are those who would argue that the **mafia** is the latest in a line of historical leeches. While there's no doubt of the organisation's power, it's not something that the casual tourist will encounter head-on although petty crime is rife in the larger cities.

The mafia is both a product and symptom of the island's poverty, corruption and bureaucratic lethargy. Sicily is poor, make no mistake, and people have emigrated to America or northern Italy for decades. It's also an island, however, of often incomparable beauty and contrasts. At its most basic it divides between a harsh, empty interior and a lush, developed coast. More specifically it consists of two major cities; **Catania**, on the east coast, of scant appeal, and **Palermo**, the capital, a far more fascinating prospect on the north coast. 'This is where Europe finally ends,' wrote D. H. Lawrence, 'beyond is Africa and Asia.' He was describing Sicily as a whole, but nowhere is the observation more true than in Palermo, where crumbling Norman and Baroque architecture contrasts with a bustling *casbah* atmosphere of twisting alleys and raucous street markets. These days, in fact, Africa seems already a part of the city.

Amongst the other towns you need to pick and choose; for overall interest, **Siracusa** stands out, once the most important city in the Greek world. It's also handy for a famous medley of Baroque towns, the most prominent of which are **Noto** and **Ragusa. Agrigento**, too, scores highly for its outstanding Greek temples, though the town – like many on the coast – is spoilt by its more modern suburbs. Places which have escaped development, however, include **Cefalù** on the north coast, perhaps the island's nicest little town (and a good beach resort into the bargain). Then there's **Taormina**, amongst the most beautiful resorts in Italy – but often crowded and expensive as a result.

Elsewhere, **Mount Etna**, Europe's foremost volcano, overshadows the north-eastern quarter of the island. Smaller volcanoes, islands this time, sprinkle the sea off the north coast, a trip to the **Aeolian Islands** rivalling an ascent of Etna itself as one of Sicily's best off-train excursions. Finally, it would be a mistake to overlook the wild and unspoiled landscapes of the Sicilian **interior**, an empty expanse of mountains and rolling plateaus centred on **Enna**.

As for **Sardinia**, it's a crime to be perfunctory, but in truth there are only three main lines on the entire island. Three main lines and one private line, which, ironically, is perhaps the absolute epitome of the quaint branch line: excruciatingly slow and old-fashioned, but gloriously scenic and fun to ride. Train buffs could well come here for this trip alone: otherwise, the skeletal rail network has to be combined with an excellent bus service if you're to explore the island under your own steam.

Routes Palermo
Messina–Milazzo–Cefalù–Palermo
Palermo–Roccapalumba–Agrigento
Agrigento–Gela–Noto–Ragusa–Siracusa
Siracusa–Noto–Ragusa
Palermo–Enna–Catania
Circumetnea: *Catania–Randazzo–Riposto*
Catania–Taormina–Messina
Sardinia
Cagliari–Mandas–Arbatax/Mandas–Sorgono

You'll be happier in the long run if you accept that trains in Sicily *are not so much a means of transport as slow but scenic ways to see the countryside. Study the timetables well and accept the inevitable delays. D. H. Lawrence summed up both the reasons for the delays and the air of resignation needed to deal with them:*

Sicilian railways are all single line. Hence, the *coincidenza*. A *coincidenza* is where two trains meet in a loop. You sit in a world of rain and waiting until some silly engine with four trucks puffs alongside. *Ecco la coincidenza!* Then after a brief *conversazione* between the two trains, *diretto* and *merce*, express and goods, the tin horn sounds and away we go happily towards the next coincidence. Clerks away ahead joyfully chalk up our hours of lateness on the announcement slate. All adds to the adventurous flavour of the journey. . . .

This understood, plan a trip around Sicily; the island lends itself more or less to a circular tour. It's one that can be followed clockwise *(to Palermo first) or* anti-clockwise *(via Etna, Catania and Siracusa). On the basis that you want to see* Palermo *first, follow* Messina–Cefalù–Palermo, *perhaps with a stopover at* Cefalù *(this is one of the island's more reliable stretches of rail).* Palermo–Agrigento *takes in the temples, after which you could wriggle slowly around the south coast to* Siracusa. *It's easier, though, to backtrack, and pick up the* Palermo–Enna–Catania *line, a great scenic route through the best of the interior. At* Catania *the private Circumetnea line makes a complete circuit of Mount Etna, with fantastic first-hand views of the volcano. Then you should pick up the fast* Catania-Siracusa *coast line and base yourself at* Siracusa. *From here the obvious trip is the line connecting some of Italy's finest Baroque towns* (Siracusa–Noto–Ragusa). *To return to* Messina *and thus to the mainland head north again, perhaps taking time out to see Taormina or put up at one of the nearby resorts* (Catania–Taormina–Messina).

Palermo

Palermo is one of Italy's most interesting cities – though not in the manner of Florence or Venice. It's not for the monuments or galleries that you come (though there's plenty to see in this respect). As with Naples, you're here for the atmosphere, a strange mixture of decaying grandeur and criminal unease. This won't, of course, be to all tastes. All Sicily's myriad social and historical strands come together here – Byzantine, Norman, Arab and Baroque architecture; cramped backstreets; slums; poverty; thieving children; beggars; frenetic crowds; manic traffic, but also a rich street culture, vibrant port, sense-assaulting markets, Arab bazaars, cheap bars, lively restaurants and all the customs, culture and colourful characters that are peculiarly Sicilian.

All these are things you need to soak up by walking. Palermo's not, however, a place where orientation is straightforward (a map from the tourist office is essential). The city's a fairly amorphous entity, the key sights widely spread – though at a pinch all bar one are within walking distance. **Corso Vittorio Emanuele** and **Via Roma** are the main streets, arteries you come back to time and again. When you get fed up with the walking, numerous buses (invariably packed) ply up and down these thoroughfares. Assuming you steel yourself, take to Palermo, and guard against rip-offs, you could spend a few days here – a couple catching the sights and soaking up the streetlife; a couple making trips to islands off Sicily's northern coast (to Ustica, say); one at Mondello, Palermo's top beach; or one visiting Monreale, a superb cathedral a few kilometres out famous for its mosaics.

Finally, it needs to be said, you'll see no visible signs of the Mafia. You will, however, have to be on constant guard for bag snatchers, pick-pockets and other bits of petty thievery. Women need to be especially careful, and everyone should avoid backstreets after dark. Locals themselves rarely venture out after 9pm.

History

Palermo's natural harbour and fine setting made it an obvious site for a city. Its name comes from the Greek *Panormos*, meaning all port, though it was never held by the Greeks. The earliest settlement, an 8th century BC trading post, was Phoenician. It was later a stronghold for the Carthaginians, Rome's North Africa-based rivals, finally falling to the Romans in 254 BC. After the fall of the Empire came the Vandals (AD 440), the Byzantines (535) and the Arabs (830).

During 240 years of Arab rule Palermo became the greatest Christian city in Europe after Constantinople. Contemporary writers constantly extolled its beauties, or recounted the wealth and vigour of its cosmopolitan population (Greeks, Lombards, Jews, Tartars, Berbers, Slavs, as well as Arabs from Spain, Syria and Egypt). In 1072, however, the Normans under Roger II took control. Nonetheless, the city continued to be at the centre of Asian, African and European trade (more money flowed to Norman coffers from Sicily than ever did from England, conquered by Roger's Norman relatives).

Palermo's history then followed the fortunes of Sicily as a whole, bandied about between the Anjous (1266), Spaniards and Bourbons, all of whom left their stamp on the city, running it to the edge of ruin in the process. Even the British ruled for a short period in 1811. It was this lack of central control, perhaps, that laid the foundations for the mafia, a powerful force for order and summary justice in an otherwise chaotic region. Mussolini almost destroyed the old-style organisation by using its own methods against it. The post-war building boom, however, provided the contracts and corruption that brought it back from the dead. Drug revenue and a thorough-going infiltration of all walks of life make it now all but omnipotent.

What to see

Cattedrale

Palermo's tawny-stoned *cattedrale* is an exotic affair, interesting more for its exuberant exterior than the chill Neoclassical interior. Amongst other things, it's the spot where the state honours its dead. General Della Chiesa, murdered by the mafia in 1982, and judges Falcone and Borsellino (similarly murdered) all had memorial services here. In the 1982 service the Archbishop of Palermo ended his sermon – one of the few to target organised crime – with the words, *Ecco il grande silenzio della morte* (Here is the great silence that is death).

Started in 1185 along Norman lines, the cathedral was spoilt by 18th-century alterations, the most evident being a large and jarring dome. The main door, though, is in a flowery Catalan–Gothic style, a 15th-century reworking of the original, likewise the Loggia dell'Incoronata on the façade's left. Otherwise much of the detail and decoration preserves its Norman flavour.

Inside, where any Norman tendency has been all but obliterated, probably its most interesting features are the **royal tombs** (two chapels in the south aisle), repositories for monarchs including Henry IV, Roger II, Frederick II and his wife, Constance of Aragon. Close by is a reliquary (1631) containing the remains of St Rosario, Palermo's patron saint. The **treasury**, to the right of the choir, is crammed with precious objects, the most beguiling an odd jewel-encrusted skull cap-cum-crown belonging to Constance (it was removed from her tomb).

Palazzo dei Normanni

If you come outside the cathedral and turn right (on Corso Vittorio Emanuele) you soon encounter a vast collection of buildings known as the Palazzo dei Normanni (or Palazzo Reale). There's been a palace or fort of some sort on the site since the city's earliest days. The Saracens built the first in the 9th century, later enlarged by the Normans, under whom it became one of the most sophisticated courts in Europe. The main façade was added by the Spaniards in the 17th century. Today most of the buildings are used by the Sicilian government.

To see anything of the state rooms you need to join a guided tour (Mon and Fri–Sat 9 am–12.30 pm; closed when parliament is in session; free). These take you round various royal apartments, the highlight of which is the **Sala di Re Ruggero** (the Hall of Roger II), a little chamber decorated with mosaics of hunting scenes. More attractive still, however, is the **Cappella Palatina**, central Palermo's undoubted artistic highlight. Built by Roger II as a private chapel (1132–40), it's the supreme example of the composite architectural style that flourished in Sicily under the Normans. The largely Romanesque interior, partly supported by old Roman columns, glitters with Byzantine-influenced mosaics describing scenes from the Old Testament. The extraordinary wooden ceiling, by contrast, is Moorish, an intricate honeycomb of exquisite carving. Alongside the high altar are an **ambo** (pulpit) and large **candelabrum**, both beautifully sculpted and studded with 12th-century mosaics.

San Giovanni degli Eremiti

Easily seen after the palazzo, San Giovanni degli Eremiti is one of the city's most picturesque places – though the surroundings are some of its poorest. This is the edge of the Albergheria quarter, a fascinating area of alleys, teeming street markets and colourful streetlife.

Built in 1132, the church is amongst Sicily's earliest pieces of Norman architecture. Most of the building retains its original appearance. Roger II personally insisted on the five ochre domes and square base, an indication of the influence of Arab architecture at the time. Equally as charming, though, are the wild gardens, a profusion of palms, shrubs and lemon trees concealing a perfect doubled-columned **cloister**.

La Martorana

Another great Norman survivor, the church of the Martorana was built by Georgios Antiochenos, an admiral of Roger II (hence its other name, Santa Maria dell'Ammiraglio). It forms one in a trio of churches gathered around Piazza Pretoria, off Corso Vittorio Emanuele, dominated by a 16th-century fountain carved with naked women (locals call this the Piazza Vergogna, the 'square of shame' after what they see as its rather salacious statues).

Started in 1143, the church received a Baroque reworking in 1588, the main additions being the curving north façade and a deluge of interior decoration. Little, though, detracts from the impact of the dome's magnificent **mosaics**, 12th-century works probably executed by Greek craftsmen. Outside the main entrance, notice a couple of separate mosaics, one showing Roger II being crowned by Christ, the other Georgios dedicating the church to the Madonna.

San Giuseppe dei Teatini

Piazza Pretoria's second church, San Giuseppe offers an antidote to the Martorana's Norman mood. Raised in 1612, it's a perfect expression of all that was good about the Baroque, the plain-faced façade concealing a riotous interior the right side of excess. In similar vein, **Santa Caterina** opposite offers another explosion of rococo decoration, though it's rarely open.

Museo Archeologico

Leave Piazza Pretoria and stroll east a short way on Corso Vittorio Emanuele. At Via Roma, the city's main crossroads, turn left and follow the street as far as the Museo Archeologico (housed in a former 16th-century convent). En route, note that in the streets off to your right – the district known as the **Vucciria** – is one of Palermo's bigger **street markets**, a great area to wander.

The **museum** groans under the weight of a superb collection, most of its exhibits taken from the western side of the island (though restorations have long been in train, so various parts of the two main floors – and courtyards – may be closed). The most famous exhibits are the **Metopes of Selinunte**, part of a valuable haul of 6th-century BC sculpture removed from Selinunte (a town and archaeological site south-west of Palermo). These carved friezes which adorned temples are collected in a single room, the best known of all being those taken from Selinunte's Temple.

Practicalities in Palermo

Tourist Office There is an information kiosk at the station. Other offices are inconveniently located well away from the city centre.
Railway station All trains run from the Stazione Centrale, Piazza G. Cesare (091/616.1806 or 656.293). It's at the southern end of Via Roma. To get to the main heart of the city walk straight up Via Roma to the *Quattro Canti*, the street's intersection with Corso Vittorio Emanuele. The station has left luggage, *albergo diurno* and foreign exchange facilities.
Buses AMAT city buses have flat fares for 1 hour, 2 hours and a day pass. Buy tickets from the booths at the station, from *tabacchi*, or shops displaying an AMAT sticker. Most buses leave from in front of the station, but the other big stops are at Piazza Castelnuovo (in the north), Viale della Libertà and Corso Vittorio Emanuele.
Taxis Take taxis from the rank in front of the station, but make sure the meter is switched on; only used licensed cabs. Most drivers are honest. Many main city squares also have ranks.
Ferries Regular boats leave from the Stazione Marittima (entry off Via Francesco Crispi) for Sardinia (Cagliari), Ustica and Naples. Hydrofoils operate to Ustica, Cefalù and the Aeolian islands. Tickets are available within the port or from travel agents. The Stazione has left luggage facilities.
Budget travel CTS, Via Garzilli 28g (091/325.752). A couple of blocks from Piazza Castelnuovo (bus from the station).
American Express Via E. Amari 40 (091/587.144).
Post Office Palazzo delle Poste, Via Roma 322, close to the Museo Archeologico.
British Consulate In Naples (081/663.514).
Hospital Ospedale Civico Regionale, Via Lazzaro (091/484.544).
Hotels Palermo has plenty of accommodation, so finding a cheap and convenient hotel is no problem, although as ever in southern cities it's sometimes worth paying a little more than usual for security and extra comforts. Most of the hotels cluster near the station, on Via Roma and Via Maqueda (the street parallel to Via Roma). More expensive options tend to lie north of Corso Vittorio Emanuele.
☆*Alessandra*, Via Divisi 99, off Via Maqueda (090/616.7009). Modern rooms and facilities.
☆*Odeon*, Via E. Amari 140, opposite the Teatro Politeama (091/332.778). Clean but slightly forlorn rooms.
☆*Orientale*, Via Maqueda 26, a few blocks

from the station (091/616.5727). Palermo's most atmospheric cheap hotel, housed in a crumbling 17th-century *palazzo*; sombre rooms but great common areas.
☆*Petit*, Via Principe di Belmonte 84 (091/323.616). Safe, peaceful and hygienic.
☆*Rosalia Conca d'Oro*, Via Santa Rosalia 7, left outside the station (091/616.4543). Cheap, slightly chaotic and not always as clean as some places, but the rooms are spacious and the owners obliging.
☆*Sud*, Via Maqueda 8 (091/617.5700). Two blocks from the station and one of the city's best budget bets. Try also the *Vittoria* in the same block (091/616.2437).
☆☆*Centrale*, Corso Vittorio Emanuele 387 (091/588.409). Central rooms with a slightly faded period charm.
☆☆*Sole*, Corso Vittorio Emanuele 291 (091/587.344). Solid old-fashioned hotel.
Camping The nearest site is the *Trinacrea* (091/530.590) on the sea at Sferracavallo (13km north-west of the city). Take bus number 28 from Piazza Castelnuovo.
Restaurants Food is superb in Palermo, sardines (*pasta con le sarde*), sword fish (*pesce spada*) and aubergines every which way being the big specialities. Anything *alla palermitana*, however, should be worth a try (and don't forget the city's famous cakes and marzipans).
Trattoria-Pizzeria Enzo, Via Maurolico, on the right as you leave the station. Undoubtedly the first choice near the station for good food, big portions and giveaway prices.
Shanghai, Vicolo de Mezzani 34, overlooking Piazza Caracciolo in the Vucciria market district. About as authentic as a Sicilian restaurant gets – tatty in an atmospheric way, filled with market traders and good, cheap food (the *Shanghai* refers to the look of the market stalls below – the food is pure Palermo).
Pizzeria Bellini, Piazza Bellini. More expensive than some places, but nice setting next to the church of La Martorana.
Hotel Patria, Via Alloro 104; take Via Paternostro off Corso Vittorio Emanuele. One of the city's most romantically sited courtyards for *al fresco* eating.
Antica Foccaceria San Francesco, Via A. Paternostro 58, off Corso Vittorio Emanuele near the church of San Francesco. Founded in 1834, this is one of Palermo's great institutions (Garibaldi is supposed to have eaten here after liberating the city). It's known for its old marble-topped tables and stomach-testing snacks – of which marinated tripe is one.

There's plenty more to keep archaeological fiends happy for hours. If you want the highlights, however, hunt out the *Ram of Syracuse* (in the bronze collection), a 3rd century BC Hellenistic work; *Hercules Overpowering a Stag*, a Roman copy of a Greek original removed from Pompeii; the *Satyr Preparing to Drink*, another Roman copy of a Greek original; and the lion's head fountains, removed from a temple at Himera (5th-century BC). The museum's open Tues–Sun 9 am–1 pm.

Galleria Regionale della Sicilia

Palermo's excellent Galleria Regionale resides in the Palazzo Abatellis on Via Alloro, close to the waterfront (Tues–Sun 9 am–1 pm). It's home to the cream of the island's medieval treasures, with sculptures downstairs, paintings upstairs. The only exception to the plan is *The Triumph of Death*, a wonderfully macabre fresco which covers the entire wall of the palace's former chapel. A 15th-century work by an unknown artist (possibly Flemish), it shows Death personified on horseback, loosing off arrows into a menagerie of victims (the artist was perhaps inspired by an outbreak of plague, a frequent occurrence in medieval Palermo). There are also plenty of first-rate Sicilian works, the painting section's real masterpieces an *Annunciation* and *Three Saints* by Antonello da Messina, one of the island's finest artists (1430–79).

Downstairs, the most mesmerising exhibit is a bust of *Eleanor of Aragon* in Room 4 by Francesco Laurana (1430–1502). Other priceless works of art include the *Malaga Vase* and a carved doorframe, both Arab-styled works.

Convento dei Cappuccini

It's definitely worth taking the bus out to see the **Convento dei Cappuccini**, one of Italy's most eerily astounding sights (take bus number 27 from Piazza Castelnuovo or Corso Vittorio Emanuele. Ask for the *catacombi* or get off at Via Pindemonte). Entombed under the old convent are some 8,000 bodies; monks, archbishops, commoners, small children, all in various states of decay and preservation. You walk up and down endless rows of corpses, all hung or propped up in macabre poses. Some still have parchment-yellow skin stretched across protruding bones. Many are wearing the clothes they died in – crumbling silks, top hats, peasant rags – creating an effect that's bizarre and comical by turns. Burying the dead thus was a Cappuchin tradition. The bodies were preserved using arsenic or quick lime, or simply left to bake in the sun. The first burial here was in the 15th century, the last in 1881. The convent is open Mon–Sat 9 am–noon and 3–5 pm. Despite the sight's increasing popularity, the monks on guard still aren't prepared for visitors. There's no admission, though they expect a small donation before you follow the corridor that leads down to the little Chamber of Horrors.

Messina – Milazzo – Cefalù – Palermo
The route

This route follows Sicily's northern (Tyrrhenian) coast, appealing in places, ravaged by modern developments in others. As the main line to Palermo it's likely to be your first taste of the island. Trains cross from the mainland to land at **Messina**, not a pretty town, usually proceeding to Palermo or Catania – meaning you probably won't need to change. At **Milazzo**, another grim place, ferries run to the **Aeolian Islands**, a volcanic archipelago whose land- and seascapes are some of Sicily's best. The only place you should stop on the mainland, however, is **Cefalù**, an excellent beach resort and historical town. It's crowded in summer, though, and accommodation may be a problem. Other good sea and sand options include the smaller resorts of Sant'Agata di Militello and Capo d'Orlando.

Trains

If you've been on a fast train from Rome or Naples the route along the Sicilian coast will be a sobering introduction to the crawling progress that characterises most of the island's trains. Nevertheless, it's Sicily's busiest piece of track, serviced by 7 fast through connections from the mainland. In addition, 10 locali *– agonisingly slow – ply the route starting at* **Messina Centrale** *(though most run only as far as Sant'Agata).*

The **fast trains** *all stop at the key points en route: Milazzo (36 km, 30 min); Capo d'Orlando (93 km, 1 hr 40 min); Sant'Agata (106 km, 1 hr 50 min); Cefalù (165k m, 3 hr); Palermo (232 km, 4 hr).*

The journey

Crossing the Straits of Messina from the mainland is one of the nicest parts of any journey south from Rome or Naples. It's appealing if only for the novelty value, never mind the views of Sicily as the ferry edges towards **Messina**. The procedure's simple if you have a through ticket: at Villa San Giovanni you sit tight on the train and the carriages are shunted on to the boat. The crossing takes no more than half an hour, but most people climb up on deck for a coffee in the boat's cheerfully dowdy bars.

Messina from a distance is attractive enough – a broad harbour and evocative-looking town – but grim in the extreme once you're off the boat. Unless circumstance forces your hand, stay on the train (or change for Taormina, Catania and the *Circumetnea*). A huge earthquake in 1908 levelled most of the old town. What survived was pounded by Allied bombs in the Second World War. Poor old **Milazzo** looks little better, its surroundings blighted by a huge oil refinery. It is, however, the main point of departure for the **Aeolian Islands** (see page 323). By now you might be wondering what's happened to Sicily's legendary beauty. The answer is that it's mainly inland, as the mountains rising to the south gradually confirm. Much of the Sicilian coast has been ravaged by housing and factories over the last 30 years.

Nevertheless, the ride definitely has its moments. The sea is an almost constant presence: orange and lemon trees dot rocky headlands, with olive groves and vines sweeping up towards the mountains. As the coast improves, resorts come thick and fast; small places for the most part, with good beaches and plenty of cheap accommodation. The first, **Capo d'Orlando**, is one of the better stops, perched on a headland and surrounded by sandy beaches (especially around San Gregorio to the east). **Sant'Agata** a few minutes beyond is a touch larger, and far more jumping in summer, though it retains the charm of its fishing village origins.

Cefalù

Cefalù, however, is the best place of all. One of Sicily's most attractive small towns, it's definitely a place to spend at least a couple of days relaxing before (or after) the rigours of Palermo. Although it receives its share of package tourists, the town's old streets and its fine beaches absorb them with no problem. Only high summer brings full hotels, a period when you may want to visit the town on a day trip. A morning would be enough to explore its sights – and still leave time for a swim.

Practicalities in Cefalù

Tourist Office Corso Ruggero 77 (0921/ 21.050). Corso Ruggero is Cefalù's main street; the office is about 100 metres south of Piazza del Duomo. It deals with accommodation and has a good map.

Railway station Viale Margherita. To reach Piazza Garibaldi, at the southern end of Corso Ruggero, turn right out of the station and follow Via Aldo Moro, Viale Margherita and Via Matteotti. It's about a ten-minute walk.

Hydrofoil In summer only a thrice-weekly hydrofoil runs from a terminal east of the town (20min walk) to Palermo, Lipari and Vulcano.

Hotels There are few cheap hotels, and few hotels of any sort in the old town. Most places are west of the headland in the modern town. Contact the tourist office in July and August, when facilities are at full stretch.

☆*Cangelosi*, Via Umberto 1, off Piazza Garibaldi (0921/21.591). A tiny 5-roomed place, and as the only budget place, likely to be full, so call in advance.

☆☆*Terminus*, Via Gramsci 2 (0921/21.034). Left of the railway station.

☆☆*La Giara*, Via Veterani 40, off Corso Ruggero (0921/21.562). Close to the beach and

comfortable rooms.

☆☆*Pensione delle Rose*, Via Gibilmanna (0921/21.885). Hit Via Mazzini from the station, then Via Umberto, which leads into Via Gibilmanna; rooms with some fine views of the town.

☆☆☆*Kalura*, Via Vincenzo Cavallaro 13 (0921/44.424). 20 minutes' walk east of the town, but a large comfortable hotel (popular with packages), redeemed by its stunning setting and private beach.

Camping The nearest site is the *Costa Ponente* (0921/20.085), 3km west of town, a 45min walk or short bus ride on the Cefalù – Lasari service (which runs from outside the station or Via Umberto nearby). It has a swimming pool and tennis courts. The smaller *San Filippo* is right alongside.

Restaurants Arkade, Via Vanni 9, off Corso Ruggero. Well-known as much for the fact that it's a Tunisian restaurant as anything else; good food, nonetheless.

Bastione, Cortile Pepe, off Via Umberto past the cathedral. The town's best all round restaurant; pizzas and particularly good seafood.

Excursion from Milazzo/Salina

The Aeolian Islands

The seven volcanic islands off Sicily's northern coast merit a holiday in their own right. They're known mainly for their beaches, wild inland scenery and mountain views. Most of all, though, they're renowned for the volcanic eruptions of Stromboli. Sadly they're becoming increasingly popular. Unless you come off-season, the big three group − Vulcano, Lipari and Stromboli − are crowded and growing ever more expensive. This said, facilities are good without being excessive, and there are usually rooms to rent during all months but August. Campsites are plentiful and bikes are available for hire in most centres. This is a sketch of what to see in the big three. Visit the others, however, Salina especially, and you'll find fewer tourists and more unspoilt beaches. Contact tourist offices for more details.

Vulcano This is the closest island to the mainland, making a good day-trip from Milazzo if you want only a taster of the islands. The last eruption here was in 1980. Mud baths and Vulcano's main crater are the reasons to come here (you can walk to the crater in an hour from the harbour, Porto di Levante). Otherwise walk to the Vulcanello, another crater, or stroll for 15 minutes from Porto towards Porto di Ponente for mudbaths and a good (but crowded) black sand beach (with campsite). Most accommodation is in Porto di Levante; rooms are affordable and reasonably abundant.

Stromboli Stromboli puts on a volcanic show about four times an hour. From June to September the island's packed with people attending its performances.

Rooms are in short supply, and those that are available tend to be rented for a minimum of three days. This means the island's best seen as a short trip from Lipari or Salina. Boats dock close to San Vincenzo, a hamlet that's merged with two others (Piscità and San Bartolo) to form an increasingly chic village known simply as Stromboli Paese ('Town'). Most of the island's accommodation is here (and is always full in July and August). The island's main beach, another black sand affair, is just north of Piscità.

A footpath leads from Piscità to the *Osservatorio*, far enough to have a view of the crater. The marked path to the top (927m) takes around another 3hr (2hr for the descent). Most bars will look after your bags. Guides are available if you prefer, but note that the signs saying ascents are illegal without them are meaningless. Many people camp near the summit. If you're camping or walking, be sure to take plenty of water.

Lipari Lipari is the largest, most varied and most beautiful of the isles. Boats run from Vulcano to Lipari Town, a picturesque spot with most of the action and accommodation (including a youth hostel, housed in the castle). The best thing to do is rent a bicycle or scooter and explore the hinterland. Cannetto is a good village, with nice pebbly beach and a fine campsite. Two kilometres away lies the well-known *Spiaggia Bianca*, one of the archipelago's nicest beaches. Other roads offer great viewpoints, rewarding scenery and plenty of walking opportunities. A reliable bus network links Cannetto and the rest of the island from Lipari Town if you don't fancy biking.

From the train you have a view of what makes Cefalù's setting special; the huge crag that looms above the town. The town takes its name from the rock, after the Greek *cephale* (head), a reference to the crag's presumed appearance. The old town crowds on to a promontory below the cliff, its Arabic honeycomb of streets as good a reason as any to spend an hour in aimless exploration. Sooner or later, though, you stumble on Piazza del Duomo, one of Italy's most enchanting main squares. Few places in Italy are as pleasant to sip a drink, shaded by palm trees and in full view of the cathedral.

Founded by Roger II in 1131, the **cathedral**'s fusion of Norman and Romanesque makes it as beautiful a building as you'll find in Sicily. According to tradition it was built by Roger in gratitude for washing up safe on Cefalù's beach during a storm. It took over a century to complete, the amber-hued façade postdated by the **interior**, completed in the 13th century. The stunning **mosaics** date from 1148, the earliest of any church mosaics in Sicily. Elsewhere the church's beauty is that of simplicity.

Just off Piazza del Duomo, Via Mandralisca leads to the **Museo Mandralisca**, a private collection of high quality (Mon–Sat 9 am–1 pm and 3.30–6 pm, Sun 9 am–noon). Amongst the articles on show are Greek ceramics, Arab pottery and archaeological fragments. The highlights are a famous *Portrait of an Unknown Man* by Antonello da Messina (1472) and a 4th-century BC Greek vase, or *krater* (notice the theme, a red-clothed fisherman disputing the price of his produce with a buyer).

The **beach** lies west of the harbour, backed by the town's modern quarter (walk along Via Vittorio Emanuele past Piazza C. Colombo). For something more strenuous, climb to the town's crag (or **Rocca**), approached by steps alongside the *Banco di Sicilia* in Piazza Garibaldi. It's 20 minutes to the Tempio di Diana, the remains of a 5th-century BC temple, and about an hour round trip if you press on to the top (where the views and countryside make the haul worthwhile). The path's obvious all the way.

Palermo–Roccapalumba–Agrigento
The route

Although this route takes you across the island from north to south – crossing some compelling countryside on the way – it's main attraction is **Agrigento**. Not for the town so much – part appealing medieval, part appalling modern – but for the Greek temples nearby, which together make up one of the greatest Greek archaeological sites in Europe. This naturally makes it a tour bus favourite, so be prepared for crowds. Alternatively, stay overnight in town and visit the ruins first thing in the morning. Either way, there's a lot to see, especially if you want to make the most of the on-site museum as well.

Beyond Agrigento you can pick up trains along the southern coast, changing at Canicatti for connections to Siracusa via Ragusa and Noto. These in turn put you on track for Catania, and thus connections to Messina or Palermo (via Enna). Alternatively, if you're in a hurry there are direct trains to Catania (5 daily) and Enna (5 daily).

Trains

There are 2 routes to **Agrigento** *from Palermo (139 km, 2 hr 10 min). Be sure to get the right one. The quickest is the* **scenic** *direct line via Roccapalumba and Aragona (9 trains daily). The other also goes via Roccapalumba but proceeds thereafter to Caltanissetta, where you change for Agrigento. This, too, offers a chance to see Sicily's wild interior. At almost 4 hours, however, it might be too much of a good thing.*

The journey

The chances are you'll be familiar with the first leg of the journey, the desultory ride along the coast from Palermo to industrial Termini Imerese: it's part of the main line from Messina to Palermo. Once the train starts to climb into the interior, however, much of the coast's squalor is left behind. The trip to Agrigento then lasts about an hour, long enough to sample the strange bare plateaus and long views that distinguish most of the island's wild hinterland (see also Palermo—Enna—Catania on page 333).

Agrigento

At Agrigento Centrale, skip the town and head straight for the **Valle dei Templi**, the Valley of the Temples. Be sure, incidentally, not to get off the train at Agrigento Bassa, still some three kilometres from the town centre. The temples and adjoining archaeological site are south of the town. Regular buses run from outside Agrigento Centrale – numbers 8, 9 and 10 all drop you at the car park which divides the eastern and western zones of the site. Note that if you first want to orientate yourself historically leave the bus earlier at the *Quartiere Hellenistico-Romano*, site of the Museo Nazionale Archeologico di San Nicola (see below). Otherwise leave it until after you have seen the site: it's about a kilometre, or ten minutes, from the main car park.

Agrigento's treasures have not been short of admirers over the centuries. The 'loveliest of mortal cities,' wrote Pindar; 'a beautiful city with stout walls,' added Virgil, rather less fulsomely. The finest tribute came from Pirandello, not surprisingly, as he was born in the town. 'Agrigento,' he observed, 'is where people eat as if they were having their last meal on earth; on the other hand they build their houses as if they were going to live in them forever.' For good measure he added, 'in other cities, between December and February you have fog, ice and, at best, a pale ray of sunshine; here the almond trees are in full flower, warmed by the breath of the African sea.'

All this is fine as far as it goes. What it doesn't say is that what once must have been the temples' idyllic setting now has to compete with Agrigento's modern and industrial skyline. Nonetheless, the temples are matchless, and the setting evocative - if you keep your eyes fixed firmly on the sea.

At the car park and *Snack Bar dei Templi* head left into the unenclosed **eastern zone**. This was the heart of the old city, founded in 582 BC by Greeks from nearby Gela. The first ruin on the right is the **Tempio di Ercole** (Herakles), eight columns (of an original 38) from the area's oldest temple (520 BC). Close by is a paleo-Christian necropolis, a labyrinth of graves and blind alleys. More impressive, however, is the tawny-stoned **Tempio di Concordia** (430 BC), the best-preserved Greek temple in the world after the Theseion in Athens. It became a Christian church in the 6th century, hence its fine state of preservation (many of the old city's other buildings were wrecked by earthquakes and early Christian vandalism). Beyond, the path follows the line of the city's old walls to the **Tempio di Giunone** (Juno), a majestic and lonely half-ruin at the edge of the site.

Returning to the car park, cross over to the site's **western zone** (9 am – 1 hr before sunset). The first temple is the **Tempio di Giove** (Jupiter), which would have been the largest Doric temple built in the Greek world. In the event it was never finished, work being halted by the Carthaginians' sack of the city in 405 BC (further damage was done in the 18th century when much of the stone was carted off to build the harbour at Porto Empedocle). Within the temple's perimeter lies a *Telemone*, one of several supporting columns sculpted into the shape of man. The other lesser ruins here include the Tempio dei Dioscuri (Castor and Pollux), actually a fake temple rebuilt in 1832 using fragments from various sources.

Back up the hill on Via dei Templi is the **Museo Nazionale Archeologico** (the bus runs past it), an overwhelming collection of artifacts removed from the old city and its environs (Tues–Sat 9 am–2 pm and 3–5 pm, Sun 9 am–1 pm; free). Amongst the things you should definitely see are numerous Greek vases (especially the *krater* in Room 15, the *Battle of the Amazons*); a *talamone*, a huge

Practicalities in Agrigento

Tourist Office Viale della Vittoria 255 (0922/ 26.922). Located close to the station – Viale della Vittoria is the street leading out of Piazza Marconi, the station forecourt.

Railway station Piazza Marconi. Buses run from here to the Valle dei Templi. For the town centre turn left out of Piazza Marconi; the third left, Via Atenea, is the main street.

Hotels Finding central accommodation shouldn't be a problem outside July and August.

☆*Concordia*, Via San Francesco 11 (0922/ 596.266). A clean and modern hotel – the best budget choice close to the station (turn left from the station and then left on Via Pirandello).

☆*Bella Napoli*, Piazza Lena 6 (0922/20.435). In a peaceful part of town off Via Bic Bac, which leads off Via Atenea at its western end (the end furthest from the station).

☆☆*Belvedere*, Via San Vito 20 (0922/20.051). close to the station, just one block east of Piazza Marconi. Clean, modern and tranquil rooms.

☆☆*Pirandello*, Via San Giovanni XXIII (0922/ 595.666). Spacious if slightly dated rooms.

Campsite The nearest site is the *Internazionale San Leone* (0922/41.612), situated on the coast 5km from town (bus number 9 from in front of the station).

Restaurants *Black Horse*, Via Celauro 8, off Via Atenea. Top-rate family-run spot, with good food, fair prices and pictures of horses all over the walls.

Atenea, Via Ficani 12 (fourth right on Via Atenea as you walk from the station end). The tourist menu and English signs may deter, but this is probably the best place for a cheap meal if finances are tight.

Forchetta, Piazza San Francesco (alongside the *Concordia* hotel). Not the cheapest place in town, but a quiet setting and some good authentic local dishes.

La Corte degli Sfizzi, Cortile Contarini. An attractive, trendy little spot in a courtyard above Via Atenea. Pizzas or full meals.

Manhattan, Salita M. Angeli 9 (up steps to the right at the start of Via Atenea near the station). The place for drinks and snacks during the day or late in the evening.

sculpted figure used to support part of a temple; lion-head water spouts removed from the temples; the *Efebo*, a marble statue of a young man; and a statuette of the *Sitting Venus*. In the grounds, pop into the 13th-century church of **San Nicola**, built on the site of a Greek sanctuary. The Gothic doorway uses pieces of ancient cornice, and inside there's a lovely Roman sarcophagus (second chapel on the right). The views of the temples from here are also some of the area's best.

Finally, if time allows, or if you're staying, give the centre of the old town a whirl. There's little specifically worth seeing, but the hilly medieval streets are pleasant to wander round.

Agrigento–Gela–Noto–Ragusa–Siracusa
The route

If you're in Agrigento this is the most obvious way – on paper – to reach **Siracusa** (Syracuse). Connections here, however, are poor, to say the least, for which reason the route's towns are best seen from Syracuse (see Siracusa–Noto–Ragusa on page 328 or Palermo–Enna–Catania on page 333). This route is given as a practical guide to getting round Sicily's south-west corner if you want to make the trip from Agrigento (a logical enough journey). For details of the towns see Siracusa–Noto–Ragusa below. Partly inland, partly on the coast, its scenic interest is less than some of the interior lines. Each of the towns, though, is a gem, thanks to the Baroque rebuilding that followed the earthquake of 1693, a cataclysm that destroyed swathes of the island. **Siracusa**, one of Sicily's most rewarding towns, deserves a couple of days, and is also the best place to stay. **Noto** is the most outstanding of the lesser towns and also a fine place to stop over – if you can find a bed. It's the most heavily promoted town in the region, making it much-visited, something to the advantage of larger but more peaceful **Ragusa**. Certain stretches of high plateau en route make for good viewing, but generally the coast is spoilt by industry and unexciting resorts.

Trains
This route may bring you face to face with the dreaded coincidenza: *the long wait for connections. There are no direct trains. You need to travel first from Agrigento to* **Canicatti** *(8 trains daily, 42 km, 50 min). At Canicatti only 3 options are available daily to get you to Syracuse. Each requires changing at Gela (81 km from Canicatti, 1 hr 30 min). From here 3 trains daily run to Ragusa (91 km from Gela, 1 hr 30 min); Noto (150 km, 3 hr) and Syracuse (183 km, 3 hr 45 min).*

Siracusa–Noto–Ragusa
The route

Siracusa (Syracuse) is an essential stop on any Sicilian itinerary, courtesy of its superb Greek remains and fascinating little medieval quarter. It's also handy for a couple of lovely beaches to the south, and as a base to visit two highly regarded towns, **Noto** and **Ragusa**. Both are crammed with Baroque architecture, Noto being the most famous, Ragusa the more peaceful. Neither has much in the way of accommodation, so aim to install yourself in Syracuse.

Trains

Syracuse *has no shortage of connections from Catania and Messina to the north. Onward connections south to Noto and Ragusa are a touch more limited (though still far better than the services from Agrigento). All trains stop at* **Noto** *(10 daily, 33 km, 30 min). Only 3 trains run through to* **Ragusa** *(112 km, 2 hr 10 min), though you gain another 2 daily connections by changing at Modica, just south of Ragusa.*

The journey

Siracusa (Syracuse)

Between about the 3rd and 5th centuries BC Siracusa was arguably Europe's greatest city, rivalled only by Athens. Today it's a vital stop on any tour of the island, mainly for its archaeological ruins, contained in the Parco Archeologico just west of the town. The modern new town is a disappointment, the old medieval centre a delight, neatly contained on a fortified island known as **Ortigia** (**Ortygia**).

The city was founded by Greeks from Corinth in 733 BC. Within 100 years it was Sicily's effective capital. By 415 BC it was strong enough to defeat the Etruscans. Athens took fright at the city's power and despatched a hostile fleet in 415 BC. Its defeat marked the highpoint of Syracuse's fortunes. In 397 BC it defeated Carthage, the other great Mediterranean power, but subsequently made the mistake of siding with the Carthaginians against the Romans. Rome besieged the city in 214 BC, and was held at bay for 13 years, partly by the war machines of Archimedes, a citizen of Syracuse. After capitulation the city declined under Roman control. The great 1693 earthquake levelled many of its Norman and Saracen buildings: Allied and Luftwaffe bombing in the Second World War took care of many more.

Parco Archeologico

It matters little either way whether you head first for the old town or the Parco Archeologico (Tues–Sun 9am–2hr before sunset). The station lies between the two, around 20 minutes' walk away from both (to find the park, pick up a map from the small information kiosk at the station). After dipping into the tourist office at the park's entrance, ignore the tawdry souvenir stands and head left for the **Ara di Ierone** II, a vast 3rd-century BC altar (198m by 23m). Used as a stage today, in the past it was the scene of sacrifices; orgies of bloodletting that saw up to 450 bulls slaughtered in a single day. Only the original base survives: the rest was filched by the Spaniards in the 16th century as building material.

Beyond the altar on the right is the **Teatro Greco**, the largest theatre in the Greek world. Built at the beginning of the 5th century BC, its 15,000 seats were cut from the living rock – though the theatre's upper tiers are now lost. Look for the carved initials at the top of the gangway (where the seats now end), the marked seats of various royal luminaries who attended performances. The Romans carried out several modifications, including the use of marble-faced seats for more privileged spectators. They also removed rows of seats at the front to make room for gladiatorial contests.

From the theatre drop down into the vegetation-covered quarry, the **Latomia del Paradiso**, a pleasant place known for the *Orecchio di Dionisio* ('Ear of Dionysius'). A large cave, it was named by Caravaggio on a visit in 1586. He was struck by the grotto's resemblance to an ear – the Dionysius bit comes from a myth that the cave's acoustic properties allowed one of the city's erstwhile rulers to overhear prisoners or conspirators kept below. The quarry provided stone for the city's monuments (there are several similar mines locally). Another grotto nearby, the **Grotta dei Cordari**, was used by the city's ropemakers. The damp air prevented rope-strands breaking under stress. Finally, hold on to your ticket to see the **Anfiteatro Romano**, a Roman amphitheatre immediately south of the main entrance. It dates from the 3rd century AD.

Museo Archeologico

The Museo Archeologico is obviously best seen in conjunction with the park (Tues–Sun 9 am–1 pm). To reach it from the park entrance take Viale Augusto which later becomes Viale Teocrito. The museum is about a kilometre down on the left, in the grounds of the Villa Landolina. Buses 5, 6, 8, 11 and 12 come here from Largo XXV Luglio in Ortigia.

Purpose-built, the *museo* is one of Sicily's newest and finest exhibition spaces. Incredibly wide-ranging, its collection covers finds from Syracuse and its environs, as well as artifacts from Gela, Agrigento and beyond (it's divided into three colour-coded sections, according to where items were found). Exhibits span Greek, Roman and early-Christian eras. The most noted is the statue of **Venus Anadiomene** (literally the 'Venus rising from the Sea'). It's a 1st century AD Roman copy of a Greek original. Also outstanding are the *kouroi*, early Greek statuettes of young men; the *Winged Victory* from the city's Temple of Athena; a marble cornice with lion-head basins; macabre theatrical masks; and a 4th-century sarcophagus from the catacombs close by.

Catacombi di San Giovanni

Roman law forbade burial inside the city limits, hence the huge network of early Christian **catacombs** that honeycomb the ground all around Syracuse. Many followed the course of old underground aqueducts, disused since Greek times (legend has it that some of the tunnels run as far as Catania). Most date from around 315 to 360 AD. In scope they're second only to the catacombs outside Rome. The only chambers open to the public, however, are under the part-ruined church of **San Giovanni**. This is off Via San Sebastiano, a short way back from the museum on Viale Teocrito.

The church was the burial place of San Marciano, Syracuse's first bishop, flogged to death by the Romans in 254. His tomb is here, part of what's thought to be the remains of Sicily's earliest Christian building. Visits to the catacombs themselves are by guided tour only (hourly on the hour Thur—Tues 10 am—noon and 4—6 pm). The tombs consist of a main gallery, broken by numerous side tunnels and niches (notice how the graves are denser around Marciano's tomb – people wished to be buried as close to a saint as possible).

Ortigia (Ortygia)

Most of your time in Syracuse should be spent in **Ortigia**, the small island that for 2,700 years has formed the heart of the city. It was here, for example, that the Athenian fleet was defeated and the Romans held at bay for 13 years (Syracuse could endure such sieges, thanks to the island's freshwater springs). Much of its appearance today is medieval and Baroque (the latter a result of the rebuilding that followed the 1693 earthquake). The main approach from the mainland is over the Ponte Nuovo to Piazza Pancali, home to the scant remains of the **Tempio di Apollo**, Sicily's oldest Doric temple (565 BC).

As ever, most pleasure's to be had wandering the streets at random. Most of the recognised sights, however, gather around **Piazza del Duomo**, the most notable of which is the duomo itself. Although fronted by a 17th-century façade, the extraordinary building is a monument to each of Syracuse's main historical epochs. 12 columns from the 5th-century BC Tempio di Atena, for example, lie embedded in walls built by the Normans (best seen in Via Minerva). Much of the interior, by contrast, was simply hacked from the old temple's *cella*. The survival of so much early material dates from the 7th century, when the temple was consecrated as a Christian church, thus pre-empting the stone-scavenging that ruined many ancient monuments (the Pantheon in Rome is another notable example of a temple saved by its conversion to Christianity).

The other thing on the island to make a point of seeing is the **Museo Regionale**, just south of the duomo at the bottom of Via Roma (Tues—Sun 9 am—1 pm). Its setting – the beautiful interior of the Palazzo Bellomo – makes a suitable backdrop for a lovely and wide-ranging collection. Most of the display is medieval, its highlights a ravishing *Annunciation* by Antonello da Messina (1474) and the *Burial of Santa Lucia* by Caravaggio. Additionally there's a lot of fine sculpture, plus a variety of silverware, fabrics, furniture, goldplate and sacred vestments.

Practicalities in Syracuse

Tourist Office There are offices at the station, San Giovanni and the Parco Archeologico. The main office in Ortigia is at Via Maestranza 33 (0931/66.932).

Railway station Via Francesco Crispi. To reach the centre (Ortigia) turn left out of the station and follow Via F. Crispi and turn left where it meets Corso Umberto I. Follow Corso Umberto I across the Ponte Nuovo to Piazza Pancali and Largo XXV Luglio on Ortigia. The station has left luggage facilities, useful if you want to see the town and archaeological park without staying overnight.

Buses Buses leave from Largo XXV Luglio in Ortigia, or from Piazza della Posta alongside.

Ferries *Tirrenia* ferries to Naples (1 weekly); Reggio di Calabria (3 weekly) and Malta (3 weekly).

Beaches The coast to the north is ravaged by industry. All the beaches are therefore south of the city. The nearest is Arenella, but it becomes crowded (to reach it take bus number 35 from Piazza della Posta). Far better is Fontane Bianche, half an hour away, also reached by regular buses from Piazza della Posta.

Youth Hostel *Ostello*, Viale Epipoli 45 (0931/711.118). A nice, relaxed hostel with double and 4-bed rooms. It's 8km from town at Belvedere (take bus number 9, 10 or 11). Be sure to call ahead first to check there's room.

Hotels Be sure to book ahead or arrive early in July and August. Most of the cheap places are around the station (not a nice area at night), though the Ortigia options are obviously preferable.

☆*Centrale*, Corso Umberto 141 (0931/60.528). Central to the new town – turn left out of the station and take the first right.

☆*Milano*, Corso Umberto 10 (0931/66.981). Close to the Porta Nuova and therefore convenient for Ortigia. Rooms are large, but the location's noisy.

☆☆*Gran Bretagna*, Via Savoia 21 (0931/68.765). By far the best choice if you manage to snap up a room; has a charming air of faded grandeur and rooms with sea views.

☆☆☆*Grand Hotel*, Viale Mazzini 3 (0931/66.729). Similar to the *Gran Bretagna*, though the rooms are of 'Thirties rather than 19th-century vintage – and prices are higher.

Noto

Only around half an hour south of Syracuse, Noto is as perfect an expression of the Baroque as you could wish for. Destroyed by the 1693 earthquake, the town was rebuilt with a lavish collection of golden-stoned churches and palaces. The plan envisaged a dual-purpose town, the residential and religio-political districts being deliberately separated. For a time it superseded Syracuse as the region's provincial capital. Thundering traffic has taken its toll on some buildings, but a (belated) restoration project launched in 1987 has begun to stop the rot.

The streets are well worth trawling, even if you normally have no time for this sort of architecture. Most of the best buildings are ranged along **Corso Vittorio Emanuele**, the main street. Along its length it widens into three piazzas, the central **Piazza Municipio** amongst the most captivating in Sicily. Here, as elsewhere, the exteriors and their superb decoration are the main attractions – the

Practicalities in Noto

Tourist Office Piazza XVI Maggio (0931/836.744). Pick up the map which indicates the town's most noted buildings.

Railway station The station is a little way south of the centre. From the forecourt take Via Principe di Piemonte uphill as far as Via Aurispa. Turn left and then third right on Via G. Zandarelli for Corso Vittorio Emanuele

(1.5km, 20min).

Hotels ☆☆*Albergo Stella*, Via F. Maiore 44 (0931/835.695). Noto's only hotel and often full as a result.

Restaurant *Trattoria del Carmine*, Via Ducezio 9. On the first street off Via Santa della Rosa from Piazza XVI Maggio.

last word in harmony: the interiors, for the most part, are disappointing. One of the more famous is the **Palazzo Villadorata**, known for its billowing balconies (it's in Via Corrado Nicolaci, first right off the Corso as you walk between Piazza Municipio and Piazza XVI Maggio.

Ragusa

If you liked Noto you'll like Ragusa, rebuilt following the same earthquake, often to the designs of the same architects (the otherwise little-known Rosario Gagliardi was the most notable). Far fewer people come here, however, and the atmosphere's more placid as a result. The train journey is also a touch more rewarding than the half hour scuttle between Syracuse and Noto. It ducks between the coast and low-hilled interior, before hauling up to Ragusa via the Irminio valley. The town divides into two – upper and newer Ragusa, and **Ragusa Ibla**, the pre-earthquake town rebuilt along Baroque lines below. Ragusa's present wealth derives from oil, the derricks, rigs and nodders all visible on the town's outskirts.

Ragusa's rewards are to be gained by walking the streets. From the station turn left and walk over the Ponte Nuovo, a bridge spanning a cleft in the ridge supporting the town: everything of note in the business-like new town lies across it, on or around Via Roma. Turn right on Corso Italia and aim to follow it and cross to Ragusa Ibla as soon as possible. The old town's a moribund spot, but the decrepitude is charming rather than squalid. Doors are locked, windows shuttered, and for much of the time you might as well be walking through a ghost town. You can easily while away an hour or so pottering around the little streets and alleys. Piazza del Duomo is the focal point, dominated by **San Giorgio**, one of the finest Baroque churches in Italy.

Practicalities in Ragusa

Tourist Office Via Natalelli 131 (0932/ 621.421). Turn left off Via Roma one block beyond Piazza della Libertà; not one of Italy's best tourist offices.

Railway station Piazza del Popolo. Turn left from the forecourt along Via Lena; Piazza della Libertà and the tourist office are 300 metres down at the end.

Hotels There's nothing in Ragusa Ibla, the only place you'd want to stay. Aim not to stay in Ragusa if possible. The little town of **Modica**, a few minutes south on the train, is a pleasant place and has a good little hotel, the *Minerva*,

Via San Domenico (0932/94.129). If you do get caught in Ragusa there are several rather pricey hotels; the best bet is the ☆☆*San Giovanni*, Via Traspontino 3 (0932/621.013). Quiet, clean and convenient for the station (take Via Leonardo da Vinci from the forecourt and turn left through Piazza dei Cappuccini at the top).

Restaurant Ibla has a couple of quiet places to eat, but the town's current favourite is the *Valle*, Via Risorgimento, close to the station (turn right from the forecourt on Viale Sicilia; Via Risorgimento is 200 metres down).

Palermo–Enna–Catania
The route

If Sicily's coastal scenery has disappointed you, this is the route to take as an antidote. It passes through the island's heart, a wonderful way to capture some of Sicily's magnificent interior landscapes. That it only passes one major town – **Enna** – gives some idea of the emptiness of the countryside en route. Enna itself, the so-called 'navel of Sicily', offers magnificent views and a few minor monuments. It's also a pleasant place to put up for the night (though the trip is possible in a day). What you want to ensure, however, is that you don't have to spend the night in **Catania**, Sicily's second city after Palermo. True, it has a few rewards if you're prepared to look. On first acquaintance, however, it's somewhere you want to leave as soon as possible.

The best onward destination is Siracusa (Syracuse) to the south (see Siracusa–Noto–Ragusa on page 328). Alternatively, you could head north to Taormina, or one of the resorts nearby. You might also want to catch the *Circumetnea*, the railway that makes a circuit around Etna. This you can do from Catania.

Trains

7 direct trains daily ply this route (243 km, 3 hr 40 min). It's a long, slow journey, and one where you should expect delays – so don't necessarily bank on making connections in **Catania**. *Breaking the journey at* **Enna** *(153 km, 2 hr 30 min) gives you most options for onward travel – that is, for making connections and avoiding a night in Catania.*

The journey

The first hour of the journey follows the same coastal stretch as the Palermo–Messina main line and the route over to Agrigento from Palermo (see Palermo–Agrigento on page 324). Little here grabs your attention, bar the mountains beginning to rise to the south and the deep green lemon groves on all sides. Ten minutes out of Palermo, look out for **Bagheria** (it has a station), for the most part a sinister and semi-derelict wasteland. For a time this was known as the 'triangle of death', having the most murders of any town or city in Italy (most of them mafia vendettas). Shortly after **Termini Imerese** the line swings south, leaving behind the despoiled coast for the suddenly pristine interior. The railway strikes off up the empty Torto valley, having shadowed a motorway and confused tangle of roads and industry virtually from Palermo.

The valley has nothing save the odd halt and dried river bed (water flows only for a brief few weeks in winter). The villages are on the hill-tops, the roads in the mountains, winding in and out of strange bare-sloped ridges and rocky escarpments. The railway is now in gripping scenery until Enna, the only snatches of civilisation being **Roccapalumba** (connections for Agrigento) and short stretches where country roads meet the line before disappearing back into the interior wilderness.

Sicilians talk of Sicily's central plateau, but to northern eyes the country is more mountain than plateau. Horizons, though, are wide, and the skies big and empty. In high summer the hills are burnt brown, the valleys patterned with the yellows and ochres of wheatfields and open pasture. In Roman times this was the 'bread-basket' of the Empire, and Sicily still produces the bulk of Italy's wheat (though, tellingly, the yields per hectare are the country's lowest). Flocks of sheep wander the slopes, tended by shepherds, kept for their milk more than their wool or meat. In spring the area's green with Edenic bounty, fields of maroon *sainfoin* dappling the fields. At other times, though, you might as well be in semi-desert; arid, windswept *High Noon* country, baked by a sun which shrivels crops, dries rivers and cracks open fields.

The Sicilian writer, Lampedusa, in his superb Sicily-set novel, *The Leopard*, describes a carriage-journey through the Sicilian interior. All the travellers had set eyes on, he wrote, 'were bare hillsides flaming yellow under the sun . . . They had passed through crazed-looking villages washed in palest blue; crossed dry beds of torrents over fantastic bridges; skirted sheer precipices which no sage or broom could temper. Never a tree, never a drop of water; just sun and dust.' If you've never seen this sort of country, it's mesmerising enough not to become monotonous, and certainly unlike anywhere else in Italy. You're also well off the beaten track, the ways of life still a good 30 years behind most of the country.

The Torto valley closes in tight to the tracks, the mountains becoming higher and steeper to either side. The railway climbs relentlessly, straining up to around 500 metres near **Vallelunga**, virtually the only settlement of any size in around an hour's travelling. Silence and stillness, disturbed only by the train, are the abiding memories of riding through these rolling hills. A tunnel finally cuts into the mood, startlingly dark and dank after the sun-filled intensity of the journey so far. **Caltanissetta**, the interior's capital, then appears to the south, spilling in tiers of modern houses from its old hill-top site. It's not a town you want to visit, though it's the interior's main rail junction. Note the connections from its Stazione Centrale and Caltanissetta-Xirbi (the station south of the town on the Palermo–Catania line). A few trains run directly to Agrigento and Syracuse via Canicatti (see Agrigento–Noto–Ragusa–Siracusa on page 327).

Enna

Enna is a far more enticing hill-town prospect than Caltanissetta, looming over the surrounding countryside from a great craggy ridge almost 1,000 metres high (making it the highest provincial capital in Italy). Its position has long consigned it to a single historical role; that of a defensive fortified citadel. This in turn, of course, has made it the target of invading armies over the centuries. Greeks,

Romans, Arabs, Normans, Lombards and Bourbons all had a go at the town, though relatively few left memorials to their passing. This said, Enna is one of the oldest settlements in Sicily, founded by the Siculi around 1250 BC, though – given its position – doubtless inhabited by Neolithic tribes earlier still (the Siculi were a tribe from mainland Italy who settled eastern Sicily – and from whom the island takes its name).

These days the town is an appealing mixture of modern and medieval, not overburdened with things to see, but redeemed by some of the island's best views and a pleasant provincial air. Arrive on a summer evening, and you also get caught up in perhaps Italy's most vigorous *passeggiata*. This walkabout centres on the town's single main street, Via Roma, and the two chief piazzas at its western end; Piazza Umberto I and Piazza Vittorio Emanuele. Orientation is extremely straightforward.

The **duomo** lies midway down Via Roma, a Gothic church (1307) with a Baroque overlay, the later decoration seen to best effect in the interior's extravagant columns and capitals. To its right is the **Museo Alessi**, home to the cathedral's treasury, a fine collection of coins, Graeco-Roman finds, gold and silverware, Byzantine paintings and miscellaneous church art (Tues–Sun 9 am–1 pm and 4–7 pm; free).

Immediately across the road, off Piazza Mazzini, is the **Museo Varisano**, a new museum devoted to local archaeological trophies dating from Neolithic to Roman times. You need to read Italian to get the most from these, but there's still enough of interest to be worthwhile – Greek vases in particular (Mon–Sat 9 am –1 pm and 4–7 pm, Sun 9.30 am–1 pm; free). Walk further down Via Roma and you come to the tree-surrounded ruins of the **Castello di Lombardia**, a well-preserved 13th-century castle built by Frederick II. It sits over the site of castles and forts that probably stretch back over 5,000 years. The crag is the town's highest point, with superlative views over the valley below to the village of Calascibetta and rolling hills beyond. On clear days Etna and its smoking summit are visible off to the east. The castle's worth a quick look (daily 9 am–1 pm; free), but this is a place to come more for the views and peaceful grassy nooks. Buy some food from the open air market (behind Piazza Umberto I) and eat your picnic here.

Just below the castle on the north side is the **Rocca di Cerere**, a huge and obvious crag, probably the site of a Greek temple to Demeter. Ceres to the Romans (hence the crag's name), Demeter was the fertility goddess and mother of Persephone. Her daughter features in one of the most famous Greek myths: Pluto's abduction of Persephone to the underworld. The event is supposed to have occurred on the shore of Lago di Pergusa, a lake just north of the town. In her rage at the abduction, Demeter prevented the corn from growing, only relenting when Zeus intervened to decree Persephone spend half her time in Sicily and half as Queen of the Underworld. Demeter then allowed the wheat to flourish, a tale of obvious relevance to an island as agricultural as Sicily.

Practicalities in Enna

Tourist Office Via Roma 413 (0935/500.544). Located 100 metres east of Piazza Umberto I.
Railway station Enna's railway station is 5km from the town centre – much too far to walk. Buses, unfortunately, only run from the station roughly hourly. If you don't want to wait, you could call a taxi from Enna or walk from the station on to the main road and hitch. Buses drop you on Viale Diaz, 300 metres west of Via Roma and the town centre.
Hotel ☆☆*Grande Albergo Sicilia*, Piazza Colaianni (0935/501.209). Large, easy-going hotel set back from Via Roma. It's the only accommodation in town, its rival, *Belvedere*, off Piazza V. Emanuele, reputedly kept shut by 'pressure from Palermo' (though check with the tourist office to see if it's managed to open). In desperation take bus number 4 from Viale Diaz to Lago di Pergusa, where there are a handful of cheap hotels on the lake shore (30min away).
Restaurant *Centrale*, Piazza VI Dicembre, signed off Via Roma near Piazza V. Emanuele. Don't be put off by the large 'Fifties-era dining room: the food's excellent and the service friendly.

Beyond Enna the train's progress is made easier by the broad-bottomed Dittaino valley. In tandem with the interior's new motorway, the line follows the river virtually all the way to **Catania**. The hills to either side are lower than earlier on the trip, and less strange in appearance, though the countryside is almost equally as empty. If you're unlucky enough to be stranded in Catania, consult the small tourist office in the station for hotel information. There's plenty of acccommodation, but aim to go upmarket – Catania's one of Italy's most crime-ridden cities. Most guides try to make out a case for the place, but there are better towns in Sicily – or Italy – to spend your time than this dirty, traffic-clogged and intimidating spot.

Circumetnea: *Catania–Randazzo–Riposto*
The route

The *Circumetnea* is a privately-owned line that encircles **Mount Etna**, one of the world's largest and most active volcanoes. Short of visiting the crater (see page 338), the railway offers the best possible views of the mountain, as well as an attractive ride through its scenic hinterland. The line, by the way, has frequently been interrupted by lava flows over the years.

Villages en route also have their plus points, though few offer much in the way of accommodation. This needn't be a problem as the line forms an (almost) circular route. Trains leave Catania, circle the volcano, and meet the main Messina–Catania FS line at Giarre-Riposto. This is just 30 kilometres from Catania. The whole trip's therefore easily done in a morning or afternoon. You could, however, travel to **Randazzo**, about half-way, and then retrace your steps. It's the closest point to the volcano and the most interesting village on the trip.

Trains

Trains do not leave from Catania's Stazione Centrale, but from the Stazione Circumetnea *on Corso Italia. When you arrive at the Centrale walk up Via della Libertà, the wide main street that leads almost directly from the station forecourt (turn left out of the station and then immediately right). The* Circumetnea *station is at the top of the street (500 metres).*

Only 5 trains daily make the full trip from Catania to Riposto (114 km, 3 hr 40 min). Another 5 run as far as Randazzo (74 km, 2 hr). Around 20 trains daily, however, connect Giarre-Riposto with Catania (30 km, 40 min). Note that Interrail cards are not valid *on the* Circumetnea *portion of the trip.*

The journey

Etna can be seen from much of Sicily, its snow-capped, gently smoking summit barely hinting at the turmoil within (despite the prominent summit, note that the volcano has over 200 separate craters). It's one of the greatest landforms in the Mediterranean, higher and more active than any other of Europe's volcanoes (and at 3,323 metres, the highest point in Italy south of the Alps). Its name comes from the Greek *aipho*, meaning 'I burn', something it's been doing since antiquity (there have been 135 eruptions since records began). Death and destruction have rained down over the centuries, most recently in 1991, most destructively in 1669 (when a 20-kilometre fissure opened in the mountain, pouring out a flood of lava that destroyed Catania). At the same time, it's proved a boon to the people who live on its slopes, its rich volcanic soils producing some of the country's finest agricultural land. Three distinct zones characterise the volcano's environs, all visible at some point from the train. Up to about 600 metres citrus trees flourish, along with almonds, walnuts and pistachio nuts. Gardens and fields overflow with fruit and vegetables. Up to around 1,500 metres vines and olives proliferate, together with dense forest cover (chestnut and various evergreens). Above the treeline is a desolation of blasted rock and endless seas of solidified lava.

All this seems a long way away as the train lumbers through Catania's moribund suburbs. Within a few minutes, however, you're coursing through olives and lemon groves. By the time you reach Paternò Etna's southern slopes are creeping into view. Paternò's castle was founded by Roger I in 1073, though mostly dates from the 13th century. It was used by the Nazis as an observation post in the Second World War, some 4,000 people being killed in the Allied bombardment to destroy it. Biancavilla ten kilometres on was settled by Albanian refugees in 1480 (one of many such villages in southern Italy). The Greek-founded village of Adrano beyond has another Roger-built castle, though the most obvious features hereabout are the orange groves on all sides.

In the 16 kilometres between Adrano and Bronte (a 30 minute stretch) you have some of your best views of Etna. Crumbling Bronte is Italy's main centre for pistachio nuts (85 per cent of national production), testament to Etna's fertility.

Look out for the remnants of the 1823 lava flow which almost destroyed the town. Eight kilometres on, at Maletto, the train has reached its highest point (pushing 1,000 metres).

Just beyond, at **Randazzo**, half the trains turn back for Catania. You could easily step into town if you're also breaking your journey. Only 15 kilometres from the summit, it's as close as you can get to the volcano by train: it's also a mildly appealing place if you want half an hour's walk and a bite to eat. Most of the buildings are built of volcanic rock – naturally – a sombre stone which lends the place a dark and gloomy air. Virtually all of them have been rebuilt since 1943, when Randazzo was devastated by the Allies (the town was an important forward base for the Germans). The main attractions are the town's three churches, each of which in turn has functioned as the duomo (medieval Randazzo had three medieval parishes, each with largely Greek, Latin and Lombard-descended inhabitants: one church was built for each). San Martino's the best, thanks to its evocatively-crumbling 14th-century campanile (the others are San Nicolò and Santa Maria).

Back on the train, the views are still outstanding, with first-hand panoramas over lava fields and land wrecked by volcanic rubble. Linguaglossa, 20 kilometres on, an unspoilt town, is the main tourist village on the volcano's northern slopes. From here on, however, the best of the views are over, and it's a fairly quiet 40 minutes down to Riposto and the end of the *Circumetnea*. To reach Giarre-Riposo's FS from the *Circumetnea* station, walk to Corso Italia and then bear uphill towards central Giarre. The station's sign-posted right after ten minutes. This is not a town to spend the night in, so plan ahead to give yourself time to move on.

Excursion from Catania/Taormina
Mount Etna: The Summit

It's reasonably easy to see Etna close-up if the railway's whetted your appetite for the volcano. The easiest way of all is to take an organised tour from Catania (trips also run from Taormina). Contact the tourist office or CIT, Via di Sangiuliano 208 (095/317.393). The tours are expensive, however, but include all transport, an accompanied ascent, and protective clothes if you need them.

Under your own steam, you can take an AST bus to the *Rifugio Sapienza*. There's only one a day, leaving from Catania's Stazione Centrale, usually at 8.05am (but check current times). It returns at around 4pm. The journey's about 40 kilometres. From the *Rifugio Sapienza* you can walk to the summit (or as near as volcanic activity allows). The hike follows a rough minibus track, and should take between 3–4hr depending on fitness (less to come down). Be sure to have sturdy footwear and plenty of warm and wet-weather gear – it's cold and always windy up here. If you don't want to walk you can take a two-hour trip by minibus (with half an hour at or near the main crater). Whichever way you go, it's an unforgettable, if occasionally surreal experience.

Catania–Taormina–Messina
The route

Taormina is Sicily's most famous resort, famed for its beautiful setting – 'the greatest work of art and nature,' said Goethe in his *Italian Journey*. The chances are you'll want to see it, though prices and high-season crowds may well prevent your staying. Various resorts nearby, however, are more affordable and have good beaches into the bargain. The best plan is probably to stay in one of these and visit Taormina as a day trip.

More generally, the route neatly completes a circuit of Sicily, leaving you well-placed at Messina to take a ferry back to the mainland. Otherwise there's little to write home about on the journey up the coast. Out of Catania, Mount Etna dominates the skyline to the west, giving way to the ridges of the Monti Peloritani beyond Taormina. On the mainland, therefore, there's always something to please the eye. Seaward, however, much of the coast – as elsewhere on the island – is spoilt by an endless procession of modern towns. If anything, things are a touch worse here, mainly because the mountains crowd everything into a narrow coastal strip: roads, motorway, railway, houses and industry. On clear days, though, you can look across the Straits of Messina for some wonderful views of the Calabrian coast.

Trains

Around 15 trains daily run between Catania and Messina (95 km, 1 hr 20 min). All of them stop at **Taormina-Giardina** *(48 km, 40 min). Of these about 10 daily continue as through trains to the mainland (so you don't have to change to catch a ferry). Of these in turn, 4 have sleeping accommodation.*

The journey
Taormina

Taormina perches high on a terrace above the sea, backed up against a mountain; 'as if it had rolled down there from the peak,' said French writer Guy de Maupassant. Behind, the town is cradled by Mount Etna. Below, it looks down over two sweeping bays, the whole ensemble creating a beautiful interplay of light, colour and matchless views. The town itself is a charming collection of tiny streets and flower-filled balconies. It's pleasure enough to walk its twisting alleys, window-shopping or stumbling on sudden squares and fleeting vistas. Sadly, it's a pleasure indulged by tourists from every corner of the globe. In high-season – which in Taormina stretches from April to September – the place is almost a caricature of itself. The streets are thronged, their charm dulled by souvenir shops. At night, flashy pizzerias compete with pounding discos, filled with glitterati attending the town's endless film and theatre festivals. Don't let this put you off – much remains unmissable – though come in March or October if at all possible.

Once you're in the old town (see Practicalities), follow any of the numerous signs to the **Teatro Greco**, Taormina's single outstanding sight (daily 9am–1hr before sunset). Built by the Greeks in the 3rd century BC, but almost completely remodelled by the Romans, the theatre commands one of the finest views imaginable (precisely the reason it was built here). Thereafter – bar a few odd Roman remnants – there's little else to see; the town is one to be explored on foot, its rewards those of views and backstreet charm. **Piazza IX Aprile** is the main centre, **Corso Umberto I** the main street. Avoid the bars here, unless you have money to spend (although perhaps one expensive coffee is worth it for the views). Try to climb to the **Castello** (for another all-round panorama), and visit the **public gardens** on Via Croce to escape the crowds.

Practicalities in Taormina

Tourist Office Palazzo Corvaia, Piazza Santa Caterina (0942/23.243). Located off Piazza Vittorio Emanuele at the eastern end of Corso Umberto I: it has an accommodation service.
Railway station Taormina-Giardini station is located on the coast well below the old town. It's a steep half hour walk to Corso Umberto I, so take one of the buses from the forecourt (they run every 15–75 mins depending on the time of day). The station has a left luggage facility if you're visiting for the day.
Buses The main bus terminal is at the lower (southern) end of Via Pirandello. Turn left from the terminal for Porta Messina and the start of Corso Umberto I.
Hotels Unless you're lucky or start looking early, don't expect to find a bed in July and August (campers should have fewer problems). Head instead to the nearby resorts of Mazzaro, Spisone, Letojanni and Giardini-Naxos. These are a few in-town options you might try – otherwise enquire at the tourist office. Bear in mind that prices soar during the summer.
☆☆*Svizzera*, Via Pirandello 26 (0942/23.790). Nice building and good views from a spotless hotel near the bus terminal at the eastern end of

Corso Umberto I.
☆☆*Villa Pompeii*, Via Bagnoli Croce 88 (0942/ 23.812). One of several reasonably-priced places on this street, which is close to the public gardens (try also the pleasant ☆☆ *Elios* at no. 98, 0942/23.431 and the *Leone* at nos. 124-6, 0942/23.878).
☆☆*Columbia*, Via Iallia Bassia 11 (0942/ 23.423). Close to the Greek theatre.
☆☆*Villa Liliana*, Via Dietro Cappuccini 4 (0942/24.373). Close to the tourist office.
☆☆*Palazzo Vecchio*, Salita Ciampoli 9 (0942/ 23.033). On one of the side alleys off Corso Umberto I.
☆☆*Friuli*, Corso Umberto 19 (0942/25.313). One of several hotels on the main street. At a similar price are the *Trinacria* at no. 99 (942/ 23.723) and the *Cuscona* at no. 238 (0942/ 23.270).
Campsite *Campeggio San Leo* (0942/24.658). Located at Capo Taormina on the cape below the town. Take any bus between the station and the old town; the site's on the right next to the *Grande Albergo Capo Taormina* (just before the bus turns left off the coast road).

Around Taormina

The closest **beaches** to Taormina are the immensely popular pebble coves at **Mazzaro**. These lie immediately east of the town and can be reached by a cable-car (*funivia*) from Via Pirandello in Taormina itself. There are actually two beaches; the more northerly *Spiaggia Mazzaro* is usually a little less crowded.

The main road above the beaches is lined with about a dozen hotels.

A little further north lies **Spisone**, a bus ride or half an hour's walk away (buses leave from the terminal in Via Pirandello). Five kilometres north is **Letojanni**, a self-contained resort, linked by five **trains** daily to Taormina (as well as by bus). The beach here is sandy – and again, popular – and there are a few hotels and a couple of campsites. Although not as inspiring as Taormina, off-season this isn't a bad place to stay.

The best spot near Taormina, however, if you don't settle in the town itself, is **Giardini-Naxos**, immediately to the south. It's a modern place, fronted by a wide, curving beach (larger and better for swimming than those at Taormina). Prices of rooms and meals are a good deal cheaper. The choice of hotels is also larger. Simply walk along the seafront for the best selection – there are dozens of places. The tourist office is on the front at Via Tysandros 76 (0942/51.010). You can walk here from Taormina-Giardini station. Regular buses run up to Taormina.

Sardinia

Cagliari–Mandas–Arbatax/Mandas–Sorgono
The route

From a practical point of view, there are few places in Europe where it makes less sense to take a train – this journey takes forever. At the same time, however, there are few lines that – beyond Mandas, at least – run through such fantastically wild countryside. Anywhere else and these lines would be run as tourist operations: steam trains still occasionally make the journey and the tracks are narrow gauge. The scenery is incomparable, the tiny hamlets en route fascinating. If you want to see old Sardinia and you're a sucker for small railways, this is the journey for you.

The route starts at **Cagliari,** Sardinia's capital – a good little city – though you could just as easily catch a ferry to Arbatax and run the trip in reverse. Whichever way you do it, read D. H. Lawrence's *Sea and Sardinia* for this route is the railway journey described in the book.

Trains

Direct trains run from Cagliari to **Sorgono** *via Mandas, though at Mandas you can change trains and pick up a branch line for* **Arbatax.** *9 trains daily (fewer on Sundays) run from Cagliari to Mandas (70 km, 1 hr 45 min). Unfortunately services beyond – through the best scenery – are very patchy. Only 2 trains daily continue to Sorgono (74 km, 2 hr 45 min); only 1 makes it to Arbatax (160 km, 4 hr), usually with a change and a wait at the halts of Lanusei or Seui. To make the Arbatax journey you usually have to catch an extremely early departure from Cagliari. 2 departures from Arbatax, however, make the return journey. Check timetables carefully.*

Cagliari

On the face of it Cagliari has everything to make it a fairly unappetising prospect: a large port, lots of industry and around a quarter of a million people. In fact it's one of the island's most pleasant cities, blessed with a compact medieval centre – easily explorable on foot – plenty of modest sights and surroundings comprised of lagoons and exquisite beaches. Its natural harbour, combined with its position at the heart of the Mediterranean, has made it an important port since time immemorial. Founded by the Phoenicians, who named it *Karalis,* it then became a Carthaginian and later a Roman colony. Decline followed the fall of Rome, but things perked up again in the 13th century with the arrival of the Pisans. Their fortifications are still some of the city's more prominent landmarks. Later

Sardinia passed to the Spanish, a generally unhappy time for Cagliari. For a while during the 18th century it belonged to Austria, eventually becoming a pawn in the machinations of the European powers. It wound up under the Italian House of Savoy in 1720. Heavy bombing in the Second World War caused considerable damage, though the rebuilding that ensued managed to leave the city's charm remarkably intact.

Orientation around the old centre is fairly straightforward. Behind the port area is Via Roma, a dual-carriageway, with Piazza Matteotti, the tourist office and the FS station at its western end (on your left as you step off the ferries). Ahead of you is the old hill-top citadel, linked to the port by Largo Carlo Felice, with Piazza Yenne and Via Manno at its head (all popular places for coffee, ice creams and people-watching).

There are two main things to see, both in the upper city. To reach them, head up Via Manno and clamber the steep streets and steps to the Bastione di San Remy (for some great views of the port and surrounding countryside). Up the narrow streets beyond you come to the **duomo**, fronted by a fake Pisan-style façade added this century. Saddled with a Baroque refit between 1660 and 1702, the interior nevertheless boasts a couple of fine pulpits, originally carved for the duomo in Pisa (they date from 1160). Visit the crypt for its set of carvings; miniature marble inlays cut into niches of rock, each concealing the remains of early Sardinian saints. The tower in the corner of the piazza, incidentally, is the **Torre San Pancrazio**. With its twin, the Torre dell'Elefante in Via dell'Università, it formed the cornerstone of the city's Pisan-built defences.

Walk north uphill to Piazza Indipendenza and you come to the **Museo Archeologico** (though note its collection is currently being transferred to the *Cittadella dei Musei* in Piazza dell'Arsenale, the square adjoining Piazza Indipendenza). This is Sardinia's premier museum, home to the cream of the island's Phoenician, Carthaginian and Roman finds. These include jewellery, amulets and bronzes, Greek urns, Egyptian artifacts and a large display of Roman glassware. The most tempting displays, however, are those dedicated to the island's ancient Nuraghic culture (dated around the second millennium BC). Most of these pieces come from the *nuraghi* mounds and tombs around the island (there are over 7,000), the most interesting a set of bronze figurines. Probably votive offerings, they mostly show warriors and hunters, together with the odd domestic scene of mothers suckling their young or shepherds with their animals. The museum is open Mon–Sat 9–1 pm and Wed, Fri and Sat 9am–1 pm and 3.30–6.30 pm.

Other sights around the city to look into include the **Roman amphitheatre**, partly closed to the public (and robbed of stone in the Middle Ages), but still able to give some idea of its original grandeur (it's also the most important Roman monument on the island). Close by is the city's **Orto Botanico**, a botanical garden with plenty of nooks to retreat from the ardours of sightseeing (daily 9 am–1 pm and also 4 pm–dusk Mon, Wed and Fri).

Practicalities in Cagliari

Tourist Office Piazza Matteotti (070/669.255).
Located off Via Roma behind the port. For the
main provincial office (the EPT), head for Piazza
Defennu 9 (070.654.811).
Railway station The FS station is in Piazza
Matteotti (9 trains daily to Olbia, Porto Torres,
Sassari and Oristano). It has a foreign exchange
facility. More importantly, however, the station
for the Cagliari–Mandas–Arbatax and
Mandas–Sorgono routes is run by the private
Ferrovie della Sardegna. Its station is in the east
of the city, in Piazza della Repubblica (070/
491.304), 20 min walk from the port.
Ferries to Sardinia Ferries are extremely busy
in July and August, though for deck passage
you should have few problems. Cabins are
booked months in advance.

Ferries for Cagliari leave on the mainland
from **Civitavecchia** (daily at 8.30pm, 13hr);
from **Genoa** (4.30 pm Tues, Thur and Sun,
21 hr); and from **Naples** (5.30 pm Tues, Fri and
Sun, 16 hr).
Buses Buses, not trains, sadly, are the way to
explore Sardinia. ARST services link most towns
to dozens of smaller villages nearby – their
Cagliari terminal is in Piazza Matteotti; PANI
services tend to connect only the major cities
and towns; their base is in Piazza Darsena (at
the opposite end of Via Roma to Piazza
Matteotti).
Beaches The city's nearest beach is at Poeto,
5km east, linked by regular buses from Piazza
Matteotti (every 5min; take services marked
with a *P* before the number). The seafront road
follows the coast along 4km of fine, sandy
beaches. You have to pay on some beaches for
showers, umbrellas and groomed sand,
although there are free beaches as well.
Hotels There's fierce competition year-round
for Cagliari's large stock of cheap
accommodation (from students and tourists
alike). Ask at the tourist office if you have
problems. Most places are close to the station,
notably on Via Sardegna, the first right off
Largo Campo Felice.
Firenze, Corso Vittorio Emanuele 50 (070/
653.678). At the top of 5 flights of stairs, but its
5 rooms are still popular so call ahead. The
Corso is the left turn off Piazza Yenne at the top
of Largo Carlo Felice.
☆*Olimpio*, Corso Vittorio Emanuele 145 (070/
658.915). Tidy, reasonably priced and often
full.
☆*Centrale*, Via Sardegna 4 (070/654.783).
Certainly convenient – and therefore usually
busy – but potentially noisy and a little
cheerless. Note the other options on this street.
☆*La Perla*, Via Sardegna 18b (070/669.446).
Clean and friendly.
☆☆*Italia*, Via Sardegna 31 (070/655.772). A
larger and more up-market choice than some in
the same street.
Restaurants Most of the city's restaurants
cluster on Via Sardegna or nearby Via Cavour.
Slightly cheaper places – mainly pizzerias – line
Via dei Mille (off Via Roma).
Da Serafino, entrances at Via Sardegna 109 and
Via Lepanto 6. A popular place with locals and
good value.
Gennargentu, Via Sardegna 60. Friendly
atmosphere and generous portions.
Antica Hostaria, Via Cavour 60. One of the
better more up-market options.

Cagliari–Mandas–Arbatax

The route

The stretch of line from Cagliari to Mandas is simply an introduction –
the line's real scenic pleasures come later. Its meandering course, though,
as it potters from village to village, is a good idea of what you can expect
of the train's excruciating pace. Low hills roll by, the Serrabus range west
of **Dolianova** one of the island's more desolate corners (there's nothing
between here and the coast some 40 kilometres away). Then the train
potters across a low plain, threading past dusty palm trees and a smattering of modern houses. Behind, old Cagliari rises proud on her rocky

bluff. Soon the train is climbing, fields giving way to the scrubby and un-cultivated uplands that dominate most of the journey. In the distance are the mountains of the Gennargentu, the train's eventual goal beyond Mandas.

If you've only time for one trip, it's hard to know which of the two lines to take beyond Mandas. Both pass through some of the wildest country in Europe; both give you onward options by bus (or by ferry, if you take the boat to the mainland from Arbatax). Lawrence settled for Sorgono, longer, and perhaps a touch more adventurous and spectacular. Either way, you can expect great looping rides around the mountains' spurs and valleys. The train seems always to be climbing, hovering around the 700 metre mark for much of both journeys. Villages are few and far between, stations appearing after long periods of utter emptiness. Many are deserted, or semi-deserted farming communities, emptied by decades of emigration. Sheep farming provides virtually the only means of survival. Until the 'Sixties, much of this area was also prime bandit country, Sardi-nia's interior being a byword for kidnappings and vendettas (less so these days, though one or two cases still make the newspapers).

The hills at first are bare moorland, later becoming increasingly wooded, scattered with swathes of hazel, oak and chestnut. Later still the landscape becomes steeper, cut by gorges and long, narrow ridges. Few places in Italy are so utterly remote. Why a railway was ever built is a mystery. Why it is still open, when so many on the island have closed, is equally puzzling. Nonetheless, it's a stunning ride, not always dramatic in the manner of Alpine rides, but unequalled for its sheer wilderness.

Practicalities

Arbatax There's a small tourist kiosk on the seafront in town, open 9 am–7 pm in summer but irregularly in winter. The tiny station's on a headland, just south of the town proper.
Tortolì 5 km before Arbatax, has a selection of hotels. The town itself has a few choices, the best a short taxi ride away; try the ☆☆☆*Cale Moresca* (0782/667.366); ☆ ☆*La Bitta* (0782/

667.080) and ☆*Supersonic* are cheaper; the last two are in the hamlet of Frailis.
Sorgono As in Arbatax, the chances are you will have to spend the night in Sorgono (though bus connections are available to Nuoro, to the north). Sorgono has 2 hotels; ☆☆*Da Nino*, Via IV Novembre (0782/60.127) and the ☆☆*Villa Fiorita* (0782/60.129).

Index

Abruzzo 229
Acquasparta 210
Aeolian Islands 314, 321
Agnelli family 53
Agostino di Duccio 225
Agrigento 314, 324–7; Museo Nazionale
  Archeologico 326–7; San Nicola church 327;
  Tempio di Ercole (Herakles) 326; Tempio di
  Giove (Jove) 326; Tempio di Guinone
  (Juno) 326
agriturismo 22
Aiguille du Midi 63
Alassio 69
Albenga 69, 70; Baptistery 69
Alberobello 305, 307
Alfedena 271, 272
Alpe di Siusi 122
Alpi Apuane 167, 198
Alto-Adige 109
Amalfi 288
Amalfi coast 284, 288
Amantea 290
Ambrose, St 81
Angelico, Fra 176, 208, 249
Aosta 49, 52, 58, 60–64; Arco di Augusto 62;
  Cattedrale 63; Porta Pretoria 62; Sant'Orso
  Church 63–4; Teatro Romano 62; Treasury
  Museum, Cattedrale 63
Aquileia 109, 147–9; Basilica 148–9; Cripta degli
  Scavi 148–9; Museo Archeologico 149; Museo
  Paleocristiano 149; Via Sacra 149
archaeological sites 24
Arezzo 169, 203–5; Castiglion Fiorentino 205;
  Pieve di Santa Maria 205; Pinacoteca 221; San
  Domenico church 205; San Francesco church
  204–5
Argentario 198, 199
Arnolfo di Cambio 246, 247
Arona 94; San Carlone statue 94
Assisi 169, 170, 218–23; Basilica di San Francesco
  220–21; Basilica of St Clare 223; Duomo 222;
  Eremo delle Carceri 223; Museo Civico 221–2;
  Piazza del Comune 221–2; Rocca 222–3; San
  Damiano church 223; Tempio di Minerva 221;
  Tesoro della Basilica 221
Aulla 198

Bagheria 333
Bagni di Tivoli 259
banks 12

Bari 274, 295, 297–300; Basilica di San Nicola
  299–300; Castello Svevo 300; Cattedrale di San
  Sabino 300
Basilicata 273, 274
Battipaglia 289
Baveno 93, 95, 96; Museo Galletti 96; Piazza del
  Mercato 96
Bellagio 102, 103
Bellinzona 99
Bergamo 80, 90–92; Cappella Colleoni 91;
  Castello 92; Cittadella 91; Galleria
  dell'Accademia Carrara 90, 92; Palazzo della
  Ragione 91; Piazza del Duomo 91; Piazza
  Vecchia 90, 91; Santa Maria Maggiore church
  91; Torre della Civica 91
Bergamo Alta 90
Bergamo Basso 90
Bernina Express (Red Train) 103, 105, 106
Bernini, Gian Lorenzo 251
Bolgheri 199
BOLOGNA 80, 109–10, 161–6; Archiginnasio
  163; Basilica di San Petronio 162; Cappella
  Bentivoglia 165; Museo Civico Archeologico
  163; Museo di Anatomia Umana 166; Palazzo
  Comunale 162; Palazzo del Re Enzo 162; Piazza
  di Porta Ravegnana 165; Piazza Maggiore 162;
  Pinacoteca Nazionale 166; San Bartolomeo
  church 165; San Domenico church 165; San
  Giacomo Maggiore church 165; San Sepolcro
  church 163; Santa Maria dei Servi church 163,
  165; Santo Stefano churches 163; SS Vitale e
  Agricola church 163; Torre degli Asinelli 165;
  Torre Garisenda 165
Bolzano 109, 117, 120–22; Castello Roncolo 122;
  Chiesa dei Domenicani 121; Duomo 120;
  Francescani, church of the 122; Piazza dell'Erbe
  121–2; Piazza Walther 120; Via dei Portici 122
Bordighera 69, 70
Bormio 106
Borromean Islands 93, 95
Borromeo, Charles 94
Bramante 250
Brenner Pass 116, 120, 123, 124
Brescia 103, 105–8; Museo Civico Romano 107;
  Museo della Chitarra 107; Piazza del Duomo
  106; Piazza della Loggia 106; Piazza della
  Vittoria 106; Pinacoteca Tosio-Martinengo 107
Brunico (Brixen) 123, 125–6
Burano Island, Venice 131, 139; Scuola dei
  Merletti 139

Caesar, Julius 232
CAGLIARI, Sardinia 342–4; Museo Archeologico
  343; Orto Botanico 343; Roman amphitheatre
  343; Torre San Pancrazio 343
Calabria 273, 294, 295
Caltanissetta 334
Camigliatello 295
Camogli 74
Campania 273, 274
camping 22
Campo Tures 125
Capo di Ponte 106, 108
Capo d'Orlando 322
Capolago 100
Capri 287
Caravaggio 241, 249
Carrara 190
Carsulae 210
Casere (Kasern) 125
Castelnuovo di Garfagnana 198
Castiglione del Lago 203, 207
Catania 313, 333, 336
Catanzaro 295
Cavour, Camillo 52
Cecina 199
Cefalù 314, 322–4; Museo Mandralisca 324
Cellini, Benvenuto 175
Certosa di Pavia 87, 89; tomb of Lodovico
  il Moro 89
Cerveteri 229, 262–3; Museo Nazionale Cerite
  263
Cervino see Matterhorn
Chamonix 58, 63
Charlemagne, Emperor 233
Châtillon 59
chemists 12
Chiarone 262
Chiasso 100
Chiavenna 103, 104
Chiusa 124
Chiusi 203
Chivasso 58
Chur, Switzerland 105
Cilento 290
Cinque Terre 52, 73, 76, 77
Circumetnea 333, 336–8
Città di Castello 211
Cividale del Friuli 109, 110, 144, 149, 152–3;
  Altar of Ratchis 152; Baptistery of Callisto 152;
  Museo Archeologico 152; Museo Cristiano 152;
  Piazzo del Duomo 152; Ponte del Diavolo 153;
  Tempietto Lombardo 153
Civitavecchia 262
climate 10
Cogne 52, 60, 61
Colico 103, 104
Collalbo 122
Colleoni, Bartolomeo 136
Columbus, Christopher 49, 51, 70, 73

Como 100–103; Museo Civico 101; Piazza
  Cavour 100; San Fedele church 101;
  Sant'Abbondio church 101
Copanello 293
Cortona 169, 203, 205–7; Fortezza Medicea 206
  –7; Museo dell'Accademia Etrusca 206; Museo
  Diocesano 206; Piazza della Repubblica 206;
  San Nicolo church 206
Cosenza 294
Courmayeur 57, 58, 63
credit cards 12
Crissolo 65
Crotone 292, 293
Cuneo 64–7
customs 11

Dante Alighieri 177
Deruta 211
Diamante 290
disabled travellers 13
Dobbiaco 110, 123, 126
Dolianova 344
Dolomites 109, 110, 116, 117, 119, 123, 126
Dolomiti di Brenta 118, 119
Domodossola 93, 96, 97
Donatello 130, 173, 175, 178
drinks 24
Doria, Andrea 71

eating 23–4
Edolo 80, 103, 105, 106, 108
Elba 199
Enna 314, 333–6; Castello di Lombardia 335;
  Museo Alessi 335; Museo Varisano 335; Rocca
  di Cerere 335

Faenza 110
Fenis 59
Ferrara 110, 154–6; Casa Romei 156; Castello
  Estense 155; Duomo 155; Museo del Duomo
  155; Palazzina di Marfisa d'Este 156; Palazzo
  Ludovico Il Moro 156; Palazzo Schifanoia 156;
  Piazza dei Diamanti 155; Pinacoteca
  Nazionale 155
Ferrovia Centrale Umbra (FCU) 209, 210, 214
Ferrovie Sud-Est (FSE) 305
Ferrovie Tranvie 107–8
Fiat 49, 53, 57, 58
Finale Ligure 69, 70; Museo Archeologico 69
FLORENCE 110, 167, 169–82; Baptistery 170,
  172–3; Bargello 170, 175; Biblioteca
  Laurenziana 176; Cappella dei Pazzi 178;
  Cappella di Filippo Strozzi 175; Cappelle
  Medicee 176; Duomo 172; Forte di Belvedere
  178; Galleria d'Arte Moderna 179; Galleria del
  Costume 179; Galleria dell'Accademia 170,
  177; Galleria Palatina 178–9; Giardino di
  Boboli 178; Loggia della Signoria 173; Medici
  tombs 176; Mercato Centrale 176; Museo degli

Argenti 179; Museo dell'Opera del Duomo
170, 173; Museo di San Marco 176;
Orsanmichele 170, 174; Palazzo Pitti 170, 178–
9; Palazzo Vecchio 173; Piazza del Duomo 170;
Piazza della Signoria 170, 173; Piazzale
Michelangelo 179; Ponte Vecchio 178; San
Lorenzo church 170, 176; San Marco church
170, 176; San Miniato al Monte church 179,
182; Santa Croce church 170, 177–8; Santa
Felicità church 178; Santa Maria del Carmine
church 170, 179; Santa Maria Novella church
170, 175–6; Santo Spirito church 179; Uffizi
170, 174–5
Foggia 295, 296, 297; Museo Civico 297
Foligno 212, 217, 218; Porta Consolare 218
Follonica 198
food 23–4
Forte di Bard 58
Forte di Marmi 190
Fortezza 123, 124
Francis, St 219–20, 223
Frascati 229, 256, 257
Friuli-Venezia Giulia 109

Gaddi, Agnolo 178
Gaddi, Taddeo 178
Galileo Galilei 177
Gallatina 311; Santa Caterina cathedral 311
galleries 24
Gallipoli 310, 311
Garfagnana 197
Gargano, the 274, 295, 297
Garibaldi, Giuseppe 52, 131
Gennaro, San 280
GENOA 51, 52, 68, 70–73, 198; Centro Storico
73; Palazzo Bianco 71; Palazzo Rosso 71–2;
Palazzo Spinola 73; San Lorenzo cathedral 73;
Santa Maria di Castello church 73; Via
Garibaldi 71–2
Ghiberti, Lorenzo 172
Ghirlandaio, Domenico 175
Giambologna (Giovanni Bologna) 175
Giardini-Naxos-Sicily 341
Giotto 109, 177–8
Gramsci, Antonio 53
Gran Sasso d'Italia 229, 267, 269
Grotte di Castellana 306
Gubbio 169

health 12–13
Herculaneum 274, 283, 284–5; Villa dei Papiri
279
hiking 116
Holy Roman Empire 233
hotels 19–21

Imperia 69
information 13
insurance 12

Ischia 287
Isola Bella 95
Isola Madre 95
Isola Maggiore 207
Issogne 59
Italian Riviera 68

Julius II, Pope 233

La Palud 63
La Spezia 75, 77, 167, 190
Ladispoli 262
Lago Trasimeno 205
Lake Como 80, 99, 100, 102, 103, 104; Villa
Carlotta 102; Villa Melzi 102; Villa Serbelloni
102
Lake Iseo 108
Lake Lugano 99
Lake Maggiore 80, 94, 96, 98
L'Aquila 229, 267–70; Beata Antonia church 270;
Fontana delle 99 Cannelle 268; Fonte Cerreto
269; Museo Nazionale d'Abruzzo 268–9; San
Bernardino church 269; Santa Maria di
Collemaggio church 270
Lateran Treaty 233
Lazio 229
Lecce 274, 302–5; Anfiteatro Romano 304;
Basilica di Santa Croce 304; Duomo 304; Museo
Provinciale 304–5; Palazzo del Governo 304;
Palazzo del Seminario 304; SS Nicola e Cataldo
church 304; Teatro Romano 304
Leonardo da Vinci 81, 85; The Last Supper 81, 85
Letojanni, Sicily 341
Levanto 77
Liguria 49, 51, 68, 69, 73
Limone Piemonte 64, 66, 67; San Pietro in
Vincoli 67
Lipari 323
Lippi, Filippino 175, 249
Locarno 96–9
Locri 292, 293
Lombards 152
Lombardy 79
Lorenzetti, Pietro 221
Lucca 167, 169, 195–7; Case Guinigi 196;
Duomo di San Martino 195; Museo Nazionale
Guinigi 196; Piazza del Anfiteatro 196; San
Frediano church 196; San Michele in Foro 195;
Tempietto 195; Tomb of Ilaria del Carretto 195
Lucera 295, 296; Museo Civico 296
Lugano 99–100; Santa Maria degli Angeli 99;
Villa Favorita 99–100
Lunigiana 198

Maderno, Carlo 250–51
Madesimo 104
Madonna di Campiglio 117–20
Maestro di San Francesco 220
Maglie 310

Malè 120
Malonno 108
Manarola 77
Mandas, Sardinia 344–5
Manzoni, Alessandro 104
maps 13
Maratea 290
Maratea Marina 290
Maremma 167, 199, 200
Margherita di Savoia 298
Marina di Bibbona 200
Martina Franca 305, 207–8; Palazzo Ducale 307
–8; San Martino church 308
Martini, Simone 220
Masaccio 175
Massa 190
Massa Marittima 167, 198, 199, 201, 202; Antico
Frantoio 201; Duomo 201; Miniera Museo 201;
Museo Civico 201
Matera 274, 300, 301–2; Duomo 32; Museo
Nazionale Ridola 301–2; San Francesco
d'Assisi church 302; San Giovanni Battista
church 302; San Pietro Caveoso church 301;
Santa Lucia alle Malve church 301; Santa Maria
de Idris church 301
Matterhorn 49, 59
Mazzaro, Sicily 340
Mazzini, Giuseppe 71, 233
Medici, Cosimo 171
Medici, Lorenzo il Magnifico 171
Menaggio 102
Messina 321
Metaponto 292
Metopes of Selinunte 318
Michelangelo 173, 175, 177, 240, 244, 249, 250,
251; The Last Judgement 244
MILAN 79–87 103; Accademia Brera 81, 84;
Castello Sforzesco 81, 84–5; Duomo 81, 82-3;
Galleria Vittorio Emanuele 83; La Scala opera
house 81, 83; Museo Civico d'Arte Antica del
Castello 84; Museo Civico d'Arte
Contemporanea 83; Museo del Duomo 83;
Museo della Scienza e della Tecnica 85; Museo
Poldi-Pezzoli 81, 83; Museo Teatrale alla Scala
83; Piazza del Duomo 81, 82–3; Pinacoteca 84;
Sant'Ambroglio church 81, 85, 87; Santa Maria
delle Grazie church 81, 85
Milazzo 321
money 11–12
Mont Blanc 49, 57, 63
Monte Baldo 117
Monte Bignone 69
Monte Generoso 100
Monte Mottarone 95
Monte Portofino 75
Monte Renon 122
Monte Rosa 49, 95
Monte Sant'Angelo 297
Monterosso 77

Monti Lessini 117
Morbegno 104–5
Mount Etna 314, 336–9
Murano island, Venice 131, 139; San Pietro
Martire church 139; Santi Maria e Donato
church 139
museums 24
Mussolini, Benito 45, 81, 233

NAPLES 273–4, 277–83; Basilica of Santa
Restituta 280; Cappella di San Severo 280, 282;
Castel Nuovo 278; Duomo 280; Museo
Archeologico Nazionale 279; Palazzo Reale di
Capodimonte 282–3; Piazza Garibaldi 278; San
Lorenzo Maggiore church 280; Sant'Anna dei
Lombardi church 279; Teatro San Carlo 278
Nardo 311
Narni 169, 212, 213–14; Piazza del Popolo 213–
14; Piazza Garibaldi 213; Ponte Augusto 213;
San Domenico church 214
Narni Scalo 213
Nicola, San 299
Noto 314, 327, 328, 331–2; Palazzo Villadorato
332; Piazza Municipio 331

Orbetello 198, 199
Orecchiella 198
Orte 212–13
Ortigia (Ortygia), Siracusa 330; Museo Regionale
330; Piazza del Duomo 330
Orvieto 170, 203, 207–9; Cappella del Corporale
208; Duomo 207–8; Museo dell'Opera del
Duomo 209; Museo Faina 208–9; Pozzo di San
Patrizio 209; San Giovenale church 209; San
Lorenzo di Arari chapel 209
Ostia Antica 229, 257–9; Decumanus Maximus
258; Piazzale delle Corporazioni 259; Porta
Romana 258; Roman amphitheatre 259; Terme
di Nettuno 258
Otranto 310–11; Duomo 310–11; San Francesco
di Paolo church 310; Santa Maria Annunziata
cathedral 310–11

Padua 109, 110, 126, 129–31; Basilica di
Sant'Antonio 129–30; Cappella degli Scrovegni
129; Eremitani church 129; Gattamelata 131;
Oratorio di San Giorgio 130; Orto Botanico
131; Piazza del Santo 129, 130–31; Pinacoteca
Civica 130; Scuola Santa 130–31
Paestum 288, 289–90
Paia a Mare 290
PALERMO 313, 315–20; Cappella Palatina 317;
Cattedrale 317; Convento dei Cappuccini 320;
Galleria Regionale della Sicilia 320; La
Martorana church 318; Museo Archeologico
318, 320; Palazzo dei Normanni 317; San
Giovanni degli Eremiti church 318; San
Giuseppe dei Teatini church 318
Palestrina 229, 260–61; Mosaic of the River Nile

261; Museo Nazionale Archeologico Prenestino
261; Tempio di Fortuna Primogenia 260–61
Palladio (Andres di Pietro della Gondola) 127,
128
Paolo 290
Papacy 233
Papal States 233
Paraggi 75
Parco Naturale dell'Argentera 64, 66
Parco Naturale dello Sciliar 122
Parco Naturale di Tessa 122
Parco Nazionale d'Abruzzo 229, 270, 271
Parco Nazionale del Gran Paradiso 49, 52, 61
Parco Nazionale delle Incisioni Rupestri
Preistorichi 106
Parco Nazionale dello Stelvio 80, 106
passports 10
Pavia 80, 87–90; Broletto (Palazzo del Comune)
88; Castello Visconteo 88; Piazza della Vittoria
88; San Lanfranco church 88; San Michele
church 88; San Pietro in Ciel d'Oro church 88;
Santa Maria del Carmine church 88
Perugia 169, 209, 211, 218, 223–7; Arco di
Augusto 225; Collegio della Mercanzia 224;
Collegio di Cambio 224; Corso Vannucci 223;
Duomo 223; Fontana Maggiore 224; Galleria
Nazionale dell'Umbria 224; Museo Nazionale
Archeologica dell'Umbria 226; Oratorio di San
Bernardino 225; Palazzo dei Priori 224; Piazza
IV Novembre 223–4; San Domenico church
225–6; San Francesco church 225; San Pietro
church 227; Sant'Agostino church 225;
Sant'Angelo church 225; Via del Aquadotto
225; Via Ulisse Rocchi 225
Pescasseroli 271
Peschici 297
Piedmont 49, 58
Piero della Francesca 212
Pinturicchio 219, 248
Pisa 167, 190–94; Baptistery 192; Campo dei
Miracoli 191; Camposanto 192–3; Duomo
192; Leaning Tower 167, 190, 191–2; Museo
dell'Opera del Duomo 193; Museo Nazionale di
San Matteo 193; Piazza dei Cavalieri 193–4;
Portale di San Ranieri 192; Santa Maria della
Spina 194
Pizzo 291
Placidia, Galla 158
Pompeii 274, 283–7
Ponte Gardena 124
Pont-St-Martin 58, 59
Portofino 73, 75, 76
Positano 288
Prato 169
Predoi (Prettau) 125
Puglia 273, 274, 292, 297, 305
Punic Wars 232
Punta Helbronner 63

Ragusa 314, 327, 328, 332
Ragusa Ibla 332
rail travel 25–48; from the Continent 15; from UK
14; international services 31–2; on the train 46
–8; public holidays 44–5; stations 36–41;
tickets and passes 16–19, 32–6; timekeeping
45; trains 25–30
Randazzo 336, 338
Rapallo 74, 76
Raphael 241, 243, 244, 245, 249
Ravello 288
Ravenna 110, 154, 156–60; Basilica di San Vitale
157; Battistero degli Ariani 158; Battistero
Neoniano 158; Mausoleo di Galla Placidia 157
–8; Museo Arcivescovile 158; Oratorio di
Sant'Andrea 158; Piazza del Duomo 158 Piazza
del Popolo 158; Tomba di Dante 158
Re 97, 98
Recco 74
Red Brigades 53
Red Train see Bernina Express
refuges 22–3
Reggio di Calabria 288, 291; Bronzi di Riace 291;
Museo Nazionale 291
registration, hotel 10–11
Republic 232
restaurants 23
Rimini 110, 154, 160–61; Piazza Cavour 160;
Tempio Malatestino 160
Riomaggiore 77
Risorgimento 52, 233
Riviera di Versilia 190
Robbia, Luca della 175
Roccapalumba 334
ROME 229–56; Ara Pacis Augustae 234; Arco di
Constantino 235; Baptistery, San Giovanni in
Laterano church 247; Bocca della Verità 248;
Campo dei Fiori 231, 251–2; Cappella Chigi
249; Cappella Paolina 249; Cappella Sistina
243, 244; Castel Sant'Angelo 240; Cathedra
Petri 251; Colonna Traiano 236; Colosseo
(Colosseum) 231, 234–5; Fontana dei Fiumi
252; Fontana di Trevi 231, 252; Fori Imperali
235–6; Foro Romano 231, 236–8; Galleria
Borghese 231; Keats and Shelley Museum 240–
41; Mercato Traiano 236; Mithraic temple 247;
Musei Capitolini 242–3; Musei Vaticani 243–
5; Museo Gregoriano Egizio 243; Museo
Gregoriano–Etrusco 243; Museo Gregorian
Profano 243; Museo Missionario Etnologico
245; Museo Pio–Clementino 243; Museo Pio
Cristiano 245; Museo Storico, Vatican museums
245; Palatino (Palatine) 238–9; Palazzo
Barberini 241; Palazzo Corsini 241–2; Palazzo
dei Conservatori 242–3; Palazzo Nuovo 242;
Palazzo-Galleria Doria Pamphili 242; Pantheon
239–40; Piazza del Campidoglio 242; Piazza di
Spagna 231, 252–3; Piazza Navona 231, 252;

Piazza Venezia 231; Pinacoteca, Vatican museums 244–5; Ponte Sant'Angelo 240; Protestant Cemetery 240; Raphael Rooms, Vatican museums 243–4; Roman Forum 231, 236–8; St Peter's 231, 250–51; San Carlino 246; San Clemente church 246–7; San Giovanni in Laterano church 247; San Luigi dei Francesci church 247–8; San Pietro in Vincoli church 251; Sant'Agnese in Agone church 252; Sant'Andrea al Quirinale church 245–6; Santa Cecilia in Trastevere church 246; Santa Maria d'Aracoeli church 248; Santa Maria del Popolo church 249; Santa Maria della Vittoria church 250; Santa Maria in Cosmedin church 248; Santa Maria in Trastevere church 249–50; Santa Maria Maggiore church 248–9; Santa Maria sopra Minerva church 249; Scala Santa 247; Sistine Chapel 243, 244; Spanish Steps 231, 252–3; Throne of St Peter 251; Tomb of Urban VIII, St Peter's 251; Villa Giulia 231, 245

Rossano 292, 293–4; Museo Diocesano 206; San Marco church 293

Rovereto 118; Museo Storico della Guerra 118

Sack of Rome 233
St Moritz, Switzerland 103, 105
Saluzzo 65; Casa Cavassa 65; Piano del Re 65; San Giovanni church 65
San Candido 117, 126
San Fruttuosa 75; San Fruttuosa di Capo di Monte, Abbey of 75
San Gimignano 167, 187–8, 189; Cappella di Santa Fina 188; Collegiata 187–8; Palazzo del Popolo 188; Sant'Agostino church 188; Torre Grossa 187
San Giovanni in Fiore 294
San Marino 154
San Michele island, Venice 139
San Remo 69
Sansepolcro 211–12
Sansovino, Andrea 249
Sant'Agata 322
Sant'Anna di Valdieri 66
Sant'Apollinare in Classe 159
Sant'Apollinare Nuovo 160
Santa Margherita Ligure 73–6
Santa Maria Maggiore 97, 98
Santa Marinella 264
Santa Severa 264
Saorge 67
Sapri 290
Sardinia 230, 262, 313, 314, 342–5
Savonarola, Girolamo 173
Sesto 126
Sestri Levante 74, 76
Sforza family 81
Sibari 292
Sicily 291, 313–41

see also under individual towns
Siena 167, 182–9; Baptistery 185; Cappella di Piazza 184; Duomo 184–5; Fonte Gaia 184; Libreria Piccolomini, Duomo 185; Museo dell'Opera del Duomo 185; Palazzo Pubblico 184; Piazza del Campo 183–4; Pincoteca Nazionale 185, 188; San Francesco church 189; Santa Maria delle Nevi church 189; Torre del Mangia 184
Signorelli, Luca 208
Siracusa 314, 327–31; Anfiteatro Romano 329; Ara di Ierone II 329; Catacombi di San Giovanni 329–30; Catomia del Paradiso 329; Grotta dei Cordari 329; Museo Archeologico 329; Ortigia (Ortygia) 330; Parco Archeologico 328–9; Teatro Greco 329; Venus Anadiomene statue 329
Social Wars 232
Sondrio 103, 105
Sorrento 274,284, 287
Soverato 292, 293
Spello 169, 218–19; Cappella Tega 219; San Lorenzo church 219; Sant'Andrea church 219; Santa Maria Maggiore church 219
Spisone, Sicily 341
Spoleto 169, 212, 214–17; Arco di Druso 215; Cappelle Erioli 216; Duomo 215–16; Museo Civico 216; Ponte delle Torri 216–17; Roman amphitheatre 215; San Ansano church 215; San Gregorio church 215; San Pietro church 217; San Ponziano church 215; San Salvatore church 215; Sant'Eufemia church 216
Stresa 93, 94–5
Stromboli 323
Sulmona 229, 265, 266–7; Annunziata church–palace 266; Duomo 267; Fontana del Vecchio 266; Piana del Fucino 265–6; Piazza XX Settembre 266; San Francesco delle Scarpe church 266

Tagliacozzo 265
Taormina 339–41; Castello 340; Corso Umberto I 340; Piazza IX Aprile 340; Teatro Greco 340
Taranto 305, 308–9; Museo Nazionale 308, 309
Tarquinia 229, 262, 264; Museo Nazionale 264
Terme di Valdieri 66
Termini Imerese 333
Terni 210, 214
Terontola 203
Tintoretto 136
Tirano 103, 105, 106
Tivoli 229, 259–60; Teatro Marittimo 260; Villa Adriana 260; Villa d'Este 259; Villa Gregoriana 260
Todi 209, 210,11; San Fortunato church 210; Santa Maria della Consolazione church 210
Torgiano 211
tourist offices 20
trains see rail travel

Trani 274, 295, 298; Duomo 298
travel insurance 12
travel to Italy 14 – 16
Tre Cime di Laveredo 126
Trentino – Alto Adige 109
Trento 117 – 120; Castello del Buonconsiglio 118;
    Museo Diocesano 118; Museo Provinciale
    d'Arte 118; Santa Maria Maggiore church 118,
    120
Trevi 169, 212, 217; Madonna delle Lacrime
    church 217; Pinacoteca 217; San Martino
    church 217; Sant'Emiliano church 217
Trieste 109, 144 – 7; Carso 147; Civico Museo
    Morpurgo 145; Colle San Giusto 144 – 5;
    Duomo 144, 145; Fortezza 144, 145; Grotta
    Gigante 147; Miramare 147; Museo di Arte e
    Storia 145; Museo Sartorio 145; Risiera di San
    Sabba 145
Tropea 274,288, 290 – 91
trulli 305, 306 – 7
TURIN 49, 52 – 7, 80; Armeria Reale 54; Basilica
    di Superga 57; Castello e Borgo Medioevale 55;
    Duomo 54; Galleria Sabauda 53 – 4; Giardino
    Reale 54; Mole Antonelliana 55; Museo Civico
    dell'Arte Antica 54; Museo dell'Automobile 57;
    Museo Egizio 53; Museo Nazionale del
    Risorgimento 54; Palazzina di Caccia di
    Stupinigi 57; Palazzo Madama 54; Palazzo
    Reale 54; Parco del Valentino 55; Piazza
    Castello 54; Porta Palatina 55; San Lorenzo
    chapel 54; Turin Shroud 54 – 5
Tuscany 110, 167, 169

Uccello, Paolo 176

Udine 110, 144, 148 – 52; Castello 150 – 51;
    Duomo 151; Galleria di Arte Moderna 151 – 2;
    Loggia del Lionello 151; Museo Civico 151;
    Museo Friuliano delle Arti e Tradizioni Popolare
    151; Oratorio della Purità 151; Palazzo
    Arcivescovile 151; Piazza della Libertà 150; San
    Francesco church 151
Umbria 167, 169, 170

Val Camonica 105, 108
Val Codera 104
Val del Gran San Bernardo 57, 60, 62
Val di Cogne 61
Val di Gressoney 57, 59
Val di Rhêmes 61
Val Pusteria 123,124
Val Tartano 105
Val Vigezza 96, 98
Valdichiana 205
Valle Aurina 123, 125
Valle d'Aosta 49, 57, 58, 61
Valle dei Templi, Agrigento 325
Valle di Valasco 66
Vallelunga, Sicily 334

Valnontey 61
Valtellina 103, 104
Valtournenche 57, 59
Vatican City 233
Velasquez 242
Veneto 109
VENICE 80, 109, 110, 126, 131 – 43; Basilica di
    San Marco 131, 133 – 4; Campanile, Piazza San
    Marco 133; Campo San Zanipolo 136 – 7;
    Colleoni statue 131, 136 – 7; Frari I 131, 135 –
    6; Galleria dell'Accademia 131, 135; Ghetto
    137 – 8; Libreria Sansoviniana 133; Lido 138 –
    9; Loggia dei Cavalli, Basilico di San Marco 133;
    Madonna dell'Orto 138; Muses Correr 133;
    Museo Vetrario, Murano 139; Pala d'Oro,
    Basilica di San Marco 134; Palazzo Ducale 131,
    134; Piazza San Marco 131, 132 – 4; Porta della
    Carta, Palazzo Ducale 134; Quaderia 133;
    Rialto 138; San Michele island 139; San Pietro
    Martire church, Murano 139; San Rocca church
    136; Santa Maria Gloriosa dei Frari church 131,
    135 – 6; Santa Maria e Donato church, Murano
    139; Scuola Grande di San Marco 137; Scuola
    Grande di San Rocco 131, 136; SS Giovanni e
    Paolo church 131, 137; Zecca 133
Ventimiglia 64, 67, 68
Venazza 77
Verona 109, 110, 112 – 16, 126; Arena 112;
    Basilica di Sant'Anastasia 114; Castelvecchio
    114 – 16; Domus Mercatorium 113; Duomo
    114; Juliet's House 113 – 14; Parco dell'Asenale
    114; Piazza dei Signori 113; Ponte Scaligero
    114; San Zeno Maggiore church 116; Scaligeri
    Tombs 113
Verres 59
Vesuvius 274, 283, 284, 285
Via Appia 289
Via Faigitelle 295
Via Flaminia 213, 218
Viadotto Solieri 66
Viareggio 190
Vicenza 109, 110, 126 – 8; Basilica 127; Duomo
    127; Loggia del Capitano 127; Museo Civico
    127 – 8; Palazzo Chiericati 127; Santa Croce
    church 127; Santo Stefano church 127; Teatro
    Olimpico 128
Villa Aldobrandini 257
Villa Rotonda (Villa Capra) 128
Villa Valmarana 128
Visconti, Gian Galeazzo 81, 82, 89
Visconti family 81, 89
Volterra 167, 198 – 203; Arco Etrusco 202; Museo
    Guarnacci 202 – 3; Ombra della Sera 202 – 3;
    Parco Archeologico 202; Piazza dei Priori 200,
    202; Pinacoteca 202; Roman theatre and bath
    complex 202
Vulcano 323

youth hostels 21 – 2